Skeletal
Biology
in the
Great
Plains

Skeletal Biology in the Great Plains

Migration, Warfare, Health, and Subsistence

Edited by Douglas W. Owsley and Richard L. Jantz

SMITHSONIAN INSTITUTION PRESS
Washington and London

© 1994 by the Smithsonian Institution

Library of Congress Cataloging-in-Publication Data
Skeletal biology in the Great Plains: migration, warfare, health, and
    subsistence / edited by Douglas W. Owsley and
Richard L. Jantz.
        p.   cm.
    Papers from a symposium held Mar. 19–21, 1989 at the
Smithsonian Institution, Washington, D.C.
    Includes bibliographical references and index.
    ISBN 1-56098-093-1
    1. Indians of North America—Great Plains—Anthropometry—
Congresses.   2. Indians of North America—Great Plains—
Mortuary customs—Congresses.   3. Indians of North
America—Great Plains—Diseases—Congresses.
4. Paleopathology—Great Plains—Congresses.   5. Great
Plains—Antiquities—Congresses.   I. Owsley, Douglas W.
II. Jantz, Richard L.
E78.G73S5   1992
978—dc20   91-14388

British Library Cataloguing-in-Publication Data is available.

Manufactured in the United States of America
00 99 98 97 96 95 94   5 4 3 2 1

Editor/Proofreader: Diane Della-Loggia
Illustrator: Karen Ackoff
Typesetter: Peter Strupp/Princeton Editorial Associates

Contents

○○○

William M. Bass. Left, Fairfax, Va., 1989. Right, explaining field methods to visitors to the Sully site, S.Dak., 1956–1958.

ooo

Dedication

The research reported in this volume is based largely on the William H. Over skeletal collection and was stimulated by its impending reburial. William M. Bass arranged for loan of the collection from the State of South Dakota to the University of Tennessee, Knoxville, from 1978 to 1985 for intensive study prior to reburial. The research reported here would not have been possible without his efforts.

In a broader sense, this volume is the culmination of Plains skeletal research begun by Bass in the 1950s. His dissertation was the first attempt at synthesis of then-existing Central Plains and Coalescent tradition skeletal samples. Subsequently, he excavated and curated the skeletal samples housed at the University of Tennessee. This collection has been extensively studied by two generations of students of Plains physical anthropology. Many of the chapters in this volume report research on skeletal material from this large collection. As a result, the Plains, formerly one of the least known areas, is now one of the most extensively studied and best understood. This increase in knowledge results directly from Bass's efforts in recovering, curating, and encouraging research on the Plains skeletal collection. The numerous theses, dissertations, and published papers resulting from this research are evidence of his willingness to make the collection available and to assist in its use.

On a more personal note, both of us have profited greatly from our association with Bill, first as students and later as colleagues. He encouraged us in our efforts and facilitated our research. He took care of numerous matters, large and small, required to mount a large project such as this one, requiring the assembly and organization of material depicting the varied approaches, methodologies, and findings of recent Plains physical anthropological research. Thus it is with deep affection and appreciation that we dedicate this volume to William M. Bass.

Richard L. Jantz and Douglas W. Owsley

○ ○ ○

Preface

What is the purpose of writing a preface to a book? The dictionary tells us that to preface is to herald or to introduce. Drs. Richard Jantz and Douglas Owsley have written an introduction that deals with the contents and coverage of this volume in some detail. So, in this preface, we prefer to herald.

This book presents the results of the labors of anthropologists, biochemists, and even an ecologist. Their contributions represent a significant addition to the corpus of scientific literature dealing with the Native Americans who have inhabited the Great Plains for centuries. More specifically, they illuminate the means by which various tribes adapted to the Plains, the subsistence strategies that they developed, their demographics and movements, their interactions with one another and eventually with the encroaching White settlers, and their conditions of health and types of disease as manifest in skeletal remains. The papers that make up this volume are based on recent research undertaken by bioarcheologists in the field and osteologists and biochemists in the laboratory. The book as a whole is a good reflection of the multidisciplinary approach to a subject. Although the papers are mainly bioarchaeological, several also deal with archaeological analysis and classification, with ethnographic and ethnohistorical information, and with isotopic paleodietary analysis. A major focus concerns the prehistoric past. Yet, human exploration, interaction, and adaptation to the plains environment were equally dynamic, if not more so, with the coming of the historic period. This volume reports on many events and factors affecting the lives of Native American peoples of the protohistoric period, and the changes and hardships they experienced secondary to Euro-American contact. The story, however, cannot end there. We are also provided with new information about the early pioneers, who tested the land and were buried in forgotten graves without epitaphs, yet whose passing marked the end of an important era in Plains history. Modern scientific techniques relying on comprehensive examination of the skeleton, as evaluated with the aid of methods such as traditional radiography, bone densitometry, tomography, scanning electron microscopy, mass spectroscopy, and the development of computerized databases, have helped fill gaps in our information, and have given us a better understanding and appreciation of the events and peoples that shaped American history in the Great Plains.

Beyond its contribution to an improved understanding of the history and culture of the Native Americans who lived on the Great Plains, so important to them and to all Americans, the book presents critical medically related knowledge that can be helpful to all humankind.

The symposium and this volume that developed out of it have been caught up in the controversy about the repatriation of Native American skeletal remains and burial artifacts. We want to make clear that we understand the emotions and demands of those who call for prompt repatriation, but, as scientists, we ask for the understanding of Native Americans. It is our hope that research, such as that described in this book, will continue to contribute to an improved understanding of Native Americans and that it will benefit them and others in the human community as well.

As scientists, we are aware that the loss of collections may hamper the continuation of research that we consider vital to the Native American community and to society at large. To prevent such a loss, it is our view that professional curation and study should precede the repatriation process. Otherwise, the education of future generations, full of questions, will be limited to our present store of knowledge and restricted by our inaccuracies and omissions. Although possessed of more advanced technological skills, they will not have the opportunity to investigate these issues and validate these observations firsthand. Gaining a better understanding of the Native American and Euro-American past through the study of skeletal remains and burial artifacts is a highly valued enterprise.

The editors greatly appreciate the efforts of the authors who have contributed to this volume. In addition, several individuals made special contributions. Diane Della-Loggia was the editor-proofreader, devoting many hours that helped insure the accuracy, consistency, and clarity of even the most difficult manuscript; Karen Ackoff prepared all illustrations through the production stage; Terence Arundel researched and drafted the maps; and Lorraine Jacoby edited the bibliographic citations. Milton Jacobs and Bertita Compton helped review early drafts of the manuscripts and managed correspondence with the authors. Princeton Editorial Associates was responsible for typesetting and indexing. We appreciate the help, guidance, and support provided by Peter Cannell, Science Acquisitions Editor for the Smithsonian Institution Press. Production costs were partly underwritten by the Department of Anthropology and the Director's Office of the National Museum of Natural History, with special thanks to Donald Ortner, Dennis Stanford, and Mary Tanner.

Examination of the William H. Over skeletal collection was sponsored by the National Science Foundation through a grant to Louisiana State University. The data were collected at the University of Tennessee. Other collections from the Iowa State Historical Society, the Office of the Iowa State Archaeologist, the Oklahoma Museum of Natural History, the Panhandle Plains Historical Society Museum, the University of Nebraska, the Nebraska State Historical Society, and the Smithsonian Institution have been used in various analyses. We greatly appreciate the efforts of Julie Droke, Billy Harrison, John Ludwickson, Rob Bozell, and Gail Potter in making these collections available. We are especially indebted to the late Robert Alex for recognizing the importance of having the W.H. Over collection systematically examined prior to reburial.

ooo

Archaeological Provenance and Burial Archaeology

CHAPTER 1

○○○

An Integrative Approach to Great Plains Skeletal Biology

DOUGLAS W. OWSLEY AND RICHARD L. JANTZ

Until the late 1950s, few archaeologists in the Plains were concerned with recovering and curating human skeletal remains (cf. Bass 1981). In South Dakota, two notable exceptions were M.W. Stirling of the U.S. National Museum (Wedel 1955) and W.H. Over of the University of South Dakota. Over, as director from 1912 to 1949 of the museum now named in his honor, and as a semiretired curator until 1952, surveyed and tested many of South Dakota's most important sites. He is acknowledged "for having been the first to investigate, record, and attempt a comprehensive interpretation of the state's prehistory" (Sigstad and Sigstad 1973:iii). His published notes and reports describe field research at more than 200 archaeological sites located in 43 counties (Over and Meleen 1941; Sigstad and Sigstad 1973). Over, with the assistance of E.E. Meleen, recovered human skeletal remains at about 15 percent of these sites. The Over Collection burials were often the only human remains recovered from some localities. For others, they represent an important addition to site collections excavated under the auspices of the Missouri Basin Project of the federal Interagency Archeological Salvage Program.

The Missouri Basin Project was created in response to the construction of four large reservoirs along the Missouri River

in North and South Dakota, which would inundate hundreds of archaeological sites. Archaeological survey and salvage investigations were undertaken by the Smithsonian Institution in partnership with the National Park Service and several universities and historical societies. Between 1946 and 1969, this program proceeded at a breakneck pace under emergency conditions (Thiessen 1992). Even so, only about 10 percent of the *known* archaeological sites were actually investigated. The primary objective was reconstruction of culture history, and most of the fieldwork involved the excavation of earthlodges. Occasionally, human remains were recovered in small numbers from some sites. Four large cemeteries, Larson (39WW2), Leavenworth (39CO9), Mobridge (39WW1), and Sully (39SL4), were excavated by crews working under the direction of William Bass. On behalf of the South Dakota Archaeological Commission and the Over Museum, W.R. Hurt partially excavated two cemeteries, Four Bear (39DW2) and Swan Creek (39WW7), and these samples were added to the Over Collection (Hurt 1957; Hurt et al. 1962).

The W.H. Over Museum Collection consisted of more than 500 skeletons from 37 prehistoric and protohistoric Plains Woodland, Middle Missouri tradition, and Coalescent tradition archaeological sites in South Dakota. In 1977, Bass arranged temporary loan and transfer of the collection to the University of Tennessee, Knoxville, for osteological analysis. Additional specimens were transferred in 1982. Several publications and dissertations resulted from this arrangement (e.g., Key 1983; Owsley 1981; Owsley and Symes 1981; Owsley et al. 1981; Puscharich 1984; Zobeck 1983). In 1985, the South Dakota Office of the State Archaeologist recalled the Over Museum human skeletal collection for reinterment, which took place in 1986.

Faced with the loss of this valuable research collection, concerned anthropologists submitted a proposal to the National Science Foundation for a final examination of the Over Collection. The objectives were systematic documentation and the application of modern biological and anthropological techniques to Plains archaeological research, thereby providing information about Plains Indian adaptations, population biology, and cultural and historical relationships. The limited time before return of the collection restricted the number of observations that could be recorded; nevertheless, the potential loss of anatomical, biomedical, and historical information was minimized through focusing on the recovery of specific types of data. The proposal was funded, and detailed osteological research for this volume began during the summer of 1985 with analysis of this collection.

Archaeologists, ethnohistorians, ethnologists, physical anthropologists, and other specialists collaborated on this multifaceted project and developed a comprehensive database. The multiple data sets that were collected contained information about archaeological provenance and chronology, bone inventories, demography (including determinations of age, sex, and race), skeletal and dental pathology, cranial and postcranial measurements, carbon and nitrogen isotope values, and taphonomic observations.

The overall composition of the collection was heterogeneous because of the biological and cultural diversity represented by the various population samples. There were differences in origins and gene pools, in activity patterns, and in events related to temporal context—especially those resulting from Euro-American contact. Some groups were nomadic hunter-gatherers, and others, semisedentary horticulturists. During the Postcontact period, several interdependent factors affected health, demography, nutrition, and sociocultural structure, including the introduction of acute infectious diseases (e.g., measles and smallpox), acquisition of the horse, and increased European presence. Semisedentary groups like the Arikara experienced increased pressure from tribes that moved into the Missouri Valley. Large-scale migrations followed the introduction of the horse, the development of a militarily oriented bison-hunting culture, and a series of intertribal wars in the eastern United States and Canada (Lehmer 1971).

Such diversity and change provide a basis for comparative research. The data can be used to examine geographic and temporal variation in cranial and postcranial morphology and the effects of Euro-American contact and exploration on demographic parameters and population health, tribal interactions and warfare, subsistence, and mortuary practices. In many cases, the human bones can be used for independent tests of archaeologically and historically derived hypotheses.

The study of the Over Museum Collection was critical to the continued application of modern biological anthropological techniques to the archaeology of the Northern Plains region. Data derived from this series were essential for testing assumptions about the prehistoric and protohistoric populations of South Dakota, and, by implication, adjacent areas. However, the Over Museum materials, by themselves, were numerically inadequate for most comparative research because of small sample sizes and the restricted spatial and temporal distribution. To investigate adequately questions about human history and adaptation on the Plains required a great deal of additional information. For the Northern Plains, this problem was partially resolved by including data from other sites, primarily those excavated as part of the River Basin Surveys program. The data sets are complementary and their combination enhanced the usefulness of both, for the River Basin Survey collections, without the Over Museum specimens, provided neither the spatial and temporal coverage nor the sample sizes needed for comprehensive bioarchaeological research.

The synthesis presented in this volume demonstrates the breadth and the methodological and technological progress of current physical anthropological research on prehistoric and protohistoric populations of the Great Plains. The general theme is Plains Indian skeletal biology, with topical emphasis on demography, paleopathology, origins, growth and development, behavior and activity patterns, subsistence strategies and dietary assessments, intertribal warfare, and the effects of Euro-American contact. The chapters are organized by topic into five major sections:

1. Archaeological Provenance and Burial Archaeology
2. Demography and Paleopathology
3. Biological Distance Relationships and Population Variation in Cranial and Postcranial Measurements
4. Subsistence Strategies and Dietary Assessments
5. Warfare on the Plains

Most papers concern Northern Plains groups, although new data derived from Central and Southern Plains samples are also presented. Furthermore, osteological research in the Great Plains is not solely limited to Native American history and biology. Direct European contact occurred earlier than historic documentation indicates, as evidenced by the identification of a Euro-American skeleton in an early eighteenth-century Native American cemetery. Migration and adaptation to the harsh Plains environment rigorously challenged later arrivals, as the study of nineteenth-century frontiersmen and Mormon farmers shows.

The first chapter in each section provides background information and introduces the chapters that follow. The authors are Donald Ortner (Part 2), Richard L. Jantz (Part 3), Larry Tieszen (Part 4), and Clayton Robarchek (Part 5). The closing chapter, by Douglas Ubelaker, is an overview that highlights the contributions of this volume. As an editor of a volume on Plains osteological research (Jantz and Ubelaker 1981), he provides perspective by noting the changes and developments in this field during the ensuing decade. For example, new analytical methods have radically changed research in skeletal biology and at a remarkable pace; hypotheses can be tested now with increasingly complex and innovative research designs.

Part 1 contains three papers that provide a foundation for the entire volume. The chapters by Donald Blakeslee and Robert Brooks discuss the ecological and sociocultural context, including chronology and cultural affiliations of the sites referenced in later papers, and introduce basic themes of this volume, such as subsistence, migrations, and warfare. The maps and tables they contain serve as reference for the entire volume.

Blakeslee undertook the formidable task of determining the cultural affiliations of the samples from the Over Museum Collection. At the beginning of this project, the archaeological context of these samples was poorly documented. Over was not a trained archaeologist, and, although his work compares well with that of his contemporaries, the records he kept are scanty by modern standards. As was common in early fieldwork (Stewart 1969), Over gave curatorial preference to the best specimens, that is, to crania and to adults. He did not keep all the skeletal remains he uncovered, only the better preserved or "more interesting" ones.

From Over's field notes, Blakeslee was able to extract the information that described individual or multiple interments in relation to type of burial (i.e., primary or secondary), placement of the body (burial position), orientation, presence of grave goods, and completeness (i.e., entire skeleton, partial,

skull only). His review alerted the team to potential biases created by preferential collecting and curatorial practices. Moreover, determination of the cultural and temporal affiliations of the sites was essential, as several studies reported here use statistical models that require a priori grouping of the specimens. Without knowledge of the archaeological parameters, such grouping would have been impossible. Specific information checked included site number and name (several were listed incorrectly in the original files), cultural affiliation, age, location of collections of artifacts, and presence of datable materials.

The skeletal biology of prehistoric populations in the Southern Plains is less well known or documented than that of those in the Northern Plains; the samples are smaller and fewer in number, and they have received less study (Owsley 1989; Owsley, Marks, and Manhein 1989). A comprehensive database is needed to facilitate analysis and enable comparison with Central and Northern Plains groups (Owsley and Jantz 1989). Brooks's review of Southern Plains cultural complexes provides the archaeological background essential for this research.

Knowledge of mortuary practices in the Northern Plains is limited, especially for certain time periods (cf. Lehmer 1971; Ludwickson, Blakeslee, and O'Shea 1981). There is some evidence for exposure of human remains prior to burial among Plains Middle Woodland groups (O'Brien 1971). Primary and, especially, secondary interments characterized the Woodland period Sonota complex, and cuts on the bones indicate that skeletonization was hastened by dissection (Bass and Phenice 1975). Archaeological data for Coalescent tradition burials have been reported for a few sites such as the Larson, Leavenworth, and Sully cemeteries (Bass, Evans, and Jantz 1971; O'Shea 1981, 1984). Some ethnohistorical accounts of burial practices are available (Orser 1980a, 1980b, 1983). The Arikara, for example, characteristically practiced primary inhumation, though occasionally there was exposure prior to burial (Ubelaker and Willey 1978). O'Shea (1984) has reported evidence of purposeful disarticulation of some skeletons among the historic Pawnee, Arikara, and Omaha. The Mandan and Hidatsa created circles of skulls as shrines to the dead of each clan.

In general, however, evidence for the intervening 1.5 millennia (i.e., Woodland to Historic) is cloudy. In the Central Plains there were charnel houses (Blakeslee and Caldwell 1979), but the pattern in the Northern Plains is not known. It is quite possible that exposure was practiced continuously in this region but that archaeologists simply have not noticed the evidence for it. In fact, potentially recoverable data from skeletons and associated artifacts that would provide information about prehistoric burial customs have received little attention. The last chapter in Part 1 is an outstanding exception that serves as a model for future investigations.

Signe Snortland's chapter uses archaeological, ethnographic, and osteological data to investigate patterning and complexity of the Jamestown Mounds site (32SN22). The approach is systematic; she begins by describing observed burial practices of the historic tribes, thus providing the foundation necessary for formal analysis and interpretation of the archaeological and osteological data. The results clearly show the benefits of interdisciplinary research and the need for precise control of stratigraphic and horizontal provenance and temporal context. Although the details are specific to this site, the broader significance of this report lies in its implications for the validity of the Woodland mound complexes that have been defined previously on the basis of generalized archaeological observations.

Examination of the Over Collection and the completion of this volume are part of a systematic research plan to link all data sets—archaeological, ethnohistorical, and osteological—to achieve a better understanding of the history and skeletal biology of the early populations of the Plains. To compile this volume, we drew on the expertise of an impressive array of specialists in Plains ethnohistory, archaeology, and physical anthropology. Although their contributions represent significant achievements in Plains studies, we must emphasize that the reburial of the W.H. Over Museum Collection has limited further progress in tracing Northern Plains prehistory. The deaccessioning of this and other major research collections will ultimately deprive humanity in general, and Native Americans in particular, of the potential medical, cultural, and other benefits that research on these remains could have produced.

We were grateful for the opportunity to conduct the final examination of the Over Collection and regret the loss of this same opportunity for future generations of researchers. Scientific methodology is founded on the principle of repeatability and validation. Moreover, advances in theory, methodology, and biotechnology have greatly increased the precision, variety, and quality of the information that can be derived from the human skeleton. New insights can be obtained by reexamining old collections with new techniques or by asking different questions that develop as new findings emerge. This natural progression is implicit in many of the chapters in this volume, for example, in information gained by reexamination of the Fay Tolton skeletal sample by Hollimon and Owsley and of bone pathology in a child from the Cotter-Hutson site reported by Mann, Owsley, and Reinhard.

The value of reexamination is most forcefully illustrated by the Four Bear remains, one of the larger skeletal samples of the Over Collection. This site on the Cheyenne River Indian Reservation was excavated by field crews that included Native Americans during the summers of 1958 and 1959 (Hurt et al. 1962). Permission had been given by the landowner, and the superintendent of the reservation offered use of the Four Bear schoolhouse as a field headquarters. The final report provided basic osteological information about the skeletal sample, including age and sex, burial positions and orientations, and some cranial measurements. By the standards of the time, this descriptive information was considered adequate, but by modern standards it is quite limited. If the burial sample had been reinterred in the 1960s, our perceptions of village demography and mortuary practices would depend on this inadequate documentation.

Data collection began with the inventory of each skeleton to determine bones present and age and sex. The results were quite different from those of the earlier study. For example, according to Hurt et al. (1962), the sample excavated in 1959 contained 42 individuals. The later analysis showed that the correct count is 51. In the first analysis, eight burials had not been recognized among commingled remains. Most of these were the remains of small children and infants, a discrepancy that reflects a basic philosophical difference in the two studies. In the 1960s the skeletal remains of children were neglected; in the 1990s such remains are essential for studies in paleodemography, paleopathology, and growth and development. The recognition and sorting of these additional subadult remains changed the mortality distribution considerably, which in turn affected interpretations based on this information.

There were other discrepancies as well. Sex assignments for Four Bear adults aged older than 15 years agreed in seven cases and differed in nine, including two individuals not assigned sex by Hurt et al. Hurt generally assessed questionable specimens as male. However, female skeletons from the Northern Plains can be rather robust, and misidentification likely. Through reexamination, some errors could be corrected because of greater experience, as well as the availability of improved craniometric and postcraniometric reference standards for the determination of sex that were not available in 1962. Furthermore, age assessments of adults were often inaccurate, and the ages of children were reported only as infant or child. New and refined techniques led to corrections and to new information. When collections are reburied, such an opportunity to restudy, revise, and correct as new techniques are developed is lost, and with it the potential for better understanding of Native American history, health, and culture.

References Cited

Bass, W.M.

1981 Skeletal Biology on the United States Great Plains: A History and Personal Narrative. *Plains Anthropologist Memoir* 17:3–18.

——, D.R. Evans, and R.L. Jantz

1971 The Leavenworth Site Cemetery: Archaeology and Physical Anthropology. *University of Kansas Publications in Anthropology* 2.

——, and T.W. Phenice

1975 Prehistoric Human Skeletal Material from Three Sites in North and South Dakota. Pp. 106–140 in The Sonota Complex and Associated Sites on the Northern Great Plains. R.W. Neuman, ed. *Nebraska State Historical Society Publications in Anthropology* 6.

Blakeslee, D.J., and W.W. Caldwell

1979 The Nebraska Phase: An Appraisal. Lincoln, Neb.: J & L Reprint Company.

Hurt, W.R.

1957 The Swan Creek Site 39WW7 Walworth County, South Dakota. Pierre, S. Dak.: Reminder.

——, Jr., W.G. Buckles, E. Fugle, and G.A. Agogino

1962 Report of the Investigations of the Four Bear Site, 39DW2, Dewey County, South Dakota. *University of South Dakota Archaeological Studies, Circular* 10.

Jantz, R.L., and D.H. Ubelaker

1981 Progress in Skeletal Biology of Plains Populations. *Plains Anthropologist Memoir* 17:43–48.

Key, P.J.

1983 Craniometric Relationships Among Plains Indians. *University of Tennessee, Department of Anthropology Report of Investigations* 34.

Lehmer, D.J.

1971 Introduction to Middle Missouri Archaeology. *U.S. Department of the Interior, National Park Service, Anthropological Papers* 1.

Ludwickson, J.K, D.J. Blakeslee, and J.M. O'Shea

1981 Missouri National Recreational River: Native American Cultural Resources. Omaha, Neb.: U.S. Army Corps of Engineers.

O'Brien, P.J.

1971 Valley Focus Mortuary Practices. *Plains Anthropologist* 16:165–182.

Orser, C.E., Jr.

1980a Relating James Mackay's "Indian Tribes" to Archaeological Manifestations of Arikara Mortuary Practices. *South Dakota Archaeology* 4:45–54.

——

1980b Toward a Partial Understanding of Complexity in Arikara Mortuary Practice. *Plains Anthropologist* 25:113–120.

——

1983 The Explorer as Ethnologist: James MacKay's "Indian Tribes" Manuscript with a Test of His Comments on the Native Mortuary Customs of the Trans-Mississippi West. *Ethnohistory* 30:15–34.

O'Shea, J.M.

1981 Social Configurations and Archaeological Study of Mortuary Practices: A Case Study. Pp. 63–88 in The Archaeology of Death. R. Chapman, K. Randsborg, and I. Kinnes, eds. Cambridge: Cambridge University Press.

——

1984 Mortuary Variability: An Archaeological Assessment. Orlando, Fla.: Academic Press.

Over, W.H., and E.E. Meleen

1941 A Report on an Investigation of the Brandon Village Site and the Split Rock Creek Mounds. *University of South Dakota Archaeological Studies Circular* 3.

Owsley, D.W.

1981 Mobridge Site Cemeteries: Controversy Concerning the Location of the Over and Stirling Burials. *Plains Anthropologist Memoir* 17:43–48.

——

1989 The History of Bioarcheological Research in the Southern Great Plains. Pp. 123–136 in From Clovis to Comanchero: Archeological Overview of the Southern Great Plains. J.L. Hofman, R.L. Brooks, J.S. Hays, D.W. Owsley, R.L. Jantz, M.K. Marks, and M.H. Manhein, eds. *Arkansas Archeological Survey Research Series* 35.

——, and R.L. Jantz

1989 A Systematic Approach to the Skeletal Biology of the Southern Plains. Pp. 137–156 in From Clovis to Comanchero: Archeological Overview of the Southern Great Plains. J.L. Hofman, R.L. Brooks, J.S. Hays, D.W. Owsley, R.L. Jantz, M.K. Marks, and M.H. Manhein, eds. *Arkansas Archeological Survey Research Series* 35.

——, M.K. Marks, and M.H. Manhein

1989 Human Skeletal Samples in the Southern Great Plains. Pp. 111–122 in From Clovis to Comanchero: Archeological Overview of the Southern Great Plains. J.L. Hofman, R.L. Brooks, J.S. Hays, D.W. Owsley, R.L. Jantz, M.K. Marks, and M.H. Manhein. *Arkansas Archeological Survey Research Series* 35.

——, G.D. Slutzky, M.F. Guagliardo, and L.M. Deitrick

1981 Interpopulation Relationships of Four Post-contact Coalescent Sites from South Dakota: Four Bear (39DW2), Oahe Village (39HU2), Stony Point Village (39ST235) and Swan Creek (39WW7). *Plains Anthropologist Memoir* 17:31–42.

——, and S.A. Symes

1981 Morphological Differences between Mandan and Historic Arikara Crania. *Plains Anthropologist Memoir* 17:49–56.

Puscharich, C.L.

1984 Metric Variation in the Arikara Pelvis. (Unpublished Ph.D. Dissertation in Anthropology, University of Tennessee, Knoxville.)

Sigstad, J.S., and J.K. Sigstad

1973   Archaeological Field Notes of W.H. Over. *South Dakota State Archaeologist Research Bulletin* 1.

Stewart, T.D.

1969   The Effects of Pathology on Skeletal Populations. *American Journal of Physical Anthropology* 30:443–450.

Thiessen, T.D.

1992   A History of the River Basin Survey and Missouri Basin Project Work Along the Missouri River. (Paper presented in the Symposium Missouri River Archaeology Protection Enhancement Considerations, Corps of Engineers, Omaha District Office, Omaha, Neb.)

Ubelaker, D.H., and P. Willey

1978   Complexity in Arikara Mortuary Practice. *Plains Anthropologist* 23:69–74.

Wedel, W.R.

1955   Archeological Materials from the Vicinity of Mobridge, South Dakota. *Bureau of American Ethnology Bulletin* 157.

Zobeck, T.S.

1983   Postcraniometric Variation among the Arikara. (Unpublished Ph.D. Dissertation in Anthropology, University of Tennessee, Knoxville.)

○ ○ ○

CHAPTER 2

The Archaeological Context
of Human Skeletons in the
Northern and Central Plains

DONALD J. BLAKESLEE

This chapter provides information about the cultural framework that yielded the human remains reported in this volume. It begins with a discussion of the theoretical problems involved in relating archaeological units to biological populations and with equating either of these to linguistic groups or sociocultural units. A sketch of the culture-historical framework introduces the time periods, climatic sequences, and geographic and cultural units. Finally, three basic themes that run throughout the volume—migrations, warfare, and subsistence—are discussed in terms of the archaeological evidence.

Theory

Before discussing what the archaeological units are, it is necessary to emphasize what they are not. Archaeologists and others commonly assume that they can equate archaeological units with societies, language units, or biological populations. This assumption is sometimes explicit, more often tacit, and quite frequently wrong. It begins with the "one society = one language" model critiqued so successfully by Hymes (1968) and adds to it assumptions of archaeological and biological

unity. The problem is compounded by combining the resulting "one society = one language = one biological population = one archaeological unit" to the tree model derived originally from philology.

The problem with the tree model is that it does not work for populations within a single species, for the historic tribes of the Plains, nor even very well for historic linguistics. The more or less continuous divergence implied by the tree model may apply to separate species, but so long as there is the possibility of gene flow between populations of a single species, there is also the possibility of biological convergence between them. For the human populations considered in this volume, a braided stream with various channels that repeatedly separate and reconverge provides a better metaphor.

For the historically documented tribes of the Plains, the tree model is hopelessly inadequate. It assumes that these political units formed by splitting from previous larger groupings. Where historic evidence is available, it points instead to tribal formation through fusion of previously independent bands and villages (Blakeslee 1975:219–225; Moore 1988).

Archaeologists are usually not cognizant of the shortcomings of the tree model in reconstructing linguistic history for their purposes. The model implies that the farther back in time one goes, the smaller the number of language groups one will find. Archaeological evidence, on the other hand, indicates that far back in time, social units were small and the communication among them limited. In such a situation, one would expect to find a great deal of linguistic diversity, not the small amount implied by unthinking use of the tree model. The problem arises because the model cannot take into account missing data—language groups that failed to survive into the historic period. A prehistorian pondering what the linguistic affiliations of an archaeological complex might have been should (but seldom does) consider that it might have been ancestral to no living language at all. Nor does he or she take into account that language replacement can take place without population replacement (Hymes 1968:39).

There is an even more basic archaeological problem: are the archaeological complexes defined well enough to allow culture-historical reconstruction? This is not the case for the burial complexes of the Northern Plains. The Sonota, Arvilla, and Devils Lake–Sourisford burial complexes are archaeological units that lack any definable cultural, political, biological, or linguistic correlates because the mounds in terms of which they were defined are accretional entities that contain the remains of several groups ("Northern Plains Woodland Mortuary Practices," this vol.). Some collections from mound sites in eastern South Dakota have sometimes been classed as Arvilla (W.H. Over State Museum, Vermillion, S.Dak.), but they contain interments of varying ages that are completely lacking in diagnostic grave offerings. They may be lumped into a unit called "Woodland B" not because they represent a single cultural or temporal entity, but merely because they share a single geographic location.

Even when the archaeological units are more appropriately defined, problems still arise. The Middle Missouri tradition gave rise in the historic period to the three bands that united to form the Mandan tribe (Ludwickson, Blakeslee, and O'Shea 1987:36) and one but not the other two of the bands that created the Hidatsa tribe (Stan Ahler, personal communication 1988). The Coalescent tradition seems to be primarily the remains of the Caddoan-speaking Arikara, but the only known village remains of the Algonquian-speaking Cheyenne (Wood 1971) and Siouan-speaking Omaha and Ponca (Howard 1970; Wood 1965) also belong to it.

Even when the archaeological units are appropriately defined, there is also the problem of sorting individual remains from multicomponent sites. The Ashland site, Nebraska, may be one example. Given the archaeological remains from the site, there is a possibility that the ossuary contains Nebraska

phase and perhaps Pawnee as well as Oneota skeletons. The Jones-Wynot and Ryan sites are known to contain human remains from several components. Most of the material from Jones-Wynot is of Saint Helena phase affiliation; the one historic skeleton is assumed to be of Omaha affiliation. Some archaeologists feel that the crania from the Ponca Fort site, Nebraska, that Jantz (1974) identified as Arikara may derive instead from the Saint Helena population that occupied the region earlier and whose ceramics were found at the site (John K. Ludwickson, personal communication 1989).

Finally, even when there is no mixing of components, the skeletal collection from a site should not be confused with a breeding population. The skeletal samples from each site are therefore samples (and not necessarily representative ones) of the breeding population.

What all this means is that there sometimes may be one-to-one relationships between polity, language, biological population, and archaeological unit, but these must always be demonstrated, not assumed.

The Culture-Historical Framework

TIME PERIODS

The temporal divisions listed in table 1 provide a framework within which the cultural sequences of both the northern and central Plains may be discussed. The table follows tradition in dividing the temporal sequence using cultural criteria (cf. Stoltman 1978:705). The only novelty is the subdivision of one of the periods into two units.

Finding a single set of terms to apply to both subareas required arbitrary decisions, as terminology varies from state to state. In Kansas, for instance, Middle Ceramic is the term applied to the period known elsewhere as Woodland. Here, the more widely used term, Woodland, is employed.

Regional differences in terminology can also arise from the existence of fundamentally different sequences. This is the case for the subdivisions of the Archaic, where very different sequences in the northwestern Plains (Frison 1978:40–62) and southeastern Plains (Chapman 1975:127–224) have led to the adoption of different definitions for Early, Middle, and Late Archaic (table 1).

A similar problem affects the subdivisions of the Woodland period. Most of the Woodland record falls into the Middle and Late Woodland periods. With a few notable exceptions, there are no well-documented equivalents of the Early Woodland complexes found farther east. Furthermore, from about the Kansas–Nebraska border south, there appear to be no clear

Table 1. Time Periods for the Northern and Central Plains

Paleo-Indian	10,000–5500 B.C.
Archaic	
Northwestern Plains	
Early	5500–2900 B.C
Middle	2900–1100 B.C.
Late	1100 B.C.–A.D. 500
Southeastern Plains	
Early	7000–5000 B.C.
Middle	5000–3000 B.C.
Late	3000–1000 B.C.
Woodland	
Early	1000–50 B.C.
Middle	50 B.C.–A.D. 350
Early Late	A.D. 350–700
Late Late	A.D. 700–950
Plains Village	
Plains Village 1	A.D. 950–1250
Plains Village 2	A.D. 1250–1700
Historic	A.D. 1700

equivalents of the Late Late Woodland complexes found in Iowa, Nebraska, and South Dakota. In Kansas, therefore, the period usually is not subdivided. The Early Late and Late Late subdivisions also have not been applied to the Northeastern Periphery, where a different Woodland tradition exists. Even though they do not apply to the whole region considered here, Benn's (1983) Early Late and Late Late subdivisions of the Woodland period are used because they allow a more precise delineation of the temporal affiliation of some of the sites discussed in this volume.

The Plains Village period is divided into two temporal units to reflect an important cultural distinction. Plains Village 1 is the time of strong cultural influences from the Mississippian center at Cahokia. The nature of the influences varied from place to place, but they are both widespread and important (Alex 1981; Anderson 1987:528; Blakeslee and Caldwell 1979; Blakeslee and Rohn 1986; Hall 1967; Henning 1967; Johnson 1973; O'Brien 1978; Wedel 1943). In the Northern Plains, Plains Village 1 is equivalent to Tiffany's (1983) Early Period. In Plains Village 2, Mississippian influences decline, and a different dynamic operates. Some complexes, such as the Nebraska phase, begin in Plains Village 1 and persist into Plains Village 2.

The Historic period is usually defined as the epoch in which historical documentation is available. Nominally the historic period on the Plains begins with the Francisco Vásquez de Coronado expedition of 1541, but documentation is both extremely scanty and time-transgressive within the area. While

recorded history began in 1541 in Kansas, it waits until 1738 in North Dakota, when Vérendrye visited the Mandan (Smith 1980). The protohistoric is usually defined as the interval between the first presence of contact material in archaeological sites and the first historic documentation of sites. It is also time-transgressive, with European trade goods appearing earlier in some regions than in others. Thus while a distinction is made between protohistoric and historic status for individual sites, the historic period defined here begins about 1700.

CLIMATIC SEQUENCE

The dominant model of Holocene climate change in the Plains is that developed by Reid Bryson and his associates

Table 2. Bryson's Climatic Sequence for the Plains

Episode	Dates	Climatic Regime
Full Glacial	?–11,050 B.C.	Cool summers, mild winters
Late Glacial	11,050–8850 B.C.	Same seasonality; a few degrees cooler than today
Pre-Boreal	8850–7580 B.C.	
Boreal	7580–5950 B.C.	Warmer summers, colder winters
Atlantic	5950–3050 B.C.	The Altithermal: drier and warmer than today
Sub-Boreal	3050–950 B.C.	Cooler in Northern Plains, drier in western Nebraska
Sub-Atlantic	950 B.C.–A.D. 350	Wetter summers, possibly stormier winters
Scandic	A.D. 350–900	Warmer; probably drier on the Northern Plains
Neo-Atlantic	A.D. 900–1150	Warmer and moister than today; wetter summers in Northern and Central Plains
Pacific I	A.D. 1150–1450	Drier, cooler in Northern and Central Plains
Pacific II	A.D. 1450–1550	Some amelioration of dryness
Neo-Boreal	A.D. 1550–1850	Colder and moister; cool summers and cold autumns
Recent	A.D. 1850–present	Modern climate

(Baerreis and Bryson 1965; Bryson, Baerreis, and Wendland 1970; Bryson and Wendland 1967; Wendland and Bryson 1974). While the details of his proposed climatic sequence have been questioned (Blakeslee 1983a, 1983b) and there are questions regarding the ways in which it has been used and abused by archaeologists, it is included here (table 2) because so many interpretations of prehistoric subsistence, migration, warfare, and health are based on it.

SPATIAL UNITS

In archaeological parlance, the Plains area is generally divided into three subareas: the Northern, Central, and Southern Plains. The dividing line between the northern and central units is generally placed at the Nebraska–South Dakota border, while the border between the Central and Southern Plains is set at the southern margin of the Kansas River system (Witty 1978). While spatial units in the Willey and Phillips (1958) system are supposed to be defined in geographic and not cultural terms, the subarea boundaries actually have been drawn where major cultural borders occur during the Plains Village period.

Within the Northern Plains subarea, three named regions exist. They are the Middle Missouri, Northwestern Plains, and Northeastern Periphery. The Middle Missouri region consists of the trench of the Missouri River from the Nebraska–South Dakota border to the North Dakota–Montana border. This definition adds the area of the Fort Randall reservoir to the Middle Missouri. Its prior omission (Lehmer 1971:26) was one of convenience; little archaeological work had been accomplished in the Fort Randall area prior to flooding of the reservoir, and the affiliations of some of what had been found was confusing. Extending west from the Middle Missouri region to the Rocky Mountains and northward into Canada is the Northwestern Plains. The Northeastern Periphery consists of the eastern Dakotas, the western prairie region of Minnesota, and the prairie portions of Manitoba and Saskatchewan.

Subdivisions of the Central Plains are those defined by Krause (1969:84–87). They are the High Plains of western Kansas and Nebraska and eastern Colorado and southeastern Wyoming, the Sand Hills of western Nebraska, the Loess Plains of central Nebraska and Kansas, and the Eastern Glaciated region of eastern Nebraska, westernmost Iowa, northeastern Kansas, and northwestern Missouri. The archaeology of the Southern Plains subarea is discussed in "Southern Plains Cultural Complexes," this volume.

THE CULTURE-HISTORICAL UNITS

The culture-historical units reviewed here are limited to those that pertain directly to the skeletal samples discussed in this volume (figs. 1–3). Readers may find summaries of the Paleo-Indian and Archaic complexes of the region elsewhere (Brown and Simmons 1987; Chapman 1975; Frison 1978). Terminological confusion exists in the literature, with some units listed as phases while equivalent units are termed variants or foci; the definitions overlap.

Only a few scattered Early Woodland sites have been excavated in the Plains area; they have yielded no human remains (table 3).

Kansas City Hopewell, found in northwestern Missouri and northeastern Kansas, is the only Middle Woodland unit discussed in this volume that exhibits strong evidence of having participated in the Hopewellian Interaction Sphere. Even so, the evidence suggests that it was peripheral to the more easterly complexes involved (Johnson 1979:90–92). The Cuesta phase (Marshall 1972; Brogan 1981), in southeastern Kansas, exhibits a different expression of Hopewell, but other Middle Woodland period units west to the Rocky Mountains generally lack such evidence, although ceramics with Middle Woodland motifs are found in a few sites of several units.

The non-Hopewellian Middle Woodland units are marked by tall subconical vessels with vertical or oblique cord-marking on the exterior surface and occasionally with horizontal cord-marking (sometimes mistaken for fabric impression) on the interior surface. Large corner-notched, side-notched, and stemmed points and the occasional boatstone suggest the use of the atlatl and dart as the primary weapon. Sites are oriented to secondary streams, and they tend to be small. The Fox Lake phase (Anfinson 1979:79) may have contributed some of the skeletons found in the W.H. Over Museum collection from northeastern South Dakota.

The Early Late Woodland was defined (Benn 1983) on the basis of three sites in Iowa and Nebraska. No phases have yet been defined for the time period in that region, but several Kansas complexes fall primarily into this time slot. They are the Grasshopper Falls phase (Reynolds 1979), the habitation sites assigned to the Schultz phase (O'Brien 1984), and the Hertha phase (Blakeslee and Rohn 1986). The same is also true of some of the post–Kansas City Hopewell sites treated by Johnson (1987), but six of the 15 sites in his sample are of Pomona, not Woodland, affiliation (cf. Brown and Simmons 1987:XIII-38). The Wolf Creek Mound skeletal remains in the W.H. Over Museum also belong to the Early Late Woodland.

Fig. 1. Selected archaeological sites in Iowa, Missouri, and Nebraska.

Early Late Woodland pottery tends to have thinner walls and more distinct shoulders than Middle Woodland wares, but overall vessel form and decorative techniques do not change much in the Central Plains. The appearance of small corner-notched points suggests the introduction of the bow and arrow, an event that Johnson (1976:14) dates about A.D. 500 in the Kansas City locality. Sites appear to be fairly ephemeral, and in the Kansas City locality, this contrasts strongly with the earlier Kansas City Hopewell pattern (Johnson 1987:395–396).

The Late Late Woodland period is marked by the introduction of cord-impressed decorative techniques in the northeastern portion of the area discussed here. They are missing from the western two-thirds of Nebraska and all of Kansas. Whether this marks a cultural boundary or whether there was a cultural hiatus over much of the region is an open question. Richard Krause (personal communication 1990) has identified some materials from north-central Kansas that belong to this period. Those ceramics lack the distinctive cord-impressed decoration found in Nebraska, Iowa, and South Dakota. In the

Northeastern Periphery, cord-wrapped stick impressions and punctates are hallmarks of Late Woodland, which is not subdivided into early and late periods.

Late Late Woodland vessels are thin walled and more globular than their predecessors, with better-defined shoulders. Bases remain subconoidal, and rims are still high compared to Plains Village rims. In Great Oasis, narrow trailed lines are used to produce some of the same motifs that are made with twisted cord impressions in Loseke Creek.

Lightly built structures predominate, but long rectangular houses are found at some Great Oasis sites (Henning 1971:128). Both corner-notched and side-notched arrow points are found. Sites on low terraces, on lakeshores, and high on secondary streams are known.

Late Late Woodland units include the Loseke Creek phase (Kivett 1952; Ludwickson, Blakeslee, and O'Shea 1987), the Sterns Creek phase (Haas 1980), Great Oasis (Ludwickson, Blakeslee, and O'Shea 1987:133–140), and the Lake Benton phase (Anfinson 1979). The unit called Truman ("Relation-

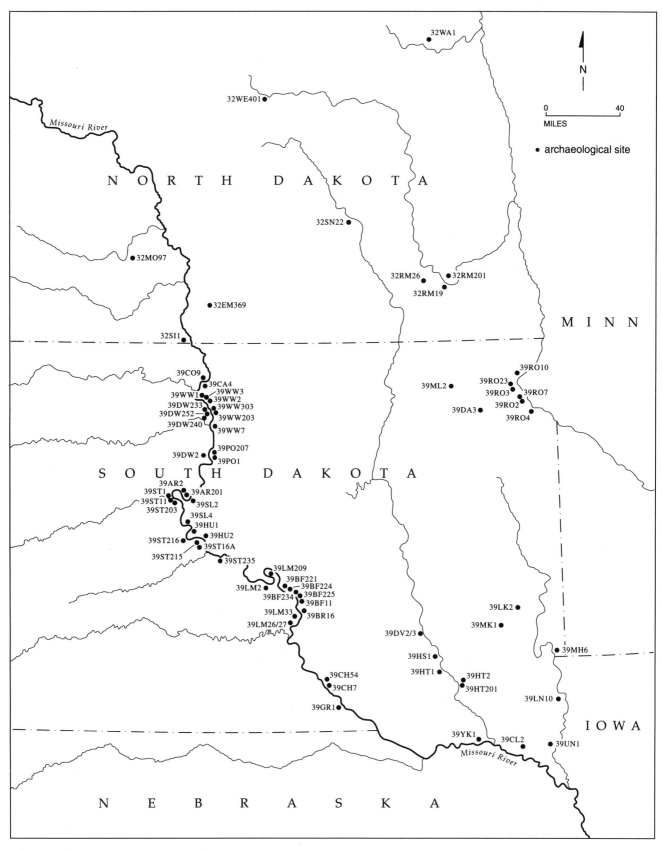

Fig. 2. Selected archaeological sites in North Dakota and South Dakota.

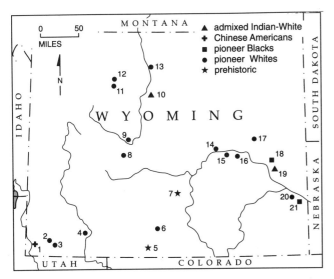

Fig. 3. Selected archaeological sites in Wyoming. 1, Red Mountain; 2, Little Muddy River; 3, Fort Bridger; 4, Green River Soldier; 5, Robber's Gulch; 6, Divide Burial; 7, Bairoil; 8, Harvey Morgan; 9, Fremont County; 10, Washakie; 11, Cody Pipe; 12, Blind Bill and Gallagher; 13, Shell; 14, Fort Casper; 15, Quintina Snoderly; 16, Glenrock; 17, Bates Creek; 18, Shawnee Creek; 19, Glendo; 20, Korell-Bordeaux; 21, Rock Ranch.

Table 3. Culture-Historical Units of the Woodland Period

Early Woodland	
Fox Lake phase	Anfinson 1979:79
Middle Woodland	
Kansas City Hopewell	Johnson 1979
Cuesta phase	Marshall 1972; Brogan 1981
Valley phase	Ludwickson, Blakeslee, and O'Shea 1987:121–125
Keith focus	Kivett 1952
Fox Lake phase	Anfinson 1979:79
Early Late Woodland	
Keith focus	Kivett 1952
Held Creek	Benn 1983
Greenwood phase	Witty 1982
Grasshopper Falls phase	Reynolds 1979
Late Late Woodland	
Loseke Creek phase	Ludwickson, Blakeslee, and O'Shea 1987:125–133
Lake Benton phase	Anfinson 1979:109
Sterns Creek phase	Haas 1980
Great Oasis	Ludwickson, Blakeslee, and O'Shea 1987:133–140

ships of the Woodland Period on the Northern and Central Plains: the Craniometric Evidence," this vol.) is a set of sites similar to the Truman Mound site (Neuman 1960), which is of Late Late Woodland affiliation. No archaeological taxon has been defined for it.

In the Plains Village and Historic periods, there are three cultural traditions in the Central and Northern Plains that are discussed in this volume. They are the Oneota, Middle Missouri, and Central Plains/Coalescent traditions (tables 4 and 5). Originally termed Upper Mississippian to reflect its geographic distribution, the Oneota tradition dominates the later prehistory of much of the upper Midwest. It extends from Missouri to Minnesota and from Illinois and Indiana to the eastern fringes of the Plains (Glenn 1974:24). The relationship of the western Oneota sites (including the Leary and Ashland sites) to the phases and horizons defined for the Prairie Peninsula is not well understood. The intrusive Oneota burials at the Hartley Fort site are of Plains Village 2 age and Orr phase affiliation (McKusick 1973:10).

Oneota sites are marked by a distinctive ceramic tradition in which the paste is usually shell tempered and the most common vessel form is a squat jar that often has trailed designs on the shoulder. Sites are fairly large villages, some of which contained long houses (McKusick 1973), although other house forms are also known (Hall 1962:17–18). Arrow points are usually of the plain triangular form, and catlinite disk pipes appear to be an Oneota invention. The direct historic approach has demonstrated that some Oneota sites are the remains of the Chiwere Siouan-speaking Iowa (Mott 1938) and Missouri (Berry and Chapman 1942), while others were left by the linguistically related Winnebago (Hall 1962; Lurie 1960). It has been suggested that both the Leary site and the Ashland site may have been created by the Chiwere-speaking Otoe (Mott 1938:277). The Dhegiha Siouan-speaking Osage (Chapman 1952:145) and Kansa (Wedel 1959) have also been tied to Oneota sites, but the known sites of the Omaha-Ponca, who also speak Dhegiha, are affiliated with the Coalescent tradition, and some late Otoe sites contain Pawnee pottery. The craniometric relationships of Oneota populations have been analyzed by Glenn (1974).

The line of cultural development that appears to have led to the Pawnee and Arikara has two names: the Central Plains tradition and the Coalescent tradition. The Central Plains tradition name applies to remains south of the Nebraska–South Dakota border and prior to the protohistoric period. The Coalescent tradition includes all the sites north of the border and all that are Protohistoric or later, regardless of location. Warren W. Caldwell (personal communication 1985) suggests dropping the term, Coalescent tradition, to reflect the continuity that exists between the two. Nevertheless, while

Table 4. Units of the Central Plains-Coalescent Tradition

Plains Village 1 Period	
Central Plains Tradition	
Nebraska phase	Blakeslee and Caldwell 1979
Smoky Hill phase	Steinacher 1976
Solomon River phase	Lippincott 1978
Classic Republican phase	Krause 1969
Related Units	
Steed-Kisker complex	O'Brien 1978
Pomona variant	Brown 1984
Plains Village 2 Period	
Central Plains Tradition	
Nebraska phase	Blakeslee and Caldwell 1979
Smoky Hill phase	Steinacher 1976
Itskari phase	Ludwickson 1978
St. Helena phase	Blakeslee 1988a
Initial Coalescent Variant	
Anoka focus	Witty 1962
Arzberger phase	Caldwell 1966
Campbell Creek phase	Smith 1977
Extended Coalescent Variant	
Shannon phase	Smith and Johnson 1968
Le Compte focus	Johnston and Hoffman 1966
La Roche focus	Hoffman 1968
Bennett focus	Stephenson 1954
Akaska focus	Hurt 1957
Historic Period	
Postcontact Coalescent Variant	
Felicia phase	Caldwell 1966; Lehmer 1971
Talking Crow phase	Lehmer and Caldwell 1966
Bad River phase	Lehmer and Jones 1968
Le Beau phase	Lehmer 1971
Heart River phase	Lehmer 1971
Lower Loup focus	Wedel 1938
Redbird focus	Wood 1965

Table 5. Units of the Middle Missouri Tradition

Early Period	
Chamberlain Variant	
Anderson phase	Lehmer 1954; Wood 1976
Grand Detour phase	Caldwell and Jensen 1969
Swanson phase	Hurt 1951; Johnson 1979
Mill Creek Variant	
Cambria phase	Knudson 1967
Big Stone phase	Haug 1981
Brandon phase	Over and Meleen 1941
Lower James phase	Alex 1981
Big Sioux phase	Henning 1968–1969
Little Sioux phase	Henning 1968–1969
Northern Extended Variant	
Clark's Creek phase	Calabrese 1972
Ft. Yates phase	Hurt 1953
Early Southern Extended Variant	
Sites in the Big Bend region	Johnson 1977
Middle Period	
Southern Extended Variant	
Thomas Riggs phase	Tiffany 1983
Northern Extended Variant	
Nailati phase	Calabrese 1972
Final Period	
Terminal Variant	
Huff phase	Lehmer 1971

some Coalescent tradition sites were created by the Arikara and Pawnee, the biological and ethnic identity of the people who created the Central Plains tradition has not been demonstrated.

Central Plains tradition sites consist of isolated farmsteads or small hamlets containing earthlodges. The pottery is mostly in the form of globular jars with direct or thickened rims. Vessels were shaped with cord-wrapped paddles, but the resulting cord-roughening was sometimes obliterated by smoothing. Artifact assemblages are substantial, indicating that sites were generally occupied for longer periods than in the preceding Woodland period. Subdivisions of the tradition in Plains Village 1 are the Nebraska phase (Blakeslee and Caldwell 1979), the Smoky Hill phase (Steinacher 1976), Solomon River Upper Republican (Lippincott 1978), and Classic Re-

publican (Krause 1969). Related but distinct units are Steed-Kisker (O'Brien 1978) and the Pomona Variant (Brown 1984). They differ from the phases of the Central Plains tradition in having less substantial dwellings and ceramics that fall outside the stylistic range of Central Plains tradition. In the case of Steed-Kisker, the pottery is of the Middle Mississippian tradition, while Pomona ceramics are an adaptation to the sub-soil clay resources of the Osage Plains (Blakeslee and Dunn 1988).

The Nebraska and Smoky Hill phases persist into Plains Village 2, and two new units, the Saint Helena (Blakeslee 1988) and Itskari (Ludwickson 1978) phases develop. The basic Central Plains lifeway continues, but changes in both lithic procurement and ceramic motifs suggest some sort of change in territoriality or boundary maintenance (Ludwickson, Blakeslee, and O'Shea 1987:161–166).

The Initial Coalescent variant begins with the intrusion of a substantial population from the Central Plains into northernmost Nebraska and along the Missouri River in South Dakota to the vicinity of Pierre. With the notable exception of the Lynch site, most work on the Initial Coalescent variant has been done in South Dakota, but preliminary reconnaissance survey indicates that there was a very substantial population along Ponca Creek in Nebraska (Steve Holen, personal communication 1987). Changes from the Central Plains tradition lifeway are limited to intense warfare, a change of house form from square with rounded corners to circular, and the addition of a few material culture traits such as grooved mauls and simple stamping on some vessels.

The Extended Coalescent variant dominated the Missouri River trench in South Dakota. A very large number of sites of this unit has been recorded, but Lehmer (1971:115) argues that the generally small size and short period of occupation of the sites have inflated the number. As might be expected with such a long linear territory, there is considerable variation within this unit, which should eventually be recognized by the definition of five or six phases.

A primary contrast between the Extended Coalescent and the Initial Coalescent is the difference in settlement patterns. Most Extended Coalescent sites are unfortified with widely spaced houses, suggestive of a return to the Central Plains tradition pattern. Most exceptions are located near the northern extremity of the Extended Coalescent territory and probably reflect episodic warfare with Middle Missouri tradition peoples who, by this time, had retreated into North Dakota. Most of these northern Extended Coalescent sites had a central fortified area to which people living in scattered houses over a wide area could flee (Lehmer 1971:116–118).

The Postcontact variant of the Coalescent tradition begins with the appearance of European trade items in the sites of the tradition. Lehmer (1971:163) offers A.D. 1675 as a beginning date, but this is merely an estimate. In the earliest protohistoric sites, there is a marked tendency for most of the trade goods to show up in burials rather than in the habitation area. Defined phases of the Postcontact Coalescent variant include Felicia (Caldwell 1966; Lehmer 1971), Talking Crow (Lehmer and Caldwell 1966), Bad River (Lehmer and Jones 1968; Hoffman 1977), Le Beau (Lehmer 1971; Lehmer and Caldwell 1966), and Heart River (Lehmer 1971). The last differs from the rest in being derived from the Middle Missouri tradition.

Protohistoric sites in the Central Plains are also assigned to the Coalescent tradition. One unit is the Redbird focus (Wood 1965), redefined as a phase by Ludwickson, Blakeslee, and O'Shea (1987:174–178). Located in northeastern Nebraska, these remains are usually assigned to the Ponca (Howard 1970; Jantz 1974; Wood 1965). The ceramics are distinct but nonetheless well within the ceramic range of the Coalescent tradition. Dwellings, which are oval to circular earthlodges, also fit the tradition, as do the nonceramic artifacts. The Ponca and the closely related Omaha were recent arrivals

in the eastern Plains, and their archaeological antecedents are not known.

The other expression of the Coalescent tradition in the Central Plains is the Lower Loup focus. Located in central Nebraska, with a few outlying sites in Kansas, this unit was demonstrated to be the cultural remains of the protohistoric Pawnee (Wedel 1938). Lower Loup is separated from the earlier Itskari phase by some sort of hiatus. The region where Lower Loup evolved from Itskari has not been documented.

The W.H. Over Museum collections included human remains from the Oacoma site, which is of Skiri band Pawnee affiliation. Ceramics from this site have Lower Loup affiliations, but the site, located in South Dakota, has generally been assigned as a somewhat aberrant member of the Talking Crow phase of the Post-contact Coalescent (Lehmer 1971:201–202). Its Skiri identity was discovered during documentary research on the Pierre-Antoine and Paul Mallet expedition of 1739 (Blakeslee 1988c). The historic dates for the site, about 1722–1750, correspond well with the archaeological age estimates for the Talking Crow phase of 1700–1750 (Lehmer 1971:202).

The Middle Missouri tradition is the cultural stream that eventually gave rise to the Mandan and Hidatsa of North Dakota. The brief summary offered here is drawn primarily from Tiffany (1983). The tradition is divided into three periods: Early, 900–1300; Middle, 1300–1550; and Late, 1550–1675.

Sites of the Early Period are scattered from eastern South Dakota and southwestern Minnesota to northwestern Iowa to the vicinity of the Black Hills. Originally, all the then-known South Dakota sites were placed in the Over focus (Over and Meleen 1941) and later in the Initial Middle Missouri variant (Lehmer 1971), while the Iowa sites were known as the Mill Creek culture. Tiffany (1983) has drawn the dividing line differently, with the Over focus sites along the Missouri River in the Chamberlain variant and the Minnesota, eastern South Dakota, and Iowa sites in the Mill Creek variant.

There are three phases of the Chamberlain variant (table 5). From north to south, they are the Anderson (Lehmer 1954), Grand Detour (Caldwell and Jensen 1969), and Swanson (Hurt 1951; Johnson 1979) phases. The Mill Creek variant includes the Lower James (Alex 1981), Brandon (Over and Meleen 1941), Cambria (Knudson 1967), and Big Sioux and Little Sioux (Henning 1968–1969) phases. There are some small fortified sites of this variant in northeastern South Dakota (Haug 1981) that have been placed in the Big Stone phase. The North Dakota state plan for archaeological preservation proposes a Northeastern Plains Village complex to account for all the Plains Village sites in the Northeastern Periphery and for associated burials now assigned to the Devils Lake–Sourisford burial complex (Signe Snortland, personal communication 1990). At least one Early Period Middle Missouri site has been reported from south of the Black Hills (Robert A. Alex, personal communication 1986), but no corresponding taxonomic unit has been established.

Early Period sites of both variants are compact villages, often fortified with a simple ditch and palisade. The houses in them are long rectangular semisubterranean structures. The villages often show evidence of lengthy habitation in the form of deep and extensive trash middens. Pottery vessels are plain or cord-roughened globular jars but are otherwise distinct from those of the Central Plains tradition. Rim forms include flaring and S-shaped types. Flat lips, sharp outer lip edges, and a sharp angle forming the neck interior set the wares of these phases apart from those of their neighbors.

The Extended Middle Missouri variant is found along the Missouri River in both North and South Dakota. There is a cluster of sites between the Bad and Cheyenne River that is separated by about 90 river miles from the rest of the sites, which extend from northernmost South Dakota to central North Dakota (Lehmer 1971:66). Only five sites, clustered between the Moreau and Grand Rivers, fill the gap. This distribution originally was reflected in the definition of two foci, Thomas Riggs in the south and Fort Yates in the north.

Archaeologists working in the area are not satisfied with Lehmer's original classification of the northern Middle Missouri sites. Stan Ahler (personal communication 1988) is developing a local sequence for the district encompassing the Knife and Heart Rivers that better reflects the local developments. All the Extended Middle Missouri sites discussed in this volume are from the southern set of sites, which Tiffany (1983) places in the Thomas Riggs phase of the Southern Extended variant. He sees it as the product of a merging of Chamberlain and Mill Creek variant peoples with some Northern Extended variant populations that were already living in the Big Bend region in Ealy Period times (Tiffany 1983:101).

Sites and houses of the Extended Middle Missouri variants were essentially like those of the Chamberlain and Mill Creek variants, but the fortification systems sometimes included bastions at intervals along the palisade (Caldwell 1964:2). Pottery vessels have simple stamped bodies, and the sharp edges of the Chamberlain and Mill Creek variants rims are missing. Arrow points of all Middle Missouri tradition variants differ slightly in shape from those of the Central Plains–Coalescent tradition in having the widest point above the side notches rather than below them.

In the Terminal Middle Missouri variant, the territorial distribution shrinks northward, with the most southerly site 10 miles below the North Dakota border. Sites of this variant are not especially numerous, but they tend to be large and well fortified. No Terminal sites are represented in the collections reported in this volume.

Following the Terminal variant, the Middle Missouri tradition was absorbed, at least taxonomically, into the (Postcontact) Coalescent tradition. The descendants of the Middle Missouri tradition continued to live apart from the more southerly populations, separated by a no man's land that spanned 100 river miles. However, in many details of material culture the two groups had indeed coalesced. All the Postcontact Coalescent populations discussed in this volume are from the southerly sites, presumably ancestral to the Arikara.

CHRONOLOGY

The dating of the cultural sequences is not precise enough to avoid interpretive confusion. The chronologies are based primarily on radiocarbon dating, with secondary reliance on stratigraphy, seriation, and dendrochronology.

The precision of radiocarbon dates is always overstated in laboratory reports. The counting error reported by them gives only the statistical uncertainty in the measurement of the single sample, not the total long-term error, which doubles the uncertainty (Taylor 1987). In real terms, about one date in three from the sites reported here should be in error by more than a century even without considering the effects of contamination, misassociation, prehistoric use of old wood, and so on.

None of the other techniques in general use has provided the desired precision, not even dendrochronology. The two pioneering attempts at applying this technique in the Plains (Weakly 1962; Will 1946) do not measure up to modern standards. The single attempt to apply modern methods (Weakly 1971) produced results that have not been accepted by the archaeologists who worked on the sites (cf. Caldwell and Snyder 1983). While ceramic seriation may have the potential to resolve some chronological questions, no one has yet demonstrated that it is possible to sequence accurately prehistoric sites that differ in age by only a decade or so.

A major effect of imprecise dating is that individual phases appear to last longer than they really did because the archaeologist cannot reject spuriously early and late dates. With the span of each phase so inflated, sequential phases appear to overlap in time (Ludwickson, Blakeslee, and O'Shea 1987: 204–208). Various scholars have proposed that Great Oasis and

Mill Creek (Henning 1981), Sterns Creek Woodland and Nebraska phase (Haas 1980), and Initial Coalescent and Initial Middle Missouri (Steinacher and Toom 1983) were contemporaneous occupants of their respective regions; others argue that they were sequential. Biometric data is one means to help resolve this problem, and Key's data ("Relationships of the Woodland Period on the Northern and Central Plains: The Craniometric Evidence," this vol.) show that Great Oasis and Mill Creek crania are very similar, which would seem to lend more support to the sequential model of their relationship than to a contemporaneous but separate cultures (and populations) model.

Table 6 lists the most important sites in the Northern and Central Plains that are discussed in this volume. The period and affiliation of the sites are provided for orientation.

Themes

MIGRATIONS

A seductively easy way to explain culture change in an archaeological sequence is to postulate that a migration occurred. For this reason and as a response to the obvious variability of the Plains climate, migration hypotheses are common in Plains archaeology.

The Woodland cultures of the Plains have antecedents in the Early Woodland complexes of the eastern woodlands, but this fact alone does not prove that they were founded by a migration or migrations from the east. Determination of their origins is confused somewhat by the incorrect assumption that any ceramics with Black Sand affinities always must be Early Woodland in age. This has affected, for instance, interpretations of the chronological placement of the Fox Lake phase of southwestern Minnesota (compare Bonney 1965, 1970 to Gibbon and Caine 1980).

The Woodland complex most likely to have derived from a migration is Kansas City Hopewell. From the beginning (Johnson 1979; Wedel 1943), the possibility of a founding migration has been given serious consideration. Judging from the ceramics, the most likely point of origin is somewhere in the vicinity of the Illinois River valley, but Stewart's original analysis of Kansas City crania showed them to be distinct from the Illinois River remains then available (Wedel 1943:219–220).

The Late Late Woodland complexes from Nebraska and South Dakota (Loseke Creek, Sterns Creek, Great Oasis) all have their closest cultural affinities to the east in Iowa, Minnesota, Illinois, and Wisconsin. This could mean that the populations that created the material remains were derived from the east.

There are several migration hypotheses concerning the origins of the Middle Missouri tradition. The first is the idea that the tradition as a whole is derived from a migration from the east. It is based on Mandan origin myths, which speak of coming from the east to the Missouri River in several movements (Bowers 1950:156–163). From an early date, the Middle Missouri tradition sites in eastern South Dakota (originally, the Over focus) were viewed as evidence for the migration (Over and Meleen 1941:2). This view presumes that the Middle Missouri populations were not descendants of earlier Woodland peoples, a position contradicted by craniometric data ("Relationships of the Woodland Period on the Northern and Central Plains: the Craniometric Evidence," this vol.).

Another migration hypothesis places the origin of the Mill Creek culture in a movement of people from the vicinity of Cahokia (Ruppé 1955:337). The rationale for this suggestion was the strong similarity between some Mill Creek ceramics and Cahokia types. However, the Mill Creek investigations demonstrated that the Cahokia-like material is not common early in the Mill Creek sequence (Henning 1968–1969:273–276). Therefore, it is likely that the Cahokian influences seen in the Mill Creek sequence reflect trade or other contact rather than population movement.

It has long been a tenet of Central Plains archaeology that there was a south to north movement of population during the Plains Village period. While there is definitely some truth to this, there is also an element of received knowledge. Gilder (1926) suggested that the Nebraska phase populations came from Mexico! While a Mexican origin has no merit whatsoever, the primary cultural descendants of the Central Plains tradition (the Pawnee and Arikara) speak Caddoan languages, and the other Caddoan languages are spoken in Oklahoma, Arkansas, Texas, and Louisiana. Hughes (1968) argues, however, that the presence of Caddoan speakers in the Plains is very ancient, and no one has offered any evidence to suggest that they entered the Plains at the beginning of Plains Village 1.

Roper (1976), in a paper that has become a classic in archaeological mathematics, used a trend-surface analysis of radiocarbon dates as evidence for a northward movement of people during this period. Her analysis has long been considered evidence for the northward movement of Plains Caddoans during Plains Village times. Since then Roper (1985) essentially retracted her original conclusions, pointing to problems in the original data.

Other expressions of the belief in a south to north movement are found in the works of Krause (1969), Calabrese

Table 6. Selected Archaeological Sites in the Northern and Central Plains[a]

Site	Name	Period	Affiliation
Iowa			
13AM103	Hartley Fort	Plains Village 2	Oneota
13PM1	Broken Kettle	Plains Village 1	Middle Missouri, Mill Creek, Big Sioux phase
13PM4	Kimball	Plains Village 1	Middle Missouri, Mill Creek, Big Sioux phase
13PW1	Council Bluffs Ossuary	Woodland or Plains Village	Woodland or Central Plains, Nebraska phase
13PW18	Haven	Middle Woodland	
13WB215	Pooler	Late Archaic to Plains Village	Mixed
Missouri			
23PL21	Pearl Mound Group	Middle Woodland	Kansas City Hopewell
23PL120	Young Mound I	Middle Woodland	Kansas City Hopewell
Nebraska			
25BO7	Loretto	Plains Village	Central Plains tradition?
25BU1	Linwood	Historic	Pawnee
25BU2	Bellwood	Historic	Pawnee
25BU4	Barcal	Protohistoric	Postcontact Coalescent, Lower Loup
25CC1	Ashland	Plains Village 2	Central Plains tradition, Nebraska phase
25CC1	Ashland	Protohistoric	Oneota
25CC62	—	—	—
25CD4	Wiseman Mounds	Plains Village 2	Central Plains tradition, St. Helena
25CD7	Jones/Wynot	Historic	Omaha?
25CD7	Jones/Wynot	Plains Village 2	Central Plains tradition, St Helena
25CD21	Burney	Late Late Woodland	Loseke Creek
25DK2	Ryan	Historic	Omaha
25DK2	Ryan	Late Late Woodland	Great Oasis
25DK9	Murphy/O'Connor	Plains Village 2	Central Plains tradition, Nebraska phase
25DK10	—	Historic	Omaha
25DK13	Maxwell	Plains Village 2	Central Plains tradition, Nebraska phase
25DO4	Havlicek Farm	Plains Village	Central Plains tradition, Nebraska phase
25DX4	—	Late Late Woodland	Loseke Creek
25FN22	Wilsonville Burial	Middle Woodland	Keith focus
25FR2	Dunn Ossuary	Woodland	—
25HK13	Massacre Canyon	Middle Woodland	Keith focus
25HW6	Coufal	Plains Village 2	Central Plains tradition, Itskari phase
25HW8	Christensen	Plains Village 2	Central Plains tradition, Itskari phase
25KX1	Ponca Fort	Protohistoric	Ponca
25KX12	Niobrara School	Late Late Woodland	Loseke Creek
25KX207B	Niobrara RR Bridge	Late Late Woodland	Loseke Creek
25MP2	McPherson	Late Archaic	—
25NC3	Wright	Protohistoric	Postcontact Coalescent, Lower Loup
25NC13	Wozney	Plains Village 2	Central Plains tradition, Itskari phase
25NC20	Genoa	Historic	Pawnee
25NH4	Whitten	Late Late Woodland	Great Oasis
25PK1	Clarks	Historic	Pawnee
25PT30	—	—	—
25PT31	Christman	Protohistoric	Postcontact Coalescent, Lower Loup
25RH1	Leary	Plains Village 2	Oneota
25RW2	Red Willow	Late Archaic	
25SD2	Leshara	Historic	Pawnee

Table 6. (*Continued*)

Site	Name	Period	Affiliation
Nebraska (continued)			
25ST12	—	—	—
25SY16	Fish Hatchery	Archaic	—
25SY67	Wallace Mound	Plains Village	Central Plains tradition, Nebraska phase
25VY3	Schultz Burial	Middle Woodland	Valley phase
25WT1	Hill/Pike	Historic	Pawnee
25WT4	Robb Ossuary	Middle Woodland	Keith focus
North Dakota			
32EM369	Linton Gravel Pit	Woodland	(Sonota)
32MO97	Bahm	—	—
32RM201	Lisbon Burial	Plains Village 1	Middle Missouri
32RM19	Wray/Alray Mound	Woodland	(Devils Lake–Sourisford)
32RM26	Fort Ransom Mound	Woodland	—
32SI1	Boundary Mounds	Woodland	(Sonota)
32SN22	Jamestown Mounds	Woodland, Plains Village	(Sonota)
32WA1	Fordville Mounds	Woodland, Plains Village	(Devils Lake-Sourisford)
32WE401	Heimdal Mound	Woodland	(Devils Lake-Sourisford)
South Dakota			
39AR2	No Heart Creek	Plains Village 2	Extended Coalescent, Le Compte
39AR201	McKensey Village	Plains Village 2	Middle Missouri, Southern Extended, Riggs phase
39BF11	Crow Creek	Plains Village 2	Initial Coalescent
39BF221	Big Bend Burials	Historic	Sioux
39BF224	Truman Mound	Late Late Woodland	(Truman)
39BF225	Sitting Crow	Woodland	—
39BF234	Old Quarry	Late Late Woodland	(Truman)
39BR16	Swanson	Plains Village 2	Middle Missouri, Mill Creek
39CA4	Anton Rygh	Plains Village 2	Extended Coalescent, La Roche
39CH7	Oldham	Late Late Woodland	Great Oasis
39CH54	Platte-Winner Bridge	Late Late Woodland	Great Oasis
39CL2	Ufford Mounds	Late Late Woodland	Great Oasis
39CO9	Leavenworth	Historic	Arikara
39DA3	Enemy Swim Lake	Woodland	(Sonota)
39DV2/3	Mitchell Mounds	Late Late Woodland, Plains Village	—
39DW2	Four Bear	Protohistoric	Postcontact Coalescent, Le Beau phase
39DW233	Swift Bird	Woodland	(Sonota)
39DW240	Grover Hand	Woodland	(Sonota)
39DW252	Arpan	Woodland	(Sonota)
39GR1	Scalp Creek	Late Late Woodland	Loseke Creek
39HS1	Bloom Village	Late Late Woodland, Plains Village 1	—
39HT1	Twelve Mile Creek	Plains Village 1	Middle Missouri, Mill Creek, Lower James phase
39HT2	Hofer Mounds	Woodland	—
39HT201	Wolf Creek Mound	Early Late Woodland	Held Creek
39HU1	Thomas Riggs	Plains Village 2	Middle Missouri, Southern Extended, Riggs phase
39HU2	Oahe Village	Protohistoric	Postcontact Coalescent, Le Beau phase
39LK2	Madison Pass Mounds	Late Late Woodland	—

(*Continued*)

Table 6. (Continued)

Site	Name	Period	Affiliation
South Dakota (continued)			
39LM2	Medicine Creek	Plains Village 1	Middle Missouri, Chamberlain or Initial Coalescent
39LM26–27	Oacoma	Historic	Skiri Pawnee
39LM33	Dinehart's Village	Protohistoric	Postcontact Coalescent
39LM209	Langdeau	Plains Village 1	Middle Missouri, Chamberlain, Grand Detour phase
39LN10	Newton Hills	Woodland	—
39MH6	Split Rock Creek	Late Late Woodland	Loseke Creek
39MK1	Montrose Mound	Woodland	—
39ML2	Fort Wadsworth Mound	Woodland	—
39PO1	Steamboat Creek Village	Protohistoric	Postcontact Coalescent, Le Beau phase
39PO207	Second Hand	—	—
39RO2	Madsen's Mounds	Woodland	—
39RO3	Buchanan Mounds	Woodland	—
39RO4	Hartford Beach Mounds	Late Late Woodland	—
39RO7	Hunters Mound	Woodland	—
39RO10	Daugherty Mounds	Woodland	—
39RO23	De Speigler	Woodland	(South Arvilla)
39SL2	Fairbanks Village	Plains Village 1	Middle Missouri, Southern Extended, Riggs phase
39SL4	Sully	Protohistoric	Extended Coalescent
39ST1	Cheyenne River	Protohistoric	Postcontact Coalescent, Bad River 2
39ST11	Fay Tolton	Plains Village 1	Initial Middle Missouri, Chamberlain, Anderson phase
39ST16A	Breeden A	Plains Village 1	Middle Missouri, Chamberlain, Anderson phase
39ST203	Black Widow Ridge	Protohistoric	Postcontact Coalescent, Bad River 1
39ST215	Leavitt	Protohistoric	Postcontact Coalescent, Bad River 2
39ST216	Buffalo Pasture	Protohistoric	Postcontact Coalescent, Bad River 2
39ST235	Stony Point	Protohistoric	Postcontact Coalescent, Bad River 2
39UN1	Arbor Hill	Woodland	—
39WW1	Mobridge	Plains Village 2	Extended Coalescent, Akaska focus
39WW1	Mobridge	Protohistoric	Postcontact Coalescent, Le Beau phase
39WW2	Larson	Protohistoric	Postcontact Coalescent, Le Beau phase
39WW3	Spiry-Eklo	Protohistoric	Postcontact Coalescent
39WW7	Swan Creek	Protohistoric	Postcontact Coalescent, Le Beau phase
39WW203	Walth Bay	Plains Village 2	Extended Coalescent, Akaska focus
39WW303	White Tail	Protohistoric	Extended Coalescent, La Roche focus
39YK1	Yankton Mounds	Middle Woodland	Valley phase
—	Fort Pierre	—	—
Wyoming			
UWFC36 w/ 48CR3595	Robber's Gulch	Prehistoric	—
48SW7101	Bairoil	Prehistoric	—
48PL56 w/ HR012	Glendo	Historic	Indian–White
—	Washakie	Historic	Indian–White
HR090–HR095	Red Mountain	Historic	Chinese-American
HR071	Rock Ranch	Historic	African-American

Table 6. (*Continued*)

Site	Name	Period	Affiliation
Wyoming (continued)			
—	Shawnee Creek	Historic	African–American
HR060	Little Muddy River	Historic	Euro-American
48UT29 w/ HR058–HR059	Fort Bridger	Historic	Euro-American
—	Green R. Soldier	Historic	Euro-American
—	Divide Burial	Historic	Euro-American
48GO54 w/ HR080	Korell-Bordeaux	Historic	Euro-American
UWFC7	Glenrock	Historic	Euro-American
—	Bates Creek	Historic	Euro-American
—	Quintina Snoderly	Historic	Euro-American
48NA209 w/ HR083–HR084	Fort Casper	Historic	Euro-American
—	Harvey Morgan	Historic	Euro-American
UWFC70-1 to UWFC70-3	Fremont County	Historic	Euro-American
—	Cody Pipe	Historic	Euro-American
—	Shell	Historic	Euro-American
—	Blind Bill	Historic	Euro-American
—	Gallagher	Historic	Euro-American

[a]Terms in parentheses are poorly known burial complexes.

(1969), and Blakeslee and Caldwell (1979). Krause created an impressionistic sequence of two phases for what is commonly called the Nebraska phase. The earlier unit, his Doniphan phase, is located farther south in eastern Nebraska than the later Douglas phase. Calabrese extended this sequence by suggesting that the Doniphan phase had its roots in the Steed-Kisker complex in the Kansas City locality.

Blakeslee and Caldwell (1979), using a ceramic seriation, also found evidence for a south to north movement during the Nebraska phase, although the details differ from Krause's sequence and do not offer support for Calabrese's hypothesis. Blakeslee (1990) has developed a model for the Nebraska phase that sees the movement as an expansion of slash-and-burn horticulturists through the forested valleys adjacent to the Missouri River.

Another postulated migration involves the origin of the Steed-Kisker complex. Steed-Kisker ceramics are of the Mississippian tradition, even though the complex itself is isolated from other Mississippian communities. Dwellings that have been excavated include some in the Mississippian tradition as well as Plains-style earthlodges. The predominance of Mississippian traits led Wedel (1943:214, 221) to suggest a population movement up the Missouri River. O'Brien (1978) also prefers this explanation for the origin of the complex,

although others view Steed-Kisker as the result of the Mississippian influence on a local Plains population.

Later in the Plains Village period, the best-documented migration in Plains archaeology occurred. It was the northward movement of the ancestral Arikara into what previously had been Middle Missouri tradition territory in southern South Dakota. The evidence for it includes archaeological patterns, craniometrics, and distributions of languages. The archaeological evidence is so clear that the distinction between ancestral Arikara and Mandan was recognized even before the salvage archaeology of the 1950s and 1960s codified it in terms of the Coalescent and Middle Missouri traditions (Sigstad and Sigstad 1973). The craniometric evidence is equally convincing (Ubelaker and Jantz 1979), and the close relationship of Arikara to the Pawnee dialects of Nebraska is without question (Parks 1979). In short, there exists the concordance between independent lines of evidence needed to demonstrate a migration.

The event is better termed an invasion than a migration. The Initial Middle Missouri populations disappeared from the region, southern Extended Middle Missouri villages were fortified, and the same is true of northern Initial Coalescent tradition sites. This is the time of the Crow Creek massacre, where the entire population of an Initial Coalescent village on this frontier was slaughtered and mutilated, with only some children and young women taken captive (Willey 1982; Zimmerman et al. 1980).

The reason behind the invasion is not understood. The most common suggestion is that a drought in the Central Plains forced populations northward into a region where cooler temperatures and lower evaporation rates allowed horticulture to be continued. However, the date of the drought in question seems to change every time the Initial Coalescent dates are revised. Lehmer (1954:148–150) originally thought that the Coalescent invasion began in the mid-sixteenth century and pointed to Weakly's (1950) evidence for a Central Plains drought of 1539 to 1564 as the cause. When the radiocarbon date from the Arzberger phase pushed the origins of the Coalescent to around 1450, the drought of 1439–1468 was thought to be a possible cause (Wedel 1961:183). Arzberger is now understood to be a late expression of the Initial Coalescent, and the Pacific I climatic episode is invoked.

Whichever drought one prefers, a basic problem with the explanation is that the Central Plains was not abandoned during this period. Saint Helena phase sites have been dated to the early 1400s (Blakeslee 1988a:10), and the Itskari phase is almost certainly contemporaneous (Ludwickson 1978). The cultural units that disappear at the right time (at the beginning of Plains Village 2) are in the Southern Plains and the southern part of the Central Plains. They are Steed-Kisker, Pomona, Smoky Hill, Solomon River Upper Republican, and Classic Republican.

The hypothesis that the same as yet unsubstantiated drought drove Central Plains tradition peoples south to initiate the Panhandle aspect (now Canark variant) in the panhandle region of Oklahoma and Texas has been discounted (Lintz 1978; Ludwickson 1978, 1979). The Buried City complex, which also occurs in the Panhandle region and is distinct from the Canark variant, does bear some ceramic similarity to the Central Plains tradition (David Hughes, personal communication 1990).

In the protohistoric and historic periods several migrations are well documented. The Cheyenne moved from Minnesota to and across the Missouri River to occupy the region around the Black Hills (Jablow 1951; Moore 1988; Schlesier 1987). The Sioux also moved westward from Minnesota to the Plains; they were already a threat to the Mandan and Assiniboine by 1738 (Smith 1980:52, 56).

A third major migration is that of the Omaha and Ponca, whose traditions place their homeland in the Ohio River valley. Late in the seventeenth century, they reached the region where South Dakota, Minnesota, Iowa, and Nebraska

come together (Fletcher and La Flesche 1911). While they are distinct from their Arikara neighbors in terms of craniometrics (Jantz 1974), ceramics from known and suspected Omaha and Ponca sites belong to the Coalescent tradition. They may also have made pottery in the Oneota tradition (Harvey 1979:227), but this has yet to be demonstrated.

Another migration of the historic period, other than that of Euro-Americans, is pertinent to the collections reported here. Two South Dakota sites, Oacoma and Oldham, located south of the Grand Detour of the Missouri in Lyman County, South Dakota, have long been known for the fact that their ceramics are of Lower Loup affiliation. That is, they belong to the ceramic tradition of the early historic Pawnee of central Nebraska. There are French documents that indicate that some Skiri Pawnee went to live with the Arikara in or shortly before 1723 (Nasatir 1952: 25). The Pawnee appear to have been visited there by the Mallet expedition of 1739 (Blakeslee 1988c). This migration may explain the later presence of some populations among the Arikara who spoke a dialect similar to Skiri (Parks 1979:203).

WARFARE

Prior to Plains Village 1, there is little in the archaeological record in the Plains suggestive of warfare. No defensive works have been found, but low intensity raiding is a possibility. The most likely type of evidence for this would be in the form of trauma to human skeletons ("Cutmarks and Perimortem Treatment of Skeletal Remains on the Northern Plains," this vol.).

In Plains Village 1, there is an apparent contrast between the Northern and Central Plains. Early Middle Missouri villages are often fortified, while early sites of the Central Plains tradition never are. As a result, there are repeated references in the literature to the peaceful conditions that prevailed in the Central Plains. An alternative view relates the different settlement patterns to the ways in which these people adapted slash-and-burn horticulture to their respective environments (Blakeslee 1987). In the Middle Missouri region, land suitable for horticulture was scarce and concentrated in defensible units; in the Central Plains it was neither scarce nor defensible, and the archaeological record reflects this. Skeletal remains rather than settlement patterns offer the best hope of measuring differences in the intensity of warfare between the two regions.

In Plains Village 2, the intensity of prehistoric warfare peaked during the invasion of South Dakota by carriers of the Coalescent tradition. Not surprisingly, northern Initial Coalescent and southern Middle Missouri tradition sites of this period are fortified. To this period belongs the Crow Creek massacre. In the ensuing interval, when the Extended Coalescent dominated South Dakota, the intensity of warfare seems to have diminished. River Basin Surveys archaeologists called it the "Pax La Roche" (Caldwell 1964:3).

It is the historic period that led to the identification of Plains Indians with intense warfare. Once again, fortified sites are found, this time in the Central as well as the Northern Plains. Multiple factors combined to generate the warfare, including the introduction of horses and guns (Mishkin 1940; Secoy 1953), the arrival of new populations from outside the Plains, epidemics that caused population losses countered partly by adoption of young captives, and the slave trade, which led to wholesale slaughter of the adult male populations of villages. The slave trade reached the Plains ahead of direct White contact for most groups. When Pierre Gaultier de Varennes La Vérendrye explored west of the Missouri River in the 1740s, he learned that the Snakes (Eastern Shoshone or Comanche) had destroyed a whole village (Smith 1980:107). In the eighteenth century, Pawnee was a synonym for slave in the Mississippi River basin (Wedel 1973). The historic period was also a time when many Euro-Americans in the region were subject to early, violent deaths ("Skeletal Injuries of Pioneers," this vol.).

SUBSISTENCE

Prior to the development of trace element and stable isotope analyses to recover information about diet, the prehistorian was dependent on settlement patterns, tool types, storage facilities, and faunal and floral remains to interpret subsistence. Given that modern recovery techniques have been applied to only a minority of Plains sites, most faunal assemblages are biased in favor of the larger species, and floral remains are sparse. Under these circumstances, comparisons of subsistence between cultural traditions and evaluations of the relative contributions of vegetable foods and meat to the diet within traditions approached the level of guesswork. Nevertheless, it is possible to trace some broad patterns for the prehistoric cultures considered in this volume.

The village tribes of the historic period made long-distance bison hunts every year (Weltfish 1965:130–237, 409–443; Wilson 1924:263–298). When in prehistory this pattern began is an open question. Holen (1983) shows that lithic acquisition by the protohistoric Pawnee was embedded in such long-distance hunts. The Skiri band obtained Smoky Hill jasper from bedrock quarries on their way to their western hunting territory, while the South Band Pawnee used bedrock

quarries of Florence chert en route to their southerly hunting grounds. Some Wichita bands also used bedrock quarries distant from their home villages. Bedrock sources may have been necessitated by the large size of the hunting bands of the historic period; the pressure of feeding a large number of people while on the trail would have forced the protohistoric villagers to use highly concentrated lithic sources (Blakeslee 1988b).

Evidence for long-distance hunts earlier than the protohistoric takes a different form. Manz and Blakeslee (1988) interpret bone element frequencies from a Saint Helena phase site as reflecting bison hunting at a distance from the habitation. The minimum number of bison from site 25DX30 was 10, but when bone tools are not considered, the count drops to one. Apparently, most bison were hunted at such a great distance from the site that it was too much work to carry home any bones other than those needed for tools. Lithics from the site suggest that such hunts may have taken place several hundred miles to the west (Padgett 1988). The pattern of lithic acquisition is very different from that reported by Holen (1983), as a wide variety of sources are represented. Since most Saint Helena sites are small compared to protohistoric villages, hunting bands may have been small as well.

Wood (1969) has proposed that long-distance bison hunts were practiced by the Classic Republican phase peoples. This is one way to explain the nonhorticultural Upper Republican sites in the High Plains of eastern Colorado (Eighmy 1984:18; Gunnerson 1987:65–74; Wood 1967). Wedel (1970), however, argues that the Upper Republican hunters had no need to travel long distances as they lived in what was prime bison hunting territory in the historic period.

This raises a separate but related issue: how far back in time can the historic distribution of bison be projected? It is very clear from even a cursory examination of the evidence that during the Woodland period bison were far more common in the Northern than in the Central Plains. In the Dakotas, bison are prominent both in habitation sites (Neuman 1975:3–34) and in mortuary sites (Neuman 1975:40, 44, 49). However, from near the Nebraska–South Dakota border all the way to the southern end of the Plains, bison are scarce in almost all Woodland period sites and in many Plains Village 1 sites. To argue that all the cultures of this large area would ignore such a prime and easily hunted food source if it were present is specious.

Sites of all periods yield a range of smaller game including rodents, birds, shellfish, and sometimes fish. In sites with few or no bison, the smaller animals appear to have contributed importantly to the diet. In sites with bison remains, any calculation of the contribution to diet will be dominated by bison (Falk 1977:155). The meaning of the smaller animals to the total subsistence picture is not well understood. They may have been supplemental tasty tidbits, important meat sources during the occasional lean season, products of the hunting activities of youngsters (Wedel 1970:241), the byproducts of protecting the gardens (Rood 1986), or any combination of these factors. Whatever their function, the remains of small game are nearly omnipresent in site collections where modern recovery techniques have been used.

Dependence on horticulture developed very slowly on the Plains. There is evidence for the intensive use of wild vegetable foods as early as Middle Archaic times in eastern Kansas. Munkers Creek phase sites (Witty 1982) yield stone knives with a sickle sheen, apparently from the harvesting of grasses. Grinding stones for the processing of seeds are also present, but there is no evidence for domesticates.

In the Late Archaic Nebo Hill phase, there is archaeological evidence suggesting slash-and-burn horticulture, but no botanical documentation has yet been found. Summer villages are in areas of upland forest, and ground stone axes and celts and chipped stone axes and hoes are found in them. Late Archaic hoes are called Sedalia diggers, and it has been suggested that they were used to harvest wild roots such as the prairie turnip (Chapman 1975:184). This is most unlikely, as historic Plains tribes that had access to metal hoes still preferred the digging stick for gathering prairie roots. With a hoe, one must cut through the thick mat of grass roots to get at the tubers; a digging stick is much easier to use.

No cultigens have yet been recovered from a Nebo Hill summer site, but the Phillips Spring site (Kay 1982:623–727), which yielded squash and gourd remains, is of the right time period and is nearby. The absence of the celts, axes, and hoes from a Nebo Hill winter camp (Blakeslee and Rohn 1986: 642–688; Deel 1985) demonstrates that these tools were used primarily during the warm season. What does one do with axes, celts and hoes, during the warm months that one does not do during the winter if not slash-and-burn horticulture? Reid's (1980, 1983) observation that the upland forest areas favored by the Nebo Hill people for summer habitation experience a temperature inversion at night, so that the frost-free season is longer than in the stream bottoms, reinforces the suspicion that horticulture was being practiced.

In the Woodland period, stone hoes disappear and are not replaced until the scapula hoe is developed in Plains Village 1 times. Axes and celts and settlement patterns that could have accommodated slash-and-burn horticulture are present in Woodland period sites. With the exception of Kansas City Hopewell and Late Late Woodland sites, botanical evidence for horticulture on the Plains is practically nonexistent and storage facilities are limited.

Adair (1988) provides a complete summary of the situation for the southern part of the area considered here. Maize, squash, and marsh elder (*Iva annua*) have been recovered from Kansas City Hopewell sites, but only in small amounts. Early Late Woodland sites generally yield no cultigens. Late Late Woodland sites differ. Kivett (1952:58) reported maize kernels from the Lawson site of the Loseke Creek phase. The Walker-Gilmore site yielded large amounts of squash and gourd remains (Haas 1980), and some Great Oasis sites contain maize in quantity (Mead 1974). If one includes Adair's Bemis Creek phase in the discussion, cultivated marsh elder may be added to the list.

In the Northern Plains, a few sites indicate that the switch to horticulture may have begun in Late Late Woodland. A mortuary site (32RY100) near Devils Lake contained a population with a high incidence of caries and interstitial grooving and indicators of poor nutrition. Another site (32RM201) yielded squash seeds and horticultural tools (Signe Snortland, personal communication 1990).

In all cases for which adequate data are available, cultigens do not loom large in the food resources of Woodland period peoples on the Plains. Wild seed plants, nuts, and a number of game species provided a broad spectrum of foodstuffs (Haas 1980) to which cultigens must have provided only a supplement.

In the Plains Village period, cultigens became more important. Maize, squashes, sunflowers, beans, and marsh elder are found widely. Differences in the subsistence adaptations of Nebraska phase and Upper Republican populations have been suggested (Wood 1969), but the major difference seems to have been between the Middle Missouri and Coalescent traditions. In Middle Missouri tradition sites, a wider variety of plants is recovered than in Coalescent tradition sites. Chenopods, amaranths, marsh elder, polygonum, and rumex seem to have been used regularly in addition to the maize, beans, squash, and sunflower found in Coalescent sites (Nickel 1977). The difference seems to have extended to hunting or at least butchering patterns (Falk 1977) as well.

References Cited

Adair, M.J.

1988 Prehistoric Agriculture in the Central Plains. *University of Kansas Publications in Anthropology* 16.

Alex, R.A.
1981 The Village Cultures of the Lower James River Valley, South Dakota. (Unpublished Ph.D. dissertation in Anthropology, University of Wisconsin, Madison.)

Anderson, D.C.
1987 Toward a Processual Understanding of the Middle Missouri Tradition: The Case of the Mill Creek Culture of Iowa. *American Antiquity* 52:522–537.

Anfinson, S.F.
1979 A Handbook of Minnesota Prehistoric Ceramics. *Occasional Publications in Minnesota Anthropology* 5.

Baerreis, D.A., and R.A. Bryson
1965 Climatic Episodes and the Dating of the Mississippian Cultures. *Wisconsin Archaeologist* 46:203–220.

Benn, D.W.
1983 Diffusion and Acculturation in Woodland Cultures on the Western Prairie Peninsula. In Prairie Archaeology. G. Gibbon, ed. *University of Minnesota Publications in Anthropology* 3.

Berry, B., and C.H. Chapman
1942 An Oneota Site in Missouri. *American Antiquity* 10:1–11.

Blakeslee, D.J.
1975 The Plains Interband Trade System: An Archaeological and Ethnohistoric Investigation. (Unpublished Ph.D. Dissertation in Anthropology, University of Wisconsin, Milwaukee.)

——
1983a Kinks in the Calibration Curve: Reassessing Radiocarbon Dates. *Transactions of the Nebraska Academy of Sciences* 11:29–36.

——
1983b Further Remarks on the Apparent and Actual Relationship between Climatic Change and Cultural Changes. *Transactions of the Nebraska Academy of Sciences* 11:29–36.

——
1987 Swidden Horticulture on the Great Plains: Explaining Plains Village Settlement Patterns. (Paper presented at the 45th Plains Conference, Columbia, Missouri).

——, ed.
1988a The St. Helena Phase: New Data, Fresh Interpretations. Lincoln: J & L Reprint.

——
1988b Tools, Trails, and Territories. (Paper presented at the Society for American Archaeology, Phoenix, Arizona.)

——
1988c The Original Santa Fe Trail: The Mallet Route of 1739. (Paper presented at the 46th Plains Conference, Wichita.)

——
1990 A Model for the Nebraska Phase. *Central Plains Archaeology:* 2(1):29–58.

——, and Warren W. Caldwell
1979 The Nebraska Phase: An Appraisal. Lincoln: J & L Reprint.

——, and Richard Dunn
1988 Identification of Subsoil Inclusions in Pomona Ceramics. Pp. 79–100 in Scanning Electron Microscopy in Archaeology. S. L. Olsen, ed. *British Archaeological Reports, International Series* 452:79–100.

——, and Arthur H. Rohn
1986 Environment and Man in Northeastern Kansas: The Hills Dale Lake Project. Kansas City: U.S. Army Corps of Engineers. Kansas City District.

Bonney, R.
1965 Evidence for Early Woodland Occupations in Southwestern Minnesota. *Minnesota Archaeologist* 27:2–48.

——
1970 Early Woodland in Minnesota. *Plains Anthropologist* 15:302–304.

Bowers, A.W.
1950 Mandan Social and Ceremonial Organization. Chicago: University of Chicago Press.

Brogan, W.T.
1981 The Cuesta Phase: A Settlement Pattern Study. *Kansas State Historical Society, Anthropological Series* 9.

Brown, K.L.
1984 Pomona: A Plains Village Variant in Eastern Kansas and Western Missouri. (Unpublished Ph.D. Dissertation in Anthropology, University of Kansas, Lawrence.)

——, and A.H. Simmons
1987 Kansas Prehistoric Archaeological Preservation Plan. Lawrence: University of Kansas.

Bryson, R.A., D.A. Baerreis, and W.M. Wendland
1970 The Character of Late-glacial and Post-glacial Climatic Changes. Pp. 53–74 in Pleistocene and Recent Environments of the Central Great Plains. W. Dort, Jr., and J.K. Jones, Jr, eds. *University of Kansas, Special Report of the Department of Geology* 3.

——, and W.M. Wendland
1967 Tentative Climatic Patterns for Some Late-glacial and Post-glacial Episodes in North America. In Land Life and Water. W.J. Mayer-Oakes, ed. *Occasional Papers of the Department of Anthropology, University of Manitoba.*

Calabrese, F.A.
1969 Doniphan Phase Origins: An Hypothesis Resulting from Archaeological Investigations in the Smithville Reservoir Area, Missouri: 1968. (Report to the National Park Service for the Department of Anthropology, University of Missouri, Columbia.)

——
1972 Cross Ranch: A Study of Variability in a Stable Cultural Tradition. *Plains Anthropologist Memoir* 9.

Caldwell, W.W.
1964 Fortified Villages in the Northern Plains. *Plains Anthropologist* 9:1–7.

——

1966 The Black Partizan Site. Smithsonian Institution. River Basin Surveys. *Publications in Salvage Archaeology* 2.

——, and Richard E. Jensen

1969 The Grand Detour Phase. Smithsonian Institution. River Basin Surveys. *Publications in Salvage Archaeology* 13.

——, and Lynn M. Snyder

1983 Dendrochronology in Plains Prehistory: An Assessment. *Plains Anthropologist* 28:33–40.

Chapman, C.H.

1952 Culture Sequence in the Lower Missouri Valley. Pp. 139–151 in Archaeology of the Eastern United States. J.B. Griffin, ed. Chicago: University of Chicago Press.

——

1975 The Archaeology of Missouri, I. Columbia: University of Missouri Press.

Deel, J.

1985 The Doherty Site (14MM27): New Views on the Late Archaic. (Unpublished M.A. Thesis in Anthropology, Wichita State University)

Eighmy, J.L.

1984 Colorado Plains Prehistoric Context. Denver: Colorado Historical Society.

Falk, C.R.

1977 Analyses of Unmodified Vertebrata Fauna Studies from Sites in the Middle Missouri Subarea: A Review. *Plains Anthropologist Memoir* 13:151–161.

Fletcher, A., and F. La Flesche

1911 The Omaha Tribe. Pp. 17–62 in *Annual Report of the Bureau of American Ethnology.*

Frison, G.C.

1978 *Prehistoric Hunters of the High Plains.* New York: Academic Press.

Gibbon, G., and C. Caine

1980 The Middle Woodland to Late Woodland Transition in Southern Minnesota. *Midcontinent Journal of Archaeology* 2:100–200.

Gilder, R.F.

1926 The Nebraska Culture Man. Omaha: Henry F. Kiser.

Glenn, E.J.

1974 Physical Affiliations of the Oneota Peoples. *Office of the Iowa State Archaeologist, Report* 7.

Gunnerson, J.H.

1987 Archaeology of the High Plains. *Bureau of Land Management, Colorado State Office, Cultural Resource Series* 19.

Haas, D.R.

1980 Walker-Gilmore: A Stratified Woodland Period Occupation in Eastern Nebraska—a Report of the 1968 Excavations. *University of Nebraska, Lincoln. Division of Archaeological Research, Technical Report* 80-22.

Hall, R.L.

1962 The Archaeology of Carcajou Point. 2 vols. Madison: University of Wisconsin Press.

1967 The Mississippian Heartland and its Plains Relationship. *Plains Anthropologist* 12(36):175–183.

Harvey, A.E.

1979 The Oneota Culture in Northwestern Iowa. *Office of the Iowa State Archaeologist, Report* 12.

Haug, J.K.

1981 Excavations at the Winter Site and at Hartford Beach Village, *1980–1981.* Rapid City, S.Dak.: South Dakota Archaeological Research Center.

Henning, D.R.

1967 Mississippian Influences on the Eastern Plains Border: An Evaluation. *Plains Anthropologist* 12:184–194.

——

1968 Ceramics from the Mill Creek Sites. *Journal of the Iowa Archaeological Society* 16:192–280.

——

1968–1969

Climatic Change and the Mill Creek Culture of Iowa. *Journal of the Iowa Archaeological Society* 15–16.

——

1971 Great Oasis Culture Distributions. Pp. 125–133 in Prehistoric Investigations. M. McKusick, ed. *Office of the Iowa State Archaeologist, Report* 3.

Henning, E.R.P..

1981 Great Oasis and the Middle Missouri Tradition. The Future of South Dakota's Past. L. Zimmerman and L. Stewart, eds. *Special Publications of the South Dakota Archaeological Society* 2.

Hoffman, J.J.

1968 The La Roche Site. Smithsonian Institution. River Basin Surveys. *Publications in Salvage Archaeology* 11.

——

1977 Archaeological Inference in Social Modelling: Social Organization in the Bad River Phase. *Plains Anthropologist Memoir* 13:21–27.

Holen, S.

1983 Lower Loup Lithic Procurement Strategy at the Gray Site, 25CX1. (Unpublished M.A. Thesis in Anthropology, University of Nebraska, Lincoln.)

Howard, J.H.

1970 Known Village Sites of the Ponca. *Plains Anthropologist* 15:109–134.

Hughes, J.T.

1968 Prehistory of the Caddoan-Speaking Tribes. (Unpublished Ph.D. Dissertation in Political Science, Columbia University, New York.)

Hurt, W.R.

1951 Report of the Investigation of the Swanson Site, 39BR16, Brule County, South Dakota, 1950. *South Dakota Archaeological Commission, Archaeological Studies, Circular* 3.

1953 Report of the Thomas Riggs Site, 39HU1, Hughes County, South Dakota, 1952. *South Dakota Archaeological Commission, Archaeological Studies, Circular* 5.

1957 Report of the Investigation of the Swan Creek Site, 39WW7, Walworth County, South Dakota, 1954–1956. *South Dakota Archaeological Commission, Archaeological Studies, Circular* 7.

Hymes, D.
1968 Linguistic Problems in Defining the Concept of Tribe. Pp. 23–48 in Essays on the Problem of Tribe. J. Helm, ed. *Proceedings of the 1967 Annual Spring Meeting of the American Ethnological Society.*

Jablow, J.
1951 The Cheyenne in Plains Indian Trade Relations, 1795–1840. *American Ethnological Society Monograph* 19.

Jantz, R.L.
1974 The Redbird Focus: Cranial Evidence in Tribal Identification. *Plains Anthropologist* 19:5–13.

Johnson, A.E.
1973 Archaeological Investigations at the Budenbender Site, Tuttle Creek Reservoir, North Central Kansas, 1957. *Plains Anthropologist* 18:271–299.

1976 A Model of the Kansas City Hopewell Subsistence-Settlement System. In Hopewellian Archaeology in the Lower Missouri Valley. A.E. Johnson, ed. *University of Kansas Publications in Anthropology* 8.

1979 Kansas City Hopewell. David Brose and N'omi Greber, eds. Hopewell Archaeology: The Chillicothe Conference. Kent, Ohio: Kent State University Press.

1987 Late Woodland Adaptive Patterns in Eastern Kansas. *Plains Anthropologist* 32:390–403.

Johnson, A.M.
1977 Testing the Modified Middle Missouri Variant. *Plains Anthropologist Memoir* 13:14–20.

Johnston, R.B., and J.J. Hoffman
1966 An Analysis of Four Survey Collections from Armstrong County, South Dakota: 39AR2 (No Heart Creek), 39AR4, 39AR5 and 39AR7. *Plains Anthropologist Memoir* 3:39–75.

Kay, M., ed.
1982 Holocene Adaptations within the Lower Pomme de Terre River Valley, Missouri. 3 vols. Kansas City, Mo.: U.S. Army Corps of Engineers, Kansas City District.

Kivett, M.F.
1952 Woodland Sites in Nebraska. *Nebraska State Historical Society Publications in Anthropology* 1.

Knudson, R.
1967 Cambria Village Ceramics. *Plains Anthropologist* 12: 247–299.

Krause, R.A.
1969 Correlation of Phases in Central Plains Prehistory. *Plains Anthropologist Memoir* 6:82–96.

Lehmer, D.J.
1954 Archaeological Investigations in the Oahe Dam Area, South Dakota, 1950–51. *Bureau of American Ethnology Bulletin* 158, *River Basin Surveys Paper* 7.

1971 Middle Missouri Archaeology. *National Park Service, Anthropological Papers* 1.

——, and Warren W. Caldwell
1966 Horizon and Tradition in the Northern Plains. *American Antiquity* 31:511–516.

——, and D.T. Jones
1968 Arikara Archaeology: The Bad River Phase. Smithsonian Institution. River Basin Surveys. *Publications in Salvage Archaeology* 7.

Lintz, C.
1978 The Panhandle Aspect and Its Early Relationship with Upper Republican. Pp. 36–55 in The Central Plains Tradition: Internal Development and External Relationships. D.J. Blakeslee, ed. *Office of the Iowa State Archaeologist, Report* 11.

Lippincott, K.
1978 Solomon River Upper Republican Settlement Ecology. Pp. 81–93 in The Central Plains Tradition: Internal Development and External Relationships. D.J. Blakeslee, ed. *Office of the Iowa State Archaeologist, Report* 11.

Ludwickson, J.K.
1978 Central Plains Tradition Settlements in the Loup River: The Loup River Phase. Pp. 94–108 in The Central Plains Tradition: Internal Development and External Relationships. D.J. Blakeslee, ed. *Office of the Iowa State Archaeologist, Report* 11.

1979 Postulated Late Prehistoric Human Movements in the Central Plains: A Critical Review. *Transactions of the Nebraska Academy of Sciences* 7:53–60.

——, D.J. Blakeslee, and J. O'Shea
1987 Missouri National Recreational River: Native American Cultural Resources. *Wichita State University Publications in Anthropology* 3.

Lurie, N.O.
1960 Winnebago Protohistory. Pp. 790–808 in Culture in History. S. Diamond, ed. New York: Columbia University Press.

Manz, K., and D.J. Blakeslee
1988 The Faunal Remains from Annie's Site and the Limitations of Subsistence Analysis. In The St. Helena Phase: New Data,

Fresh Interpretations. D.J. Blakeslee, ed. Lincoln: J & L Reprint.

Marshall, J.O.
1972 The Archaeology of Elk City Reservoir: A Local Archaeological Sequence in Southeast Kansas. *Kansas State Historical Society, Anthropological Series,* 6.

McKusick, M.B.
1973 The Grant Oneota Village. *Office of the Iowa State Archaeologist Report* 4.

Mead, B.E.
1974 Seed Analysis of the Meehan-Schell Site (13BN110), a Great Oasis Site in Central Iowa. (Unpublished M.A. Thesis in Anthropology, University of Wisconsin, Madison.)

Mishkin, B.
1940 Rank and Warfare among the Plains Indians. *American Ethnological Society Monograph* 3.

Moore, J.
1988 The Cheyenne Nation: A Social and Demographic History. Lincoln: University of Nebraska Press.

Mott, M.
1938 The Relation of Historic Indian Tribes to Archaeological Manifestations in Iowa. *Iowa Journal of History and Politics* 36:227–314.

Nasatir, A.P.
1952 Before Lewis and Clark: Documents Illustrating the History of the Missouri, 1785–1804. St. Louis: St. Louis Historical Documents Foundation.

Nickel, R.K.
1977 The Study of Archaeologically Derived Plant Materials from the Middle Missouri Subarea. *Plains Anthropologist Memoir* 13:53–58.

Neuman, R.W.
1960 The Truman Mound Site, Big Bend Area, South Dakota. *American Antiquity* 26:78–92.

——
1975 The Sonota Complex and Related Sites on the Northern Great Plains. *Nebraska State Historical Society Publications in Anthropology* 6.

O'Brien, P.A.
1978 Steed Kisker and Mississippian Influences on the Central Plains. Pp. 67–80 in The Central Plains Tradition: Internal Development and External Relationships. D.J. Blakeslee, ed. 67–80. *Office of the Iowa State Archaeologist Report* 11.

——
1984 Archeology in Kansas. *University of Kansas, Museum of Natural History, Public Education Series* 9. Lawrence.

Over, W.H., and E.E. Meleen
1941 A Report on an Investigation of the Brandon Village and the Split Rock Creek Mounds. *University of South Dakota Museum. Archaeological Studies Circular* 3.

Padgett, W., III.
1988 The Lithic Assemblage from House 2, 25DX30. In The St. Helena Phase: New Data, Fresh Interpretations. D.J. Blakeslee, ed. Lincoln: J & L Reprint.

Parks, D.R.
1979 The Northern Caddoan Languages: Their Subgrouping and Time Depths. *Nebraska History* 60:214–239.

Reid, K.C.
1980 Nebo Hill: Archaic Political Economy in the Riverine Midwest. (Unpublished Ph.D. Dissertation in Anthropology, University of Kansas, Lawrence.)

——
1983 The Nebo Hill Phase: Late Archaic Prehistory in the Lower Missouri Valley. Pp. 11–39 in Archaic Hunters and Gatherers in the American Midwest. J. Phillips and J. Brown, eds. 11–39. New York: Academic Press.

Reynolds, J.D.
1979 The Grasshopper Falls Phase of the Plains Woodland. *Kansas State Historical Society, Anthropological Series* 7.

Rood, R.J.
1986 Faunal Remains from Anasazi Sites in the Yellowjacket District, Southwestern Colorado. (Paper presented at the 44th Plains Conference, Denver.)

Roper, D.C.
1976 A Trend-surface Analysis of Central Plains Radiocarbon Dates. *American Antiquity* 41(2):181–189.

——
1985 Some Comments on Kvamme's Re-examination of Roper's Trend Surface Analysis. *Plains Anthropologist* 30:259–262.

Ruppé, R.
1955 Archaeological Investigation of the Mill Creek Culture in Northwestern Iowa. *American Philosophical Society Yearbook* 335–338.

Schlesier, K.H.
1987 The Wolves of Heaven: Cheyenne Shamanism, Ceremonies and Prehistoric Origins. Norman, Okla.: University of Oklahoma Press.

Secoy, F.R.
1953 Changing Military Patterns on the Great Plains. *American Ethnological Society Monograph* 21.

Sigstad, J.S., and J.K. Sigstad
1973 Archaeological Field Notes of W.H. Over. *Research Office of the South Dakota State Archaeologist Bulletin* 1.

Smith, C.S.
1977 The Talking Crow Site. *University of Kansas Publications in Anthropology* 7.

——, and A.E. Johnson
1968 The Two Teeth Site. Smithsonian Institution. River Basin Surveys. *Publications in Salvage Archaeology* 8.

Smith, G. Hubert
   1980 The Explorations of the Vérendryes in the Northern Plains, 1738–1743. W. R. Wood, ed. Lincoln: University of Nebraska Press.
Steinacher, T.L.
   1976 The Smoky Hill Phase and Its Role in the Central Plains Tradition. (Unpublished M.A. Thesis in Anthropology, University of Nebraska, Lincoln.)
———, and D.L. Toom
   1983 Archaeological Investigations at the Whistling Elk Site (39HU242), 1978–1979. *University of Nebraska, Division of Archaeological Research, Technical Report* 83–04.
Stephenson, R.L.
   1954 Taxonomy and Chronology in the Central Plains–Middle Missouri Area. *Plains Anthropologist* 1:15–21.
Stoltman, J.B.
   1978 Temporal Models in Prehistory: An Example from Eastern North America. *Current Anthropology* 19(4):703–746.
Taylor, R.E.
   1987 Radiocarbon Dating: An Archaeological Perspective. Orlando, Fla.: Academic Press.
Tiffany, J.A.
   1983 An Overview of the Middle Missouri Tradition. In Prairie Archaeology. G.E. Gibbon, ed. *University of Minnesota Publications in Anthropology* 3.
Ubelaker, D.H., and R.L. Jantz
   1979 Plains Caddoan Relationships: The View from Craniometry and Mortuary Analysis. *Nebraska History* 60:249–259.
Weakly, H.
   1950 Dendrochronology and Its Climatic Implications in the Central Plains. In Proceedings of the Sixth Plains Archaeological Conference, 1948. University of Utah Anthropological Papers 11.

   1962 Dendrochronology and Archaeology in Nebraska. *Plains Anthropologist* 7:138–146.
Weakly, W.F.
   1971 Tree Ring Dating and Archeology in South Dakota. *Plains Anthropologist Memoir* 8.
Wedel, M. Mott
   1973 The Identity of La Salle's *Pana* Slave. *Plains Anthropologist* 18:203–217.
Wedel, W.R.
   1938 The Direct Historical Approach in Pawnee Archaeology. *Smithsonian Miscellaneous Collections* 97(7).

   1943 Archaeological Investigations in Platte and Clay Counties, Missouri. *U.S. National Museum Bulletin* 183.

———
   1959 An Introduction to Kansas Archaeology. *Bureau of American Ethnology Bulletin* 174.

———
   1961 Prehistoric Man on the Great Plains. Norman, Okla.: University of Oklahoma Press.

———
   1970 Along the Trail—Some Observations on Two House Sites in the Central Plains: An Experiment in Archaeology. *Nebraska History* 51:225–252.
Weltfish, G.
   1965 The Lost Universe: The Way of Life of the Pawnee. New York: Basic Books.
Wendland, W.M., and R.A. Bryson
   1974 Dating Climatic Episodes of the Holocene. *Quaternary Research* 4:9–24.
Willey, P.
   1982 Osteology of the Crow Creek Massacre. (Unpublished Ph.D. Dissertation in Anthropology, University of Tennessee, Knoxville.)
Willey, G.R., and P. Phillips
   1958 Method and Theory in American Archaeology. Chicago: University of Chicago Press.
Wilson, G.L.
   1924 The Horse and Dog in Hidatsa Culture. *Anthropological Papers of the American Museum of Natural History* 15(2).
Witty, T. A., Jr.
   1962 The Anoka Focus. (Unpublished M.A. Thesis in Anthropology, University of Nebraska, Lincoln.)

———
   1978 Along the Southern Edge: The Central Plains Tradition in Kansas. Pp. 56–66 in The Central Plains Tradition: Internal Development and External Relationships. D.J. Blakeslee, ed. *Office of the Iowa State Archaeologist, Report* 11.

———
   1982 The Slough Creek, Two Dog and William Young Sites, Council Grove Lake, Kansas. *Kansas State Historical Society, Anthropological Series* 10.
Wood, J.J.
   1967 Archaeological Investigations in Northeastern Colorado. (Unpublished Ph.D. Dissertation in Anthropology, University of Colorado, Boulder.)
Wood, W.R.
   1965 The Redbird Focus and the Problem of Ponca Prehistory. *Plains Anthropologist Memoir* 2.

———
   1969 Conclusions. Two House Sites in the Central Plains: An Experiment in Archaeology. *Plains Anthropologist Memoir* 6.

——
    1971 Biesterfeldt: A Post-Contact Coalescent Site on the Northeastern
         Plains. *Smithsonian Institution Contributions to Anthropology* 15.

——
    1976 Fay Tolton and the Initial Middle Missouri Variant. *Missouri
         Archaeological Research Series* 13.

Zimmerman, L., T. Emerson, P. Willey, M. Swegel, J. Gregg, P.
Gregg, E. White, C. Smith, T. Haberman, and P. Bumsted
    1980 The Crow Creek Site (39BF11) Massacre: A Preliminary
         Report. (Report to the U.S. Army Corps of Engineers,
         Omaha District.) Vermillion: University of South Dakota
         Archaeology Laboratory.

CHAPTER 3

○ ○ ○

Southern Plains Cultural Complexes

ROBERT L. BROOKS

This chapter presents an archaeological background to Southern Plains cultural complexes discussed in subsequent chapters of this volume. It covers the Plains Village and Protohistoric periods. Information on those complexes not included in this discussion can be found in Hofman et al. (1989), Bell (1984), Blakeslee (1978), and Wedel (1961).

Environment

While the boundaries of the Southern Plains are not sharply defined, particularly at the peripheries, the area is considered here as including the plains region lying south of the Arkansas river valley in Kansas and extending southward to include most of the western two-thirds of Oklahoma, north-central Texas and the Texas panhandle, the eastern foothills of New Mexico, and southeastern Colorado (fig. 1). It is essentially an area of rolling prairie grasslands, with timbered areas being restricted to the stream valleys. The northern boundary is marked by the Arkansas River valley, which delimits the Southern Plains from the Central Plains. The eastern margins are marked by the appearance of more varied topography and woodlands, which are the habitat of the various groups associated with the Caddoan area.

The area of the Southern Plains contains 450,000 to 500,000 square kilometers and has been described as a "land of sun and wind and grass" (Wedel 1961). Descriptions of the environment have been prepared by Fenneman (1931), Thornbury (1965), and Hunt (1974). The climate of the Southern Plains is subhumid to semiarid continental with 50 centimeters or less annual precipitation. The region is characterized by dramatic fluctuations in seasonal rainfall patterns, rapid changes in daily temperatures, and high evapotranspiration rates during the summer months. In the winter months (November through March), it is relatively dry due to cold air masses working their way south from the Arctic. Most precipitation comes between the months of April and September as cool dry air from the north collides with moist, warm air from the Gulf of Mexico or as a consequence of thermal heating in the summer months. In many cases, this precipitation occurs in thunderstorms, which may also contain high winds and large hail.

In the central portion of the Southern Plains is a series of southeasterly sloping high plateaus. Local relief on these plateaus is slight and has been created principally by wind erosion, which has resulted in the formation of numerous playa lakes and isolated dune areas (Reeves 1966; Walker

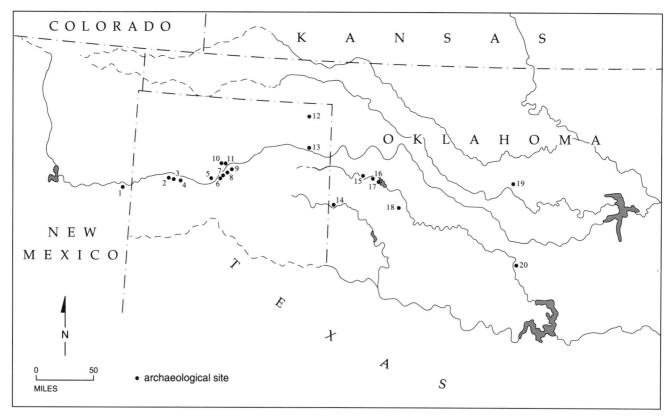

Fig. 1. Selected archaeological sites of the Southern Plains. 1, Congdon Butte; 2, Landegrin Mesa; 3, Saddleback Mesa; 4, Mesa Alamosa; 5, Footprint; 6, Alibates 28; 7, Antelope Creek 22 and 22A; 8, Lookout Ruin; 9, Mathews; 10, Arrowhead Peak; 11, Big Blue Cemetery; 12, Handley Ruins; 13, Parcell; 14, Edwards I; 15, Wickham #3; 16, Cotter-Hutson; 17, Heerwald; 18, McLemore; 19, Nagle; 20, Grant.

1978). Much of this area is drained by the headwaters of the North Canadian, Washita, Red, Brazos, and Colorado rivers. Native vegetation in the subarea consists of short grasses, sage, yucca, and mesquite. Cottonwoods and willows are found along major stream drainages, and scrub vegetation (e.g., juniper, post and blackjack oak) are found along major escarpments and canyon walls. In this subarea, bison and various small game animals were available.

The eastern boundary of the Southern Plains extends from the Arkansas River valley south to the eastern end of the Edwards Plateau in central Texas. In the northern portion of the area, the landscape is dominated by slightly rolling plains, whereas along the Edwards Plateau, geologic features such as canyons, mesas, and deeply entrenched stream valleys occur. The eastern boundary of the Southern Plains experiences greater annual precipitation than the other subareas with the quantity increasing to the south and east. In the southern half of this area is found the Cross Timbers natural region, consisting of mixed grass uplands interspersed with scrub forests of pin and blackjack oak, elm, and cedar. Because of the deeper and more fertile floodplain soils, alluvial valleys exhibit decid-

uous forests of oak, walnut, hickory, and pecan, as well as a variety of less dominant canopy and understory species. Animals including bison, deer, elk, turkey, and numerous small game were present.

The western border of the Southern Plains ranges from outwash materials in southeastern Colorado, to volcanic areas, mesas, and deeply dissected plateaus in eastern New Mexico, to the Pecos River Valley to the south. Much of the periphery of the subarea contains east-sloping valley bluffs and the Llano Estacado. This is the most desertlike area of the Southern Plains. Bunch grass, sage, and mesquite are the dominant vegetation in upland settings, while cottonwoods and willow grow along stream channels. Game animals in the subarea include bison and antelope and in canyon areas, mule deer and turkey.

CLIMATE

Climatic and geomorphological conditions on the Southern Plains during the Plains Village period have been documented (Bond 1966; Bryson, Baerreis, and Wendlund 1970; Hall 1982,

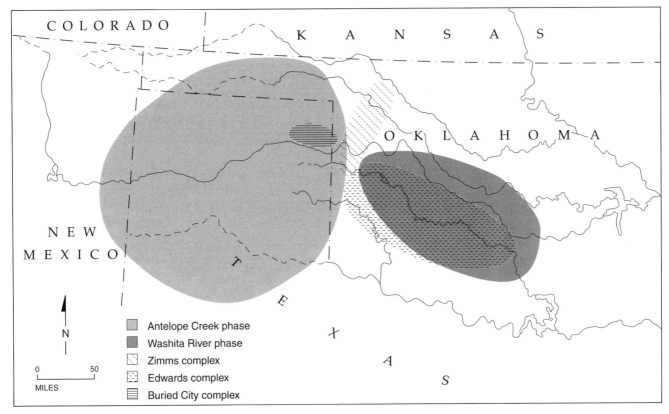

Fig. 2. Cultural complexes of the Southern Plains.

1983; Reid and Artz 1984; and Taylor 1986). Changes in climatic conditions and resultant geomorphological processes brought about significant adaptations in Plains Village cultures. Although previous paleoenvironmental research has focused on a diversity of settings ranging from canyons to alluvial valleys, some correspondence can be established between the results of the various studies. In general, the period approximately 800–550 B.C. to 50 B.C. can be viewed as a period of drier conditions. This climatic subperiod was followed by wetter conditions until approximately A.D. 850. From then until roughly A.D. 1500–1600, the climate was drier and somewhat warmer. These changes had a profound affect on the settlement pattern and the subsistence activities of Plains Village societies.

The Plains Village Period

Beginning around A.D. 800, societies of farming people began establishing themselves on the Southern Plains (Wedel 1959). Remains of their villages are found primarily along major stream drainages where fertile floodplain soils fostered the development of simple gardening economies that were sup-plemented by a strong reliance on hunting and the collecting of edible wild plants. Based on this mixed, but stable subsistence economy, numerous Plains Village societies developed on the Southern Plains.

Although differences exist among these Plains Village societies, they share a general way of life that contrasts with that of groups inhabiting adjacent regions. One feature that distinguishes these Plains groups is their utilization of bison. The bison not only provided a bountiful supply of meat but also materials for clothing, bedding, and containers. The bones were used to make a variety of tools and ornaments. Bison remains dominate the bone refuse and debris at village sites, with deer and other animals reflecting a secondary importance.

This emphasis on the bison was complemented by the hunting of other game and the collection of shellfish, the collection of wild plants, and the growing of garden crops. Corn and beans are well documented in the archaeological record, but squash, tobacco, and other crops were probably grown as well. These diverse resources contributed to a broader economic base, which meant survival at times when crop failure or a scarcity of shifting bison herds threatened normal supplies.

Village sites for these societies were small, most ranging from 0.2 to 1.6 hectares. They are found along both major streams and tributary creeks close to a reliable water supply and alluvial soils amenable to tilling with bison bone hoes and digging sticks. Frequently, several small settlements were clustered close together, suggesting a scattered, almost rural community comprised of several family groups. In other situations, a larger site appears as the central community with scattered homesteads located up and down the river valley. Relatively isolated sites also occur. These settlements are characterized by residential dwellings, storage and refuse pits, sheet midden deposits, and occasional burials or a cemetery.

The sociopolitical organization of these Southern Plains villagers is thought to have been egalitarian with power based on achievement and leadership abilities. However, some historic Plains societies exhibited evidence of social stratification and ranking, and this pattern may also have been true of prehistoric groups (Holder 1970:23–87).

The principal groups considered here include the Antelope Creek phase of Texas and Oklahoma, the Buried City complex of the Texas panhandle, the Zimms complex of western Oklahoma, and the Washita River phase of western and south-central Oklahoma (fig. 2).

THE ANTELOPE CREEK PHASE

Settlements of the Antelope Creek phase are found in the panhandle areas of Texas and Oklahoma between the Canadian and Arkansas river drainages. This distinct cultural expression is best distinguished by the use of stone slab masonry in the construction of houses and storage facilities. These structures range from single-family dwellings up to compound multiroomed apartments, resembling single-story pueblos.

ORIGINS

The origins of the Antelope Creek phase remain obscure except for their roots within older, indigenous Plains Woodland populations. In general, the Antelope Creek sites appear as the most divergent of the Southern Plains villages. This is largely due to their utilization of stone slab architectural construction and differences in the artifact assemblage, primarily in ceramics.

RESEARCH AND DATES

Krieger (1946), Suhm, Krieger, and Jelks (1954), Watson (1950), Campbell (1969), Schneider (1969), and Lintz (1978,

1982, 1986) have provided summary data on Antelope Creek phase sites. Over 25 sites have been studied and reported upon (Lintz 1986). Lintz (1986) has presented over 50 radiocarbon dates and four archaeomagnetic dates taken from 16 different sites and has defined a temporal range for Antelope Creek of approximately A.D. 1200 to 1500. Lintz (1986) has suggested that the period can be further refined into early and late subphases. These dates make the Antelope Creek phase contemporaneous with the Washita River phase and the Zimms and Buried City complexes.

SETTLEMENT PATTERNS

Antelope Creek phase sites include temporary camps, possibly bison kill and processing stations, isolated farmsteads or hamlets, and villages. Settlements often contain several house units forming a scattered community. They are marked by stone slab masonry that formed the wall base, arranged as single units or compound multiple structures. In size they range from single family dwellings up to compound multiroomed apartments(containing as many as 30 rooms), resembling single-story pueblos. By the later part of the phase, there is a transition from multiroom structures to more single room units. Other village features include storage pits, masonry granaries, shallow pits, midden areas, and burials. Cemeteries or burials were also present usually on high ridges or outlying areas from the settlement.

The residential dwellings feature the use of large stone slabs for wall construction. Additional features include a passageway entrance, a depressed central floor channel, four central support posts, a central hearth, benches, sometimes an altar on the west end of the structure, and floor pits. The altars are thought to have been used for ceremonies or rituals.

SUBSISTENCE

The subsistence economy of Antelope Creek phase groups was based on the growing of tropical cultigens, the collection of edible wild plants, and hunting. In general, dietary practices were similar to those of western groups of the Washita River phase where hunting probably played an equal or greater role than horticulture. Because of the high meat yield, hunting activities focused on bison, although deer and antelope were also taken (Duffield 1970; Lintz 1986). The meat diet was supplemented by smaller game such as cottontail and jackrabbit, prairie dog, ground squirrel, gopher, rat, bobcat, raccoon, badger, and fox. Amphibians and reptiles (ornate box turtles, snapping turtles and frogs), fish, and migratory birds (ducks and geese) were also exploited. Mussels were collected from streams and rivers. Farming consisted primarily of gardening activities along the fertile terrace of the major streams. Tropical cultigens such as popcorn and flint corn and beans were grown. In addition, wild plants including hackberry, mesquite, buckwheat, grasses (chenopodium and amaranth), cattail, sand plum, persimmon, prickly pear, and Indian mallow were collected (Green 1967; Kellar 1975; Christopher Lintz, personal communication 1989). These resources illustrate the use of a variety of habitats including the river valley as well as upland prairies.

TECHNOLOGY

Artifacts manufactured of chipped stone are most commonly made of chert derived from the Alibates quarries north of Amarillo, Texas. Chert items include projectile points, numerous scrapers, knives, drills or perforators, crude hoes, and preforms or unfinished items. Arrowpoints are the most plentiful projectile points, although dart points do occur. Typical arrowpoints are triangular forms with or without side notches (Fresno, Washita, and Harrell types). Corner notched and other forms occur, but they are not abundant at most sites. Chert end and side scrapers made from flakes are common and indicate an extensive skin dressing activity. Knives occur in various forms such as ovate and narrow curved forms, but the alternate-beveled diamond-shaped knife is most typical of these sites. Some notched or corner-tanged knives made from flakes are also present. Perforators or drills occur in several varieties: simple pin-shaped drills, T-shaped drills, and flake drills. They are typically of small diameter and delicate in construction. Although rare, some sites have produced double-bitted notched implements of quartzite, possibly used as hoes or axes.

Implements of ground stone include grinding basins, manos, abraders, hammerstones, ornaments, pipes, and celts. The milling stones typically have oval-shaped basins for grinding by a rotary motion with a small hand stone. Trough-type metates similar to those in the Southwest are more rare. Wedge-shaped manos are present, suggesting that the metate was well known. There are also some bedrock mortars and sharpening stones at some sites where rock outcrops were handy. Sandstone abraders for smoothing arrowshafts or sharpening bone tools are also common. Stone ornaments include small disk-type beads and small turquoise pendants. Stone pipes are represented by equal-armed elbow pipes, which usually have a barrel shaped-expanding bowl. The stone celt is found occasionally, but it appears to be a trade item derived from the Washita River or Caddoan peoples living to the east.

Tools and implements made from bone are also common at Antelope Creek villages. Bison and deer bones were preferred although other animal bones were sometimes used. Bone artifacts include the bison scapula hoe, bison tibia digging stick tips, scapula knives, beamers made from bison bone, hide grainers made from the bison femur head, notched ribs or the musical rasp, arrowshaft wrenches, bone awls, antler flakes, antler tapping tools, spatulas, and tubular bone beads. Bone awls are probably the most plentiful bone artifact, and these occur in several varieties: split-bone awls, splinter awls, turkey-bone awls, split rib awls, and rib-edge awls. Certain varieties were specifically prepared with a square cross-section and all four sides carefully smoothed. Perforated awls or needles also occur but are rare. Rattles made from whole turtle shells are also reported.

Mussel shells occur in the middens and were sometimes used for scrapers, spoons, or shredders. Occasional specimens have notched or denticulate edges and were probably used as shredders or sawlike tools. Mussel shell was also used for small shell pendants and flat perforated disk beads. Imported shells include olivella and conch shell. There are also some specimens of conch shell, apparently columella sections, which were drilled for tubular-shaped beads.

In addition to items of clay, there are a few additional artifacts such as small pieces of hematite and limonite, which were used as a source for pigments. Shaped pieces of microcline are found at some sites along with mica and flakes of obsidian. There are known samples of basketry manufactured with a plaited, twined, or coiled technique.

Clay was used for several purposes with pottery being the most commonly manufactured item. Perforated pottery disks made from sherds, daub with grass impressions, short tubular pipes, and clay beads are reported, but the tubular pipes and beads are uncommon.

The pottery is represented by two types: Borger Cordmarked and Stamper Cordmarked. Differences between the two are minor with Stamper Cordmarked offering greater variations in the rim form, simple decoration, and common presence of mica in the paste. The vessels are typically a globular jar form with a rounded base; the rims are straight, either vertical or with a slight outward flare. The bodies are covered with cordmarks, usually placed vertically except in the basal sections of the vessel. The paste has been tempered with crushed rock, commonly quartz, and sand but may also have mica, bone, or other materials present. Shell tempering appears to be absent. Decoration is minimal and is more likely to occur on the Stamper Cordmarked variety; it includes lip notches, fingernail punctates, raised fillets parallel to the rim, and incisions. These are limited to the neck or rim area, usually forming a single row of design elements extending around the circumference of the vessel. Small lip tabs rarely occur, but handles remain unreported.

Southwest pottery trade sherds occur at many of the Panhandle sites. These are typically a black-on-white ware or examples of the glazed wares from northeastern New Mexico. Examples of Abiquiu Black-on-gray, Aqua Fria Glaze-on-red, Cieneguilla Red-on-yellow, St. Johns Polychrome, Rowe Black-on-white, and Lincoln Black-on-red are reported and evaluated by Baerreis and Bryson (1966).

SOCIAL AND POLITICAL ORGANIZATION

Little is known concerning the political organization of Antelope Creek phase people. Traditionally, it has been argued that Plains societies were egalitarian with status based on personal achievements rather than ascribed status through kinship ties. However, this evaluation was based principally on societies that had become nomadic bison hunters and had experienced considerable economic and social change. Prehistoric village farmers such as those of the Antelope Creek phase may have had a different social organization based on more circumscribed social and political networks. The labor required to build multiroom apartments of stone and to develop an agriculturally based economy would have required somewhat greater levels of complexity and logistical cohesiveness (Binford 1980). Because Antelope Creek phase groups were involved in agricultural production, it is likely that their societies were structured and organized through matrilineal kinship ties (Lowie 1954:89–94).

There is some information concerning trade with Puebloan societies to the west. It is suspected that bison meat and hides were traded to Southwest groups for ceramics, obsidian, turquoise, and possibly additional supplies of corn. This has been argued because similar trading was present in the Protohistoric period (Baugh 1986; Speilman 1983). There are also some indications of trade and exchange with Caddoan-speaking groups to the east.

Warfare or intergroup conflict also played a role in Antelope Creek society. There is evidence for a moderate level of conflict during this period in the Texas panhandle. However, it is unclear whether this represents a pervasive pattern or infrequent occurrences.

SITES

Twelve sites affiliated with the Antelope Creek phase are discussed in this volume (table 1) (Lintz 1982, 1986). The Antelope Creek 22 site is located on a relatively high bench

Table 1. Southern Plains Archaeological Sites Treated in This Volume

Sites	References
Antelope Creek 22, 41HC23	Holden 1930; Baker and Baker 1939, 1941
Antelope Creek 22A, 41HC23	Johnson 1939; Duffield 1970
Alibates 28, 41PT11	Duffield 1970; Baker and Baker 1939, 1941
Arrowhead Peak, 41HC19	Green 1967
Footprint, 41PT25	Green 1967
Big Blue Cemetery, SARE-242	Davis 1969
Saddleback Mesa, 41OL1	Holden 1933; Green 1967
Landegrin Mesa, 41OL2	Texas Historical Commission 1984
Lookout Ruin, 41HC29	Lowrey 1932
Mesa Alamosa, 41OL8	Marmaduke and Whitsett 1975
Congdon Butte, LA1994	Moorehead 1931
Mathews, 41HC21	Jack Hughes 1962
Handley Ruins, 41OC1	Eyerly 1912; Hughes and Jones-Hughes 1987; Moorehead 1931
Parcell, Panhandle Plains Mus. A227	Jack Hughes 1962
Wickham #3, 34RM29	Wallis 1984
Heerwald, 34CU27	Shaeffer 1966; Drass, Baugh, and Flynn 1987
Cotter-Hutson, 34CU41	Keith, Snow, and Snow 1971
McLemore, 34WA5	Pillaert 1963
Grant, 34GV2	Sharrock 1961
Nagle, 34OK4	Brues 1957; Sharrock 1957
Edwards I, 34BK2	Baugh 1982

on the west side of Antelope Creek. The site consists of contiguous rooms extending over some 800 square meters.

The numerous investigations at Antelope Creek resulted in the excavation of some 1,134 square meters. In total, 25 rooms were partially or totally excavated. From this work, it was determined that seven household units were present with four building episodes occurring during the occupation span of the settlement. In addition to the typical artifact assemblage of chipped and ground stone and bone tools, ornaments, and ceramics, one burial was recovered.

Antelope Creek 22A is the designation for a set of contiguous rooms found approximately 45 meters east of Antelope Creek 22 at the base of the bluff. Approximately 229 square meters were excavated at 22A. This work revealed the presence of five rooms and a stone-lined cist. Sixteen burials were recovered.

Alibates 28 consists of a large contiguous room structure located on the north rim of the escarpment overlooking

Alibates Creek. In addition to the contiguous room unit, there were several isolated rooms and cists. Both rectangular structures and circular structures with burials were identified.

Over 5,500 square meters were excavated at Alibates 28, uncovering 50 rooms and 15 burials. Five radiocarbon dates are available for the site. Corrections for these dates from the Museum Applied Science Center for Archaeology, University Museum, University of Pennsylvania (MASCA) place the range of occupation from A.D. 1200 to approximately 1410 (Ralph, Michael, and Han 1974). Alibates 28 appears to have experienced sequential building episodes. Unit I, the northern set of rooms, dates to the earlier building episodes, with those in Unit II being constructed somewhat later and having greater interaction with Puebloan groups.

The Arrowhead Peak site is located on a small, prominent butte 45 meters above the Canadian River and near its juncture with Bugbee Creek. The site consists of a contiguous room structure, an isolated room, and midden area. In total, some 140 square meters were excavated with nine rooms and a midden area being studied. One MASCA-corrected radiocarbon date from Arrowhead Peak places occupation of the site between A.D. 1240 and 1400.

Saddleback Mesa, on a stream tributary to the Canadian River, covers 474 square meters, including 38 rooms and a number of cists (circular storage features). The rooms were tiered across the site; rooms at the southeast end were higher and smaller than rooms at the northwest extension. Extensive midden deposits yielded a diversity of tools and faunal remains. These consist of typical Antelope Creek phase chipped stone, ceramic, and bone tool assemblages (Haynes 1932; Holden 1933).

No radiocarbon dates are available for Saddleback Mesa. The artifact assemblage and architectural style are consistent with those found at other Antelope Creek phase sites within the Canadian River valley.

The Footprint site is situated on a small terrace remnant at the mouth of Big Canyon some 15 meters above and 600 meters south of the Canadian River's main channel. A total of 115 square meters was excavated. The most revealing aspect of the work at the site was the recovery of a complex set of burials from Room (House) I. The remains of at least seven individuals were recovered from three separate burial pits. The pits may contain some intermixed remains. In addition to remains in the burial pits, other remains are present on the house floor with 11 detached crania ("trophy skulls") present on the last floor of the house. These data have been interpreted as the consequences of intergroup conflict ("Warfare on the Southern Plains," this vol.).

Three radiocarbon assays were run on the Footprint site. MASCA corrections for these dates place occupation of the site between A.D. 1180 and 1520.

Big Blue Cemetery is located along the west rim of Big Blue Creek. Excavations over 37 square meters documented the presence of four separate individuals and a stone slab concentration that failed to contain any remains. Although burial furniture found in association with the burials indicates that the Big Blue Cemetery is affiliated with the Antelope Creek phase, the site or sites within the Big Blue Creek valley that the graves were associated with could not be determined.

Landegrin Mesa is located on a high mesa overlooking the Canadian River in Oldham County, Texas. A total of around 200 square meters has been excavated at the site. This work has documented the presence of 12 to 14 rooms and numerous construction episodes. Approximately 50 radiocarbon dates exist for Landegrin Mesa. MASCA corrections for these dates place occupation of the mesa between A.D. 1150 and A.D. 1500.

Lookout Ruin is located on a high mesa in the middle of the Antelope Creek floodplain in Hutchinson County, Texas. The site is one kilometer south of Antelope Creek 22. The Lookout Ruin investigations resulted in the identification of a three-room structure, a small rectangular structure, and two stone cists. Material remains are analogous to those found at other nearby Antelope Creek settlements.

Mesa Alamosa is located atop a high mesa along the Canadian River valley breaks near Landegrin Mesa. The site contains a contiguous room structure and perhaps other features. No excavations have been conducted at this site.

The Congdon Butte site is yet another settlement atop a high mesa overlooking the Canadian River valley. It is in eastern New Mexico.

The Mathews site is situated on the west bank of John's Creek, a tributary of the Canadian River. The Mathews site is a multiroom structure affiliated with the Antelope Creek phase. Materials recovered from the site, with the exception of some decorated ceramics, are those typically found in Antelope Creek assemblages. Although it is difficult to determine it is estimated that at least a dozen burials were removed from the cemetery area at Mathews (Hughes 1962). Unfortunately, the Mathews site has been essentially destroyed by vandals.

THE BURIED CITY COMPLEX

The Buried City complex refers to a particular cultural expression found along Wolf Creek, a tributary of the North Canadian (Beaver) River in the northeast corner of the Texas panhandle. The complex also apparently extends into Ellis County in western Oklahoma.

RESEARCH AND DATES

This complex has been identified as separate from the Antelope Creek phase (Hughes and Hughes-Jones 1987). Important sites of the Buried City complex include: Gould Ruins, Buried City or the Handley Ruins (Eyerly 1912; Moorehead 1931), Courson B, and Kit Courson (Hughes and Hughes-Jones 1987). Sites of this complex have been reported for other portions of the northeast Texas panhandle. A series of sites along Wolf Creek in Ellis County, Oklahoma, may also relate to these developments (Drass and Turner 1989). Seven radiocarbon dates from the Courson B site place the temporal range of the Buried City complex from A.D. 1150 to 1330. Thus, these remains are roughly contemporaneous with the earlier part of the Antelope Creek phase.

SETTLEMENT PATTERN

In view of the preliminary nature of the information on the Buried City complex, detailed discussion of settlement and community patterns must await further survey data. To date, only hamlets and villages have been identified. With one exception (Gould Ruins), all structures at these sites represent single units without interior dividing walls. Individual structures may consist of four or five houses up to 20 or more dwellings. Most villages appear to be placed well away from the creek adjacent to the valley wall (Hughes 1986).

The architecture of structures along Wolf Creek is similar to Antelope Creek phase houses; however, a major difference is the absence of vertical slabs for the walls. Instead, boulders of caliche are used as foundation. This technique is somewhat reminiscent of some Apishapa phase structures in southeastern Colorado. Houses of the Buried City complex also contain larger benches and altars than those found in Antelope Creek phase houses and may cover areas up to 65 square meters.

Other features normally associated with houses include straight-sided refuse-filled storage pits and semicircular or D-shaped rooms attached to the southeast corner of the dwellings.

Little information is available on burial practices. A few adults and one child have been excavated from the village at Courson B. Additional burials have been reported from along the valley rim. These data suggest a pattern of loosely flexed interments with no particular orientation of the body. In contrast to the Antelope Creek phase, burials of the Buried City complex appear to contain greater variety in grave goods.

SUBSISTENCE

Subsistence practices have not been well documented. However, the presence of bison tools modified for agricultural activities reflects the cultivation of crops such as corn, beans, and squash. A subsistence pattern similar to that practiced by people of the Antelope Creek phase is suspected, but with greater emphasis on hunting and gathering since there is less availability of fertile floodplain soils.

TECHNOLOGY

The material inventory is similar to that of the Antelope Creek phase. Lithic artifacts and debris include typical side-notched and unnotched triangular arrowpoints comparable to Washitas and Fresnos. Diamond-beveled knives, flake drills, a variety of bifacial and unifacial scraper forms, and an assortment of other stone tools are also present. Alibates does not commonly occur, indicating that people of the Buried City complex were not involved in the Southern Plains trade network that included the Antelope Creek phase.

Ground stone items have been found—poorly formed metates made of local sandstone and simple manos of quartzite. Several pieces of amazonite used for pendants and inlays have also been recovered.

Bone tools are those common to other Plains Village tradition cultures. Included are bison scapula hoes, bison skull hoes, bison tibia digging sticks, bison scapula smoothers, deer metapodial awls, and deer mandible sickles. Marine shell items are rare. However, mussel shell pendants do occur at some sites.

Ceramics differ significantly from those found at Antelope Creek phase villages. Ceramics are typically sand tempered with minor amounts of bone, shell, and clay. The most common vessel form is a large globular jar with an occasional rounded form. Many vessels are thick, poorly fired, and exhibit a soft paste. Unlike Antelope Creek wares, many of the sherds from the Buried City complex exhibit decoration in the form of single, double, and triple rows of fingernail impressions around the vessel neck, chevron designs, and crenulated rims. Other design elements include appliqué and fillet, punctation, incising, strap handles, fabric- and corncob-impressed surfaces, and in one case, a polished surface. Ceramics from the Buried City sites are thought to bear their greatest similarities to pottery found at Upper Republican sites in west central Kansas (Hughes 1986).

SOCIAL AND POLITICAL ORGANIZATION

Although little is known of the political organization of the Buried City complex, it is likely that it operated at a simpler level than that of the surrounding Antelope Creek phase groups. There are two reasons for less structure. First, the society has fewer residences and a greater emphasis on hunting and gathering. Second, there is an absence of the interaction with external groups that is noted for Antelope Creek societies. In general, there was little logistical need for a highly organized society.

One burial reported for the Gould Ruins potentially contained embedded arrowpoints. Otherwise little documentation for conflict can be found.

SITES

The Handley Ruins are located on a high terrace overlooking Wolf Creek in Ochiltree County, Texas. The site consists of a multiroom structure bearing similarities to Antelope Creek phase settlements. Investigations at the Handley Ruins resulted in the identification of a number of rooms and refuse areas. In addition, a number of burials were excavated (Moorehead 1931).

The Parcell site is located on the north side of the Canadian River on a ridge above an intermittent stream and its juncture with the Canadian River. Although the records are incomplete, it appears that the cemetery held at least 10 burials. Materials found at the Parcell site are those typically found at Panhandle aspect sites. However, there was no evidence of stone slab architecture. Because of the site's proximity to the area containing the Buried City complex, it has been included here as representative of this cultural expression. In fact, Parcell cannot be clearly established as representing either Antelope Creek or Buried City.

THE ZIMMS COMPLEX

Sites of the Zimms complex are found primarily in Roger Mills County in western Oklahoma, although one site has been recorded in Woodward County in the northwestern part of the state. In general, the complex appears to fall between the Washita River and the North Canadian River drainages. Zimms complex sites are distinguished by an Antelope Creek phase type of house floor plan (without stone slab masonry) and a material inventory similar to that of the Washita River phase.

ORIGINS

Origins of the Zimms complex are poorly understood. It may stem in part from Woodland developments in the Texas panhandle and western Oklahoma. Work on the Buried City complex in Ochiltree County, Texas, is also suggestive of ties to this cultural manifestation (Hughes and Hughes-Jones 1987).

RESEARCH AND DATES

Summaries of the Zimms complex are presented by Flynn (1986), Moore (1984), and Drass and Moore (1987). Documented sites of the Zimms complex include Zimms (34RM72) (Flynn 1984), New Smith (34RM400) (Brooks, Moore, and Owsley 1991), and Hedding (34WO1) (Shaeffer 1966). Examination of burials from Wickham #3 (Wallis 1984) has revealed this to be another likely Zimms complex site.

Four radiocarbon dates and one archaeomagnetic date from the Zimms site and two radiocarbon dates from New Smith indicate a range for the Zimms complex between A.D. 1265 and 1425. Thus, the Zimms complex is contemporaneous with the Antelope Creek and Washita River phases.

SETTLEMENT PATTERN

Settlements consist of small hamlets or isolated homesteads situated on high terraces or ridge toes above principal tributary streams rather than major river valleys. Sites documented contain only one or two houses.

The nature of the dwellings serves to identify the Zimms complex as a distinct cultural expression. Houses excavated at the Zimms and Hedding sites are semisubterranean structures with central, depressed floor channels and a raised floor platform on the west wall. Instead of the stone slab masonry found in Antelope Creek sites, the walls were plastered with daub. Similar structural design elements are present at the Footprint site.

One other noteworthy feature of Zimms complex settlements is the presence of specialized mortuary practices. This pattern consists of the placement of deceased individuals in a shallow pit, sometimes leaving a shroud or tapestry over the burial, the construction of a grass arbor over the burial, and subsequent burning of the arbor. There are a number of shallow pits filled with small quantities of faunal remains surrounding the arbors, suggesting some type of ritual feast associated with the deaths.

SUBSISTENCE

Subsistence activities for Zimms complex groups are thought to reflect the standard Plains Village horticultural pattern, but operating at a less intensive scale. Because of the small size of the settlements, tropical cultigens may comprise less of the diet with greater reliance on animal protein and edible wild plants. Evaluations of skeletal remains from the New Smith and Wickham #3 sites found fewer caries than in adjacent groups (Antelope Creek and Washita River phases), suggesting less reliance on a starchy diet.

TECHNOLOGY

Chipped stone artifacts include unnotched (Fresno) and side-notched (Washita, Harrell) triangular arrowpoints and a limited number of larger dart point styles. Other tool forms consist of diamond-beveled and ovate bifacial knives, unifacial end and side scrapers and knives, and marginally modified flakes. Bifacial drills have also been reported. Although Alibates and local chert gravels are commonly used for tool manufacture, some Florence A chert from the Flint Hills region of north-central Oklahoma is also found.

Ground stone pieces are limited but include manos, grinding basins, sandstone abraders, and diorite celts.

Bone tools consist of bison scapula hoes, bison tibia digging sticks, deer bone metapodial awls, and antler tine arrowpoints.

Ceramics at Zimms complex sites bear strong resemblances to wares found at Washita River phase sites. The dominant pottery type is Quartermaster Plain, a thin compact pottery tempered with shell, limestone, fossiliferous shale, and occasionally grit (Moore 1984). Vessel forms are not well documented, but they are probably similar in shape to those found at other southern Plains Villages. Decoration consists of nodes, rim tabs, and fillet strips. Other pottery found in smaller percentages included Lee Plain and Lindsay Cordmarked. There is also some evidence of ceramic trade wares. A few sherds apparently from the Caddoan area (East Incised?) as well as one Taos Black-on-white sherd from New Mexico have been found at the Zimms and New Smith sites.

SOCIAL AND POLITICAL ORGANIZATION

Because Zimms complex settlements are typically small, it is likely that their political organization would be less structured than that of more aggregated societies such as the Washita River and Antelope Creek phases. However, the Zimms com- plex exhibits elaborate mortuary practices, which may indicate an elaborate set of rituals for their society.

SITES

One site affiliated with the Zimms complex is discussed in this volume, the Wickham #3 site in Roger Mills County. Wickham #3 is located on a high terrace of the Washita River. Three burials uncovered there were placed in shallow pits with a tapestry or mat placed over them. An overlying arborlike structure was then burned. This pattern is very similar to that found at the New Smith site, some 18 kilometers northeast of Wickham #3.

THE WASHITA RIVER PHASE

The Washita River phase has been designated for a series of village sites located along the Washita River in south-central and west-central Oklahoma (Bell 1984; Hofman 1978). These sites are found chiefly along the Washita River in Garvin, Grady, Caddo, Custer, Washita, and Roger Mills counties, although villages are to be found around the peripheries of this region, including the South Canadian River valley to the north and the Wichita and Arbuckle mountain areas to the south.

ORIGINS

Origins of the Washita River phase people remain obscure. Some evidence suggests their roots reside in Plains Woodland cultures. It is much more likely, though, that their most direct relationship lies with preceding Custer phase populations. In either case, the ultimate source would be Plains Woodland groups adapted to a Southern Plains environmental setting.

RESEARCH AND DATES

A large number of Washita River phase settlements are known for Oklahoma with the total number probably being in excess of 200 sites (Bell 1984a; Brooks 1987; Drass, Baugh, and Flynn 1987; Hofman 1978; Pillaert 1963; Richards 1971; and Sharrock 1961). Because of differences in material assemblages and subsistence activities from east to west along the Washita River drainage, it has been suggested that two subphases can be documented (Brooks 1989). However, it is not known whether these subphases may reflect culturally distinct groups.

Approximately 25 radiocarbon and archaeomagnetic dates are available for approximately 10 sites. Reevaluations and corrections for these dates place the range of the Washita River phase between A.D. 1250 and 1450 (Brooks 1987; Drass and Swenson 1986). It is likely that the Washita River phase can be divided into an early and a late subphase.

SETTLEMENT PATTERN

Washita River phase settlements consist of villages of 5 to 20 houses occurring along principal streams and rivers. These villages are often found spaced from 2.4 to 3.2 kilometers apart along the Washita River proper. Village remains include wattle and daub houses, sheet middens, house middens, storage and refuse pits, and cemeteries.

SUBSISTENCE

Horticultural products were probably the mainstay of the diet, particularly in the more eastern sites. Tropical cultigens include corn, beans, and squash. In addition to agricultural products, the diet of the Washita River people included animal protein from bison, deer, antelope, and numerous small mammals. Fish and mussels were obtained from the Washita River and smaller streams. It can be documented that numerous edible wild plants such as marsh elder, sunflower, chenopodium and amaranth, and sand plum were eaten. There are indications that some plants such as creeping cucumber and morning glory were used for medicinal and ritual purposes.

Although the Washita River phase is relatively homogeneous, diversity in subsistence activities can be recognized from the eastern margin (Garvin and McClain counties) to the western periphery (Roger Mills and Custer counties). The western area emphasizes greater reliance on bison while the eastern sites are more agriculturally oriented. It was initially thought that this shift represented a gradual cline trending east to west. However, evidence from the skeletal collection at the McLemore site in western Oklahoma attests to the fact that the Washita River phase people were heavily dependent on a complex carbohydrate diet such as that found in agricultural societies (Douglas Owsley, personal communication 1989). There are two explanations for this disparity: (1) there was a rather abrupt change from corn to greater reliance on bison, and (2) both subsistence strategies were employed, depending on economic and social variables.

TECHNOLOGY

Artifacts of chipped stone include projectile points, scrapers, drills, knives, and a few miscellaneous items. The projectile points are small-sized arrow points, most commonly simple notched or plain triangular forms. There is considerable variation in form, and numerous identified types do occur (e.g., Fresno, Washita, Harrell, Scallorn, Morris, Bonham, Huffaker, and others). Some larger dart points (e.g., Gary, Williams) also occur, but they appear to be atypical. Scrapers are abundant, in a variety of forms: small end scrapers, side scrapers, pointed scrapers, and simple flake scrapers. Drills or perforators are present, with several forms being represented. Chipped-stone knives include ovate, triangular, and diamond-shaped alternate-beveled forms, the diamond shape the most characteristic although it is less common in the eastern part of the study area. Numerous retouched flakes were apparently also used as knives. Rough unfinished or preform materials, cores, flakes, and other flaking debris are also represented in a minor quantity. Analysis of chert materials from which these tools were made indicates use of not only local river and upland gravel but also materials derived from outside the region: Frisco chert from near Fittstown in Pontotoc County, Kay County (Florence A) chert from north-central Oklahoma, and Alibates dolomite from quarries near Amarillo, Texas (although this material can also be found as river gravel in western Oklahoma).

Ground-stone artifacts include celts, pipes, sandstone arrowshaft smoothers, awl abraders and hones, milling basins and metates, mortars, manos and mullers, small stone balls, perforated stone disks, and hammerstones. The most common items are manos and milling basins for food preparation, and the sandstone abraders or hones for finishing arrows or bone tools. Milling basins include both rotary grinding basins and trough metates as well as mortars. Oval manos are apparently used with grinding basins whereas loaf-shaped forms are used with the southwestern-style metates. Stone celts are generally small, almost round in cross-section, and carefully made, usually of ferriferous sandstone or igneous rock such as diorite or granite. Stone pipes are typically a small equal-armed elbow pipe with a slightly bulbous bowl, although one example from the Lee I site has a stem projection beyond the bowl. Stone disks with several perforations and small stone balls are represented at some sites, and trade articles sometimes occur (for example, ear spools derived from Caddoan groups to the east).

There is a variety of artifacts manufactured from bone, most commonly from bison or deer. The bison scapula hoe and skull hoes or scoops are typical digging or gardening tools. The scapula hoes have a characteristic half-socket or large groove for attaching the handle. The bison skull hoes have been cut from the horn core and adjacent portions of the frontal bone of the skull; the horn core forms the handle with the attached skull sections forming the blade. Additional digging implements include socketed bison tibia digging-stick tips, bison ulna picks, and chisel-shaped tools.

Bone awls or perforators are common and occur in a variety of forms. Perhaps the most abundant type is an awl made from a split deer cannon bone (metatarsal). Other types include awls made from split, splintered, or whole bones, rib-edge awls, flat split rib awls, bird bone awls, and fish spine awls. Perforated awls or needles have not been found. There are also flat, spatulate-shaped bone tools that display polish from use, possibly in weaving or basket making.

Additional bone artifacts include the deer jaw sickle, deer bone arrowshaft wrenches, beamers, knives or cutting tools made from sections of the bison scapula, and notched bone rasps.

Hollow bones and tubes are also common; more rare are deer toe tinklers, small bone balls, flat bone pendants, and fishhooks. Antler was used for handles, chipping tools or flakers, and other minor purposes. One specimen has been cut and worked as if to form part of an antler headdress. Other unique items include a bone arrow-cock and pieces of a bracelet or curved ornament.

Mussel shells (maple-leafs, black sands, and pimplebacks) are frequently found in the middens of Washita River phase sites. Shell was used as a tempering agent in pottery and was also made into flat, disk-shaped, and tubular beads as well as for spoons and scrapers. Small disks of shell and other unidentified items that may have served as decorative attachments or insets on wood have been found. Simple shell pendants and small circular gorgets also occur, and one gorget from the McLemore site was made of conch shell. Whole shells, especially small snail or olivella shells, were used for beads.

Miscellaneous stone items include hematite, limonite, steatite, and selenite. Some of these were certainly utilized for pigments, while others, such as the selenite (McLemore site, Burial #34), may have been kept as a curiosity.

In addition to its use in ceramics, clay was normally used as daub in house construction, and small loaf-shaped rolls of raw clay are sometimes found in storage pits or with burials. Human figurines made of clay, and occasionally modeled or decorated to provide some anatomical detail, have been found at a few sites. Other clay items include perforated disks made from pottery sherds, simple elbow-type pipes, thick-walled clay cups having a corncob-roughened exterior, and cone-shaped objects thought to have functioned as pot supports, and pottery vessels.

Pottery sherds are common at Washita River village sites. The most typical ware is plain surfaced or cordmarked. In the eastern part of the region, the most common types are Nocona Plain, Lee Plain, and Lindsay Cordmarked. The types Stafford Plain and Stafford Cordmarked are found in the more western sites. Some trade sherds and even whole vessels occur more rarely as imports.

The pottery has a variety of tempering materials including shell, caliche, crushed rock, sand, and bone. The typical vessels are globular or vase-shaped jars having a small rounded or flattened disk-shaped base. The rims may be straight or they may flare outward slightly. Bowls and bottles have been recovered, especially from sites in the eastern part of the region. Decorations other than cordmarking are not plentiful but include both loop and strap handles, small vertical lip tabs, lugs, appliquéd fillets and nodes, incising, and punctations. Some slipped sherds may represent replication of Sanders-type pieces from the east (Ferring and Perttula 1986). Trade wares include a human effigy bowl, animal figures attached to the rim of bowls, and types that are from the Caddoan area.

SOCIAL AND POLITICAL ORGANIZATION

Plains Village societies may have had greater social and political complexity than the nomadic or seminomadic Plains groups encountered in historic times. Evidence from Washita River phase settlements is indicative of a greater logistical organization than that traditionally associated with Plains Village societies. Washita River phase settlements are sizable, containing 10 to 20 houses and populations from approximately 75 to 150 people. Villages were distributed approximately every 3.2 kilometers along the river. Undoubtedly all villages were not contemporaneous. However, these population and settlement estimates point to large numbers of Washita River phase people living in close proximity. The presence of sedentary aggregated groups necessitates a political structure capable of decision-making beyond the single settlement. It has been suggested by Bell (1984a) that the Washita River phase had a community-level type of structure. In community social organization, political decision-making is vested in a group that is organized at a multisettlement level (Warren 1972). These officials may gain their position through achievement or through inheritance.

Washita River phase groups' interaction with rank-level Caddoan societies living in eastern Oklahoma would also have required greater sociopolitical organization. Especially during the Spiro phase (A.D. 1250–1450), the complexity of the Caddo was reflected by ranking priestly elites and large ceremonial mound complexes in eastern Oklahoma, western Arkansas, and northeastern Texas. They had an extensive trade network ranging from the Rocky Mountains to the Gulf Coast of Mexico and from the Great Lakes to Baja California. In dealing with these priestly rulers, some Washita River phase political leaders undoubtedly would have to assume greater leadership roles.

Both these factors point to a need in Washita River phase society for some degree of centralized decision-making and leadership beyond the egalitarian roles typically ascribed to Plains societies.

SITES

The Heerwald, Cotter-Hutson, McLemore, and Grant sites fall within roughly contemporaneous times.

The Heerwald site (formerly called Shahan II, 34CU7) is located on a terrace of Turkey Creek in Custer County, Oklahoma. The site consists of a scatter of village debris occurring over an area of some 56,400 square meters. Sixty-six features, including one burial with three individuals and 13 possible houses, were documented. Two MASCA-corrected radiocarbon dates place occupation of the site between A.D. 1325 and 1430.

The Cotter-Hutson site is situated on a second terrace of Oak Creek in Custer County. Investigations in 1969 resulted in the recovery of a limited number of artifacts, a child's burial (Burial 1), and an adult mandible. Cotter-Hutson represents the thin scatter of a Plains Village occupation over an unspecified area. Three trash pits contained thick cordmarked and plain-surfaced pottery; Young, Scallorn, Washita, Fresno, and Harrell arrowpoints, unifacial scrapers; manos and metates; elbow pipes; shell disk beads; a second child's burial (Burial 2) (Keith, Snow, and Snow 1971); and a dog burial. These recovered materials fall within the western variety of the Washita River phase. Although dates are lacking, Cotter-Hutson should fall A.D. 1250–1450.

The McLemore site is located on a terrace on the north side of Cobb Creek, a tributary of the Washita River. Excavations of approximately 280 square meters documented the presence of one house, 28 storage or trash pits, one cache pit, and 48 burials containing 59 individuals (Lopez 1970). Three corrected radiocarbon assays place occupation of the site between A.D. 1070 and 1362.

The Grant site is located on a terrace of the Washita River. Excavation of between 2,475 and 3,300 square meters yielded the partial remains of one house, 5 hearths, 29 storage or trash pits, and 19 individuals within 10 burials. One radiocarbon sample from the site was subsequently dated with a MASCA-corrected date of A.D. 1245–1395.

OTHER VILLAGE FARMING SOCIETIES

There are other sites in the Southern Plains that reflect the existence of additional cultural complexes. One of these is the Nagle site, situated on a low terrace adjacent to the North Canadian River. Nagle is a cemetery rather than a habitation site. Materials found with the 16 burials include ear spools, a pottery jar and bowl, and a sandstone abrader. The cemetery at Nagle is viewed as representing the remains of a refuge population of Spiro phase Caddoans (perhaps a lineage) from eastern Oklahoma, perhaps the Spiro Mounds site. Although only one of the individuals recovered exhibits evidence of traumatic death, it is suspected that others in this population were victims of intergroup conflict (see "Warfare on the Southern Plains," this vol., for additional discussion of the Nagle site remains). No dates are available for the Nagle site but the remains probably fall within A.D. 1250 to 1450, the span of the Spiro phase in eastern Oklahoma.

The Protohistoric Period

The Protohistoric period on the Southern Plains begins with Francisco Vásquez de Coronado's entrada across the region in 1541 and lasts until roughly 1800 (Baugh 1986; Bell 1984b; Hofman 1989). During this time, aboriginal societies on the Southern Plains had infrequent and brief contact with Europeans resulting in an extremely limited historical record. Thus, most information on protohistoric Native American cultures has been derived from the archaeological record (Baugh 1982; Bell, Jelks, and Newcomb 1967; Hartley and Miller 1977; Odell 1989; Wedel 1959).

Although all Protohistoric societies can be identified by their emphasis on bison hunting, two distinct, but not necessarily mutually exclusive, patterns have been recognized for the Southern Plains (Lowie 1954). In the eastern portions of the region, there occur coalesced semisedentary village farmers who are historically identified with tribes such as the Pawnee, Wichita, Kansa, and Osage. The eastern villagers lived in sizable settlements of between 100 and 150 houses, which were situated on the terraces of principal streams. Subsistence activities consisted of the growing of corn, beans, and squash. During the fall and winter, a few people remained in the villages while most residents mounted major bison hunting expeditions to supplement the maize diet. Small game was also hunted throughout the year. These village societies often served as the middlemen in trading relationships between other Indians and Whites. This placed them at risk in terms of exposure to European diseases.

Nomadic hunters and traders who are historically linked with the Apache and Comanche inhabit the western areas of the Southern Plains. Dwellings of these groups were typically the transportable tepee. Village size may have equaled that of the coalesced villagers although these Indians routinely moved their settlements in following the bison herds. These nomadic bison hunters traded their bison hides and meat for agricultural goods (corn and beans) to supplement the meat diet. Because of their less sedentary lifeway, the bison hunters were less susceptible to the European diseases, and they eventually gained numerical superiority over their village counterparts as a consee of the demise of villages brought about by contact with White society.

Although a number of Protohistoric societies can be identified for the Southern Plains, the only group to be discussed here is the Edwards complex of western Oklahoma.

EDWARDS COMPLEX

The Edwards complex refers to a series of sites in western Oklahoma along the Salt Fork of the Red River and tributaries of the Washita River. Although Baugh (1986) has collapsed the Edwards complex and the Wheeler complex into the Wheeler phase, Hofman (1989) does not think that the cultural complexes merit combining under one taxonomic label. In fact, existing data on the Edwards and Wheeler complexes more strongly support maintenance of two separate and distinct labels for these cultural entities.

ORIGINS

Origins of the Edwards complex are unclear. While this protohistoric cultural complex may reflect movement into the area by Athapaskan-speaking groups such as the Apache, the Edwards complex may also demonstrate continued presence in the area of sedentary villages of the Wichita or related subgroups. Another consideration raised by Robert G. Campbell (Lee Johnson, personal communication 1989) is that protohistoric western Oklahoma complexes are possibly those of the Tawakoni Wichita.

RESEARCH AND DATES

The initial definition of the Edwards complex was based on the similarity of remains found at the Edwards I, Taylor (34GR9), and Duncan (34WA2) sites in western Oklahoma. Summaries of this cultural complex have been presented by Baugh (1982, 1986) and Hofman (1984, 1989). Radiocarbon dates for the Edwards complex place occupation between A.D. 1500 and 1650.

SETTLEMENT PATTERN

Settlements of the Edwards complex consist of small villages located along major streams or principal tributaries. The number of dwellings present in a settlement is not accurately known. Best estimates would place the number of dwellings between 5 and 20. These houses appear to be of wattle and daub construction with no evidence of the floor channels characteristic of the previous Antelope Creek phase. Of special interest in the construction of Edwards complex settlements is the presence of circular enclosures (ditches) measuring approximately 50 meters in diameter that surround the sites. These ditches are interpreted as fortification trenches. Despite the "distinctiveness" created by construction of these fortifications, only a small number of Edwards complex settlements have been identified. In addition to the presence of "villages," some evidence exists for bison kills or processing stations in the region (Brooks and Flynn 1988).

SUBSISTENCE

Corn has been identified at the Duncan site. However, the quantity of corn is quite small. In addition, no deep storage pits or horticultural tools (e.g., bison scapula hoes, innominate hoes, or horn core hoes) have been found at Duncan, the site that has had the most extensive work. Skeletal remains of Edwards complex people are also lacking. Therefore, the Edwards complex cannot be assumed to be a horticultural society.

TECHNOLOGY

Lithic tools are dominated by small triangular arrowpoints lacking notches (70% Fresnos) with other forms less prominent. Despite the abundance of Garza arrowpoints at some Texas panhandle protohistoric sites, they are extremely rare in Oklahoma. Drills and scrapers are also characteristic. Scrapers are rather small compared to the large items found in historic Wichita villages. The lithic assemblage includes obsidian from principally the Jimenez Mountains of New Mexico.

Ground-stone tools consist of manos and metates, celts, and sandstone abraders. Catlinite pipes are also found at some sites. Ornaments include turquoise disk-type beads and pendants.

Bone artifacts include bison tibia digging sticks and fleshers. Although bison scapula hoes have been found at sites with Edwards complex components, it is not known whether these are protohistoric remains or those of earlier Plains Village people. Awls made from deer and turkey also occur. Bone ornaments include tubular beads as well as one example of engraved bone from the Duncan site. The shell ornaments most commonly found are disk beads and gorgets. Some of the shell is olivella from Baja California.

Clay artifacts are predominantly pottery although some pipes, pipe fragments, other tools, and ornaments were also found. Pottery is represented by a number of indigenous and trade wares. The indigenous pottery includes a black sandy paste ware similar to Scott Plain ceramics found in Kansas or Lovitt Plain from Nebraska. A micaceous plain ware has been identified as Perdido Plain (Baugh 1982). Little Deer ceramics comprise the local decorated wares. Included among the decorated Little Deer specimens are appliqué strips, fingernail punctations, incising, brushed surfaces, neck banding, and carinated rims.

Trade wares from both the Caddoan area and the Southwest have been documented at Edwards complex sites. A diversity of Caddoan pottery is present. Identified types include Avery Engraved, Ripley Engraved, Sanders Engraved, Sanders Plain, Taylor Engraved, Womack Engraved, Maydelle Incised, Keno Trailed, Nash Neck Banded, and Canton Incised. However, some of the Caddoan wares may be replicas based on the analysis of Caddoan sherds found at earlier Plains Village sites in western Oklahoma. Southwestern sherd types include Wiyo Black-on-White, Pecos Glaze V and VI, Pecos or Picuris Plain Red, Ocate and Cimarron micaceous wares, and polychromes (Baugh 1982).

SOCIAL AND POLITICAL ORGANIZATION

The social and political organization of the Edwards complex is not well understood. Historic bison hunting groups documented for the Southern Plains were typically nomadic and maintained group coherence through egalitarian means. However, the presence of fortification trenches around Edwards complex settlements suggests that more complex organization would have been required to mobilize the necessary labor for construction of such fortifications. The use of these villages also indicates a greater degree of sedentariness than that found with nomadic hunters and gatherers. Generally, increased sedentariness also brings about increased need for logistical organization.

Trade relationships intensified significantly during the Protohistoric period on the Southern Plains, and the Edwards complex is no exception. There is trade for obsidian from New Mexico. Other trade networks existed with Wichita (?)

groups in north-central Oklahoma and south-central Kansas for Florence A or Kay County chert. More detailed descriptions of this trade can be found in Speilman (1983).

Warfare or intergroup conflict also apparently increased during the period. Both the Edwards I and Duncan sites, as well as others in west Texas (e.g., the Bridwell site, 41CB27, a Garza complex occupation) have circular entrenchments, which are thought to represent defensive fortifications. There is also considerable ethnohistoric documentation of conflict between groups such as the Wichita and Apache, the Osage and the Wichita, and Southwestern groups and Athapaskan-speaking groups (Wedel 1982; John 1975).

SITE

One site pertaining to the Edwards complex and the Protohistoric period is discussed in this volume. This site is the Edwards I site, located on a terrace of the North Fork of the Red River in Beckham County, Oklahoma. The site consists of a surface scatter of materials covering some 10 acres of area enclosed by a circular ditch that is believed to have functioned as a fortification.

References Cited

Baerreis, D.A., and R.A. Bryson
1966 Dating the Panhandle Aspect Cultures. *Bulletin of the Oklahoma Anthropological Society* 14:105–116.

Baker, E., and J.A. Baker
1939 (Third) Quarterly Report (1939) West Texas State College–WPA Archaeological Project. (Manuscript on file, Panhandle Plains Historical Museum, Canyon, Tex.)

———
1941 Final Report WPA–West Texas State Archaeological Project 9249. (Manuscript on file, Panhandle Plains Historical Museum, Canyon.)

Baugh, T.G., ed.
1982 Edwards I (34Bk2): Southern Plains Adaptations in the Protohistoric Period. *Oklahoma Archeological Survey, Studies in Oklahoma's Past* 8.

———
1986 Culture History and Protohistoric Societies in the Southern Plains. Pp. 167–187 in Current Trends in Southern Plains Archaeology. T.G. Baugh, ed. *Plains Anthropologist Memoir* 21.

Bell, R.E.
1984a The Plains Villagers: The Washita River. Pp. 307–324 in Prehistory of Oklahoma. R.E. Bell, ed. New York: Academic Press.

——
1984b Protohistoric Wichita. Pp. 363–378 in Prehistory of Okla-homa. R.E. Bell, ed. New York: Academic Press.

——, ed.
1984c Prehistory of Oklahoma. New York: Academic Press.

——, E.B. Jelks, and W.W. Newcomb, ed.
1967 A Pilot Study of the Wichita Indian Archaeology and Ethnohistory. (Report submitted to the National Science Foundation, Washington.)

Binford, L.R.
1980 Willow Smoke and Dog's Tails: Hunter Gatherer Settle-ment Systems and Archaeological Site Formation Processes. *American Antiquity* 45:4–20.

Blakeslee, D.J, ed.
1978 The Central Plains Tradition: Internal Development and External Relationships. *University of Iowa, Office of the State Archaeologist, Archaeological Report* 11.

Bond, T.A.
1966 Palynology of Quarternary Terraces and Floodplains of the Washita and Red Rivers, Central and Southeastern Okla-homa. (Unpublished Ph.D. Dissertation in Geology, Uni-versity of Oklahoma, Norman.)

Brooks, R.L.
1987 The Arthur Site: Settlement and Subsistence Structure at a Washita River Phase Village. *Oklahoma Archeological Survey, Studies in Oklahoma's Past* 15.

——
1989 Village Farming Societies. Pp. 71–91 in From Clovis to Comanchero: Archaeological Overview of the Southern Great Plains. J.L. Hofman, R.L. Brooks, J.S. Hays, and D.W. Owsley, eds. *Arkansas Archeological Survey Research Series* 35.

——, and P. Flynn
1988 Tx-71: A Late Prehistoric Bison Processing Station in the Oklahoma Panhandle. *Plains Anthropologist* 33:467–487.

——, M.C. Moore, and D. Owsley
1991 New Smith, 34RM400: A Plains Village Mortuary Site in Western Oklahoma.

Brues, A.
1957 Skeletal Material from the Nagle Site. *Bulletin of the Okla-homa Anthropological Society* 5:101–106.

Bryson, R.A., D.A. Baerreis, and W.M. Wendlund
1970 Tentative Climatic Patterns for Some Late Glacial and Post-glacial Episodes in Central North America. Pp. 271–298 in Life, Land, and Water. W.J. Mayer-Oakes, ed. Winnepeg: University of Manitoba Press.

Campbell, R.G.
1969 Prehistoric Panhandle Culture on the Chaquaqua Plateau, Southeast Colorado. (Unpublished Ph.D. Dis-sertation in Anthropology, University of Colorado, Boulder.)

Davis, E. M.
1969 A Diary of the 1969 TAS Field School at Lake Meredith in the Panhandle. *Texas Archaeology* 13(2):7–17.

Drass, R.R., and M.C. Moore
1987 The Linville II Site (34Rm-492) and Plains Village Mani-festations in Far Western Oklahoma. *Plains Anthropologist* 32:404–418.

——, and F.E. Swenson
1986 Variation in the Washita River Phase of Central and West-ern Oklahoma. *Plains Anthropologist* 31:35–50.

——, and C.L. Turner
1989 An Archeological Reconnaissance of the Wolf Creek Drainage Basin Ellis County, Oklahoma. *Oklahoma Archeo-logical Survey, Archeological Resources Survey Report* 35.

——, T.G. Baugh, and P. Flynn
1987 The Heerwald Site and Early Plains Village Adaptations in the Southern Plains. *North American Archaeologist* 8:151–190.

Duffield, L.F.
1970 Some Panhandle Aspect Sites in Texas: Their Vertebrates and Paleoecology. (Unpublished Ph.D. Dissertation in Anthro-pology, University of Wisconsin, Madison.)

Eyerly, T.L.
1912 The Buried City of the Panhandle. *The Archaeological Bulle-tin* 3:1–5.

Fenneman, N.M.
1931 Physiography of the Western United States. New York: McGraw-Hill.

Ferring, C. R., and T. Perttula
1986 Defining the Provenance of Red-slipped Pottery from Texas and Oklahoma by Petrographic Methods. (Un-published manuscript, Oklahoma Archeological Survey, Norman.)

Flynn, P.
1984 An Analysis of the 1973 Test Excavations at the Zimms Site (34RM72). Pp. 215–290 in Archaeology of the Mixed Grass Prairie, Phase I: Quartermaster Creek. T.G. Baugh, ed. *Oklahoma Archaeological Survey, Archeological Resources Survey Report* 20.

——
1986 Analysis of Test Excavations at the Zimms Site (34RM72), Western Oklahoma. Pp. 129–140 in Current Trends in Southern Plains Archaeology. T.G. Baugh, ed. *Plains Anthro-pologist Memoir* 21.

Green, F.E.
1967 Archeological Salvage in the Sanford Reservoir Area. *Na-tional Park Service Report* 14-10-0333-1126. Alibates Na-tional Monument, Amarillo, Texas.

Hall, S.A.
1982 Late Holocene Paleoecology of the Southern High Plains. *Quaternary Research* 17:391–407.

1983 Geology and Holocene Sediments and Buried Trees of Carnegie Canyon. Pp. 15–46 in The Geomorphology and Archaeology of Carnegie Canyon, Ft. Cobb Laterals Watershed, Caddo County, Oklahoma. C. Lintz and S.A. Hall, eds. *Oklahoma Conservation Commission, Archaeological Research Report* 10.

Hartley, J.D., and A.F. Miller

1977 Archaeological Investigations of the Bryson-Paddock Site, an Early Contact Period Site on the Southern Plains. *Oklahoma River Basin Survey, Archaeological Site Report* 32.

Haynes, G.H.

1932 A report on the excavations of Saddleback Ruin. (Unpublished Masters Thesis in Anthropology, Texas Tech University, Lubbock.)

Hofman, J.L.

1978 The Development and Northern Relationships of the Archaeological Phases in the Southern Plains Subarea. Pp. 6–35 in The Central Plains Tradition: Internal Development and External Relationships. D.J. Blakeslee, ed. *University of Iowa, Office of the State Archaeologist, Archaeological Report* 11.

1984 The Western Protohistoric: A Summary of the Edwards and Wheeler Complexes. Pp. 347–362 in Prehistory of Oklahoma. R.E. Bell, ed. New York: Academic Press.

1989 Protohistoric Culture History on the Southern Plains. Pp. 91–101 in From Clovis to Comanchero: Archaeological Overview of the Southern Great Plains. J.L. Hofman, R.L. Brooks, J.S. Hays, and D.W. Owsley, eds. *Arkansas Archeological Survey Research Series* 35.

——, R.L. Brooks, J.S. Hays, and D.W. Owsley, eds.

1989 From Clovis to Comanchero: Archeological Overview of the Southern Great Plains. *Arkansas Archeological Survey Research Series* 35.

Holden, W.C.

1930 The Canadian Valley Expedition of March, 1930. *Bulletin of the Texas Archaeological and Paleontological Society* 2:21–32.

1933 Excavations at Saddleback Ruin. *Bulletin of the Texas Archaeological and Paleontological Society* 5:39–52.

Holder, P.

1970 The Hoe and the Horse on the Plains: A Study of Cultural Development Among North American Indians. Lincoln: University of Nebraska Press.

Hughes, D.T.

1986 The Courson 1986 Archeological Project. (Paper presented at the Annual Meeting of the Texas Archaeological Society, Laredo.)

——, and A. Hughes-Jones

1987 The Courson Archeological Projects, 1985 and 1986. Perryton, Texas: Innovative Publishing.

Hughes, J.

1962 Field Trip Record, April 15, 1962. (Notes on file, Panhandle Plains Museum, Canyon, Tex.)

Hunt, C.B.

1974 Natural Regions of the United States and Canada. San Francisco: W. H. Freeman.

John, E.A.H.

1975 Storms Brewed in Other Men's Worlds, the Confrontations of Indians, Spanish, and French in the Southwest, 1540–1795. College Station, Tex.: Texas A&M University Press.

Johnson, C.S.

1939 A Report on the Antelope Creek Ruin. *Bulletin of the Texas Archeological and Paleontological Society* 11:190–203.

Keith, K.D., C.C. Snow, and J.B. Snow

1971 A Child's Skeleton from Western Oklahoma. *Bulletin of the Oklahoma Anthropological Society.* 20:115–131.

Keller, J.E.

1975 Black Dog Village. *Texas Highway Publications in Archaeology Report* 5.

Krieger, A.D.

1946 Culture Complexes and Chronology in Northern Texas. *University of Texas Publication* 4640.

Lintz, C.

1978 Panhandle Aspect and Its Early Relationship with Upper Republican. Pp. 36–55 in The Central Plains Tradition: Internal Development and External Relationships. D. Blakeslee, ed. *University of Iowa Office of the Iowa State Archaeologist, Archaeological Report* 11.

1982 An Overview of the Antelope Creek Focus. Pp. 37–56 in *Transactions of the 17th Regional Archaeological Symposium for Southeastern New Mexico and Western Texas.*

1986 Architecture and Community Variability within the Antelope Creek Phase. *Oklahoma Archeological Survey, Studies in Oklahoma's Past* 14.

Lopez, D.R.

1970 The McLemore Cemetery Complex: An Analysis of Prehistoric Burial Customs. *Bulletin of the Oklahoma Anthropological Society* 19:137–150.

Lowie, R.H.

1954 Indians of the Plains. Lincoln: University of Nebraska Press.

Lowrey, E.J.

1932 The Archaeology of the Antelope Creek Ruins. (Unpublished Master's Thesis in Anthropology, Texas Tech College, Lubbock.)

Marmaduke, W.S., and H. Whitsett

1975 Reconnaissance and Archaeological Studies in the Cana-
dian River Valley. *Canadian Breaks, A Natural Area Survey* 7.
Austin: Division of Natural Resources and Environment,
University of Texas.

Moore, M. C.

1984 A Reconnaissance of Quartermaster Creek. Pp. 51–214 in
Archaeology of the Mixed Grass Prairie Phase I: Quarter-
master Creek. T.G. Baugh, ed. *Oklahoma Archeological Survey,
Archeological Resources Survey Report* 20.

Moorehead, W.K.

1931 *The Archaeology of the Arkansas River Valley.* Andover: Andover Press.

Odell, G.H.

1989 Final Report on Archaeological Excavations Conducted
Between May and July, 1988 at the Lasley Vore Site (34Tu-
65), Jenks, Oklahoma. (Report submitted to the Kimberly-
Clark Corporation, Greenville, S. Carolina.)

Pillaert, E.

1963 The McLemore Site of the Washita River Focus. *Bulletin of
the Oklahoma Anthropological Society* 11:1–113.

Ralph, E.K., H.N. Michael, and M.C. Han

1974 Radiocarbon Dates and Reality. *Archaeology of Eastern North
America* 2(1):1–20.

Reeves, C.C.

1966 Fluvial Lake Basins of West Texas. *Journal of Geology* 74:269–
291.

Reid, K.C., and J.A. Artz

1984 Hunters of the Forest Edge: Culture, Time, Process in the
Little Caney Basin (1980, 1981, and 1982 Field Seasons).
Oklahoma Archeological Survey, Studies in Oklahoma's Past 13.

Richards, M.K.

1971 The Lee Site, a Late Prehistoric Manifestation in Garvin
County, Oklahoma. *Bulletin of the Oklahoma Anthropological
Society* 20:1–82.

Schneider, F.E.

1969 The Roy Smith Site, Bv-14, Beaver County, Oklahoma.
Bulletin of the Oklahoma Anthropological Society 18:119–179.

Shaeffer, J.B.

1957 The Nagle Site, Ok-4. *Bulletin of the Oklahoma Anthropological Society* 5:93–100.

——

1966 Salvage Archaeology in Oklahoma, Vol. 2: Papers of the
Oklahoma Archaeological Salvage Project, Nos. 18–21.
Bulletin of the Oklahoma Anthropological Society 14:1–86.

Sharrock, F.W.

1961 The Grant Site of the Washita River Focus. *Bulletin of the
Oklahoma Anthropological Society* 9:1–66.

Spielman, K.A.

1983 Late Prehistoric Exchange Between the Southwest and
Southern Plains. *Plains Anthropologist* 28:257–272.

Suhm, D.A., A.D. Krieger, and E.B. Jelks

1954 An Introductory Handbook of Texas Archeology. *Bulletin of
the Texas Archaeological Society* 25.

Taylor, J.W.

1986 A Canyon in Western Canadian County: Archaeological
and Geomorphological Clues from Non-Destructive Testing. *Bulletin of the Oklahoma Anthropological Society* 35:69–
134.

Texas Historical Commission

1984 Completion Report (Project: Landegrin Mesa). (Report
submitted to the National Register of Historic Places.
Project No. 48-84-OJB-48.11.)

Thornbury, W.P.

1965 *Regional Geomorphology of the United States.* New York: John
Wiley and Sons.

Walker, J.R.

1978 Geomorphic Evolution of the Southern High Plains. *Bay-
lor Geological Studies Bulletin* 35.

Wallis, C.S., Jr.

1984 Summary of Notes and Earlier Analyses of the Wickham
#3 Site, 34Rm-29, Roger Mills County, Oklahoma. *Bulle-
tin of the Oklahoma Anthropological Society* 33:1–29.

Warren, R.

1972 The Community in America. New York: Rand McNally.

Watson, V.

1950 The Optima Focus of the Panhandle Aspect: Description
and Analysis. *Bulletin of the Texas Archeological and Paleontological Society* 21:7–68.

Wedel, M.

1982 The Wichita Indians in the Arkansas River Basin. Pp. 118–
134 in Plains Indian Studies: A Collection of Essays in
Honor of John C. Ewers and Waldo Wedel. D.H. Ubelaker
and H.J. Viola, eds. *Smithsonian Contributions to Anthropology*
30.

Wedel, W.

1959 The Kansa. *Bureau of American Ethnology Bulletin* 174.

——

1961 Prehistoric Man on the Great Plains. Norman, Okla.: University of Oklahoma Press.

CHAPTER 4

○○○

Northern Plains Woodland Mortuary Practices

J. SIGNE SNORTLAND

Analysis of mortuary practices is one of the few means available to archaeologists for investigating the outcome of purposeful behavior in prehistoric cultures (O'Shea 1981:3). Mortuary analysis links disposal treatment to social structure and organization (Goldstein 1981:54). In this chapter historic period Northern Plains tribal funerary behavior is examined to identify factors essential to the interpretation of prehistoric mortuary practices. With the factors thus identified, a Northern Plains Woodland cemetery, the Jamestown Mounds site (32SN22), is analyzed to reveal burial patterns, called mortuary variables, and to reconstruct mortuary events. Identified variables are compared with Hopewell and Sonota burial practices. The results are used to review critically defined Northern Plains burial complexes. This analysis reveals the complexity involved in the construction of burial mounds and, more importantly, the necessity of interdisciplinary studies to maximize the interpretation of human cemeteries. The partnership of archaeology and physical anthropology forms the foundation of this approach.

To explain variations in burial modes and associated cultural materials, archaeologists on the Northern Plains have defined three burial mound complexes: Sonota, Arvilla, and Devils Lake.arch–Sourisford (fig. 1). These complexes are dif-ferentiated by geographic boundaries, artifact trait lists, and temporal delimiters.

The Sonota complex consists of mounds containing large, oval, subfloor, straight-walled burial chambers holding multiple individuals (Neuman 1975). These mounds appear to have been constructed about A.D. 1–600. Artifacts include conical textile-impressed or plain ceramics, Besant projectile points, exotic shells, freshwater shell artifacts, few copper ornaments, pigments, and a full range of chipped stone tools, ground stone tools, and worked bone tools and ornaments. The most distinctive feature of the complex is the association of bison crania or articulated bison skeletons with the central burial chamber.

The Arvilla complex is identified by linear and circular mounds with subsoil pits holding disarticulated primary and secondary burials (Jenks 1932; Johnson 1973). Grave goods range from utilitarian to ornamental. The complex dates from A.D. 500 to 900 but may have persisted for a longer period in the Red River drainage of Manitoba (Johnson 1973:66).

The Devils Lake–Sourisford complex is defined by the presence of exotic items such as incised miniature vessels, whelk shell gorgets, tubular pipes, columella shell beads, and incised stone tablets (Syms 1979:283). Burial mode has yet to

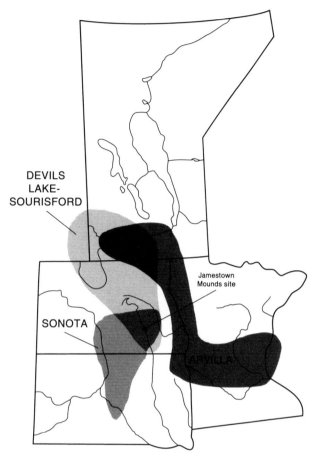

Fig. 1. Geographical boundaries of the Sonota, Arvilla, and Devils Lake–Sourisford burial complexes following Neuman (1975), Johnson (1973), and Syms (1979).

be defined as few of these mounds have been professionally excavated. Radiocarbon dates from three mounds and two occupation areas range from A.D. 900 to 1400.

Burial Practices During the Historic Period

The purpose of examining historic mortuary behavior is to identify behavior patterns that aid in interpretation of the archaeological record. The ethnographic data reveal that variations in orientation of the head, position of the corpse, types of burial goods, and use of ocher appear to have depended upon a variety of factors including age, sex, and social position. Burial goods interred with the deceased included a greater variety than the archaeological record suggests. Perishables such as food and clothing were often used as burial offerings, and among some groups the food was consumed by the mourners, left for the poor, or eaten by scavenging animals

(Bushnell 1927). Burial practices varied among Northern Plains tribes, but there were also many similarities.

SIOUX

According to Catlin (1973:10), the Sioux "often deposit their dead on trees, and on scaffolds; but more generally bury in the tops of bluffs, or near their villages." When a member of the tribe dies "after the autumnal leaves have fallen," they "deposit the remains upon a scaffold, not to be removed until the leaves have unfolded in spring, and if a death occur after the leaf-buds have burst, the remains of the dead are likewise deposited, not to be removed until the leaves have fallen in autumn" (Comfort 1873:389). The scaffolded remains were later buried in the ground during the warm season (Pond 1986:162–164). With the Sisseton Sioux a person "was only buried in the ground as a mark of disrespect in consequence of the person having been murdered, in which case the body would be buried in the ground, face down, head toward the south and with a piece of fat in the mouth" (Bushnell 1927:24). The Sisseton also placed weapons and medicine bundles beside the body of a warrior and oriented his head to the south. Women and children's faces were painted red and cooking utensils were placed with the body instead of weapons. A kettle of cooked food was placed at the head of a child's grave (Bushnell 1927:25). The Yankton scaffolded the dead, except "those who die in battle are buried on the spot" (Bushnell 1927:28). Scaffolded bodies were wrapped in hide or cloth and personal effects were placed with them. The son of a Yankton chief was buried in the ground in a standing posture (Bushnell 1927:28).

MANDAN

The Mandan "never bury the dead, but place the bodies on slight scaffolds . . . and they are there left to moulder and decay. . . . When the scaffolds on which the bodies rest, decay and fall to the ground, the nearest relations having buried the rest of the bones, take the skulls . . . and place them in circles of an hundred or more" (Catlin 1973:89–90). Children who died before they were named were placed in trees or buried apart from other members of the tribe (Bowers 1973:98). Murder victims were buried face down (Bowers 1965:171). Scaffold burial was a recent change. The Mandan said that "the Lord of Life [First Creator] has, indeed, told us that we come from the ground, and should return to it again; yet we have lately begun to lay the bodies of the dead on stages, because we love them, and would weep at the sight of them" (Wood 1967:18).

The dying person decided whether he would rather be buried or exposed on a scaffold; "in earlier times earth burials were more common" (Bowers 1973:99). Circumstances also dictated the form of burial. During smallpox epidemics, traditional funerary forms were not followed. During the 1837 smallpox epidemic at Fort Clark, an observer reported "several Men, Women, and Children that has been abandoned in the Village, are laying dead in the lodges, some outside of the Village, others in the little river, not entered" (Abel 1932:128).

HIDATSA

The Hidatsa recognize a number of methods of dealing with the dead and remember a time when burials were placed in the ground. They had been to Devils Lake where they had "seen the burial mounds of their old people who formerly lived there" (Bowers 1956:170). Informants spoke of "traditions of earth burials made in mounds or mounds built over the burial in the outline of the individuals 'spirit god'" (Bowers 1965:171). Both scaffolding and burial were practiced during the Historic period. When a man died, his pipe, weapons, personal bundle, and pigments were placed with the body. If a person died away from the village, a year later the skull was collected and returned to the village (Bowers 1965:169–171).

ARIKARA

Orser (1980:116) summarizes Arikara mortuary practices as follows: "[They] usually buried their dead in a sitting . . . or extended . . . posture, wrapped in either a buffalo robe or other skin . . . covered with wood." The body would be facing west. Scaffolding a corpse prior to interment may have been an older mortuary practice among the Arikara, who "abandoned the old method of scaffolding their dead" (Orser 1980:114). Scaffolding appears also to have been practiced when death occurred during the winter (Orser 1980:118). Upon occasion, old graves were reopened to include additional burials. "We found thirty-one new graves, and we found that several old ones had been opened, and the surface set thick with prickly pears to conceal the new dirt" (Orser 1980:115).

Burial goods described by observers include bow and arrows, pipes, fire steel flint, utilitarian objects, vermilion, bison hides, and hair from the heads of mourners. "If the deceased has left a son, he receives his father's medicine apparatus; if not, it is buried with him in the grave" (Orser 1980:115).

ASSINIBOINE

The Assiniboine practiced scaffolding, although this did not appear to be the preferred method:

If the death happen in the winter-season, and at a distance from the burial-ground of the family, the body invariably accompanies all the wanderings and journeys of the survivors, till the spring, and till their arrival at the places of interment. In the mean time, it is everywhere rested on a scaffold, out of the reach of beasts of prey. The grave is made of a circular form, about five feet deep, and lined with bark of the birch, or some other tree, or with skins. A seat is prepared, and the body is placed in a sitting posture, with supporters on either side. The Body and its accompaniments are covered with bark, the bark with logs, and the logs with earth (Henry 1969:310).

Another early observer, Henry Kelsey in 1690, describes the funeral ceremony after one of his Assiniboine guides died. He notes evidence of cremation and states: "Last night death ceased & this morning his body was burned according to their way they making A great feast for him yt did it now after yt ye flesh was burned his Bones were taken & buried wth Loggs set up round of about ten foot Long so we pitcht today near 14 Miles & came to they holding it not good to stay by ye Dead" (quoted in Hanna 1976:6).

PLAINS OJIBWA

The historic Plains Ojibwa practiced at least four forms of burial. In the winter the dead were wrapped in a hide and placed on a scaffold or in a tree. In seasons when the ground was thawed, simple inhumation was practiced, or a shallow grave was excavated and the body interred in an extended position. The body was wrapped in a hide and covered with poles, the hole was filled with earth, and a protective cover of rocks was layered over the grave. The most common type of grave until 1910 was the "house type" in which an individual was placed in a sitting position at one end of a pit, and a gable roofed structure was constructed over the grave. A small hole was cut in the wall opposite the corpse, and for four days offerings were inserted through the hole and left on a shelf nailed beneath it (Howard 1977:226–227).

To summarize, these ethnographic accounts demonstrate changes through time in mortuary practices, as well as variations within single components. Although the accounts emphasize the widespread use among Northern Plains tribes of scaffolding or exposure of the deceased, this was not the only mode of dealing with the dead. Most historic groups either remembered burial in the ground or still practiced interment as an alternative funerary mode. The selection of the particular form of disposal depended on a variety of factors. The most prevalent of these are age or social affiliation, gender, and circumstances of death. Likewise, time of year and distance from burial grounds were also considered. Consequently, a number of cultural and environmental factors were involved in the selection of a particular practice. Although some changes in practices are temporally related, variations within a component are culturally determined.

Methods of Mortuary Analysis

Mortuary analysis employs a number of quantifiable variables that identify patterning in the burials (Buikstra 1976; Goldstein 1981). These descriptors record the physical representation of the burials in the archaeological context. Six mortuary variables have been selected to define patterns in the Jamestown sample: burial mode, including disposition of the burial and degree of articulation; burial preparation; number of individuals per burial; burial orientation; burial locus; and burial associations, which includes number of types of burial goods and nonlocal goods.

Observed patterns are examined with respect to nine burial factors. These factors are the social, cultural, and environmental mechanisms that explain the reasons for the patterns observed in the archaeological record as defined by the variables. The factors are derived from the ethnographic data and from other studies of mortuary practices (Bartel 1982; Binford 1971; Brown 1981; Buikstra 1976; Goldstein 1981; Saxe 1970; Tainter 1978; Ucko 1969). A society may practice more than one type of burial depending on a variety of circumstances (Binford 1971). The burial factors considered include social status, social affiliation (i.e., tribe, clan, etc.), age, gender, environmental constraints, distance to cemetery (from place of death), number of deaths, circumstances of death, and temporal change.

Jamestown Mounds Site

The Jamestown Mounds site provides an opportunity to apply this approach to mounds found on the Northern Plains. The site is situated on a high terrace overlooking the confluence of the James River with Pipestem Creek within the city limits of Jamestown, North Dakota (fig. 1). Site 32SN22 consists of the cemetery; 32SN207 is the adjacent area occupied by the builders and subsequent users of the cemetery. Originally composed of an interconnected complex of nine linear, seven

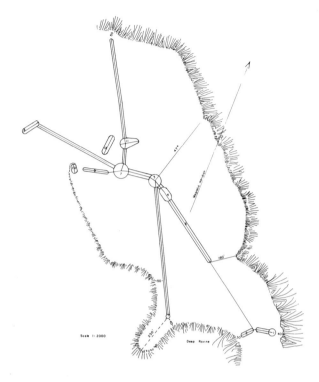

Fig. 2. Jamestown Mounds site (Lewis 1883).

conical, and two oblong mounds (fig. 2), the cemetery was reduced by modern construction to six partial mounds.

The site probably was first recorded by Thomas (1873), who may have excavated part of one of the conical mounds. Land examiners from the Northern Pacific Railroad also excavated a mound in the vicinity (Foster 1878). T.H. Lewis (1883) produced the only complete map of the mound complex (fig. 2). By 1952, much of the complex had been cultivated and only three mounds were recorded (Cain 1952). These mounds were mapped in 1974 (Fox 1987; Schneider and Vehik 1976).

Emergency salvage excavation of three mounds (Mounds A, A1, and B) recovered a minimum of 75 individuals (Snortland 1987; Williams 1985). Four temporal components were identified (Components I, II, III, and IV); table 1 presents the radiocarbon dates for these. The stratigraphy of the mounds indicated three stages of mound construction: Components I, III, and IV. Component II was a period when central burial chambers (ossuaries) were reused, but without any apparent addition of fill to the mound structures (fig. 3).

PROBLEMS WITH SITE ANALYSIS

Destruction of the Jamestown Mounds site prior to archaeological excavation resulted in an irrevocable loss of data. Only

Table 1. Radiocarbon Dates from Sites 32SN22 and 32SN207

Site/Mound	Provenance	SHSND No.	Lab No.	Sample Type	Uncorrected A.D.	Calendar Date Range[a]
32SN22/A1	F-12, ossuary	82-T-10	Tx-4732	Bone	110 ± 180	25 B.C.–A.D. 395
32SN22/A2	F-23, ossuary	82-T-14	Tx-4745	Bone	160 ± 90	A.D. 90–340
32SN22/A2	F-9, cache pit	82-T-12	Tx-4734	Bone	380 ± 240	A.D. 240–640
32SN22/A2	F-23, ossuary	82-A-2	Beta-5407	Wood	440 ± 120	A.D. 410–650
32SN22/A2	F-23, ossuary	82-T-4	Tx-4727	Wood	600 ± 90	A.D. 600–770
32SN22/A1	F-12, ossuary	82-T-9	Tx-4731	Bone	580 ± 170	A.D. 540–790
32SN22/A1	F-12, ossuary	82-T-2	Tx-4725	Wood	610 ± 70	A.D. 636–766
32SN22/A1	F-12, ossuary	82-A-1	Beta-5406	Wood	750 ± 70	A.D. 689–897
32SN22/A1	F-14, pit	83-B-1	Beta-6570	Bone	930 ± 70	A.D. 897–1031
32SN22/A1	F-1(1981), pit	82-T-13	Tx-4735	Bone	980 ± 90	A.D. 970–1170
32SN22/B	F-1, ossuary	82-T-8	Tx-4744	Bone	30 ± 120	50 B.C.–A.D. 230
32SN22/B	F-1, ossuary	82-T-5	Tx-4728	Charcoal	50 ± 70	A.D. 15–215
32SN22/B	F-7, pit	82-T-11	Tx-4733	Bone	190 ± 200	A.D. 30–460 A.D. 477–529
32SN22/B	F-4, pit	83-B-2	Beta-6571	Bone	80 ± 60	A.D. 785–962
32SN22/B	F-25, pit	82-T-15	Tx-4743	Bone	990 ± 210	A.D. 890–1260
32SN207/B	F-3, hearth	82-T-3	Tx-4726	Charcoal	650 ± 100	A.D. 650–810 A.D. 845–852
32SN207/D	F-4, cache pit	82-T-6	Tx-4730	Charcoal	640 ± 140	A.D. 600–890
32SN207/D	F-6, hearth	82-T-1	Tx-4724	Charcoal	830 ± 70	A.D. 809–1000
32SN207/D	F-22, cache pit	82-T-6	Tx-4729	Charcoal	1110 ± 270	A.D. 940–1395

[a]Corrected by Stuiver and Pearson (1986).

three mounds were excavated systematically. Thus, the total number of individuals buried in the Jamestown mortuary complex can only be approximated. Given that linear mounds on the Northern Plains seldom contain human remains, that the contents of oval mounds are unknown, and that approximately 25 people were buried in each of the three excavated conical mounds, it is estimated that a total of 175 individuals could have been buried in the seven conical mounds. The analyzed individuals, therefore, would represent 43 percent of the total estimated burial population.

Damage to mounds resulted in problems in attribution. When cultural materials from Mounds A1 and A2 could not be clearly differentiated, the two mounds were designated Mound A.

The interpretation of scattered burials, in which bones are disarticulated, presents a particular problem. Scattered burials can represent a particular mode of interment, as interpreted in this study, or a processing stage in an overall multiple-stage burial program, or some other disposition mode that has been subsequently disturbed. Evidence of a multiple-stage program is indicated by two relatively empty cache pits found near the central ossuaries. Although the cache pits contained few

pieces of cultural material, both held small fragments of human bone. Empty cache pits associated with ossuaries are interpreted as former burial pits emptied to fill an ossuary (Kivett 1953:127) similar to the Huron Feast of the Dead (Trigger 1990:126–131). In a multiple-stage program, the body was buried and then moved, or exposed on a scaffold, defleshed, and buried again. Other combinations were also possible. However, scattered burials can also result from postdepositional disturbances.

The interpretation of the central ossuary in Mound B presents another problem. This feature was excavated previously (Foster 1878; Thomas 1873:655–656). If materials were removed from the ossuary, the significance of the single female associated with multiple artifacts in the central burial chamber becomes questionable.

The greatest problem in mortuary analysis is small samples. Whenever possible, components were separated during this project, resulting in small samples in each component. With further research at additional sites, it is anticipated that components from similar time periods can be combined to increase sample sizes.

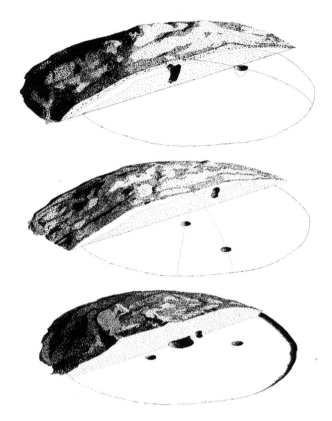

Fig. 3. Schematic representation of stratigraphy of Mound B (32SN22). Top, Component IV; center, Component III; bottom, Component I. This mound was not used during Component II.

MORTUARY VARIABLES

BURIAL MODE

Six forms of burial modes are identified based on disposition of the burial and degree of articulation: bundle, dissected, scattered, flexed-lying, flexed-sitting, and prone. The first three are secondary interments. The last three are primary interments varying only in placement of limbs and posture.

Bundle burials are composed primarily of a tight cluster of disarticulated long bones and crania, presumably as a result of transportation from a scaffold and interment in a bag or basket. Exposure is reflected by the absence of smaller elements and weathering of bones.

Dissected disposition refers specifically to the intentional separation of articulated elements and is distinguished from secondary interments by evidence of purposeful disarticulation, such as cutmarks near articular surfaces.

Scattered burials are disarticulated, secondary interments characterized by weathered elements; bones generally lack signs of dissection. Unlike bundle burials, the bones are not grouped into a cluster and are frequently composed of a few isolated elements.

Flexed-lying burials are primary interments situated on a side or back with knees bent and legs pulled up into the midsection. Arms are also in a flexed position.

Flexed-sitting burials are primary interments in an upright fetal position with knees bent and drawn up to the chest.

Prone individuals are interred face (ventral side) down as a primary interment. In the Jamestown prone case, the arms point down into the underlying soil and the knees are bent with the lower legs extending upward.

Table 2 lists burial modes in each of the components. Numbers are based on minimum number of individuals (Williams 1985). Position of individuals in each feature is illustrated in figure 4. In general, if there were more than one primary interment in a single grave feature, both bodies were in the same position. In most cases, pits containing primary interments included isolated elements from other individuals.

BURIAL PREPARATION

Evidence of burial preparation consists of ocher stains on bone, cut marks, postmortem alteration of elements, disarticulation, rearticulation, and partial cremation. Red or yellow

Table 2. **Burial Modes in Each of the Mound Components**[a]

Mode	Component I		Component II		Component III		Component IV		Total
	N	%	N	%	N	%	N	%	
Bundle	1	2.2	2	18.2	2	16.7	0	0	5
Dissected	28	60.9	0	0	0	0	0	0	28
Flexed-lying	1	2.2	1	9.1	3	25.0	1	16.7	6
Flexed-sitting	3	6.3	1	9.1	2	16.7	0	0	6
Prone	1	2.2	0	0	0	0	0	0	1
Scattered	12	26.1	7	63.6	5	41.7	5	83.3	29
Total	46	99.9	11	100.0	12	100.1	6	100.0	75

[a]Percentages do not add up to 100 due to rounding.

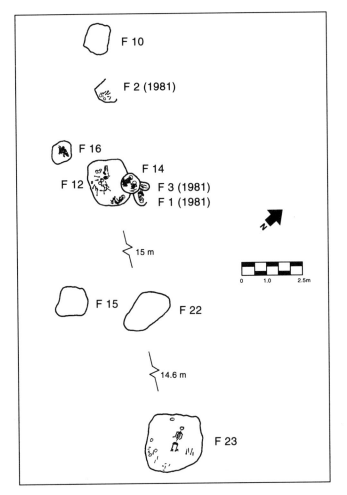

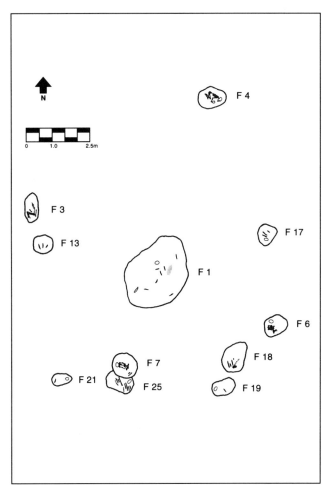

Fig. 4. Burial positions of individuals interred in Mound A (32SN22)(left) and Mound B (32SN22)(right). Circles are disarticulated crania and lines represent disarticulated long bones.

ocher stains bones from 11 Mound A individuals and 10 Mound B burials (table 3). Cut marks are visible on only three Mound A adults and are not apparent on Mound B burials. Possible postmortem cranial alteration takes the form of crushed parietals on two skulls from the Mound A1 ossuary. Although the parietals could have been crushed by the weight of grave fill, similar alterations are noted in other Woodland sites and probably represent intentional postmortem activity (cf. Obey 1974:19). Disarticulation, a characteristic of both scattered and dissected burial modes, is the most frequent type of burial preparation; 48 cases in Mound A and 14 in Mound B were observed. Rearticulation is rare and is found in only three instances, once in Mound A and twice in B. Cremation, an unexpected form of burial preparation, was identified in 11 Mound A individuals and possibly one Mound B case (Williams 1985:3.21, 3.22).

NUMBER OF INDIVIDUALS PER BURIAL

The burials are divided into two types: ossuary and small pit grave. An ossuary is a large pit containing four or more individuals, commonly referred to as a central burial chamber. A small pit grave is not so large and contains one to three interments. Three ossuaries were uncovered in the Jamestown Mounds. The largest, in terms of number of interments, was in the center of Mound A1, which held 28 individuals in the lower level and two in the upper. The ossuary in Mound A2 had 12 interments with approximately nine in the lower level and three in the upper. In contrast, only one partial individual was uncovered in the Mound B ossuary. It is classified as an ossuary due to its large size and because it appeared to have been previously excavated. The number of individuals in small pit graves in

Table 3. Evidence of Burial Preparation at Jamestown Mounds by Age and Sex[a]

Preparation	Total Subadult		Total Adult		Unknown Gender		Adult Male		Adult Female	
	N	%	N	%	N	%	N	%	N	%
Mound A										
Ocher	4	10.2	7	18.9	1	5.3	2	20.0	4	50.0
Cut Marks	0		3	8.1	2	10.5	0		1	12.5
Cranial Alteration	0		2	5.4	2	10.5	0		0	
Dissection	33	84.6	15	40.5	10	52.6	4	40.0	1	12.5
Rearticulation	1	2.6	0		0		0		0	
Cremation	1	2.6	10	27.0	4	21.1	4	40.0	2	25.0
Total	39	100.0	37	99.9	19	100.0	10	100.0	8	100.0
Mound B										
Ocher	5	35.7	5	38.5	1	16.7	1	100.0	3	50.0
Cut Marks	0		0		0		0		0	
Cranial Alteration	0		0		0		0		0	
Dissection	7	50.0	7	53.8	5	83.3	0		2	33.3
Rearticulation	2	14.3	0		0		0		0	
Cremation	0		1(?)	7.7	0		0		1(?)	16.7
Total	14	100.0	13	100.0	6	100.0	1	100.0	6	100.0

[a]Percentages do not add up to 100 due to rounding.

Mound A ranged from one to four and averaged 2.6 individuals. The number of occupants of Mound B pit graves also ranged from one to four and averaged 1.9.

BURIAL ORIENTATION

None of the individuals is positioned toward the northeast or south: one is oriented toward the east, two toward the southeast, two toward the west, one toward the southwest, and six toward the north and northwest. Orientation was determined by the placement of the superior end of the vertebral column or cranium, if present. Because the location of the cranium and the vertebral column of bundle burials often gave conflicting results, orientation was measured only on primary interments. Sample size was small due to the exclusion of secondary interments, which necessitated combining components.

BURIAL LOCUS

Burial locus refers to the location of a grave within a mound. Three loci are identified: central burial chamber, subfloor pit, and mound fill pit. A central burial chamber is the ossuary located under the apex of a mound beneath the original ground surface. Subfloor pits are small pits also constructed beneath the original ground surface but are situated under the periphery of the mound (fig. 4). These

are contemporaneous with the central burial chambers. Mound fill pits are small pits that intrude into the mound stratum of the previous component. Subfloor pits are found only in Mound B.

Burial mode varies by locus. All dissected burials and a single prone burial are located in central burial chambers; no flexed-sitting burials are associated with these chambers. Burials in subfloor pits generally are flexed-sitting or scattered, and the majority of mound fill interments are secondary. Flexed-lying individuals also are found in mound fill. The majority of individuals (57%) were interred in the central burial chambers, 11 percent in subfloor pits, and 32 percent in mound fill (table 4).

Table 4. Burial Mode by Locus

Mode	Central Chamber Component I	Subfloor Pit Component I	Mound Fill Pit Components II–IV
Bundle	1	0	2
Dissected	28	0	0
Scattered	12	4	15
Flexed-lying	1	1	4
Flexed-sitting	0	3	3
Prone	1	0	0
Total	43	8	24

Table 5. Artifact Associations in Mound A[a]

| Item | Locus | | | | Individual | | | |
	Central I	Md Fill II	Md Fill III	Md Fill IV	Subadult	Adult U	Adult M	Adult F
Abrader								
Biface	1		1					1
Bone artifacts—other	2							
Bone tube		1						
Ceramics	1							1
Copper	1					1		
Hide	1							
Horn gorget								
Limestone rock								
Mano/metate								
Projectile point	1							
Groundstone, round								
Groundstone, tabular								
Shell, *Anculosa*								
Shell, columella		1	1	1	1		1	1
Shell, *Marginella*	1							
Shell, gorget								
Shell, pendant		1						
Shell, washer-shaped								
Textile	1				1	1		
Uniface	2	1	1					1
Total	11	4	3	1	2	2	1	4

[a]Md = Mound, U = unidentified gender, M = male, F = female. Counts represent number of associations, not numbers of artifacts.

Table 6. Artifact Associations in Mound B[a]

| Item | Locus | | | | Individual | | | |
	Central I	Subfloor I	Md Fill III	Md Fill IV	Subadult	Adult U	Adult M	Adult F
Abrader		1						1
Biface			1					
Bone artifacts—other		1	1	1	1		1	
Bone tube	1	1						2
Ceramics		1	2	2		1		2
Copper								
Drill								
Groundstone, round	1	2			1			2
Groundstone, tabular		1						
Hide								
Horn gorget			1				1	
Limestone rock	1	1	2		1	1		2
Mano/metate	1	1						2
Projectile point								
Shell, *Anculosa*		3			2			1
Shell, columella	1	1						1
Shell, *Marginella*		1						2
Shell, gorget		1						1
Shell, pendant		2			1			1
Shell, washer-shaped		1			1			
Textile								
Uniface			1	1				
Total	5	18	8	4	8	2	2	17

[a]Md = Mound, U = unidentified gender, M = male, F = female. Counts represent number of associations, not numbers of artifacts.

BURIAL ASSOCIATIONS

Utilitarian and nonutilitarian objects were found in association with burials (tables 5–6). Some of the items were manufactured from local materials, but many of the worked shell artifacts were made from exotic species. Nonlocal mollusks include *Busycon contrarium, Marginella apicina,* and *Anculosa praerosa.* Artifact association refers to the presence of an artifact in a grave. A direct association with a single person is noted as an individual count. A composite artifact with many pieces, such as a necklace, is counted as one association. Twenty-one types of artifact associations are identified.

Artifact associations reveal a number of changes through time (tables 5–6). Most obvious is the decrease in the number of associated artifacts. In Mound A, the decrease in artifacts was gradual but distinct. In Component I, 11 associations were noted, Component II had four, Component III three, and Component IV one. In Mound B, number of associations also decreased through time, from 23 in Component I to eight in Component III, and four in Component IV. The types of artifacts also changed temporally. In Mound B exotic artifacts were found only in Component I; in Mound A, fewer exotic artifacts were recovered, and only columella were found in the later components.

BURIAL FACTORS

SOCIAL STATUS

Social status is the most frequently cited factor to explain burial mode variability. Status is reflected in "unequal access to certain types of burial treatment, locality of final interment, and items included as part of the grave furniture" (Buikstra 1976:41). Among the Hopewell more males showed evidence of postmortem processing, exclusive interment in central burial chambers, and conspicuous displays of exotic artifacts (Buikstra 1976).

Although the number of skeletal remains identifiable to gender is small, comparison of the Buikstra (1976) model with burial data from the Jamestown Mounds reveals a marked contrast. No form of burial treatment is exclusively associated with males in the Jamestown sample. In fact, more subadults and females show evidence of burial preparation, except that more males than females were cremated (table 3). Similarly, burial in the central burial chamber was not limited exclusively to males; the only identified individual in the disturbed central ossuary in Mound B is female (table 7).

Vehik (1982) observes similarities between Sonota (contemporary with Components I and II of the Jamestown

Table 7. Age-Sex Distribution of Individuals at Jamestown Mounds by Locus of Final Interment

	Subfloor Pit	Mound Fill	Central Ossuary
Adult male			
A	0	2	8
B	0	1	0
Adult female			
A	0	2	4
B	1	1	1
Unknown gender			
A	0	3	1
B	2	4	0
Total adult			
A	0	7	13
B	3	6	1
Subadult			
A	0	6	29
B	5	5	0

Mounds) and Hopewell burial practices; however, her data demonstrate even closer comparisons with Jamestown. Vehik (1982, 1983) suggests that fewer females (n = 19) than males (n = 39) were buried in Sonota central features, and that burial of females or juveniles in the central pit seemed to require the presence of an adult male. However, 20 of the adults buried in Sonota central burial chambers could not be sexed, and most of the central interments were subadults (n = 96). This finding is similar to Components I and II of the Jamestown Mounds where more males (n = 8) than females (n = 5) and more subadults (n = 29) than adults (n = 14) were in central ossuaries.

Burial in Sonota peripheral subfloor pits shows a similar distribution. More Sonota adult males (n = 4) than females (n = 2) are in peripheral pits. Jamestown Component I peripheral subfloor pits contain one female, two adults of unknown gender, and five subadults (table 7). Young adults are conspicuously absent from both Sonota and Jamestown samples, an absence that, among the Sonota, Vehik (1982:177) interprets as deliberate exclusion because of low status. Williams (1985:4.6–4.8) suggests that this absence can represent a population experiencing an infectious disease.

Distribution of burial goods in the Jamestown Mounds is also similar to Sonota and does not clearly correlate with burial preparation and burial locus, the other two Hopewellian indicators of status. Although most Mound A artifact associations are in the central burial chamber, the majority of Mound B artifacts are from peripheral subfloor

Table 8. Relative Status of Individuals as Indicated by Grave Good Associations

Feature	Associations	Number of Individuals	Burial Number	Sex	Age	Relative Status
Mound A						
1 (81)	0	2	—	—	—	Low
2 (81)	2	4	—	—	—	Low
3 (81)	2	1	46	—	1.5–2.5	Medium
12	1	30	—	—	—	Low
14	1	4	—	—	—	Low
16	1	2	—	—	—	Low
23	3	12	—	—	—	Low
Mound B						
1	2	1	6	F	+23	Medium
3	1	1	7	—	15–23	Low
4	1	3	—	—	—	Low
6	6	2	3	—	9–11	High
7	8	4	4	F	16–23	High
13	0	1	13	—	16–30	Low
17	0	1	33	—	35–45	Low
18	0	3	—	—	—	Low
19	0	1	37	—	6–12	Low
21	1	1	38	—	1–1.5	Low
25	1	2	34	F	+40	Low

pits (tables 5–6). Burial goods are most often associated with females (n = 21), secondarily with subadults (10), and least often with males (n = 3). Most Jamestown exotic materials were associated with females or subadults; in only one case was imported shell found in association with a male. In Vehik's Sonota sample, the only exotic artifacts directly associated with specific individuals were those found with children (Vehik 1982:176).

Braun (1979) suggests that burial goods are grouped into two types: those found in middens and burials; and those found exclusively in burials. He argues that goods found only in burials are markers of prestige. The other materials could be included in feature fill if soil from an occupation area was used to backfill burial pits.

Burial artifacts absent in the occupation area (Site 32SN207) include antler or bone tubes, mortuary vessels, limestone rocks, copper, round ground stones, tabular ground stone, hide, horn gorgets, shell artifacts, and textiles. Table 8 presents an inventory of grave goods. In all cases, if the quantity of artifacts is high, so is the variety, and vice versa.

Following Braun (1979), relative status is calculated by grouping burials into arbitrary status categories according to the number of artifact associations. The arbitrary status categories are low, zero or one association; medium, two or three associations; and high, greater than three associations. Using this technique only two high-status Jamestown individuals are identified. One is a 16- to 23-year-old female; the second is a 9- to 11-year-old subadult (sex unknown). Two individuals could be interpreted as having medium status: a 1.5- to 2.5-year-old and a 23+-year-old female. Because the adult was recovered from a disturbed pit, the artifact associations are questionable. The remaining burials (89.3%) are of relatively low status. Furthermore, there is a difference in relative status between Mound A and Mound B. Both of the high-status individuals and one medium-status individual were buried in Mound B. Conversely, Mound A individuals are grouped into a low-status category except for one medium-status individual.

If Braun's (1979) indicators of status are accepted, then high-status males are absent at Jamestown. They may have been buried elsewhere. If this hypothesis is true, high-status males are lacking from all Sonota mounds because adult males generally are not directly associated with exotic burial goods (Vehik 1982; 1983). However, such a situation is unlikely.

Instead, the lack of status symbols associated with Sonota male burials probably reflects a cultural difference between Hopewell and Plains groups. Among historic Plains peoples a person did not necessarily inherit high status; he was expected to earn it through deeds of generosity, leadership, and participation in ceremonies (Meyer 1977:70). "Giveaways" of possessions earned a person prestige, and those of high status had the fewest material goods (Grobsmith 1979:124). The data suggest that this practice had prehistoric roots.

The Jamestown data do not fit the Hopewell status model. Inclusion in central burial chambers is not limited to a particular group of people. Both genders and most age groups, except young adults, are represented. Furthermore, the overall ratio of artifacts to individuals is low in the central burial chambers. Postmortem processing also cuts across age groups and genders. If the historic Plains custom of giveaways has a prehistoric origin, burial goods cannot be considered as a reliable marker of status.

SOCIAL AFFILIATION

Although social affiliation as a factor in burial mode variability is difficult to identify archaeologically, it has been demonstrated in the ethnographic record. For example, the Omaha bury symbols of the clan in the grave of a clan member (O'Shea, 1981:43), but unless that symbol remains in the archaeological record and is recognized as a clan symbol, the relationship is lost. Three possible symbols of social affiliation were recovered from the Mound A1 and A2 ossuaries: a polished raccoon (*Procyon lotor*) cranium, a partial skeleton of a domesticated dog (*Canis familiaris*), and raven (*Corvus corax*) leg bones. The dog skeleton displayed cutmarks on the atlas, tibia, and mandible. These are the only nonhuman, nontool faunal remains recovered from burial pits that appear to have been intentionally positioned in a grave. These species are not found in the faunal assemblage from the occupation area and are probably not the remnants of food.

AGE

All age groups are represented in the Jamestown sample. Age was a criterion used in determining the form of some burial modes. The burial mode of subadults differs from adults in that the majority of subadults (91.1%) are not articulated (table 9), but this correlation is probably attributable more to poor preservation of the less durable, cartilaginous young bone than to cultural factors. Subadult burials show evidence of postmortem burial preparation, with 40 cases of dissection, three instances of rearticulation, and one partial cremation (table 3). Only subadult burials were rearticulated.

Subadults not only were interred with adults but also were buried alone. In Mound B, subadults are divided equally between interment in subfloor pits and mound fill. The majority of individuals in central burial chambers in Mound A were subadult (table 7). Vehik (1982:178) indicates that age was a primary factor in excluding young adults from burial in Sonota mounds, and young adults also are conspicuously absent from the Jamestown sample.

GENDER

Binford (1971:20) uses the Human Relations Area Files to identify burial factors among four subsistence categories: hunters and gatherers, shifting agriculturalists, pastoralists, and settled agriculturalists. Within those four groups he finds that sex is frequently a criterion affecting mortuary variables and that among hunters and gatherers it is the primary criterion. The Jamestown sample is no exception. Gender appears to be a factor at least in burial mode, although the sample is small. Burial mode by age and sex demonstrates some variation by gender (table 9). All the flexed-sitting burials are either female

Table 9. Burial Mode by Age and Sex

Mode	Subadult	Unknown Gender	Adult Male	Adult Female	Total
Bundle	2	2	0	1	5
Dissected	21	0	6	2	29
Flexed-lying (indeterminate side)	1	0	0	0	1
Flexed-lying, right	0	1	1	1	3
Flexed-lying, left	0	0	1	0	1
Flexed-sitting	3	0	0	3	6
Prone	0	0	0	1	1
Scattered	18	9	1	1	29
Total	45	12	9	9	75

Table 10. Orientation of Site 32SN22 Burials

Burial	Feature	Orientation	Age Group	Gender	Component
1	4	NW	Subadult	Indeterminate	III
2	4	SE	Adult	Male	III
7	3	N	Adult	Indeterminate	I
4	7	W	Adult	Female	I
3	6	W	Subadult	Indeterminate	I
31	16	E	Adult	Indeterminate	II
9b	12	N	Adult	Female	II
12	14	N	Adult	Female	III
11	14	NW	Adult	Female	III
44	1(1981)	SE	Adult	Female	III
46	3(1981)	SW	Subadult	Indeterminate	IV
42	23	NW	Adult	Female	I

or subadult; the only prone adult is female. The female sample is the only group where articulated burials are in the majority. Other gender or age groups usually had unarticulated elements.

Burial preparation varies between genders (table 3). Ocher is more common to females than males, but more males than females are dissected or cremated. Distribution in the three loci also demonstrates some differentiation by sex. Only females and subadults were buried in subfloor pits. The only identified individual remaining in the disturbed Mound B central burial chamber is female (table 7), which directly contrasts with Hopewellian mounds where burial in central chambers is limited to males (Buikstra 1976:34). Flexed-sitting females tend to be associated with exotic burial goods. The only identifiable male in Mound B was located in mound fill. In Mound A, males, as well as females, were found in central burial chambers. Both genders were interred in Mound A fill.

Orientation demonstrates no clear pattern, but it could be gender-related. The variations do not appear to be temporally based but may show some relation to gender (table 10). Females tend to be oriented toward the north or northwest (n = 4). The only adult identifiable as male is oriented southeast, but an adult female has the same orientation. Saxe (1971) suggests that orientation was related to solar traverses linked with interment during seasonal hunter-gatherer subsistence movements.

ENVIRONMENTAL CONSTRAINTS

Interment versus exposure was seasonally determined among most Northern Plains historic groups. Although theoretically it would be possible to construct a mound by

building fires to thaw enough soil to erect an earthwork, a great expenditure of effort or an extended period of time would be required. Mound building was more likely a warm weather activity pursued when the resource base would support a group living for a period of time in the immediate vicinity of the cemetery (Thompson 1980). Many secondary interments found in the mounds may reflect season of death rather than a deliberate two-part burial program involving exposure before burial.

DISTANCE TO CEMETERY

Another explanation for secondary interments may be related to distance to burial grounds from the place of death. If, for example, death occurred during the summer and the group was too far from a desirable burial ground, burial would be delayed until the group returned to the cemetery area. If a decision was made to transport the dead person to a place of burial immediately, processing probably would be required. As was reported in 1824 of a Siouan Indian, "On his arrival, he found that the corpse had already made such progress towards decomposition, as rendered it impossible for it to be removed. He then undertook, with a few friends, to clean off the bones; all the flesh was scraped off and thrown into the stream; the bones were carefully collected into his canoe, and subsequently carried down to his residence" (Bushnell 1927:21). Processing such as this would produce a dissected, bundle, or scattered burial, with evidence of dissection. The ossuaries could represent spring interment of all the people who had died over a hard winter or those who had died some distance from the mounds and had been transported to the burial ground.

The variable degree of weathering between individual interments supports this possibility.

NUMBER OF DEATHS

If multiple deaths occurred within a limited time period, the individuals might have been buried together. Most Jamestown graves contained more than a single individual. In the case of a catastrophic event causing the death of a large number of people, traditional burial practices are often abandoned. The smallpox epidemics along the Upper Missouri River in the nineteenth century necessitated changes in funerary behavior when the number of dead exceeded the living. The smallpox epidemic at Fort Clark resulted in the abandonment of the dead (Abel 1932). Williams (1985) suggests that the Mound A1 ossuary may have resulted from an infectious disease episode because all the individuals are in similar condition. In contrast, the Mound A2 ossuary varies in bone preservation and burial modes; therefore, it probably does not reflect a catastrophic event.

CIRCUMSTANCES OF DEATH

Historic accounts document that circumstances of death often dictate burial mode. The Mandan and Sisseton Sioux buried murder victims face down. Mandan children who died before they were named were scaffolded in trees or interred apart from those who had names. Yankton Sioux who died in battle were not scaffolded in the general cemetery but were buried on the spot. Other groups treated victims of suicide, childbirth, and lightning differently from people who died from other causes (Binford 1971).

Circumstances of death could explain some of the variation in burial treatment at Jamestown. Individuals interred in Component I of the Mound A1 ossuary may have died during an epidemic. All the individuals in this ossuary are dissected, and some display cutmarks, charring, and crushed parietals. Disarticulated crania were placed on top of partially articulated postcranial remains in a concentration on the floor of the ossuary. One individual was pregnant at death and may have died during childbirth (Williams 1985:3.6–3.7); however, her manner of burial did not differ from the other individuals in the Mound A1 ossuary.

The concentration of partially dissected bodies in good condition found in the Mound A1 ossuary contrasts with burial mode in the other undisturbed Mound A2 ossuary where most individuals were exposed before interment, resulting in weathered bones in scattered or bundle burials. One

exception in the Mound A2 ossuary is an adult female who was buried in a prone position, which could suggest she was murdered.

Two adult females in unusual circumstances were not given uncommon burial treatment. One was shot in the lower back with an arrow that may have been fatal (Williams 1985:3.50–3.51). Her skull is charred and cracked; cutmarks on neck and femora indicate that the body was processed or mutilated. The other female suffered from degenerative arthritis and possibly tuberculosis, which may have contributed to her death (Williams 1985:3.52; Williams and Snortland-Coles 1986). The two woman were buried side by side in flexed-sitting positions similar to other females and subadults.

TEMPORAL CHANGE

Table 2 illustrates changes in burial modes through time. Bundle burials form a small percentage of all burials, and by Component IV these are absent. Dissected burials are restricted to Component I in the Mound A1 ossuary but comprise a large percentage of burials from that level. Flexed-lying interments increase through time, but flexed-sitting decreases and is missing from Component IV. Prone position is restricted to a single occurrence in Component I. Scattered secondary burials are noted in all levels; in Component IV, 83.3 percent of all burials are secondary scattered burials, indicating that most individuals were exposed to the elements on a scaffold or in some other manner prior to interment. Variation in burial positions decreases through time with a corresponding increase in the percentage of secondary scattered burials. Although all six types of burial positions are represented in Component I, Components II and III have four, and Component IV has only two.

Archaeological evidence mirrors the ethnographic record. For example, groups such as the Arikara, Mandan, and Hidatsa changed mortuary practices through time, and older informants could remember practices no longer in use. Scaffolding or tree burial followed by interment of defleshed bones was practiced historically. Some of those same groups recalled that long ago their ancestors interred directly into the ground, and the Hidatsa remembered burial in mounds (Bowers 1965).

The overall decrease in exotic artifact associations may be attributed to a decrease in exchange, a change in customs regarding burial goods, an increase in scaffolding, or a combination of the three. Skeletal biology of the Jamestown population indicates that these people did not migrate into the area from the east from the source of the exotics (Williams 1985), and distance to the source areas precluded procurement during seasonal movements. The presence of exotic items indicates some exchange occurred possibly with Hopewellian trading networks. If exotic materials were obtained primarily through trade with Hopewellian groups, this may account for the drop in exotics after Component I because Component II postdates Hopewell. The decrease in exotic burial goods in Component II may reflect declines in the Hopewellian trading A.D. 400 (Buikstra 1976; Syms 1976). The persistent use of columella as a burial good even into Component IV suggests continuation of a limited amount of exchange.

Another explanation for the decrease in burial goods takes into consideration the type of mortuary artifact selected. "Grave goods do not always reach the grave" (Chapman and Randsborg 1981:18). If burial goods were perishable or were consumed or inherited during the funeral ceremony, they would not be interred with the body. Finally, one of the most significant factors is the increase in scaffolding as opposed to primary burial. If goods were exposed with the body, many would be lost during transport or by weathering.

MORTUARY EVENTS

Combining the results of the preceding mortuary analysis with description of features, radiocarbon dates, and burial goods, the sequence of mortuary events at the Jamestown Mounds is reconstructed. The radiocarbon dates cited in the text are corrected using Stuiver and Pearson (1986).

COMPONENT I

Mortuary events began during the Middle Woodland period with the exposure of a minority of the dead on scaffolds or in trees. The period of exposure varied, depending on the season in which death occurred; those who died in the fall were scaffolded longer than those who died in the spring. During the warm season, Native Americans physically similar to Sonota people moved to a temporary campsite on a high terrace near the confluence of the James River and Pipestem Creek (site 32SN207) and began constructing a mortuary complex by stripping sod from a circular area. An oval central burial chamber was excavated in the center of the stripped area, and an unknown number of individuals were placed in it circa 50 B.C.–A.D. 230, including at least one adult female. Burial goods included in the central chamber of Mound B were bison remains, columella tubes, four groundstone tools, a wild grape seed (cf. *Vitis*), soft limestone, and a copper crescent.

About the same time, a female and a partially rearticulated child were interred in flexed-sitting positions in separate, small, subsurface pits at Mound B. The pits were approximately equidistant from the central chamber and encircled it. The child and adult primary interments were covered with more burial goods than any other individuals in the mortuary complex (washer-shaped shell disks, *Anculosa* beads, *Marginella* beads, columella tubes, trapezoidal shell pendants, musselshell gorgets, groundstone tools, soft limestone rocks, an antler tube, and red ocher), possibly during a funeral giveaway ceremony. The selection of the flexed-sitting burial position was based on the gender and age of the deceased, and rearticulation was related to age of the individual. Additional incomplete burials were placed in the pits with the primary interments. A partially decomposed adult, who was exposed prior to burial, was interred with red ocher in a flexed-lying position in a third peripheral pit. An infant was buried with an *Anculosa* bead and a bison rib in a fourth small, subfloor pit. Glacial till obtained from the nearby living area was piled over the graves to begin Mound B.

During the same period (25 B.C.–A.D. 395) an epidemic swept through the population killing at least 28 people, mostly infants, children, and old adults, as well as a pregnant woman. Some of these people, generally the males, were partially cremated and were exposed for a relatively short period of time. After a deep, cylindrical pit (Mound A1 ossuary) was dug into a glacially deposited hill east of Mound B, it was lined with animal hides and the partially dissected bodies of the epidemic victims, including both sexes, were laid on the bottom of the ossuary. Two polished raccoon crania, possibly symbols of a social affiliation, were placed in the grave. Isolated human crania were grouped together and placed in a central position on top of dismembered bodies. The ossuary was covered with a low tumulus (Mound A1).

A third ossuary (Mound A2) was begun A.D. 90–340 east of the Mound A1 ossuary to inter people who died over a much longer period of time than those in Mound A1 ossuary. The bottom of this cylindrical pit was lined with a partially charred, unidentifiable material. An adult bundle burial wrapped in charred textile was laid on the material with a copper tinkler, *Marginella* beads, fragments of two bifaces and a uniface, and the partial remains of a subadult. The burials were covered with sand. An adult female, whose burial disposition suggests that she was murdered, was placed face down with an infant on top of bundle burial. Her arms extended down into the sand below; her knees were bent and her feet pointed upward. After her body was covered with sand, a modified partial dog skeleton (social affiliation symbol) and scattered remains of at least one child and an adult were laid on top.★ The grave was backfilled with glacial till.

In general, dissected and prone burials occurred only in Component I, and the greatest variety of burial positions were represented. Unlike Hopewell mounds, both genders and most age groups were interred in central burial chambers with very few burial goods. The greatest variety and quantity of burial goods were placed in Component I small, peripheral burial pits associated with subadults or females.

COMPONENT II

Three small, peripheral pits were excavated into the edge of Mound A1 and near Mound A2 ossuary to bury an undetermined number of people or to prepare bodies for burial. One pit was then used circa A.D. 240–650 to store or dispose of six unmodified bison (*Bison bison*) scapulae and a radius. These were cached as potential digging tools. Later (circa A.D. 410–650; 600–770), the Mound A2 ossuary was reopened, and a layer of wood planks was placed over the previous interments and burned. At least two scattered child burials and numerous fragmentary human bones from scaffolded bodies were later positioned on the layer of wood. Some of these individuals were buried originally in three adjacent small pits and then were transferred to this ossuary during a ceremony that possibly resembled the Huron Feast of the Dead. Northern raven (*Corvus corax*) leg bones, symbols of social affiliation, were included in the ossuary.

About the same period (A.D. 540–790; 636–766; 689–897) Mound A1 ossuary was reopened and an oak post was placed in the center of the crania concentration, which was covered with soil. An infant, lying on a hide or mat, was interred in the ossuary, and another layer of soil was added to cover the body. Near the top of the ossuary an adult female was positioned on her right side in a flexed-lying position, and the ossuary was refilled.

Two small pits were excavated into Mound A1. After extended exposure, partial remains of two children and two adults were buried in a small pit with a single columella tube, a trapezoidal shell pendant, and a fragment of a uniface. The weathered condition of the shell ornaments indicates that these artifacts were exposed with the bodies. After a polished bone tube was laid on the bottom of a small pit, a young adult in a flexed-sitting position and a secondary interment of

another young adult were situated in the grave. The grave was sealed with two ocher-coated granitic boulders. Dirt was piled over all of the Mound A1 graves to form a second level. A similar mound was constructed to cover the Mound A2 ossuary and associated features, but modern disturbance precludes determination of the boundaries of this earthwork.

In all, fewer exotic burial goods were included in Component II graves, possibly due to the decrease in trade after the decline in Hopewell culture around A.D. 400. Fewer people were buried in Component II (n = 11) as compared to Component I (n = 46), and Mound B was not used at all. This was the final period that ossuaries were used.

COMPONENT III

An adult male who died A.D. 785–962 was buried in Mound B on his left side in a flexed position. An infant and a child lying together with a trapezoidal horn gorget, and an ocher-covered beaver (*Castor canadensis*) incisor were placed in the small, oval, peripheral grave that intruded into the northern edge of the mound. Burial positions of the two children are indeterminate because of poor preservation.

A small grave was dug into the center of Mound A1 and partially into the northeastern edge of ossuary. The bodies of five people were placed into the grave; three were exposed for an extended period of time before interment and were decomposed. The fourth individual was a young adult female (A.D. 897–1031) who had been shot in the back and was buried with the arrowhead lodged in her spinal column. Before she was interred her legs were removed by cutting around the femoral proximal articulations. Her left arm was also disarticulated and her body was arranged in flexed-sitting position. Sitting in a flexed position beside her was an older female who apparently suffered from tuberculosis (Williams and Snortland-Coles 1986). Columella beads, a biface, and a uniface were laid on and around the body of the older female before the grave was covered with earth.

Two other intrusive pits were excavated into the edges of Mound B, and three adult bundle burials were interred in them. In one of these graves, a bundle burial was laid on the bottom beside a Sandy Lake mortuary vessel and was covered with an ocher-coated limestone slab and two granitic rocks. The upper surface of the slab was used as a platform for another bundle burial. Radiocarbon dates indicate death occurred about A.D. 890–1260. After all the graves were closed, soil was piled over the graves to increase the height and width of Mound B.

About the same time (A.D. 970–1170), an old adult female stained with red ocher was placed on her right side in a

---

*Because of inadvertent mixing of levels during osteological analysis, an additional two adults and four children cannot be assigned to either component but are possibly part of this episode.

flexed-lying position in a small grave that intruded into the top of Mound A1.

In general, the number of interments are similar in Component II (n = 11) and Component III (n = 12), but ossuaries were not reused during Component III. Burial positions were also similar in the two components. Graves were limited to small, peripheral pits. Grave goods were sparse, and the only exotic materials were columella.

COMPONENT IV

Sometime after Component III ended, people returned to the Jamestown Mounds to add an intrusive burial to the top level of Mound A1 and to continue construction of Mound B. Component IV marks the culmination of the use of the mounds for mortuary purposes. Prior to interment, three deceased adults and four children were exposed for a long period of time resulting in extremely weathered, incomplete skeletal remains. All these individuals were buried in Mound B and were covered with a final mound layer. The only unquestionable burial good was a uniface. Based on the recovery of a side-notched projectile point, the linear mound that connected Mounds B and C and continued northward to the terrace edge (fig. 2) was also built during this time period.

The only Component IV burial in Mound A1 was a flexed, primary interment of an infant buried near the mound apex. The child was laid on his or her right side, with three columella beads. Construction of the grave disturbed the edge of another small grave.

Component IV is undated because of the fragmentary nature of the bone. This component represents only a marginal use of the cemetery compared to preceding periods. Overall the decline in the number of people buried here and the lessened quantity and quality of burial goods reflects an increasing use of scaffolding.

Conclusion

Careful examination of the three Northern Plains mortuary complexes—Sonota, Arvilla, and Devils Lake–Sourisford—in relation to the information recovered from the Jamestown Mounds and to ethnographic data reveals problems with the complexes as defined. In reference to the Sonota complex, Neuman (1975:94) states that "the vast majority of the human interments were placed in a single, centrally located subfloor burial pit; however, sometimes others were deposited on the mound floor, and also within the mound-fill matrix." Neu-

man had few radiocarbon dates to determine a time range for the complex and therefore anticipated a limited time span: "Obviously the Grover Hand Mound 1 date of A.D. 1300 is much too late for the material it is to represent; and, to my mind, the Boundary Mound 3 date of 250 B.C. is too early. The other nine assays . . . seem acceptable." However, projectile points from Sonota include Besant, corner-notched, small side-notched (Boundary Mound 1), and triangular (Neuman 1975:91; Wood 1960:77), showing a temporal range similar to that represented by the discarded radiocarbon dates. In view of the multiple components in the Jamestown Mounds, these data support the interpretation of multiple components in Sonota complex mounds.

Arvilla has been redefined a number of times (Jenks 1932; Johnson 1973; Syms 1982; Wilford 1941, 1955) but still suffers from a mixing of components and a comparative lack of radiocarbon dates. Many of the mounds described by Johnson (1973) held intrusive burials recovered from mound fill; yet, during analysis the skeletons and artifacts were lumped together. Syms's (1982:162) attempt to distinguish Arvilla from Devils Lake–Sourisford by a comparison of traits identified the following characteristics for Arvilla: textile-impressed, miniature Woodland vessels; fewer imported shells, except for columella, and more local clam shells; few tubular bone artifacts; ceramic elbow pipes; and higher frequency of Natica beads and fewer washer-shaped beads. Distinctions between the two complexes are unclear. As Syms (1982:152) states, "Even the most common items appear at less than half of the sites."

The weakness of Devils Lake–Sourisford definition is that it is based primarily on extensive artifact trait lists that include many artifacts found in all three burial complexes. Several "diagnostic" Devils Lake–Sourisford artifacts, such as trapezoidal pendants and washer-shaped shell disks, were recovered from Jamestown site's Component I, which predates Devils Lake–Sourisford complex by 800 years. Many diagnostic artifacts are not common to all the sites included in the complex. Much of the data are from secondary sources and unprovenienced collections. A review of field maps, which were not available to Syms (1979), reveals that most of the Heimdahl Mound whelk shell gorgets diagnostic of this complex were found in mound fill 0.55 meter above the skeletons and separated from the burials by an uninterrupted stratum (Johnson 1931). The diagnostic vessel from the Moose Bay Burial Mound was found in a pit that intruded into the top of an existing mound (Hanna 1976:16), yet the entire mound was classified as belonging to this complex. The radiocarbon date for the Moose Bay mound was collected from the central burial chamber, which predates the diagnostic vessel (Hanna 1976:22).

Osteological analysis by Key (1983:93) indicates that "the northern Woodland groups (Sonota, South Arvilla and Devils Lake–Sourisford) define a tight cluster somewhat distinct from the Central Plains groups (Keith, Valley, and Loseke Creek)." Sonota and Arvilla are so similar that it is difficult to distinguish between them, but Devils Lake–Sourisford tends toward Great Oasis, which possibly is a reflection of small sample size rather than of actual differences (Patrick J. Key, personal communication 1989). Williams's (1975:3.61) biological distance analysis of Jamestown, Sonota, Arvilla, Mandan, Hopewell, and Archaic site populations demonstrates that the Jamestown females cluster closely with Sonota females and have slightly less association with Archaic females. Arvilla forms a loose association with Mandan, but Hopewell is distinct from all the Northern Plains peoples. Although diagnostic artifacts from the Jamestown Mounds and radiocarbon dates indicate some affiliation and contemporaneity with Arvilla and Devils Lake–Sourisford, genetically the population is closest to Sonota. Thus, it is evident that the Woodland mounds were used by people who were related biologically and that a mound-building or at least that a mound-using tradition continued throughout the Woodland period on the Northern Plains.

In summary, the complexes are based on incomplete data and are supported by few radiocarbon dates. Because most mounds have more than one component, the lack of vertical and horizontal controls has resulted in a mixture of time periods. Even if radiocarbon dates were available, mounds often were assigned to a complex on the basis of one or two dates. Multiple radiocarbon dates on single features have shown that central burial chambers were reused for a span of some 600 years, and a single mound served as a place of interment for 1,300 years. Mounds cannot be dated completely with one or two samples from a single level, nor can they be assigned to a complex on the basis of diagnostic artifacts recovered from mound fill.

The three complexes, as currently defined, are based primarily upon archaeological data; relatively little osteological evidence is incorporated. Archaeological interpretation of a human cemetery created without adequate supporting physical anthropological analysis is questionable. Although these complexes may be regarded as representing overgeneralized archaeological patterns, it is unlikely that the excavated cemeteries contain individuals from one biological population.

References Cited

Abel, A.H., ed.
1932 Chardon's Journal at Fort Clark, 1834–1839, Descriptive of Life on the Upper Missouri, of a Fur Trader's Experiences Among the Mandans, Gros Ventres, and Their Neighbors; of the Ravages of the Small-Pox Epidemic of 1837. Pierre: State of South Dakota, Department of History.

Bartel, B.
1982 A Historical Review of Ethnological and Archaeological Analyses of Mortuary Practice. *Journal of Anthropological Archaeology* 1:32–58.

Binford, L.R.
1971 Mortuary Practices: Their Study and Their Potential. Pp. 6–30 in Approaches to the Social Dimensions of Mortuary Practices. J.A. Brown, ed. *Society for American Archaeology Memoirs* 25.

Bowers, A.W.
1965 Hidatsa Social and Ceremonial Organization. *Bureau of American Ethnology Bulletin* 194.

——
1973 Mandan Social and Ceremonial Organization [1950]. Chicago: University of Chicago Press.

Braun, D.P.
1979 Illinois Hopewell Burial Practices and Social Organization: A Re-Examination of the Klunk-Gibson Mound Group. Pp. 66–79 in Hopewell Archaeology: The Chillicothe Conference. D.S. Brose and N. Greber, eds. Kent, Ohio: Kent State University Press.

Brine, A., and G.L. Fox
1987 Unmodified and Modified Molluscan Remains. In The Jamestown Mounds Project, Vol. 1. J. S. Snortland, ed. Bismarck: State Historical Society of North Dakota.

Brown, J.A.
1981 The Search for Rank in Prehistoric Burials. Pp. 25–37 in The Archaeology of Death. R. Chapman, I. Kinnes, and K. Randsbord, eds. New York: Cambridge University Press.

Buikstra, J.
1976 Hopewell in the Lower Illinois Valley: A Regional Approach to the Study of Human Biological Variability and Prehistoric Behavior. *Northwestern University Archaeological Program. Scientific Papers* 2.

Bushnell, D.I.
1927 Burials of the Algonquian, Siouan and Caddoan Tribes West of the Mississippi. *Bureau of American Ethnology Bulletin* 83.

Cain, H.T.
1952 Smithsonian Institution River Basin Survey Site Form for Site 32SN22. (Manuscript in files of Archaeology and Historic Preservation Division, State Historical Society of North Dakota.)

Catlin, G.
  1913 North American Indians. Vol. 1. Philadelphia: Leary Stuart.

——

  1973 Letters and Notes on the Manners, Customs, and Conditions of North American Indians, Written During Eight Years' Travel (1832–1839) Amongst the Wildest Tribes of Indians in North America. New York: Dover Publications.

Chapman, R., and K. Randsborg
  1981 Approaches to the Archaeology of Death. Pp. 1–24 in The Archaeology of Death. R. Chapman, I. Kinnes, and K. Ransborg, eds. New York: Cambridge University Press.

Comfort, A.J.
  1873 Indian Mounds near Fort Wadsworth, Dakota Territory. *Annual Report of the Board of Regents of the Smithsonian Institution.* Washington: U.S. Government Printing Office.

Densmore, F.
  1979 Chippewa Customs. Minneapolis: Minnesota Historical Society Press.

Foster, E.H.
  1878 Pre-historic Men. *Jamestown Alert* July 25:1.

Fox, G.L.
  1987 Historical Research. In The Jamestown Mounds Project, Vol. 1. J.S. Snortland, ed. Bismarck: State Historical Society of North Dakota.

Goldstein, L.G.
  1981 One-dimensional Archaeology and Multi-dimensional People: Spatial Organization and Mortuary Analysis. Pp. 53–70 in The Archaeology of Death. R. Chapman, I. Kinnes, and K. Randsborg, eds. New York: Cambridge University Press.

Grobsmith, E.S.
  1979 The Lakota Giveaway: A System of Social Reciprocity. *Plains Anthropologist* 24(84):123–132.

Hanna, M.G.
  1976 The Moose Bay Burial Mound, EdMq-1. *Saskatchewan Museum of Natural History Anthropological Series* 3.

Henry, A.
  1969 Travel and Adventures in Canada and the Indian Territories, Between the Years 1760 and 1776. Edmonton: Hurtig.

Howard, J.H.
  1977 The Plains-Ojibwa or Bungi, Hunters and Warriors of the Northern Prairies with Special Reference to the Turtle Mountain Band. *Reprints in Anthropology* 7.

Jenks, A.E.
  1932 The Problem of the Culture from the Arvilla Gravel Pit. *American Anthropologist* 34(3):455–466.

Johnson, E.
  1973 The Arvilla Complex. *Minnesota Prehistoric Archaeology Series* 9.

Johnson, J. A.
  1931 Chart Showing the Central Portion of an Indian Mound. (Manuscript in files of archaeology and Historic Preservation Division, State Historical Society of North Dakota.)

Key, P.J.
  1983 Craniometric Relationships Among Plains Indians: Culture-historical and Evolutionary Implications. *University of Tennessee, Department of Anthropology, Report of Investigations* 34.

Kivett, M.F.
  1953 The Woodruff Ossuary, a Prehistoric Burial Site in Phillips County, Kansas. *Bureau of American Ethnology Bulletin* 154.

Lewis, T.H.
  1883 Letter, T.H. Lewis to A.J. Hill, September 26, 1883, and Accompanying Sketch Maps, Plan Maps, and Survey Notes of the Jamestown Earthworks. (Manuscript, Record Group #30.C.11.1B in files of Minnesota State Historical Society Archives, St. Paul, Minnesota.)

Meyer, R.W.
  1977 The Village Indians of the Upper Missouri: The Mandans, Hidatsas, and Arikaras. Lincoln: University of Nebraska Press.

Neuman, R.W.
  1975 The Sonota Complex and Associated Sites on the Northern Great Plains. *Nebraska State Historical Society Publications in Anthropology* 6.

Obey, W. A.
  1974 The Arvilla People. *The Minnesota Archaeologist* 33(3–4):1–33.

Orser, C.E.
  1980 Toward a Partial Understanding of Complexity in Arikara Mortuary Practice. *Plains Anthropologist* 25(88):113–120.

O'Shea, J.
  1981 Social Configuration and the Archaeological Study of Mortuary Practices: A Case Study. Pp. 39–52 in The Archaeology of Death. R. Chapman, I. Kinnes, and K. Randsborg, eds. New York: Cambridge University Press.

Pond, S.W.
  1986 The Dakota or Sioux in Minnesota as They Were in 1834. St Paul: Minnesota Historical Society Press.

Saxe, A.A.
  1970 Social Dimensions of Mortuary Practices. (Unpublished Ph.D. Dissertation in Anthropology, University of Michigan, Ann Arbor.)

Schneider, F., and R. Vehik
  1976 Archaeological Surveys in the Garrison Diversion Unit, North Dakota. Section I: Archaeological Survey of the Proposed Route of the New Rockford Canal; Section II: Archaeological Survey of Bank Stabilization Areas Along the James River and of the Proposed Oakes Canal and Irrigation Areas. (Manuscript in files of Archaeology and Historic Preservation Division, State Historical Society of North Dakota, Bismarck.)

Snortland, J.S., ed.
  1987 The Jamestown Mounds Project, Vol. 1. Bismarck: State Historical Society of North Dakota.

Stuiver, M., and Gordon Pearson

1986   High-Precision Calibration of the Radiocarbon Time Scale, A.D. 1950–500 B.C. *Radiocarbon* 28(2B):805–838.

Syms, E.L.

1976   Indigenous Ceramics and Ecological Dynamics of Southwestern Manitoba: 500 B.C.–A.D. 1800. (Unpublished Ph.D. Dissertation in Anthropology, University of Calgary, Edmonton, Alberta.)

———

1979   The Devils Lake–Sourisford Burial Complex on the Northeastern Plains. *Plains Anthropologist* 24(86):283–308.

———

1982   The Arvilla Burial Complex: A Re-assessment. *Journal of the North Dakota Archaeological Association* 1:135–166.

Tainter, J.A.

1978   Mortuary Practices and the Study of Prehistoric Social Systems. Pp. 106–137 in Advances in Archaeological Method and Theory 1. M.B. Schiffer, ed. New York: Academic Press.

Thomas, C.

1873   Ancient Mounds of Dakota. *Sixth Annual Report of the U.S. Geological Survey of the Territories.*

Thompson, M.

1980   Connoisseurs of Caviar. *The Nebraska Anthropologist* 5:107–119.

Trigger, B.G.

1990   The Huron, Farmers of the North. Fort Worth, Texas: Holt, Rinehart and Winston.

Tyron, G.W.

1873   Strepomatidae (American Melanians): Land and Freshwater Shells of North America, *Smithsonian Miscellaneous Collections* 253(4).

Ucko, P.J.

1969   Ethnographic and Archaeological Interpretation of Funerary Remains. *World Archaeology* 1:262–281.

Vehik, S.C.

1982   Social Determinants of Middle Woodland Mortuary Practices on the Northeastern Plains Periphery: A Consideration of Hopewellian Relationships. *Journal of the North Dakota Archaeological Association* 1:167–180.

———

1983   Middle Woodland Mortuary Practices along the Northeastern Periphery of the Great Plains: A Consideration of Hopewellian Interactions. *Midcontinental Journal of Archaeology* 8(2):211–255.

Wilford, L.A.

1941   A Tentative Classification of the Prehistoric Cultures of Minnesota. *American Antiquity* 6(3):231–249.

———

1955   A Revised Classification of the Prehistoric Cultures of Minnesota. *American Antiquity* 21(2):130–142.

Williams, J.A.

1985   The Jamestown Mounds Project, Vol. 2: Skeletal Biology. Bismarck: State Historical Society of North Dakota.

———, and J.S. Snortland-Coles

1986   Pre-contact Tuberculosis in a Plains Woodland Mortuary. *Plains Anthropologist* 31(113):249–252.

Wood, W.R.

1960   The Boundary Mound Group (32SI-1): An Eastern Woodland Complex in North Dakota. *Plains Anthropologist* 5(10):71–78.

———

1967   An Interpretation of Mandan Culture History. *Bureau of American Ethnology Bulletin* 198.

○○○

PART 2

Demography and Paleopathology

CHAPTER 5

○ ○ ○

Descriptive Methodology in Paleopathology

DONALD J. ORTNER

The quality of scientific and scholarly research in any discipline rests on the methods that are used to investigate problems important to that discipline. Both paleodemography and paleopathology are affected by methodological limitations that place very real constraints on the types of research. Ignoring these constraints leads to serious risks of making statements that overextend the methods and have a high probability of being wrong or, perhaps even more serious, right but for the wrong reasons.

Developing an appropriate methodology is often very time consuming and rarely brings the professional rewards engendered by conducting and publishing research using a well-established, although perhaps inadequate, research methodology. Despite this strategic problem, it is time for paleodemographers and paleopathologists to take a very hard look at methodology. Are some of the current methods inadequate or inappropriate for the type of conclusions being made? What are their inherent limitations? Are there ways to improve the methodology?

I know very little about the archaeology of the Plains; my knowledge of paleodemography is also limited. I do have some knowledge of human skeletal paleopathology, and for that reason I will focus on some of the methodological issues in that subdiscipline. The specifics may be somewhat different in other specialty areas, but the problems and principles are similar.

The fundamental methodology in paleopathology is descriptive and classificatory. That is, the first questions about a skeletal abnormality are what is it and how does it relate to normal bone tissue and to other skeletal abnormalities? Careful description and classification are basic to everything else that is done in paleopathology; however, it is not the ultimate objective of research. It represents a vital preliminary step in answering the next question: what does it mean? Given the presence of a certain category of disease in a population, what, for example, was its impact on the process of biological adaptation in that population? This and other questions cannot be answered with any scientific reliability unless description and classification have been done well.

Historical and Theoretical Background

There is a very substantial literature on paleopathology going back at least 150 years. Much of the earliest work was done by scholars who were medically trained. Often they understood clinical descriptive and classificatory systems and applied these to abnormalities apparent in archaeological skeletons. Unfortunately, the medical emphasis on diagnosis (classification) is apparent in many of these publications, and this is often attempted with minimal stress on careful description. If the diagnosis is correct, one can, of course, use the data for the next stage of research, that is, attempting to understand the significance of the presence of disease in a population.

It is often the case that the diagnosis appears to be inadequate. The researcher is in the uncomfortable position of ignoring the report or having to accept the author's classification without the option for independent evaluation of the criteria contributing to the diagnosis. Either possibility is, frankly, bad science. For example, the literature on Old World archaeology and physical anthropology contains reports that attribute descriptive lesions of the spine to tuberculosis (Ortner and Theobald 1993). In some cases the associated descriptive data clearly indicate that such a diagnosis is at least problematic. More often the descriptive detail needed to evaluate the diagnostic classification is lacking or inadequate, and there is insufficient data to know if the opinion expressed is valid or not. The skeletal response to tuberculosis is similar to several other infectious conditions that can affect the spine (Morse 1961:491; Ortner and Putschar 1981:148–149). This problem is further complicated by the fact that both trauma and neoplasm can produce similar results. This rather generalized response of skeletal tissue to disease is typical of most other orthopedic diseases and is a significant limitation in paleopathology. Careful description is an essential step in keeping misclassification to a minimum.

Good description and classification are far more challenging tasks than is apparent in the literature on paleopathology. Currently the tools for achieving this objective are inadequate. Some archaeologists admit to similar problems in that discipline. Physicians in both orthopedic pathology and radiology have invested and continue to invest very substantial resources in refining their descriptive and classificatory systems. Specialists in paleopathology must begin to do the same.

Descriptive Methodology

Good description of skeletal paleopathology begins with an understanding of the basic abnormal conditions that can occur. One also requires a terminology that is appropriate to the features that can be observed. Terminology in skeletal paleopathology has largely been borrowed from orthopedic radiology and pathology; however, there are subtle aspects of dry-bone pathology that exhibit features that are beyond the experience of virtually all radiologists and most orthopedic pathologists. Therefore, terms must be used and, if necessary, developed to describe more effectively the unique features seen in pathological archaeological skeletons.

The most fundamental rule in good description is to make a clear distinction between description and classification. Calling a destructive lesion of the spine tuberculosis (or Pott's disease) is not good description. The two critical and basic elements in describing a skeletal abnormality are: what is the nature of the abnormality or lesion and where is the abnormality or lesion located?

There are two broad descriptive categories of dry-bone disease. The first of these involves some type of disturbance in the growth and development process that results in the abnormal size and shape of one or more bones. This category includes conditions, often congenital, that result in dwarfism or gigantism. Several combinations of skeletal abnormality occur. For example, in achondroplasia, the long bones are shorter than normal but normal in bone-shaft diameter. Osteogenesis imperfecta tarda results in long bones that are normal in length but subnormal in bone-shaft diameter. In pituitary dwarfism the dimensions of all the bones are proportionately smaller than normal.

The second descriptive category of dry-bone disease included conditions that affect one or more bones that otherwise have developed normally but have secondary abnormal conditions superimposed on or in them. In this category there are conditions that stimulate abnormal bone tissue formation, abnormal bone tissue destruction, and both formation and destruction. One should emphasize that these descriptive categories are not mutually exclusive or discrete. Specific cases may have features of all categories. The location within a bone and the distribution pattern throughout the entire skeleton is crucial information in classification.

An additional dimension of good description is to provide some indication of the speed with which abnormal bone is formed or destroyed. Proliferative lesions of bone vary from those that form slowly to lesions that form bone tissue rapidly. In general, smooth, dense, compact abnormal bone tissue is formed slowly and usually is the result of chronic disease processes. Porous abnormal fiber bone is less well organized and is formed more rapidly (fig. 1). Large projections of abnormal fiber bone, often arranged in a lumpy cauliflowerlike or sunburst pattern, are

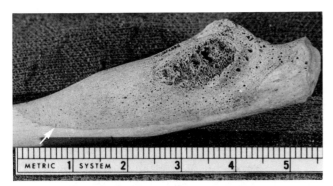

Fig. 1. Fiber bone formation in the proximal, medial right ulna of a child about six years of age at time of death. Multiple bones are involved in this case, and disseminated hematogenous osteomyelitis is a strong possibility. Note the boundary between normal compact bone and porous fiber bone (arrow). The fiber bone is fairly well organized but has a central area where bone formation is more aggressive and poorly organized. (National Museum of Natural History catalog No. 379345; scale in centimeters.)

Fig. 3. Large, coalescing lytic lesions in the calvarium of an adult male from an archaeological site on St. Lawrence I., Alaska. The large lytic focus exhibits formation of reactive bone that has sealed off the diploe (arrow). The adjacent, smaller lytic focus shows no evidence of repair of the exposed diploe. (National Museum of Natural History catalog No. 280091.)

formed very rapidly (fig. 2). It is typically indicative of an aggressive pathological process such as a neoplasm.

Destructive lesions in bone tissue also reflect the speed of skeletal response to pathology. Destructive lesions that have well-defined margins lined with dense compact bone are the result of a relatively slow chronic process (fig. 3). In X-ray films, lesions of this type have a dense, light (radiolucent) zone surrounding the lytic focus. Destructive lesions that have well-defined margins but no compact bone lining are faster and more aggressive or have not had time for bony repair. In an X-ray film these lesions will have a definite edge at the margin of the lytic focus but no evidence of a remodeled, dense border. Destructive lesions

whose margins are poorly defined are the most aggressive and rapidly forming lesion of this type. The X-ray film shows a density gradient at the boundary of the lytic focus rather than a well-defined margin.

Another complication in describing destructive lesions in archaeological bone cases is that while there may be no evidence of bone repair on an X-ray film, one may see such evidence at the microscopic level. An important descriptive distinction to make in archaeological specimens may be between destructive lesions in which the pathological process inhibits any repair and those in which repair is evident, if only at the microscopic level. In at least some cases of human skeletal paleopathology, this distinction will be possible.

An example of a destructive disease process in which there has been no reactive repair is seen in an adult female skull from Peru, dated to between A.D. 500 and 1530. Only the skull, lacking the mandible, is available for study. The most striking feature in the specimen is the presence of multiple lytic foci (fig. 4). In the X-ray film, there is no evidence of reparative bone adjacent to any destructive focus in the skull. A small piece of bone tissue, which included a lytic focus, was removed from the posterior portion of the cranium. The sample was carefully cleaned with an ultrasonic cleaner, compressed air, and, using a dissecting microscope, a needle and fine tweezers. The specimen was photographed at increasing magnifications using a scanning electron microscope (fig. 5).

Howship's lacunae are the scalloped depressions in bone tissue surfaces associated with the destruction of bone tissue by cells (osteoclasts). They are apparent on virtually all surfaces within the lytic focus. There is no evidence of reactive repair at any site within this tissue sample.

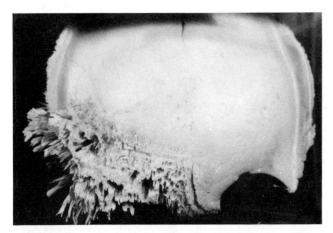

Fig. 2. Aggressive and rapid fiber bone formation in the right supraorbital region of the skull in a 14-month-old male. Bone formation stimulated by metastases of adrenal neuroblastoma. [The Royal College of Surgeons of Edinburgh, Scotland, catalog No. 1VUH (1).]

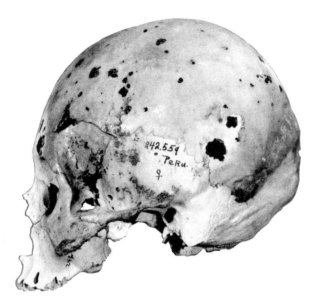

Fig. 4. Multiple scalloped lesions of the skull in an adult female from an archaeological site in Caudivilla, Peru. Multiple myeloma is a diagnostic option. Lesions, distributed throughout the calvarium, vary from pinhole size to as much as 15 mm in diameter. (National Museum of Natural History catalog no. 242559.)

A modern anatomical specimen provides a contrast at the microscopic level. It is the skeleton of a white female aged 79 years at the time of death. All bones are much lighter than normal indicating abnormal loss of bone mass (osteoporosis). A fragment of trabecular bone was removed from a rib and treated similarly to the specimen from the Peruvian

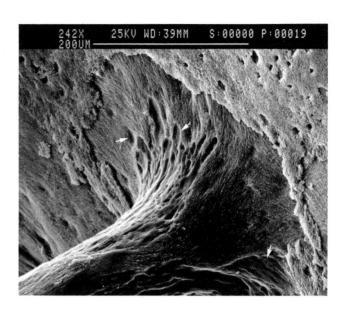

Fig. 6. Scanning electron microscope photograph of a trabeculum and the adjacent bone plate in the rib of a 79-year-old white female with osteoporosis. The trabeculum is in the lower central and left portion of the field. New fiber bone formation is apparent in the upper portion of the field and particularly the upper right corner. Normal, rugose bone surface is seen at the boundary between the trabeculum and the bone plate. Scalloped areas of osteoclastic destruction are apparent in the trabeculum and continue into the bone plate (black arrows). There is evidence of early stages of refill of the destructive process in several of the Howship's lacunae (white arrow). (National Museum of Natural History catalog No. 382085, Terry Collection No. 793R.)

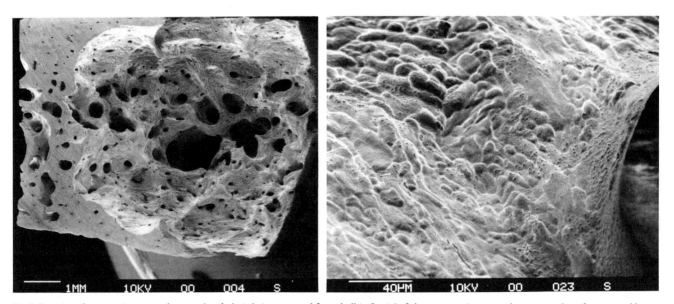

Fig. 5. Scanning electron microscope photographs of a lytic lesion removed from skull in fig. 4. Left, low-power view; note the very rough surfaces created by osteoclastic destruction of bone tissue. Right, higher-power view of one of the surfaces. There is no evidence of any repair of the destroyed surface.

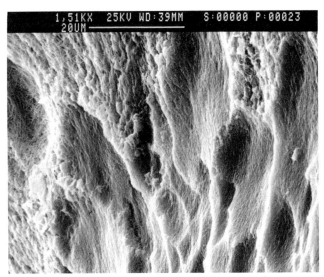

Fig. 7. Higher power of Howship's lacunae. Note the evidence of a network of new collagen fibers lining the surface of the lacunae (arrow) highlighted in fig. 6.

case. Photographs of a trabeculum were taken at increasing magnifications.

The photograph taken at low magnification (fig. 6) shows the trabeculum as it merges with a larger plate of bone tissue. The normal, rugose surface is interrupted by large areas of bone destruction. Also apparent is an area with a layer of new fiber bone. At higher power one can also see evidence that demonstrates early stages of repair in one of the Howship's lacunae (fig. 7) as collagen fibers are laid down as an irregular fibrous network in the depression of the lacunae. In this specimen evidence of cellular (osteoblast) repair is abundant even though it is inadequate to maintain normal tissue density and would not be apparent in a clinical radiograph.

The distinction between these two destructive processes is one that is rarely made in clinical practice but provides significant cellular information in archaeological cases. In the Peruvian specimen, for example, the lack of any evidence of cellular repair lends weight to a diagnostic option of one of a few neoplastic conditions that inhibit repair, such as multiple myeloma (Glasko 1986:28).

Conclusions

Currently, skeletal paleopathology is seriously limited because it is unable to provide the data that is needed to clarify some of the important questions in human microevolution and biocultural adaptation. For example, what was the impact of major social change, such as the emergence of agriculture and

the development of urbanism, on human biology including disease? Some valiant attempts have been made to explore problems in paleopathology on this level (e.g., Cohen and Armelagos 1984); however, the base of solid data is very thin in terms of quantity and quality. This must and can improve.

The recovery of human DNA from archaeological tissues (Paabo 1987) and immunoglobulins from archaeological bone tissue (Tuross 1991) represents a major potential methodological breakthrough whose utility will be clarified in the next decade. In the meantime, skeletal paleopathologists need to make a major effort to improve the precision of the terminology and the descriptive methods in the analysis of skeletal samples. Biochemistry and molecular biology may provide important new tools, but these methods will be even more effective if skeletal paleopathologists have a better base of anatomical data to compare with biochemical data.

In descriptive methodology, paleopathologists need to evaluate carefully every feature that can be studied, including those obtained using radiological, anatomical, and histological methods. Paleopathologists must integrate their methodology with existing methods in medical disciplines, but without limiting their observations to features known to specialists in those disciplines. Paleopathologists have something unique to contribute to the understanding of skeletal disease. The major components of their methodology will be a careful and consistent description of the type and pattern of pathological conditions in skeletons. These findings must be related to the experience of orthopedic specialists as much as possible.

Another cautionary note is that one needs to be careful in interpreting features seen in archaeological materials. Remember that, in a case of skeletal paleopathology, one is viewing conditions at a single point in time in what would have been a complex and ongoing process. Since an individual can die at any stage of skeletal disease, an archaeological specimen may reflect the bony response to disease at any stage from the earliest, initial reaction to the end-stage response.

There are other problems in paleopathology including the need for a much more adequate theoretical context for research (Ortner 1991). However, a more effective descriptive methodology would permit the exploration, with greater clarity, of the implications of different categories of disease in a given population. There are three basic options for interpreting the evidence of the presence or absence of disease in a skeletal sample: a person can die before the skeleton is affected as the result of a virulent disease process, an inadequate or inappropriate immune response to disease or some combination of both; the patient can recover before the skeleton is affected; and the disease process reaches a type of equilibrium with the host in which the disease process becomes chronic and the host survives long-term, perhaps with some loss of biological function. The last option implies an intermediate but relatively effective immune response by the host.

Most often in skeletal infectious disease what is visible is evidence of chronic disease with intermediate virulence of the parasite and a relatively good immune response by the host. The implication of this is one of the poorly understood but crucial paradoxes of skeletal paleopathology, that is, evidence of skeletal disease may, in fact, be evidence of fairly good adaptation and good immune response. That is to say, people with skeletal disease may be healthier than individuals in a skeletal sample who died without skeletal involvement. Murray (1990), working with archaeological skeletal samples from Arkansas, indicates that historic period material had a lower mean age at death than earlier materials from sites dated to the prehistoric through early historic period. She argues that the reduction in age at death in the more recent skeletal sample was due to the introduction of European diseases. An additional interesting observation is that the incidence of skeletal disease decreased in the later-period skeletal samples. This finding illustrates the importance of considering the biological processes that result in bone pathology. It is also important to recognize that not everyone showing evidence of skeletal disease is unable to function at least minimally. There is a very substantial amount of biological and cultural redundancy in most human populations that allow successful adjustments to be made despite the presence of endemic disease. Think it through very carefully, but above all describe in detail what you see before making an attempt to classify the problem or condition seen in a skeleton.

Commentary on the Chapters on Demography and Paleopathology

The reports that follow in this section on paleodemography and paleopathology provide some useful insights on the current and potential value of archaeological skeletal studies. They also demonstrate the importance of careful attention to research methodology and good descriptive analysis.

Trimble explores the microevolutionary dimensions of viral epidemics, particularly smallpox, in the early historic period. He reviews some of the factors that affect the impact of epidemic disease on a human population including the infectious agent and the environment of the host as broadly defined. One of the factors that could have received greater emphasis is the cultural and biological backup systems that attenuate the effect of the disease agent. It is clear, in the case

of the nineteenth-century smallpox epidemics, that social relationships (trade) were a factor, but chance factors also seem to have been at work. Culturally patterned living conditions as well as the negative attitudes of the Plains Indians toward preventative therapy were crucial. Morbidity and mortality were enhanced by the breakdown in social organization resulting from the inability to plant and harvest crops, which led to widespread malnutrition and starvation. This was exacerbated by raids from nomadic groups and the inability of decimated sedentary agriculturists to resist. Trimble's report provides evidence of just how vulnerable complex societies are to epidemic disease and to the devastating consequences disease can have on human societies.

Williams reports on the demography and paleopathology of a substantial sample (N = 402) of Archaic and Woodland skeletons from the Northern Plains. He presents data on the prevalence of four skeletal disease categories—degenerative arthritis, trauma, inflammation, and metabolic or developmental abnormalities. Evidence of skeletal degenerative arthritis includes marginal overgrowths of bone of the joints, breakdown of subchondral bone (usually seen as porosity of the joint surface), and breakdown of articular cartilage (expressed as eburnation or polishing of the joint surface). The relationship of these skeletal manifestations of degenerative arthritis to clinical symptoms is not well known. Some evidence of arthritis was common in the skeletal sample, but severe manifestations were rare. This suggests that arthritic joint problems were probably minimal.

Trauma was uncommon, and most of what occurred is attributed to accidental causes rather than interpersonal aggression. Evidence of bone inflammation was found in 7 percent of the total sample. As in all archaeological samples, adults are unlikely to exhibit evidence of childhood trauma, so the prevalence of trauma is likely to be underestimated. Williams raises the possibility that some of the inflammatory lesions of the lower leg may have been ossified hematomas associated with scurvy. This is very doubtful in adult material where, in contrast with infants and children, the periosteum is very tightly attached to the diaphyseal surface and unlikely to be involved with a hematoma that can ossify. A more conservative interpretation is simple inflammation following trauma that activates a periosteal response, including the apposition of additional bone, in the area of inflammation. Evidence of inflammation associated with infection is rare, but Williams notes that a strong case can be made for tuberculosis in at least two individuals.

Williams correctly emphasizes the difficulties in the diagnosis of metabolic and developmental diseases. Much of his discussion regarding this broad category of disease is focused on evidence of porotic hyperostosis and the common assumption that this is evidence of anemia. What one sees in skeletal remains are porous lesions of the skull vault and orbital roof that, in some cases, also involve an increase in bone thickness. Many diseases can cause this general condition, including anemia. A diagnosis of anemia is highly problematic unless there is clear evidence of enlarged spaces for hematopoietic marrow. Porosity of the skull surfaces without involvement of the marrow should not be attributed to anemia without further confirming evidence.

Schermer, Fisher, and Hodges provide a helpful review of the literature on the paleopathology of treponematosis and skeletal evidence for this disease in a small prehistoric skeletal sample from western Iowa. The sample is from three sites, one of which is probably dated to the Early Woodland, another to the Middle Woodland. The third is not dated with confidence although a Woodland date seems likely. The burials are secondary and mixed, making the diagnosis of skeletal lesions even more challenging.

The authors argue that the lesions seen in several cases fit the pattern associated with treponematosis. They contend that, of the three treponemal syndromes that can affect the skeleton, the most likely candidate is endemic syphilis. They base this conclusion on two lines of evidence. The first is that Woodland populations in this area are thought to consist of small hunting and gathering groups and, in Old World villages, endemic syphilis is more common in small groups than venereal syphilis where both are endemic. They also argue that the bones of the skull are rarely involved in their sample and that this is more likely to be the case with endemic syphilis. The authors recognize that establishing the specific syndrome of treponematosis on the basis of this type of evidence is risky. I agree with them and suggest that, given the known current geographical distribution for endemic syphilis, venereal syphilis may be a more conservative explanation.

The chapter on the evidence of respiratory disease in archaeological skeletal samples by Kelley et al. suggests the importance of looking very carefully at fairly subtle evidence of disease in the skeleton. Ribs have received minimal attention in the literature on paleopathology. Kelley et al. argue that the evidence of inflammatory lesions on ribs can be used as an indicator of infectious disease. The authors lean heavily on clinical data in interpreting their findings, but they seem somewhat equivocal. They note that pneumonia tends to be more common in the right lung and tuberculosis more common in the left. Their data show no side difference in the Plains sample, and on that basis a distinction between pneu-

monia and tuberculosis could not be made. They argue that clinical evidence of skeletal involvement in pneumonia is rare. The problem with that conclusion is that clinical evidence is largely based on radiology and lesions of the type used in this chapter are not likely to be observed in clinical chest X-rays.

Somewhat more convincing is the observation that tuberculosis tends to affect the upper lung and pneumonia the lower quadrants of the lung. The lesions in the sample were on the upper ribs. What remains unclear is what other infectious conditions can result in inflammatory lesions of the ribs and what is their pattern of involvement? The various expressions of inflammation of the pleura (pleurisy) are of obvious importance in differential diagnosis. Nevertheless, Kelly et al. have called attention to a type of lesion that may reflect inflammation of other tissues of the chest.

Mann, Owsley, and Reinhard report on evidence suggestive of infection and neoplasm in the skeletons of two Native American children (3 to 5 years of age), one from Nebraska and the other from Oklahoma. Through detailed descriptions, the authors report on osseous changes manifested by otitis media, mastoiditis, and postcranial lesions suggestive of histiocytosis X and tuberculosis (infection). Although the lesions in the child from Nebraska likely reflect histiocytosis X, a disease of unknown origin, other dieseases including metastatic neuroblastoma, lymphoma, and osteomyelitis are also considered. The child from Oklahoma presents strong evidence of tuberculosis based on resorptive lesions of the vertebral bodies (vertebra plana) and left elbow, and periostitis on the visceral surface of at least one rib. This example, first studied in 1971, underscores the importance of preserving human skeletons for future examination and serves to show what may be learned through advances in skeletal pathology.

Willey and Hoffman discuss of therapeutic or prophylactic procedures in dental disease among North American skeletal samples. They observe that the significance of interproximal grooves seen in archaeological dentitions from many geographical areas is still being argued. Willey and Hoffman base their findings on the study of 74 skulls in the skeletal collection of the W.H. Over Museum. The sample, subsequently reburied, included skeletons from various time periods excavated from archaeological sites in South Dakota. The authors provide data to support their opinion that interproximal grooves are the result of a therapeutic procedure to relieve the discomfort of dental disease. They note that the root of the black sampson plant is still used by many contemporary tribes for dental pain. It has a mild anesthetic effect that would relieve local pain from inflamed gums or caries. The authors note that there is no obvious link between the use of black sampson root and dental grooves. Despite this, they argue that interproximal grooves are most likely the result of using plant materials to bring relief to local pain.

Gill's report on evidence of trauma in Plains pioneer skeletons demonstrates the value of skeletal research in clarifying historical traditions. For many people, the pioneers of the Old West evoke an immediate image of hard and dangerous living, tough people and violent death—often at the hands of another person. Gill recognizes this popular tradition but points out that the supporting evidence is often ephemeral. He makes a distinction between the early pioneers (who depended on a mixed economy including hunting, mining and cattle herding) and later settlers with an economy based more on agriculture. His sample of the former category does support the popular image. Evidence of violence in the agriculturist sample was significantly less. Fourteen of seventeen adults in the early pioneer sample showed evidence of skeletal trauma. Six of the seventeen died a violent death. The age at death was in the 20- to 40-year range, and most of the individuals in the sample were very robust males.

References Cited

Cohen, M.N., and G.J. Armelagos
  1984 Paleopathology at the Origins of Agriculture. Orlando, Fla.: Academic Press.
Glasko, C.S.B.
  1986 Skeletal Metastases. Stoneham, Mass.: Butterworths.

Morse, D.
  1961 Prehistoric Tuberculosis in America. *American Review of Respiratory Diseases* 83:489–503.
Murray, K.A.
  1990 The Population-disease Experience Among Native Americans: Bioarcheological Evidence from Arkansas. *American Journal of Physical Anthropology* 81:273. (Abstract of paper.)
Ortner, D.J
  1991 Theoretical and Methodological Issues in Paleopathology. In Human Paleopathology: Current Syntheses and Future Options. D.J. Ortner and A.C. Aufderheide, eds. Washington: Smithsonian Institution Press.
——, and W.G.J. Putschar
  1981 Identification of Pathological Conditions in Human Skeletal Remains. Washington: Smithsonian Institution Press.
——, and G. Theobald
  1993 Diseases in the Pre-Roman World. In Cambridge World History of Human Disease, Pt. 5. K.F. Kiple, ed. New York: Cambridge University Press.
Paabo, S.
  1987 Molecular Genetic Methods in Archaeology: A Prospect. *Anthropologischer Anzeiger* 45: 9–17.
Tuross, N.
  1991 Recovery of Bone and Serum Protein from Human Skeletal Tissue: IgG, osteonectin and albumin. In Human Paleopathology: Current Syntheses and Future Options. D.J. Ortner and A.C. Aufderheide, eds. Washington: Smithsonian Institution Press.

CHAPTER 6

○ ○ ○

The 1837–1838 Smallpox Epidemic on the Upper Missouri

MICHAEL K. TRIMBLE

Until the 1960s and early 1970s, theoretical orientations embraced by many anthropologists for explicating disease effects on given populations revolved almost exclusively around the ideas of scholars who were closely identified with a single sector of concern, the sociocultural (Ashburn 1947; Bruner 1961; Cockburn 1963; Jacobs 1974; Jarcho 1964). Both the strengths and weaknesses of these sociocultural orientations lie in their basic empirical generalizations. Their strength is that they are useful for summarizing and ordering large numbers of specific time-place-people observations. On the other hand, their explanatory power is poor.

During the 1960s and 1970s, the epidemiological orientation crystallized. This paradigm has a biological rather than a sociocultural focus, and it cannot readily be delineated by reference to a single author. However, explicit theoretical statements are most often associated with Alland (1966, 1970), Armelagos and McArdle (1975), Black (1966), Black et al. (1974), and Crosby (1972). Important empirical contributions have been made by several authors: Black (1966), Cockburn (1971), Dobyns (1963, 1966, 1983), Dunn (1968), Fine (1975), Livingstone (1958), McCracken (1971), and Wiesenfeld (1967).

The epidemiological paradigm is broadly concerned with dimensions of disease that are often treated as dependent variables, that is, how do the variables of biology, culture, and environmental pressure influence the process and distribution of disease? Within this broad framework, human beings are seen as evolutionarily unique, utilizing and transmitting culture as a highly efficient instrument for adapting to and controlling their environments. Human adaptation is, however, a mutually interactive cultural and biological process with references to given environmental parameters. Thus, the scope of the epidemiological paradigm encompasses communities and populations, the behavior of human groups and of microbiota, the perceptions of the disease and primary environmental features, and the definitions of diseases.

Variables and Core Factors for Assessing Epidemics

Attempts to assess the introduction and spread of an epidemic within a population must address mutual relations between the general variables of disease, biology, culture, environment, and the "core factors" associated with these variables. For

Table 1. Variables and Core Factors in the Spread of Disease

Disease	Culture	Biology	Environment
Pathogenicity and virulence	Nutrition	Adaptation and genetic resistance	Climatic factors
Infectivity and transmission	Sanitation	Age	Mode of transmission
Invasiveness	New technology	Sex	Seasonality
Stability of pathogen	Density	Acquired resistance	
	Acculturation		
	Cognitive system (as it relates to disease)		
	The medical practitioner		

present purposes, disease variables include the traditional notion involving organic pathogens as well as the notion of "insult" (Audy 1971). "Insults" are physical, chemical, psychological, social, and infectious stimuli that adversely affect the individual's (or population's) adjustment to an environment. Insults may originate externally or internally.

Cultural variables are those concepts and techniques used by individuals or populations to control their environment. Central to this definition is the notion that not every concept or technique is "survival-worthy." Through time, cultural traits that were once survival-worthy or neutral to a population's health and continuity can become detrimental.

Biological variables are defined as the sum of the changes occurring in the genetic composition of individuals that allow the species to adjust to environmental change. If adjustment does not occur, the species may not survive. Survival is governed by endogenous and exogenous factors. Exogenous factors include environmental pressures and stimuli of varying intensities. Endogenous factors involve the degree of genotypically controlled plasticity within individuals, which in turn can condition the response to environmental stimuli. Environmental variables include the effects of geographical location and climate upon living populations.

Therefore, general variables that address disease, culture, biology, and environment must be evaluated when assessing the impact of an epidemic on a population. Naturally, these variables are composed of a number of "core factors" that describe or affect each variable and that represent the minimal units of observation necessary for evaluating the spread of an epidemic. Some "core factors" can be discussed or grouped under more than one variable. This notion supports a major point: the process of the spread of disease is inextricably intertwined in an articulated network of cultural, biological, and environmental variables. Table 1 lists the primary factors to be considered when evaluating the spread of disease within a population.

The History of the 1837–1838 Epidemic

In 1837, a smallpox epidemic swept through the Northern Plains. Although not the first, this epidemic was one of the most devastating outbreaks in North America. The entire Missouri River Trench became "one great grave yard" (National Archives, microfilm roll 884).

The epidemic in the upper Missouri region began almost simultaneously at three widely separated places. By July 1, 1837, the disease had broken out and was rapidly spreading among the Yankton and Santee Sioux Indians at Sioux Agency, the government annuity house near Fort Pierre (fig. 1) (Trimble 1979:73). Cases of the disease were reported at the American Fur Company's trading post, Fort Union, at the mouth of the Yellowstone River, almost 1,000 miles upstream a few days later (Abel 1932:294; Larpenteur 1962:132). On July 14, the first recorded death occurred in the Indian village at Fort Clark, another trading post down the Missouri River, near the mouth of Knife River (Abel 1932:121). Within weeks, the pestilence spread to the Assiniboine and Blackfeet around Fort Union, and to the Mandan, Arikara, and Hidatsa near Fort Clark (Meyer 1977).

Within three months, smallpox was spreading "with the greatest destruction possible," in the words of Jacob Halsey, an eyewitness at Fort Union (Abel 1932:394). Ten out of every 12 Indians in Halsey's area were dead. Although he had been unable to keep pace with the number of victims, he presumed that at least 700 Blackfeets and perhaps 800 Assiniboines were dead (Abel 1932:394–395). Alexander Culbertson, another eyewitness, estimated that more than half the Assiniboine tribe fell victim to the disease and that about two-thirds of the Blackfeet tribe were dead (DeVoto 1947:289–291). By winter these large and powerful Indian tribes along the headwaters of the upper Missouri were reduced to tiny, starving remnants (Ewers 1961:72).

Fig. 1. Tribes on the upper Missouri River vaccinated for smallpox in 1832 with the locations of trading posts/annuity houses.

Downstream at Fort Clark, the toll from the disease was even more dreadful. By August 11, François Chardon, the clerk at the fort, had recorded in his daily journal that the Mandans were dying so fast that it was impossible to keep a record (Abel 1932:126). Smallpox spread to the Arikara and

Hidatsa, and they died as rapidly as the Mandan. On September 19, Chardon recorded that 800 Mandans were dead (Abel 1932:132) and that in one of the Mandan villages near the fort, only 14 people out of a former population of more than 600 were left alive. By the end of the month, he speculated that the disease had destroyed seven-eighths of the Mandan tribe, and one-half of the Arikara and Hidatsa (Abel 1932:137–138).

By early spring, the epidemic died out. In its aftermath, as many as 17,000 people were dead (DeVoto 1947:294–295).

These data permit the following generalizations. A smallpox epidemic persisted over a three- to seven-month period along the Missouri River from Fort Leavenworth in present-day Kansas to Fort Union on the headwaters of the Missouri. There appears to be a rough patterning associated with the direction of the outbreaks—south to north—and the degree of severity among tribal groups. Severe mortality associated with this epidemic left several cultural groups as nonfunctional social units.

This summary represents the depth of understanding achieved by published accounts.

MODE OF INTRODUCTION

To explore the concept of "patterning," the second level of inquiry involves establishing the modes and points of introduction of the virus. This research allows easier modeling of the epidemic process for the Northern Plains area and helps clarify regional epidemic sequences.

The introduction and rapid dissemination of this epidemic can be traced to, and was a function of, the Euro-American fur trade (Trimble 1979:69–84). The crew of the steamboat *St. Peters* experienced an outbreak of smallpox while on a provisioning tour up the Missouri River to fur trading posts and U.S. government agencies. The virus infected almost all the passengers aboard the vessel (National Archives, microfilm roll 883). An epidemic of this type usually would not spread as rapidly over such a wide geographic area; however, the steamboat captain refused to quarantine the crew and passengers because he feared delays in the schedule (Meyer 1977:92–99). As a consequence, the localized smallpox outbreak on board the *St. Peters* was rapidly transported upriver.

Passengers capable of transmitting the disease disembarked and came into contact with Indians at the successive docking points (Trimble 1979:74–77). At Council Bluffs Agency (fig. 1), members of the Otoe, Omaha, and Pawnee are reported to have been exposed (National Archives, microfilm roll 883). The next stop, at Sioux Agency, exposed the Yankton and Santee Sioux. There was a stop at Fort Pierre, but there is no mention of which groups were exposed (National Archives, microfilm roll 883). At Fort Clark, smallpox apparently was introduced among the Mandan, Hidatsa, and Arikara by

two Arikara women who disembarked to visit relatives (Meyers 1977:97–99; Trimble 1979:38–42).

The final groups directly infected with smallpox from the *St. Peters's* passengers were the Blackfeet and Assiniboine who were awaiting trading goods and government annuities at Fort Union (DeVoto 1947).

In seven weeks (first week of May to third week of June 1837), smallpox was introduced into almost every major tribe living on or near the Missouri Trench. Through continued intertribal contact, the initial introduction developed into the 1837–1838 epidemic on the Great Plains.

VARIABLES

What factors were the key elements in determining why this disease became epidemic? What accounts for the varying morbidity and mortality estimates between tribes?

Epidemiological investigations should consider four major theoretical variables: disease, biology, culture, and environment. By examining these variables, their core factors, and associated interrelationships during a disease crisis a better understanding of the crucial elements involved in each epidemic can be isolated. This approach provides an explanatory framework that identifies key elements distinguishing individual epidemic episodes as well as summarizing variable causes. Epidemics can only be understood through multivariate analysis where examination of associations of variables suggest disease causation and cultural response. In an attempt to define more clearly why the disease became epidemic and to identify the factors contributing to its virulence, the data are considered using this four-variable framework.

DISEASE

Smallpox is a highly contagious disease characterized by chills, pains, and high fever during the initial symptom phase. This phase is followed by the appearance of skin eruptions covering the face, hands, and often the entire body. After passing through various stages of formation, the eruptions finally dry, usually leaving pockmarks. This advanced phase is followed by a lengthy and precarious recuperation period. Two varieties of the disease have high mortality rates (Stimson and Hodes 1956).

The virus can be transmitted through contact with an infected person, or with clothing, bedding, dust, or other objects or possessions of victims of the disease. A patient with smallpox is capable of passing the virus to others almost immediately after the first symptoms appear until several weeks after recuperation begins. As in all contagious situations, overcrowding, unsanitary conditions, and a debilitated state of individual physical health accelerate the spread and intensity of smallpox (Bower and Piliant 1954:85–90).

BIOLOGICAL

A person who contracts the disease and lives acquires life-long immunity. Other preventives for the disease are isolation, quarantine, variolation, and vaccination. Variolation involves transferring scab material from a patient recovering from smallpox to a healthy individual. Care must be taken to insure that the patient is recovering at the time the scabs are obtained as success depends on the donor's antigenic response to the disease. Antibodies are concentrated in the last loci of the infection, the scabs. Transferring the scabs also transfers antibodies; the healthy individual will contract only a mild case of smallpox and thereafter be immune.

Vaccination uses material taken from a patient who has cowpox, a mild disease of cows with a low communicability rate in humans. Exposure to cowpox confers immunity to smallpox. Developed in the 1790s by Edward Jenner, vaccination soon became preferred to that of variolation because of the lower risk of death for vaccinated individuals and the reduced chance of beginning an epidemic (Dixon 1962).

On the Great Plains, however, where supplies of vaccine were difficult to obtain, variolation was the main technique used to immunize Indians. In fact, this technique was the main immunization tool on the Plains until at least the mid-nineteenth century (Ferch 1983:2–6, 1984:4–6).

CULTURAL

The 1837–1838 epidemic was extremely virulent, and there can be little doubt that either or both of the virulent strains of variola smallpox were present. Other conditions in the villages of both the nomads and the horticulturists undoubtedly contributed to the intensity and spread of the disease. One of these conditions was the living accommodations of the Indians; the other was their debilitated physical condition.

Both the horticulturists—Arikara, Mandan, and Hidatsa—and nomads—Sioux, Iowa, and Otoe—were semisedentary. The horticulturists lived part of the year in large earthlodge villages located along major rivers or streams where they farmed. The earthlodges were semisubterranean circular structures with log frameworks covered with willow mats overlaid with a thick coating of earth and sod and dirt floors. The lodges varied in size from about 20 to more than 30 feet

in diameter with a side entrance and a smoke hole in the center of the roof. Because of the construction, material, and design, these lodges were cool and damp during the summer, and warm and damp during the winter. Generally, the lodges were closely spaced in the villages, sometimes hardly allowing room for one person to pass between them. In 1834, the Mandan village adjoining Fort Clark contained approximately 60 earthlodges clustered in an area with a diameter of about 200 yards (Thwaites 1906, 15:349–350).

As many as 15 to 25 people could live in each lodge along with dogs and even horses (Thwaites 1959, 1:219, 258, 298). Euro-American visitors were dismayed by the filth, stench, and crowded conditions. One visitor noted the location of the toilet as immediately outside the lodge door (Coues 1897, 1:332ff). Cooking facilities were in the center where the entire household and visitors shared both food and eating utensils (Coues 1897, 1:328). In the summer, the horticulturists left for the High Plains to live in skin tents while hunting for meat for the winter months.

The nomads lived in portable skin tents almost year round. These tents were generally 10–20 feet in diameter, contained a central hearth for cooking and heating, and housed 7–10 individuals (Abel 1932). The nomadic groups spent the summer months on the Plains hunting bison and collecting provisions for the winter. During the winter months they camped in the river bottoms, moving only when fuel and animal resources became depleted (National Archives, microfilm rolls 883–884). Their lifeway insured greater freedom of movement than the horticulturists who, while sharing similar summer and winter hunting patterns, were tied to their earthlodges since they returned each fall to harvest their crops.

ENVIRONMENTAL

François Chardon, the clerk at Fort Clark in 1837–1838 and a major source on the horticulturists, recorded limited environmental data (Abel 1932). Although his journal lacks the finer points of meteorological reporting, such as precise temperature, amount of rainfall, and wind speed, Chardon reported general weather observations (presence or absence of rain, wind strength, and extremes of temperature). Chardon's journal makes it possible to model weather conditions prior to the outbreak of smallpox. These observations are of considerable interest because they suggest that climate and general environmental conditions affected living patterns within the Indian villages, which in turn probably intensified the severity of the epidemic.

The month of May 1837 was cold and wet, with rain recorded for almost one-third of the month. The wetness of the season hardly abated as June was recorded as being "soggy." During the last 10 days of June, it rained three more times, turned quite cold once, and Chardon recorded "smokey weather" as a result of the firing of the prairies for two other days. July was unusually damp, with rain recorded for six days during the first two weeks. After the first reported death from smallpox on July 14, the rains continued, and the burning prairies frequently filled the sky with thick smoke (Abel 1932:120–124).

Beginning as early as March, Chardon recorded an increasing shortage of food for both the Mandan and Hidatsa (Abel 1932:102, 104). Game was scarce, indicating that the effects of prolonged hunting of bison and other game were leading to depletion of nearby animal populations (Coues 1897, 1:336–337). Food shortages during May reached an acute stage: in entries for that month, Chardon wrote of Indians and himself starving for seven days. This situation continued during June (Abel 1932:110–120). During this month, Chardon recorded his tally of fur inventories made in preparation for the arrival of the company steamboat, the *St. Peters*. The area's game depletion was dramatically indicated by the low fur intake for the season. The shortage of food remained critical through July. The eruption of the smallpox epidemic disrupted the traditional hunting patterns and plunged the area into famine (Abel 1932:116–120).

Analysis of Differential Morbidity and Mortality

Given these observations, several reasons explain why this disease became such a virulent epidemic while exhibiting variable morbidity and mortality rates among tribes. First, smallpox is highly contagious. Unless the initial host is placed in isolation or the general population has acquired immunity through past contact or inoculation, one case can rapidly develop into an epidemic. Not only were the initial victims unquarantined, but also there were many Indians living along the upper Missouri River who lacked immunity, acquired or conferred, to the disease. The long period of communicability provided the potential (which was realized) for prolonged transmission of the disease. Thus, the initial outbreak became an areal epidemic.

Knowledge of vaccination and variolation practices existed, and, if employed on a wide scale, could have had an enormous effect. However, the archival evidence for morbidity and mortality rates strongly suggest that no large-scale inoculation

programs had ever taken place among the Upper Missouri tribes. A major obstacle was the traditional unwillingness of Plains tribes to submit to a medical intervention they felt would endanger their lives (National Archives, microfilm rolls 883, 884). Generalized conferred immunity did not exist for most tribes as of 1837.

The second reason for differential morbidity rates of smallpox is that the large, nucleated communities of the horticulturists proved to be a disadvantage. Nucleated communities not only increased the chances of an epidemic but also facilitated this one. In such an environment, a virus could easily be transmitted through an entire village in a number of days. Planting and harvesting schedules requiring close cooperation between family groups were disrupted, guaranteeing nutritional stress, and increased mortality. Chardon's description of the horticulturists' experiences with smallpox in 1837–1838 supports this conclusion (Abel 1932).

Conversely, the nomadic populations of the Plains were built on a foundation of self-sufficiency requiring cooperation of fewer family groups. These bands only united to become tribes—and hence large population groups—during corporate endeavors such as the summer bison hunt. When an epidemic struck a tribe or even a band, it dissolved into small family units to escape the disease. This strategy diminished the impact of an epidemic. Dispersing behavior, thus, had the effect of a general quarantine. Morbidity and mortality were often confined to small bands, reducing the chances of transmission to other nomadic groups. The community disruption caused by the loss of agricultural specialists associated with the village tribes was not a factor among nomadic groups.

The living practices of the nomads and horticulturists provide data that help explain the differential morbidity and mortality among these groups. The horticulturists were more likely to experience a crowd-disease epidemic because of nucleation in households and within the earth-lodge villages. Transmission rates are greatly enhanced when large numbers of people interact within a small area. Village permanence additionally increased the chances of an epidemic's being introduced. Most of the horticulturists' villages were visited regularly by Euro-Americans and native groups for trading. The villagers were continuously exposed to microbes carried by visiting traders. In contrast, the nomadic groups visited trading posts but did not live in proximity to them. Their nomadic life insured fewer contacts with potential pathogens. The smaller number of inhabitants housed in their portable living quarters, as well as their ability to disperse, provided fewer chances for the spread of an acute crowd infection.

Third, the environmental variables must be considered. Chardon's diary reported inclement weather for the horticulturists' villages during June and July. The concentration of large numbers of people compelled to stay indoors because of the rain during a time when the epidemic was being transmitted, but was not yet clinically apparent, contributed to the overall infection rate. Chardon also states that game was scarce. The increased numbers of nutritionally stressed individuals affected survival rates once the epidemic began. Not only were potentially recovering patients deprived of high-quality protein, but the problem was compounded because fewer healthy individuals were available for hunting and foraging when food was needed most. Many survivors died from starvation (Abel 1932).

The aforementioned variables are crucial to discussions of the morbidity and mortality suffered by the Indian tribes of the Plains in 1837–1838. However, questions remain as to why there was such a disproportionate fatality rate among populations of the upper Missouri, as opposed to Indians of the lower Missouri. Research (Ferch 1983, 1984; Unrau 1989) has revealed that selective vaccination programs took place among Indians who either inhabited the lower Missouri or interacted with Euro-Americans in that area (fig. 1).

Formal vaccination programs were initiated in autumn 1831 and summer and autumn 1832 under the auspices of the U.S. government. John Dougherty, the senior Indian agent at the Council Bluffs Agency (National Archives, microfilm roll 750), administered the programs and contracted physicians. The most ambitious program took place in 1832, its goal to vaccinate as many Indians as possible on the Missouri River. However, bureaucratic delays contributed to the failure of this program. The campaign scheduled for May 1832 did not begin until August. As a result, many tribes were out on the High Plains hunting and missed the opportunity to be vaccinated. Nonviable vaccine matter brought about further delays (National Archives, microfilm roll 750).

However, despite flaws in the administration of the program, parts of the Iowa, Otoe, Omaha, and Pawnee as well as Yankton, Yanktonai, and Teton Sioux (approximately 3,500 people) were vaccinated. At that time of year, these Indians were living on the lower Missouri River below Fort Pierre. Because of delays, the tribes of the upper Missouri—the Mandan, Hidatsa, Arikara, Assiniboine, Cree, and Blackfeet—were not vaccinated. This meant that the lower Missouri River groups had a reduced probability of experiencing an epidemic when exposed to the smallpox virus. Conversely, those groups that had not acquired immunity through vaccination or recent epidemic episodes experienced higher mor-

bidity and mortality rates. The nomadic groups of the lower Missouri River, especially the Sioux, were the main beneficiaries of the vaccination program and suffered the lowest mortality of the major Plains tribes (Trimble 1992). The Yankton, Yanktonai, and Teton were disproportionately vaccinated, and in terms of conferred immunity among the Plains tribes, they clearly were at an advantage during the 1837–1838 epidemic. The upper Missouri River horticulturists and nomads lacked this immunity, resulting in high morbidity and mortality.

Cultural Consequences

The impact of this epidemic on the tribal life of the Northern Plains Indians (primarily the Mandan, Hidatsa, Arikara, and Assiniboine) was enormous. The high mortality destroyed family relationships, which were the backbone of their collective tribal existence. It took almost two generations before these relationships were rejuvenated (Lehmer 1971, 1977a, 1977b). The sudden loss or depletion of cooperative units—crucial for success in hunting, trading, and farming—further divided and isolated the surviving tribes. Efficiency in these endeavors was greatly impaired, leading to an immediate inability to compete successfully, especially in economic spheres, with rival groups.

Other effects of the epidemic permanently altered the culture of the Northern Plains Indians. The loss of large numbers of Mandan, Hidatsa, and Arikara upset the balance of power, resulting in a realignment of tribal boundaries and shifts in tribal allegiances. The surviving Mandan, culturally shattered, were forced to coalesce with the Hidatsa and later with the Arikara for survival. The intertribal trading system on the upper Missouri River was destroyed by the decline of the Mandan and Hidatsa, the principal brokers of the system, which forced the remaining tribal fragments to depend, to a greater extent, upon the White traders and their goods.

Equally important was the loss of tribal power embodied in its warriors. With reduced manpower, the horticulturists lost the ability to defend traditional territories from raiding and poaching. Surviving villages became isolated garrisons, unable to defend their populace or crops from the nomadic Sioux tribes. The nomadic groups came to view and to use the once powerful horticulturists' villages as resources for human or material goods.

The epidemic also influenced the political fortunes of the Northern Plains Indians. The decimation of the hunter-warrior classes reduced the food-obtaining capabilities of the tribes and ultimately forced a split of northern Plains Indians into two major allegiance groups. Those who chose to depend more on food obtained through government annuities moved closer to trading posts and Indian agencies. With the passage of years, the receipt of doles and assistance became a way of life, in return for which these Indians forfeited their independence. This dependence weakened their bargaining position during later negotiations for land. Ultimately, these groups became the first "reservation Indians" in the area.

Because they sustained fewer losses from disease, the nomadic tribal groups were able to marshal the power necessary to sustain traditional lifeways. They eventually moved farther west into areas where game was more plentiful. As a result of the horticulturists' collapse, these nomadic populations became the most powerful aboriginal groups residing on the Plains. Once the village tribes were shattered and disorganized, the nomadic groups became the favored trading partners of certain Euro-American fur trading companies. The net effect of the nomadic groups' movement west was to remove some bands from the approaching wave of westernization, thereby allowing them to retain their independence for several decades. These groups became the "unfriendly Indians" against whom the United States waged war during the last half of the nineteenth century.

Conclusions

The use of ethnohistoric data for developing accurate cultural histories for human populations has a long tradition in anthropology. Properly practiced, ethnohistory can be instructive within the limits of the discipline. However, ethnohistoric data can be profitably employed for more than developing independent culture histories. Used in conjunction with paradigms from complementary disciplines, ethnohistoric data can describe and model cultural process as well.

This examination of the Plains smallpox epidemic of 1837–1838 demonstrates the utility of such an approach. By combining ethnohistoric data with general paradigms from epidemiology, not only the individual histories and effects of the epidemic among tribes are illustrated but also the process is modeled on a regional basis.

In this analysis, a general history of the epidemic on the Plains was reconstructed using ethnohistoric data. Next, epidemiological paradigms of disease causation and transmission were used to generate and define analytical topics, in an effort to identify the processes behind the virus's spread as well as its potential cultural consequences. With these analytical topics, ethnohistoric and epidemiological data can be examined to allow the acceptance, rejection, or modification of the original propositions. Finally,

following full analysis of all data, generalizations regarding the introduction, spread, and effect of smallpox among aboriginal populations living in the Plains in 1837–1838 could be posited. In addition, a number of potential cultural responses to acute crowd infections could be modeled, given differences in population immunity. Ethnohistory, used carefully and creatively, can be an explanatory as well as a predictive discipline.

References Cited

Abel, A.H., ed.
  1932 Chardon's Journal at Fort Clark, 1834–1839. Pierre: South Dakota State Department of History.
Alland, A., Jr.
  1966 Medical Anthropology and the Study of Biological and Cultural Adaptation. *American Anthropologist* 68:40–51.
——
  1970 Adaptation in Cultural Evolution: An Approach to Medical Anthropology. New York: Columbia University Press.
Armelagos, G.T., and A. McArdle
  1975 Population, Disease and Evolution. Pp. 1–10 in Population Studies in Archaeology and Biological Anthropology. A. Swedland, ed. *Memoirs of the Society for American Archaeology* 30.
Ashburn, P.M.
  1947 The Ranks of Death. F.D. Ashburn, ed., New York: Coward McCann.
Audy, J.R.
  1971 Measurement and Diagnosis of Health. P. Sheppard, ed. Boston: Houghton-Mifflin.
Black, F.L.
  1966 Measles Endemicity in Insular Population: Critical Community Size and its Evolutionary Implication. *Journal of Theoretical* Biology 2:207–211.
——, W.J. Hierholzer, F. DePinheiro, A.S. Evans, J.P. Woodall, E.M. Opton, J.E. Emmons, B.S. West, J.G. Edsall, W.G. Downs, and G.D. Wallace
  1974 Evidence for Persistence of Infectious Agents in Isolated Human Populations. *American Journal of Epidemiology* 100: 230–250.
Bower, A.G., and E.B. Pilant
  1954 Communicable Diseases, 7th ed. Philadelphia: W.B. Saunders.
Bruner, E.M.
  1961 Mandan. Pp. 187–278 in Perspectives in American Indian Culture Changes. E. Spicer, ed. Chicago: University of Chicago Press.
Cockburn, A.
  1963 The Evolution and Eradication of Infectious Disease. Baltimore, Md.: John Hopkins University Press.
——
  1971 Infectious Diseases in Ancient Populations. *Current Anthropology* 12:42–54.

Coues, E., ed.

1897 New Light on the Early History of the Greater Northwest: The Manuscript Journals of Alexander Henry and of David Thompson, 1799–1814. New York: Francis P. Harper.

Crosby, A.W., Jr.

1972 The Columbian Exchange: Biological and Cultural Consequences of 1492. Westport, Conn.: Greenwood.

Dixon, C.W.

1962 Smallpox. London: Churchill.

De Voto, B.

1947 Across the Wide Missouri. Boston: Houghton Mifflin.

Dobyns, H.F.

1963 Indian Extinction in the Middle Santa Cruz River Valley, Arizona. *New Mexico Historical Review* 38:163–181.

——

1966 Estimating Aboriginal American Population: An Appraisal of Techniques with a New Hemispheric Estimate. *Current Anthropology* 7:395–416, 440–444.

——

1983 Their Number Become Thinned. Knoxville, Tenn.: University of Tennessee Press.

Dunn, F.L.

1968 Epidemiological Factors: Health and Disease in Hunter-Gatherers. Pp. 221–228 in Man the Hunter. R. B. Lee and I. DeVore, eds. Chicago: Aldine.

Ewers, J.C.

1961 Five Indian Tribes of the Upper Missouri: Sioux, Arikaras, Assiniboines, Crees, Crows. (Written by Edwin Thompson Denig.) Norman, Okla.: University of Oklahoma Press.

Ferch, D.L.

1983 Fighting the Smallpox Epidemic of 1837–38: The Response of the American Fur Company Traders. *The Museum of the Fur Trade Quarterly* 19:2–6.

——

1984 Fighting the Smallpox Epidemic of 1837–38: The Response of the American Fur Company Traders. *The Museum of the Fur Trade Quarterly* 20:4–9.

Fine, D.E.M.

1975 Vectors and Vertical Transmission: An Epidemiologic Perspective. *Annals of the New York Academy of Science* 266:173–194.

Jacobs, W.R.

1974 The Tip of the Iceberg: Pre-Columbian Indian Demography and Some Implications for Revisionism. *William and Mary Quarterly* 31:123–132.

Jarcho, S.

1964 Some Observations on Disease in Prehistoric America. *Bulletin of the History of Medicine* 51:585–593.

Larpenteur, C.

1962 Forty Years a Fur Trader. E. Coues, ed. Minneapolis, Minn.: Ross and Haines.

Lehmer, D.J.

1971 Introduction to Middle Missouri Archaeology. *National Park Service Anthropological Papers* 1.

——

1977a The Other Side of the Fur Trade. Pp. 91–104 in Selected Writings of Donald J. Lehmer. Lincoln, Neb.: J & L Reprint.

——

1977b Epidemics Among the Indians of the Upper Missouri. Pp. 105–111 in Selected Writings of Donald J. Lehmer. Lincoln, Neb.: J & L Reprint.

Livingstone, F.B.

1958 Anthropological Implications of Sickle-Cell Gene Distribution in West Africa. *American Anthropologist* 60:553–562.

McCracken, R.D.

1971 Lactase Deficiency: An Example of Dietary Evolution. *Current Anthropology* 12:479–517.

Meyer, R.W.

1977 The Village Indians of the Upper Missouri, the Mandans, Hidatsas and Arikaras. Lincoln: University of Nebraska Press.

Stimson, P.M. and H.L. Hodes

1956 A Manual of the Common Contagious Diseases. 5th ed. Philadelphia: Lea and Febiger.

Thwaites, R.G., ed.

1906 Early Western Travels, Vols. 14, 22–24. Cleveland, Ohio: A.P. Clark.

——

1959 Original Journals of the Lewis and Clark Expedition, 1804–1806. New York: Antiquarian Press.

Trimble, M.K.

1979 An Ethnohistorical Interpretation of the Spread of Smallpox in the Northern Plains Utilizing Concepts of Disease Econology. (Unpublished Masters Thesis in Anthropology, University of Missouri, Columbia.)

——

1992 The 1832 Inoculation Program on the Missouri River. In Disease and Demography in the Americas. Washington: Smithsonian Institution Press.

Wiesenfeld, S.L.

1967 Sickle-Cell Trait in Human Biological and Cultural Evolution. *Science* 157:1134–1140.

Microfilm Sources

Letters Received by the Office of Indian Affairs: Upper Missouri Agency, 1824–1881. Record Group 75. Microcopy No. 234, Roll No. 750 (1824–1851), Washington, D.C.: National Archives.

Letters Received by the Office of Indian Affairs: Upper Missouri Agency, 1824–1881. Record Group 75. Microcopy No. 234, Roll No. 883 (1824–1835). Washington, D.C.: National Archives.

Letters Received by the Office of Indian Affairs: Upper Missouri Agency, 1824–1881. Record Group 75, Microcopy No. 234, Roll No. 884, pp. 0270–0396, National Archives, Washington.

○ ○ ○

CHAPTER 7

Disease Profiles of Archaic and Woodland Populations in the Northern Plains

JOHN A. WILLIAMS

The year 1946 initiated a new phase in Northern Plains archaeology, especially along the Missouri Trench. In that year construction was begun on five dams that flooded most of the Missouri river in the Dakotas (Helgevold 1981; Lehmer 1971). During the ensuing years "salvage" and "contract" archaeology became commonplace. Through the Smithsonian Institution–sponsored River Basin Surveys numerous sites were identified (Cooper and Stephenson 1953; Huscher and McNutt 1958; Lehmer 1971), but only a small percentage were actually test excavated, including many cemeteries. Even those sites that were "salvaged" received limited sampling, which resulted in continued exposure of archaeological materials and burials due to shoreline erosion, for example, at Anton Rygh (39CA4) and Mobridge (39WW1).

With the availability of large skeletal samples from the Plains and elsewhere emerged the anthropological subdiscipline of bioarchaeology. Human osteology had progressed from a purely descriptive examination of the human skeleton to the integrated study of human osteological remains in an archaeological and environmental context. At first, the focus of attention was on sites along the Missouri Trench. These sites

and accompanying cemeteries are better documented (Hughey 1980), and bioarchaeological research has emphasized a problem-oriented approach (Bass 1981). This research includes studies of skeletal growth and dental calcification (Jantz and Owsley 1984a, 1984b; Merchant and Ubelaker 1977), craniometric relationships, genetic affiliation, temporal changes and microevolution (Jantz 1972, 1973, 1976, 1977; Key 1983; Key and Jantz 1981; Owsley and Jantz 1978; Owsley et al. 1981), and paleodemography and paleopathology (Gregg and Gregg 1987; Gregg, Steele, and Clifford 1965; Gregg et al. 1981; Owsley and Bass 1979; Owsley, Berryman, and Bass 1977; Palkovich 1981; Steele, Gregg, and Holzhueter 1965).

Although significant progress has been made in delineating the bioarchaeology of the Village peoples of the Missouri Trench, the Archaic and Woodland periods of the Northern Plains remain understudied. The osteological and dental data derived from the cemeteries excavated in this region (Fox and Williams 1982; Williams 1982, 1985a, 1985b) and from those excavated earlier were used to establish basic health profiles for prehistoric peoples. The purpose of this chapter is not to describe individual examples of disease but to summarize information pertaining to certain disease classifications. From these compilations, inferences on disease and the quality of prehorticultural life in the Northern Plains may be drawn.

Archaeological Sites

Twenty-nine sites from North Dakota (Cole 1967, 1968a, 1968b; Hlady 1950; Fox 1980; Fox and Williams 1982; Wilford 1970; Williams 1982, 1985a, 1985b, 1990), South Dakota

(Johnson 1973; Williams 1988), and northwestern Minnesota (Johnson 1973; Scott and Loendorf 1976; Williams 1990) were included in this study. Most of the samples (79%) are from the Northeastern Plains with the remainder from the Middle Missouri Plains (table 1). Radiocarbon age determinations were available for nine sites. Using these dates, as well as artifacts and depositional context, workers have identified three as Archaic—Pipestem Creek (32SN102), the Bahm site (32MO97), and the Wolbaum site (32BA100). The Lisbon site

Table 1. Site Demographic Profiles

Site	Minimum Number of Individuals	Adults	Juveniles	Males	Females
21MA1	4	2	2	1	1
21MA6	1	1	0	1	0
21MA10	9	5	4	3	2
21NR2	2	1	1	0	1
21PL6	13	13	0	6	7
21PL13	11	4	7[a]	1	3
21RL1	17	8	9	4	4
21TR2	5	2	3	0	1
32BA100	1	1	0	1	0
32BA403	1	1	0	1	0
32CV401	1	0	1	0	0
32GF1	47	22	25	8	12
32GF4	4	4	0	0	0
32GF19	28	18	10	7	7
32GF305	8	4	4	1	0
32GF308	11	6	5	0	1
32MO97	19	9	10	4	5
32NE301	3	2	1	1	0
32RM201	1	1	0	0	1
32RY100	30	16	14[b]	9	7
32SN19	17	14	3	4	5
32SN22	75	27	48[c]	9	11
32SN102	4	3	1	1	2
32WA1 (Fordville except Blasky)	4	2	2	0	0
32WA1 (Blasky)	7	4	3	2	2
32WA32	1	1	0	1	0
39HU203	1	1	0	1	0
39LM256	7	4	3	2	2
39RO23	70	49	21	28	18
Total	402	225	177	96	92

[a]Includes 2 late-term fetuses.

[b]Includes 1 late-term fetus.

[c]Includes 4 late-term fetuses.

(32RM201) and the Devils Lake site (32RY100) have tentatively been identified as Initial Middle Missouri. These sites were included because radiocarbon dates placed them at the interface of the terminal Late Woodland and the Initial Middle Missouri. All remaining sites are of Woodland association. The number of interments ranges from a single individual at six sites to a maximum of 75 individuals at the Jamestown Mounds (32SN22).

Demography

A total of 402 individuals were included in this study (table 1). Of these, 225 were adults (≥16 years) and 177 were juveniles (<16 years), including seven late-term fetuses. Twenty-four individuals, 13 adults and 11 juveniles, were recovered from the three Archaic sites. This small and poorly preserved sample makes it difficult to draw specific conclusions concerning the skeletal pathology of Archaic populations. Thus, for the purpose of this study the Archaic and Woodland samples were pooled and collectively represent a pre-Village sample.

Although the total number of individuals in the combined sample was relatively large, only 62 involved primary burials (table 2). Sixty-four burials represented secondary bundle interments. The majority of burials, 296, were of an undescribed burial mode. Among these were 62 burials recovered from commingled ossuaries. As a result very few burials involved complete skeletons (table 3).

A high percentage of adults were sexed (83%), 96 males and 92 females. However, due to small site samples, incomplete skeletons, and the frequent lack of association between sexed adult crania and pelvises on the one hand and unsexed infracranial elements on the other, no attempt was made to delineate sex differences in the incidence of disease.

The lack of complete skeletal representation is illustrated by a tabulation of the numbers of major adult appendicular bones (table 4). Although 225 adults were identified in this series, of the major long bones, the left humerus and right femur were represented by the highest individual counts. The os coxa was the least frequent major bone. Less than half (n = 90) of the adults were represented by an intact cranium. Only 75 adults possessed more than 40 percent of the infracranial skeleton, defined here as the major appendicular long bones. Even fewer, 48 adults, possessed an intact vertebral column. Juvenile skeletons were less complete and less well preserved. The single most common intact juvenile long bone, the left humerus, was present in only 28 percent of the burials. The larger, denser bones were most likely to be interred and preserved. Because complete skeletons were uncommon, the

Table 2. Burial Types by Site

Site	Primary	Secondary	Unknown
21MA1	2	0	2
21MA6	0	1	0
21MA10	1	0	9
21NR2	2	0	0
21PL6	2	4	7
21PL13	6	0	5
21RL1	1	13	3
21TR2	1	0	4
32BA100	1	0	0
32BA403	1	0	0
32CV401	1	0	0
32GF1	17	0	30
32GF4	0	0	4
32GF19	4	11	13
32GF305	1	1	2
32GF308	0	0	11
32MO97	0	0	19[a]
32NE301	0	0	3
32RM201	1	0	1
32RY100	4	5	21
32SN19	0	0	17
32SN22	12	17	46[b]
32SN102	1	0	3
32WA1 (Fordville except Blasky)	0	0	4
32WA1 (Blasky)	0	0	7[a]
32WA32	1	0	0
39HU203	1	0	0
39LM256	0	0	7
39RO23	4	12	54
Total	62	64	296

[a]Ossuary.

[b]33 individuals in either of two ossuaries.

data must be evaluated in terms of accurate bone counts of appropriate skeletal elements. Disease incidence was tallied not only by individual but more appropriately by the incidence per bone or bone group.

Disease Profiles

Five disease categories were included in this study: osteoarthritis, trauma, inflammation, metabolic and developmental disorders, and dental pathology. These categories were chosen for two reasons. First, the pathological conditions comprising

Table 3. Skeletal Inventories for Each Site

Site	Adult Crania	Maxilla or Mandible with Permanent Dentitions	Infracranial Skeleton (at least 40%)	Intact Vertebral Column
21MA1	1	2	2	2
21MA6	1	1	0	0
21MA10	5	5	2	0
21NR2	0	0	0	0
21PL6	8	12	4	1
21PL13	2	2	5	3
21RL1	5	6	9	0
21TR2	0	0	1	1
32BA100	1	1	1	0
32BA403	0	0	1	0
32CV401	0	0	1	0
32GF1	17	19	20	10
32GF4	0	0	0	0
32GF19	6	9	6	3
32GF305	1	1	1	1
32GF308	0	0	0	0
32MO97	5	9	3	1
32NE301	1	1	1	0
32RM201	1	1	1	1
32RY100	4	7	10	6
32SN19	0	3	3	1
32SN22	9	14	10	8
32SN102	3	2	1	1
32WA1 (Fordville except Blasky)	0	0	0	0
32WA1 (Blasky)	1	2	0	0
32WA32	1	1	1	1
39HU203	1	1	1	1
39LM256	4	4	1	0
39RO23	13	22	16	15
Total	90	125	101	56

these categories are relatively common and leave relatively unambiguous traces in the skeleton. Second, when taken together, these five categories create a composite profile of general health and the quality of life. Less common conditions, such as neoplasias, which did not fall into one of these categories, as well as those for which a firm diagnosis was not possible, were excluded from this compilation.

OSTEOARTHRITIS

Osteoarthritis is a progressive breakdown of the joint articular cartilage. As the cartilage loses its integrity, osteolytic activity (erosion and pitting) may develop over the center of the joint

surface. At the same time osteophytes form along the joint margin. This differential action causes the joint to degrade in the center and build up along the margins. In terminal stages of cartilage destruction, bone-to-bone contact develops together with the formation of dense sclerous bone and eburnation (polishing) of the articular surface (Ortner and Putschar 1981; Steinbock 1976).

Eighty adults (36% of all adults) showed some manifestation of osteoarthritis (table 5). All levels of degenerative arthritis were encountered among these individuals. The largest group, 45 percent of the total cases, was classified as mild, displaying porous degeneration of the joint surface with no marginal lipping. Only 17 percent were classified as severe,

Table 4. Major Intact Bone Tabulation

Element	Left	Right	Total
Adult			
Humerus	110	103	213
Radius	81	95	176
Ulna	90	87	177
Os coxa	68	68	136
Femur	103	110	213
Tibia	97	91	188
Fibula	79	78	158
Juvenile			
Humerus	49	36	85
Radius	24	31	55
Ulna	29	25	54
Femur	41	37	78
Tibia	40	34	74
Tibula	19	10	29

Fig. 1. Severe degenerative joint disease of the right humeral head in an adult male from the Bahm site.

displaying marked marginal lipping and in some instances eburnation of the joint surface (fig. 1). Due to the large number of different affected joints and the lack of complete representation of all skeletal elements, joint incidence was reduced to three categories: upper appendicular (shoulder, elbow, wrist), lower appendicular (pelvis, knee, ankle), and other. This last category included the temporomandibular and the arthrodial joints of the vertebral column. Every major joint was affected. The most common were the shoulder and elbow and load-bearing joints of the pelvis and knee, with a nearly even distribution among the upper and lower appendages. Trauma may be considered a factor in the incidence of degenerative joint disease, but, as with vertebral osteophytosis, simple aging is a more likely cause (Gregg and Gregg 1987; Ortner and Putschar 1981; Steinbock 1976).

Vertebral osteophytosis was also frequent with at least 34 adult cases (of the 225) having been identified (table 6). Taken in the context of skeletal representation, 71 percent (34/48) of all adults represented by a vertebral column displayed some level of vertebral osteophytosis. As is characteristic for this condition (Ortner and Putschar 1981; Steinbock 1976), the weight-bearing lumbar region was the most common focus (79% of all adults displaying vertebral osteophytosis), followed by the cervical and thoracic vertebrae. Although some cases

Table 5. Frequencies of Osteoarthritis by Site

Site	Number Affected	Upper Appendicular	Lower Appendicular	Other
21MA1	1	—	—	1
21MA6	1	—	—	1
21MA10	2	2	—	—
21PL6	5	2	2	2
21PL13	3	3	2	1
21RL1	5	5	5	3
32BA403	1	1	1	—
32GF1	8	7	6	—
32GF19	6	2	2	3
32GF305	1	1	—	—
32MO97	2	2	2	—
32NE301	1	—	1	—
32RM201	1	1	—	—
32RY100	6	4	4	—
32SN19	4	2	2	—
32SN22	11	11	11	1
32WA1	4	1	2	2
32WA32	1	1	1	—
39HU203	1	1	—	1
39LM256	2	—	2	—
39RO23	14	13	8	2
Total	80	59	51	17

Table 6. Frequencies of Vertebral Osteophytosis by Site

Site	Number Affected	Cervical	Thoracic	Lumbar	Sacral
21MA1	1	—	1	1	—
21PL6	1	—	—	1	—
21PL13	2	1	—	1	—
32GF1	4	2	2	4	1
32GF19	2	—	1	2	1
32RY100	2	1	2	1	1
32SN19	1	1	1	1	—
32SN22	12	6	7	8	1
32WA32	1	1	1	1	—
39LM256	1	1	—	—	—
39RO23	7	5	2	7	—
Total	34	18	17	27	4

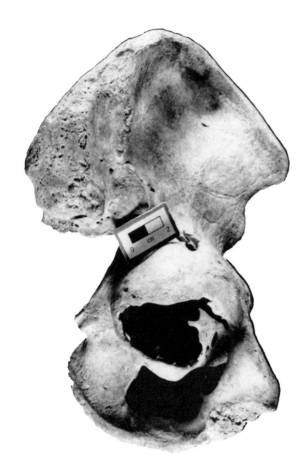

Fig. 2. Intrapelvic protrusion (protrusio acetabuli) of the left os coxa of an adult male from the Colony Mound site.

the Inkster site (32GF19), a fractured left clavicle is so poorly resolved that a pseudoarthrosis was formed (Williams 1982). In this particular case severe active periostitis is evident in the lower legs, implying that the trauma that created this fracture may have had more serious systemic consequences. At the multicomponent Jamestown Mounds, four ankylosed thoracic vertebrae were recovered from a central ossuary in Mound A. A radiograph demonstrated that the middle two vertebrae (T8? and T9?) are wedge shaped, the probable result of compression fracture. The ankylosis was a secondary response stabilizing this injury. This case was the only observed vertebral fracture.

A highly unusual form of fracture trauma was observed in a 25-year-old male from the Colony Mound site (32GF305). Here intrapelvic protrusion (protrusio acetabuli) of the left acetabulum took place (fig. 2). Although this may have been idiopathic, a unilateral focus, the presence of an internally displaced secondary acetabulum, and limited arthritic degeneration of the femoral head point to recent trauma as the most likely origin (Turek 1984).

Unresolved subluxations (dislocations) were very rare. Extensive secondary articular facets were formed in only two cases, a left shoulder and a mandible. These modifications indicated that a significant amount of time elapsed since the dislocation was incurred.

The most common expression of trauma (31 cases), and the least severe, involved the formation of bone spurs (enthesophytes). Reaction to ligament or muscle tears can cause calcification of the inflamed tissue (Zimmerman and Kelley 1982). The most common locations were the calcaneal tuberosity and the proximal tibio-fibular articulation (table 7). Several muscles and ligaments attach to the calcaneal tuberosity, significantly the long plantar ligament and the plantar aponeurosis. Together these maintain the antero-posterior tarsal arch. The presence of bone spurs on the calcaneal tuberosity implies that these ligaments were frequently inflamed. Of the 13 tibio-fibular spurs, 12 were on the proximal fibula. This converts to an 8 percent incidence when the total number of intact fibulae is considered. These locations indicate that the knee and heel were subject to repeated minor trauma. The site distribution of these spurs is noteworthy (table 7). Although tibio-fibular spurs were fairly evenly distributed among the eight sites in which they were present, the 11 heel spurs were found in three sites. These sites comprise 41 percent (92/225) of the total adult skeletal sample and 32 percent (20/62) of the primary burials, indicating that the distribution of these bone spurs probably reflects a more complete sampling of skeletal elements. The site distribution of calcanei provides a better

were severe, only one case involved ankylosis. However, the underrepresentation of vertebrae among these samples may have biased the distribution.

TRAUMA

Evidence of trauma was uncommon although 22 broken bones were observed. These fractures were distributed as follows: six crania, one mandible, two vertebrae, three ribs, one clavicle, three radii, three ulnae, one os coxa, one femur, and one fibula. Of these, 15 (68%) were poorly resolved and displayed some degree of angular distortion, ankylosis of adjacent bones (i.e., tibia and fibula), or loss of bone length. Excluding the skull, 11 fractures (68%) involved the upper torso. This distribution suggests that the arms and thorax were more common than the legs as foci of infracranial fracture trauma. Two Colles's fractures of the radius display marked posterior deflection of the distal surface. In an example from

Table 7. Bone Spur Frequencies by Site

Site	Calcaneal	Tibio-fibular	Other
21MA10	—	1	—
21PL6	—	2[a]	—
21RL1	—	—	1
32GF1	—	2	2
32GF308	—	1	—
32NE301	—	1[b]	1
32RY100	2	—	—
32SN19	—	2	—
32SN22	4	3	1
32WA32	—	2[a]	—
39RO23	5	—	2
Total	11	13	7

[a]Bilateral.

[b]Proximal tibia.

illustration of this observation. Calcanei were recovered from 17 sites for a total of 103 left and right elements. The three sites with recorded calcaneal spurs represent 58 calcanei or 56 percent of the total, with a per bone incidence of 11 percent. It appears then that the presence and distribution of this

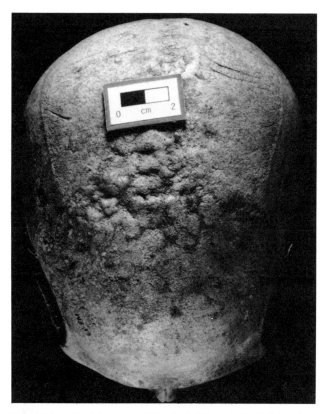

Fig. 4. Unhealed scalping on an adult male skull from the Blasky Mound.

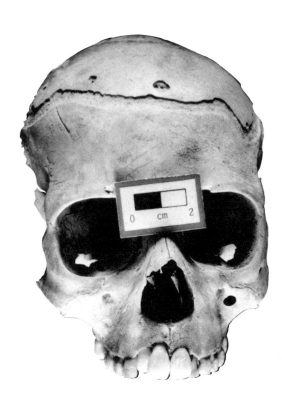

Fig. 3. Unhealed scalping in a juvenile from the Bahm site.

particular trauma was due to sample size and completeness and not to sample differences.

Three putative cases of aggression trauma were noted. The first is an apparent unhealed scalping that preceded the time of death by a significant interval of time. This case, from the Bahm site, involves a 10-year-old (fig. 3). An adult from this site also displays cuts consistent with scalping. However, as there is substantial evidence for defleshing at this site, it is not clear whether these cuts resulted from that mortuary practice. The second example also involves scalping. The calvarium of an adult male from the Blasky Mound (32WA1) has a coarse irregular appearance. The margins of this lesion are moderately hypervascularized. Several deep, partially healed cuts are present on the posterior margin of the parietals. The occurrence of well-demarcated sclerous tissue indicates the presence of an active osteomyelitic lesion at the time of death (fig. 4) (Ortner and Putschar 1981). The third instance of apparent aggression trauma, from the Jamestown Mounds, involves a projectile point injury of the lower spine of a 17-year-old female. A projectile point was discovered between the sacrum and the fifth lumbar vertebra at the time of excavation. The absence of sclerous tissue formation at the injury site suggests that the trauma occurred perimortem (Williams 1985a).

INFLAMMATION

Twenty-eight cases of osteitis were observed, a 7 percent (28/422) incidence. Twenty-three cases involved nonspecific periostitis (table 8), a response to local injury (traumatic or infectious) or to a hematogenous infection originating at some other point in the body. None of these cases involved the formation of sequestra or involucrum, the characteristic facies of osteomyelitis (Ortner and Putschar 1981; Steinbock 1976). Nineteen of the twenty-three cases minimally involved the tibia whereas seven cases involved the fibula (table 9). Fourteen of the tibial foci were bilateral as were four of the fibular foci. The lower legs are common foci for hematogenous infection. This predilection may be due to their low position in the circulatory system or to their cooler temperature through reduced surrounding tissue mass (Ortner and Putschar 1981). Hematomas resulting from physical trauma are also more likely to occur on the tibia due to the reduced tissue mass on the anterior surface (Gregg and Gregg 1987). The remaining four cases involved other appendicular bones: the humerus, radius, ulna, and femur. The bilateral cases and those involving multiple bone foci, in all probability, reflect systemic hematogenous infection or other systemic disease. For adults the per-bone incidence rate for the tibia (26/188) is 14 percent and for the fibula (5/158) it is 3 percent. The juvenile per-bone incidence rates for these bones are similar,

Table 8. Cases of Nonspecific Periostitis by Site

Site	Adult	Juvenile
21PL6	2	—
21PL13	1	—
21RL1	2	—
32BA403	1	—
32GF1	—	2
32GF19	1	3
32MO97	1	—
32NE301	1	—
32RY100	1	2
32SN19	1	—
32SN22	2	—
32WA32	1	—
39RO23	2	—
Total	16	7

Table 9. Distribution of Nonspecific Periostitis by Site

Site	Tibia	Fibula	Other
21PL6	+[a]	—	—
	+[a]	—	—
21PL13	+[a]	—	Bilateral femora
21RL1	+[a]	+	Bilateral ulnae, right radius
	+[a]	+	Bilateral humeri and radii, right ulna
32BA403	+	+	—
32GF1	+[a]	+[a]	Bilateral femora
	—	—	Left femur
32GF19	—	—	Left ulna
	+	—	—
	+	+[a]	—
	—	—	Right femur
32MO97	+[a]	—	Bilateral femora
32NE301	+[a]	—	—
32RY100	+[a]	—	—
	+[a]	—	—
	+	—	Left femur
32SN19	+[a]	—	—
32SN22	+	—	—
	+[a]	—	—
32WA32	+[a]	+[a]	—
39RO23	+[a]	+[a]	—
	—	—	Bilateral femora
Total	19	7	10

[a]Bilateral.

9 percent (7/74) and 7 percent (2/29), respectively. The majority of cases (19) were mild and inactive and did not involve a significant increase in cortical thickness. These cases very likely reflect healed inflammation in the process of osteoclastic remodeling. The remaining four cases were judged to be active, displaying moderate to severe cortical thickening or recent osteosclerotic activity or both. One in particular, a 30- to 35-year-old female recovered from the Red Lake River Mounds (21RL1), displays moderate systemic periostitis of the appendicular skeleton. These lesions, especially those of the tibiae, have multiple foci with well-marked margins of active osteosclerosis. These point to the presence of multiple hematomas (fig. 5). The pattern of these lesions suggests the possibility of scurvy as an explanation (J. Gregg, personal communication 1989; Steinbock 1976). However, the cause of this condition remains undetermined.

The remaining five cases reflect evidence of a specific infection, skeletal tuberculosis. Two appear unequivocal. The first is a previously reported unilateral necrotic lesion of the acetabulum of a 40-year-old female from the Jamestown

Fig. 5. Possible multiple ossified subperiosteal hematomas on a left tibia of an adult female from the Red Lake Mounds.

Mounds (Williams and Snortland-Coles 1986). The second is an example of Pott's disease in an 11-year-old from the Late Woodland Arvilla site (32GF1) (Johnson 1973). The child has necrosis of the vertebral column with gibbus formation and kyphosis (fig. 6). The skeleton also displays systemic active periostitis of the appendicular skeleton, probably a secondary reaction to the tuberculosis and not part of the primary vertebral lesion. Three additional examples are more ambiguous. These comprise isolated necrotic lesions. None displays any evidence of sclerous remodeling. Two, from the Late Woodland De Spiegler site (39RO23), involve single lumbar vertebrae. The third is a partial os coxa recovered from the Woodland site (32SN19). This bone fragment displays massive erosion of the articular surface of the acetabulum, together

with deep lytic cavities in the eroded surface. Given their isolated nature and the absence of more definite indicators, these three cases must remain open to other diagnoses, including postmortem diagenesis.

Associated with these examples of bone inflammation is unique evidence of a specific parasitic infection, a probable hydatid cyst recovered from the burial matrix of a 45-year-old female at the Jamestown Mounds (Williams 1985a, 1985c). The nematode parasite of hydatid disease is associated with hunting societies, in which it is normally found in canid hosts and only incidentally infects humans.

METABOLIC AND DEVELOPMENTAL DISORDERS

Unlike the previous categories, metabolism-dependent pathology is more subtle with a greater range of possible manifestations, some of which are associated with disturbances in growth and development. This disease pattern appears less significant and less dramatic among prehorticultural populations in which diet was more varied and therefore potentially better balanced (Lallo, Armelagos, and Mensforth 1977). In terms of direct indicators of metabolic stress this was the case for this series of population samples.

Twenty-two cranial lesions were provisionally identified as metabolism-dependent. Following Mann and Murphy (1990) these cases were placed into one of three categories: ectocranial porosis (pitting of the cranial vault without cortical thickening); porotic hyperostosis (pitting of the cranial vault with cortical thickening); and cribra orbitalia (porosity of the superior orbits) (table 10). The etiology of these lesions is not fully known, and several diseases are implicated (El-Najjar 1976; Lallo, Armelagos, and Mensforth 1977; Mensforth et al. 1978).

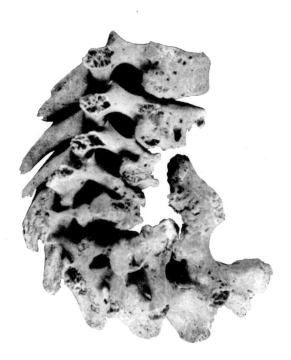

Fig. 6. Pott's disease in a juvenile from the Arvilla site.

Table 10. Occurrence of Porotic Cranial Lesions by Site

Site	Ectocranial Porosis	Porotic Hyperostosis	Cribra Orbitalia
21MA1	—	1	—
21MA6	—	1	—
21MA10	2	1	1[a]
21PL6	2	—	—
21PL13	—	—	1
32GF19	—	—	1[a]
32RY100	5	2	1
32SN22	—	—	2[a]
39RO23	—	1	1[a]
Total	9	6	7

[a]Juvenile.

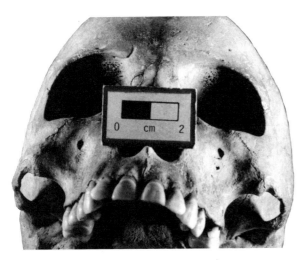

Fig. 7. Cribra orbitalia in an adolescent female from the Peter Lee Mound.

Table 11. Number of Vertebral Defects by Site

Site	Lumbo-sacral	Spondylolysis	Spina Bifida
21MA1	1	—	—
21PL6	1	—	1
32GF1	4	3	—
32GF19	1	—	—
32GF305	1	—	—
32NE301	—	—	1
32RM201	1	1	—
32RY100	2	—	—
32SN22	—	2	—
32WA32	—	—	1
39HU203	—	—	1
39RO23	5	3	1
Total	16	9	5

Of these, iron deficiency anemia is the most commonly identified cause (Steinbock 1976; Stuart-Macadam 1985, 1987). The most frequent lesion expression, mild to moderate ectocranial porosis, accounted for 10 percent of the adult crania. Pitting was observed on the frontal, parietal, and, less frequently, the occipital bones. The greatest degree of pitting was on the frontal immediately anterior to bregma and on the parietals along the margins of the sagittal suture. In the cases of porotic hyperostosis, bossing of the cranial vault anterior to bregma and along the sagittal margins was also evident. Radiographs of these crania indicated a moderate degree of diploic hypertrophy, and in a few cases a faint hair-on-end appearance. Six of the seven cases of cribra orbitalia are juvenile, representing 8 percent (6/76) of all juvenile frontal bones. Only one case, an adolescent female from the Peter Lee Mound (21PL13), displays spongy hypertrophy of the superior orbits (fig. 7). This individual also has a fused vertebral column and generalized osteoporosis. The cause of these conditions, and whether they are associated with, or secondary to, the cribra orbitalia, is undetermined. The remaining cases of cribra orbitalia involve minor pitting of the superior orbits. Sclerous scar tissue on the superior orbits of a partial adult cranium is suggestive of healed cribra orbitalia; however, other metabolic conditions such as scurvy cannot be ruled out (Ortner and Putschar 1981).

Although not directly metabolism-dependent, three vertebral defects may also reflect a developmental disturbance: lumbo-sacral transitional vertebra, spondylolysis, and spina bifida (table 11). All three conditions have fairly high frequencies when the relatively small number of vertebral columns and sacra are taken into account. The five cases of spina bifida,

out of a total of 49 sacra, have a per-bone frequency of 10 percent. With only 56 intact vertebral columns, the 16 lumbo-sacral transitional vertebrae have a per–vertebral column frequency of 28 percent, whereas that of spondylolysis is 16 percent. Because isolated vertebrae were not tallied, these frequencies are probably inflated. However, single vertebrae or other incomplete vertebral columns were uncommon, and the degree of error is considered to be low.

DENTAL PATHOLOGY

Partial or complete dentitions of 111 adults were found. Several categories of dental pathological conditions were recorded: periodontitis, abscess, enamel hypoplasia, and caries. Because the deciduous dentition was poorly represented, all cases of dental disease, unless otherwise stated, apply to permanent teeth and adults.

Periodontal disease is an inflammation of the gingival tissue and the alveolar bone (cf. Bhaskar 1981; Carranza 1984; Grant, Stern, and Everett 1979; Shafer, Hine, and Levy 1983). This inflammation originates primarily from bacterial utilization of nutrients trapped in the periodontium. In addition to the characteristic infradental pockets and craters, alveolar resorption occurs. The tooth roots are exposed as the alveolar bone recedes apically, weakening alveolar attachment. Periodontal disease is the most common cause of tooth loss in later life. Abscessing is another consequence of advanced periodontitis. Although a deficiency of calcium or an excess of phosphorus in the diet may play a role in periodontal disease, no clear associations have been made (Costa 1982; Grant,

Table 12. Frequencies of Periodontitis Expression by Site[a]

Site	Mild 1.0–2.9 mm	Moderate 3.0–4.9 mm	Severe 5.0+ mm
21MA1	2	1	—
21MA6	—	1	—
21MA10	3	1	1
21PL6	6	3	—
21PL13	1	—	—
21RL1	4	1	2
32BA100	—	1	—
32CV401	1	—	—
32GF1	4	4	3
32GF19	5	4	2
32GF305	1	—	—
32MO97	4	3	3
32NE301	1	—	—
32RM201	—	1	—
32RY100	6	3	2
32SN19	1	1	1
32SN22	4	3	2
32WA1	2	2	1
39HU203	1	—	—
39LM256	—	1	2
39RO23	6	9	7
Total	52	39	26

[a]Edentulous dentitions are excluded.

Stern, and Everett 1979; Patterson 1984). Highly processed diets, leading to a lessened ability to control oral hygiene, are more likely to result in periodontitis.

Periodontal disease can be assessed in a variety of ways that consider morphological changes in the alveolar bone, that is, the formation of infrabony pockets and craters, and alveolar resorption (Costa 1982; Patterson 1984). This study recorded the degree of alveolar resorption (table 12). Periodontitis, as measured by the level of periodontal resorption, was present in every adult. The degree of periodontitis was fairly evenly distributed from mild to moderate to severe.

Dental calculus is implicated in the incidence of periodontitis. Calculus is the calcified accumulation of plaque deposits. Supragingival calculus deposits ranging from mild to severe were observed in the dentitions of 66 percent (67/101) of adults. That more individuals were not observed with calculus deposits is probably a reflection of postmortem tooth loss. Not unexpectedly, those individuals with mild deposits also displayed little or no periodontal resorption whereas the opposite was true for those individuals with severe deposits.

Apical abscessing, another common dental condition, was observed in over half (53/101) of all adult dentitions. These ranged from a single abscess in 19 individuals to a high of 18 in one individual from the De Spiegler site. One abscess included perforation of the maxilla and subsequent sinus (antrum) involvement.

The level of tooth trauma in a population is in direct proportion to the levels of food processing and abrasive particles in the diet (Wallace 1974). Horticultural diets are generally highly processed and low in abrasive quality. Pre-horticultural Archaic and Woodland populations therefore display higher levels of tooth trauma than do horticultural societies (Patterson 1984; Williams 1985b). Such damage can result in exfoliation of the traumatized tooth. Thirty-three individuals displayed chipped or fractured teeth.

Enamel hypoplasia or chronologic enamel aplasia is generally defined as any macroscopic defect in the enamel surface (Pindborg 1970; Sarnat and Schour 1941, 1942). Hypoplastic defects can range from minor depressions in the enamel surface, with no dentin exposure, to a complete disruption of the enamel. These defects appear either as bandlike depressions (linear enamel hypoplasia) or as pits on contralateral teeth. Numerous causal agents have been linked to the presence of hypoplasia. Specific and nonspecific infections are commonly implicated in cases in which antibiotic treatment is unavailable (Sweeney et al. 1969). High fever, whether of infectious origin or not, has been associated with hypoplasia in laboratory studies (Kreshover 1944; Kreshover and Clough 1953). Vitamin deficiencies and malnutrition have also been cited as causes (Cook and Buikstra 1979; Giro 1947; Sarnat and Schour 1941, 1942). In general, any major systemic alteration enhances the probability of a hypoplastic episode.

The appearance of a hypoplastic line or pit on a particular tooth is a function of the timing of enamel deposition (El Najjar, DeSanti, and Ozebek 1978; Giro 1947; Kreshover 1944; Massler, Schour, and Poncher 1941; Orban 1957; Pindborg 1970; Sarnat and Schour 1941, 1942). The deciduous teeth are good indicators of systemic stress during the prenatal and early neonatal stages (Blakey and Armelagos 1985). The permanent dentition covers a longer period of time, not beginning mineralization until after birth, and continuing to form through six to eight years of age. The permanent dentition is therefore a good indicator of early childhood stress. The majority of enamel hypoplasia occurs during the first two years of life, diminishing by the fourth year. Usually only one class of tooth is affected, marking a short period of systemic stress. If the stress is severe and of a long duration, the hypoplastic events may be reflected on several teeth.

Like dental trauma, linear enamel hypoplasia was low in frequency. Twenty-five individuals displayed one or more

Table 13. Linear Enamel Hypoplasia Episode Distribution

Episode Years (±0.2)	Number of Individuals[a]
1.5	1
2.0	—
2.5	9
3.0	12
3.5	7
4.0	8
4.5	7
5.0	6
5.5	1
Total	51

[a]Excluding duplications within the same individual and 5 unrecorded cases at sites 32GF1 and 39RO23.

Table 14. Frequencies of Dental Caries by Site

Site	Number Affected	Pit or Fissure	Smooth	Radicular
21MA1	1	4	—	—
21MA6	1	2	—	—
21PL6	2	5	—	—
21PL13	3	2	—	3
21MA10	2	3	—	—
32GF1	2	5	—	2
32MO97	2	4	—	—
32RM201	1	2	—	—
32RY100	7	9	2	3
32SN22	3	1	—	4
32WA1	1	1	—	—
39HU203	1	2	—	—
39RO23	1	1	—	—
Total	27	41	2	12

hypoplastic episodes. All were mild in expression and did not involve dentin exposure. These hypoplastic events affected the permanent maxillary and mandibular central incisors and canines exclusively. The central incisors and canines mineralize during the first six to six and one-half years of life, the most stressful period for the growing child. Therefore, these teeth are common sites for hypoplastic defects (Goodman, Armelagos, and Rose 1980). Where contralateral teeth were present, both displayed the same banding pattern.

In cases in which multiple hypoplastic episodes existed, the spacing between them ranged from 0.2 to 2.0 years. Goodman, Armelagos, and Rose (1980) theorize that a yearly spacing of hypoplastic episodes corresponds with a seasonal stress, possibly related to maize horticulture. Hypoplastic spacing of less than one year is more often found among Woodland populations. Episodes per person varied from one to four. Using intervals of 0.5 years (table 13), the highest number of episodes (55%, n = 28) fell within the range of 2.5 to 3.5 years, possibly marking a period of weaning stress (Goodman et al. 1987; Goodman, Armelagos, and Rose 1984). Stresses at the youngest age—1.0 year—were recorded only in the juveniles and subadults as these hypoplastic episodes occur high (near the occlusal edge) on the tooth crown and were lost to attrition by young adulthood.

Dental caries is a complex infectious disease of the external surface of the tooth. Various bacteria, primarily *Streptococcus* spp., produce decalcifying acids, which, if left unchecked, cause dissolution of the enamel and dentin (Bhaskar 1981; Legler and Menaker 1980; Morhart and Fitzgerald 1980). A high caries incidence has long been recognized as a character-

istic feature of a processed food diet. Carious lesions are infrequent among prehorticultural societies, in which coarse, low-carbohydrate foods are relatively noncariogenic (Patterson 1984). Physiological and possibly external environmental factors may also be related to caries incidence (Curzon 1983; Curzon and Cutress 1983; Hildebolt et al. 1988). Schneider (1986), in a study of lower Great Lakes populations, reports that zinc, copper, and iron when present in enamel have a cariostatic effect whereas nickel has a cariogenic effect. Results such as these suggest that diet may play a multifaceted role in the production of carious lesions.

Carious lesions were categorized on the basis of location: pit or fissure, located in the grooves and pits of the occlusal surface; smooth surface, located on the sides of the crown; and radicular or root caries usually near the cemento-enamel junction (Legler and Menaker 1980; Ostrom 1980). Carious lesions were low in frequency in these population samples (table 14). The largest single number of lesions and the largest number of affected individuals came from the Devils Lake site.

Patterns of Bone Pathology and Disease

A major difficulty encountered in interpreting compilations of regional pathology is the lack of comprehensive comparative data. The majority of studies in paleopathology have focused on specific pathological conditions and limited population samples (Gregg et al. 1981; Williams 1985c). Few broad summaries exist (Morse 1978). Gregg and Gregg (1987) published more than two decades of documentation of paleopathological evidence from North and South Dakota. Although the majority of their samples were derived from post-Woodland populations, their text serves as a basic outline for this region.

OSTEOARTHRITIS

As is the case for prehistoric populations in general, arthritis was the most commonly identified nondental pathological condition (Ortner and Putschar 1981; Steinbock 1976). Although the distribution of degenerative joint disease among the various load-bearing joints was similar, Gregg and Gregg (1987) report a significantly lower overall frequency (2.3% to 7.1%) in both Woodland and Village samples. Vertebral osteophytosis had a similar pattern but again a higher frequency (71% versus 10.6% to 28.2%) in this study. Two explanations exist for this discrepancy. First, it is possible that some cases of diagenesis have been misinterpreted as mild (porous degeneration) degenerative joint disease. Second, the difference in frequencies reflects the mortality in the demographic pattern of the 225 adults comprising this series of samples. In cases in which age could be accurately determined, 49 percent (110 adult skeletons) were 30 years of age or older. This finding points to a bias in these samples toward older individuals.

TRAUMA

The various forms of trauma were infrequent and similar in frequency to those reported by Gregg and Gregg (1987). The only comparative differences exist in Village sites such as Larson and Crow Creek, where high levels of aggression trauma have been recorded (Gregg et al. 1981). All other frequency differences compared to Gregg and Gregg, such as those of calcaneal bone spurs, appear to be due to the small and incomplete skeletal samples comprising this study. Of significance were the putative cases of scalping. If correctly diagnosed, these push back the antiquity of this practice on the Northern Plains to Woodland if not Archaic times.

INFLAMMATION

As reported by Gregg and Gregg (1987), nonspecific periostitis was uncommon and associated with either localized trauma or systemic disease (e.g., infection). The incidence of periostitis was lower than that reported by Bass and Phenice (1975) for three Middle Woodland Sonota cemeteries of north-central South Dakota. This may be a function of sampling or it might imply that regional, and perhaps temporal,

differences exist in disease profiles for nonspecific bone inflammation. Osteomyelitis was nonexistent except for one case associated with antemortem scalping. The cases of specific infection, putative cases of tuberculosis, establish the presence of this disease by the Late Woodland on the northern Plains. Whether this disease already existed on the Plains or was acquired via trade from eastern populations is unknown (Williams and Snortland-Coles 1986). The single case of a probable hydatid cyst illustrates a normally overlooked dimension of paleopathology in which characteristic bone involvement does not take place.

METABOLIC AND DEVELOPMENTAL DISORDERS

Excluding two speculative instances of scurvy, the evidence of metabolic conditions was limited to three cranial lesions: ectocranial porosis, porotic hyperostosis, and cribra orbitalia. With one exception all the cases were mild. The etiology of these lesions is not fully established, and several diseases are implicated (El-Najjar 1976; Lallo, Armelagos, and Mensforth 1977; Mensforth et al. 1978). Of these, iron deficiency anemia is the most often attributed cause (Steinbock 1976; Stuart-Macadam 1985, 1987). One potentially significant aspect of these cases is that all but two occur in Middle and Late Woodland northeastern Plains population samples. This observation may indicate that the transition to maize horticulture, coupled with the appearance of iron deficiency anemia, may have first occurred in the eastern half of the northern Plains and then progressed westward (Lallo, Armelagos, and Mensforth 1977; Mensforth et al. 1978).

Two neural arch defects (spondylolysis and spina bifida) and lumbo-sacral transitional vertebrae were recorded. The frequencies of these defects were similar to those reported for the Plains and other North American locations (Bennett 1972; Bradtmiller 1984; Gregg and Gregg 1987). Although the etiology of these anomalies is not the same, there is evidence to suggest that spondylolysis and lumbo-sacral transitional vertebrae may form a complex of neural arch and spinal defects (Bennett 1972; Bradtmiller 1984; Stewart 1956). For these defects the separation of environmental and genetic factors is difficult. Spina bifida, for example, is listed as a mendelian trait with dominant inheritance (McKusick 1988), with distinct population associations (Post 1966). Other evidence suggests that dietary zinc deficiency may be a contributing factor (Bergmann, Makosch, and Tews 1980; Soltan and Jenkins 1982; Wolley 1988). Spondylolysis, although considered to be of traumatic origin, likewise has distinct familial patterns (Merbs 1989; Wiltse, Widell, and Jackson 1975).

The distribution of these defects was skewed toward the eastern Late Woodland samples, among which intact vertebral columns were more prevalent. With one exception, every site where intact vertebral columns were present displayed one or more of these vertebral defects. Although sampling is a factor, it is by no means the only one. Thirteen vertebral columns (23%) were recovered from the Jamestown Mounds yet only two vertebral anomalies (both spondylolysis) were present in this sample. It is possible that these defects are indicative of a regional developmental stress, perhaps nutritional or metabolic in nature. For spondylolysis an alternative explanation may lie in an age-cumulative incidence pattern (Bradtmiller 1984; Bridges 1989; Stewart 1931). Although some spondylolysis did occur in older adults (40+ years) there was no definite trend indicating age as a factor. Furthermore, comparison of the three largest cemetery populations (Arvilla, Jamestown Mounds, DeSpiegler), accounting for 63 percent of the intact vertebral columns, showed similar demographics at older age intervals. If a genetic etiology is correct, these same sample distributions might reflect a common gene pool rather than a common environmental substrate. Extrapolating these frequencies to the populations at large indicates that these mild and asymptomatic developmental defects were very common.

DENTAL PATHOLOGY

The permanent dentition was the second most common skeletal element in these samples. Although often neglected in bioarchaeological research, the teeth are important in paleopathology as an indicator of population stress and dietary adaptation (Goodman, Armelagos, and Rose 1980; Patterson 1984; Smith 1984). Comparative data for the northern Plains are lacking.

Periapical abscesses were frequent and represent bacterial infection of the tooth pulp and necrosis of the surrounding periapical tissue. For an infection to occur, physical exposure of the pulp usually must take place. Extensive carious lesions and excessive occlusal attrition are common causes of pulp exposure. One or both of these conditions were present among these individuals.

Caries were low in frequency, an expected consequence of a prehorticultural subsistence pattern consisting of coarse, low-carbohydrate foodstuffs. The highest single incidence of caries was recorded at the Devils Lake site. This caries incidence, together with other reported skeletal conditions, suggests that this particular skeletal sample may be part of a population undergoing the transition to horticulture (Williams 1985b).

For a prehorticultural subsistence pattern, dental trauma was less frequent than expected. However, as damaged teeth are more prone to caries, abscess, and premortem loss, this unusually low rate may be a reflection of exfoliation as well as enamel attrition.

Patterson (1984) reports that hypoplasia is equally common among prehorticultural and horticultural populations of the Great Lakes region. In the Illinois valley the number of hypoplastic episodes increased with the transition from the Middle to Late Woodland and to the Mississippian (Cook and Buikstra 1979; Goodman, Armelagos, and Rose 1980, 1984). The data derived from the Great Lakes and Illinois valley are not directly comparable. The northern Plains populations have a lower overall and age-dependent incidence. This lower incidence suggests that these populations were not experiencing the same level of nutritional and metabolic stress as contemporary Woodland and later maize-dependent eastern populations. Given a high level of crown attrition, coupled with antemortem and postmortem tooth loss, it was impossible to determine the true extent of hypoplasia or temporal trends.

SUMMARY

Using the criteria of these five disease categories, the overall health of these population samples was good, in direct contrast to that of the later Village populations (Gregg and Gregg 1987; Gregg et al. 1981). Although arthritis was a common ailment, few cases were severe enough to have been debilitating. Trauma and infection were both low in frequency. Some of the observed cases—those involving probable skeletal tuberculosis and scalping—are significant. Dental disease was typical of a prehorticultural subsistence pattern. Periodontal inflammation was a serious factor in oral health, but caries and linear enamel hypoplasia were relatively rare. When taken together, these health profiles can be extrapolated to form a summary statement about prehorticultural disease. Because major chronic pathological contributors to mortality were lacking in these population samples, causes of death were therefore most likely acute and deadly. The nature of these nonspecific mortality factors awaits future definition.

References Cited

Bass, W.M.

1981   Skeletal Biology of the United States Plains: A History and Personal Narrative. *Plains Anthropologist Memoir* 17, 2:3–18.

——, and T.W. Phenice
1975 Prehistoric Human Skeletal Material from Three Sites in North and South Dakota. Pp. 106–140 in The Sonota Complex and Associated Sites on the Northern Great Plains. R.W. Neuman. ed. *Publications in Anthropology* 6.

Bennett, K.A.
1972 Lumbo-sacral Malformations and Spina Bifida Occulta in a Group of Proto-historic Modoc Indians. *American Journal of Physical Anthropology* 36:435–440.

Bergmann, K.E., G. Makosch, and K.H. Tews
1980 Abnormalities of Hair Zinc Concentration in Mothers of Newborn Infants with Spina Bifida. *American Journal of Clinical Nutrition* 33:2145–2150.

Bhaskar, S.N.
1981 Synopsis of Oral Pathology. 6th ed. St. Louis, Mo.: C.V. Mosby.

Blakey, M.L., and G.J. Armelagos
1985 Deciduous Enamel Defects in Prehistoric Americans from Dickson Mounds: Prenatal and Postnatal Stress. *American Journal of Physical Anthropology* 66:371–380.

Bradtmiller, B.
1984 Congenital Anomalies of the Lower Spine in Two Arikara Skeletal Series. *Plains Anthropologist* 29:327–333.

Bridges, P.S.
1989 Spondylolysis and Its Relationship to Degenerative Joint Disease in the Prehistoric Southeastern United States. *American Journal of Physical Anthropology* 79:321–329.

Carranza, F.A., Jr., ed.
1984 Glickman's Clinical Periodontology. 6th ed. Philadelphia: W.B. Saunders.

Cole, K.
1967 The Colony Mound, 32GF305: A Test Excavation of 1967. *University of North Dakota, Department of Sociology and Anthropology Field Reports in Archaeology* 4.

——
1968a The Turtle River Survey. *University of North Dakota, Department of Sociology and Anthropology, Field Reports in Archaeology* 5.

——
1968b Miscellaneous Sites in Eastern North Dakota. *University of North Dakota, Department of Sociology and Anthropology Field Reports in Archaeology* 6. Grand Forks.

Cook, D.C., and J.E. Buikstra
1979 Health and Differential Survival in Prehistoric Populations: Prenatal Dental Defects. *American Journal of Physical Anthropology* 51:649–664.

Cooper, P.L., and R.L. Stephenson
1953 Appraisal of the Archaeological Resources of the Oahe Reservoir, North and South Dakota. (Report for the Missouri Basin Project) Washington: Smithsonian Institution.

Costa, R.L., Jr.
1982 Periodontal Disease in the Prehistoric Ipiutak and Tigara Skeletal Remains from Point Hope, Alaska. *American Journal of Physical Anthropology* 59:97–110.

Curzon, M.E.J.
1983 Epidemiology of Trace Elements and Dental Caries. Pp. 11–30 in Trace Elements and Dental Disease. M.E.J. Curzon and T.W. Cutress, eds. Boston: John Wright.

——, and T.W. Cutress, eds.
1983 Trace Elements and Dental Disease. Boston: John Wright.

El-Najjar, M.Y.
1976 Maize, Malaria, and the Anemias in the Pre-Columbian New World. *Yearbook of Physical Anthropology* 20:329–337.

——, M.V. DeSanti, and L. Ozebek
1978 Prevalence and Possible Etiology of Dental Enamel Hypoplasia. *American Journal of Physical Anthropology* 48:185–192.

Fox, R.
1980 1978–1979 Cultural Resource Investigations Along the Middle Sheyenne River Valley Including Lake Ashtabula and a Portion of the Sheyenne River. No. 1 Omaha, Neb.: U.S. Army Corps of Engineers.

——, and J.A. Williams
1982 The Pipestem Burial: An Archaic Interment from Southeastern North Dakota. *North American Archaeologist* 3:51–77.

Giro, C.M.
1947 Enamel Hypoplasia in Human Teeth: An Explanation of Its Causes. *Journal of the American Dental Association* 34:310–317.

Goodman, A.H., G.J. Armelagos, and J.C. Rose
1980 Enamel Hypoplasias as Indicators of Stress in Three Prehistoric Populations from Illinois. *Human Biology* 52:515–528.

——
1984 The Chronologic Distribution of Enamel Hypoplasias from Prehistoric Dickson Mounds Populations. *American Journal of Physical Anthropology* 65:259–266.

——, A.H., L.H. Allen, G.P. Hernandez, A. Amador, L.V. Arriola, A. Chavez, and G.H. Pelto
1987 Prevalence and Age at Development of Enamel Hypoplasias in Mexican Children. *American Journal of Physical Anthropology* 72:7–19.

Grant, D.A., I.B. Stern, and F.G. Everett, eds.
1979 Periodontics in the Tradition of Orban and Gottlieb. 5th ed. St. Louis, Mo.: C.V. Mosby.

Gregg, J.B. and P.S. Gregg
1987 Dry Bones: Dakota Territory Reflected. Sioux Falls, S.Dak.: Sioux Printing.

Gregg, J.B., J.P. Steele, and S. Clifford
1965 Ear Disease from the Sully Burial Site. *Plains Anthropologist* 10:233–239.

Gregg, J.B., L.J. Zimmerman, J.P. Steele, H. Ferwerda, and P.S. Gregg
1981 Ante-mortem Osteopathology at Crow Creek. *Plains Anthropologist* 25:287–300.

Helgevold, M.K.

1981 A History of South Dakota Archaeology. *Special Publication of the South Dakota Archaeological Society* 3.

Hildebolt, C.F., S. Molnar, M. Elvin-Lewis, and J.K. McKee

1988 The Effect of Geochemical Factors on Prevalences of Dental Diseases for Prehistoric Inhabitants of the State of Missouri. *American Journal of Physical Anthropology* 75:1–14.

Hlady, W.M.

1950 Mound C, Fordville Mound Group, Walsh County, North Dakota: Its Excavation and Archaeology. *North Dakota History* 17:253–260.

Hughey, D.V.

1980 An Overview of Great Plains Physical Anthropology. Pp. 52–67 in Anthropology on the Great Plains. W.R. Wood and M. Liberty, eds. Lincoln: University of Nebraska Press.

Huscher, H.A. and C.H. McNutt

1958 Appraisal of the Archaeological Resources of the Big Bend Reservoir, South Dakota. (Report for the Missouri Basin Project.) Washington: Smithsonian Institution.

Jantz, R.L.

1972 Cranial Variation and Microevolution in Arikara Skeletal Populations. *Plains Anthropologist* 17:20–35.

——

1973 Microevolutionary Change in Arikara Crania: A Multivariate Analysis. *American Journal of Physical Anthropology* 38:15–26.

——

1976 Discriminant Function Analysis. Pp. 32–33 in Fay Tolton and the Initial Middle Missouri Variant. W.R. Wood, ed. *Missouri Archaeological Society Research Series* 13.

——

1977 Addendum to Murrill's Analysis. P. 165 in The Talking Crow Site: A Multicomponent Earthlodge Village in the Big Bend Region, South Dakota, by C.S. Smith. *University of Kansas Publications in Anthropology* 9.

——, and D.W. Owsley

1984a Long Bone Growth Variation in the Northern and Central Plains. *American Journal of Physical Anthropology* 63:13–20.

——

1984b Temporal Changes in Limb Proportionality Among Skeletal Samples of Arikara Indians. *Annals of Human Biology* 11:157–163.

Johnson, E.

1973 The Arvilla Complex. *Minnesota Prehistoric Archaeology Series* 9.

Key, Patrick J.

1983 Craniometric Relationships Among Plains Indians: Culture-Historical and Evolutionary Implications. *University of Tennessee, Department of Anthropology Report of Investigations* 34.

——, and R.L. Jantz

1981 A Multivariate Analysis of Temporal Changes in Arikara Craniometrics: A Methodological Approach. *American Journal of Physical Anthropology* 55:247–259.

Kreshover, S.J.

1944 The Pathogenesis of Enamel Hypoplasia: An Experimental Study. *Journal of Dental Research* 23:231–238.

——, and O.W. Clough

1953 Prenatal Influences on Tooth Development, II: Artificially Induced Fever in Rats. *Journal of Dental Research* 32:565–577.

Lallo, J.W., G.J. Armelagos, and R.P. Mensforth

1977 The Role of Diet, Disease, and Physiology in the Origin of Porotic Hyperostosis. *Human Biology* 49:471–485.

Legler, D.W., and L. Menaker

1980 Etiology, Epidemiology and Clinical Implications of Caries. In The Biologic Basis of Dental Caries. L. Menaker ed. Hagerstown, Md.: Harper and Row.

Lehmer, D.J.

1971 Introduction to Middle Missouri Archaeology. *U.S. Department of the Interior, National Park Service, Anthropological Papers* 1.

McKusick, V.

1988 Mendelian Inheritance in Man. 8th ed. Baltimore: Johns Hopkins University Press.

Mann, R.W., and S.P. Murphy

1990 Regional Atlas of Bone Disease: A Guide to Pathologic and Normal Variation in the Human Skeleton. Springfield, Ill.: Charles Thomas.

Massler, M., I. Schour, and H.G. Poncher

1941 Developmental Pattern of the Child as Reflected in the Calcification Pattern of the Teeth. *American Journal of Diseases of Children* 62:33–67.

Mensforth, R.P., C.O. Lovejoy, J.W. Lallo, and G.J. Armelagos

1978 The Role of Constitutional Factors, Diet, and Infectious Disease in the Etiology of Porotic Hyperostosis and Periosteal Reactions in Prehistoric Infants and Children. *Medical Anthropology* 2:1–59.

Merbs, C.F.

1989 Spondylolysis: Its Nature and Anthropological Significance. *International Journal of Anthropology* 4:163–169.

Merchant, V.L. and D.M. Ubelaker

1977 Skeletal Growth of the Protohistoric Arikara. *American Journal of Physical Anthropology* 46:61–71.

Morhart, Robert, and Robert Fitzgerald

1980 Microbial Aspects of Dental Caries. Pp. 297–312 in The Biologic Basis of Dental Caries. Lewis Menaker, ed. Hagerstown, Md.: Harper and Row.

Morse, D.

1978 Ancient Disease in the Midwest. *Illinois State Museum Reports of Investigation* 15.

Orban, B.J.
1957 Oral Histology and Embryology. 9th ed. St. Louis, Mo.: Mosby.

Ortner, D.J., and W.G. Putschar
1981 Identification of Pathological Conditions in Human Skeletal Remains. *Smithsonian Contributions to Anthropology* 28.

Ostrom, C.A.
1980 Clinical Cariology. In The Biologic Basis of Dental Caries. L. Menaker ed. Hagerstown, Md.: Harper and Row.

Owsley, D.W., and W.M. Bass
1979 A Demographic Analysis of Skeletons from the Larson Site (39WW2), Walworth County, South Dakota: Vital Statistics. *American Journal of Physical Anthropology* 51:145–154.

Owsley, D.W., and R.L. Jantz
1978 Intracemetery Morphological Variation in Arikara Crania from the Sully Site (39SL4), Sully County, South Dakota. *Plains Anthropologist* 23:139–147.

Owsley, D.W., H.E. Berryman, and W.M. Bass
1977 Demographic and Osteological Evidence for Warfare at the Larson Site, South Dakota. *Plains Anthropologist* 22:119–131.

Owsley, D.W., G.D. Slutzky, M.F. Guagliardo, and L.M. Deitrick
1981 Interpopulation Relationships of Four Post-Contact Coalescent Sites from South Dakota: Four Bear (39DW2), Oahe Village (39HU2), Stony Point Village (39ST235), and Swan Creek (39WW7). *Plains Anthropologist Memoir* 17:31–42.

Palkovich, A.
1981 Demography and Disease Patterns in a Protohistoric Plains Group: A Study of the Mobridge Site (39WW1). *Plains Anthropologist Memoir* 17:71–84.

Patterson, D.K.
1984 A Diachronic Study of Dental Paleopathology and Attritional Status of Prehistoric Ontario Pre-Iroquois and Iroquois Populations. *National Museum of Man, Mercury Series, Archaeological Survey of Canada Paper* 122.

Pindborg, J.J.
1970 Pathology of the Dental Hard Tissues. Philadelphia: W.B. Saunders.

Post, R.H.
1966 Pilot Study: Population Differences in the Frequency of Spina Bifida Occulta. *Eugenics Quarterly* 13:341–352.

Sarnat, B.G., and I.S. Schour
1941 Enamel Hypoplasia (Chronologic Enamel Aplasia) in Relation to Systemic Disease: A Chronologic, Morphologic, and Etiologic Classification. *Journal of the American Dental Association* 28:1989–2000.

——
1942 Enamel Hypoplasia (Chronologic Enamel Aplasia) in Relation to Systemic Disease: A Chronologic, Morphologic, and Etiologic Classification. *Journal of the American Dental Association* 29:67–75.

Schneider, K.N.
1986 Dental Caries, Enamel Composition, and Subsistence Among Prehistoric Amerindians of Ohio. *American Journal of Physical Anthropology* 71:95–102.

Scott, G.T., and L.L. Loendorf
1976 Karlstad Ossuary 21MA10. Grand Forks, N.Dak.: University of North Dakota.

Shafer, W.G., M.K. Hine, and B.M. Levy
1983 A Textbook of Oral Pathology 4th ed. Philadelphia: W.B. Saunders.

Smith, B.H.
1984 Patterns of Molar Wear in Hunter-gatherers and Agriculturalists. *American Journal of Physical Anthropology* 63:39–56.

Soltan, M.H., and D.M. Jenkins
1982 Maternal and Fetal Plasma Zinc Concentration and Fetal Abnormality. *British Journal of Obstetrics and Gynaecology* 89:56–58.

Steele, J.P., J.B. Gregg, and A.M. Holzhueter
1965 Paleopathology in the Dakotas. *South Dakota Journal of Medicine* 18:17–29.

Steinbock, R.T.
1976 Paleopathological Diagnosis and Interpretation. Springfield, Ill.: Charles Thomas.

Stewart, T.D.
1931 Incidence of Separate Neural Arch in the Lumbar Vertebrae of Eskimos. *American Journal of Physical Anthropology* 16:51–62.

——
1956 Examination of the Possibility That Certain Characters Predispose to Defects in the Lumbar Arch. *Clinical Orthopedics* 8:44–46.

Stuart-Macadam, P.
1985 Porotic Hyperostosis: Representative of a Childhood Condition. *American Journal of Physical Anthropology* 66:391–398.

——
1987 Porotic Hyperostosis: New Evidence to Support the Anemia Theory. *American Journal of Physical Anthropology* 74:521–526.

Sweeney, E.A., J. Cabrera, J. Urritia, and L. Mata
1969 Factors Associated with Linear Hypoplasia of Human Deciduous Incisors. *Journal of Dental Research* 48:1275–1279.

Turek, S.L.
1984 Orthopaedics: Principals and Their Application. 4th ed. Philadelphia: Lippincott.

Wallace, J.A.
1974 Approximal Grooving of Teeth. *American Journal of Physical Anthropology* 40:385–390.

Wilford, L.A.
1970 Burial Mounds of the Red River Headwaters. *Minnesota Prehistoric Archaeology Series* 5.

Williams, J.A.
1982 The Inkster Burial. 32GF19: Skeletal Biology of a Northeastern Plains Woodland Population. *Journal of the North Dakota Archaeological Association* 1:181–215.

1985a Volume II: Skeletal Biology. In The Jamestown Mounds Project. J.S. Snortland, ed. Bismarck: State Historical Society of North Dakota.

1985b Site 32RY100: Skeletal Biology of the Infracranial Skeleton and Related Parameters. (Report submitted to the State Historical Society of North Dakota, Bismarck.)

1985c Evidence of Hydatid Disease in a Plains Woodland Burial. *Plains Anthropologist* 30:25–28.

1988 *Analysis of Miscellaneous Human Osteological Remains Recovered from Multi-County Areas of South Dakota.* Omaha, Neb.: U.S. Army Corps of Engineers.

1990 Miscellaneous Human Skeletal Remains from North Dakota and Northwestern Minnesota. *University of North Dakota Department of Anthropology Contribution* 253.

——, and J.S. Snortland-Coles

1986 Pre-contact Tuberculosis in a Plains Woodland Mortuary. *Plains Anthropologist* 31:249–252.

Wiltse, L.L., E.H. Widell, and D.W. Jackson

1975 Fatigue Fracture: The Basic Lesion in Isthmic Spondylolisthesis. *Journal of Bone and Joint Surgery* 57:17–22.

Wolley, A.M.

1988 Prehistoric Zinc Nutrition: Archaeological, Ethnographic, Skeletal, and Chemical Evidence. (Unpublished Masters Thesis, University of Nebraska, Lincoln.)

Zimmerman, M.R., and M.A. Kelley

1982 Atlas of Human Paleopathology. New York: Praeger.

CHAPTER 8

○○○

Endemic Treponematosis in Prehistoric Western Iowa

S.J. SCHERMER, A.K. FISHER, AND D.C. HODGES

Treponematosis is an infectious disease of four clinically distinct syndromes: yaws, endemic syphilis or treponarid, venereal syphilis, and pinta. Hudson (1958, 1965) and others have argued that all four syndromes are caused by the same microorganism, *Treponema pallidum*. Hackett (1963) believed that, although the four are closely related, three separate microorganisms—*T. pallidum* (venereal and endemic syphilis), *T. pertenue* (yaws), and *T. carateum* (pinta)—are involved. Varying hygienic conditions and cultural and climatic factors can have a modulating effect on the basic infection. The effects of these factors on the evolution of the disease have been extensively discussed (Brothwell 1981; Hackett 1963; Hudson 1958, 1965; Steinbock 1976).

Skepticism about the existence of treponemal disease in prehistoric America has prevailed since the nineteenth century. Although the focus of attention has been on venereal syphilis, the pre-Columbian existence of nonvenereal treponemal infections has also been debated. The controversy continued to flourish largely because of the lack of discriminating criteria applied to the diagnosis of bone lesions in skeletal material, lack of precise methods for determining the archaeological age of suspected lesions, and lack of widespread reporting of results (El-Najjar 1979; Ortner and Putschar 1981; Steinbock 1976). Progress in paleopathologic studies has encouraged more sophisticated and more detailed methods of examination so as to reduce mistaken diagnoses. Baker and Armelagos (1988) reviewed the available documentary and osteological evidence on treponemal disease from both the Old and the New World. The reported evidence for pre-Columbian New World treponemal infections has increased dramatically since the late 1970s, strengthening the argument that the disease was endemic in the New World before European contact.

Evidence for treponemal infection in the prehistoric Plains region, however, is limited. One Kansas City Hopewell skull has been described with changes suggestive of treponematosis (Stewart and Quade 1969). A comprehensive review of Plains skeletal pathologies led Gregg and Gregg (1987:61) to conclude that "nothing suggesting treponemal infections was in Middle Plains Woodland skeletons" and, presumably, pre-

Woodland as well. The Crow Creek site, radiocarbon dated to the mid-fourteenth century, is cited as the only pre-Columbian evidence (Gregg and Gregg 1987:62). Walker (1983:499) also concludes that evidence for treponemal infections in small hunting and gathering groups of the Plains is "meagre to non-existent." He notes resorptive changes in the clavicle, manubrium, and thoracic vertebrae as suggestive of a possible syphilitic aortic aneurysm at a Late Archaic period site (515 B.C. ± 85) on the Northern Plains. Bony changes suggestive of possible treponematosis in prehistoric western Iowa were noted (Anderson and Thompson 1977:14; Fisher 1980, 1983). This chapter reexamines that evidence, providing a more detailed description of the lesions and supporting a differential diagnosis of endemic treponematosis. In addition, evidence from another western Iowa site is discussed.

Skeletal Involvement in Treponemal Diseases

Of the four syndromes of treponematosis, only pinta leaves no recognizable signs in the skeletal structures. Pinta is clinically expressed as essentially a dermatological disorder. Although the other three syndromes also have prominent dermatological expressions, they are characterized individually by varying degrees of involvement of other organ systems. Although skeletal involvement is possible in cases of yaws, endemic syphilis, and venereal syphilis, lesions in bone do not always develop in these disorders. It has been estimated that bone lesions occur in approximately 10 to 20 percent of patients with untreated venereal syphilis, in about 5 percent of cases of yaws, and in from 1 to 5 percent of cases of endemic syphilis (Steinbock 1976). Other researchers (Cook 1976, 1984; Jackson, Boone, and Henneberg 1986; Powell 1988) have found a much larger proportion of their skeletal study populations exhibiting lesions suggestive of treponemal infections. It has been suggested that this difference may be explained by differences between radiographic or clinical assessments and direct assessments of dry bone (Baker and Armelagos 1988: 725). The difference may also be due to the nature of skeletal collections, in which only a small, possibly unrepresentative, sample of the larger population is recovered. The lesions produced in individual bones by any of these diseases are so similar that it may be difficult or impossible to distinguish among them. The distribution of lesions in several bones of a single skeleton offers the greatest prospect of a differential diagnosis.

The fundamental nature of bone change in treponematosis is low grade, chronic inflammation that results in the production of new bone tissue on the subperiosteal surface and within the medullary space. Apposition of new bone to the cortical surface leads to the production of nodular masses that distort the normal external contours and dimensions of individual bones, whereas apposition of bone on the walls of the medullary canal may drastically reduce the medullary space. Goff (1967) has called attention to increased weight of some syphilitic bones following the addition of bone tissue on the cortex and on the walls of the medullary space. Occasionally, nodular areas of bone that have developed on a cortical surface may undergo local necrosis with loss of bone substance at those points. Structural alterations of the teeth are known to occur only in congenital syphilis.

Detailed patterns of bone change in treponemal disease have been studied meticulously by Hackett (1976) with the objective of establishing criteria by which identification of the disease in skeletal material can be made with greater confidence. The anatomic details of the changes he has emphasized include surface plaques of new bone, striated new bone, pitting from the addition of plaques upon striated bone, nodes and enlargements (particularly of long bones), nodes with rugose surface patterns, superficial cavitation, and bone apposition on the anterior portion of the tibia. Although other diseases may induce similar bony changes, the lesions are usually associated with other pathological features that help to differentiate them from treponematosis. Hackett's diagnostic criteria for treponemal infections were used in evaluating the periosteal changes reported in this study.

Archaeological Sites

POOLER SITE

The Pooler site (13WB215), one and one-half acres approximately one-half mile south of the Des Moines River, occupies a northeast-southwest–oriented ridge on the generally flat uplands above the river (Abbott and Schermer 1983; Fisher 1981; Young 1981).

Five individuals were recovered from a bundle burial in an isolated pit labeled Feature 1. A small, side-notched projectile point and a few shell-tempered sherds suggest a late Late Woodland to post-Woodland, possibly Oneota, burial.

A single flexed burial was recovered from Feature 2, Mound 3. Very limited and highly fragmented charred remains were recovered from the fill surrounding the flexed burial. Reexamination of these fragments suggests the presence of three subadults rather than the two identified by Young (1981). A rim sherd recovered with the primary burial suggests a late Middle Woodland to early Late Woodland interment.

At least 10 individuals were recovered from a small ossuary, Feature 6, Mound 2, clustered at the bottom of a shallow basin. Although both Archaic and Woodland projectile points were found at the site, it was originally believed (Abbott and Schermer 1983) that the site was not used as a cemetery until the Middle Woodland period. Radiocarbon bone collagen dating of Feature 6 has extended the use of the site as a cemetery to Late Archaic or Early Woodland, 610 B.C.

Bone preservation in Feature 6 was fair to good, but there was extensive breakage. The ossuary contained the remains of at least eight adults and two subadults. Assignment of various elements to particular individuals was hampered by disarticulation, intermingling, and missing bones, making it difficult to determine accurately the age and sex of adults. Estimations of age were made by assessing degenerative changes in the auricular surface of the innominate (Lovejoy et al. 1985), cranial suture closure, and degenerative changes in long bones. Estimations of sex were made on the basis of combined sexually dimorphic characteristics of the crania, mandibles, long bones, and innominates. A minimum number of males and females in various age categories was then compiled. Five adult males and three adult females are represented: two males, 25–35 years of age; two males and one female, 35–45 years of age; two females, 45–55 years of age; and one possible male, probably middle-aged. The two subadults were also represented by incomplete remains: one, 7–9 years of age and one, 15–17 years of age.

HAVEN SITE

The Haven site (13PW18) is located on the summit of a loess bluff overlooking the Missouri floodplain. In 1971 approximately four burials, reportedly composed of two adult females, one adult male, and one subadult, were removed (Anderson and Thompson 1977:7, 8) but disappeared. A left femur and a left and right tibia were recovered in 1977 from the same location. It is unknown whether these remains belonged to one of the originally recovered individuals or if they represent a fifth individual. A radiocarbon date of A.D. 140 has been established for the site based on bone collagen.

COUNCIL BLUFFS OSSUARY

Councis Bluffs Ossuary (13PW1) is located on a bluff overlooking the Missouri River floodplain. Parts of 10 skeletons were salvaged there (Ruppé 1957). A mass burial was found on the slope below the crest of the bluff, at about one foot below the surface. Individual flexed burials were found farther down the slope, about 100 feet from the mass grave, about two feet below the surface. No radiocarbon date is available from this site. Bone preservation was good, but identification of individual skeletons was hampered by intermingled and missing bones. Five adults—one male and two females, 20–35 years of age; one male and one female, 35–50 years of age—were represented. Subadults—one 13–15 years and four 1–5 years of age—were also present (Schermer 1993).

CULTURAL AFFILIATION

The dates for the Feature 6 burials from Pooler fall within the dates for Late Archaic in the Plains area in general. These bundle burials, though, appear to have been placed as part of mound construction or an additive stage of mound construction; thus, on the basis of this Woodland diagnostic criterion, the burials may be considered Early Woodland. In western Iowa, a paucity of data for the Late Archaic–Early Woodland transition makes it difficult to place the Feature 6 date within one or the other. Very little is known about Early Woodland in Iowa in general but especially in western Iowa (Tiffany 1986). The similarity to the earlier Archaic period is reflected in the sparse occupations of suspected Early Woodland sites. The composition of Early Woodland and early Middle Woodland period components at the M.A.D. sites (13CF101–102) are not appreciably different from the underlying aceramic (and possibly Late Archaic) component (Benn 1982:38). Evidence from the Hanging Valley site (13HR28), a Middle Woodland burial site, suggests the presence of an admixture of Late Archaic and Woodland traits even into the Middle Woodland period in western Iowa (Tiffany et al. 1988). That these Pooler site, Feature 6, individuals were members of a small mobile hunter-gatherer population can be assumed.

The burials from the Haven site, with a date of A.D. 140 ± 80 years, fall within the Middle Woodland period, about A.D. 1 to 300–400 (Alex 1980:123; Benn 1982:42). Evidence from the Hanging Valley site dating to A.D. 190 ± 190 (Tiffany et al. 1988) suggests that small, mobile hunter-gatherer groups were probably still the norm in western Iowa during this period.

No dates were available and no definite cultural affiliation could be assigned for the burials from Council Bluffs Ossuary. The field notes suggest a multicomponent site with burials from each component and indicate that both primary burials and ossuary burials were recovered. The field notes suggest that the primary burials were "probably" Woodland, but no evidence was recorded for this assertion. Glenwood (Nebraska phase) potsherds were recovered from the "upper" grave, and four distinct burials were excavated in the "Glenwood level" (Eischen 1957). The remains themselves have lost their contextual information but are probably Woodland to post-Woodland in age.

Pathologic Changes

POOLER SITE

No periosteal proliferative responses were observed in any of the bones from Features 1 or 2.

In Feature 6, bones from at least four of the eight adults showed surface irregularities produced by new subperiosteal bone formation (tables 1–3). Periosteal reactive bone and cortical thickening were most extreme in the tibiae. Tibiae 1 and 2, Fibula 1, and Femora 9 and 10 were found in close approximation in the ossuary, exhibit similar widespread periosteal changes, and possibly belong to the same individual. Fibula 7 and Ulna 4 also possibly are from this same individual. The other three individuals are identified by Tibia 3, Tibia 6, and Tibiae 7 and 12.

TIBIAE

Twelve tibiae were recovered, with periosteal changes observed on six. Tibiae 1 (right) and 2 (left) appear to be paired based on metric and morphological similarity. This individual was a male, 25–35 years of age. Similar widespread periosteal changes were seen in both tibiae. Both bones were complete with changes affecting the entire shaft but no involvement of the articular ends. The shaft circumferences were enlarged by expansive periosteal bone, which was characterized by coarse striations and pitting. Frequently, the added bone was in the form of small, parallel, closely spaced ridges, oriented approximately in line with the long axis of the shafts. As earlier ridges were covered by later formations, the grooves between them were converted into tunnels, the mouths of which often gave the bone surface a porous or pitted appearance (fig. 1). A bowed appearance, due to anterior subperiosteal bone apposition, was pronounced in side view (fig. 1, center). Periosteal reaction was still active at the time of death, especially on the medial surfaces of both bones. Several erosive pits suggestive of superficial cavitations were observed in the expanded surface of Tibia 2. None was observed in Tibia 1. Radiographs of both tibiae showed pronounced cortex thickening and slight narrowing of the medullary cavity (fig. 1, bottom).

A second individual, a middle-aged to older adult male, was represented by Tibia 3, an incomplete shaft. Periosteal reaction resulted in moderate rugose nodes and expansions (healed) on

Table 1. Postcranial Elements Exhibiting Periosteal Reaction at the Pooler Site, Feature 6

Element		Total/with Periosteal Reaction[a]	Suggestive of Treponematosis[a]
Femur	l	6/2	1 (2)
	r	8/2	1 (2)
Tibia	l	7/4	3 (4)
	r	5/2	2
Fibulae	l	4/2	1
	r	7/3	1 (2)
Humeri	l	5/1	0
	r	7/0	0
Radii	l	6/2	0
	r	6/3	0 (3)
Ulnae	l	5/0	0
	r	5/3	2 (3)
Clavicle	l	4/1	0 (1)
	r	4/0	0
Carpals		9/0	0
Metacarpals		19/0	0
Phalanges (hand)		21/0	0
Tarsals		15/0	0
Tali	l	1/0	0
	r	1/1	0
Calcanea	l	2/0	0
	r	2/0	0
Metatarsals		22/1	0
Phalanges (foot)		16/0	0
Vertebrae			
Cervical		13/0	0
Thoracic		10/0	0
Lumbar		8/0	0
Ribs		44[b]/1	0
Total		262/26	11 (20)

[a]Numbers in parentheses indicate total including possible but nondiagnostic cases.

[b]Plus 136 rib fragments.

the lateral surface of the bone with slight expansion and irregularity on the posterior surface. The medial surface of the middle third of the shaft was characterized by active striated and pitted expansions. The radiograph showed cortex thickening as well as narrowing of the medullary cavity. This bone was abnormally heavy in weight.

A third individual, a middle-aged to older adult female, was represented by Tibia 6, a shaft only. Periosteal changes were limited for the most part to the medial, medio-posterior, and medio-anterior surfaces with a nodelike appearance interspersed with general expansion. There were no noticeable

Table 2. Cranial Periosteal Reactions at the Pooler Site, Feature 6

Element		Total/with Periosteal Reaction	Suggestive of Treponematosis[a]
Frontal		6/0	0
Parietal	l	6/0	0
	r	6/0	0
Temporal	l	5/0	0
	r	5/0	0
Occipital		7/0	0
Zygomatic	l	2/0	0
	r	2/0	0
Maxilla	l	6/0	0
	r	5/1	0 (1)
Nasal cavity		6/2	0 (1)
Total		56/3	0 (2)[b]

[a]Numbers in parentheses indicate total including possible but nondiagnosed cases.

[b]From the same cranium.

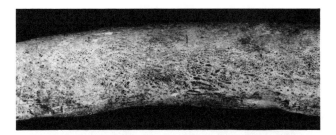

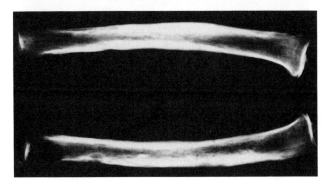

Fig. 1. Top, right tibia with coarse striations and plaquing, giving a pitted appearance. Center, left tibia with bowed appearance due to anterior subperiosteal bone apposition. Bottom, radiograph of Tibia 1 and Tibia 2, Pooler site, Feature 6. Note thickened cortex, both subperiosteal apposition and narrowing of medullary cavity.

Table 3. Periosteal Changes at the Pooler Site, Feature 6, and Hackett's (1976) Proposed Diagnostic Criteria for Treponemal Infections (Long Bones)

		Nondiagnostic Periosteal Response	Nodes or Expansions[a] with Plaques	Finely Striate[b] Nodes or Expansions	Coarsely Striate[b] and Pitted Expansions	Rugose Nodes or Expansions			Superficial Cavitation on Nodes
						Slight	Moderate	Gross	
Femora	l	1					1		
	r	1					1		
Tibiae	l		1			1	1		1
	r							1	1
Fibulae	l				1				
	r		1					1	
Radii	r	1	2						
Ulnae	r	1			1				1
Clavicle	l	1							
Total	5	4		2	1	3	2	3	

[a]Not considered a diagnostic criterion by Hackett.

[b]"On trial" diagnostic criteria.

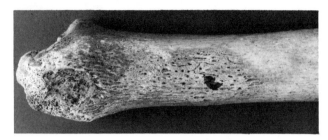

Fig. 2. Right tibia. Note subperiosteal node with superficial cavitation. Pooler site, Feature 6.

striations. The periosteal response was not active at the time of death; the bone surface appeared smooth but with a roughened, rugose appearance. The medial expansions from anterior to posterior in the distal third of the shaft exhibited plaques or bridges of bone applied to the original bone surface and on top of previous expansions. The radiograph showed cortex thickening, but the medullary cavity was not noticeably narrowed.

Tibiae 7 and 12 are possibly paired and represent a fourth individual, a young adult male. Only the proximal half of Tibia 7 was recovered. Periosteal plaque formation on the medial surface adjacent to the nutrient foramen was localized and active. There were small, scattered, localized areas of finely striated bony apposition. Part of a coarsely striated and pitted node was present on the lateral surface at the postmortem break near midshaft. On the medio-anterior midshaft surface a large erosive depression or pit extended into the cortex but did not perforate the medullary canal. Periosteal reaction had begun along the superior border of the lesion. From the radiograph, there appears to have been very slight medullary apposition adjacent to the depression. Tibia 12 was a complete bone. There were localized areas of active striations and plaque formation on the medial surface. A large striated node with superficial cavitation was also present on the medial surface in the distal one-eighth to one-fourth of the shaft (fig. 2). Additional localized areas of striations and plaques over striations, giving a finely pitted appearance, were present on the lateral and posterior surfaces. The radiograph shows only localized and very slight cortical thickening with no noticeable narrowing of the medullary cavity.

FIBULAE

Eleven fibulae were recovered, with periosteal changes observed on five. Fibulae 1 and 7 appear to be paired based on metric and morphological similarity. Fibula 1 was complete.

All surfaces of the entire shaft exhibited gross periosteal changes. The expanded medial surface was fairly smooth and appeared mostly healed but with coarse striations still visible. Active periostitis characterized the rest of the bone. The distal two-thirds of the shaft was grossly expanded with a rough undulating surface, distinct striations, and plaquing. A distinct subperiosteal node was present near the proximal end of the shaft. The radiograph showed cortex thickening and slight narrowing of the medullary cavity. Fibula 7 was also complete. Gross and active periostitis was limited to the distal half to two-thirds of the shaft. All surfaces exhibited gross, coarsely striated and pitted expansions. The shaft was greatly expanded with a very rugose and pitted appearance. The radiograph showed cortex expansion with Weber's line, indicating the demarcation between the original cortical surface and the subsequently formed bone, still visible.

Fibula 6 was complete. Active periosteal reaction had resulted in small localized nodes on the medial surface of the middle third of the shaft. The new bony growth was striated, with plaquing giving a pitted appearance.

Both Fibula 3 and Fibula 4 were incomplete and showed only localized periostitis with slight expansions. The periosteal reaction of Fibula 4 appeared to be related to an antemortem fracture near the distal end of the shaft. The fracture had healed but with a slight malalignment.

FEMORA

Fourteen femora were recovered with periosteal changes observed on four. Femur 4 was a shaft only and exhibited only slight irregularity of the anterior surface, which was healed at the time of death. Femur 7, a shaft only and from a different individual, also exhibited only slight periosteal reaction, which had healed by the time of death.

Two complete femora, labeled 9 (fig. 3) and 10, appeared to be paired based on metric and morphological similarities. Similar periosteal changes were seen in both. Changes were

Fig. 3. Left femur showing rugose periosteal thickening of distal third of shaft. Pooler site, Feature 6.

mainly restricted to the distal halves of the shafts but were most pronounced in the distal third, involving all surfaces. The shafts appeared thickened, most prominently on the posterior surfaces. Active periostitis was present on the posterior surface of Femur 9 but was mostly inactive on Femur 10 except along the linea aspera. The bone surfaces were characterized by coarse striations and pitting. Radiographs of both showed thickened cortex and slight narrowing of the medullary cavity.

ULNAE

Three of the 10 ulnae were affected with periostitis. Ulna 2 exhibited the most severe reaction (fig. 4). The radiograph shows some destruction of the original cortex, which had not yet opened through the node to the new surface. The surface of Ulna 4 exhibited coarse striations and pitting with a slight rugose appearance. Cortical thickening was diffuse. Ulna 1 was less affected, with a slightly roughened thickening of the distal shaft and the medial surface of the proximal one-quarter of the shaft.

RADII

Five of the 12 radii exhibited slight periosteal changes. One of these, Radius 5, was probably related to an antemortem fracture with subsequent healing. Three radii (4, 10, and 12) had localized areas of fine periosteal plaque. The other radius (Radius 1) also had minor changes with very slight swelling and roughness at midshaft.

CLAVICLES

Only one of the eight clavicles showed any periosteal reaction. The shaft of this clavicle was slightly thickened in several small, localized areas.

The only cranial involvement was on the frontal process of the right maxilla of Cranium A in the form of a localized, pitted, periosteal apposition of new bone (fig. 5). The maxilla was part of an almost complete skull that showed no lesions of

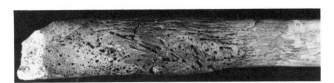

Fig. 4. Right ulna with coarse striations and plaquing. A large periosteal node on the medial surface is just distal to the midshaft. Pooler site, Feature 6.

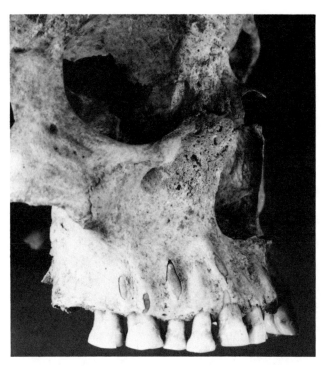

Fig. 5. Periosteal reaction on frontal process of right maxilla. Also present in adjacent interior nasal cavity. Pooler site, Feature 6.

the cranial vault bones. The skull could not be related with certainty to any particular skeleton.

Examination of the limited remains of the two subadults did not find any evidence of periosteal reactions.

HAVEN SITE

The three leg bones recovered appeared to be part of the same skeleton because they were found close together, they had similar dimensions, all showed signs of chronic periostitis, and all were unusually heavy when compared to the weight of normal bones from prehistoric burials in similar soils. The size of the bones and their fused epiphyses indicated that the individual was an adult (Fisher 1980). Distortion of the diameters of the bones precluded an identification of sex.

The surface of the femur had a granular texture created by the presence of small, roughly parallel, longitudinally oriented ridges and tiny irregular osseous plaques. Many plaques viewed under slight magnification appeared to have clearly defined, abrupt margins that suggested apposition upon a prior cortical surface. Most of the tibial surfaces also were covered with subperiosteal new bone, but in greater amounts than the femur. The appositional character of the new bone—most abundant over the distal two-thirds of the shafts—was

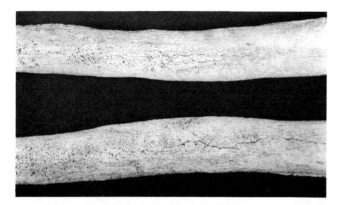

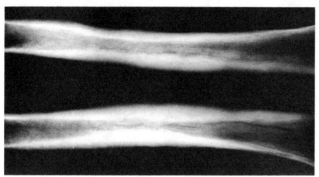

Fig. 6. Tibiae from the Haven site. Top, Lateral view with appearance of anterior bowing caused by subperiosteal bony apposition. Bottom, Radiographs of same bones showing increased thickness of cortex, both subperiosteally and endosteally.

readily apparent without magnification in several areas where the margins of the abnormal masses were separated from the underlying cortex, although most of the new bone appeared continuous with the original surface. The new bony growth was striated, with plaquing giving a pitted appearance. The rather considerable amount of new bone that had been laid down on the middle part of the shafts had transformed the normally sharp and fairly straight anterior tibial border into a rounded and broadened shape that protruded gently anteriorly. Similar processes had converted the normally triangular cross-sectional shape of the tibia into an enlarged and irregular cylindrical structure in the distal third of the shaft. Radiographs demonstrated increased thickness of the tibial cortex throughout much of the diaphyses but less so in the metaphyseal area (fig. 6). Weber's line could be seen in the posterior portion of the distal third of the right tibia. Increased endosseous bone formation had occurred mainly in the distal two-thirds of the shafts with consequent reduction of the medullary cavity. Focal areas of cortical radiolucency, indicative of resorption, were not observed in either the periosteal or endosteal surfaces. Histologic examination showed no ab-

normality of the cortex other than an obvious reduction of the diameters of what was visually estimated to be approximately one-half the Haversian canals.

COUNCIL BLUFFS OSSUARY

A minimum of 10 individuals (five adults and five subadults) was represented in the collection available for examination. As with the other two sites, the most severe periosteal reactions were found on the tibiae and fibulae (tables 4–5). Three of the five adult tibiae exhibited widespread, gross, rugose changes. Two of these appear to be paired based on metric and morphological similarities and belonged to one of the younger

Table 4. Adult Postcranial Elements Exhibiting Periosteal Reaction at Council Bluffs Ossuary

Element		Total/With Periosteal Reaction	Suggestive of Treponematosis
Femur	l	2/1	0
	r	3/1	0
Tibia	l	2[a]/1	1
	r	3/3	2
Fibula	l	2[b]/2[b]	2
	r	1/1	1
Humeri	l	2[a]/0	0
	r	4/0	0
Radii	l	1/0	0
	r	3/0	0
Ulnae	l	3[a]/0	0
	r	2/0	0
Clavicle	l	2/0	0
	r	1/0	0
Metacarpals		2/0	0
Tarsals		1/0	0
Tali	l	2/0	0
	r	1/0	0
Calcanea	l	3/0	0
	r	2/0	0
Metatarsals		6/0	0
Vertebrae			
Cervical		1/0	0
Thoracic		14/0	0
Lumbar		8/0	0
Ribs		11[c]/0	0
Total		82/9	6

[a]One is less than half present.

[b]One is shaft fragments (2), unable to side, default to left.

[c]Plus 9 fragments.

Table 5. Adult Cranial Periosteal Reactions from Council Bluffs Ossuary

Element		Total/With Periosteal Reaction
Frontal		6[a]/0
Parietal	l	5/0
	r	5/0
Temporal	l	5/0
	r	4/0
Occipital		5/0
Zygomatic	l	2/0
	r	3/0
Maxilla	l	4/0
	r	3/0
Nasal cavity		2/0

[a]One may be a juvenile.

adult females. Both tibiae showed diaphyseal expansion with coarse striations and plaques of periosteal reactive bone. Some healing had taken place. The left tibia of this pair also had rough proliferative bony apposition along the interosseous crest area (fig. 7). The third tibia, the proximal two-thirds of a right tibia belonging to the older adult female, had a pronounced bowed appearance. Widespread periosteal reactive bone covered all surfaces of the shaft except the posterior surface. The expansion had a smoothed, nodular appearance with pitting visible on the lateral surface near the midshaft. The medullary cavity was markedly narrowed.

All three fibulae examined had diffuse periostitis. Two fibulae appeared to be paired and probably belonged to the same individual as the paired tibiae. Both had gross, widespread, periosteal changes. The left fibula had rough proliferative

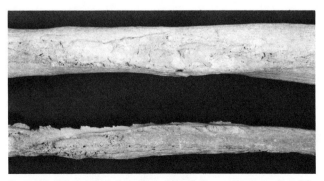

Fig. 7. Left tibia and fibula from Council Bluffs Ossuary. Note rough proliferative bony apposition along interosseous crests.

bony apposition along the interosseous crest area, similar to that on the left tibia. The distal half of the right shaft was moderately expanded with a smoothed but slightly nodular appearance. Slight striations were still visible in the distal quarter of the shaft. Coarsely striated subperiosteal bone covered the proximal half of the shaft. The third fibula consisted of two portions of shaft, both exhibiting widespread expansion with a smoothed but rugose appearance.

Two femora exhibited very slight localized periostitis. One showed abnormal bony apposition along the linea aspera. One small shaft fragment from a femur or tibia was slightly striated. All other skeletal portions available for observation appeared normal except for osteoarthritic changes.

The five subadults from Council Bluffs Ossuary were also examined. One of the younger children was represented by a pair of femora; another by pairs of femora, tibiae, and humeri; the third by pairs of femora and tibiae; and the fourth by a tibia and clavicle fragment. No periostitis was observed on any of these bones. The older juvenile was represented by pairs of clavicles, femora, and fibulae; a right ulna; and a left humerus. Unfortunately, no tibiae were recovered for this individual. Small, localized, periosteal apposition was observed on the lateral surface of the distal quarter of the shaft of the right femur. The pair of fibulae consisted of one relatively complete bone and the proximal half of the shaft of the other. The periosteal changes in each had resulted in a distinct nodal swelling in the proximal quarter of the shafts. Although the lesions were partially healed, coarse striations and plaquing were still visible. The posterior surface of the distal third of the shaft of the left humerus was swollen, with a roughly smoothed appearance, suggestive of a healed lesion. In addition to the subadult long bones, one calva was recovered. Although badly warped, the bone appeared normal. Only eight subadult teeth were available for examination. All appeared normal.

Conclusions

The affected long bones from the Pooler site exhibited various degrees of striation and pitting, surface plaques, rugose nodes and expansions, and superficial cavitation. Of the 20 postcranial bones with periosteal changes cited as possible evidence of treponemal infection, 11 fit Hackett's (1976) diagnostic criteria for treponematosis (table 3). In addition, four were characterized by nodes or expansions with plaques, not considered diagnostic but present in many of the treponemal cases Hackett examined. Five of the 20 bones exhibited nondiagnostic periosteal response that could not be used alone to diagnose treponemal disease. Narrowing of the medullary cavity by endosteal apposition was observed radiographically in those bones exhibiting the greatest subperiosteal alteration. The tibiae from three individuals gave the appearance of anterior bowing due to the proliferation of new periosteal bone along the anterio-medial and anteriolateral aspects of the shafts. Periosteal changes were limited to the shafts of the long bones only and did not involve the articular ends. Hackett's analysis showed that these changes are more frequently associated with treponemal disease than with nontreponemal bone disease. Only one bone, an incomplete tibial shaft, was abnormally heavy in comparison to normal tibiae.

All three bones from the Haven site had been affected by a diffuse periostitis and were abnormally dense. Periosteal new bone—striated, woven, and porous—could be seen on the cortical surfaces. Anterior apposition of new periosteal bone gave a bowed appearance to both tibiae. The medullary cavities of all three bones had been reduced by endosteal encroachment. Since only the shafts had been recovered, it is not known if articular ends were involved in the osteoblastic response. The affected bones from Council Bluffs Ossuary exhibited similar cortical expansion with striated and plaquelike subperiosteal bone deposition. Articular surfaces were not involved.

The abnormalities observed in the bones from the Pooler site, the Haven site, and Council Bluffs Ossuary have been described for yaws, endemic syphilis, and venereal syphilis. Lesions are multiple and, where bones could be paired, occur bilaterally in the long bones. The character of the lesions in all these bones was generally similar. The common feature was the evidence of productive periostitis, sometimes resulting in nodular expansions of the long bone shafts. The prominent "saber shin" tibia was observed in bones from all three sites. In more severe cases, endosteal bone apposition resulted in a reduced medullary cavity. The appositional nature of the expansions was discernible by both inspection and radiography. The pelvis, ribs, and hand and foot bones were normal. There were no vertebral changes except for slight to severe osteoarthritis.

Radiographic examination showed that the thickening of the long bone diaphyses was dense bone rather than the lacelike structure of active Paget's disease. Absence of sequestrum and cloaca formation, lack of joint involvement, multiple bone lesions, and a somewhat regular outline to the new bone formation make a diagnosis of pyogenic osteomyelitis unlikely (Steinbock 1976). The multiple lesions affecting long bone shafts, the absence of involvement of the vertebral col-

umn, hip, and knee, the lack of joint involvement, and the fact that the predominant reaction was osteoblastic rule out a diagnosis of tuberculosis. The possibility of these changes being confused with those produced by Paget's disease, tuberculosis, or pyogenic osteomyelitis is negated by contrary radiographic and histologic findings, by the pattern of skeletal involvement, and by the generalized nature of the periostitis. Therefore, there appears to be substantial evidence to support a diagnosis of treponematosis.

As Steinbock (1976), Hackett (1976), and Ortner and Putschar (1981) discuss, it is difficult to differentiate among yaws, endemic syphilis, and venereal syphilis because similar or identical lesions can occur in all three. The incidence of skeletal involvement and the specification of type and location of lesions do differ somewhat. Steinbock (1976) has cited numerous reports on the location of bone lesions in treponematosis. Those lesions produced by yaws and endemic syphilis share a similar skeletal distribution. Involvement in order of decreasing frequency occurs in the tibia, fibula, ulna, and radius and to a lesser extent in the other bones. In venereal syphilis, the tibia is more frequently involved than any other long bone but lesions on the fibula are relatively rare. Steinbock (1976) and Ortner and Putschar (1981) note that involvement of the skull is less common and less destructive in yaws than in venereal syphilis. The characteristic syphilitic caries sicca rarely, if ever, occurs in yaws (Ortner and Putschar 1981:181). Cranial involvement is rare in endemic syphilis, although destruction of the nasal-palatal region does occur frequently (Steinbock 1976:138).

At the Pooler site, tibiae were the bones most frequently affected, followed by fibulae, ulnae, femora, radii, clavicles, and maxilla. The only cranial involvement was the localized periosteal expansion on the frontal process of a maxilla. Whether this reaction was in response to treponemal infection or another, local infection is uncertain. The distribution of bone lesions from Pooler is more characteristic of yaws or endemic syphilis than of venereal syphilis and follows closely the distribution of lesions described by Powell (1988) of treponematosis at Moundville, Alabama. Powell argues, as Cook (1976) did, that the evidence suggests that this prehistoric treponemal syndrome has features reminiscent of both yaws and endemic syphilis.

Although the evidence for pre-Columbian treponemal disease has increased dramatically, most of it is from relatively late, sedentary, agricultural groups (Baker and Armelagos 1988). Because of the epidemiology of nonvenereal treponemal infections, the disease could have been present in small Archaic and Woodland hunting and gathering groups. Steinbock (1976) cites a survey of 322 Bosnian villages in which the prevalence of endemic syphilis was inversely proportional to the size of the population. The frequency of the disease was greatest when the population was less than 200. Hudson (1965) reported that endemic treponematosis could maintain itself in small, endogamous populations. Jackson, Boone, and Henneberg (1986) inferred possible seasonal aggregation from the high incidence of skeletal lesions indicative of infectious disease, including treponematosis, in a nonsedentary Texas hunter-gatherer group. Sites providing the earliest evidence suggestive of treponemal infections have been radiocarbon-dated at 3300 B.C. (the Tick Island Archaic site, Florida) (Bullen 1972) and 3350 B.C. (Indian Knoll, Kentucky) (Brothwell and Burleigh 1975:393). In Illinois, Late Archaic Red Ocher burials at the Morse site, 1500–1000 B.C. (Morse 1978), and Late Archaic burials at the Klunk site (Cook 1984; Morse 1978) contain individuals exhibiting bone lesions suggestive of treponemal infection. A comparison of the proportion of infected Archaic individuals at the Klunk site with the patterns seen in Illinois Middle and Late Woodland series suggests that treponematosis was present in the Archaic, but at significantly lower levels than in later periods (Cook 1984:259). There is limited evidence suggestive of treponemal infection at a Late Archaic site on the Northern Plains (Walker 1983).

Other western Iowa burial sites that have been extensively studied produce no evidence of treponemal disease. At the Turin Gravel Pit (13MN2) (2770 B.C. ± 250), four individuals (1 adult, 3 subadults) were examined, but no periosteal changes were observed (Fisher et al. 1985). At Lewis Central School site (865 B.C. ± 80), a minimum of 25 Archaic individuals (19 adults, 6 subadults) were examined. Only one radius and one ulna showed superficial areas of reactive bone, suggestive of localized chronic inflammatory lesions of the adjacent soft tissues of undetermined cause (Anderson et al. 1978). Seven Middle Woodland individuals (2 adults, 5 subadults) were examined from the Hanging Valley site. Although these individuals were nutritionally stressed, there was no evidence of treponemal infection (Tiffany et al. 1988). Nutritional status is less critical in resistance to endemic treponematosis than in resistance to other infectious diseases (Hackett 1951; Myers 1951; Powell 1991). There was no evidence of treponemal infection in any of the individuals from the later Woodland or late prehistoric burials at the Pooler site. Comparison of craniometric characteristics among the three burial populations showed dissimilarity (Abbott and Schermer 1983). Although this craniometric variability could be due to small sample size with the comparison of individuals rather than

population means, the dissimilarity could also be the result of changes through time of the populations that used the site, suggesting the later burials were unrelated to the earlier Feature 6 individuals suffering from treponemal disease.

In summary, at least four of eight adults from the Late Archaic–Early Woodland component at the Pooler site appear to have been affected by treponemal infection—two males 25–35 years of age, and one male and one female 35–50 years of age. Neither of the two subadults appeared to be affected. Although only some bones display the presence and widespread nature of diagnostic lesions highly suggestive of treponematosis and can thus be cited as "classic" examples of the disease, those individuals showing lesser forms of involvement may represent different stages of the disease. The pathological changes seen at Pooler cannot be regarded as a matter of chance, but rather are suggestive of what might be expected of a nonlethal communicable disease in a small, mobile prehistoric population.

Only limited remains from one adult individual from the Haven site were available for examination, so the prevalence of treponemal disease at that site remains unknown. That this one individual did suffer from treponemal infection is possible considering the nature of the proliferative periosteal changes seen in all three bones.

Limited, commingled remains of a minimum of 10 individuals were available from Council Bluffs Ossuary. Two of the five adults, both female—one 25–30 years of age, the other 35–50 years of age—and one of five subadults, 13–15 years of age and of indeterminate sex, exhibited changes suggestive of treponemal infection.

Bone lesions recorded from burials at these three western Iowa sites conform to judiciously selected criteria that characterize treponemal disease. The chance that these lesions may have been produced by pyogenic osteomyelitis, tuberculosis, or Paget's disease is quite low because radiographic and histologic evidence and the locations and distribution of these lesions do not conform to the usual diagnostic characteristics of these alternatives. These pieces of evidence justify a diagnosis of treponematosis. Frequencies of skeletal element involvement for one local population suggest that the type of treponematosis observed may be yaws or endemic syphilis.

Radiocarbon evidence supports the conclusion that endemic treponematosis probably existed in Iowa as early as 610 B.C. The groups affected by this disease apparently were small populations whose subsistence economies probably focused primarily on hunting and gathering. The extent of extraregional contacts or intergroup interaction and aggregation is unknown. Evidence for treponemal infection is lacking in samples from earlier (Archaic) and later (Late Woodland and late prehistoric) populations in the region, although few sizable skeletal series have been examined. The evidence clearly points to the existence of pre-Columbian treponemal infection in the eastern Plains.

References Cited

Abbott, L.R., and S. Schermer
   1983   The Pooler Site (13WB215). *Office of the Iowa State Archaeologist. Research Papers* 8(3).
Alex, L.M.
   1980   Exploring Iowa's Past: A Guide to Prehistoric Archaeology. Iowa City: University of Iowa Press.
——, and D. Thompson
   1977   A Cultural Resource Survey of the Proposed Site of the Pottawattamie County Landfill. *Office of the Iowa State Archaeologist. Research Papers* 2(8):7–8,14.
Anderson, D.C., M. Finnegan, J. Hotopp, and A.K. Fisher
   1978   The Lewis Central School Site (13PW5): A Resolution of Ideological Conflicts at an Archaic Ossuary in Western Iowa. *Plains Anthropologist* 23(81):183–219.
Baker, B.J., and G.J. Armelagos
   1988   The Origins and Antiquity of Syphilis: Paleopathological Diagnosis and Interpretation. *Current Anthropology* 29(5):7O3–737.
Benn, David W.
   1982   Woodland Cultures of the Western Prairie Peninsula: An Abstract. Pp. 37–52 in Interrelations of Cultural and Fluvial Deposits in Northwest Iowa. E.A. Bettis, III and D.M. Thompson, eds. Vermillion, S.Dak.: The University of South Dakota Archeological Laboratory.
Brothwell, D.
   1981   Microevolutionary Change in the Human Pathogenic Treponemes: An Alternative Hypothesis. *International Journal of Systematic Bacteriology* 31(1):82–87.
——, and R. Burleigh
   1975   Radiocarbon Dates and the History of Treponematoses in Man. *Journal of Archaeological Sciences* 2:393–396.
Bullen, A.K.
   1972   Paleoepidemiology and Distribution of Prehistoric Treponemiasis (Syphilis) in Florida. *Florida Anthropologist* 25:133–174.
Cook, D.C.
   1976   Pathologic States and Disease Process in Illinois Woodland Populations: An Epidemiologic Approach. (Unpublished Ph.D. Dissertation, University of Chicago, Chicago.)
——
   1984   Subsistence and Health in the Lower Illinois Valley: Osteological Evidence. Pp. 235–269 in Paleopathology at the Origins of Agriculture. M.N. Cohen and G.J. Armelagos, eds. Orlando, Fla.: Academic Press.

Eischen, R.P.
   1957   Archaeology Laboratory Report. (Unpublished report on file, Office of the Iowa State Archaeologist, Iowa City, Iowa.)
El-Najjar, M.Y.
   1979   Human Tremonematosis and Tuberculosis: Evidence from the New World. *American Journal of Physical Anthropology* 51:599–618.
Fisher, A.K.
   1980   Human Bones from the Haven Site, 13PW18, with Changes Suggestive of Treponemal Infection. (Unpublished paper on file, Office of the Iowa State Archaeologist, Iowa City, Iowa.)
——
   1981   Human Bones from the Pooler Site (13WB215). *Office of the State Archaeologist. Research Papers* 6(1)1–4.
——
   1983   Possible Treponemal Disease in Prehistoric Iowa. (Paper presented at 1983 Plains Conference, Rapid City, South Dakota.)
——, W.D. Frankforter, J.A. Tiffany, S.J. Schermer, and D.C. Anderson
   1985   Turin: A Middle Archaic Burial Site in Western Iowa. *Plains Anthropologist* 30(109):195–218.
Goff, C.W.
   1967   Syphilis. Pp. 279–294 in Diseases in Antiquity. Don Brothwell and A.T. Sandison, eds. Springfield, Illinois: Charles C. Thomas.
Gregg, J.B., and P.S. Gregg
   1987   Dry Bones: Dakota Territory Reflected. Sioux Falls, South Dakota: Sioux Printing.
Hackett, C.J.
   1951   Bone Lesions of Yaws in Uganda. Oxford, England: Blackwell Scientific Publications.
——
   1963   On the Origin of the Human Treponematoses. *Bulletin of the World Health Organization* 29:7–41.
——
   1976   Diagnostic Criteria of Syphilis, Yaws and Treponarid (Treponematoses) and of Some Other Diseases in Dry Bones. Berlin: Springer-Verlag.
Hudson, E.H.
   1958   Treponematoses—or Treponematosis? *British Journal of Venereal Diseases* 34:22–23.
——
   1965   Treponematosis and Man's Social Evolution. *American Anthropologist* 67:885–901.
Jackson, B.E., J.L. Boone, and M. Henneberg
   1986   Possible Cases of Endemic Treponematosis in a Prehistoric Hunter-Gatherer Population on the Texas Coast. *Bulletin of the Texas Archeological Society* 57:183–193.

Lovejoy, C.O., R.S. Meindl, T.R. Pryzbeck, and R.P. Mensforth
1985 Chronological Metamorphosis of the Auricular Surface of the Ilium: A New Method for the Determination of Adult Skeletal Age at Death. *American Journal of Physical Anthropology* 68:15–28.

Morse, D.
1978 Ancient Disease in the Midwest. 2d rev. ed. *Illinois State Museum Reports of Investigations* 15.

Myers, J.A.
1951 Tuberculosis Among Children and Adults. 3d ed. Springfield, Ill.: C.C. Thomas.

Ortner, D.J., and W.G.J. Putschar
1981 Identification of Pathological Conditions in Human Skeletal Remains. *Smithsonian Contributions to Anthropology* 28.

Powell, M.L.
1988 Status and Health in Prehistory: A Case Study of the Moundville Chiefdom. Washington: Smithsonian Institution Press.

——
1991 Endemic Treponematosis and Tuberculosis in the Prehistoric Southeastern United States: The Biological Costs of Chronic Endemic Disease. In Human Paleopathology: Current Syntheses and Future Options. D.J. Ortner and A.C. Aufderheide, eds. Washington: Smithsonian Institution Press.

Ruppé, R.J.
1957 Unpublished Fieldnotes on file at Office of the State Iowa Archaeologist, Iowa City, Iowa.

Schermer, S.J.
1993 Analysis of Human Remains from the Council Bluffs Ossuary, 13 PW1, Pottawattomie County, Iowa. *Office of the State Archaeologist. Research Papers* 18(1):195–220.

Steinbock, R.T.
1976 Paleopathological Diagnosis and Interpretation. Springfield, Ill.: C.C. Thomas.

Stewart, T.D., and L.G. Quade
1969 Lesions of the Frontal Bone in American Indians. *American Journal of Physical Anthropology* 30:89–110.

Tiffany, J.A.
1986 The Early Woodland Period in Iowa. Pp. 159–170 in Early Woodland Archaeology. K.B. Farnsworth and T.E. Emerson, eds. Kampsville, Ill.: Center for American Archaeology.

——, S.J. Schermer, J.L. Theler, D.W. Owsley, D.C. Anderson, E.A. Bettis III, and D.M. Thompson
1988 The Hanging Valley Site (13HR28): A Stratified Woodland Burial Locale in Western Iowa. *Plains Anthropologist* 33(120):219–259.

Walker, E.G.
1983 Evidence for Prehistoric Cardiovascular Disease of Syphilitic Origin on the Northern Plains. *American Journal of Physical Anthropology* 60:499–503.

Young, M.A.
1981 Analysis of Human Skeletal Remains from the Pooler Site, 13WB215. *Office of the State Archaeologist. Research Papers* 6(3).

○○○

CHAPTER 9

Respiratory Disease Among Protohistoric and Early Historic Plains Indians

MARC A. KELLEY, SEAN P. MURPHY, DIANNE R. LEVESQUE, AND PAUL S. SLEDZIK

The depopulation of Native Americans living along the Missouri River during the eighteenth and nineteenth centuries resulted from a dramatic series of events including a variety of introduced and endemic infectious diseases (Kelley 1980; Palkovich 1981; Ramenofsky 1982). This report focuses on the frequency of pulmonary disease among four archaeological sites with particular emphasis on periosteal reactions restricted to the visceral surface of the ribs. Kelley and Micozzi (1984) reported on these lesions using known cause-of-death skeletal remains from the Hamann-Todd Collection in the Cleveland Museum of Natural History. In that study, the ribs of 445 early twentieth-century American Whites and Blacks (primarily from the lower socioeconomic strata) in which the stated cause of death was tuberculosis were examined. More specifically, nearly 80 percent of these individuals died of pulmonary tuberculosis. Approximately 9 percent exhibited localized, mild periosteal reactions on the inner surfaces of varying numbers of ribs. The left ribs were favored, and a preference was noted for mid-upper rib involvement. Kelley and Micozzi also examined the skeletal remains of 385 individuals who died of pneumonia

(both lobar and bronchopneumonia), concluding that rib lesions rarely resulted from pneumonia. This study represents continued and in-depth diachronic analysis of these lesions in skeletal remains of Plains Indians from late prehistoric and early historic times. The primary objective was to determine the frequency of rib periostitis in four Arikara Indian skeletal collections.

Sites and Collections

Four South Dakota archaeological sites were selected for analysis: Sully (39SL4), Mobridge (39WW1), Larson (39WW2), and Leavenworth (39CO9). Mobridge and Sully were multicomponent sites occupied for two to three generations (table 1). Multicomponent sites can be particularly useful for detecting evolving demographic and pathologic patterns.

Collectively, there are nearly 2,000 individuals represented from these sites. Only those with at least one-half of the ribs preserved were included for analysis. Fetal and infant remains under one year of age were excluded. The highly active remodeling and vascular bones of young infants make it

Table 1. Archaeological Sites

Site Name	Archaeological Variant	Date Range
Mobridge F1	Extended Coalescent	A.D. 1600–1650
Mobridge F2	Postcontact Coalescent	1675–1700
Sully A	Extended Coalescent	1650–1675
Sully B	Postcontact Coalescent	1679–1733
Sully D	Extended Coalescent	1650–1675
Sully E	Postcontact Coalescent	1675–1700
Larson	Postcontact Coalescent	1679–1733
Leavenworth	Historic Arikara	1802–1832

Source: Key 1983:130–132.

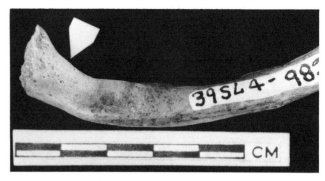

Fig. 2. Enlarged and pitted periosteal reaction in neck region of rib (Sully Feature 421, B96).

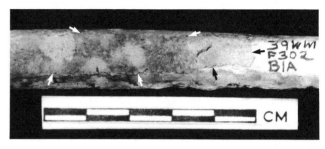

Fig. 3. Plaquelike periostitis (arrows) covering rib (Mobridge Feature 302, B1A).

difficult or impossible to detect the subtle periosteal lesions under investigation. A final sample of 740 individuals from these four sites was deemed acceptable for analysis. Using diagrammatic aids, rib lesions were recorded by side, location, and number of ribs affected. Age and sex estimates for Sully, Larson and Leavenworth were provided by Douglas Owsley; age and sex for Mobridge were estimated by Marc Kelley.

A total of 46 (6.2%, N = 740) individuals were identified as exhibiting periostitis of varying severity on the inner surfaces of the ribs. Figures 1–4 illustrate the typical appearance of these lesions in the Arikara material. In figure 1, the mildest form, bone reaction is barely visible on the fifth rib. Figure 2 exhibits a more distinct enlargement in the neck region of a rib. Figure 3 presents the most common manifestation of rib inflammation, a plaquelike periostitis that flakes off easily. Severe inflammation with a swollen and pitted appearance is shown in figure 4. The histologic appearance of a typical rib lesion is illustrated in figure 5. The deposition of new bone over the original cortical bone is clearly visible.

With regard to the location of rib lesions, 87 percent (40/46) of the Arikara cases were unilateral, 13 percent bilateral. Figure 6, based on data derived from a nineteenth-century clinical series consisting of 1,131 cases of pneumonia and 250 cases of pulmonary tuberculosis (Stokes 1844), gives the distribution of left, right, and bilateral lung involvement for tuberculosis and pneumonia. The Arikara rib lesion pattern is also depicted in figure 6. Pneumonia is more prevalent in the right lung, tuberculosis in the left lung. The Arikara rib lesions

Fig. 1. Mild expression of periostitis (arrows) on fifth rib (Sully Feature 421, B122B).

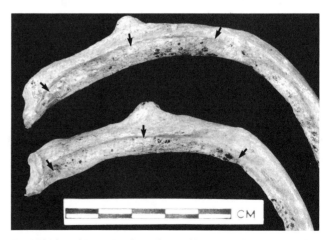

Fig. 4. Thickened (arrows) and pitted cortical bone extending over several upper ribs (Sully Feature 421, B122B).

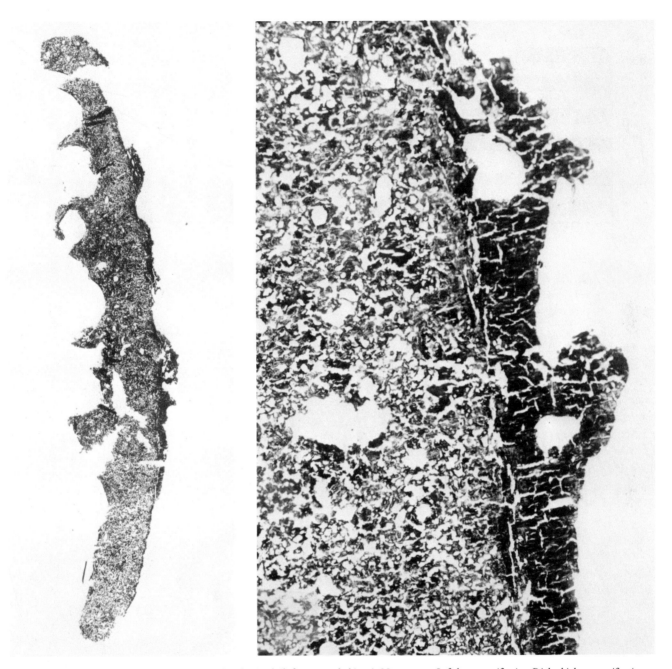

Fig. 5. Magnification of partially decalcified, sectioned, and stained rib from an early historic Narragansett. Left, low magnification. Right, higher magnification of same sectioned rib, showing newly deposited bone overlying original cortical bone (Kelley, Sledzik, and Murphy 1987).

are fairly evenly distributed by side with no statistically significant preference observed.

The periostitis may localize in the neck region, central region, or spread extensively over both these regions of the rib. When multiple ribs exhibit inflammation, the same portion of each rib is consistently involved. Placing the ribs in anatomical order gives the distinct impression that the zone of

bony inflammation corresponds to an underlying lesion of the lung or pleura.

The number of ribs affected ranged from 1 to 12 with a mean of 4.6 ribs per individual. Table 2 provides a detailed breakdown of the mean number of ribs affected by site and component, and the percent of individuals with rib lesions from each sample. Sully components A and D are treated as

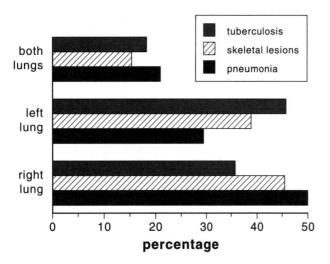

Fig. 6. Side preference for pneumonia and tuberculosis based on a nineteenth-century clinical series (Stokes 1844). The Arikara skeletal lesions are included.

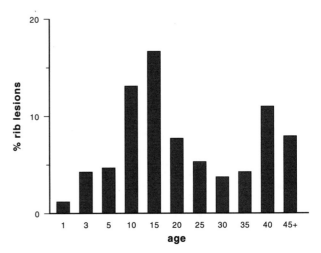

Fig. 7. Breakdown by rib for the Plains Indians identified in this series as exhibiting periosteal reaction.

one sample, as are B and E since they represent essentially contemporaneous occupations. Note that the percent of individuals displaying rib lesions at the Mobridge F1 and F2 components is identical. The Sully components exhibit similar percentages. On the other hand, the mean number of ribs affected does show a tendency to increase through time (Mo 1 vs. Mo 2; t = 1.62, df = 13, p < .10; Sully A and D vs. Sully B and E; t = 1.50, df = 13, p < .10). Simple regression analysis plotting the mean number of ribs affected against date of occupation reveals no significant relationship (r^2 =.321; p = .24). Overall, the rib lesion rates are tightly clustered with a range of 4.3 to 8.6 percent for these four sites.

Pair-wise comparisons using the chi-square statistic for all 15 possible combinations of these sites and components indicate no significant differences at the .05 level.

An examination of the Arikara osteological material indicates that periostitis tends to localize on the middle and upper ribs (fig. 7). This pattern is similar to that observed by Kelley and Micozzi (1984). Pulmonary tuberculosis generally affects the upper lung (Anderson 1948:260; Stokes 1844:410), while the pneumococcal pneumonias show a preference for the lower quadrants (Stokes 1844; Heffron 1939; Cecil, Baldwin, and Larsen 1926). Thus, if rib periostitis is a response to subadjacent soft tissue inflammation, then it follows that most Arikara lung lesions were localized in the mid to upper lobes.

Figure 8 presents the percentage of individuals in each age category (exclusive of fetuses and neonates less than a year old) that exhibit inflammation of the ribs found in these sites. A low rate is observed for the early childhood years, followed

Table 2. Descriptive Statistics by Site

Site Name	Mean No. Ribs Affected (standard deviation)	No. Individuals with Rib Lesions	Percentage
Mobridge F1	2.8 (0.82)	5/76	6.6
Mobridge F2	5.4 (3.40)	10/152	6.6
Sully A, D	3.4 (1.67)	9/128	7.0
Sully B, E	5.7 (4.46)	6/70	8.6
Larson	6.0 (2.73)	12/244	4.9
Leavenworth	4.0 (1.00)	3/70	4.3
All Sites	4.6	46/740	6.2

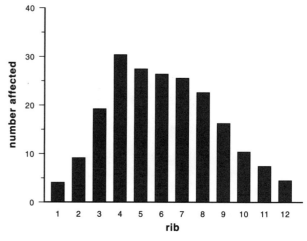

Fig. 8. Breakdown by age for individuals from Arikara samples exhibiting rib lesions.

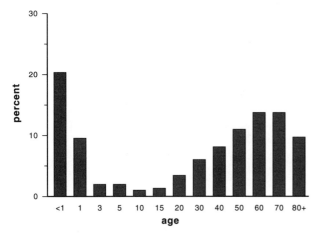

Fig. 9. Breakdown by age for individuals admitted with pneumonia during the preantibiotic era (Heffron 1939).

by a marked increase in adolescence. Rates dip during early adulthood and rise steadily from middle age onwards. It is impossible to establish whether an association exists between the rib lesions and the cause of death, but it is insightful to examine the age-at-risk statistics for common respiratory ailments.

In fig. 9 the age distribution of hospital admissions (>45,000) for pneumonia between 1921 and 1930 is presented (Heffron 1939). It is clear that early infancy and old age categories were at greatest risk in preantibiotic times. The adolescent group was largely spared.

Figure 10 illustrates the age-at-risk profiles for tuberculosis and pneumonia based on hospital admissions data (Heffron 1939) and the Arikara series. Comparing the age distribution of the hospital admissions for tuberculosis to that of the

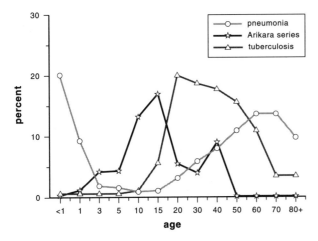

Fig. 10. Morbidity curves for pneumonia, tuberculosis, and the Arikara series.

Arikara series, a high adolescent peak is observed for both groups. This contrasts sharply with the low adolescent rates observed for pneumonia.

Interpretation

The detection of periostitis extending along the inner surfaces of the ribs in four large series of eighteenth and early nineteenth century Arikara Indians is consistent with the findings of Kelley and Micozzi (1984) in terms of appearance, location, and frequency. The lesions were encountered in 4–9 percent of all skeletons examined. There is some evidence to indicate that the periostitis rate may reach even higher levels in some samples. In a systematic survey of more than 1,600 individuals from the Terry Collection (National Museum of Natural History, Department of Anthropology), rib lesions were observed in nearly 22 percent (Charlotte Roberts, personal communication 1989). The Terry Collection consists primarily of lower-socioeconomic-status individuals, which suggests that under some conditions rib lesions can be quite common.

In the present study, the authors have identified only two respiratory conditions that existed at sufficient frequencies in the preantibiotic era that could account for such lesions: pulmonary tuberculosis and pneumonia (either lobar or bronchopneumonia). Pneumonia is a general term describing inflammation of the lung tissues. Pneumonia-causing bacteria and viruses may reach the lung via the airways or bloodstream. Infection via the respiratory tract is more common. Bacteria (including tuberculosis), viruses, mycoplasma, and fungi are known etiologies (Oswald and Fry 1962). The majority of bacterial pneumonias are caused by *Streptococcus pneumoniae,* which affects three males to every one female (Hoeprich 1972:311–313). Pneumonia can affect persons of any age, but in preantibiotic times it was more prominent in infants and older adults (Heffron 1939: fig. 10). Skeletal involvement of any kind is a rare complication of pneumonia (Hoeprich 1972; Jaffe 1972). When it is observed, it takes the form of septic arthritis (Hoeprich 72:317). Jaffe (1972:1049) states that 0.3 percent of pneumonia patients develop septic arthritis. Tuberculosis, on the other hand, tends to involve the skeletal system in chronic cases.

Which species of bacteria and viruses predictably elicit bone response in humans? Martin and White (1972:1190) list the causes of bacterial osteomyelitis as *Staphylococcus aureus* (80%), streptococcus sp. (10%), and salmonella sp. (5%). The remaining 5 percent result from miscellaneous bacteria including *Hemophilis influenzae,* Brucella sp., *Streptococcus pneumoniae,* Pseudomonas sp., and Bacteroides sp. Among the viruses capable of producing osteomyelitis are smallpox and rubella—neither of which is characterized by rib or pulmonary involvement (Ortner and Putschar 1981:227–229).

Tuberculosis may be an acute or chronic disease caused by either *Mycobacterium tuberculosis* (human type) or *Mycobacterium bovis* (bovine type). Other species known as "environmental mycobacteria" may also produce tuberculosislike disease (Clark et al. 1987). It is probably safe to assume that bovine tuberculosis via domesticated cattle was not yet present among eighteenth-century Arikara and that the human type, or pulmonary tuberculosis, accounted for the majority of the rib, spine, and other skeletal lesions observed. Infection via bison is a very unlikely possibility (Cockburn 1963:221; Van der Hoeden 1964:15).

The pathogenesis of human tuberculosis is complex, and a brief review of the subject is in order. When the tubercle bacilli enters the body (usually through inhalation of infectious droplets) for the first time, this is known as primary or first-infection tuberculosis. This may occur at any age but typically occurred in children in past centuries. The bacilli localize into one or several points in the lungs where they multiply and usually lead to tubercle formation. From the lungs, some bacilli will disseminate to the lymph nodes in the center of the chest where they also produce inflammation and enlargement (Burnet and White 1975). Collectively, the lung and lymph node lesions are referred to as the primary tuberculosis complex (Myers 1959:198). Typically, these lesions become encapsulated by fibrous or bony tissue, and thereafter the patient appears healthy. However, in some cases this primary complex fails to heal, and the bacilli continue to spread with high fatality rates arising from miliary tuberculosis, tubercular pneumonia, or meningitis. Reinfection or reactivation tuberculosis may occur months, years, or decades after the primary infection. In the past, children who survived the primary infection often experienced new risks upon entering adolescence, early adulthood, or even old age (Burnet and White 1975; Fishberg 1932:43; Pagel et al. 1964:472; Segal 1941:113). Resorption of the capsules or reexposure to the bacillus may lead to a more severe reaction than the primary complex due to the sensitization process. Figures 11 and 12 illustrate documented cases of pulmonary cavitations arising from secondary tuberculosis in wet tissue preparations. It will be noted that lung involvement can be quite extensive. It would seem that a variety of stressors—malnutrition, alcoholism, and associated illness—may promote reinfection and reactivation. Tuberculosis is unusual because the human defense mechanism is much more effective against primary infection than subsequent attacks (Myers 1959:211).

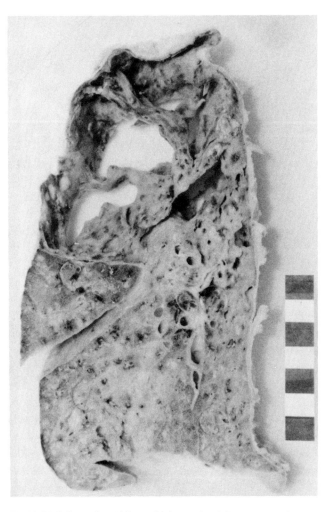

Fig. 11. Right lung of a middle-aged white male exhibiting acute pulmonary tuberculosis. Disease active at time of death. Note large cavitation. (Armed Forces Institute of Pathology 20484.)

In Table 2, it was noted that the percentage of individuals with rib lesions was essentially stable at Mobridge and Sully sites where multigenerational components existed. This pattern is consistent with the natural history of tuberculosis. Numerous historical accounts have demonstrated precipitous increases in tuberculosis rates subsequent to war, malnutrition, social disruption, crowded prison conditions, alcoholism, and the like (Burnet and White 1975; Dubos and Dubos 1952; Dubos and Hirsch 1965; Lester 1981:976; Segal 1941:115). Psychological stress has also been implicated, but this is difficult to quantify. There is an abundance of examples documenting the increase in the rate of tuberculosis following social disruption. During both World Wars, the mortality rate from tuberculosis rose dramatically in several European countries including England, Switzerland, and the Netherlands

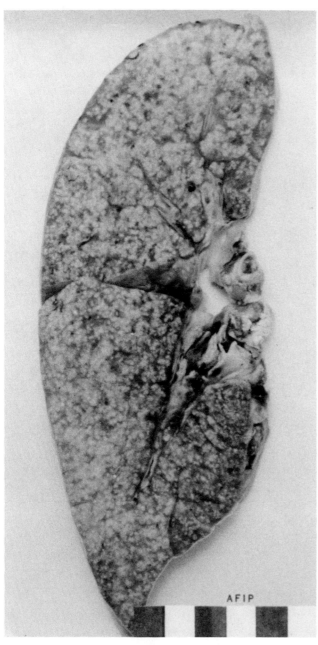

Fig. 12. Complete right lung of middle-aged white male exhibiting miliary tuberculosis. Specimen is permeated with whitish nodules, 1–2 mm in diameter. (Armed Forces Institute of Pathology 85525.)

(Dubos and Dubos 1952:234–235). Other forms of social disruption such as that seen in the late nineteenth-century Canadian Indians of the Qu'Appelle Valley Reserve exacted the highest toll of tuberculosis mortality ever recorded— 9,000 per 100,000 at its peak (Dubos and Dubos 1952:191). In another setting, tuberculosis claimed a death toll of 4,000 per 100,000 among Blacks in prisons in Pennsylvania and

Maryland in the early nineteenth century (Dubos and Dubos 1952:265). While table 2 supports the conclusion that tuberculosis morbidity and mortality remained high for several generations, the increasing number of ribs affected per individual over time might be interpreted (with the exception of Leavenworth) as increasing chronicity and resistance.

The eighteenth-century Arikara would also seem to be a classic example of a culture experiencing social upheaval with subsequent high morbidity and mortality from tuberculosis. However, it is certain that in addition to tuberculosis, other diseases, including smallpox, measles, treponemal infection, and gastrointestinal disorders contributed to the Arikaras' poor health. Palkovich (1981) examined two components at the Mobridge site and concluded that the demographic profiles were significantly different. She concluded that tuberculosis, treponemal infection, and a malnutrition-anemia condition accounted for this disparity. We agree that a demographic disparity exists, but it is almost certainly not due to the disorders suggested by Palkovich. Tuberculosis has caused high mortality for centuries among Europeans, Asians, and Africans under the appropriate conditions. It is highly unlikely that the Arikara (at Mobridge, in this case) would have adapted culturally and genetically to tuberculosis in the matter of one or a few generations. A much more likely explanation would be the introduction of viral infections, such as smallpox and measles, which would take a high toll among the first generation of Arikara to be exposed. Those who were exposed and survived would be subsequently immune. Those who were not exposed, or were born into the next generation, would be vulnerable to subsequent outbreaks. Thus, it follows that a smaller reservoir of susceptible hosts would be available by the time the Mobridge 2 component was in use and would account for the demographic disparity. In our view, the viral infections lead to a form of social disruption that exacerbated the lethal role of tuberculosis among these Indians.

A strong case has been made for a method of detecting respiratory ailments utilizing rib lesions. It would appear that the great majority of these cases are the result of pulmonary tuberculosis. This conclusion is based on the age distribution of individuals with rib lesions, the location within the rib cage of such lesions, and review of the medical literature and pathogenesis of tuberculosis versus other respiratory ailments. The medical literature is devoid of any mention of a common rib inflammation or pulmonary disease association. In dry bone, these lesions are readily detectable, but they would go completely undetected with conventional radiography in the living patient as well as during routine autopsies. The streptococcal pneumonias may produce bony response in the ribs, but this would be a rare occurrence.

Given the postcontact dates assigned to the Plains Indian samples examined here, this report does not resolve questions pertaining to the antiquity or prevalence of tuberculosis among pre-Columbian New World inhabitants. Nonetheless, these lesions do shed light on questions dealing with the dynamics of Indian-White contact during the eighteenth century, the attendant sociocultural disruption, and the impact of pulmonary tuberculosis.

References Cited

Anderson, W.A.D.
  1948   Pathology. St. Louis: C.V. Mosby.
Burnet, M., and D.O. White
  1975   Natural History of Infectious Disease. 4th ed. New York: Cambridge University Press.
Cecil, R.L., H.S. Baldwin, and N.P. Larsen
  1926   Clinical and Bacteriologic Study of 2000 Typed Cases of Lobar Pneumonia. *Transactions of American Physicians* 41:208.
Clark, G.A., M.A. Kelley, J.M. Grange, and C. Hill
  1987   The Evolution of Mycobacterial Disease in Human Populations: A Reevaluation. *Current Anthropology* 28(1):45–62.
Cockburn, A.
  1963   The Evolution and Eradication of Infectious Diseases. Baltimore: The Johns Hopkins Press.
Dubos, R., and J. Dubos
  1952   The White Plague: Tuberculosis, Man and Society. Boston: Little, Brown.
——, and J.G. Hirsch
  1965   Bacterial and Mycotic Infections of Man. 4th ed. Philadelphia: J.B. Lippincott.
Fishberg, M.
  1932   Pulmonary Tuberculosis. Vol. 1, Philadelphia: Lea and Febiger.
Heffron, R.
  1939   Pneumonia. New York: The Commonwealth Fund.
Hoeprich, P.D.
  1972   Bacterial Pneumonias. In Infectious Diseases. P.D. Hoeprich, ed. New York: Harper and Row.
Jaffe, H.L.
  1972   Metabolic, Degenerative and Inflammatory Disease of Bones and Joints. Philadelphia: Lea and Febiger.
Kelley, M.A.
  1980   Disease and Environment: A Comparative Study of Three Early American Indian Skeletal Populations. (Unpublished Ph.D. Dissertation, Case Western Reserve University, Cleveland, Ohio.)
——, and M.S. Micozzi
  1984   Rib Lesions and Chronic Pulmonary Tuberculosis. *American Journal of Physical Anthropology* 65:381–386.
——, P.S. Sledzik, and S.P. Murphy
  1987   Health, Demographics, and Physical Constitution in 17th-Century Rhode Island Indians. *Man in the Northeast* 34:1–25.
Key, P.J.
  1983   Craniometric Relationships Among Plains Indians. *University of Tennessee, Department of Anthropology Report* 34.
Lester, W.
  1981   Tuberculosis. In Medical Microbiology and Infectious Diseases. A.I. Braude, ed. Philadelphia: W.B. Saunders.
Martin, R.R., and A.C. White
  1972   Osteomyelitis. Pp. 1189–1198 in Infectious Diseases. P.D. Hoeprich, ed. New York: Harper and Row.
Myers, J.A.
  1959   Tuberculosis. In Diseases of the Chest Including the Heart. J.A. Myers, ed. Springfield, Ill.: C.C. Thomas.
Ortner, D.J., and W.G.J. Putchar
  1981   Identification of Pathological Conditions in Human Skeletal Remains. *Smithsonian Contributions to Anthropology* 28.
Oswald, N.C., and J. Fry
  1962   Diseases of the Respiratory System. Philadelphia: F.A. Davis.
Pagel, W.F., A.H. Simmonds, N. MacDonald, and E. Nassau
  1964   Pulmonary Tuberculosis. 4th ed. New York: Oxford University Press.
Palkovich, A.M.
  1981   Demography and Disease Patterns in a Protohistoric Plains Group: A Study of the Mobridge Site (39WW1). In Progress in Skeletal Biology of Plains Populations. R.L. Jantz and D.H. Ubelaker, eds. *Plains Anthropologist Memoir* 17:71–84.
Ramenofsky, A.
  1982   The Archaeology of Population Collapse: Native American Response to the Introduction of Infectious Disease. (Unpublished Ph.D. Dissertation, University of Washington, Seattle.)
Segal, J.
  1941   Diseases of the Respiratory Tract. New York: Oxford University Press.
Stokes, W.
  1844   Diseases of the Chest. 2d ed. Philadelphia: E. Barrington and G.D. Haswell.
van der Hoeden, J.
  1964   Zoonoses. Amsterdam: Elsevier.

○ ○ ○

CHAPTER 10

Otitis Media, Mastoiditis, and Infracranial Lesions in Two Plains Indian Children

ROBERT W. MANN, DOUGLAS W. OWSLEY, AND KARL J. REINHARD

One disease condition that is common to nearly all children is otitis media, also known as middle ear disease. Although most people speak of it as a middle ear "infection," other causes such as neoplasm (tumor) can result in manifestations and symptoms mimicking an infectious process. This paper presents findings related to osseous lesions in two Indian children, approximately three to five years of age, who died with otitis media and infracranial lesions. Through macroscopic and radiographic analysis, it is possible to show that one child probably suffered from tuberculosis and the other from histiocytosis X. From an epidemiological and historical perspective, these determinations in skeletons from the Plains contribute to improved understanding of the evolution of infectious and tumorous disease in North America.

The two children reflect different skeletal manifestations of otitis media and infracranial lesions. Although the differential diagnosis of disease in archaeological skeletons must be tempered with caution, the morphology and distribution of bone lesions in these children provide evidence for distinguishing infectious from tumorous disease. These cases serve two basic purposes: first, to provide detailed descriptions of the lesions, and second, to stimulate new thought and perspectives on the epidemiology, history, and geographic distribution of infectious and tumorous diseases in the Plains. In addition, these unusual examples demonstrate the contribution of skeletal remains to improved understanding of disease in prehistoric populations.

Otitis Media

Otitis media is a disease of the middle ear that commonly occurs secondary to an infectious process (frequently during the winter) in the upper respiratory tract (Casselbrant et al. 1985; Henderson et al. 1982). Clinical studies have shown that susceptibility varies by age and racial affiliation. Otitis media is common in infants after the neonatal period (birth to 28 days), with declining incidence after the first year of life. A study of 2,565 children living in Boston, Massachusetts, revealed that 9 percent had at least one episode of otitis media by age three months, and 65 percent experienced the condition by 24 months of age (Teele et al. 1984). Using otoscopy (examining the ear with an instrument), 205 of 970 infants (21.1%) in a neonatal pathology ward were diagnosed as having otitis media (Pestalozza 1984).

High frequencies of otitis media have been reported in Indians (Jaffe 1969; Gregg, Steele, and Halzhueter 1965), Eskimos (Kaplan, Fleshman, and Bender 1973), and Australian aborigines (Hudson 1986). In fact, otitis media has been listed as the leading disease among Indian and Eskimo groups since 1969 (Wiet et al. 1980). Conversely, American Whites (Wiet 1979) and Blacks (Griffith 1979) experience low frequencies of this disease. Anatomic (morphology of the Eustachian tube) and genetic factors might be responsible for racial differences in the incidence (Daniel et al. 1988).

Some researchers have attributed the prevalence of middle ear disease in Indian and Eskimo groups to poor socioeconomic conditions (Cambron, Galbraith, and Kong 1965; Reed, Struve, and Maynard 1967). However, subsequent researchers, including Reed and colleagues, have failed to demonstrate a relationship between the prevalence of otitis media and climate, family size, sanitary conditions, or crowding (Ferrer 1985; Shaw et al. 1981; Van Cauwenberge 1985). As noted by Tos, Poulsen, and Borch (1979), otitis media does not seem to be a "poor man's" disease.

A general decrease in the severity of acute otitis media has occurred since the 1970s in many industrialized nations. Possible factors responsible for this decrease include prompt medical treatment, better general health, improved social conditions, lower virulence of responsible organisms, and treatment with antibiotics (Phelps and Lloyd 1990; Scott and Jackler 1989). In the past, the condition seems to have been more severe and frequently complicated by acute labyrinthitis, acute mastoiditis (inflammation often followed by destruction of the mastoid antrum or process), or intracranial sepsis (Phelps and Lloyd 1990). A 10-year (1974 to 1983) study in Israel found that, although still a serious and potentially lethal disease, acute mastoiditis is an infrequent complication of acute otitis media (Rosen, Ophir, and Marshak 1986).

The pathogenesis of otitis media usually follows an event, such as allergy or infection, that causes congestion of the respiratory mucosa, obstruction of the isthmus, and accumulation of mucosal secretions of the middle ear (Bluestone and Klein 1988). In individuals with low resistance or in whom the infection has reached a state of high virulence, the disease quickly spreads throughout the temporal bone, resulting in a local inflammatory response and generalized systemic changes (Pendergrass, Parsons, and Hodes 1956). Proliferation of bacteria in the middle ear leads to suppurative (producing pus) and symptomatic otitis media. Mastoid disease, a possible sequela to otitis media, has been associated with pneumonia, influenza, tuberculosis, and exanthemata. The spread of bacteria (e.g., *Staphylococcus aureus*) may result in hearing loss, osseous lesions, and rapid destruction of the mastoid antrum and air cells (mastoiditis), tegmen tympani, and surrounding bone within a few days. Perforation of the tegmen or pyramid may lead to epidural abscess and death despite antibiotic therapy (Stanievich et al. 1981).

Prehistoric and historic archaeological examples of otitis media have been reported from Egypt (Moodie 1931), Iran (Rathbun and Mallin 1977), Arizona (Titche et al. 1981), Tennessee (Dowd 1989), and North and South Dakota (Gregg, Steele, and Halzhueter 1965). Gregg and colleagues (1965) found evidence of altered pneumatization in approximately 47 percent of 417 temporal bones (dry specimens) from South Dakota. This frequency suggests a high infection rate during infancy and early childhood.

Histiocytosis X

Histiocytosis X (the X signifying of unknown origin) is the terminology used as a comprehensive category for three conditions: eosinophilic granuloma, Hand-Schuller-Christian disease, and Letterer-Siwe disease. These conditions are commonly believed to be expressions of the same basic pathologic process. Eosinophilic granuloma is the mildest form of the disease, which may present as single or multiple osseous lesions. Hand-Schuller-Christian disease is the most varied form, presenting as chronic disseminated osseous lesions seen predominantly in children, although it may be found in adolescents and, rarely, adults. Letterer-Siwe disease is the acute form and has a poor prognosis (Resnick and Niwayama 1988). It is most commonly seen in children below the age of three years. Histiocytosis X occurs primarily in infants, children, and young adults and is more common in males by a ratio of nearly 2:1 (Barnes and Peel 1990). Aural and temporal bone involvement are common during the course of the disease.

Tuberculosis

Tuberculosis is disseminated by two sources of infection: inhalation or ingestion of the human (*Mycobacterium tuberculosis*) or bovine (*Mycobacterium bovus*) form of the tubercle bacillus. In the past, the second form was responsible for approximately 20 percent of all skeletal cases, especially in children (Resnick and Niwayama 1988). Skeletal tuberculosis (Pott's disease of the spine), a condition most familiar to paleopathologists, is one manifestation of the disease. Invasion of the temporal bone by tubercle bacilli may result in tuberculous otitis media, a condition rarely encountered in modern groups (only 10 cases in children were reported between 1960 and 1977; MacAdam and Rubio 1977). The tubercle bacillus is present universally and, although everyone is exposed to it at one time or another, not everyone contracts the disease. Factors including host immunity, age, general hygiene, nutrition, sanitation, population size (e.g., crowding), and geography affect the incidence and virulence of tuberculosis (Buikstra 1981; Daniel 1981).

The frequency of tuberculosis, although disproportionately distributed throughout the world, has declined dramatically with the advent of chemotherapy. The rate of tuberculosis in the United States decreased steadily until 1985, at which time it leveled off, but in 1986, the trend reversed (Rieder et al. 1989). Incidences of smear-positive pulmonary tuberculosis by continent are highest for Africa (165/100,000) and Asia (110/100,000) and lowest for North America (7/100,000) (Styblo and Rouillon 1981). Nearly four million new infectious cases of tuberculosis develop worldwide each year. Although skeletal tuberculosis can affect individuals at any age, it is rare in the first year of life. The interval between 5 and 14 years is the "favored age" for tuberculosis in children (Smith and Marquis 1987).

In 1985, of 1,261 patients in the United States with childhood tuberculosis, 36.2 percent were Black, 27.3 percent were Hispanic White, 20.1 percent were non-Hispanic White, 12.7 percent were Asian or Pacific Islander, and 3.7 percent were Native American (Hayden, Bloch, and Snider 1987). Of the 22,170 known-race patients with tuberculosis in the United States, 397 (2%) were Indians and Eskimos. The incidence for this group was 25 per 100,000, or 4.4 times the rate for Whites (5.7 per 100,000) (Gregg 1987). Although Native Americans accounted for high frequencies of reported tuberculosis cases in Alaska (71%) and South Dakota (62%), these groups comprise only 14 percent and 7 percent of the Alaska and South Dakota populations, respectively. Lester (1986) reports that tuberculosis has an inverse relationship to the standard of living within a society. The frequency of the disease increases during times of social catastrophe and decreases with improvements in the standard of living and nutrition. Historically, Indian and Eskimo children have been at high risk for contracting tuberculosis.

Mycobacterial tuberculosis of the musculoskeletal system occurs from hematogenous (blood stream) spread and usually involves the spine (Pott's disease) or a single bone or joint (Day et al. 1991). The joints of the lower limb are more commonly affected than those of the upper limb. Examples of skeletal tuberculosis have been reported from prehistoric and historic archaeological sites in North America (Buikstra 1981).

Sites Represented by the Two Skeletons

The 25DK10 cemetery was located on a 300-foot high bluff overlooking the floodplain of the Missouri River one mile northwest of the Big Village site (25DK5) in Dakota county, Nebraska. Looters discovered this and other Omaha cemeteries and were collecting burial artifacts. University of Nebraska archaeologists alerted to this destruction organized two salvage crews in the late 1930s and early 1940s to excavate burials and preserve skeletal remains and artifacts from further plundering (Reinhard et al. 1990). The more than 60 skeletons recovered represented historic Omahas of both sexes and all ages buried about 1780 to 1820. Bone preservation was excellent, although many burials had been disturbed by previous excavations and by burrowing animals. One of the examples described in this report, a child aged 4.5 to 5.5 years and designated Individual 1 (Burial 47), came from this site.

The child was buried in an extended, supine position and shared a single burial pit with another subadult. The burial pit, which had been disturbed by looters, measured 26 inches long and 16 inches wide. The skeleton, found 68 inches below surface, is nearly complete (missing only portions of the hands and feet) and well preserved. Staining resulting from copper salts is visible on both temporals and on most of the long bones of the arms and the fibulae. Green staining on the temporal bones and mummified adhering soft tissue (portions of the ears) resulted from copper coil ear ornaments. As was typical of many Omaha burials from 25DK10, a large number of burial objects were placed with this individual, including seven copper bracelets, 14 copper pendants, one silver pendant, five copper coils, one lead band, one iron handle, a pail lid, and trade beads.

Age was determined by the degree of dental development (Moorrees, Fanning, and Hunt 1963a, 1963b) and lengths of the long bones (Merchant and Ubelaker 1977). The crowns of the first permanent molars are complete and the roots are approximately half developed, suggesting 4.5 to 5.5 years of age. A maximum length measurement of the right femur is 180 millimeters, which is consistent with the estimated age based on the dentition.

During a salvage operation at the Cotter-Hutson site (34CU41) in Custer County, Oklahoma, Don G. Wyckoff of the Oklahoma archaeological Survey recovered the skeleton of a child of 2.5 to 3.5 years of age (Burial 2, designated

Individual 2 in this report). Artifacts from the surface and associated refuse pits included cordmarked and plain pottery with caliche and grit temper, grinding stones and milling basins, shell disk beads, and small projectile points of the Young, Scallorn, Washita, Fresno, and Harrel types (Keith, Snow, and Snow 1971). The site was occupied by people of the Custer focus, a prehistoric farming and hunting-gathering culture of western Oklahoma (Bell and Baerris 1951; Buck 1959). Radiocarbon dates for other Custer focus sites indicate dates between A.D. 800 and 1100 (Bell 1968; Brooks 1989). The flexed burial was found lying on its left side in a small circular refuse pit. All major bones were recovered with the exception of the hands and feet.

An age estimate was based on the stage of dental development of both the deciduous and permanent teeth. Complete crown and partial root formation of the permanent first molars (6-year molars) suggest an age of 2.5 to 3.5 years (Moorrees et al. 1963a, 1963b). These teeth are still within their bony crypts and have not fully erupted through the jaw. The deciduous teeth show mild attrition and no carious lesions.

Skeletal Pathology of Individual 1

Individual 1 exhibits mixed lesions in the cranium, mandible, ribs, vertebrae, and long bones. The temporals have resorptive lesions that had caused considerable erosion of both ear canals (fig. 1). The left temporal bone has a resorptive defect measuring 34 by 14 millimeters involving the petrous process (tympanic plate and antrum entirely destroyed) and mastoid process, with destruction of the bone superior and posterior to the external auditory meatus (fig. 1, bottom). The ectocranial margin of the defect is remodeled, beveled, and ringed with irregular scar tissue that is radiographically visible as sclerosis. Internally, there is evidence of mild osseous remodeling in the form of irregular scar tissue along the margin of the defect. Radiographs of the mastoid process exhibit coalescence of the air cells. There is no endocranial or ectocranial evidence of active fibrous bone. The extent of osseous remodeling (healing) indicates a prolonged condition. The squamosal suture is nearly completely obliterated, a condition possibly related to infection.

The right temporal bone also shows resorption of the petrous process, with complete destruction (by otitis media) of the tympanic plate and mastoid antrum. The external auditory meatus is eroded and the meatal opening is enlarged superiorly. The defect measures 24 by 10 millimeters, with an irregular, porous margin of reactive bone superior and poste-

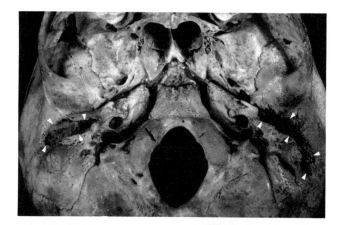

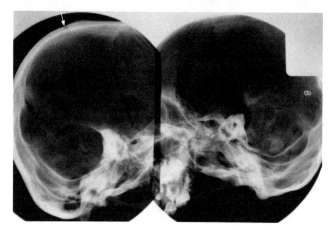

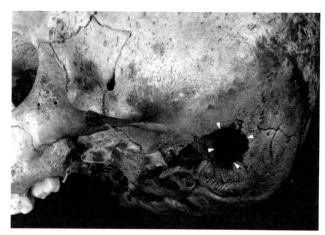

Fig. 1. Bilateral mastoiditis in Individual 1 showing (top) resorption (arrowheads) of both auditory canals. Center, radiograph showing resorptive lesions in the temporal bones (otitis media) and lytic lesion in the right parietal (arrow). Bottom, large resorptive lesion (arrowheads) in the left temporal bone.

rior to the external auditory meatus. The mastoid process is not noticeably affected. The squamosal suture is completely obliterated.

The occipital exhibits marrow hyperplasia (porotic hyperostosis), which is commonly attributed to anemia (Angel 1964, 1966; Macadam 1989). The right parietal exhibits what superficially appears to be asymmetrically positioned porotic hyperostosis. The "spongy" lesions are most pronounced in the occipital and right parietal, with mild involvement along the lambdoidal suture. The right parietal also exhibits a small perforating lesion (fig. 2), measuring 12 by 6 millimeters (outer cortex) and 4 by 2 millimeters (inner cortex), located near the vertex, approximately 3 centimeters lateral to the sagittal suture. This ovoidal lesion has a mildly raised external margin of reactive bone, sclerosis, and is bounded anteriorly by an irregularly shaped but well-demarcated mound of spongy bone. When viewed ectocranially, the defect is inwardly beveled and exhibits mild vascularization (tiny pits reflecting an increase in the number of blood vessels).

A radiograph (fig. 3) of the right parietal reveals that the outer table of bone beneath the spongy bone is intact, and there is no evidence of diploic expansion (that is, porotic hyperostosis). Macroscopic and radiographic examination of the right parietal indicates that the area of raised bone is more consistent with a periosteal (inflammatory), rather than a diploic, reaction to the adjacent lytic lesion, possibly reflecting a hemangioma. The orbital plates exhibit mild cribra orbitalia, a pitting and thickening condition frequently attributed to anemia. Mild porosity is also visible on both cheekbones.

In regard to the mandible, the right condyloid process is slightly larger than the left and exhibits a small resorptive lesion (probably healed) at the anterior margin of the articular

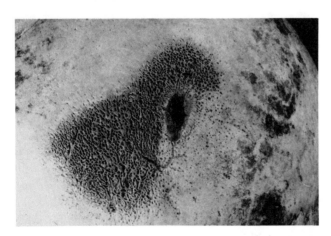

Fig. 2. Close-up of the lytic lesion and porous reactive bone in the right parietal (Individual 1).

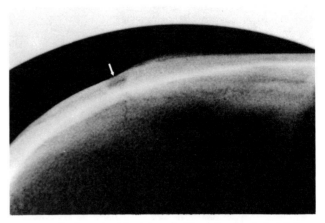

Fig. 3. Lateral radiograph of the right parietal bone showing the lytic lesion (arrow) bounded anteriorly by periosteal reactive bone (Individual 1).

capsule. The circular lesion measures 4 by 3 millimeters, lacks sclerosis, and has a well-defined margin and a smooth floor. The depth of the lesion measures 2 millimeters and is confined to the cortex. The neck of the right ramus is thicker (healed periostitis) mediolaterally than the left neck.

The infracranial skeleton exhibits numerous active focal areas of osteolysis and laminated ("onionskin") periosteal new bone. Laminated reactive bone is created by concentric planes of ossification beyond the cortex interspersed with radiographically lucent zones between the new bone lamellae (Ragsdale, Madewell, and Sweet 1981). Affected bones are the tibiae, fibulae, ulnae, right humerus and radius, left ribs 4, 7, 9, and 10, and right ribs 2, 4, 7, 8, 11, and 12. Vertebrae C6, T12, L1, and the arches of three lower thoracic vertebrae (numbers unknown) also exhibit lesions. The ribs and tibiae best represent laminated new bone. The scapulae, clavicles, os coxae, and hands and feet were unaffected as were the epiphyseal plates.

Ten left and nine right ribs are present for examination. Of these, four left (nos. 4, 7, 9, and 10) and six right ribs (nos. 2, 4, 7, 9, 11, and 12) (fig. 4) exhibit active periostitis and/or multiple lytic, expansatile lesions. The lesions affect both the inner (visceral) and outer surfaces of the ribs, with perforation mostly confined to the outer surfaces. Laminated new bone has resulted in mediolateral thickening and "clubbing" of the vertebral segments of three left (nos. 7, 9, and 10) and three right (nos. 8, 11, and 12) ribs.

Most affected is the fourth right rib, which exhibits five ovoidal cortical perforations, four of which are in the inner surface, confined to a 12-millimeter area and a small sequestrum (loose dead-bone fragment) in the medullary cavity. The smallest perforation is on the outer surface, which lacks evidence of periostitis. The perforations are associated with active

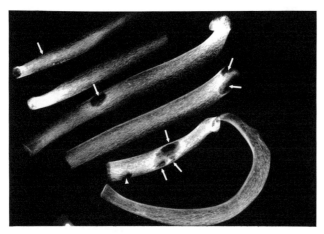

Fig. 4. Right ribs (Individual 1) showing periostitis and multiple resorptive lesions (arrows; arrowhead indicates postmortem breakage).

periostitis, in some instances resulting in eccentric expansion of the outer cortex, with concomitant perforation of the inner surfaces in the right fourth rib and eleventh left rib. The lytic lesions in the cortex range in size from 3 to 7 millimeters.

The right seventh rib also exhibits a large resorptive lesion situated a few centimeters posterior to its midshaft. The rib is broken and missing bone (postmortem) at the posterior margin of the lesion. The ovoidal expansatile lesion is located along the inferior half of the outer surface of the rib, measures 13 by 8 millimeters, and is surrounded by a narrow "capsule" of cortical bone. The medial cortex exhibits 2 millimeters of laminated new bone. The lesion has a smooth, dense floor, and the inner cortex opposite the larger lesion exhibits an ovoidal resorptive lesion measuring 5 by 3 millimeters. The macroscopic appearance of the defects indicates osteolysis, originating either in the medullary cavity or on the inner cortex, followed by outer involvement of the rib cortices.

Seven vertebrae exhibit resorptive lesions of either the centrum or arch (fig. 5). Of 18 vertebrae present for examination, three exhibit moderate to severe destruction of the bodies, and four have lytic lesions in the arches. Lytic lesions are present in the cervical, thoracic, and lumbar vertebrae.

Of the cervical vertebrae, only C6 shows destruction of the anterior body. The lesion, which was confined largely to the right half, destroyed approximately half the body. The margins of the defect are irregular, with little evidence of remodeling. Approximately 6 millimeters of bone remain along the posterior centrum.

Three lower thoracic vertebrae (numbers indeterminate) present lytic lesions in the vertebral arches. Lesions are visible in two right vertebral arches and one left. One vertebra shows

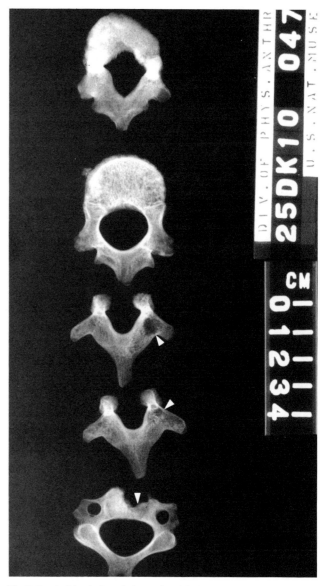

Fig. 5. Cervical (top), thoracic (second and third), and lumbar (fourth and fifth) vertebrae showing resorptive lesions (arrowheads) of the bodies and arches (Individual 1).

destruction of the right superior articular facet; the right inferior articular facet is destroyed in a second vertebra. The twelfth thoracic vertebra shows extensive destruction and flattening (vertebra plana) of the inferior body and mild cortical resorption of the pedicles (the superior end-plate of the opposing first lumbar vertebra also exhibits mild destruction). The bodies present no evidence of sclerosis. The lesion resulted in a groove extending anteroposteriorly that would have involved the posterior longitudinal ligament and, possibly, the spinal cord.

Lumbar vertebra 1 shows mild destruction of the superior end-plate and reactive bone encircling the left Hahn's cleft, the vascular opening in children's vertebral bodies. A cauliflower-shaped extension of bone measuring 3 millimeters is located anterior to this cleft. The right inferior vertebral arch exhibits active periostitis. The third lumbar vertebra has a small perforation with an irregular and raised margin in the inferior surface of the arch near its convergence.

The cortex of the right tibia is thickened anteriorly and exhibits vascularization and laminated periosteal new bone. Macroscopically, the outer cortex suggests only a mild, active periosteal response; however, radiographs reveal an ill-defined intramedullary lucency (early-stage lesion) bounded laterally by laminated new bone in the proximal third of the shaft. The lesion exhibits minimal sclerosis, has mildly eroded the endosteum (that is, scalloping), and does not communicate with the outer cortex. The lucency measures 20 by 12 millimeters and is oriented along the long axis of the shaft. The left tibia exhibits an ill-defined intramedullary radiolucency near the midshaft, periosteal new bone, and increased vascularization, also confined to the anterior shaft.

The diaphyses of both humeri show active periostitis along the posterior and lateral surfaces of the distal shafts. The pattern of periosteal new bone is symmetrical, and the new bone is loosely attached, pitted, and darker in color than the surrounding normal cortex. There is a separate island of periostitis on the medial portion of the diaphysis of the right humerus immediately above its midshaft. This new bone is also immature and easily flakes away from the underlying cortex. The circumference of the left humeral diaphysis is smaller than that of the right humerus (most visible on radiograph). Radiographic examination reveals an ovoidal, eccentric, intramedullary resorptive lesion measuring 15 by 6 millimeters near the medial cortex of the left humerus (fig. 6). The lesion has a narrow radiopaque margin, with a narrow sclerotic band encircling the defect.

The proximal diaphysis of both ulnae and anterior midshaft of the right radius (in supination) are thickened and exhibit localized periostitis and vascularization. The margin of periosteal new bone on the right radius has remodeled and is indistinct (healed and faded), whereas those on the ulnae are distinct from the surrounding bone. The radius and ulnae exhibit eccentric (that is, confined to one surface) thickening and expansion of their diaphyses. A radiograph of the right radius reveals two resorptive intramedullary lesions measuring 8 by 5 millimeters and 8 by 2 millimeters at the midshaft (fig. 7). The lesions exhibit no sclerosis beneath the areas of periosteal new bone. The lesions resulted in focal resorption

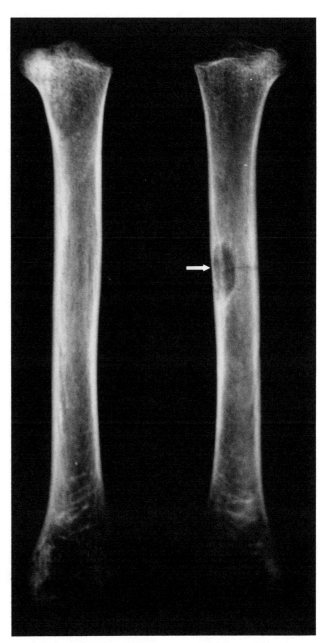

Fig. 6. Humeri of Individual 1 with an intramedullary resorptive lesion (arrow) in the cortex of the left humerus (breakage across the lytic lesion is artifactual).

of both the medullary cavity and endosteal surface (scalloping) of the diaphysis. Neither lesion perforated the outer cortex. The bones of the right forearm (radius = 114 millimeters, ulna = 115 millimeters) are longer than those of the left forearm (radius = 111 millimeters, ulna = 113 millimeters), and the humeri are equal in length. The left radius and both ulnae present no evidence of resorptive lesions.

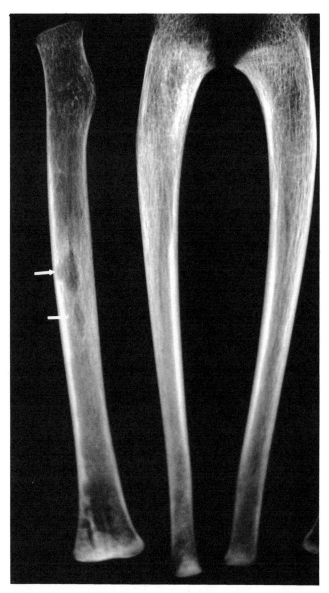

Fig. 7. Radiograph of the ulnae and right radius with two intramedullary lytic lesions (arrows) (Individual 1).

The distal halves of the fibulae are thickened and porous. Involvement of the diaphyses is eccentric, with no evidence of draining sinuses. The pattern of periostitis is symmetrical and confined to the medial surfaces opposing the tibiae. Radiographs reveal no evidence of resorptive lesions.

CORTICAL THICKNESS AND BONE DENSITOMETRY

Plain-film radiographic examination of the long bones for pathological features gave the impression of some cortical thinning (osteopenia). Therefore, the possibility of decreased bone mass was assessed quantitatively through measurements of cortical thickness and densitometry of the femur.

Densitometric measurements of certain appendicular bones are often used as a means of identifying osteoporosis. Osteoporosis is a condition of decreased bone mass as a result of any of a number of metabolic, disease, or nutritional factors. Loss of the bone in the axial skeleton is disproportionately greater than in the appendicular skeleton (Frost 1963). Thus, if visible changes are evident in the long bones, the loss of volume is more dramatic in other areas of the skeleton.

Table 1 presents radiographically determined measurements of cortical thickness for the 25DK10 child and for nine other children from three protohistoric Northern Plains village sites. These children were selected for comparison solely on the basis of age and comparability of femur length (an approximate diaphyseal length of 177 millimeters). Standardized posterior-anterior and lateral views were taken of each femur using a Kodak, Lanex, fine, single-screen cassette and Kodak single-emulsion ortho M film. Three measurements were determined for each view: T (total subperiosteal diameter), M (medullary cavity width), and C (cortical thickness calculated as C = T − M) (after Garn 1970). The medullary cavity width at midshaft is absolutely and relatively larger in both projections compared to the reference sample. The average cortical thickness of the control sample in both dimensions is exactly 1 millimeter larger than noted for Individual 1.

Measurements of bone mineral content (BMC) were determined for each femur at the midshaft and the femoral neck using a digital bone densitometer (table 2) (Norland Corporation Model 1768, with collimator #4 and a bone edge search threshold setting of 75%; Norland Corporation 1986). The densitometer determines bone mineral content using a single photon absorption technique. A collimated beam of monoenergetic photons passes through the bone, and the resulting transmission attenuation is monitored with a photon detector. The absorption curve is integrated to obtain a value related to the total bone mineral per unit length of the bone being scanned. The data reported in the printout are the bone width (BW), the bone mineral content in grams per centimeter (BMC), and the ratio BMC/BW (grams/cm²). The BW measurement represents the width dimension of the bone being scanned and is approximately equivalent to the value of T, as measured in the posterior-anterior view with plain-film radiography. The ratio BMC/BW is a measure of density of the bone. The densitometer was calibrated by scanning a calibration phantom having a known BMC.

Four scans were taken at each site and averaged to obtain the best estimates for the two sites on each femur. The values

Table 1. Femoral Cortical Thickness and Mineral Content Measured by Radiography

	N	Femur Length Mean (mm) S.D.	Midshaft Radiography Posterior-Anterior View		
			T Mean (mm) S.D.	M Mean (mm) S.D.	C Mean (mm) S.D.
25DK10	1	177.0	12.1	8.1	4.0
39CA4 (n = 1)	9	177.4	12.6	7.6	5.0
39SL4 (n = 5)		15.0	0.7	0.6	0.7
39WW1 (n = 3)					

			Medio–Lateral View		
			T Mean (mm) S.D.	M Mean (mm) S.D.	C Mean (mm) S.D.
25DK10	1		12.6	8.4	4.2
39CA4 (n = 1)	9		13.4	8.2	5.2
39SL4 (n = 5)			1.0	0.6	0.7
39WW1 (n = 3)					

Table 2. Femoral Cortical Thickness and Mineral Content Measured by Densitometry

	N	Femur Length Mean (mm) S.D.	Midshaft Densitometry		
			BW Mean (mm) S.D.	BMC Mean (g/cm) S.D.	BMW/BW Mean (g/cm^2) S.D.
25DK10)	1	177.0	12.6	0.78	0.62
39CA4 (n = 1)	9	177.4	12.9	1.02	0.79
39SL4 (n = 5)		15.0	0.7	0.14	0.09
39WW1 (n = 3)					

			Femoral Neck Densitometry		
			BW Mean (mm) S.D.	BMW Mean (g/cm) S.D.	BMC/BW Mean (g/cm^2) S.D.
25DK10	1		18.9	0.71	0.37
39CA4 (n = 1)	8		18.2	0.92	0.51
39SL4 (n = 4)			0.11	0.14	0.10
39WW1 (n = 3)					

for Individual 1 appear in table 1, compared to the overall mean values for the nine reference femora. (No femoral neck scan was taken for one control specimen because of postmortem breakage in the neck region.)

As table 2 shows, the midshaft and femoral neck values for BMC and BMC/BW of Individual 1 are nearly two standard deviations less than the age-matched reference sample. In fact, for both scan sites, Individual 1 has the lowest values recorded in this series. The range varied between a low of 0.62 (midshaft BMC/BW for Individual 1) and a high of 0.92; the femoral neck low was 0.37 (BMC/BW for Individual 1), compared to a high of 0.70. These density measurements parallel the pattern described for the cortical thickness data. Figure 8 shows a midshaft scan of the 25DK10 femur and four reference specimens using computed tomography. The two-dimensionsal images of the tomogram illustrate individual differences in cross-sectional areas of the cortical bone and the medullary cavity. Note that the 25DK10 femur is completely circular, lacking development of the linea aspera, a prominent muscle attachment site on the posterior femur.

The femur of this child exhibits a thinner cortex, sparce trabeculae, and diminished mineral content relative to other children of similar age and stature. These physical signs reflect osteoporosis of the skeleton. This condition can be attributed to several factors related to the disease process including poor nutrition and inactivity. As the disease progressed, the child experienced a loss of appetite resulting in reduced nutritional intake and increased immobility. Reduced cortical thickness and enlarged medullary cavities due to increased endosteal resorption are characteristic of malnutrition and malabsorption (Garn 1970). Furthermore, histomorphometric and bone densitometry studies of paraplegics and bedridden patients have demonstrated significant losses of trabecular and cortical bone within relatively short periods of time (Chantraine, Nusgens, and Lapiere 1986; Mazess and Whedon 1983; Stout

1982). Immobilization results in muscle atrophy, lower bone mineral density, cortical porosity, and greater endosteal diameters (Doyle, Brown, and Lachance 1970; Smith and Gilligan 1989). Loss of compact bone occurs at a slower rate than for trabecular bone. Both increased osteoclastic resorption and decreased bone formation are responsibile for bone loss with immobilization.

Skeletal Pathology of Individual 2

The skull exhibits a resorptive defect (that is, exaural abscess) measuring 5 by 4 millimeters in the outer temporal cortex immediately superior to the right mastoid process (illustrated in Owsley 1989:132). This lesion communicates with a second perforating lesion in the tegmen and the mastoid process, signifying mastoiditis. The defect in the outer vault has an irregular margin and is bordered by porous reactive bone measuring approximately 1.5 centimeters in diameter (some bone may have been destroyed postmortem). A radiograph reveals a lucency in the mastoid antrum surrounded by dense (sclerotic) bone. The mandible is macroscopically normal.

A gross pathologic and radiographic examination (Keith, Snow, and Snow 1971) suggests that the premortem changes in the right temporal bone could have resulted from a coalescent mastoiditis or a cholesteatoma, leading to an epidural abscess. Meningitis and subdural empyema frequently accompany epidural abscesses, each of which usually causes the death of the untreated patient. Any of these complications could have resulted in death.

The distal left humerus exhibits a large resorptive lesion in the metaphysis and coronoid and radial fossae (fig. 9). The defect is roughly confined to the area within the articular capsule, measures 17 by 14 millimeters, and has smooth, sloping borders. When viewed from below, the lesion has an irregular and porous floor of reactive bone with perforation into the medullary cavity. The cortex superior to the lesion is healed and thickened anteroposteriorly (2.5 millimeters thicker than the right humerus). Radiographs reveal regional sclerosis (thickened reactive bone) associated with the resorptive lesion (fig. 10).

The proximal left ulna exhibits two ovoidal resorptive lesions measuring 9 by 6 millimeters and 8 by 5 millimeters. The larger (cortical) defect is situated immediately superior to the radial notch, and the smaller defect is on the semilunar notch. The smaller lesion has eroded the subchondral bone (the articular surface) and exposed the trabeculae. There is no evidence of inflammation or sclerosis associated with the defects. Although the lesion above the radial notch was con-

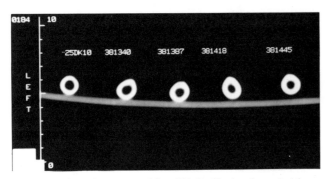

Fig. 8. Computerized tomogram of the midshafts of five length-matched femora including Individual 1 (25DK10). The femora are in a prone position.

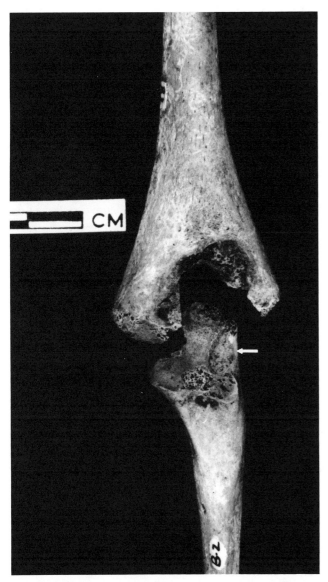

Fig. 9. Left humerus and ulna of Individual 2 with a large resorptive lesion in the metaphysis (arrow points to a healed ovoidal lesion in the ulna).

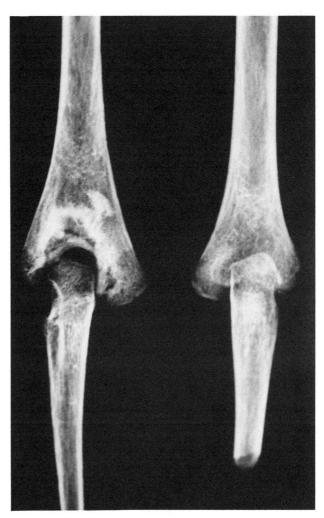

Fig. 10. Radiograph of the humeri showing resorption and sclerosis (dense white areas) in the left humerus (Individual 2).

fined to the cortex, the subchondral lesion may have communicated with the medullary cavity.

The left fifth rib (fig. 11), although fragmentary, has subperiosteal new bone (periostitis) along its inferior (visceral) surface. The immature new bone is situated approximately 3.5 centimeters from the vertebral end and is porous and loosely attached to the underlying cortex.

Two vertebrae (probably thoracic) exhibit nearly complete destruction of the bodies. The trabeculae are thickened, and all that remains of the bodies are thin end-plates (one each). The pattern and extent of osseous destruction are nearly identical. It is likely that these were opposing vertebrae.

The remainder of the skeleton revealed no other lesions, although this child also shows pronounced osteoporosis. The approximate length of the femur was 165 millimeters (estimated because of postmortem breakage). Posterior-anterior and lateral radiographs were taken of the femora of Individual 2 and of four Plains Village children (three from South Dakota and one from Oklahoma, with an average femur length of 160 millimeters). The midshaft measurements are as follows:

| | Posterior-Anterior View | | | Lateral View | | |
	T	M	C	T	M	C
Individual 2	10.6	8.6	2.0	9.4	6.9	2.5
Reference (n = 4)	11.8	7.4	4.4	12.3	7.7	4.6

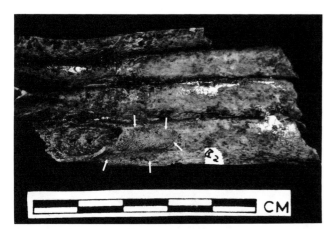

Fig. 11. Patchy periostitis (arrows) along the visceral surface of the left fifth rib (Individual 2).

Individual 2 has smaller total subperiosteal diameters (T), especially as measured in the lateral view, and a proportionately larger medullary cavity (M). The cortical thickness (C) is less than half that of the reference sample.

Interpretation of Skeletal Lesions

For Individual 1, the gross and radiographic features include a smooth-walled, beveled, lytic lesion in the right parietal, vertebra plana of the twelfth thoracic vertebra, multifocal lytic lesions, with minimal sclerosis of the ribs and long bones, laminated periosteal new bone formation, and otitis media. The amount of temporal destruction indicates that the child was deaf. The distribution and appearance of the lesions strongly suggest disseminated histiocytosis X (Langerhans cell histiocytosis), frequently referred to as Hand-Schuller-Christian disease when observed in children more than two years old. Involvement of the temporals, resulting in otitis media, could reflect aural histiocytosis, cholesteatoma, or other infection (Dorfman 1989). The presence of minimal sclerosis and rapid periosteal new bone suggests that the disease process was, at the minimum, of a few months' duration. Although disseminated histiocytosis X is the preferred diagnosis, metastatic neuroblastoma, lymphoma, and osteomyelitis (pyogenic, salmonella, or spirochetal) are other possibilities in young children with multiple lytic lesions of bone.

The lesions in Individual 2 consist of otitis media in the righ temporal bone, multiple resorptive lesions in the left humerus and ulna, and periosteal new bone along the left fifth rib. Erosion of the lateral cortex of the mastoid and petrous processes, combined with sclerosis of the mastoid antrum, indicates a chronic infectious process such as a cholesteatoma

rather than coalescent mastoiditis (Keith, Snow, and Snow 1971). The proliferation of stratified squamous epithelium (skin) in the middle ear forms a cholesteatoma. Accumulation of the cholesteatoma gives rise to an enlarged mass capable of producing osseous erosion, labyrinthitis, facial paralysis, intracranial suppuration, and death.

Resorptive lesions in the left elbow, left fifth rib, and two vertebrae suggest a disseminated infection consistent with tuberculosis. According to Steindler (1952), the focus of tuberculosis of the elbow joint is frequently located at the upper end of the ulna, around the olecranon fossa. A focus in the articular surface of the humerus is less common, and in the radius it is the exception. Reportedly, tuberculosis of the elbow is prevalent in adults, with less than one third of 19 clinical cases (elbow tuberculosis) from early twentieth-century North America being noted in children under 15 years of age (Steindler 1952). Because of similar radiographic features, and in the absence of biopsy, chronic pyogenic osteomyelitis of the elbow must also be considered (Silverman 1985).

The periosteal rib lesion provides further evidence to suggest that the child suffered from tuberculosis rather than a nonspecific osteomyelitis. Rib lesions of the kind seen in this child strongly suggest pulmonary tuberculosis, as similar rib lesions are rarely associated with pneumonia (Kelley and Micozzi 1984). Pneumonia is more prevalent in the right lung and tuberculosis in the left lung ("Respiratory Disease Among Protohistoric and Early Historic Plains Indians," this vol.) (as is the case for Individual 2). Tuberculous otitis media has been found to occur clinically as a complication of the pulmonary infection (Pendergrass, Parsons, and Hodes 1956).

It is difficult to ascertain the sequence of infection in this child. The first question one might ask is whether the infracranial lesions were primary or secondary sites of infection. That is, which lesions occurred first, those in the left forearm, the rib, or the temporal bone? Both the mastoid disease and the lesions in the left arm represent longstanding conditions in that both sites exhibit considerable remodeling (compared with that of known duration in other dry-bone specimens). The child was able to mount an immune response to the infection for a period of at least a few months.

The rib lesion, although seemingly of more recent origin than the other skeletal lesions, might represent an early response to pulmonary tuberculosis. Periosteal lesions on the visceral surface of the uppermost ribs may be the first discernible evidence of tuberculosis ("Respiratory Disease Among Protohistoric and Early Historic Plains Indians," this vol.). The rib lesion in this child might represent an early site of pulmonary inflammation, with involvement of the right temporal bone and left elbow following. Two observations support this hypothesis: tuberculous otitis media is more likely to be secondary to a pulmonary lesion, rather than isolated (not pulmonary) (Phelps and Lloyd 1990), and tuberculous otitis media has a tendency to cause less sclerosis than chronic mastoiditis of nonspecific origin (Pendergrass, Parsons, and Hodes 1956).

Conclusion

The two children described in this report serve as examples of the variability and "natural" course of untreated otitis media, tuberculosis, and tumor in prehistoric and historic North America. Individual 1 probably suffered from several disorders. Histiocytosis X affected many elements in the cranial and infracranial skeleton. The otitis media resulted either from the histiocytosis X or some infectious process involving viral or bacterial agents. Whatever the cause of otitis media in this individual, the child became deaf. Periostitis present on many bones could represent another infection, although such an infection cannot be determined unambiguously from dry specimens. The presence of cribra orbitalia and porotic hyperostosis is indicative of anemia. Finally, the loss of cortical bone suggests that the child suffered from reduced food intake and immobility for a period before death.

For the contemporary Omaha, who encouraged and permitted this analysis, the examination of ancestral remains is important in tracing the origin of disease conditions still present in the tribe. This study, for example, not only documents otitis media, a problem that persists among modern Native Americans, but also demonstrates that the problem is of long standing, among both the Omaha and preceding peoples.

The finding of both otitis media and histiocytosis X in Individual 1 has implications for the reconstruction of the Omaha health care system of 200 years ago. The skeletal collections from Omaha cemeteries contain cases of both trauma-induced pathology, such as fractures and gunshot wounds, and conditions of infectious etiology, such as osteomyelitis. Although individuals who suffered trauma often survived and healed well (as shown by skeletal remains), lesions of infectious origin appear to have been active at death, as in the case of Individual 1. This finding suggests that certain infectious conditions could not be treated so effectively as trauma. Individual 1 suffered from a tumorous condition, probably complicated by bacterial infection. That the osteolytic activity in Individual 1 progressed to the extreme shows that long-term care for sick and dying individuals was available, in spite of overwhelming odds against recovery.

The pattern of osseous lesions in Individual 2 strongly suggests tuberculosis and provides evidence for comparison with other skeletons from the New World. When first examined in 1971, both the otitis media (infectious) and resorptive (tubercular) lesions in the elbow were described using radiography and gross examination. The resulting report, combining the expertise of both physician and anthropologist, did not suggest tuberculosis in the differential diagnosis, although much was known about skeletal tuberculosis at that time. Two observations are relevant to the revised interpretation presented here: (1) identification of periosteal rib lesions often associated with tuberculosis, and (2) presence of two vertebrae with severe erosion of the centra (Pott's disease) that were previously overlooked. Both findings led to reevaluation of disease possibilities. Omission of the vertebral data by the previous researchers does not reflect neglect or lack of expertise, but instead subsequent diagnostic advances developed by both the clinical and anthropological communities. Keith, Snow, and Snow (1971:125) were cognizant of the importance of a comprehensive skeletal analysis when they wrote: "For this reason, the authors have attempted to make this particular analysis as comprehensive as time and space allowed. The desirability of more complete skeletal studies is quite evident, for these studies are the bases of paleodemography which endeavors to reconstruct the population picture of prehistoric man." Twenty years later, researchers had the opportunity to gain additional information. This example highlights the importance of long-term curation of large and diverse skeletal samples as a basis for increased understanding of morbidity and mortality among peoples of North America in the preantibiotic era.

Mark Kransdorf, Therese Bocklage, and Jeno I. Sebes provided opinions on differential diagnosis and confirmation of the diseases. Alison Galloway and Rachel Power provided background information and determined the femur mineral content of Individual 1 using the densitometer. Fran Albrecht was responsible for the radiographs. The CT scan was provided by the University of Iowa Hospitals and Clinics. Examination of the skeleton from 34CU41 was made possible by Julie Droke, Collections Manager for the Oklahoma Museum of Natural History, University of Oklahoma. The research was facilitated by the Omaha tribe.

References Cited

Angel, J.L.

    1964   Osteoporosis: Thalassemia? *American Journal of Physical Anthropology* 22:369–374.

——

    1966   Porotic Hyperostosis, Anemias, Malarias and Marshes in Prehistoric Eastern Mediterranean. *Science* 153:760–763.

Barnes, L., and R.L. Peel
1990 Head and Neck Pathology: A Text/Atlas of Differential Diagnosis. New York: Igaku-Shoin.

Bell, R.E.
1968 Dating the Prehistory of Oklahoma. *Great Plains Journal* 7:42–52.

——, and D.A. Baerreis
1951 A Survey of Oklahoma Archaeology. *Bulletin of Texas Archaeological and Paleontological Society* 22:7–100.

Bluestone, C.D., and J.O. Klein
1988 Otitis Media in Infants and Children. Philadelphia: W.B. Saunders.

Brooks, R.L.
1989 Village Farming Societies. Pp. 71–90 in From Clovis to Comanchero: Archaeological Overview of the Southern Great Plains. J.L. Hofman, R.L. Brooks, J.W. Hays, D.W. Owsley, R.L. Jantz, M.K. Marks, and M. H. Manhein. Fayetteville, Ark.: Arkansas archaeological Survey.

Buck, A.D.
1959 The Custer Focus of the Southern Plains. *Bulletin of the Oklahoma Anthropological Society* 7:1–31.

Buikstra, J.E.
1981 Introduction. Pp. 1–25 in Prehistoric Tuberculosis in the Americas. J.E. Buikstra, ed. Evanston: Northwestern University Archaeological Program.

Cambron, K., J.D. Galbraith, and G. Kong
1965 Middle Ear Disease in Indians of the Mount Currie Reservation, British Columbia. *Canadian Medical Association Journal* 93:1301–1305.

Casselbrant, M.L., L.M. Brostoff, E.I. Cantekin, M.R. Flaherty, D.C. Bluestone, W.J. Doyle, and T.J. Fria
1985 Otitis Media with Effusion in Preschool Children. *Laryngoscope* 95:428–436.

Chantraine, A., B. Nusgens, and M. Lapiere
1986 Bone Remodeling During the Development of Osteoporosis in Paraplegia. *Calcified Tissue International* 38:323–327.

Daniel, T.M.
1981 An Immunochemist's View of the Epidemiology of Tuberculosis. Pp. 35–48 in Prehistoric Tuberculosis in the Americas. J.E. Buikstra, ed. Evanston: Northwestern University Archaeological Program.

Daniel, H.J. III, R.T. Schmidt, R.S. Fulghum, and L. Ruckriegal
1988 Otitis Media: A Problem for the Physical Anthropologist. *American Journal of Physical Anthropology* 31:143–167.

Day, L.J., E.G. Bovill, Jr., P.G. Trafton, H.A. Cohen, and J.O. Johnston
1991 Orthopedics. In Current Surgical Diagnosis and Treatment. 9th ed. L.W. Way, ed. Norwalk, Conn.: Appleton & Lange.

Dorfman, H.D.
1989 Bone Diseases. In Diagnostic Surgical Pathology. S.S. Sternberg, ed. New York: Raven.

Dowd, J.T.
1989 The Anderson Site: Middle Archaic Adaptation in Tennessee's Central Basin. *Tennessee Anthropological Association, Miscellaneous Paper* 12.

Doyle, F., J. Brown, and C. Lachance
1970 Relation Between Bone Mass and Muscle Weight. *The Lancet* 1(643):391–393.

Ferrer, H.P.
1985 The Epidemiology of SOM in School and Preschool Children. P. 28 in Abstracts from the International Symposium on Acute and Secretory Otitis Media. J. Sade, ed. Tel-Aviv: Tel-Aviv University.

Frost, H.M.
1963 Bone Remodelling Dynamics. Springield, Ill.: C.C. Thomas.

Garn, S.M.
1970 The Earlier Gain and the Later Loss of Cortical Bone. Springfield, Ill.: C.C. Thomas.

Gregg, J.B.
1965 Ear Disease in the Indian Skulls at the Museum of the State Historical Society of North Dakota. *North Dakota History* 32:233–242.

——, J.P. Steele, and A.M. Halzhueter
1965 Roentgenographic Evaluation of Temporal Bones from South Dakota Indian Burials. *American Journal of Physical Anthropology* 23:51–61.

Gregg, M.B., ed.
1987 Tuberculosis Among American Indian and Alaskan Natives: United States. *Morbidity and Mortality Weekly Report* 36:493–495.

Griffith, T.E.
1979 Epidemiology of Otitis Media—An Interracial Study. *Laryngoscope* 89:22–30.

Hayden, C.H., A.B. Bloch, and D.E. Snider
1987 Tuberculosis Among Children: United States, 1985. *Annual Review of Respiratory Disease* Suppl. 135:A74.

Henderson, F.M., A.M. Collier, M.A. Sanyal, J.M. Watkins, D.L. Fairclough, W.A. Clyde, and F.W. Denny
1982 A Longitudinal Study of Respiratory Viruses and Bacteria in the Etiology of Acute Otitis Media with Effusion. *New England Journal of Medicine* 306:1377–1383.

Hudson, H.M.
1986 Evaluation of Trends in Middle Ear Disease Among Australian Aborigines. *Biometrics* 42:159–169.

Jaffe, B.F.
1969 The Incidence of Ear Disease in the Navajo Indians. *Laryngoscope* 79:2126–2134.

Kaplan, G.J., J.K. Fleshman, and T.R. Bender
1973 Long-term Effects of Otitis Media: A Ten-Year Cohort Study of Alaskan Eskimo Children. *Pediatrics* 52:577–585.

Keith, K.D., C.C. Snow, and J.B. Snow, Jr.
1971 A Child's Skeleton from Western Oklahoma. *Oklahoma Anthropological Society Bulletin* 20:115–131.

Kelly, M.A., and M.S. Micozzi
1984 Rib Lesions in Chronic Pulmonary Tuberculosis. *American Journal of Physical Anthropology* 65:381.

Lester, W.
1986 Tuberculosis. In Infectious Diseases and Medical Microbiology. 2d ed. A.I. Draude, C.E. Davis, and J. Fierer, eds. Philadelphia: W.B. Saunders.

MacAdam, A.M., and T. Rubio
1977 Tuberculous Otomastoiditis in Children. *American Journal of Diseases of Children* 131:152–156.

MacAdam, P.S.
1989 Porotoc Hyperostosis: Relationship Between Orbital and Vault Lesions. *American Journal of Physical Anthropology* 80:187–193.

Mazess, R.B., and G.D. Whedon
1983 Immobilization and Bone. *Calcified Tissue International* 35:265–267.

Merchant, V.L., and D.H. Ubelaker
1977 Skeletal Growth of the Protohistoric Arikara. *American Journal of Physical Anthropology* 46:61–72.

Moodie, R.
1931 Roentgenographic Studies of Egyptian and Peruvian Mummies. *Field Museum of Natural History, Anthropology Memoirs* III. Chicago.

Moorrees, C.F.A., F.A. Fanning, and E.E. Hunt, Jr.
1963a Formation and Resorption of Three Deciduous Teeth in Children. *American Journal of Physical Anthropology* 21:205–213.

———
1963b Age Variation of Formation Stages for Ten Permanent Teeth. *Journal of Dental Research* 42:1490–1502.

Norland Corporation
1986 Digital Bone Densitometer Model 2780 Operators' Manual. Fort Atkinson, Wisc.: Norland Corporation.

Owsley, D.W.
1989 The History of Bioarchaeological Research in the Southern Great Plains. Pp. 123–136 in From Clovis to Comanchero: Archaeological Overview of the Southern Great Plains. J.L. Hofman, R.L. Brooks, J. W. Hays, D.W. Owsley, R.L. Jantz, M.K. Marks, and M. H. Manhein. Fayetteville, Ark.: Arkansas Archaeological Survey.

Pendergrass, E.P., S.J. Parsons, and P.J. Hodes
1956 The Head and Neck in Roentgen Diagnosis. 2nd ed. Springfield, Ill.: C.C. Thomas.

Pestalozza, G.
1984 Otitis Media in Newborn Infants. *International Journal of Pediatric Otorhinolaryngology* 8:109–124.

Phelps, P.D., and G.A.S. Lloyd
1990 Diagnostic Imaging of the Ear. 2nd ed. London: Springer-Verlag.

Ragsdale, B.D., J.E. Madewell, and D.E. Sweet
1981 Radiologic and Pathologic Analysis of Solitary Bone Lesions. Pt. II: Periosteal Reactions. *Radiologic Clinics of North America* 19:749–783.

Rathbun, T., and R. Mallin
1977 Middle Ear Disease in a Prehistoric Iranian Population. *Bulletin of the New York Academy of Medicine* 53:901–905.

Reed, D., S. Struve, and J.E. Maynard
1967 Otitis Media and Hearing Deficiency Among Eskimo Children: A Cohort Study. *American Journal of Public Health* 57:1657–1662.

Reinhard, K.J., K.N. Sandness, S. Parks, G. Toth, and S. Moorhead
1990 Progress Report of Skeletal Analysis Related to LB 340 Legislation. (Manuscript on file, University of Nebraska, Lincoln.)

Resnick, D. and G. Niwayama
1988 Diagnosis of Bone and Joint Disorders. 2nd ed. Philadelphia: W.B. Saunders.

Rieder, H.L., G.M. Cauthen, G.D. Kelly, A.B. Bloch, and D.E. Snider, Jr.
1989 Tuberculosis in the United States. *Journal of the American Medical Association* 262:385–389.

Rosen, A., D. Ophir, and G. Marshak
1986 Acute Mastoiditis: A Review of 69 Cases. *Annals of Otology, Rhinology and Laryngology* 95:222–224.

Scott, T.A., and R.K. Jackler
1989 Acute Mastoiditis in Infancy: A Sequela of Unrecognized Acute Otitis Media. *Otolaryngology. Head and Neck Surgery* 101:683–687.

Shaw, J.R., N.W. Todd, M.H. Goodwin, and C.M. Feldman
1981 Observations on the Relation of Environmental and Behavioral Factors to the Occurrence of Otitis Media Among Indian Children. *Public Health Report* 96:342–349.

Silverman, F.N.
1985 The Limbs. Pp. 361–944 in Caffey's Pediatric X-Ray Diagnosis. 8th ed., F.N. Silverman, ed. Chicago: Year Book Medical.

Smith, E. L., and C. Gilligan
1989 Mechanical Forces and Bone. Pp. 139–173 in Bone and Mineral Research/6. W.A. Peck, ed. New York: Elsevier Science.

Smith, M.H.D., and J.R. Marquis
1987 Tuberculosis and Other Mycobacterial Infections. Pp. 1342–1387 in Textbook of Pediatric Infectious Diseases. 2nd ed. R.D. Geigin and J.D. Cherry, eds. Philadelphia: W.B. Saunders.

Stanievich, J.F., C.D. Bluestone, J.A. Lima, R.H. Michaels, D. Rohn, and M.Z. Effron

    1981   Microbiology of Chronic and Recurrent Otitis Media with Effusion in Young Infants. *International Journal of Pediatric Otorhinolaryngology* 3:137–143.

Steindler, A.

    1952   Post-Graduate Lectures on Orthopedic Diagnosis and Indications, III. Springfield, Ill.: C.C. Thomas.

Stout, S.D.

    1982   The Effects of Long-term Immobilization on the Histomorphology of Human Cortical Bone. *Calcified Tissue International* 34:337–342.

Styblo, K., and A. Rouillon

    1981   Estimated Global Incidence of Smear-positive Pulmonary Tuberculosis: Unreliability of Officially Reported Figures on Tuberculosis. *Bulletin of the International Union Tuberculosis* 56:118–126.

Teele, D.W., J.O. Klein, B.A. Rosner, and the Greater Boston Otitis Media Study Group

    1984   Otitis Media with Effusion during the First Three Years of Life and Development of Speech and Language. *Pediatrics* 74:282–287.

Titche, L., R. Wachter, S. Coulthard, and L. Harries

    1981   Mastoiditis in Prehistoric Arizona Indians. *Arizona Medicine* 38:712–714.

Tos, M., G. Poulsen, and J. Borch

    1979   Etiologic Factors in Secretory Otitis. *Archives of Otolaryngology* 105:582–588.

Van Cauwenberge, P.

    1985   Character Acute and Secretory Otitis Media. Pp. 3–11 in Acute and Secretory Otitis Media. J. Sade, ed. Amsterdam: Kugler.

Wiet, R.J.

    1979   Patterns of Ear Disease in the Southwestern American Indian. *Archives of Otolaryngology* 105:381–385.

——, J. Stewart, G. DeBlanc, and D. Weider

    1980   Natural History of Otitis Media in the American Native. *Annals of Otology, Rhinology and Laryngology* 89:14–19.

Wood, W.D., K.R. Burns, and S.R. Lee

    1986   The Mt. Gilead Cemetery Study: An Example of Biocultural Analysis from Western Georgia. Athens, Ga.: Southern Archaeological Services.

CHAPTER 11

○ ○ ○

Interproximal Grooves, Toothaches, and Purple Coneflowers

P. WILLEY AND JACK L. HOFMAN

Noncarious, artificially produced grooves between the teeth have been noted on Plains Indian teeth (Ubelaker, Phenice, and Bass 1969). Interproximal grooves are widespread geographically and through time. Grooves occur in early hominids from Ethiopia (Boas and Howell 1977), fossil remains across most of the Old World (de Lumley 1973; Frayer 1991; Frayer and Russell 1987; Perez, DeArsuaga, and Bermudez de Castro 1982; Puech and Cianfarini 1988; Senyurek 1940; Siffre 1911; Turner 1988; Vallois 1945; Weidenreich 1937), and in later specimens from the Old World (Frayer and Russell 1987; Lukacs and Pastor 1988; Formicola 1988). They have been reported from Australia (Brown and Molnar 1990; Campbell 1925) and South America (Eckhardt and Piermarini 1988). In North America, grooves have been reported from California (Schulz 1977), the Great Basin (Larsen 1985), the Southeast (Ubelaker, Phenice, and Bass 1969) and the Plains (Berryman, Owsley, and Hendersen 1979; Ubelaker, Phenice, and Bass 1969).

The cause of groove formation is disputed, variously attributed to therapeutic or palliative use of a probe (Berryman, Owsley, and Hendersen 1979; Frayer 1991; Ubelaker, Phenice

and Bass 1969), sucking grit between teeth during swallowing (Wallace 1974), antemortem chemical erosion (Brothwell 1963; Pindborg 1970; Sognnaes 1959), processing nondietary objects (Brown and Molnar 1990; Eckhardt 1990; Schulz 1977), a habitual or compulsive practice (Berryman, Owsley and Hendersen 1979), or combinations of these causes. In the Middle Missouri region most grooves are associated with dental and periodontal disease (figs. 1–2), and the orientation, location, and morphology of the grooves argue for the use of a toothpicklike probe inserted repeatedly between the teeth. Those grooves, when associated with diseased tissue, appear to be therapeutic or palliative. Those not associated with diseased tissues have been interpreted as resulting from idiosyncratic, compulsive, or habitual practice.

Despite the association of some grooves with diseased dental and periodontal tissues and the presumption of therapeutic or palliative treatments, previous investigators have failed to examine the plants used for these purposes. Although there are many plants indigenous to the Plains that have palliative properties, the one most widespread geographically and most frequently mentioned in ethnographic accounts is black sampson (*Echinacea angustifolia*).

147

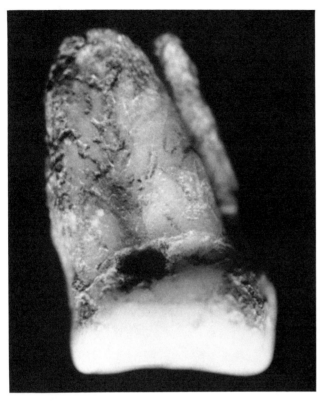

Fig. 1. Interproximal groove and carious lesion on distal surface of a right maxillary second molar. Note calculus on tooth.

The mild anesthetic qualities of the black sampson roots, rather than being topical, are general within the oral cavity. For instance, placing a small portion of the root next to the cheek and gum not only numbs that location but also fairly rapidly numbs the tip of the tongue. This observation suggests

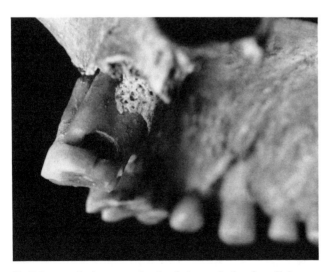

Fig. 2. Interproximal groove and carious lesion on distal surface of left maxillary first molar. Note alveolar resorption.

that some of the healthy teeth with grooves—presumed to indicate idiosyncratic behavior or object manipulation not associated with palliative effects—might result from a general anesthetic effect directed at nearby inflamed tissues.

W.H. Over Museum Skeletal Material

MATERIALS AND METHODS

The skeletal remains from the William H. Over Museum, Vermillion, South Dakota, are an excellent sample. The collection, buried in 1986, was large, well-preserved, and from several periods.

Previous studies have implied that, unless the grooves are in diseased teeth, associated with alveolar resorption or other diseased soft tissue, no palliative or therapeutic influences were being exerted. This assumption needs to be reevaluated in light of the known general effects of documented palliative plants. The health of the grooved tooth and periodontal tissues was examined, as was the health of the two adjacent teeth in the same dental row, the occlusally opposed teeth to these three, and overall oral health.

Adult dentitions (maxilla and mandible) were selected for examination. Specimens from major sites (those having good documentation and 10 or more individuals) that retained more than half their maxillary and mandibular teeth were included. Specimens from minor sites (having few individuals and less documentation) and missing more than half their teeth were omitted. The sites, cultural identification, and number of specimens examined are summarized in table 1.

The teeth were examined in natural light for grooves. The presence or absence of each tooth was noted. The teeth and periodontal area were examined for carious lesions, abscesses, antemortem loss, calculus, and alveolar resorption. Although carious lesions, abscesses, and antemortem loss were identified easily, the presence and degrees of calculus development and alveolar bone resorption could be assessed only in general terms for a few specimens.

Identification of grooves was based on shape. Concavities with U-shaped cross-sections found between the crowns of adjacent teeth near the cemento-enamel juncture were considered grooves. Contrary to some reports, polish or sheen in the grooves was often not visible macroscopically, although striations were frequently observed. Another issue is the similarity of the standard maxillary premolar morphology to grooves. A shallow, natural "groove" occurs frequently near the cemento-enamel juncture of the maxillary premolars, especially the distal surfaces. To avoid misidentification of

Table 1. W.H. Over Museum Dentitions

Tradition and Site	Females Total/With Grooves	Males Total/With Grooves	Total
Plains Woodland Tradition			
39DV2	0/0	1/1	1
39HS1	1/0	0/0	1
39HT2	1/0	1/1	2
39LH10	1/0	0/0	1
39MH6	1/0	3/1	4
39RO2	0/0	1/0	1
39RO4	1/0	2/2	3
39RO10	4/0	4/2	8
39UN1	1/0	1/0	2
Total	10/0	13/7	23
Coalescent Tradition			
39CO9	1/0	4/2	5
39CA4	0/0	2/1	2
39DW2	7/1	2/0	9
39HU2	0/0	1/1	1
39LM26-27	1/0	0/0	1
39LM33	2/0	1/0	3
39ST1	0/0	1/0	1
39ST235	4/0	2/0	6
39WW1	3/0	6/0	9
39WW7	2/0	6/3	8
Total	20/1	25/7	45
Middle Missouri Tradition			
39HT1	2/0	0/0	2
39LM2	0/0	1/0	1
39SL2	1/0	2/0	3
Total	3/0	3/0	6
Total	33/1	41/14	74

these features as interproximal grooves, only those specimens with striations or markedly enlarged grooves were identified as grooves. All possible grooves were reinspected using a 6× binocular microscope, and only those grooves passing the second inspection were included in subsequent analyses.

Once the individual teeth were inspected for grooves and health, the assessments were combined for analytical purposes. An overall evaluation of oral health was made. A dentition was considered healthy if there were three or fewer teeth with carious lesions or periodontal areas indicating abscesses or antemortem loss. If the individual had four or more of these maladies in any combination, the dentition was considered diseased. A tooth was considered healthy if it lacked carious

lesions, abscesses, and alveolar resorption but was considered diseased if any of these conditions were present. These criteria were applied to teeth adjacent to the grooved tooth with the additional criterion of antemortem loss. If an adjacent tooth was missing antemortem, it was considered diseased. Health of teeth across the occlusal plane from a grooved tooth was assessed. The corresponding tooth and one on each side of it were inspected, and if any of the three teeth were diseased or the location indicated antemortem loss, the occlusal area was considered diseased. Thus, for adjacent and occlusally opposed teeth, pathological conditions active at death as well as inferred previous disease conditions were identified.

Several statistical tests were applied to these data to evaluate relationships between grooves and age, sex, side, culture, subsistence, or tradition. Binomial Z-tests were applied to the groove distribution by side (left-right), jaw (mandible-maxilla), and anterior-posterior positions. Chi square and Fisher Exact tests were applied to the other variables using standard computer programs (SAS Institute 1985). Fisher Exact test results were used when chi square assumptions were violated.

Sex and age were determined using standard techniques. Sex was identified using cranial morphology and, when available, postcranial morphology. Age was determined as old or young from the dental remains alone. The progression of dental attrition from molar to molar and antemortem tooth loss were used, with the division between young and old being approximately 35 years. Dental age was preferred over skeletal age, in this case, because the progression of attrition and tooth loss were more important variables than estimated chronological age.

RESULTS

Altogether 74 (33 female and 41 male) dentitions were analyzed; the number of teeth and their health status are presented in table 2. Some teeth display more than one condition (for example, adjacent and occlusal teeth afflicted), and these teeth are tallied twice or more. Thus, the numbers presented are number of observations, not necessarily minimum number of teeth. Calculus is recorded only for teeth, with interproximal grooves, that are otherwise healthy.

Thirty-two interproximal grooves were present in the dentitions of 15 of the individuals (figs. 1–2). The number of grooves by individual ranged from one (eight individuals) to six (one individual), with one being the most frequent.

Statistical tests for side, mandible-maxilla, and anterior-posterior location differences were calculated using all 32 grooves separately. There was no preference for left

Table 2. Health of W.H. Over Museum Teeth

	I1	I2	C	PM1	PM2	M1	M2	M3	Total
Tooth									
Maxilla—no interproximal grooves									
Healthy	75	84	112	103	94	101	93	74	736
Carious lesions	0	0	5	6	5	10	7	8	41
Alveolar abscess	0	1	6	10	4	16	9	6	52
Antemortem loss	3	4	2	4	9	19	14	13	68
Total	78	89	125	123	112	146	123	101	897
Maxilla—interproximal grooves present									
Healthy	0	0	0	0	0	1	3	1	5
Carious lesions	0	0	0	1	3	1	3	1	9
Alveolar abscess	0	0	0	1	0	0	0	0	1
Adjacent teeth afflicted	0	0	0	3	5	1	4	0	13
Occlusal teeth afflicted	0	0	0	1	2	1	3	0	7
Healthy, missing data	0	1	0	0	1	0	0	0	2
Calculus	0	0	0	0	0	0	0	1	1
Total	0	1	0	6	11	4	13	3	38
Mandible—no interproximal grooves									
Healthy	85	101	108	113	119	116	119	105	866
Carious lesions	0	2	3	2	4	5	4	2	22
Alveolar abscess	4	0	2	4	3	7	3	2	25
Antemortem loss	9	2	1	2	7	18	13	15	67
Total	98	105	114	121	133	146	139	124	980
Mandible—interproximal grooves present									
Healthy	0	0	0	0	0	0	0	0	0
Carious lesions	0	0	0	1	0	0	0	0	1
Alveolar abscess	0	0	0	0	1	1	0	0	2
Adjacent teeth afflicted	0	0	1	0	0	0	0	0	1
Occlusal teeth afflicted	0	0	1	1	0	0	0	0	2
Calculus	0	0	0	0	1	1	0	0	2
Total	0	0	2	2	2	2	0	0	8
Total	176	195	241	252	258	298	275	228	1,923

(n = 16) or right (n = 16) side. There were many more grooved maxillary teeth (n = 28) than mandibular teeth (n = 4) (Z = 4.243, $F[Z]$ = 0.9999, $P < 0.0001$). Posterior teeth (n = 30) were more frequently grooved than anterior teeth (n = 2) (Z = 3.651, $F[Z]$ = 0.9998, $P < 0.001$).

Statistical tests for sex and age differences in grooving were performed using the same 74 dentitions. Males had more grooves than females (χ^2 = 10.954, df = 1, $P < 0.001$). This difference in grooves by sex was not related to oral health because there was no difference in overall mouth health between the sexes (χ^2 = 0.001, df = 1, $P < 0.974$). As expected, there was a difference in the frequency of grooving by age (χ^2 = 4.141, df = 1, $P < 0.05$). Older adults (42 indi-

viduals total, 12 with grooves) had proportionately more grooves than the younger ones (32 individuals total, 3 with grooves). This result was expected because the overall oral health of the older adults was poorer than that of the younger adults (χ^2 = 25.699, df = 1, $P < 0.0001$).

The association of grooves with oral disease was evaluated. Ten of the 32 grooves were associated with teeth having carious lesions. Ten of the 32 grooved teeth also had resorbed alveolar bone. Fourteen of 30 grooved teeth had diseased teeth or sockets adjacent to them; the other two were omitted due to missing adjacent teeth or alveolar bone. Nine of 27 grooves were occlusally opposite from diseased teeth or sockets; the other five instances had missing observations such as missing teeth or alveolar bone. When all pathological conditions were combined, 22 grooves of 30 were on diseased teeth, associated with resorbed alveolar bone, adjacent to diseased teeth or sockets, occlusally opposite from diseased teeth or sockets, or characterized by some combination of these conditions; two grooves were excluded from this overall assessment because of incomplete observations or questionable disease assessments. The records of the remaining eight grooves were inspected for other indications of disease, and three of these grooved teeth were associated with calculus. The other five grooves—four of them in a single individual—were associated with healthy tissues. Therefore, there were at least five of the 32 grooves that cannot be explained by palliative attempts associated with oral disease. Looking at the dentitions as a whole, there was no association of overall oral disease (four or more diseased teeth or alveoli) and grooves ($\chi^2 = 1.579$, df = 1, $P < 0.208$).

The dentitions were tested for difference in grooving by subsistence and cultural tradition. There was no difference between the frequency of grooved dentitions in the predominantly foraging Plains Woodland and the more horticulturally oriented Plains Villager samples (Fisher Exact two-tailed test, $P < 0.221$). This result was surprising because the overall oral health of the two subsistence orientations is statistically different ($\chi^2 = 4.264$, df = 1, $P < 0.039$), with the Woodland sample being healthier. One intriguing aspect of these data was that more of the grooves in the Woodland sample were associated with healthy tissues than in the Villager sample. There was no difference in the frequency of grooved dentitions between the Middle Missouri and Coalescent traditions (Fisher Exact two-tailed test, $P < 0.572$), as might be expected given the similar subsistence base of these populations. But it should be noted that the Middle Missouri sample available for study was quite small and may not fully represent the geographic and temporal norms of the Middle Missouri tradition as a whole.

INTERPRETATION

Many of the results of this study compare well with previous studies of interproximal grooves from the Northern Plains (e.g., Berryman, Owsley and Hendersen, 1979; Ubelaker, Phenice, and Bass 1969). The grooves were relatively common, and if one groove occurs in a dentition, then other grooves were frequently present (7 of 15 of the individuals have multiple grooves). Also as in previous studies, maxillary teeth were more frequently affected than mandibular teeth, the posterior teeth were more frequently grooved than the anterior ones, males had a higher frequency of grooves than

females, and most of the grooves were associated with diseased teeth and alveoli, although there is no association of overall oral disease and grooves.

There is, however, a general association of locations with pathological conditions and locations with grooves. The disproportionate number of interproximal grooves on the posterior maxillary dentition fits the general association of grooves and oral disease. The posterior dentition is less accessible for oral hygiene and less naturally cleaned than the anterior dentition. Thus, the posterior dentition is more prone to disease than the anterior. In the W.H. Over Museum sample, the posterior dentition has a higher incidence of dental conditions than the anterior. Omitting the teeth with grooves to simplify the comparison, the combined maxillary and mandibular anterior teeth had 7.2 percent (44 of 609 observations) pathological conditions, in contrast with the posterior dentition, which had 18.2 percent (231 of 1,268 observations). These differences are statistically significant ($\chi^2 = 39.76$, df = 1, $P < 0.001$).

Inspection of the difference between maxillary and mandibular health reveals a similar finding. Again omitting the teeth with grooves, the mandibular dentition (that with the fewer grooves) has 11.6 percent (114 of 980 observations) pathological conditions, whereas the maxillary teeth have 17.9 percent (161 of 897 observations). This difference, too, is statistically significant ($\chi^2 = 14.941$, df = 1, $P < 0.001$). So the higher frequency of dental problems in the maxilla and the posterior dentitions contrasted with the mandibular and anterior dentitions supports in a general way the association of grooves with dental disease.

Why males more commonly have interproximal grooves than females is speculative. Perhaps there existed some consistent, even if minor, differences in diet or dental hygiene. The difference in groove distribution by sex might be explained by the use of different plants by the two sexes. In southern Ghana, for instance, men tend to use harder, more bitter chewing sticks whereas children and women tend to use different plants that are softer and milder (Adu-Tutu et al. 1979). Possibly a similar sex pattern of harder-softer plant use was present on the Northern Plains. It is also possible that the males of the Middle Missouri Region had more time to engage in such grooming and hygiene activities than did the females. According to at least one historic account (Tabeau 1939:148), the women were occupied throughout the day while the males relaxed in the village. Perhaps such periods of inactivity were conducive to oral care and "treatment" of dental maladies.

Another noteworthy result is the lack of difference in the frequency of grooves by side of the mouth. This result is germane to the idiosyncratic explanation of grooves. It has been suggested that some grooves were produced by idiosyncratic behavior not associated with ameliorating the discomfort associated with dental disease. By extension of this explanation, a predilection for the dominant, presumably right, side might be expected. This expectation is not found even with the few grooves associated with healthy tissues, indicating random grooving by side. Furthermore, if purely habitual actions or compulsive behavior were responsible for formation of the grooves, there would be more grooves on anterior rather than posterior teeth because of the greater accessibility of anterior teeth. Such a pattern was not found. In fact, most grooves are located in relatively hard-to-reach locations.

This pattern also brings into question another explanation offered for interproximal grooves. Some authors (Brown and Molnar 1990; Eckhardt 1990; Lukacs and Pastor 1988; Schulz 1977) have suggested that manipulating or processing nondietary objects, such as sinews and fibers, caused at least some of the grooves. Certainly there is good ethnographic data in support of this hypothesis (reviewed by Larson 1985; Lukacs and Pastor 1988; Molnar 1972; Schulz 1977). This explanation is appropriate for occlusal grooves and some of the interproximal grooves present in the anterior teeth because these teeth are more accessible. If the grooves were produced while manipulating objects, there should be a disproportionate number on one side of the dentition, presumably the dominant, right side, although it is also possible that they might occur bilaterally. In the specimens from the W.H. Over Museum collection, none of these expectations is fulfilled: the grooves tend to be in the interproximal surfaces of the posterior dentition and evenly distributed by side. Producing grooves through manipulating objects is a poor explanation for most of the grooves documented in this study.

Unexpected results include the similar frequency of dental grooves in the W.H. Over Museum material by chronological period, by subsistence economy, and between archaeological traditions. The Plains Woodland and Plains Villager samples have similar frequencies, documenting the fact that this practice had time-depth and that the incidence did not change through time. This continuity could be taken as support for the idiosyncratic interpretation. The Middle Missouri and Coalescent traditions also have similar groove frequencies, but there is little basis, in terms of subsistence and economy, for assuming that differences should occur between these samples.

Of note is the expected correlation between frequency of interproximal grooves and age. This pattern may obscure differences in economy and cultural tradition. The increasing likelihood of dental maladies with age probably resulted in increased use of palliatives by older individuals regardless of culture group or economy. Also, it may take many months or years for the grooves to develop, depending upon the nature of their formation.

Medicinal Plants and Oral Health

Plants have been employed in dental hygiene and treatment of dental disease worldwide. The geographic distribution of plant use with dental disease is extensively documented.

For example, chewing sticks are used as a dentifrice by many rural people across the Old World, Oceania, and the Americas (Elvin-Lewis 1979). In East Tennessee some rural people still use sweet gum (*Liquidambar styraciflua*) and black gum (*Nyssa sylvatica*) twigs (Lewis and Elvin-Lewis 1977). Sweet and black gum, like many plants preferred for chewing sticks, have medicinal properties that prevent or delay dental disease. Pharmacological studies of chewing sticks on a worldwide basis frequently demonstrate antibiotic, analgesic, anticariogenic, antipyretic, and antiinflammatory properties (Elvin-Lewis 1979).

When oral health deteriorates, plants are used in palliative or therapeutic treatment of disease. Many plants used to treat oral diseases, like those used for oral hygiene, have been shown empirically to have beneficial properties (Elvin-Lewis 1986).

A number of plants were used to treat oral, throat, and tooth disorders among Plains Indians. Ethnobotanical surveys, conducted primarily during the early twentieth century, inventoried medicinal plant use among a few groups (table 3). Despite the variety of plants with documented usage, this list probably excludes many plants that were in use at the time of Euro-American contact, given the late period when the surveys were conducted and the limited number of tribes involved. Among the documented species that were used for dental maladies or as mouth and throat aids among Plains Indians, species of purple coneflowers (*Echinacea* spp.) were most widely and commonly reported. More than 10 tribal groups are known to have used black sampson for various medicinal purposes, usually including treatment of toothache (table 4). Because purple coneflowers were consistently regarded by Plains Indians as useful for the treatment of dental problems, black sampson has been studied in detail. Given the known (though imperfect) relationship between interproximal grooves and dental disease, and the documented use of purple coneflowers in aboriginal treatment of such disease, the relevance of purple coneflowers to the study of oral hygiene and the interproximal grooves in the W.H. Over Museum skeletal collection from the Northern Plains is evident.

Table 3. Plants Used by Plains Indians for Throat and Mouth Medicine

Scientific Name	Common Name	Tribe or Group
Oral aids		
Echinacea angustifolia	Black sampson	Cheyenne, Montana state Indians
Juniperus virginiana	Red cedar	Kiowa
Mirabilis nyctaginea	Four-o'clock	Pawnee
Prunus americana	American plum	Cheyenne
Throat aids		
Achillea lanulosa	Woody yarrow	Cheyenne
A. millefolium	Common yarrow	Cheyenne
Artemisia mexicana	Sagebrush	Kiowa
Balsamorrhiza sagittata	Balsam root	Cheyenne
Echinacea angustifolia	Black sampson	Cheyenne, Kiowa, Sioux
Echinacea spp.	Purple coneflower	Comanche
Juniperus communis	Juniper	Cheyenne
J. horizontalis	Juniper	Cheyenne
J. scopolorum	Juniper	Cheyenne
Osmorhiza chilensis	Cicely	Blackfeet
Oxytropis lagopus	Locoweed	Blackfeet
Perideridia gairdneri	Yampa	Blackfeet
Physaria didymocarpa	Twinpod	Blackfeet
Zanthoxylum americanum	Prickly ash	Comanche
Toothache remedy		
Acorus calamus	Sweet flag	Teton Sioux, Omaha, Pawnee, Ponca
Balsmorrhiza sagittata	Balsam root	Cheyenne
Echinacea angustifolia	Black sampson	Cheyenne, Omaha, Pawnee, Ponca, Teton Sioux
E. pallida	Pale coneflower	Cheyenne
Echinacea sp.	Purple coneflower	Comanche
Glycyrrhiza lepidota	American Licorice	Pawnee, Teton Sioux
Rhus aromatica	Fragrant sumac	Cheyenne
Salix sp.	Willow	Kiowa
Zanthoxylum americanum	Prickly ash	Comanche

Source: Moerman 1986: table 2.

Table 4. Aboriginal Medicinal Uses of Black Sampson

Tribe	Condition Treated	Source
Cheyenne	Neck pain; sore mouth, gums, or throat; toothache	Grinnell 1905
Teton Sioux	Burns, headache, enlarged glands, snakebite, stings, toothache	Gilmore 1919
Fox	Fits, stomach cramps	Smith 1928
Kiowa	Coughs, sore throat	Vestal and Schultes 1939
Montana State Indians	Rattlesnake bites	Blankinship 1905
Omaha	Burns, septic, snakebite, stings, sore eyes, enlarged glands, toothache	Gilmore 1913, 1919
Pawnee	Burns, headache, enlarged glands, snakebite, stings, toothache	Gilmore 1919
Ponca	Burns, enlarged glands, stings, snakebite, toothache	Gilmore 1919
Teton Sioux	Bowel pain, tonsilitis, toothache	Densmore 1918
Winnebago	Burns, headache, enlarged glands, toothache	Gilmore 1919

Source: Moerman 1986:156–158.

BLACK SAMPSON

Black sampson (fig. 3) was frequently used on the Plains to obtain relief from toothache, sore throat, and painful gums. Perhaps the popularity of this plant is related, in part, to its broad geographical distribution, which extends from Saskatchewan, Minnesota, and Montana to southern Texas. Its east-west distribution is more limited, stretching from Minnesota and Iowa in the east to Montana, Wyoming, and Colorado in the west (McGregor 1968:figure 1). Black sampson typically grows on dry, sometimes rocky, prairies and barrens

Fig. 3. Purple coneflower approaching full bloom. Scale on top edge of compass is 5 cm. Photograph taken June 23, 1988, Sherman County, Nebr.

(McGregor 1968). It blooms in late spring and early summer. Following blooming, the durable stem and dried efflorescence commonly remain attached to the root of this perennial plant for many months. This persistence enhances the ability to identify the plant and locate the root throughout the year, not only during the plant's blooming period.

There were many aboriginal medicinal uses for black sampson (table 4). Nearly all documented tribes used the plant for oral and throat ailments. The specific manner in which the plant was used, which portions of the plant were used, and how it was prepared, were omitted from these ethnobotanical accounts, but it is clear that the root was used by the Cheyenne, Fox, Kiowa, Montana Indians, Omaha, and Teton Sioux. *E. angustifolia* has been most frequently cited as being used among Plains tribes, although *E. purpurea* is also often mentioned.

The medicinal properties of black sampson found their way into Euro-American pharmacology, presumably passed from American Indian informants. According to Foster's (1985:14–21) review of *Echinacea* medicinal history, the first published mention was by Clapp (1852), who cited its value in treating gonorrhea and other diseases. However, inclusion of the plant in standard medical practice was delayed about 30 years. An eclectic doctor who had been marketing "Meyer's Blood Purifier," which included *E. angustifolia,* brought the plant to the attention of a prominent pharmacist in the 1880s. The medicinal properties of black sampson were enthusiastically endorsed by eclectic medical practitioners while being shunned by the "regular" medical doctors. By 1920, members of both the American Medical Association and the U.S. Department of Agriculture denounced the use of the plant. At the same time it was the most widely sold American medicinal plant. It was used to treat syphilis, gonorrhea, wounds, diphtheria, cholera, blood poisoning, boils, carbuncles, abscesses, inflamed glands, meningitis, neoplasms, skin disorders, tonsillitis, stings, and snake bites; it was believed to stimulate digestion, circulation, liver function, the lymphatic system, and endocrine functions.

Pharmacological and chemical research since 1950 (Foster 1985:21–25) has substantiated some of the earlier claims. Substances from the *Echinacea* plants have been found to be slightly antibiotic against streptococci (Koch and Uebel 1953) and *Staphylococcus aureus* (Stoll, Renz, and Brack 1950); to inhibit hyaluronidase while stimulating white blood cells, macrophages, and regeneration of connective tissue (Koch and Uebel 1953, 1954; Kuhn 1953); to enhance leukocyte production (Foster 1985); to promote blood clotting (Nikol'skaya 1954) and wound healing (Bonadea, Bottazzi, and Lavazza 1971); to improve bacterial skin infections (Foster

1985); to prevent influenza (Wacker and Hibig 1978); to stimulate the immunological system, and perhaps to be effective in treating some cancers and infectious diseases. The chemical composition of *E. angustifolia* has been summarized by Foster (1985:24–25). Although the list of uses and tested or "verified" properties is impressive, the main point is that the plant has properties that make it well suited for use in aboriginal herbal remedies for problems such as toothache.

Black sampson is used today as a popular medicine among some rural people and modern herbalists. For instance, some Teton Sioux Indians on Pine Ridge Reservation and other people in southwest South Dakota use the plant for toothaches, and it is among the most popular ingredients of cures used by modern herbalists, at least in one health food store (Cynthia Reed, personal communication 1988). In traditional herbal medicine, the plant is used as a blood purifier, and it has gained popularity as a stimulant for the autoimmune system.

Roots of *E. angustifolia* were collected from three places in Kansas, two in Nebraska, and one in Texas in summer 1986 and 1988 by the authors. Most of the roots were tasted fresh, and those samples not consumed in the field were air dried in paper sacks with no other special attention. All plants were assumed to be *E. angustifolia* because they were collected outside the range of the other *Echinacea* species.

After the roots, stems, leaves, and flowers of black sampson were tasted, the root was found to be the most effective part of the plant. The fresh flower was less effective and the stems and leaves had little apparent effect. When the root was taken orally and either chewed or sucked, it produced a numbing sensation, both in the location where the root was held and more generally throughout the mouth. When the root was placed between the cheek and gum, for instance, it numbed not only that spot but also the tip of the tongue, the lips, and, to a lesser extent, the throat. These taste tests were based on relatively small pieces of the plant used for short periods of time. Originally, it seemed likely that the stems might have been intensively used, as the stem diameter on most plants is comparable to the size of many interproximal grooves. The abrasive nature of the stem surface (due to opal phytoliths) might also contribute to the formation of interproximal grooves. However, the minimal reaction gained from chewing *E. angustifolia* stems leaves this possibility in doubt. It may be that stem portions were used in a toothpicklike fashion in conjunction with a root quid.

Experimentation may enable a more accurate assessment of whether the stems could produce interproximal grooves comparable to those documented on aboriginal dentitions. Abrasions have been produced under laboratory conditions using commercially made toothbrushes, extracted teeth, and a specially designed machine (Harry Mencer, personal communication 1990). This experimental situation could be modified using a variety of plants and plant parts instead of the toothbrushes and the microabrasion in the grooves thus produced could be compared with that in the aboriginal grooves. The results of such experiments might eliminate some plants, plant parts, or other objects from the list of possible candidates for materials producing the aboriginal grooves. However, identification of plant species through such experimentation is unlikely. The possibility that plant opal phytoliths may be present in the dental calculus or plaque on surfaces of, or adjacent to, interproximal grooves or that dental boluses (impacted plant particles) may be present in cavities adjacent to the grooves is an important one that requires further investigation. Such study may lead to a more direct evaluation of the use of specific medicinal plants or other materials in association with dental grooves.

There has been much archaeological emphasis on prehistoric plant use. Most commonly the archaeological concern is for plants that were used for food, structures, utensils, or fires. Nevertheless, it is clear from historic accounts that plants were used for a great variety of purposes. Gilmore (1919), in his classic work on aboriginal plant use in the Missouri River region, noted the use of plants for a wide variety of purposes and objects. He also documented the importance of plants as medicinal treatments. If plants were used as intensively in prehistory as they were in the first two decades of the twentieth century, then many plant uses are not directly observable in the archaeological record. The association of dental grooves and plants may be one of the few archaeological or osteological indicators of plant use for health purposes.

Conclusion

Interproximal grooves in geographic prehistoric teeth have been found across a wide area and through time. Most grooves are associated with diseased teeth or periodontal tissues.

Historic accounts indicate that black sampson (*Echinacea angustifolia*) was used by Plains Indians to relieve toothaches. Present-day herbalists and mainstream medical practitioners employ it for a variety of purposes, and experimental work suggests that its mild anesthetic would relieve some pain associated with dental discomfort. Although it cannot be demonstrated that black sampson produced the grooves observed on the teeth from the W.H. Over Museum collection, it is likely that it or some similar palliative plant was employed in many instances of dental distress. Because there are some interproximal grooves where no dental or periodontal disease was observed, the possibility remains that habitual or compulsive behavior was the reason for the formation of some grooves.

The work of the following people enriched the research on the Over Museum skeletal collection and purple coneflowers: Bob Alex; Stan Roth; Ron McGregor; Eldon, Frank, and Marion Willey; Cynthia Reed; Harry H. Mincer; Jan Simek; Stephen P. Langdon; and Mike Logan.

References Cited

Adu-Tutu, M., Y. Afful, K. Asante-Appiah, D. Lieberman, J.B. Hall, and M. Elvin-Lewis
1979   Chewing Stick Usage in Southern Ghana. *Economic Botany* 33:320–328.

Berryman, H.E., D.W. Owsley, and A.M. Hendersen
1979   Non-carious Interproximal Grooves in Arikara Indian Dentitions. *American Journal of Physical Anthropology* 50:209–212.

Blankinship. J.W.
1905   Native Economic Plants of Montana. *Montana Agricultural College Experiment Station Bulletin* 56. Bozeman.

Boas, N.T., and F.C. Howell
1977   A Gracile Hominid Cranium from Upper Member G of the Shungura Formation, *American Journal of Physical Anthropology* 46:93–108.

Bonadea, I., G. Bottazzi, and M. Lavazza
1971   Echinacin B, an Active Polysaccharide from Echinacea. *Rivista Italiana della Essenze, dei Profumi e delle Piante Officinali* 53:281–295.

Brothwell, D. R.
1963   The Macroscopic Dental Pathology of Some Earlier Human Populations. Pp. 271–288 in Dental Anthropology. D.R. Brothwell, ed. Oxford: Pergamon Press.

Brown, T., and S. Molnar
1990   Interproximal Grooving and Task Activity in Australia. *American Journal of Physical Anthropology* 81:545–553.

Campbell, T.D.
1925   Dentition and Palate of the Australian Aboriginal. Adelaide, Australia: Hassel.

Clapp, A.
1852   Report on Medical Botany. *Transactions of the American Medical Association* 5:698–906.

de Lumley, M.-A.
1973   Anteneandertaliens et Neandertaliens du Bassin Mediterranéen Occidentale Européen. *Etudes Quaternaires* 2:1–626.

Densmore, F.
1918   Teton Sioux Music. *Bureau of American Ethnology Bulletin* 61. Washington.

Eckhardt, R.B.
1990   The Solution for Teething Troubles. *Nature* 343:578.
——, and A.L. Piermarini
1988   Interproximal Grooving of Teeth: Additional Evidence and Interpretation. *Current Anthropology* 29:668–670.

Elvin-Lewis, M.
1979   Empirical Rationale for Teeth Cleaning Plant Selection. *Medical Anthropology* 3:431–458.

——
1986   Therapeutic Rationale of Plants Used to Treat Dental Infections. Pp. 48–69 in Plants in Indigenous Medicine and Diet: Biobehavioral Approaches. N.L. Etkin, ed. Bedford Hills, N.Y.: Redgrave Publishing.

Formicola, V.
1988   Interproximal Grooving of Teeth: Additional Evidence and Interpretation. *Current Anthropology* 29:663–664.

Foster, S.
1985   Echinacea Exalted! The Botany, Culture, History, and Medicinal Uses of the Purple Coneflower. 2nd ed. Brixey, Miss.: Ozark Beneficial Plant Project.

Frayer, D.W.
1991   On the Etiology of Interproximal Grooves. *American Journal of Physical Anthropology* 85:299–304.
——, and M.D. Russell
1987   Artificial Grooves on the Krapina Neanderthal Teeth. *American Journal of Physical Anthropology* 74:393–405.

Gilmore, M.R.
1913   A Study of Ethnobotany of the Omaha Indians. *Collections of the Nebraska State Historical Society* 17:314–357.

——
1919   Uses of Plants by the Indians of the Missouri River Region. Pp. 43–124 in *33rd Annual Report of the Bureau of American Ethnology*. Washington. (Reprinted: University of Nebraska, Lincoln, 1977.)

Grinnell, G.B.
1905   Some Cheyenne Plant Medicines. *American Anthropologist* 7:37–43.

Koch, E., and H. Uebel
1953   Experimental Studies Concerning the Local Action of *Echinacea purpurea* on Tissues. *Arzneimittel-Forschung* 3:16–19.

——
1954   Experimental Studies on the Local Influence of Cortisone and Echinacin upon Tissue Resistance Against Streptococcus Infection. *Arzneimittel-Forschung* 4:551–560.

Kuhn, O.
1953   Echinacea and Phagocytosis. *Arzneimittel-Forschung* 3:194–200.

Larsen, C.S.
1985   Dental Modifications and Tool Use in the Western Great Basin. *American Journal of Physical Anthropology* 67:393–402.

Lewis, W.H., and M. Elvin-Lewis
1977   Medical Botany. New York: John Wiley and Sons.

Lukacs, J.R., and R.F. Pastor
1988   Activity-induced Patterns of Dental Abrasion in Prehistoric Pakistan: Evidence from Mehrgarb and Harappa. *American Journal of Physical Anthropology* 76:377–398.

McGregor, R.L.
1968   The Taxonomy of the Genus *Echinacea* (compositae). *University of Kansas Science Bulletin* 48:113–142.

Moerman, D.E.
1986   Medicinal Plants of Native America. *University of Michigan Museum of Anthropology, Technical Reports* 19.

Molnar, S.
1972   Tooth Wear and Culture: A Survey of Tooth Functions Among Some Prehistoric Populations. *Current Anthropology* 13:511–526.

Nikol'skaya, B.S.
1954   The Blood-clotting and Wound-healing Properties of Preparations of Plant Origin. *Trudy Vsesoyuznyi Obshchestva Fiziologov, Biokhimikov i Farmakologove Akad. Nauk S.S.S.R.* 2:194–197.

Perez, P.J., J.L. De Arsuaga, and J.M. Bermudez de Castro
1982   Atypical Toothwear in Fossil Man. *Paleopathology Newsletter* 39:11–13.

Pindborg, J.J.
1970   Pathology of the Dental Hard Tissues. Philadelphia: W.B. Saunders.

Puech, P.F., and F. Cianfarani
1988   Interproximal Grooving of Teeth: Additional Evidence and Interpretation. *Current Anthropology* 29:665–668.

SAS Institute
1985   SAS User's Guide. Version 5 Edition. Cary, N.C.: SAS Institute.

Schulz, P.D.
1977   Task Activity and Anterior Tooth Grooving in Prehistoric California Indians. *American Journal of Physical Anthropology* 46:87–92.

Senyurek, M.S.
1940   Fossil Man in Tangier. *Papers of the Peabody Museum of Archeology and Ethnology, Harvard University* 16:1–27.

Siffre, A.
1911   Note sur une Usure Spéciale des Molaires du Squelette de La Quina. *Bulletin de la Société Préhistorique Française* 8:741–743.

Smith, H.H.
1928   Ethnobotany of the Meskwaki Indians. *Public Museum of Milwaukee Bulletin* 4:175–326.

Sognnaes, R.F.
1959   Microradiographic Observations on Demineralization Gradients in the Pathogenesis of Hard Tissue Destruction. *Archives of Oral Biology* 1:106–121.

Stoll, A., J. Renz, and A. Brack
1950   Antibacterial Substances, II: Isolation and Constitution of Echinacoside, a Glycoside from the Roots of *Echinacea angustifolia*. *Helvetica Chimica Acta* 33:1877–1893.

Tabeau, P.A.
1939   Tabeau's Narrative of Loisel's Expedition to the Upper Missouri. A.H. Abel, ed. Norman: University of Oklahoma Press.

Turner, C.G., II
1988   Interproximal Grooving of Teeth: Additional Evidence and Interpretation. *Current Anthropology* 29:664–665.

Ubelaker, D.H., T.W. Phenice, and W.M. Bass
1969   Artificial Interproximal Grooving of the Teeth in American Indians. *American Journal of Physical Anthropology* 30:145–150.

Vallois, H.V.
1945   L'Homme fossile de Rabat. *Comptes Rendus de l'Académie des Sciences* 221:669–671.

Vestal, P.A., and R.E. Schultes
1939   The Ecomonic Botany of the Kiowa Indians. Cambridge, Mass.: Botanical Museum.

Wacker, A., and A. Hibig
1978   Virus Inhibition by *Echinacea purpurea*. *Planta Medica* 33:89–102.

Wallace, J.A.
1974   Approximal Grooving of Teeth. *American Journal of Physical Anthropology* 40:385–390.

Weidenreich, F.
1937   The Dentition of Sinanthropus pekinensis: A Comparative Odontography of the Hominids. *Paleontologia Sinica* 101:1–121.

○○○

CHAPTER 12

Skeletal Injuries of Pioneers

GEORGE W. GILL

Folklore holds that life on the western American frontier was rigorous and violent. It creates a picture of lone male adventurers or small groups of explorers moving westward first, followed by pioneer settlers often traveling as entire families. Both pioneer elements, but particularly the early explorers, are assumed to have experienced more physical hardship and violent episodes than citizens living in the context of their own culture in established communities. Such impressions, drawn more from oral tradition than from written history, are hard to confirm or refute. In fact, most of the earliest explorers on the western frontier were plainsmen, mountainmen and settlers totally unknown to history. Therefore, to gain a balanced perspective on the culture history of the frontier, and particularly to understand the lifeways of countless numbers of unknown pioneers, anthropological information as well as written history must be used. Historic archaeology has been used often in this way, to round out history; human osteology, much less often. As a means of documenting violent episodes, human osteology is an excellent tool.

Human osteology and burial archaeology are also excellent sources of information on many other past human activities and conditions, such as health, mortality, and mortuary practices.

Methods and Samples

METHODS

A standard University of Wyoming three-page osteological data form has been completed for each individual skull or skeleton in all three pioneer samples. For each complete, adult specimen this includes 92 measurements and 55 observations of both discrete and continuous anthroposcopic traits. A complete skeletal inventory and record of pathological conditions is also included. Photographs and X-rays have been obtained as required. In most cases of skeletal trauma and skeletal pathology, personnel from the medical sciences have been consulted—orthopedic surgeons, orthodontists, paleopathologists, and radiologists. In all gunshot cases ballistics personnel from the Wyoming State Crime Laboratory, Cheyenne, have been consulted.

Basic determinations for age, sex, race, and stature have been made according to standard procedures as outlined in the basic references. For instance, in this study sex is determined from both metric and nonmetric assessments of pelvic morphology, the cranium, femora, and humeri (Bass 1987; Krogman and Iscan 1986; Stewart 1979).

Ages for infants and children are established by long bone lengths (Johnston 1962), dentition (Schour and Massler 1944), and the formation and fusion of long bone epiphyses and vertebral elements (Anderson 1962; Krogman and Iscan 1986). Age at death for adults is established by evaluation of the pubic symphysis (McKern and Stewart 1957; Stewart 1979), morphological changes in the distal extremities of the ribs (Iscan, Loth, and Wright 1984, 1985), and dental attrition (Ubelaker 1989).

Racial affinities are determined by both anthroposcopic and metric criteria of mostly the skull and teeth (Gill 1986; Gill et al. 1988; Krogman and Iscan 1986; Stewart 1979). Living stature is calculated here using the appropriate Trotter formulae (Stewart 1979). Treatment of skeletal trauma and other pathological conditions is discussed below with the results of these examinations.

SAMPLES

A sample of 31 pioneers from Wyoming (table 1) exists as a result of accidental discoveries and relocations of grave sites. Most are a part of the University of Wyoming Human Osteology Collections, Laramie (those in table 1 with human remains numbers or forensic case numbers), but a few have been reburied. Others are curated in other museum collections in Wyoming.

The few interments listed in table 1 excavated by University of Wyoming anthropologists possess complete burial records and in most cases have been reported (Gill 1976, 1987, 1988; Gill and Smith 1989; Gill et al. 1984). The only exception is the Fort Bridger site material, which is less well preserved than the rest. A photograph of a cranial injury of one of these (Ft. Bridger 2) has been published (Moore et al. 1980:73).

Complete records also exist for Quintina Snoderly (table 1), a woman who died on the Oregon Trail in 1852 near present-day Casper, Wyoming. She was crushed beneath a wagon overturned in the current while crossing the Platte River (Buff 1990).

The Red Mountain cemetery sample from southwestern Wyoming (table 1) was excavated by Wyoming State Crime Laboratory personnel and also has accompanying records. The six individuals from that site are, according to local historians, Chinese-American construction workers on the transcontinental railroad line of 1868 or early miners. The remains are unquestionably Mongoloid, and the well-preserved clothing from the graves supports Chinese origin.

The Fremont County pioneers were recovered by the Fremont County Coroner's Office and are nicely preserved

skeletons. Most others in table 1 are less well preserved and the interments less well documented than those just mentioned. Two from the Trail Town Museum in Cody, Wyoming (Blind Bill and Gallagher) were gunfighters killed in 1894 and have been reinterred in the historic cemetery at TrailTown.

The University of Wyoming osteology files contain full records on two other pioneer samples as well: 33 skeletons from the earliest pioneer Mormon cemetery in Salt Lake Valley, Utah (late 1840s and early 1850s); and 13 burials of West Texas pioneers from two boothill graveyards (Coffey and Trigger Boothill cemeteries) near Ballinger, Texas (1870s). The former sample was excavated by archaeologists with the Office of Public Archaeology, Brigham Young University, Provo, and subcontracted to Wyoming for osteological analysis in 1987 (with transfer to the Wyoming Physical Anthropology Laboratory for one year). The Texas sample was excavated by archaeologists with Mariah Associates, Inc., Albuquerque, New Mexico, in May 1989 as part of a reservoir project survey, excavation, and relocation. The human osteology analysis on this project was likewise subcontracted to University of Wyoming, but with all work conducted at a field laboratory near the site. Both the early Mormons and the Texas pioneers have been reburied. Osteology reports are available for both populations (Gill 1989a, 1989b; Tigner-Wise 1989).

Analysis

DEMOGRAPHY

As seen in fig. 1, the demographic profiles of the three pioneer samples differ significantly. Particularly the Salt Lake Valley pioneers differ from the two groups of Plains pioneers (which are combined on the graphs). Two-thirds of the Mormon cemetery sample consists of individuals below the age of two years, while only one-third of the Texans are of that age, and none of the Northwestern Plains sample. Except for the one child, the Wyoming sample is almost all adults in their 20s, 30s, or early 40s. The oldest seems to be the Glenrock male from along the Oregon Trail, or perhaps the Black woman from Shawnee Creek. The Texas sample, like many cemetery populations of the nineteenth century, is somewhat bimodal (older adults and the very young).

The sex ratios of the Texas and Wyoming samples are noticeably skewed by an over abundance of males, and yet the Salt Lake Valley sample is comprised primarily of females. No adult females occur in the small Texas sample, and of the 29 Wyoming non-Indians (excluding the two admixed Indi-

Table 1. Human Osteological Profile of Wyoming Pioneers

Name: Site/Individual	Specimen Number	Age	Sex	Race	Stature	Completeness	Pathology
Harvey Morgan[a]	—	25 yrs	M	Caucasoid	—	Skull only	Scalping (19 cut marks); wagon hammer mutilation (piercing cranium)
Quintina Snoderly[b]	—	43–55 yrs	F	Caucasoid	165.1 ± 3.55 cm (5' 5")	Nearly complete	Perimortem fractures of vertebrae, spinous processes, transverse processes (T-8–L-3)
Blind Bill[c]	—	30–36 yrs	M	Caucasoid	165.4 ± 3.74 cm 5' 5⅛")	Nearly complete	Perimortem gunshot trauma (fractured right scapula and right 5th rib)
Gallagher[c]	—	30–36 yrs	M	Caucasoid	184.5 ± 4.57 cm 6' 1")	Complete (mummy)	Gunshot trauma
★John Sharp (Ft. Bridger 1a)	HR058	37 yrs	M	Caucasoid	—	Fragmentary	Dental caries, fillings, abscesses. Anomalous canines; possible old fracture of right clavicle
★Ft Bridger 1b	HR059	22–24 yrs	M	Caucasoid	165.1 ± 2.99 cm (5' 5")	Nearly complete	Spina bifida; dental caries, abscess
★Ft. Bridger 2 (Little Muddy River Burial)	HR060	29–36 yrs	M	Caucasoid	175.9 ± 3.27 cm (5' 9¼")	Skull complete; partial postcranial	Scar (100 mm long) on frontal bone with penetration and "uplift" (saber cut?)
Glenrock (Oregon Trail)	UWFC7a	65+ yrs	M	Caucasoid	172.6 ± 2.99 cm (5' 8")	Skull complete; partial postcranial	Broken nose; destroyed mental eminence (partial healing); possible loss of right eye (destroyed right orbit, partial healing)
Glenrock Child	UWFC7b	5–6 yrs	—	Unknown	—	Skull nearly complete; partial postcranial	None evidenced
★Glendo Burial	HRO12	26–33 yrs	F	Caucasoid/ American Indian	159.4 ± 3.55 cm (5' 2¾")	Nearly complete	One small cavity
★Rock Ranch Burial	HRO71	24–30 yrs	M	Negroid	169.2 ± 3.78 cm (5' 6½")	Fragmentary	Multiple gunshot trauma (cranial and postcranial)
★Korell-Bordeux 15	HRO80	31–37 yrs	M	Caucasoid	185.2 ± 2.99 cm (6' 1")	Nearly complete	Multiple gunshot trauma (cranial and postcranial); rib fractures
Ft. Caspar S	HRO83	28–38 yrs	M	Caucasoid	173.6 ± 4.05 cm (5' 8½")	Nearly complete skull, fragmentary postcranial	Old rib fracture (left 2nd); dental caries, abscesses
Ft. Caspar N	HRO84	26–38 yrs	M	Caucasoid	173.1 ± 3.37 cm (5' 8¼")	Fragmentary	Dental caries
Red Mountain 1	HRO90	42–45 yrs	M	Mongoloid	159.3 ± 3.24 cm 5' 2¾")	Broken skull, partial postcranial	Dental caries, abscesses
Red Mountain 2	HRO91	26–34 yrs	M	Mongoloid	159.8 ± 3.27 cm (5' 3")	Skull complete; partial postcranial	Dental caries, abscesses
Red Mountain 3	HRO92	34–42 yrs	M	Mongoloid	159.6 ± 3.24 cm (5' 3")	Nearly complete	Abscesses, alveolar resorption; slight arthritis
Red Mountain 4	HRO93	26–34 yrs	M	Mongoloid	161.1 ± 3.25 cm (5' 3½")	Nearly complete	Caries, abscesses; slight arthritis

(Continued)

Table 1. (*Continued*)

Name: Site/Individual	Specimen Number	Age	Sex	Race	Stature	Completeness	Pathology
Red Mountain 5	HRO94	25–30 yrs	M	Mongoloid	161.0 ± 3.24 cm (5′ 3¼″)	Nearly complete	Perimortem cut marks (ribs); broken humerus (antemortem); dental caries, abscesses
Red Mountain 6	HRO95	42–48 yrs	M	Mongloid	164.4 ± 3.24 cm (5′ 4¾″)	Nearly complete	Caries and abscesses; slight arthritis
Green River Soldier[d]	—	25–33 yrs	M	Caucasoid	171.7 ± 2.99 cm (5′ 7¾″)	Nearly complete; missing mandible	Broken nose; caries
Cody Pipe[e]	—	35–45 yrs	M	Caucasoid	—	Skull only	"Pipe" groove in anterior teeth (left side)
Cody No Pipe[e]	—	30–35 yrs	M	Caucasoid	—	Skull only	None evidenced
Shawnee Creek Skull[f]	—	50+ yrs	F	Negroid	—	Skull only	None evidenced
Bates Creek[f]	—	25–38 yrs	F	Caucasoid	—	Skull only	None evidenced
Shell Burial[c]	—	50+ yrs	M	Caucasoid	—	Skull only	Depressed fracture (left frontal); abscesses, tooth loss
Washakie County	UWFC45	26–35 yrs	M	Caucasoid/ American Indian	167.8 + 4.05 cm (5′ 6″)	Skull, partial skeleton	Anomalous incisor tooth (impacted)
Fremont County 1	UWFC70-1	35–43 yrs	F	Caucasoid	157.6 + 3.55 cm (5′ 2¼″)	Nearly complete	Abscess and dental caries; slight arthritis
Fremont County 2	UWFC70-2	50+ yrs	M	Caucasoid	173.5 + 2.99 cm (5′ 8½″)	Nearly complete	Double fracture (left tibia, fibula); filled teeth, loss of teeth, abscesses; slight arthritis
Fremont County 3	UWFC70-3	45–55 yrs	M	Caucasoid	164.6 + 2.99 cm (5′ 5″)	Nearly complete	Fracture of left humerus and left ribs 10 and 11; dental caries, abscesses; slight arthritis
*Divide Burial	—	22–24 yrs	M	Caucasoid	176.7 + 2.99 cm (5′ 9½″)	Nearly complete	Maxillary fracturing and tooth loss (edentulous maxilla)

[a]Pioneer Museum, Lander, Wyo.

[b]Casper College, Casper, Wyo.

[c]Trail Town Museum, Cody, Wyo.

[d]Western Wyoming College, Rock Springs, Wyo.

[e]Buffalo Bill Historical Center, Cody, Wyo.

[f]Wyoming Pioneer Memorial Museum, Douglas, Wyo.

*Indicates burials excavated by University of Wyoming personnel under Gill's direction.

ans) the sample is 82.8 percent adult male and 13.7 percent adult female (no infants/newborns and 3.5 percent children). In marked contrast, the Salt Lake Valley sample is 87.9 percent females and infants/newborns, and only 6.1 percent males (and 6.1 percent children and adolescents).

Even though quite narrow in age and sex distribution, the Northwestern Plains sample is much more varied in racial composition than the Salt Lake Valley sample (table 1, fig. 1) and also in patterns of skeletal trauma. The small Texas sample appears to parallel quite closely the Wyoming population in these two areas, with one admixed adult male (possibly Hispanic) and a wide range of severe skeletal injuries and other signs of a rigorous and violent life (for example, recovered bullets, fractures).

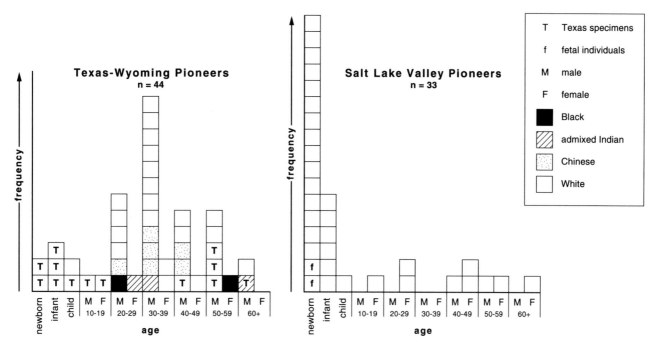

Fig. 1. Age at death for the skeletal populations of Texas and Wyoming and the Salt Lake Valley, Utah.

INDIVIDUAL PROFILES

Of the 77 pioneers from the broader study (Wyoming, Texas, and Utah) four individuals from the Northwestern Plains (Wyoming) sample have been selected for this report. Selection has been based largely upon the extent and complexity of the skeletal traumas.

HARVEY MORGAN

Harvey Morgan was a 25-year-old White frontiersman living at Camp Brown in 1870, at the present-day town site of Lander, Wyoming. On June 27 he and two companions embarked upon what was to be a brief sojourn from the fort. As they were riding in their wagon, they were ambushed by Indians; all three were killed. The scene of the massacre was discovered within approximately two hours after the Indians had left. A detachment from Camp Brown was dispatched the next day to retrieve the bodies for burial and make a report of the incident. The men had apparently been fortified behind their wagon, which was badly shot up. Harvey Morgan was known in the region as an expert marksman, and according to reports over 200 spent cartridges from his rifle were recovered at the site, suggesting that perhaps he had done the most damage to the raiding party. It has been assumed that once all ammunition was gone the three Whites were overtaken and

killed. Two of the three were scalped and Harvey Morgan's body mutilated. According to the account on file with the Fremont County Pioneer Association, "The ground was literally packed down around the scene of battle by thousands of moccasin tracks. The Indians had ridden in a circle around the whites while fighting, and had a beaten track. There seems to have been a large war party." The account goes on to say that, "after they had killed the whites, they scalped Jerome Mason and Harvey Morgan and then cut the skin across the back of Morgan's neck and split the skin down the entire length of his back, and skinned the hide back about three inches on each side and took out the sinews of the back. They then drove the wagon hammer [also called the queen pin] through his head with the neckyoke" (Farlow 1913).

The remains of the three men were buried along a stream at Camp Brown, and over the years the grave locations were lost. In 1908 the body of Morgan was discovered. It was clearly identifiable with the wagon hammer still in place. A fourth mutilation may have been done to Morgan's body and not reported in the official military documents. By this account, Morgan had also had his genitals cut from his body and placed in his mouth (Henry Hudson, personal communication 1980).

The skull of Harvey Morgan (fig. 2) is all that remains for study today, even though earlier accounts speak of "the body of Morgan" being in the possession of the Fremont County

Fig. 2. Harvey Morgan cranium. Left parietal shows the exit wound of the wagon hammer and two cut marks probably related to the scalping (bracketed with arrows).

Pioneer Association. From the skull alone, two of the four mutilations can be documented. The skull has had plaster poured inside to secure the hammer, which had loosened over the years as the cranial bones dessicated. A photograph (copyright 1913) of the cranium taken before the plaster was added shows the hammer in exactly the same position as today. This curatorial approach has rendered examination of entry and exit wounds much more difficult, but appears not to have altered appreciably, if any, the original position of the hammer.

Besides the hammer entry and exit wounds there are 19 cut marks associated with the scalping, and some severe radiating fracture lines caused by the hammer mutilation.

The longest cut marks are three across the frontal bone (38 millimeters, 58 millimeters, and 41 millimeters), perfectly horizontal and parallel and beginning 66 millimeters above the right orbit. The one highest on the frontal bone is 29 millimeters below point bregma. Another parallel cut mark just above and lateral to the uppermost of these long cuts is similar but shorter (23 millimeters). Six other shorter cut marks (from 7 millimeters to 23 millimeters) occur at the same level above the left eye, and are oriented in approximately the same horizontal position.

Two parallel marks 26 mm long may be seen 5 millimeters above the nuchal line on the left side of the occipital, and 2 millimeters above these a smaller (9 millimeters long) cut mark exists. Only two are visible on the right parietal, near the hammer entry. The longest is a 32-milli-meter cut mark 13 millimeters below the hammer entry and 29 millimeters above the temporal suture. The other line, about half that length, closely parallels and intersects the longer line (creating more of a "double line" than two separate lines).

Three additional scalping marks occur on the left parietal in the vicinity of the exit of the hammer tip. Two of these are visible in fig. 2, and these are indicated by arrows. The longest (48 millimeters) parallels the superior fracture line and has its inferior tip obliterated by the hammer exit. A shorter, double-cut mark, 20 mm long, is nearly perpendicular to the long, superior cut mark and may be seen in fig. 2 between the hammer exit and the temporal suture (28 millimeters below the hammer exit).

Figure 2 shows three radiating fractures from the hammer exit wound. Fracture lines 1 and 3 clearly represent perimortem fractures, as does the first 30 millimeters of fracture line 2. An extension of fracture line 2 may be a postmostem dry crack. The largest fractures are associated with the hammer entry. One (21-millimeter) fracture line extends from the entry wound diagonally across both parietals, traversing the sagittal suture. A wider, heavier fracture divides the right parietal inferiorly (as well as the right temporal). This 75-millimeter-long crack separates the right auditory meatus from the mandibular fossa by 27 millimeters (normally about 10 millimeters). A third large fracture (85 millimeters long) extends from the entry wound to the sagittal suture.

FORT BRIDGER 2

The skull of Fort Bridger 2 (fig. 3) comes from a pioneer grave that was eroding from the banks of the Little Muddy River near Fort Bridger, Wyoming. Most of the skeleton was recovered during excavations in spring 1978 by an archaeological crew consisting of University of Wyoming archaeology-osteology students and Fort Bridger Museum personnel. Osteological analysis has shown the individual to be a White man between 29 and 36 years of age who had suffered a severe blow to the frontal area sometime prior to death.

The grave was located between the riverbank and the original frontier-period Union Pacific Railroad grade. According to historians at the Fort Bridger historical site, the grave was that of a railroader working on the transcontinental line in 1868. Allegedly a gravestone once existed at the site, which revealed the 1868 date, but was removed from the threatened site a few years prior to our salvage excavation.

Figure 3 shows a rather straight scar 100 millimeters long, extending diagonally from just above the right orbit (where the wound was deepest) to a terminal point 53 millimeters above the left orbit. Endocranial examination shows that the first 40 millimeters (over the right eye), which never fully closed, did penetrate the inner table of the frontal bone.

Radiographic analysis reveals very little if any fracture line beyond the first 40 millimeters, so perhaps only the periosteum was affected over the last 60 mm of the scar. A clear ridging occurs beyond the open 40-millimeter scar but no noticable fracture line.

This trauma may represent a Civil War injury, perhaps a saber wound. The age of the individual at death, the degree of healing (fully healed), and the year of death (1868) all tend to point to the Civil War, or at least to the war years. The long, straight aspect of the wound itself, without displacement or depressed fracturing, also suggests an instrument such as an ax or saber. The possibility of a fracture by a blow from a blunt instrument, or object, cannot be entirely ruled out. However, a radiating fracture line from such a blow from a blunt object would tend *not* to follow a perfectly straight line. Also, at the most distal extremity of the scar (45 millimeters above the left eye) it looks as though some "lifting" occurred. According to paleopathologist Ellis R. Kerley (personal communication 1978), most Civil War saber cut marks show a "lifting" of the bone of the outer table of the skull. Thus, the most likely conclusion regarding the cause of this severe skeletal trauma is that it was a cut wound from a long (or very wide), sharp instrument. The lack of fracturing and the lack of deep depression to the outer table of the frontal bone, plus the suggestion of lifting at the terminus of the wound, also suggest a saber as the instrument.

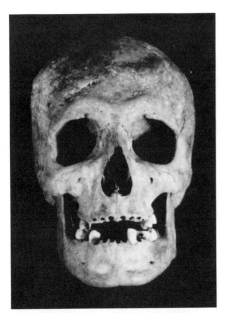 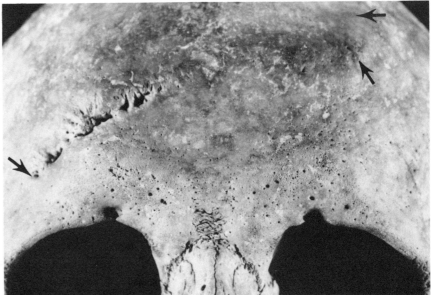

Fig. 3. Fort Bridger 2 cranium, which exhibits a 100-mm scar across the frontal bone. The frontal bone shows the traumatic lesion. The deepest penetration (beginning at the left arrow) broke through the inner table of the skull and never fully closed. The right arrows bracket the terminus of the lesion, which seems to represent "uplift" of the outer cranial table.

ROCK RANCH SLAVE

The historical Rock Ranch, located four miles west of Torrington, Wyoming, in the earliest days of its establishment was a trading post as well as ranch. A former plantation owner from Missouri established the ranch–trading post and brought Black slaves there in the 1850s.

In autumn 1980 excavations at the site led to the discovery of a human skeleton buried inside the corner of a former ranch building. According to local stories a Black slave from the early days of the Rock Ranch trading post was killed and buried under the floor of a building on the ranch (Donald Housh, personal communication 1980). The interment did clearly fit two of the three points of the story. It came from inside the corner of an old building (Gill 1988, burial photographs), and the bones themselves show that the person had been killed (fig. 4). The remaining question was whether the remains represented those of a Negroid individual.

Clearly the Rock Ranch remains are those of a non-Indian based upon the form of the incisor teeth (not even trace shoveling) and the type and degree of wear on the teeth. Furthermore, a small gold filling on the lingual surface of the upper, lateral incisor would be most unusual for an American Indian from that period (Gill 1988). Regarding the distinction between Caucasoid and Negroid classification, clearly the majority of diagnostic features come out strongly on the Negroid side. Among the 15 traits of this partial skeleton indicative of American Blacks are procumbent anterior teeth suggesting marked alveolar prognathism, low cranial vault, narrow cranial breadth and postbregmatic depression (Krogman and Iscan 1986); smooth cranial architecture with high bone density as evidenced by the texture of the outer cranial table, and a protuberant occipital form (Bass 1987); undulating supraorbital ridges in combination with a rounded frontal bone and sharp upper orbital margins (Krogman and Iscan 1986); distinctive "Negroid" angle and form of the mastoid process (Gill 1986); and a nearly dolicocranic cranial index (Krogman and Iscan 1986). Some shape features of the mandible resemble those often seen on male Blacks, but rarely on male Whites (unless advanced in age), that is, narrow corporal thickness to the mandible in combination with an oblique gonial angle (Gill 1986).

The partial skeleton appears to represent the remains of a Black male, 24–30 years old, and of average stature (Gill 1987) who met death from multiple gunshot wounds and was buried beneath the floor of a building at the Rock Ranch.

The multiple gunshot injuries sustained at or near the time of death of this individual were from at least three bullets. One of these, lodged in the centrum of a lumbar vertebra (L3), is from a .44 caliber weapon (Gill 1987:105). The point of entry of another large caliber projectile is evident through the right parietal bone (fig. 4). No definite exit wound exists for that particular entry wound, although fractured bone is present at the cranial base which does suggest exit. Another projectile

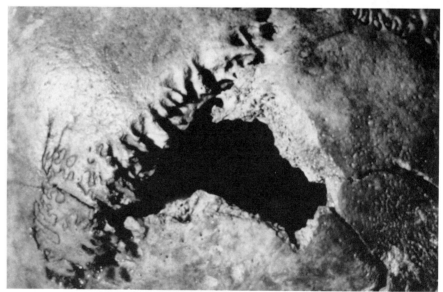

Fig. 4. Gunshot entry wound of the right parietal of the Rock Ranch slave (HR071) and exit wound of the occipital bone.

entered between the eyes (illustrated in Gill 1988:fig. 6) and did continue through the brain to exit below the lambdoidal suture line on the left side of the squamosal portion of the occipital (fig. 4). The frontal entry wound is only partly preserved and difficult to study, but would seem to be of a smaller caliber (11-millimeter-diameter opening) (Gill 1987: 105).

The injury profile of this individual, regarding the multiple gunshot wounds, is unusual and could lead to at least two possible interpretations. The possibility of an execution-style killing, involving more than one weapon, is a clear possibility (Gill 1987). This is suggested by the varying angles of entry and possibly different bullet sizes. Also, the number of "killing" shots is more than required. An ambush with a final round between the eyes is also a possibility.

KORELL-BORDEAUX 15

During archaeological excavations in autumn 1980 at the Korell-Bordeaux site near Lingle, Wyoming, and within the perimeter of a small Plains Indian burial ground, the grave of a White frontiersman was found (Gill 1987; Gill et al. 1984). In brief, the grave (fig. 5) was located on the edge of a bluff above the site of the old Bordeaux Trading Post. It was a part of the larger Korell-Bordeaux site located on Korell family property three miles west of the town of Lingle.

Explorations at this site were in response to a proton magnetometer survey that indicated a grave site location. This survey had followed disinterment of 13 graves from the Korell land, which were discovered during earth-moving operations, and which seem to represent one or more small Plains Indian cemeteries. These burials, well endowed with Euro-American and Plains Indian artifacts, were probably associated with the Bordeaux Trading Post, which was just north of the cemetery along the North Platte River, and the Oregon Trail, which passed below the bluff and next to the trading post (Korell 1981). Other historic sites in the immediate vicinity that could relate to the grave site are Fort Laramie, the Gratten Massacre site, the Pony Express route, the Mormon Trail, and the Rock Ranch trading post.

The tall, robust frontiersman of approximately 34 years of age was killed in 1869 or 1870, judging from the dates and degree of wear on some nickels in a coin pouch around his neck. It looks as though he had been married and lost his wife shortly before his death, as evidenced by a black ring of mourning next to his German silver wedding band. He was very clearly Caucasoid, from all skeletal criteria (Gill et al. 1984), and likely of British descent based upon certain physi-

Fig. 5. Grave site of Korell-Bordeaux 15 (HR080). The face is obscured by a wide-brimmed black hat.

cal traits and cultural associations (particularly the mourning jewelry). His remains were laid to rest next to the graves of several American Indians. The Plains Indians were in coffins, but this White plainsman was buried without a coffin (fig. 5). Burial was with boots on, a large-brimmed black hat placed over the face, and what seems to have been buckskin pants, a shirt with small buttons and a jacket with large metal buttons (Gill 1987; Gill et al. 1984).

This individual had also sustained multiple gunshot wounds (fig. 6). One projectile (.44 or .45 caliber) entered the cranium above the left eye and exited low on the right site of the occipital bone. The points of entry and exit provide an angle of trajectory that shows that the firearm was held well above the head of the victim when fired (Gill et al. 1984). This at first seems unusual for a victim who was about six feet one inch tall, but is possibly explained by another wound to the hip (fig 6). A shattered proximal femur with clear perimortem fracturing apparently represents another gunshot injury caused by a large caliber weapon (Gill 1987:105).

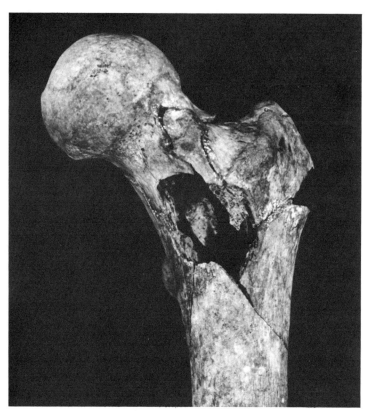

Fig. 6. Gunshot entry wounds, above the left eye and to the proximal left femur of HR080. The hip was shattered by the large caliber round, which severed the head and neck from the diaphysis.

The presence of the severe trauma to the hip, considered in conjunction with the high angle of entry of the cranial gunshot wound, suggests a logical sequence of events. Among the various possibilities, the sequence that appears most probable is a gunshot wound to the hip which brought the large frontiersman to the ground, then a second shot above the left eye at close range, fired from a position above the wounded man's head (Gill et al. 1984:235). Ribs 10–12 on the right side of the man's chest were broken and partly healed at the time of death.

Interpretation

Large numbers of lone males and all-male groups first penetrated the wilderness of the trans-Mississippi West, to be followed by settler groups that included women and children. This explains why the skeletal samples of most populations of western pioneers from unmarked graves (which are usually the oldest graves) tend to be skewed heavily toward adult males. As shown in fig. 1, the sample of Northwestern Plains pioneers from Wyoming consists of 25 males, 5 females, and

only one child (no infants). The Texas population is much less skewed from a normal population curve but seems to tend in somewhat the same direction regarding the preponderance of adult males. Standing in marked contrast to both the Wyoming and Texas pioneer samples is the Salt Lake Valley Mormon population, which is 69.7 percent infants and newborns and reveals three adult females for every adult male. This would seem to be due in part to the Mormom pattern of settlement, which was to move entire communities of men, women, and children to Salt Lake Valley to immediately settle and farm. The high percentage of women and children in the Mormon sample undoubtedly reflects also their practice of polygyny.

The ages of the adult Texans at the time of death are quite consistent which those of the two male Mormon pioneers (late middle-age to old age) from the Salt Lake Valley study. Both populations contrast markedly with the Wyoming sample, which shows much younger ages at death. The average age at death for the Wyoming pioneers was 36 years, as opposed to 55.5 years for the adult male Texans and Mormons. This and other characteristics of the Wyoming sample suggest a very high percentage of unsettled, lone travlers (hunters, trappers, and soldiers). This interpretation is consistent with not only the narrow range of ages, but also the skewed sex ratio, the type and extent of traumatic injury, and the number of violent deaths.

Dental health of the Wyoming pioneers seems to be normal for a nineteenth-century frontier population. Almost no fillings are to be found, but rather some unattended caries (usually small) and occasional abscesses. The caries frequency for the pioneer Whites from Wyoming is 20 percent (Tigner-Wise 1989). The sample of frontier Blacks is too small to compare with the Whites, but the historic Chinese from the Red Mountain cemetery (not yet fully studied with regard to dental pathology) appear to be overall in much worse condition (some extremely large caries and multiple abscesses). The American Indians from the Northwestern Plains, on the other hand, are in overall much better condition dentally than the Whites or any of the other historic populations (except for their extreme dental attrition, particularly in the region of the Red Desert in southern Wyoming).

Clearly the healthiest teeth among the pioneer Whites are among the Texas pioneers. The samples from the Coffey and Trigger Boothill cemeteries show a 1.8 percent caries frequency. This is a much lower frequency than among most civilized agriculturists (generally 10–27 percent) and is comparable to prehistoric hunters and gatherers (Turner 1979). Curiously, three out of five of the adult Texans also show edge-edge occlusion, another trait of hunter populations (and a rare condition among modern Whites). One of the Wyoming frontiersmen also shows edge-edge bite and marked attrition, resembling the Texas cattlemen and prehistoric hunters. It is possible that the chewing of tough food, such as jerky, from early childhood might be an explanation for these unexpected occlusion patterns. The lower caries frequency is more complex and probably results from a combination of various environmental factors (diet, water supply) and perhaps genetic ones.

Equally surprising is the extremely high caries frequency of 54 percent among the Salt Lake Valley pioneers. All adults in that population were badly afflicted. Severe problems with dental health (like this but rarely so severe) are relatively common among horticulturists who rely heavily upon starchy foods and less on meat in their diet (Turner 1979). The Wyoming pioneers (trappers, hunters, railroaders) relied less upon bread, cereals, and other starchy products from the farm than did the Mormon farmers, and much more on bison, deer, and other meat sources.

These variations in diet probably account for at least some of the differences in dental health between the two groups. The Texans were largely ranchers and cattle drovers with presumably a high meat content in their diets as well. They also appear to have come from frontier families as children (unlike the Mormons and perhaps the majority of the Wyoming pioneers), with tough food in their diets from a much earlier age (judging from the patterns of occlusion and severe wear).

Aside from the dental problems of particularly the Mormons, skeletal evidences within all three pioneer samples for chronic diseases are very few. The Mormon sample suggests the most, with not only the high infant death rate, but some transverse lines (Harris lines) of growth arrest on the infant long bones and some cases of cribra orbitalea (Gill 1989a; Tigner-Wise 1989). Such things seem to occur when growth and development is disrupted by childhood disease or malnutrition. In the Mormon sample these effects seem to be at a fairly normal level for the mid-nineteenth century, when childhood diseases were very common and often quite devastating. Even the high infant mortality rate seen in the Mormon pioneer sample (almost 70%) is not, according to Tigner-Wise (1989), too far out of the ordinary for North American populations of the 1840s and 1850s.

Many traumatic injuries and signs of violence are evidenced on the bones of the Wyoming pioneers. If one omits from the sample those of a different cultural background (admixed Caucasoid/American Indians and the historic Chinese), and those specimens that are largely incomplete (skull only), as well as the one partial child's skeleton, an exceedingly high percentage of individuals (82.4%) show signs of skeletal trauma (14 of the 17 specimens). At least six of these (Morgan, Snoderly, Gallagher, Blind Bill, Korell-Bordeaux 15, and the Rock Ranch slave) died a violent death (35.3%). Furthermore, all five males of that sample were killed by other human beings. Gunshot trauma probably accounts for all violent deaths, even though Harvey Morgan's exact cause of death at the hands of the Plains Indian war party is not precisely known (arrows, war clubs, gunshot, the wagon hammer?).

In marked contrast, the pioneer Mormon sample shows no signs of violence to the skeleton and only one individual with skeletal trauma (one of the two adult males reveals a severe double fracture of the radius and ulna, successfully healed). The settled life of farmers, leading a well-organized religious life (in marked contrast to the Wyoming frontier) probably accounts for these differences. Of course, the radically different sex ratios may contribute as well, since among the Wyoming pioneers the females rarely show injury either, and in no case do they show signs of human violence on the skeleton.

Among the Texas pioneers a significant number of skeletal traumas and signs of violence are evidenced as well. Even though the adult sample is small, it suggests a frequency of trauma somewhat comparable to that for the Wyoming pioneers. However, a few contrasts are also suggested. The Wyoming remains seem to exhibit a few more signs of violence from fighting and warfare, while the Texas skeletons show more blunt force trauma (possibly injuries associated with the herding of livestock, paricularly as conducted from horseback) (Gill 1989b). Common to the Texans are traumatic injuries to the dorsal skeleton (such as spinous processes of vertebrae and proximal ribs) covering wide areas over the back, as if caused by trampling from cattle or horses. Blade wounds and recovered bullets were found in this small sample as well. The variations between these two Plains populations (Northwestern Plains and Southern Plains) may eventually prove to be slight as sample sizes grow.

Regarding stature and general robusticity, all three samples of pioneer Whites seem to be similar to each other and to differ somewhat from White population averages. Stature is probably slightly above the average for the late 1800s. The Wyoming White males average 173.5 centimeters or just under five feet eight and one-half inches (n = 12). The Texas drovers (n=6) average the same (174.0 centimeters) and the two Mormon males slightly less (171.8 centimeters). By pooling the two Caucasoid females from Wyoming with the five Mormon females an average of 163.6 4centimeters (almost 5 feet four and one-half inches) (n = 7) is obtained. The sample of Blacks is insufficient to allow any generalization as to stature, and the six Oriental males average about 160.9 centimeters.

Robusticity among the male Whites on the frontier is noteworthy than stature. The males of all three frontier samples are quite robust, particularly in the arms (humeral head diameters of 51–55 millimeters) and cranial architecture (large supraorbital tori, robust nuchal lines). This kind of variance toward greater robusticity among pioneers, as opposed to the populations from which they come, has been the subject of discussions among physical anthropologists. For instance, Hrdlicka (1925:1) characterized the North American founding fathers as being, "on the whole, rather above than below the average in sturdiness and energy, for in those times the coming over meant considerable cost as well as hardship, and the weaklings either stayed behind or were rapidly eliminated under the strenuous conditions." It appears that the western pioneers of North America were generally more robust than their close cousins inhabiting the more settled regions of the eastern United States. In order to substantiate these inferences about the western pioneers, the existing skeletal sample will need to be increased.

Other more remarkable anthropometric findings among the pioneer Whites have been found in addition to these variations in stature and robusticity. Cranial size and craniofacial proportions are of particular interest. So far the female sample is a bit small for study, but among the males clear trends exist. The males of all three samples of pioneer Whites have long, large crania and long faces. The cranial capacity averages for all three samples are above 1520 cc. These large rugged skulls also average in the dolichocranic range. Faces too are long and narrow (Gill 1989a, 1989b; Tigner-Wise 1989). These patterns of size, shape, and rugosity of the cranium, in conjunction with the long faces and a propensity (at least for some) toward edge-edge occlusion are of interest, but the reasons for this morphological pattern are not entirely clear, and the relatively small sample sizes should be kept in mind. Certainly the limited evidence at hand suggests an exciting working hypothesis that the western pioneers differed significantly from parental populations in ways predictable according to natural selection theory. Perhaps even the remarkable evidences for skeletal trauma and the violent episodes in the lives of these early Whites on the frontier all fit within the same emerging picture of them as a quite select group.

Summary

The pioneer skeletons from the Northwestern Plains in Wyoming show an unusual amount of skeletal pathology as a result of traumatic injury. The same may be true for West Texas drovers, judging from a single small sample. Violent episodes among the earliest pioneers appear to have been quite common. Over one-third of the frontier Whites from Wyoming died a violent death at the hands of other human beings. This profile of injury, conflict, and early death among largely young adult male frontiersmen differs markedly from the pattern seen among the Salt Lake Valley pioneers of Utah, who followed a farming way of life. Most American Indian samples from the Northwestern Plains likewise show considerably less skeletal injury than the early Wyoming Whites. A single possible exception is the Red Desert sample of the early Late Prehistoric period where brutal homicides and attempted homicides are documented skeletally (Gill 1991).

Generally, the Plains Indian samples show much less severity in their skeletal traumas and fewer of them (frontal depressions and broken noses). These skeletal traumas among the Northwestern Plains Indians, among females as well as males, seem in most cases to be the result of some form of domestic violence (Combs 1990; Nashelsky 1984), and may have sometimes been inflicted ritually in public (Wright 1984). The pioneer White females show none of these signs of violence to their crania.

A number of reasons account for the contrasts between the Plains Indians and the White frontiersmen in skeletal trauma. For one thing the White frontiersmen appear from all evidence and from historical accounts, to be a select group and not an average sampling from the Euro-American population at large. The Northwestern Plains Indian sample appears, on the other hand, to be a normal cross-section of the total population. Furthermore, the weapons utilized within the Euro-American culture during this early period on the plains were more devastating than most weapons available to the Indians and would tend to leave more marks of violence upon the skeleton. Also a reasonable percentage of the White males making up the frontier sample may have been Civil War veterans carrying injuries incurred during an unusually brutal period of warfare. Additionally, the pioneer Whites represent individuals exposed to the harshness of the frontier and beyond the protection provided by their civilization in the eastern United States.

Other intriguing osteological findings that seem to support the idea that the pioneers in the West were a select and somewhat unique element are the indications of unusual skeletal size and robusticity among the males as well as large cranial sizes and rather extreme craniofacial proportions (long narrow skulls and faces). Even though only 77 pioneer skeletons have been studied (and only 32 adult males and 11 adult females), the findings do justify a tentative hypothesis of significant skeletal variations as well as unusal levels of violence indicated on the bones. Possible explanations for the osteometric variations could be natural selecton (such as selective migration and/or differential survival), immediate ancestry (local racial variants producing the pioneers), certain direct actions of the environment (especially regarding dental occlusion), or combinations of these factors.

This study suggests that violent episodes were probably commonplace on the western frontier. More appears to have been happening on the Great Plains than can be gleaned from history books.

References Cited

Anderson, J.E.
1962 The Human Skeleton. Ottawa: National Museums of Canada.
Bass, W.M.
1987 Human Osteology: A Laboratory and Field Manual of the Human Skeleton. 3rd ed. Columbia: Missouri Archaeological Society.

Buff, C.M.
1990 The Excavation of an Oregon Trail Burial. *The Wyoming Archaeologist* 33(3–4):51–62.
Combs, E.A.
1990 Prehistoric Plains Indian Skeletal Injuries: An Examination and Analysis. Unpublished manuscript on file, Department of Anthropology, University of Wyoming, Laramie.
Farlow, E.J.
1913 Photograph and one-page manuscript. Fremont County Pioneer Museum, Lander, Wyoming.
Gill, G.W.
1976 The Glendo Skeleton and Its Meaning in Light of Postcontact Racial Dynamics in the Great Plains. *Plains Anthropologist* 21(72):81–88.
—— 1986 Craniofacial Criteria in Forensic Race Identification. In Forensic Osteology. K.J. Reichs, ed. Springfield, Ill.: Charles C. Thomas.
—— 1987 Human Skeletons from the Rock Ranch and Korell-Bordeaux Sites. *The Wyoming Archaeologist* 30(3–4):103–107.
—— 1988 A Partial Human Skeleton from the Rock Ranch Site, Southeastern Wyoming. (Unpublished manuscript on file, Department of Anthropology, University of Wyoming, Laramie.)
—— 1989a Osteological Analysis of the Salt Lake Valley Pioneers. (Report submitted to the Office of Public Archaeology, Brigham Young University, Provo, Utah.)
—— 1989b Analysis of Skeletal Remains from the Coffey and Trigger Boothill Cemeteries, Stacy Reservoir Project, Ballinger, Texas. (Report submitted to Mariah Associates, Inc., Albuquerque, New Mexico.)
—— 1991 Human Skeletal Remains on the Northwestern Plains. In Prehistoric Hunters of the High Plains, G.C. Frison, ed. 2nd ed. San Diego: Academic Press.
——, J.W. Fisher, Jr., and G.M. Zeimens
1984 A Pioneer Burial Near the Historic Bordeaux Trading Post. *Plains Anthropologist* 23(15):229–238.
——, and C.S. Smith
1989 The Divide Burial from Near Wamsutter, Sweetwater County, Wyoming. *The Wyoming Archaeologist* 32(3–4):61–80.
——, S.S. Hughes, S.M. Bennett, and B.M. Gilbert
1988 Racial Indentification from the Midfacial Skeleton with Special Reference to American Indian and Whites. *Journal of Forensic Sciences* 33(1):92–99.

Hrdlička, A.

1925 *The Old Americans*. Baltimore, Md.: Williams & Wilkins.

Iscan, M.Y., S. Loth, and R.K. Wright

1984 Age Estimation from the Rib by Phase Analysis: White Males. *Journal of Forensic Science* 29(4):1094–1104.

———

1985 Age Estimation from the Rib by Phase Analysis: White Females. *Journal of Forensic Sciences* 30(3):853–863.

Johnson, F.E.

1962 Growth of the Long Bones of Infants and Young Children at Indian Knoll. *American Journal of Physical Anthropology* 20(3):249–254.

Korell, A.

1981 Comments on the Korell-Bordeaux Site. *The Wyoming Archaeologist* 24(1):28–34.

Krogman, W.M., and M.Y. Iscan

1986 The Human Skeleton in Forensic Medicine. 2nd ed. Springfield, Ill.: Charles C. Thomas.

McKern, T.W., and T.D. Stewart

1957 Skeletal Age Changes in Young American Males. *Quartermaster Research and Development Center, U.S. Army, Nartick, Massachusetts, Technical Report* EP-45.

Moore, L.G., P.W. VanArsdale, J.E. Glittenberg, and R.A. Aldrich

1980 The Biocultural Basis of Health. St. Louis, Mo.: C.V. Mosby.

Nashelsky, M.B.

1984 A Survey of the Traumatic Injury Seen on the Skeletal Remains of a Sample of Prehistoric Northwestern Plains Indians. (Senior Honors Research Paper, Department of Anthropology, University of Wyoming, Laramie.)

Schour, I., and M. Massler

1944 Development of the Human Dentition. Chart. Chicago: American Dental Association.

Stewart, T.D.

1979 Essentials in Forensic Anthropology. Springfield, Ill.: Charles C. Thomas.

Tigner-Wise, L.F.

1989 Skeletal Analysis of a Mormon Pioneer Population from Salt Lake Valley, Utah. (Unpublished Masters Thesis, University of Wyoming, Laramie.)

Turner, C.G., II

1979 Dental Anthropological Indications of Agriculture Among the Jomon People of Central Japan. *American Journal of Physical Anthropology* 51(4):619–636.

Ubelaker, D.H.

1989 Human Skeletal Remains; Excavation, Analysis, Interpretation. 2nd ed. Washington, D.C.: Taraxacum.

Wright, M.P.

1984 The Physical Abuse of Plains Indian Women: An Ethnographic Overview. (Unpublished manuscript on file, Department of Anthropology, University of Wyoming, Laramie.)

ooo

Biological Distance Relationships and Population Variation in Cranial and Postcranial Measurements

○○○

CHAPTER 13

The Social, Historical, and Functional Dimensions of Skeletal Variation

RICHARD L. JANTZ

Metric data are perhaps the most fundamental data in biological anthropology. Measurements have proven extremely adaptable to questions and methods available at any given time. Measurement arose initially to aid in forming the discrete categories thought to exist in nature (Hursh 1976). Measurement, primarily of crania, began in earnest in the mid-nineteenth century when it was used to justify notions of racial superiority (Gould 1981). The Frankfurt conference, held in 1882, and conferences in Monaco in 1906 and Geneva in 1912 led to standardized measurements, many of which continue to be used (Hrdlicka 1939).

Two sets of developments have interacted to stimulate use of metric data to investigate anthropological questions. First is the development of multivariate statistical procedures, culminating in Mahalanobis's generalized distance and Fisher's discriminant functions (Howells 1984). The computational burden of these statistics prevented their widespread application until the development of electronic computers and statistical packages. Since then, anthropologists, often working with statisticians, have employed a bewildering array of statistical tools to draw out the biological meaning of metric variation.

Second, microcomputers and readily available software allow development and efficient management of large data bases (Jantz and Moore-Jansen 1988; Schwidetzky 1984). This technology in turn allows specification of more complex models to explain morphometric variation. For crania, the basic idea that morphometric similarity implies genetic similarity has been augmented by formal models allowing testing of specific hypotheses. These studies include attempts to infer large-scale immigration patterns and regional population structure (Sokal and Uytterschaut 1987), differentiation via genetic drift (Scuilli and Mahaney 1991), postmarital residence patterns (Konigsberg 1988), and within-sample heterogeneity (Key and Jantz 1990).

At the same time, it is becoming clearer that skeletal structures, both cranial and postcranial, are subject to a great many environmental responses requiring new classes of models. Functional models have been infrequently employed to explain cranial variation. Reduction in cranial size has been attributed to lower demands associated with agriculture (Larsen 1982). Craniofacial restructuring has been attributed to changes in masticatory demands associated with agriculture (Carlson and Van Gerven 1977), and Guagliardo (1982) has shown cranial response to dental wear.

The chapters in this section are grouped together by virtue of employing metric techniques to address questions of skeletal variation in the Plains. Most of them fit into and extend the framework described above. The first four chapters utilize cranial measurements, but in different ways and to different ends.

Key's chapter continues the long Plains tradition of using cranial measurements to infer evolutionary and hence historical relationships among groups. This tradition begins with Bass's (1964) monograph attempting to synthesize craniometric data of Pawnee, Arikara, and Central Plains crania. Bass's conclusion that Central Plains crania were only remotely related to the later Caddoan-speaking Pawnee and Arikara sets the stage for physical anthropology to contribute to questions of continuity versus replacement in the Plains. As skeletal samples became available from more populations, such questions were examined in greater detail (Jantz 1973; Jantz, Owsley, and Willey 1978), culminating in Key's (1983) exhaustive synthesis of around 1,000 Plains crania. Key's synthesis led to the formation of a comprehensive Plains craniometric data base, which has found numerous applications in Plains craniometric research.

Key's focus on Woodland craniometric variation attempts to remedy the long neglect Woodland groups have experienced compared to the more numerous and better-preserved samples from Coalescent populations. Relying on an extensive battery of measurements and appropriate dimension-reducing procedures, he is able to address questions of biological continuity regarding both predecessors and successors of Woodland populations in the Plains. In spite of small samples, Key's results are coherent and yield a number of patterns, some of which support relationships derived archaeologically, and some of which suggest alternatives to archaeological hypotheses. In particular, the craniometric evidence strengthens arguments concerning continuity from Woodland to Plains Village traditions.

Historical inferences requiring identification of individual crania are less common than those relying on intergroup relationships. However, when populations come into contact, the ability to identify migrants is of obvious value. Such applications have profited from progress in forensic techniques, where identification of ethnic origin of individual skeletons is the goal (Gill and Rhine 1990). In the Plains, identification of Arikara crania in a Ponca site constitutes one of the few examples of successful implementation of this technique (Jantz 1974). The technique also has obvious application in repatriation examinations, where ethnic identity often becomes a central issue. For example, a cranium found near Genoa, Nebraska, was labeled "Indian skull/Pawnee" (Stuhr Museum of the Prairie Pioneer, Grand Island, Neb.: 62-706-65). Morphological examination identified it as clearly White, preventing its inappropriate repatriation as a Native American.

Euro-American contact is documented historically in the Plains, but to date no one had succeeded in identifying a Euro-American cranium in a protohistoric Native American cemetery. It has not even been possible to say much about the genetic consequences of White admixture (Jantz 1973), presumably because the number of migrants was small, at least prior to 1800. Jantz and Owsley's identification of a Euro-American cranium in an early Arikara site illustrates the potential of applying forensic techniques to identify ethnic origin of individual crania. It provides evidence for the physical presence of Euro-Americans at a time earlier than firmly documented by historical records. Such a finding has clear relevance to historical questions concerning the early fur traders and will obviously bear on the opportunity for direct introduction of communicable diseases into the Plains. The need for communication between biological anthropologists and historians is well illustrated. It should be emphasized that the morphological evidence was the only direct evidence available. There was no archaeological indication that Euro-Americans might have been present at Swan Creek. The element composition of the teeth (Schneider and Blakeslee 1990) provides valuable corroboration but by itself is unable to suggest an origin for an outlying value.

Social inferences from craniometric data in the Plains have taken the form of attempting to identify various occupations of multicomponent sites (Owsley and Jantz 1978; Owsley et al. 1981). Byrd and Jantz's chapter applies that approach to the Leavenworth site, testing a specific hypothesis concerning the social composition of the village (Bass, Evans, and Jantz 1971). The social implications of craniometric variation offer fertile ground for testing social hypotheses that have been generated from other evidence (Hoffman 1977; Schneider and Blakeslee 1990).

Cole and Cole's chapter is the last one to deal with craniometrics. It does so in a way that has been totally ignored in the Plains and indeed in modern populations generally. Their concern with the functional determinants of brow ridge morphology transfers a model developed in the paleoanthropology literature (Smith and Ranyard 1980) to changes in subsistence patterns. The ambiguity of their results must stem from inadequate understanding of brow ridge response to functional stress. The Plains may not be the best place to test such hypotheses due to the special character of Plains agriculture.

A great deal of attention has been devoted to identification of skeletal markers that reveal various interactions between the population and the environment. Many of these employ paleopathological or biochemical techniques and thus appear in other sections of the volume. Metric techniques seem to offer the most promising results in the area of inferring function from postcranial variation. The Plains offers a different cultural and environmental context within which to view functional responses. The samples available represent transition from hunting and gathering to settled village life. Within the Coalescent there is the further transition brought about by introduction of the horse. There is, presumably, a great deal of variation in activity patterns among the populations. Zobeck's (1983) extensive analysis has shown that interpopulation variation in the Northern Plains is considerably less than that seen in the cranium.

The papers by Ruff and by T. Cole offer parallel perspectives on variation in lower limb bone morphometrics among these populations. Ruff applies engineering principles to femur cross-sections. His samples were unfortunately limited to the Over collection material from the Northern Plains and to the Southern Plains. T. Cole, on the other hand, has focused on the more extensive material from the Northern Plains using traditional metric features of the lower limbs. In neither paper do the results support predictions of bone response to subsistence change such as those seen in the Southeast (Ruff, Larsen, and Hays 1984). The authors argue that no significant changes in activity patterns accompanied subsistence changes in the Northern Plains. The heavy reliance of Plains villagers on hunting, unique among North American subsistence systems (Lehmer and Wood 1977), supports this idea.

The Southern Plains femur cross-sections, characterized by extreme anterior-posterior elongation, present a considerable challenge to the functional model of femur shape and its relationship to subsistence and activity. The challenge to prehistorians requires a mobility model consistent with the extreme femur morphology and substantially different from that seen in the Northern Plains. The aberrant cross-sections have been identified by Owsley and Jantz (1989) using traditional measurements. Their analysis yields a clear separation of Northern and Southern Plains agriculturists in femur cross-sections. Notably lacking at this point is analysis of data from the Central Plains. Incorporation of Central Plains long-bone dimensions is necessary before there is any hope of formulating a model that will account for variation in geometrical properties of long bones in the Plains generally.

The last chapter in the metric section is primarily a methodological contribution, addressing the issue of assigning age to American Indian children from the dentition. Utilization of children's skeletons for inferences about growth variation has been hampered by the necessity of applying inappropriate dental age criteria. Data on dental development in living Native American populations exist (Trodden 1982) but are limited to the permanent dentition, whereas the majority of children's skeletons in archaeological samples possess deciduous teeth. Lovejoy, Russell, and Harrison (1990) approach the problem by assuming that American Indian dental precocity is progressive; Jantz and Owsley's analysis suggests the opposite. The precise nature of developmental patterning in American Indian dentition is unlikely to be settled from skeletal samples. However, it should be evident that far more can be done with skeletal samples by way of testing developmental hypotheses.

References Cited

Bass, W.M.
    1964 The Variation in Physical Types of the Prehistoric Plains Indians. *Plains Anthropologist Memoir* 1.

——, D.R. Evans, and R.L. Jantz
    1971 The Leavenworth Site Cemetery: Archaeology and Physical Anthropology. *University of Kansas Publications in Anthropology* 2.

Carlson, D.S., and D.P. Van Gerven
    1977 Masticatory Function and Post-pleistocene Evolution in Nubia. *American Journal of Physical Anthropology* 46:495–506.

Gill, G.W., and S. Rhine, eds.
    1990 Skeletal Attribution of Race. *Maxwell Museum of Anthropology Anthropological Papers* 4.

Gould, S.J.
    1981 The Mismeasure of Man. New York: Norton.

Guagliardo, M.F.
    1982 Craniofacial Structure, Aging and Dental Function: Their Relationships in Adult Human Skeletal Series. (Unpublished Ph.D. Dissertation in Anthropology, University of Tennessee, Knoxville.)

Hoffman, J.J.
    1977 Archaeological Inference in Societal Modeling: Social Organization of the Bad River Phase. In Trends in Middle Missouri Prehistory: A Festschrift Honoring the Contributions of Donald J. Lehmer. W.R. Wood, ed. *Plains Anthropologist Memoir* 13.

Howells, W.W.
    1984 Introduction. Pp. 1–11 in Multivariate Statistical Methods in Physical Anthropology. G.N. Van Vark and W.W. Howells, eds. Dordrecht, The Netherlands: D. Reidel.

Hrdlicka, A.
    1939 Practical Anthropometry. Philadelphia: The Wistar Institute of Anatomy and Biology.

Hursh, T.M.
    1976 The Study of Cranial Form: Measurement Techniques and Analytical Methods. Pp. 465–489 in The Measures of Man:

Methodologies in Biological Anthropology. E. Giles and J.S. Friedlaender, eds. Cambridge, Mass.: Peabody Museum Press.

Jantz, R.L.

1973   Microevolutionary Change in Arikara Crania: A Multivariate Analysis. *American Journal of Physical Anthropology* 38:15–26.

——

1974   The Redbird Focus: Cranial Evidence in Tribal Identification. *Plains Anthropologist* 19:5–13.

——, D.W. Owsley, and P. Willey

1978   Craniometric Relationships of Central Plains Populations. Pp. 144–156 in The Central Plains Tradition: Internal Developments and External Relationships. D.J. Blakeslee, ed. Iowa City: Office of the State Archaeologist.

——, and P.H. Moore-Jansen

1988   A Data Base for Forensic Anthropology: Structure, Content and Analysis. *University of Tennessee, Department of Anthropology, Report of Investigations* 47.

Key, P.J.

1983   Craniometric Relationships Among Plains Indians. *University of Tennessee, Department of Anthropology, Report of Investigations* 34.

——, and R.L. Jantz

1990   Statistical Assessment of Population Variability: A Methodological Approach. *American Journal of Physical Anthropology* 82:53–59.

Konigsberg, L.W.

1988   Migration Models of Prehistoric Postmarital Residence. *American Journal of Physical Anthropology* 77:471–482.

Larsen, C.S.

1982   The Anthropology of St. Catherines Island, 3: Prehistoric Human Biological Adaptation. *Anthropological Papers of the American Museum of Natural History* 57:157–270.

Lehmer, D.J., and W.R. Wood

1977   Buffalo and Beans. Pp. 85–89 in Selected Writings of Donald J. Lehmer. *Reprints in Anthropology* 8. Lincoln, Neb.: J and L Reprint.

Lovejoy, C.O., K.F. Russell, and M.L. Harrison

1990   Long Bone Growth Velocity in the Libben Population. *American Journal of Human Biology* 2:533–540.

Owsley, D.W., and R.L. Jantz

1978   Intracemetery Morphological Variation in Arikara Crania from the Sully Site (39SL4), Sully County, South Dakota. *Plains Anthropologist* 23:139–147.

——, and R.L. Jantz

1989   A Systematic Approach to the Skeletal Biology of the Southern Plains. Pp. 136–156 in From Clovis to Commanchero: Archaeological Overview of the Southern Great Plains. J.L. Hofman, R.L. Brooks, and D.W. Owsley, eds. *Arkansas Archeological Survey Research Series* 35.

——, G. Slutzky, M.F. Guagliardo, and L.M. Deitrick

1981   Interpopulation Relationships of Four Post-contact Coalescent Sites from South Dakota: Four Bear (39DW2), Oahe Village (39HU2), Stony Point Village (39ST235) and Swan Creek (39WW7). In Progress in Skeletal Biology of Plains Populations. R. L. Jantz and D. H. Ubelaker, eds. *Plain Anthropologist Memoir* 17:31–42.

Ruff, C.B., C.S. Larsen, and W.C. Hayes

1984   Structural Changes in the Femur with the Transition to Agriculture on the Georgia Coast. *American Journal of Physical Anthropology* 64:125–136.

Schneider, K.N., and D.J. Blakeslee

1990   Evaluating Residence Patterns from Prehistoric Populations: Clues from Dental Enamel Composition. *Human Biology* 62:71–83.

Schwidetzky, I.

1984   Data Banks and Multivariate Statistics in Physical Anthropology. Pp. 283–288 in Multivariate Statistical Methods in Physical Anthropology. G.N. Van Vark and W.W. Howells, eds. Dordrecht, The Netherlands: D. Reidel.

Scuilli, P.W., and M.C. Mahaney

1991   Phenotypic Evolution in Prehistoric Ohio Amerindians: Natural Selection versus Random Genetic Drift in Tooth Size Reduction. *Human Biology* 63:499–511.

Smith, F.H., and G.C. Ranyard

1980   Evolution of the Supraorbital Region in Upper Pleistocene Fossil Hominids from South-central Europe. *American Journal of Physical Anthropology* 53:589–610.

Sokal, R.S., and H. Uytterschaut

1987   Cranial Variation in European Populations: A Spatial Autocorrelation Study at Three Time Periods. *American Journal of Physical Anthropology* 74:21–38.

Trodden, B.J.

1982   A Radiographic Study of the Calcification and Eruption of the Permanent Teeth in Inuit and Indian Children. *Archaeological Survey of Canada Paper* 112.

Zobeck, T.S.

1983   Postcraniometric Variation Among the Arikara. (Unpublished Ph.D. Dissertation in Physical Anthropology, The University of Tennessee, Knoxville.)

○○○

CHAPTER 14

Relationships of the Woodland Period on the Northern and Central Plains: The Craniometric Evidence

PATRICK J. KEY

The people who inhabited the Great Plains during the Woodland period left their mark upon the landscape. The extensive earthworks and burial mounds they left behind in the Dakotas, Nebraska, Kansas, and Missouri were a source of wonder to the early European settlers. The early interpretations of the earthworks as the remains of everything from semimythic Moundbuilders, to Toltecs, lost tribes of Israel, and wandering Welshmen has given way to a more reasoned appreciation of the capabilities of indigenous Americans. Yet this history of excavation and interpretation continues to have problems, notably in provenience and dating. Many of the Woodland materials currently housed in museums and historical societies were excavated under very poor conditions. Human skeletal material in particular is often poorly provenienced. Postcranial remains are often missing from the collections, as are females and subadults in general. Few of the early excavators were aware that a burial mound might represent a complex, multicomponent accretionary sequence rather than a single stage event.

These ambiguities have created problems in interpretation. Many Woodland archaeological designations are poorly defined. Dating is a particular problem. There are remarkably few radiocarbon dates from Woodland sites, and whole complexes are sometimes dated on tenuous ceramic associations. It is common to see estimates of dates for Woodland complexes differing by 400 to 500 years among various workers.

Analytical Methodology

This study is based upon subsamples of a Plains Indian craniometric data base consisting of 80 variables taken on some 1,000 individuals. In the present case, 127 individuals were analyzed. Various multivariate statistical techniques were employed, but the results reported here are all based upon discriminant functions calculated from principal component scores extracted from a pooled within-groups correlation matrix. The scores were calculated for the data base as a whole and not just for the individuals employed here (Key 1983). The scores have been centered on the grand sex means of the data base as a whole and all sex effects dropped from subsequent analyses.

Discriminant function analysis is a well-known multivariate technique that defines axes of variability maximizing the differences between groups. Discriminant analysis requires having an a priori group structure and weighing the contribution of groups relative to sample size. The sample size scaling involves two considerations. On one hand, it means that groups with large sample sizes can dominate the space and define all the major axes of variation to the exclusion of poorly sampled groups. On the other hand, it prevents the oddities of sampling variance in small groups from distorting the results. One hopes that the small groups at least estimate their population means effectively.

A larger concern is the need to define groups a priori. This leads to a certain circularity in that the results are usually interpreted in terms of the groups that went into the analysis to begin with. The discriminant functions will maximize the variability among these groups, no matter how poorly defined they may be.

Since a group structure is necessary, the groups are defined in terms of the smallest possible archaeological unit that can encompass closely related sites. It was necessary to pool sites together in order to get sample sizes large enough to run the analysis and to minimize the sheer complexity of it. The unit employed here is the burial complex, although this is a somewhat nebulous term often used interchangeably with "phase" and "composite" in the literature. In some of the analyses presented here, Paleo-Indian and Archaic samples are considered as groups and compared with the Woodland. These units are not equivalent, of course, but the scarcity of individuals from these early time periods presented no alternative.

Another problem worth noting is that not all the groups possibly interacting on the various time horizons are present in the analysis. Apparent relationships between groups in the present sample may actually be reflections of external events, unknown in the present context. This is effectively an insurmountable problem since the scope of possible interactions during the Woodland period might conceivably encompass the entire North American continent.

Cultural Overview

The beginning of the Woodland period is traditionally marked by the appearance of pottery in archaeological assemblages. This event occurs much earlier in the Eastern Woodlands than it does on the Plains, a condition that led many people to suggest that the Plains Woodland represents a migration of Woodland groups from the east (Wilmeth 1972:153). Plains Woodland sites tend to be located along the terraces of major rivers and their tributaries, situations that reproduce in miniature the forest belts of the eastern

United States. However, the Plains Woodland lifeway of small nomadic bands exploiting migratory resources is in marked contrast to the sedentary horticulturalism of the Eastern Woodlands. Others prefer to see the Woodland as a diffusion of ceramic technologies and burial ceremonialism into indigenous Archaic groups (Benn 1980).

Early Woodland materials from the Plains are very sparse. It appears that a basically Archaic lifeway persisted there until the Middle Woodland period, beginning around 50 B.C.

There are a number of Middle Woodland complexes, although not all are represented here.

MIDDLE WOODLAND

The Kansas City Hopewell complex is a Middle Woodland configuration dating from about 50 B.C. to A.D. 300 with unquestionable influences from the large Hopewell centers in the Illinois and Ohio River valleys (O'Brien 1971; Wedel 1943, 1961:89). Wilmeth (1972:153) has suggested that it is the cultural and biological base from which the Keith and Valley complexes emerged, although others would dispute this, viewing it as an isolated Hopewellian outlier.

The Valley complex is distributed throughout the eastern glaciated region of the Central Plains (Hill and Kivett 1940; Kivett 1952). It dates from about A.D. 1–700 (Ludwickson, Blakeslee, and O'Shea 1981:122; O'Brien 1971:175). The dates suggest that Valley was contemporary with Kansas City Hopewell. The complex is usually defined through the presence of Valley cord-roughened pottery.

The Keith complex occurs throughout the High Plains region of western Kansas and Nebraska and interleaves into the Loess Plains region of the Central Plains (Hill and Kivett 1940; Kivett 1953; Wedel 1961:90). Its usage here includes the Ash Hollow focus. Dates for the Keith complex are rare and contradictory, but it is generally viewed as contemporaneous with Valley. It is usually defined on the basis of Harlan cord-roughened pottery and large numbers of shell disk beads associated with ossuary burials (Kivett 1953:130–137).

The Sonota complex is a widespread mortuary complex distributed over the Middle Missouri and Northeastern Plains. It is characterized by burials in large conical mounds, often with large quantities of bison bone, Knife River Flint, and occasional exotic artifacts. Sonota exhibits profound evidence of bison ceremonialism and may in fact be related to the Besant bison hunters of the Northwestern Plains. The complex dates from about A.D. 1 to 600 (Neuman 1975).

Other Middle Woodland groups not represented here include the Laurel complex on the Canadian Plains, the Fox Lake complex on the Northeastern Plains, and the Cuesta and Grasshopper Falls complexes on the Central Plains of Kansas. Other groups possibly interacting on this time horizon are the Besant and Avonlea of the Northwestern Plains.

LATE WOODLAND

In some areas, the Late Woodland seems to represent a break from the Middle Woodland, in others it is an elaboration of trends established earlier. A variety of Late Woodland materials are known from the Plains. The Loseke Creek complex extends over most of the eastern glaciated region of the Central Plains and into the Fort Randall region of the Middle Missouri. The Loseke Creek individuals analyzed here are from the Fort Randall region. The dating of Loseke Creek is unclear, although it is generally considered to be older than the Sterns Creek complex in southeastern Nebraska. An estimated date of A.D. 700–800 is suggested by Ludwickson, Blakeslee, and O'Shea (1981:127). Sterns Creek is not represented here.

The details of Late Woodland manifestations in the Middle Missouri have not been worked out with any precision. Some limited material from this area is grouped into the Truman complex based on the presence of distinctive Truman Plain Rim pottery. Radiocarbon dates for Truman pottery are in the A.D. 600–800 range (Neuman 1960, 1967:479).

On the Northeastern Plains, the Arvilla complex appears about A.D. 500–600. It persists until about 900 in the Prairie Lakes region and until about 1100 in the Red River Valley of North Dakota and Manitoba (Johnson 1973). Syms (1982: 162–163) would extend this date to 1400 in the north, although this seems very late. All the Arvilla individuals analyzed here are from five mounds on the shore of Lake Traverse in Roberts County, South Dakota; therefore the term South Arvilla is used.

An important Late Woodland complex not represented here is Blackduck, distributed over most of Manitoba and points east. Blackduck appears to be ancestral Algonquian (Syms 1977:106), although this has not been demonstrated biologically. Another Late Woodland complex not represented here is the Schultz from the Central Plains of Kansas.

TERMINAL WOODLAND

Those Woodland complexes that appear to overlap with Plains Village configurations have been grouped into a Terminal Woodland variant. This is a very complex time period on the Plains, with evidence of mass migrations, cultural innovations, and complex cultural interactions.

The Devils Lake–Sourisford complex is a configuration distributed throughout the Northeastern Plains (Syms 1979). It is characterized by large and elaborate earthworks and the presence of Mississippian-derived "Southern cult" artifacts associated with the burials (Howard 1953). Syms (1979) suggests this complex may be ancestral Siouan with dates from about 900 to as late as 1400.

Great Oasis is a problematical complex included here with the Terminal Woodland. On economic and ceramic grounds it is generally viewed as transitional between the Woodland and Plains Village patterns (Johnston 1967:53–72). The degree to which Great Oasis people practiced agriculture is the subject of some debate, as is their relationship to Plains Village manifestations such as the Mill Creek and Over phases (Ludwickson, Blakeslee, and O'Shea 1981:133–140) and to Mississippian groups such as Cambria and various Oneota groups. Great Oasis is distributed over much of the Prairie-Plains border and up the Middle Missouri as far as the Big Bend (Henning 1971:125–133). It appears to date between about 950 and 1120 (Ludwickson, Blakeslee, and O'Shea 1981:218; Tiffany 1981:62).

Finally, if Syms's dates are correct, the northern components of the Arvilla complex should also be included in the Terminal Woodland.

Study Samples

Large and well-documented samples for all the Plains Woodland groups were not available for this analysis. Samples for some groups simply do not exist; others have been reburied; and some have not been measured. The samples employed in this analysis are presented in table 1.

Individuals in these samples have been subject to various analyses to determine relationships among the Woodland groups, relationships of the Woodland groups to their predecessors, and relationships of the Woodland groups to the Initial variant of the Middle Missouri tradition. Ongoing research will focus on Woodland relationships to other early plains villagers and to historic tribes of the region.

The analysis that follows is based upon relatively small samples. Although the results appear unambiguous, they

Table 1. Groups, Group Symbols and Sample Sizes

Tradition	Phase	Symbol	Number
Paleo-Indian	Paleo-Indian	P	8
Archaic	Archaic	A	17
Woodland			
Middle	Kansas City Hopewell	H	4
	Valley	V	2
	Keith	K	8
	Sonota	S	17
Late	Truman	T	3
	Loseke Creek	L	12
	South Arvilla	R	22
Terminal	Great Oasis	G	10
	Devils Lake–Sourisford	D	11
Initial Middle Missouri	Anderson	N	3
	Mill Creek	M	4
	Over	O	4
	Grand Detour	E	2
Total			127

should be viewed in the light of concerns about sample size and provenance.

Results

PALEO-INDIAN, ARCHAIC, WOODLAND, AND KANSAS CITY HOPEWELL

The first analysis is an examination of Woodland relationships to earlier Paleo-Indian and Archaic samples and to Kansas City Hopewell. Table 2 presents the overall results for this analysis (along with all subsequent analyses), and table 3 presents the significant discriminant functions for all the analyses. The Wilks's lambda reported in table 2 is a Multivariate Analysis of Variance (MANOVA) for the group effect, and it indicates that highly significant group heterogeneity is present. That is, it is highly unlikely that the groups are members

of the same population. Table 3 indicates that four significant discriminant functions were extracted, accounting for 73.28 percent of the common variance.

Figure 1 plots the group centroids along the first three functions. Subsequent analyses will reveal some of the finer points of this plot but the highlight here is the distinction between Kansas City Hopewell and the rest of the sample. This group occupies an extreme position on both the second and third functions. This is an impressive distinction, since there are only four Kansas City Hopewell individuals in the sample. These results strongly suggest that Kansas City Hopewell is not a Plains group biologically, at least insofar as the sample employed here.

WOODLAND AND KANSAS CITY HOPEWELL

The next analysis examines Kansas City Hopewell and Woodland relationships without the presence of the Paleo-Indian and Archaic (table 3).

Although the overall level of heterogeneity is lower, and three significant functions were extracted instead of four, the plots are very similar to the previous analysis. Figure 2 displays the group centroids on the three significant functions. Once again, the extreme position of the Kansas City Hopewell sample is self-evident. In light of these results, the Kansas City Hopewell individuals have been dropped from the subsequent analyses in order to examine more subtle aspects of Plains Woodland relationships.

WOODLAND GROUPS

An analysis of the Woodland groups without Paleo-Indian, Archaic, or Kansas City Hopewell indicates that the groups are still highly heterogeneous, although the levels have come down substantially from previous analyses (table 2). Two significant functions were extracted, accounting for 60.62 percent of the common variance (table 3).

The plot of individuals on the two significant functions (fig. 3) presents a consistent pattern of relationships that will

Table 2. MANOVAs for the Group Effect

Analysis	Wilks's Lambda	Chi-Square	Degrees of Freedom	Probability
Paleo-Indian, Archaic, Woodland, Kansas City Hopewell	0.03168	334.845	210	0.00000
Woodland, Kansas City Hopewell	0.03031	255.226	168	0.00002
Woodland Groups	0.04252	219.463	147	0.00010
Paleo-Indian, Archaic, Woodland	0.04104	298.570	189	0.00000
Woodland, Initial Middle Missouri	0.01317	348.538	231	0.00000

Table 3. Significant Discriminant Functions

No.	Eigenvalue	Relative Percentage	Cumulative Percentage	Canonical Correlation	Chi-square	Degrees of Freedom	Probability
Paleo-Indian/Archaic/Woodland/Kansas City Hopewell							
1	1.40334	30.80	30.80	0.76414	249.79	180	0.00045
2	0.71729	15.74	46.54	0.64629	197.34	152	0.00785
3	0.66898	14.68	61.22	0.63311	147.65	126	0.09102
4	0.54950	12.06	73.28	0.59551	105.17	102	0.39491
Woodland/Kansas City Hopewell							
1	1.76178	35.92	35.92	0.79870	181.07	140	0.01110
2	0.90889	18.53	54.45	0.69003	133.87	114	0.09847
3	0.72569	14.80	69.25	0.64848	94.04	90	0.36457
Woodland							
1	1.76232	39.48	39.48	0.79874	148.85	120	0.03811
2	0.94368	21.14	60.62	0.69679	102.66	95	0.27781
Paleo-Indian/Archaic/Woodland							
1	1.44756	34.04	34.04	0.76904	214.88	160	0.00249
2	0.77897	18.32	52.36	0.66172	161.02	133	0.04940
3	0.60948	14.33	66.69	0.61537	116.02	108	0.27072
Woodland/Initial Middle Missouri							
1	2.17383	34.96	34.96	0.82760	255.56	200	0.00483
2	1.09698	17.64	52.60	0.72327	195.96	171	0.09264
3	0.68688	11.05	63.65	0.63811	153.86	144	0.27169

hold up throughout all the subsequent analyses and in fact has been present in the analyses shown so far. The Middle Woodland complexes from the Central Plains (Valley and Keith complexes) cluster tightly along with Great Oasis from the Terminal Woodland. This configuration is displaced away from a cluster of Northern Plains groups: the Middle Woodland Sonota complex and its geographical counterpart from the Terminal Woodland, the Devils Lake–Sourisford complex. The Late Woodland Loseke Creek and South Arvilla complexes constitute a third cluster distinct from these previous

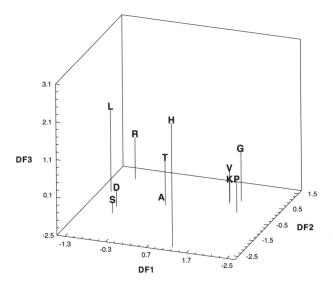

Fig. 1. Plot of the group centroids along the first three discriminant functions for the Paleo-Indian, Archaic, Woodland, and Kansas City Hopewell samples. Key to letters for all figures is in table 1.

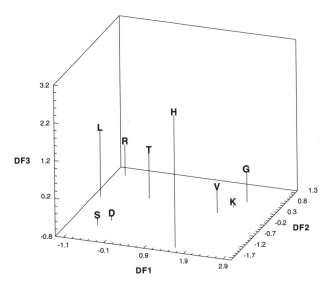

Fig. 2. Plot of the group centroids along the first three discriminant functions for the Woodland and Kansas City samples.

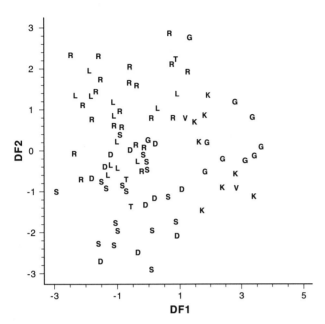

Fig. 3. Plot of the individuals along the first two discriminant functions for the Woodland sample.

groups. The Late Woodland Truman complex does not clearly align itself with any of these groups. This is a sample of only three individuals.

A plot of the group centroids along the two significant functions reiterates these relationships (fig. 4). There are essentially three clusters evident: a Central Plains cluster, a North-

ern Plains cluster, and a cluster made up of groups from the Prairie-Plains border area. These clusters cross-cut time lines, suggesting biological continuity within a given geographical region. It is interesting that the Loseke Creek and South Arvilla complexes from the Prairie-Plains border area are quite distinct from the Central Plains groups (the Valley and Keith) even though their geographical extents overlap considerably. Great Oasis from the Terminal Woodland aligns itself unequivocally with the Central Plains groups, strongly suggesting biological continuity with these groups. This implies some population movements in the Prairie-Plains border area during the transition from the Late Woodland to the Terminal Woodland. This area has a very complex archaeological history, and it is truly unfortunate that more samples are not available.

PALEO-INDIAN, ARCHAIC, AND WOODLAND

The next analysis reintroduces the Paleo-Indian and Archaic samples into the analysis to examine Woodland relationships in light of their predecessors. Table 2 indicates that significant heterogeneity has been introduced, but the plots indicate that the structure of Woodland relationships has not changed.

Figure 5 plots individuals along the first two functions. (The third function, although significant, does not draw any

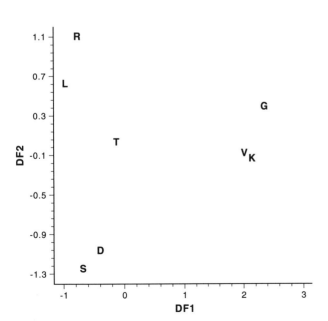

Fig. 4. Plot of the group centroids along the first two discriminant functions for the Woodland sample.

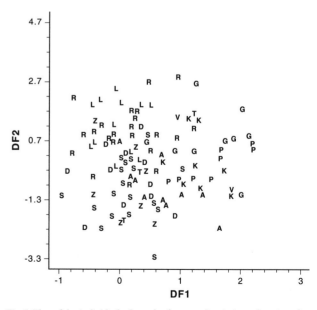

Fig. 5. Plot of the individuals along the first two discriminant functions for the Paleo-Indian, Archaic, and Woodland samples. The Archaic group has been separated into a Northern Plains (Z) group and a Central Plains (A) group.

clear distinctions). Note that the underlying pattern of Woodland relationships still holds. The Central Plains cluster aligns very closely with the Paleo-Indians in the present sample, while the Archaic individuals seem to disperse throughout the space. Given that the Central Plains and Northern Plains complexes appear as distinct groups in the Middle Woodland, one might expect this dichotomy to be reflected in the preceding Archaic period. This is indeed the case. The Archaic sample employed here is made up of individuals from both the Northern and Central Plains. The Northern Plains individuals are clearly aligned with the later Woodland groups from that area, while the Central Plains individuals are displaced in the direction of the Central Plains Woodland, although they are not fully in that camp. Five of the seven Northern Plains Archaic individuals are from a North Dakota site radiocarbon dated to late in the Archaic sequence, so their alignment with the Northern Plains Woodland is not surprising. All except one of the Paleo-Indians are from the Central Plains, and their alignment with the Central Plains Woodland makes sense, although it is difficult to generalize considering the enormous time periods involved.

WOODLAND AND INITIAL MIDDLE MISSOURI

A final analysis examines Woodland relationships to phases of the Initial Middle Missouri variant of the Plains Village tradition. This analysis was done primarily to investigate the relationship of Great Oasis to the various Middle Missouri groups, although other interesting patterns are evident.

Figure 6 plots individuals along the three significant functions, and fig. 7 plots the group centroids. Once again, the previous pattern of Woodland relationships holds (although the first function has been reflected on its axis, a statistical artifact of no consequence). Note how closely the Mill Creek phase resembles Great Oasis. These groups cluster tightly and align themselves with the Central Plains Woodland groups. The Over phase, an Initial Middle Missouri group from the lower James River, also aligns closely with the Central Plains Woodland. The Anderson phase, an Initial Middle Missouri group located in the Bad-Cheyenne region of the Middle Missouri, aligns closely with the Northern Plains Woodland, and the Truman complex, a Middle Missouri group from the Late Woodland. A distinct outlier is the Grand Detour phase from the Big Bend region of the Middle Missouri. This group occupies an extreme position on the first two functions. Ideally, it should align with the Anderson phase, but it is a small sample of only two individuals and may be subject to sampling or provenience problems.

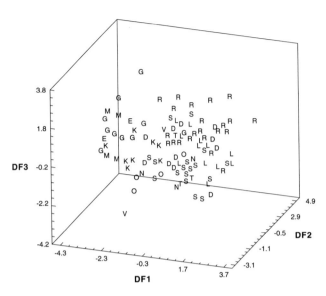

Fig. 6. Plot of the individuals along the first three discriminant functions for the Woodland and Initial Middle Missouri samples.

These results are interesting for several reasons. First, Great Oasis and Mill Creek are very similar, suggesting a close biological relationship between them. Second, the Over phase also clusters with the Central Plains Woodland, once again suggesting an affinity. Third, the Anderson phase from the Missouri Trench aligns itself with the Truman complex and with the Northern Plains Woodland groups, not with the Central Plains groups. This suggests that even though the Anderson phase is an Initial Middle Misouri group, it is more like a Northern Plains group biologically. Therefore, it is

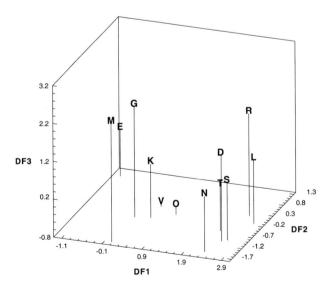

Fig. 7. Plot of the group centroids along the first three discriminant functions for the Woodland and Initial Middle Missouri samples.

tempting to view the Initial Middle Missouri developments along the Missouri Trench more as a cultural diffusion into the area rather than Lehmer's (1971:97–105) suggested migration of people from the Prairie-Plains border area.

Of course, these results are based upon very small samples. It is unfortunate that more samples are not available from this crucial time period to try to unravel these complex relationships.

Conclusions

Although much of the picture remains unclear due to the absence of some important groups in the present analysis, some definite patterns have emerged. During the Middle Woodland there were at least three distinct biological configurations on the upper Plains. Kansas City Hopewell is the most distinctive of these. It is probably not a Plains group biologically and would resemble the Illinois Hopewell rather closely. A second group is the Keith and Valley complexes on the Central Plains. Wilmeth (1972) had combined these two into the Orleans composite, and this makes sense craniometrically. This configuration is distinct from the Sonota complex which covers most of the Northern Plains in this period.

There is some suggestion that the regional dichotomy evident in the Woodland emanates from the Archaic period. Those individuals from Archaic sites on the Northern Plains cluster with later Northern Plains Woodland groups, and Central Plains Archaic individuals associate with the Central Plains Woodland. However, most of the Northern Plains Archaic sample is from very late in the Archaic sequence.

The biological continuity on the Northern Plains appears to extend into the Terminal Woodland as well. The Devils Lake–Sourisford individuals align very closely with the earlier Sonota.

Evidence for biological continuity on the Central Plains is less clear. The Late Woodland Loseke Creek and South Arvilla complexes are quite distinct from their Middle Woodland counterparts, even though the geographical ranges of the various groups overlap considerably. Therefore it is tempting to view these Late Woodland groups as a migration of new people into the area. If this is the case, their ultimate origin remains an open question.

Great Oasis, from the Terminal Woodland, covers most of the area occupied earlier by Loseke Creek and South Arvilla, yet it is fundamentally distinct from them. Instead, it is clearly aligned with groups that occupied this same region even earlier, in the Middle Woodland. This again suggests that Loseke Creek and South Arvilla are a separate population, and that biological continuity on the Central Plains stems from the Keith and Valley complexes into Great Oasis.

Great Oasis is also very similar to the Mill Creek phase of the Initial Middle Missouri and to a lesser extent with the Over phase. These relationships suggest a continuity from the Central Plains Woodland groups, through Great Oasis and into the early Plains Village period.

The Anderson phase, on the other hand, more closely resembles the Woodland groups from the Missouri Trench and the Northern Plains. This suggests that at least some of the Initial Middle Missouri developments may represent a diffusion of ideas into indigenous groups and not a migration of new people.

In summary, the results reported here argue for a long-term biological continuity in various regions of the Plains. This is especially true for the Northern Plains, where the same biological population may have been in place at least since the Archaic.

References Cited

Benn, D.W.
  1980 Diffusion and acculturation in Woodland cultures on the Western Prairie Peninsula. (Paper presented at the 38th Plains Conference, Iowa City.)

Hill, A.T. and M. Kivett
  1940 Woodland-like Manifestations in Nebraska. *Nebraska History* 21(3):143–243.

Henning, D.R.
  1971 Great Oasis Cultural Distributions. Pp. 125–133 in Prehistoric Investigations. M. McKusick, ed. *Office of the State Archaeologist Report* 3.

Howard, J.
  1953 The Southern Cult on the Northern Plains. *American Antiquity* 19(2):130–138.

Johnson, E.
  1973 The Arvilla Complex. *Minnesota Historical Society, Prehistoric Archaeology* 9.

Johnston, R.B.
  1967 The Hitchell Site. *Smithsonian Institution River Basin Surveys, Publications in Salvage Archeology* 3.

Key, P.J.
  1983 Craniometric Relationships Among Plains Indians: Culture-Historical and Evolutionary Implications. *University of Tennessee, Department of Anthropology, Report of Investigations* 34.

Kivett, M.F.
  1952 Woodland Sites in Nebraska. *Nebraska State Historical Society Publications in Anthropology* 1.

———
  1953 The Woodruff Ossuary, a Prehistoric Burial Site in Phillips County, Kansas. *Bureau of American Ethnology Bulletin* 154.

Lehmer, D.J.

1971 Introduction to Middle Missouri Archaeology. *National Park Service, Anthropological Papers* 1.

Ludwickson, J., D. Blakeslee, and J. O'Shea

1981 Missouri National Recreational River: Native American Cultural Resources. Report to the Interagency Archeological Services, Denver.

Neuman, R.W.

1960 The Truman Mound Site, Big Bend Reservoir Area, South Dakota. *American Antiquity* 26(1):78–92.

1967 Radiocarbon Dated Archaeological Remains on the Northern and Central Great Plains. *American Antiquity* 32(4):471–486.

1975 The Sonota Complex and Associated Sites on the Northern Great Plains. *Nebraska State Historical Society Publications in Anthropology* 6.

O'Brien, P.J.

1971 Valley Focus Mortuary Practices. *Plains Anthropologist* 16: 165–182.

Syms, E.L.

1977 Cultural Ecology and Ecological Dynamics of the Ceramic Period in Southwestern Manitoba. *Plains Anthropologist Memoir* 12.

1979 The Devils Lake–Sourisford Burial Complex on the Northeastern Plains. *Plains Anthropologist* 24(86):283–308.

1982 The Arvilla Burial Complex: A Re-assessment. *Journal of the North Dakota Archaeological Association* 1:135–166.

Tiffany, Joseph A.

1981 A Compendium of Radiocarbon Dates for Iowa Archaeological Sites. *Plains Anthropologist* 26(91):55–73.

Wedel, W.R.

1943 Archeological Investigations in Platte and Clay Counties, Missouri. *U.S. National Museum Bulletin* 183.

1961 Prehistoric Man on the Great Plains. Norman, Okla.: University of Oklahoma Press.

Wilmeth, R.H.

1972 The Woodland Sequence in the Central Plains. (Unpublished Ph.D. Dissertation, University of Michigan, Ann Arbor.)

CHAPTER 15

○ ○ ○

White Traders in the Upper Missouri: Evidence from the Swan Creek Site

RICHARD L. JANTZ AND DOUGLAS W. OWSLEY

Physical anthropology has made consistent contributions to historical inference in the Northern Plains. Much of this effort involves assessing craniometric relationships among archaeologically defined samples. Although craniometric analyses frequently support archaeological hypotheses, such as the idea of continuity between the Woodland and Middle Missouri traditions (Key 1983), they sometimes call hypotheses into question, such as the relationship of Mill Creek to Middle Missouri tradition and Mandan groups (Owsley, Morey, and Turner 1981). Occasionally, such analyses lead to the identification of foreign crania in a site sample, for example, the presence of Arikara females among the Ponca at the Ponca Fort site, Nebraska (25KX1) (Jantz 1974).

A biological effect of contact among various groups in the Northern Plains was gene flow. Temporal change in cranial morphology seen in Arikara crania has been attributed to gene flow from the Mandan (Jantz 1973; Key 1983). With the increasing presence of Euro-American traders in the upper Missouri, there was opportunity for interbreeding with Caucasians. Ethnohistoric accounts have documented specific instances of White resident traders marrying Indian women and

raising families (Wood and Thiessen 1985:42). The opportunity for sexual contact of a more casual nature has also been documented (Ronda 1984:63–64; Wood and Thiessen 1985:68–69). Craniometric consequences of gene flow between Euro-Americans and Native Americans have been difficult to identify, leading Jantz (1973) to conclude that its magnitude must have been relatively small, at least prior to the early nineteenth century.

This chapter offers evidence for the presence of a White male, presumably a trader, at the Swan Creek site and describes the biological and historical implications of this evidence. The ethnicity of this individual is unknown but is presumed to be French or Spanish since both groups were present in the upper Missouri at an early date.

Skull 2198 at Swan Creek

Swan Creek, South Dakota (39WW7), is a multicomponent Coalescent tradition village site that dates from 1675 to 1725 (Hurt 1957; Key 1983; Owsley et al. 1981). In the multivariate analysis of crania from Swan Creek to explore its multicomponent nature, a distinct outlier was found. This cranium

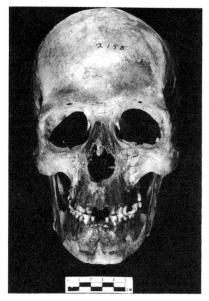 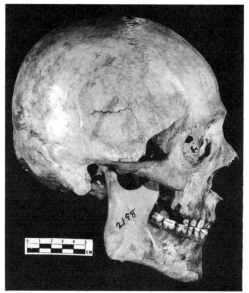 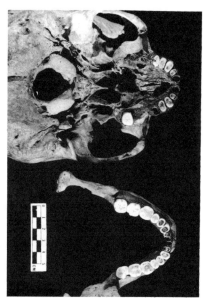

Fig. 1. Three views of skull 2198 from the Swan Creek site.

in overall morphological configuration was Caucasoid rather than Mongoloid. Figure 1 shows this skull (specimen 2198), which is from a skeleton excavated by W.H. Over. The circumstances of its burial do not appear different from those for others at Swan Creek. It was one of five skeletons found "more or less jumbled together and extended as low as six feet below the surface" (Sigstad and Sigstad 1973:311). Skull 2198 is complete, exhibiting no breakage and missing only teeth. Unfortunately, the remaining tooth crowns are too worn to allow examination of crown or cusp morphology. The postcrania include 11 left and 5 right ribs; 3 cervical, 12 thoracic, and 5 lumbar vertebrae; and a right calcaneus.

Skull 2198 is that of a male, aged 40 to 50 years. Sex criteria, including size, brow ridge and nuchal crest development, mastoid size, and blunt orbital margins make sex determination virtually certain. The assessment of age was based on the degree of dental attrition and amount of obliteration of the cranial vault and maxillary sutures. The sutures of the vault are closed endocranially and partially closed ectocranially. The degree and pattern of maxillary suture obliteration on the hard palate substantiate an age estimate of middle age or older (40+ years). Some vertebrae exhibit osteophytosis, a condition commonly accompanying middle to old age.

The cranium exhibits three healed depression fractures on the vault. The largest fracture is ovoidal, measuring 11 by 19 millimeters, and is located above the left eye orbit, medial to the temporal line. A second ovoidal fracture measuring 11 by 9 millimeters is on the posterior portion of the right parietal bone, medial to the temporal line. The smallest frac-

ture is U-shaped (nearly circular), measuring 6 by 5 millimeters, and is located low on the right parietal bone near the coronal suture. All three fractures involved only the outer table of the vault, are well healed, lack radiating fractures, and were not life-threatening.

The right corpus of the mandible exhibits a roughly circular lingual cortical defect, commonly referred to as Stafne's defect (Stafne 1942), in the retromolar area. The defect measures 10 by 10 by 2 millimeters (length, width, and depth) and has a well-defined, gently sloping border and an irregularly surfaced floor. This defect, situated at the most distal portion of the mylohyoid groove, has eroded the lingual cortex nearly to the point of perforating the buccal cortex. Gross morphological examination and position of the defect are consistent with lingual cortical mandibular defects frequently found on contemporary clinical radiographs. The most likely cause of this developmental (not pathological) defect is pressure erosion of the corpus by the submandibular salivary gland or salivary lymph node. Stafne's defect is usually found in adult males, ranging in incidence from 1 in 78 (Langlais, Cottone, and Kasle 1976) to 1 in 276 (Karmiol and Walsh 1968).

Traditional anthroposcopic observations used in forensic anthropology for race identification indicated that skull 2198 was atypical of Swan Creek crania. Table 1 lists a number of craniofacial traits; most observations for 2198 are characteristic of Whites. The cranial index is mesocranic (cranial index = 77.1, cf. Bass 1987), the sagittal outline is high and rounded, alveolar prognathism is greatly reduced, the palate has a triangular parabolic shape, and the malars are small in size with

Table 1. Craniofacial Trait Variations with Classification of Skull 2198 Italicized

Characteristics	American Indian	Caucasoid
Cranial form	Medium-broad	*Medium*
Sagittal outline	Medium-low	sloping frontal
Nose form	Medium	*Narrow*
Nasal bone size	Medium/large	*Large*
Nasal profile	*Concavo-convex*	Straight
Nasal spine	Medium, tilted	*Prominent, straight*
Facial prognathism	Moderate	*Reduced*
Malar form	Projecting	*Reduced*
Palatal form	Elliptic	*Parabolic*
Orbital form	*Rhomboid*	*Rhomboid*
Zygomaxillary suture	Angled	*Curved*

Source: Gill 1986.

slight projection. The nasal bones are prominent with a narrow nasal aperture (nasal index = 43.6, leptorrhine form).

MORPHOMETRIC ANALYSIS

Race determination from cranial measurements was initially assessed using the White/Indian and White/Black formulas developed by Giles and Elliot (1962). As illustrated in fig. 2, the result of this classification based on eight standard measurements was identification as White. However, the Giles and Elliot method is frequently inaccurate when applied to American Indian crania, and especially those from the Northwestern Plains (Ayers, Jantz, and Moore-Jansen 1990; Birkby 1966;

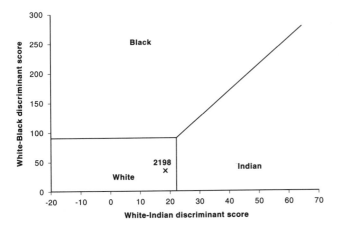

Fig. 2. Race determination of skull 2198 from the Giles and Elliot (1962) discriminant function.

Fisher and Gill 1990; Snow et al. 1979). The high frequency of misclassification obtained in validation trials has been attributed in part to morphological variation among Indian populations and to use of an ancient reference sample (the Archaic period Indian Knoll from Kentucky) as the basis for the White/Indian formulas.

Because of the need for a reliable craniometric technique for distinguishing between American Indians and Whites, Gill (1984) developed a method using measurements of the midfacial region. These measurements quantify differences in midfacial projection, prominence of the nasal bones, angularity of the frontal processes of the maxillae, and interorbital breadth. Caucasian crania generally show narrower faces, higher nasal bridges, and greater midline projection than Indian crania.

Six measurements, taken with a simometer (a modified coordinate caliper), are used to calculate three indices that provide the basis for discrimination. The technique is considered accurate, with a frequency of correct classification of 85 percent or better (Curran 1990; Gill and Gilbert 1990; Gill et al. 1988).

Skull 2198 classifies as White on all three indices (maxillofrontal = 40.9, zygoorbital = 49.1 and alpha = 71.0). The corresponding sectioning points are 40, 38, and 60, with race identified as White when at least two of the indices have greater values (Gill et al. 1988). These classification results provide strong evidence that the individual was Caucasian (G. Gill, personal communication 1989). However, the accuracy of the method varies somewhat among Plains Indian tribes, with the frequency of misclassification particularly high for Arikara males. None has misclassified as strongly Caucasoid as 2198. In fact, for the alpha and zygoorbital indices, none of the North American Indians tested to date has attained higher values.

Further assessments necessary to limit the possibility of misidentification require comprehensive multivariate discriminant analysis using appropriate reference samples and selected vault and facial measurements and angles.

Detailed comparison of the metric profile of skull 2198 is complicated by the paucity of craniometric data from French or Spanish samples of a similar time period. The best available sample is about 300 crania composed of seven subsamples from various parts of France (Savayarden, Auvergnaten St. Nectaire, Gallots-Bretons, Bas-Bretons, St. Jean de Luz, Cimet de l'Ouest, and Cimet de la Cité) (Frizzi 1910). Specific dates for the subsamples, except for a general date of 1500–1900 (Schwidetzky and Rösing 1984), were not obtainable. The 10 measurements presented by Schwidetzky and Rösing were used along with comparable dimensions from the Postcontact Coalescent Larson site to estimate a discriminant function that maximizes the classification for these two samples. Because the Larson crania are a large sample of Le Beau phase crania contemporaneous with the Le Beau component at Swan Creek (C. Johnson, personal communication 1982), this series provides an appropriate Northern Plains calibration sample. Le Beau phase sites such as Larson and Swan Creek represent Arikara populations (Owsley et al. 1981).

Fisher's discriminant for two groups was estimated as $z = W^{-1}d$, where z is the vector of discriminant weights, W is the within-sample covariance matrix, and d is the difference vector between sample means. Since only means are available from the French sample, the covariance matrix was estimated using the Larson cranial measurements. The resulting discriminant weights can be used to classify the crania from the Swan Creek site. This approach avoids using Swan Creek crania to estimate the function.

Data from a Berg sample from southern Austria are also available. These crania were measured by Howells (1973), and the data are nearly comparable to the Larson and Swan Creek measurements. Howells's sample (56 males and 53 females) dates from the seventeenth to nineteenth centuries (Guagliardo 1982). These dates bracket the Larson and Swan Creek sites.

The Euro-American/Northern Plains Indian discriminant functions were calculated with the Berg and Larson samples. The software SAS PROC STEPWISE was used to determine the best discriminant models from the 70 variables available. Variables were entered using the MAXR criterion with the number of steps set to 15. As PROC STEPWISE is a multiple regression procedure, the discriminant model is achieved by using a dummy variable for group, "0" and "1" for Berg and Larson, respectively.

The classification probabilities are evaluated using both posterior and typicality probabilities. Posterior probabilities evaluate classification based on the assumption that the unknown specimen comes from one of the calibration samples (Campbell 1984). In reality, the specimen may be different from both calibration samples. The typicality probability evaluates a specimen's probability of being different from each multivariate mean. This value is obtained by referring the D^2 of a specimen from a calibration sample to a chi square table with degrees of freedom equal to the number of variables (Campbell 1984).

European versus Indian Analysis

The means for the French and Larson calibration samples are shown in table 2, along with the measurement vector for skull 2198. The 10 dimensions shown in table 2 were selected by Schwidetzky and Rösing (1984) for comparability, allowing synthesis of a large number of European cranial samples, but they are unselected as far as Native American–French differences are concerned. Measurement definitions for the French series are from Martin (1956; see also Moore-Jansen and Jantz 1986, for English translations); the Larson and Swan Creek samples were measured according to Howells's (1973) method. Only two dimensions are significantly affected there-

Table 2. Larson and French Means for 10 Dimensions Used in the Discriminant Function

Measurement	Larson Site	French	2198	Coefficients
Maximum length	182.083	176.692	178[a]	0.0160
Basion-bregma height	134.550	128.00	128[a]	0.5086
Maximum breadth	140.600	143.846	137	−0.3887
Minimum frontal	93.617	96.538	110[a]	−0.5192
Bizygomatic breadth	140.450	128.920	131[a]	1.2089
Nasion-prosthion height	73.283	65.692[b]	78	1.0070
Nasal height	54.867	53.923	53[a]	−0.7655
Nasal breadth	25.967	24.462	23[a]	0.9652
Orbit height	35.700	34.154	33[a]	0.2118
Orbit breadth	40.683	39.615[b]	42	−0.5958

[a]Indicates measurement closer to French mean.

[b]2 mm subtracted from published sample means.

Table 3. French-Indian Discriminant Statistics

Group	Mean Score	Standard Deviation	Misclassification
French	149.8497	—	—
Larson site	178.0483	5.3102	1/60
Swan Creek	174.944	7.5187	3/23
Sectioning Point	163.949		

by, nasion-prosthion height and orbit breadth. In both, the measurements taken according to Martin are greater by 2–3 millimeters. An approximate correction for technique difference called for subtracting 2 millimeters from the French sample means.

Arikara-French differences in the sample means show Indian crania to be wider in the face but narrower in the vault. The Arikara sample is also higher in the vault and face than the French sample. For seven of the 10 dimensions listed in table 2, skull 2198 measures closer to the French mean. Table 2 also provides the discriminant coefficients required to calculate discriminant scores.

Table 3 presents the French, Larson, and Swan Creek sample means on the linear discriminant function, their standard deviations, and numbers of misclassifications. Only one Larson cranium misclassifies as French, but three from Swan Creek are so classified. The Swan Creek mean is slightly closer to the French mean than is that of Larson, and the variability is higher.

Figure 3 shows the distribution of discriminant scores for the Larson and Swan Creek crania. Table 4 gives the discriminant scores and classification statistics for the Plains Indian crania identified as French by the function. Skull 2198 has the lowest score and a correspondingly high probability of classifying as French on both posterior and typicality probabilities. The typicality probability with Larson shows that the skull cannot be reliably excluded from that sample. The cranium from Burial 53 is only slightly closer to the Larson mean, and thus it also has high probabilities of classification as French. A third skull, labeled "Bass," which was donated by a local collector, falls slightly below the sectioning point, and thus exhibits only marginally higher probabilities of being French.

Berg-Larson Analysis

Table 5 gives the variable names, means, and standard deviations of 19 variables used in discriminating the Larson and Berg reference samples. The measurements of skull 2198 are also given. The subsets of variables that best discriminate the Larson and Berg males were compared, using models with 2 through 14 variables. After step 14, additional variables entered were no longer significant at a probability of less than .05. Therefore, the 14-variable model was accepted as the best subset with which to discriminate the Berg and Larson samples. The Indian-Caucasian differences identified by the stepwise analysis reflect several craniofacial complexes. The most important for discrimination is midfacial size and robusticity, for which the Arikara have larger values for zygomaxillary breadth, minimum cheek height, and inferior malar length. Frontal curvature is also important, with Indians possessing flatter frontals, as seen in a larger frontal angle and a lower frontal subtense. Vault breadths exhibit a complex pattern of variation. Indians are narrower in the posterior vault dimension biasterionic breadth and the anterior vault dimension stephanic breadth, but wider in biauricular breadth. Other dimensions discriminating the two groups reflect specific aspects of cranial variation: foramen magnum length and mastoid breadth are smaller in Native Americans; interorbital breadth is larger in the European sample.

The Berg, Larson, and Swan Creek samples were classified on all functions from two to 14 variables to determine classification performance over the range of models. Table 6 shows the mean and variance of the discriminant scores for the three samples and the classification performance. All Berg crania are classified correctly on all except the two-variable model. All Larson crania are correctly classified on six-variable and subsequent models. The Swan Creek sample has two or more crania classified as Caucasian on models using up to 11 measurements. Skull 2198 misclassifies with the European sample, and after step 11 is the only one to do so. The mean discriminant score for Swan Creek is displaced toward the European mean and is more variable than either Larson or Berg.

Table 7 gives the discriminant score for skull 2198, the D^2 from the Larson and Berg calibration samples, and the posterior and typicality classification probabilities. The sectioning point is approximately 0.5 for all functions. The discriminant score for 2198 ranges from 0.408 (step 3) to 0.091 (step 7); the last is close to the Berg mean of 0.070 for that step. After the five-variable model, the posterior probability of Caucasian is 1 and that of Native American 0, to three decimal places. The typicality probabilities indicate that for the early models 2–5, skull 2198 could not be excluded from Larson, even though its probabilities with Berg are much higher. However, on models using six to nine variables, the skull can be excluded

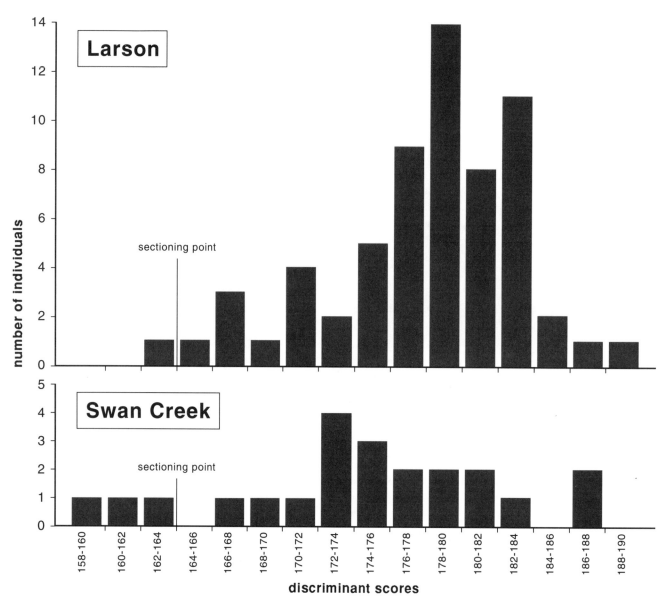

Fig. 3. Distribution of French-Larson discriminant scores for Larson and Swan Creek male crania.

Table 4. Classification Statistics for Swan Creek Crania Identified as French by the French-Indian Discriminant Function

Skull	Score	D² from		Posterior Probability		Typicality Probability	
		French	Larson	French	Larson	French	Larson
2198	159.126	3.052	12.698	0.992	0.008	0.98	0.25
Burial 53	161.382	4.716	9.851	0.929	0.071	0.90	0.50
Bass	162.979	6.113	8.054	0.725	0.275	0.80	0.60

Table 5. Means and Standard Deviations of 19 Variables Entering the Stepwise Function Discriminating Larson and Berg Males

Code Variable Name	Larson		Berg		
	Mean	Standard Deviation	Mean	Standard Deviation	2198
Biauricular breadth	129.50	4.11	127.52	5.42	122
Basion-prosthion length	100.45	4.04	93.75	5.70	91
Biasterionic breadth	106.07	3.72	113.61	4.34	107
Mastoid breadth	11.50	1.60	13.11	1.46	17
Orbit height	35.70	2.01	33.75	1.83	33
Interorbital breadth	21.47	1.97	22.88	2.50	24
Zygomaxillary breadth	103.15	4.46	93.29	4.31	93
Inferior malar length	36.43	3.08	35.70	3.38	41
Malar subtense	10.12	1.39	10.54	1.50	15
Minimum cheek height	24.50	1.93	23.14	2.46	21
Bistephanic breadth	109.20	5.33	122.73	6.11	116
Frontal chord	112.15	3.43	111.05	3.99	117
Frontal subtense	23.28	2.03	27.05	2.56	26
Parietal fraction	54.57	6.47	58.50	4.49	60
Foramen magnum length	36.65	2.72	38.98	3.08	30
Frontomalare radius	79.05	2.79	76.96	3.12	86
Nasion angle, basion-bregma	77.02	2.77	76.50	3.28	76
Frontal angle	134.63	3.11	127.70	3.75	130
Parietal angle	132.70	3.83	132.59	4.21	133

Table 6. Discriminant Score Means, Variances and Misclassification Rates for Larson, Berg, and Swan Creek Male Crania

Step	Larson		Berg		Swan Creek		Misclassifications		
	Mean	Variance	Mean	Variance	Mean	Variance	Larson	Berg	Swan Creek
2	0.873	0.055	0.136	0.043	0.788	0.061	5/60	1/56	4/23
3	0.899	0.047	0.108	0.036	0.813	0.061	3/60	0/56	4/23
4	0.911	0.040	0.096	0.036	0.823	0.062	3/60	0/56	4/23
5	0.918	0.039	0.088	0.032	0.819	0.052	3/60	0/56	2/23
6	0.930	0.031	0.075	0.032	0.765	0.072	0/60	0/56	3/23
7	0.935	0.027	0.070	0.032	0.776	0.071	0/60	0/56	2/23
8	0.941	0.022	0.063	0.032	0.803	0.054	0/60	0/56	3/23
9	0.945	0.021	0.059	0.030	0.764	0.050	0/60	0/56	3/23
10	0.948	0.020	0.056	0.029	0.784	0.041	0/60	0/56	2/23
11	0.951	0.019	0.053	0.028	0.775	0.040	0/60	0/56	2/23
12	0.953	0.019	0.050	0.026	0.791	0.033	0/60	0/56	1/23
13	0.955	0.018	0.048	0.025	0.791	0.035	0/60	0/56	1/23
14	0.956	0.020	0.047	0.022	0.831	0.036	0/60	0/56	1/23

Table 7. Discriminant Score for Skull 2198 at Each Step and Its D^2, Posterior, and Typicality Probability from Larson and Berg

Step	2198 score	Larson			Berg		
		D^2	Posterior	Typicality	D^2	Posterior	Typicality
2	0.318	6.249	0.042	0.05	0.676	0.958	0.75
3	0.408	5.789	0.052	0.15	2.155	0.948	0.50
4	0.339	8.583	0.013	0.10	1.556	0.987	0.80
5	0.293	10.981	0.004	0.05	1.175	0.996	0.90
6	0.109	21.394	0.000	0.01	0.037	1.000	0.99
7	0.091	24.201	0.000	0.01	0.015	1.000	0.99
8	0.291	15.756	0.000	0.05	1.936	1.000	0.98
9	0.155	24.631	0.000	0.01	0.363	1.000	0.99
10	0.249	20.045	0.000	0.02	1.538	1.000	0.99
11	0.222	22.797	0.000	0.02	1.217	1.000	0.99
12	0.312	18.365	0.000	0.10	3.066	1.000	0.99
13	0.358	16.667	0.000	0.20	4.498	1.000	0.98
14	0.378	15.915	0.000	0.30	5.237	1.000	0.98

from Larson at the .05 probability level or below. Considerable reorganization occurs in the discriminating set at step 6 in the stepwise selection of variables. The variables included at that step had a dramatic effect on the classification assessment of skull 2198.

Possibility of Hybrids at Swan Creek

The evidence supports the contention that cranium 2198 is that of a Caucasian male. If he was a resident trader (the most likely explanation for his presence) or captive, there might be hybrid offspring present at Swan Creek. Detecting such persons craniometrically would be difficult; presumably they would be intermediate morphometrically but slightly more likely to classify as Arikara rather than European because of the shared environment. The distribution of Swan Creek discriminant scores was examined from this perspective. As hybrids could be of either sex, the distribution of discriminant scores in both sexes was considered.

Females from Berg and Larson were subjected to the stepwise procedure described for males. After 15 steps, all variables entered remain significant at .05 or less. The 15-variable female function includes the following: cranial length, zygomatic breadth, biasterionic breadth, nasion-prosthion height, mastoid breadth, orbit height and breadth, interorbital breadth, zygomaxillary breadth, bistephanic breadth, occipital subtense and fraction, foramen magnum length, nasion radius, and simotic angle. The function differs in certain details from that for males but agrees in selecting midfacial breadth, robusticity, and vault breadth as

the principal variables for discriminating between Europeans and Native Americans.

Figure 4 shows the distribution of male (14-variable model) and female (15-variable model) calibration samples and the Swan Creek sample. In both sexes, the function classifies all Larson and Berg crania into their correct groups and all Swan Creek crania as Indian, with the exception of male skull 2198. Several male and female crania fall closer to the sectioning point than do any of the Larson crania; thus the mean discriminant score for both sexes has moved in the direction of Caucasian and the variation is greater.

Interpretation

Before addressing the implications of the discovery for the biological and cultural history of the Northern Plains, two points bearing on the analytical reliability must be considered. The first is the effect of interobserver variation on the measurements. There is considerable interobserver variation in craniometric results, and such variation is typical of some of Howells's dimensions (Utermohle and Zegura 1982). The Berg sample was measured by W.W. Howells; the Larson and Swan Creek samples by P.J. Key. Minor variations in technique between Key and Howells could exaggerate Indian-European differences of the calibration samples. Classification of the Swan Creek crania, and 2198 in particular, should be biased toward the Indian calibration sample as these crania were measured by Key.

The second consideration is the plastic response of crania to environmental or functional factors. Such responses are

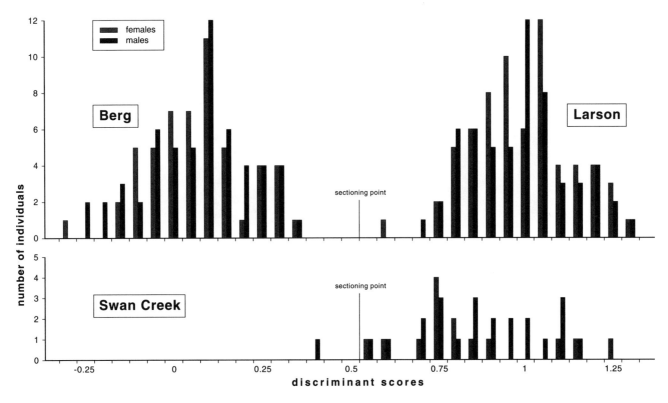

Fig. 4. Distribution of Berg-Larson discriminant scores for Berg, Larson, and Swan Creek crania for males and females.

presumably greatest during ontogeny and would be reflected in the functions developed from the calibration samples. The person represented by skull 2198 probably grew up in a European or Euro-American setting. However, by all indications, he had spent considerable time among the Indians. Thus any environmental bias would also be conservative in testing the hypothesis that he is Caucasian. The bias would be even stronger for any hybrids that might be present.

These results have implications for discrimination of Caucasian and Native American crania. The analysis of Swan Creek crania was based on the best calibration samples and measurement sets available; two samples were required. The French sample, with 10 standard measurements available, is most closely matched ethnically to early Euro-Americans who might have been present in the upper Missouri as early as the seventeenth century. The Berg sample, somewhat less desirable as an ethnic match, allowed a much more fine-grained metric analysis because of the availability of additional measurements. The Berg-Larson discriminant function is more efficient than the French-Larson function, demonstrating that the unconventional measurements employed by Howells are capable of higher discriminatory power than the more traditional ones. These issues have been addressed (Gill

1984; Key and Jantz 1981). The results also confirm the role of midfacial morphology in discriminating Caucasian–Native American differences.

Figure 5 is a facial approximation of skull 2198, created by the combination of computer graphics and video image capture technology. It provides an indication of what the Euro-American from the Swan Creek site might have looked like in life.

An assessment of the significance of these findings depends on both the skull's association with the Swan Creek site and cemetery and a reliable date for the site. Over's notes are not detailed, but there seems no reason to doubt that he obtained the cranium from the cemetery area often associated with the Swan Creek site. Over excavated at least 30 burials from the main cemetery between the years 1920 and 1940, and 60 more were excavated during the University of South Dakota's 1954–1956 field seasons. Hurt (1957:14) observes that Over apparently excavated nearly all the graves marked by surface depressions.

The association of Swan Creek burials with different occupations of the site is complex. Hurt (1957) identified four occupations at Swan Creek, termed A, B, C, and D. Occupation A, the earliest, is assigned to Akaska, an Extended Coales-

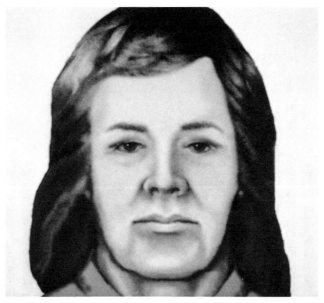

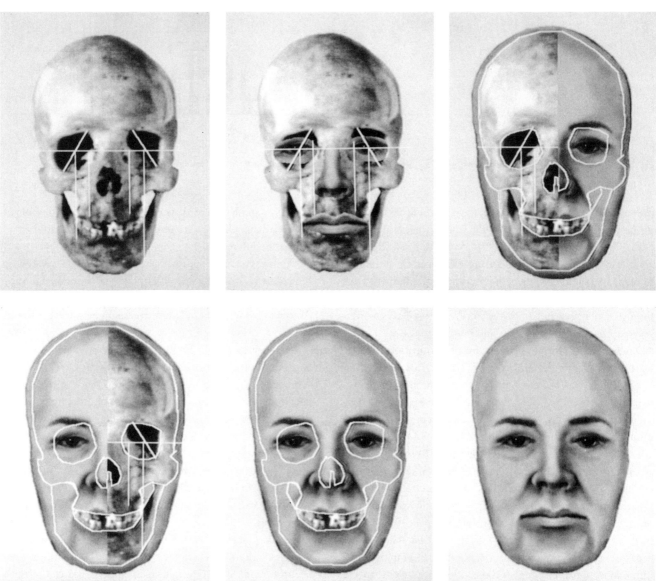

Fig. 5. Facial approximation of skull 2198. The hairstyle is that of men of this era. Computer "aging" techniques were used to make the facial features appear to be those of a man 40–50 years of age. (Image developed by Emily Craig.)

cent phase. Occupations B–D are assigned to Le Beau, a Postcontact Coalescent variant. Hurt (1957) observed two burial patterns at Swan Creek, primary and secondary, with the secondary frequently intrusive into the primary. This observation led Hurt to associate the secondary with Le Beau and the primary with Akaska.

The idea that the two burial patterns mark different tribal, ethnic, or temporal groups is appealing but unsupported by research. Ubelaker and Willey (1978) have shown that both secondary and primary burial practices occur in sites associated with the Arikara. Craniometric analysis of Swan Creek burials also shows no evidence for differentiation between the two burial types (Owsley et al. 1981). Therefore, the apparently disarticulated state of burial 2198 cannot be used to associate it with any particular Swan Creek occupation.

The dating of the two occupations is on somewhat firmer ground. Hurt (1957) dates occupation A at 1675, occupation B at around 1700, and occupations C and D at between 1700 and 1725. These dates are supported by ceramic seriation. Grange (1981) obtained dates of 1690 ± 44 years and 1717 ± 33 years for Swan Creek A and B, respectively. C. Johnson's (personal communication 1982) midpoint ceramic dates are 1675 for Swan Creek B and 1690 for Swan Creek C and D. The rarity of Euro-American trade materials at Swan Creek makes a date later than 1750 unlikely (Orser and Owsley 1982). A single blue glass bead is the only artifact that definitely can be identified as Euro-American in origin.

Support for the foreign origin of skull 2198 has emerged from Schneider's (Schneider and Blakeslee 1990) analysis of dental element composition. The Swan Creek analysis identified an extreme outlier (see Schneider and Blakeslee 1990: fig. 5), which turned out to be a tooth from skull 2198 (K. Schneider, personal communication 1990). The element composition of 2198 allows the conclusion that his teeth formed in an environment different from that of any other Swan Creek individuals.

The earliest well-documented European contact with the Arikara villages in the upper Missouri was the La Vérendrye expeditions of 1742 and 1743 (Wood and Thiessen 1985). However, ethnohistorians have suspected that French fur traders contacted the Arikara by the end of the seventeenth century. Wedel (1979:191) refers to accounts of French traders living with the Pawnee in 1700 and speculates that some may have kept to the Missouri mainstem instead of turning west up its tributaries. Etienne Veniard, Sieur de Bourgmont, a French Canadian, is said to have reached the Arikara villages at the junction of the Cheyenne River in 1714 (Berry 1978:42). Spanish presence in the upper Missouri in the early eighteenth century is also likely. Spanish traders were reported on the Missouri buying buffalo leather in 1706 and in present South Dakota in 1714 (James Hansen, personal communication 1992).

The osteological evidence presented here supports the view that Euro-American resident traders were in the Arikara villages around the Grand River by the early eighteenth century and perhaps earlier. A more precise estimate is not possible because of problems in dating the site and associating the burial with a specific component.

Hurt's (1957:25) observation that the Swan Creek village experienced a reduction in population is of particular interest in relation to these findings. It has been argued that disease-induced depopulation occurred in the Middle Missouri sub-area as early as the 1600s (Ramenofsky 1982, 1987). Owsley's (1992) demographic analysis of several Postcontact Coalescent tradition populations reports high mortality rates early in the seventeenth century. This pattern probably relates to the introduction of acute crowd infections. Disease pressure became intense during the early eighteenth century, as indicated in the mortality profiles of sites such as Larson. Ramenofsky's argument is that disease pathogens were passed over aboriginal trade routes preceding the arrival of Euro-American traders. The presence of Euro-Americans at the Swan Creek village means that disease pathogens could have been directly carried in by the early eighteenth century.

George Gill helped with the assessment of racial characteristics and metrics using the simometer. W.W. Howells, Harvard University, allowed use of his Berg data. R.W. Mann provided information about stafne defects. This research was supported by a grant from the National Science Foundation (BNS-8510588).

References Cited

Ayers, H.G., R.L. Jantz, and P.H. Moore-Jansen
1990 Giles and Elliot Race Discriminant Functions Revisited: A Test Using Recent Forensic Cases. Pp. 65–71 in Skeletal Attribution of Race. G.W. Gill and S. Rhine, eds. Albuquerque: University of New Mexico, Maxwell Museum of Anthropology.

Bass, W.M.
1987 Human Osteology: A Laboratory and Field Manual. 3rd ed. *Missouri Archaeological Society* 2.

Berry, J.J.
1978 Arikara Middlemen: The Effects of Trade on an Upper Missouri Society. (Unpublished Ph.D. Dissertation in Anthropology, Indiana University, Bloomington.)

Birkby, W.
1966 An Evaluation of Race and Sex Identification from Cranial Measurements. *American Journal of Physical Anthropology* 24:21–28.

Campbell, N.A.

1984   Some Aspects of Allocation and Discrimination. Pp. 177–192 in Multivariate Statistical Methods in Physical Anthropology. G.N. Van Vark and W.W. Howells, eds. Dordrecht, Holland: D. Reidel.

Curran, B.K.

1990   The Application of Measures of Midfacial Projection for Racial Classification. Pp. 55–57 in Skeletal Attribution of Race. G.W. Gill and S. Rhine, eds. Albuquerque: University of New Mexico, Maxwell Museum of Anthropology.

Fisher, T.D., and G.W. Gill

1990   Application of the Giles and Elliot Discriminant Function Formulae to a Cranial Sample of Northwestern Plains Indians. Pp. 59–63 in Skeletal Attribution of Race. G.W. Gill and S. Rhine, eds. Albuquerque: University of New Mexico, Maxwell Museum of Anthropology.

Frizzi, E.

1910   Der Franzosenschädel im Vergleich mit dem von Bayern, der Schweiz und Tirol. Korrespondenzblatt Deutsche Gesellschaft für Anthropologie, Ethnologie und Urgeschichte 41:5–8.

Giles, E., and O. Elliot

1962   Race Identification from Cranial Measurements. Journal of Forensic Sciences 7:145–157.

Gill, G.W.

1984   A Forensic Test Case for a New Method of Geographical Race Determination. Pp. 329–339 in Human Identification: Case Studies in Forensic Anthropology. T.A. Rathbun and J.E. Buikstra, eds. Springfield, Ill.: C.C. Thomas.

———

1986   Craniofacial Criteria in Forensic Race Identification. Pp. 143–159 in Forensic Osteology: Advances in the Identification of Human Remains. K.J. Reichs, ed. Springfield, Ill.: C.C. Thomas.

———, and B.M. Gilbert

1990   Race Identification from the Midfacial Skeleton: American Blacks and Whites. Pp. 47–53 in Skeletal Attribution of Race. G.W. Gill and S. Rhine, eds. Albuquerque: University of New Mexico, Maxwell Museum of Anthropology.

———, S.S. Hughes, S.M. Bennett, and B.M. Gilbert

1988   Racial Identification from the Midfacial Skeleton with Special Reference to American Indians and Whites. Journal of Forensic Sciences 33:92–99.

Grange, R.T., Jr.

1981   Ceramic Formula Dating of the Arikara. Pp. 31–55 in Method and Theory in Plains Archaeology: A Volume Dedicated to Carlyle S. Smith. A.E. Johnson and L.J. Zimmerman, eds. Special Publication of the South Dakota Archaeological Society 8.

Guagliardo, M.F.

1982   Craniofacial Structure, Aging and Dental Function: Their Relationships in Adult Human Skeletal Series. (Unpublished Ph.D. Dissertation in Anthropology, University of Tennessee, Knoxville.)

Howells, W.W.

1973   Cranial Variation in Man: A Study by Multivariate Analysis of Patterns of Differences Among Recent Human Populations. Papers of the Peabody Museum of Archaeology and Ethnology, Harvard University 67:1–259.

Hurt, W.R.

1957   Report of the Investigation of the Swan Creek Site 39WW7, Walworth County South Dakota. Pierre, S.Dak.: Reminder.

Jantz, R.L.

1973   Microevolutionary Change in the Arikara Crania: A Multivariate Analysis. American Journal of Physical Anthropology 38:15–26.

———

1974   The Redbird Focus: Cranial Evidence in Tribal Identification. Plains Anthropologist 19:5–13.

Karmiol, M., and R.F. Walsh

1968   Incidence of Static Bone Defect of the Mandible. Oral Surgery, Oral Medicine, Oral Pathology 26:225–228.

Key, P.J.

1983   Craniometric Relationships Among Plains Indians: Culture-Historical and Evolutionary Implications. University of Tennessee. Department of Anthropology Report of Investigations 34.

———, and R.L. Jantz

1981   Temporal Change in Arikara Craniometrics. American Journal of Physical Anthropology 55:247–284.

Langlais, R.P., J. Cottone, and M.J. Kasle

1976   Anterior and Posterior Lingual Depressions of the Mandible. Journal of Oral Surgery 34:502–509.

Martin, R.

1956   Lehrbuch der Anthropologie. Vol. 3. K. Saller, ed. Rev. 3rd ed. Stuttgart, Germany: Gustav Fischer Verlag.

Moore-Jansen, P.H., and R.L. Jantz

1986   A Computerized Skeletal Data Bank for Forensic Anthropology. Knoxville: University of Tennessee, Department of Anthropology.

Orser, C.E., and D.W. Owsley

1982   Using Arikara Osteological Data to Evaluate an Assumption of Fur Trade Archaeology. Plains Anthropologist 27:195–204.

Owsley, D.W.

1992   Demography of Prehistoric and Early Historic Northern Plains Populations. Pp. 75–86 in Disease and Demography in the Americas. J.W. Verano and D.H. Ubelaker, eds. Washington: Smithsonian Institution Press.

———, D.F. Morey, and W.B. Turner

1981   Inferring History from Crania: Biological Distance Comparisons of Mill Creek and Early Middle Missouri Tradition Crania with Mandan and Arikara Population Samples. *Plains Anthropologist* 26:301–310.

——, G.D. Slutzky, M.F. Guagliardo, and L.M. Deitrick

1981   Interpopulation Relationships of Four Post-contact Coalescent Sites from South Dakota: Four Bear (39DW2), Oahe Village (39HU2), Stony Point Village (39ST235) and Swan Creek (39WW7). *Plains Anthropologist* 26:31–42.

Ramenofsky, A.F.

1982   Disease and the Archaeology of Population Collapse: Native American Response to European Contact. (Unpublished Ph.D. Dissertation in Anthropology, University of Washington, Seattle)

——

1987   Vectors of Death. Albuquerque: University of New Mexico Press.

Ronda, J.P.

1984   Lewis and Clark Among the Indians. Lincoln: University of Nebraska Press.

Schneider, K.N., and D.J. Blakeslee

1990   Evaluating Residence Patterns Among Prehistoric Populations: Clues from Dental Enamel Composition. *Human Biology* 62:71–83.

Schwidetzky, I., and F.W. Rösing

1984   Vergleichend-statistische Untersuchungen zur Anthropologie der Neuzeit (nach 1500). *Homo* 35:1–49.

Sigstad, J.S., and J.K. Sigstad, eds.

1973   The Archaeological Field Notes of W.H. Over. *South Dakota State Archaeologist Research Bulletin* 1.

Snow, C.C., S. Hartman, E. Giles, and F.A. Young

1979   Sex and Race Determination of Crania by Calipers and Computer: A Test of the Giles and Elliot Discriminant Functions in 52 Forensic Science Cases. *Journal of Forensic Sciences* 24:448–460.

Stafne, E.C.

1942   Bone Cavities Situated Near the Angle of the Mandible. *Journal of the American Dental Association* 29:1969–1972.

Ubelaker, D.H., and P. Willey

1978   Complexity in Arikara Mortuary Practice. *Plains Anthropologist* 23:69–74.

Utermohle, C.J., and S.L. Zegura

1982   Intra- and Interobserver Error in Craniometry: A Cautionary Tale. *American Journal of Physical Anthropology* 57:303–310.

Wedel, M.M.

1979   The Ethnohistoric Approach to Plains Caddoan Origins. Toward Plains Caddoan Origins: A Symposium. *Nebraska History* 60:183–196.

Wood, W.R., and T.D. Thiessen

1985   Early Fur Trade on the Northern Plains. Norman, Okla.: University of Oklahoma Press.

○○○

CHAPTER 16

Osteological Evidence for Distinct Social Groups at the Leavenworth Site

JOHN E. BYRD AND RICHARD L. JANTZ

Archaeologists employ various lines of evidence for testing hypotheses about social organization. Deetz (1965) and Longacre (1964), for example, have used ceramic data to infer residence patterns. However, there are problems in using artifactual data to infer behavior that is only indirectly related to the artifacts, as Allen and Richardson (1971) have noted.

Many types of social behavior and events have biological consequences, allowing hypotheses about them to be tested with biological data. In the Plains, several attempts have been made to identify ethnic or archaeological affinities of multicomponent cemeteries (Owsley and Jantz 1978; Owsley, Bennett, and Jantz 1982; Owsley et al. 1981). Outside the Plains, skeletal variation has been used to infer postmarital residence patterns (Lane and Sublette 1972; Konigsberg 1988). Element composition of dentition (Schneider and Blakeslee 1990) may also be useful in inferring patterns of mate exchange.

In this chapter metric data are used to infer the social composition of the Leavenworth site (39CO9), South Dakota.

The Leavenworth cemetery is located on rugged hills overlooking a terrace where two villages once stood. Excavations at the site have been conducted since the early nineteenth century (Bass, Evans, and Jantz 1971; Wedel 1955; Krause 1972). The Leavenworth cemetery consists of five distinct areas designated A, B, C, D, and E by Bass, Evans, and Jantz (1971). O'Shea (1984) hypothesized that the spatial segregation of the cemetery areas reflected former band distinctions. The inhabitants of the site, which was occupied 1804–1832, have been identified as historic Arikara by archaeological as well as ethnohistoric data (Krause 1972).

Hypotheses

The hypotheses to be tested require some elaboration because they have been formulated from several lines of evidence. The first is linguistic. Parks (1979a; 1979b) has examined ethnohistoric accounts and linguistic data concerning Caddoan-speaking groups on the Plains and concluded that the inhabitants of the Leavenworth villages spoke two major dialects. Parks's (1979a:236) interpretation is that there was a "major social and linguistic contrast" at the Leavenworth villages. "Some groups were more properly Arikara, while others were more like the Panian groups to the South."

Linguistic and social divergence of this magnitude is likely to be accompanied by detectable biological differentiation.

The second line of evidence is ethnohistoric. Pierre-Antoine Tabeau, a French trader who lived at the Leavenworth villages 1802–1805, provided information about the Arikara inhabitants (Abel 1939). Based on Tabeau's writings, it is believed that the site was settled by Arikara groups from the nearby Grand-Moreau region and the more southerly Bad-Cheyenne region after these people suffered a number of disasters including epidemic diseases and raids from other native groups (Abel 1939).

The third line of evidence is archaeological. Two postcontact Coalescent tradition phases, the Bad River phase (Hoffman and Brown 1967; Lehmer and Jones 1968) and the Le Beau phase (Hurt 1957; Lehmer 1971), have been identified as culminating in the historic Arikara. Both phases date from 1675 to 1780. The two phases have been referred to as "Left Bank" (Le Beau) and "Right Bank" (Bad River) Arikara (Hoffman 1977:21) because of their separate spatial distributions. Ceramics from the respective phases are similar but distinct. Bad River sites contain a majority of Stanley ware, with minority representations of Colombe Collared and Talking Crow types; Le Beau sites contain Stanley and Talking Crow along with a large proportion of a hybrid form between the two (Lehmer and Jones 1968; Lehmer 1971). A minority representation of Le Beau S-Rim also characterizes Le Beau phase sites (Lehmer 1971). Lehmer (1971) refers to the two phases as regional expressions of the same basic culture.

Ceramics recovered from the Leavenworth site have been reported in Krause (1972). Prior to Krause's report, Hoffman and Brown (1967) suggested that the ceramics at Leavenworth closely resembled those of the Bad River sites to the south. Krause saw similarities between Leavenworth and the Buffalo Pasture site of the Bad River phase (cited in Lehmer and Jones 1968). However, a comparison between the list of ware types reported for Leavenworth in Krause (1972) and the ware types that characterize the respective phases (Lehmer 1971) suggests that the Leavenworth site is at least as closely tied to Le Beau manifestations as to Bad River. Specifically, the presence of Le Beau ware and Le Beau S-Rim ware in the assemblages from the two villages points to a relationship with the Le Beau phase. The large proportion of Stanley Braced Rim ware along with a small representation of Colombe Collared Rim ware indicates a relationship with the Bad River phase. This diversity of ceramic types at Leavenworth is interpreted here as further evidence that the villages were occupied by groups from both the Bad-Cheyenne and the Grand-Moreau regions.

The affinity Bad River sites exhibit with more southern sites indicates that they may have retained stronger links with the Pawnee than the Le Beau phase sites. For purposes of generating hypotheses, the Bad River and Le Beau phase sites are identified as antecedents of the two major social divisions at the Leavenworth site.

The final line of reasoning is biological. Key and Jantz (1990) have shown that the Leavenworth cemetery exhibits greater variation than the single-component Larson site, and more variation than the Bad River sites considered together. They also showed that Leavenworth cemetery areas are significantly heterogeneous, reflecting social (i.e., mating or former mating) subdivisions.

The convergence of the linguistic, archaeological, and biological data yield testable hypotheses about the inhabitants of the Leavenworth site: (1) that the Leavenworth site was inhabited by descendents of both Bad River and Le Beau people, and (2) that these social divisions used discrete burial areas.

Materials and Methods

Crania from five Le Beau and five Bad River phase sites were used to construct Le Beau and Bad River samples. The sites and sample sizes are listed in table 1. Metric data were obtained from a Plains craniometric data base assembled by Key (1983). Fifteen measurements (see Howells 1973) were selected by stepwise discriminant analysis, separately by sex. Variables chosen for males and females were then combined and centered and sexes analyzed together. The following variables were used: maximum frontal breadth (XFB), basion-prosthion length (BPL), mastoid height (MDH), interorbital breadth (DKB), dacryon subtense (DKS), M1 alveolus radius

Table 1. Sites and Sample Sizes Included in Derivation of Discriminant Function

Phase	Site	Name	N
Le Beau	39CO31	Nordvold 1	4
Le Beau	39DW2	Four Bear	12
Le Beau	39HU2	Oahe Village	4
Le Beau	39WW1	Mobridge F2	88
Le Beau	39WW2	Larson	127
Bad River	39ST1	Cheyenne River	16
Bad River	39ST203	Black Widow Ridge	8
Bad River	39ST215	Leavitt	5
Bad River	39ST216	Buffalo Pasture	11
Bad River	39ST235	Stony Point	8

(AVR), bregma radius (BRR), zygomaxillare angle (SSA), glabello-occipital length (GOL), biasterionic breadth (ASB), supraorbital projection (SOS), zygomaxillare radius (ZMR), nasion angle, ba-pr (NAA), frontal angle (FRA), and occipital angle (OCA). Descriptive statistics for these variables by phase are presented in Key (1983).

The first analytical procedure was to discriminate the Le Beau and Bad River samples. This was accomplished using PROC DISCRIM in the SAS package (SAS 1985). The procedure yields a linear function that separates the Le Beau phase sample from the Bad River phase sample. The function was then used to obtain discriminant scores for Leavenworth crania. Leavenworth scores were used to classify the Leavenworth crania and to evaluate craniometric variation among cemetery areas.

William H. Over's field notes (Sigstad and Sigstad 1973) are sufficiently clear to indicate that his burials came from areas designated A and B by Bass, and to place specific burials in these areas. Accordingly, Over's burials were assigned to Bass's areas A or B.

One of the most difficult problems was assigning crania excavated by Stirling (Wedel 1955) to burial areas designated by Bass. Apparently, Stirling's field notes contained a map showing the location of his excavations. This can be inferred from a map prepared by Maurice Kirby (see Bass, Evans, and Jantz 1971) that shows locations of Stirling's burials. Judging from Kirby's map, Stirling dug in both area B and area C. Most of the burials in the sample analyzed probably were taken from area C, as Bass's excavations yielded relatively few burials from area C. Bass, Evans, and Jantz (1971:34) specifically refer to encountering previously excavated pits in area C. Accordingly, the two crania from Bass's area C have been grouped with those from Stirling's excavation to create the analytical units consisting of Bass's area A (13 crania), B (18 crania), and Stirling/C (16 crania).

Results

The first question examined was the degree of metric differentiation between Le Beau and Bad River phase crania. The Mahalanobis D^2 between the two phases is 2.12, a difference that is significant ($F_{1,267} = 5.35$, P < .05), but it is apparent that the two distributions overlap considerably, yielding a correct classification rate of 75.74 percent for Le Beau an 70.83 percent for Bad River.

Table 2 gives the discriminant function coefficients associated with each variable and the correlation of each variable with the discriminant score. The latter constitute structure

Table 2. Discriminant Function for Separating Le Beau and Bad River Phase Individuals

Measure	Coefficient	Correlation	
		LeBeau	Bad River
GOL	−0.12834	−0.19	−0.08
ASB	0.12639	0.44	0.38
SOS	−0.6864	−0.51	−0.38
ZMR	0.17621	0.13	0.33
NAA	0.00937	−0.11	−0.06
FRA	0.14682	0.32	0.51
OCA	−0.15089	−0.21	−0.01
XFB	0.0494	0.19	0.33
BPL	−0.08097	−0.16	−0.08
MDH	−0.10719	−0.32	−0.27
DKB	0.02339	0.22	0.12
DKS	0.13678	0.00	0.34
AVR	0.08772	0.01	0.30
BRR	0.05919	0.08	0.14
SSA	0.04917	0.28	0.30
Constant	−0.7013		

coefficients and allow morphological interpretation of the nature of morphometric difference between the two phases. The correlations suggest the following: Bad River crania are broader both posteriorly and anteriorly (ASB and XFB), frontals are flatter (FRA), maxillae are less projecting (SSA), and mastoids are smaller (MDH).

The hypothesis that the Leavenworth site population was composed of descendants of Bad River phase and Le Beau phase populations was tested by calculating discriminant scores for each of the Leavenworth crania using the Le Beau-Bad River discriminant function. Means and standard deviations are shown in table 3. Several observations are noteworthy. The Leavenworth mean lies between the means for Bad River and Le Beau, but clearly closer to that of Le Beau. The Leavenworth range is somewhat greater than for either Bad River or Le Beau, resulting in a higher standard deviation. The hypothesis that Leavenworth crania are more variable than Le Beau phase crania was tested by comparing variances of the discriminant scores. This procedure yields an F ratio of 1.39, with 47 and 235 degrees of freedom. The one-tailed probability is 0.057. Of 47 Leavenworth individuals, 15 or 32 percent have scores assignable to the Bad River population and 32 or 68 percent were classified as Le Beau.

The hypothesis arguing that individuals buried in the different cemetery areas at Leavenworth are spatially patterned in a manner that reflects their relationship with the Bad River and Le Beau phases was tested by classifying crania from each

Table 3. Le Beau Phase, Bad River Phase, and Leavenworth Site Discriminant Scores

Population	N	Mean	Standard Deviation
Le Beau Phase	235	−1.0499	1.41
Bad River Phase	48	1.0055	1.49
Leavenworth site	47	−0.7229	1.67

Table 4. Classification of Leavenworth Crania on Bad River–Le Beau Discriminant Function by Cemetery Area[a]

	Leavenworth Cemetery Areas					
	A		**B**		**Stirling/C**	
Phase	N	%	N	%	N	%
Bad River	3	23.1	2	11.1	10	62.5
Le Beau	10	76.9	16	88.9	6	37.5
Mean discriminant score	−0.78		−1.47		0.16	
Standard deviation	1.71		1.50		1.47	

[a]$\chi^2 = 10.94$, df = 2; $P < .005$. F = 4.66, df = 2.44; $P < .05$.

cemetery area into Le Beau and Bad River phases. Table 4 shows the classification results and also gives the discriminant score means for each Leavenworth area. The chi-square test for homogeneity clearly shows variation among areas in LeBeau-Bad River classification rates. The mean discriminant scores also show signficant variation among areas.

Stirling/C is the only area showing affinity with the Bad River phase. A majority of its crania classify as Bad River and the mean discriminant score is displaced toward the Bad River mean. Crania from areas A and B classify strongly with Le Beau and their discriminant scores are most similar to Le Beau.

Interpretation

O'Shea (1984) has discussed the trend from single to multiple burial areas among the historic Arikara and Pawnee, suggesting that the multiple burial areas in the later sites represent an attempt to maintain distinctive features of corporate group membership such as bands. At Leavenworth, the discrete burial areas are the only evidence for horizontal structuring (O'Shea 1984:220). Results showing significant interarea variation in cranial metrics, as well as the results of Key and

Jantz (1990), support the hypothesis that the Leavenworth village was an amalgamation of formerly heterogeneous breeding populations. Variation among social groups apparently persisted, in spite of the likelihood of intermarriage at Leavenworth.

It is clear from the ethnohistorical record that eighteenth-century Arikaras were divided into a large number of villages, perhaps as many as 43. The villages apparently were organized into seven to ten bands (Parks 1979b). The five burial areas at Leavenworth may be an attempt to mark the existence of band-level divisions of the Arikara. Unfortunately, the samples were adequate for only three of the five areas, and there was no a priori basis for testing Leavenworth cemetery area association with specific bands, for these are archaeologically unidentifiable. Therefore, testing was limited to the hypothesis that there were two major subdivisions of the Arikara, as argued by Parks (1979b), and that these two subdivisions are recognizable archaeologically as the Bad River and Le Beau phases. The results show that Bad River and Le Beau phase crania can be discriminated. Classification of these Leavenworth crania showed that they derived from both the Bad River and Le Beau phases. Further interpretations are limited somewhat by the absence of a coherent picture of relationships between Le Beau and Bad River populations and of how each contributed to the historic Arikara. Lehmer and Jones (1968) suggest that Leavenworth may ultimately be considered Bad River 4, implying continuity with the earlier Bad River phases. As Johnston (1982:42) has emphasized, the unspecified contribution of Le Beau sites to historic Arikara requires further analysis of this problem, taking into account the similarity of Leavenworth crania to Le Beau rather than to Bad River crania, as earlier archaeological interpretations would have predicted. Why Leavenworth crania should be morphologically closer to Le Beau crania is not yet clear, but the following two considerations may be relevent.

First, relative population sizes of the two phases differ. It is possible that the Le Beau population was considerably larger than that of Bad River, and that Leavenworth's composition reflects these differing proportions. The numbers of sites of the two phases appear to be about equal, although Le Beau sites have a larger geographic distribution. More Le Beau burials have been excavated than Bad River burials, probably reflecting a more systematic salvage effort in the Grand-Moreau region. Alternatively, southern populations may have experienced greater devastation from epidemic diseases than more northern populations, leaving more Le Beau survivors to take up residence at the Leavenworth villages.

Second, the Leavenworth cemetery inadequately reflects the composition of the village. It was pointed out in the initial analysis of the Leavenworth cemetery (Bass, Evans, and Jantz 1971) that there were many fewer burials than the known population of the villages should have produced. The situation remains unclear. No other burial location is yet known, nor any other reason why the cemetery would be deficient in burials. Both the cemetery as a whole and each of the burial areas have a normal demographic profile, indicating that certain classes of individuals, such as infants, were not systematically excluded from burial in the cemetery. Consequently, the possibility that descendents of the Bad River population were underrepresented in the cemetery cannot be excluded.

One final note concerns the conclusion of Bass, Evans, and Jantz (1971) that the Leavenworth crania were more homogeneous than those of several comparative series, a result the opposite of what this analysis shows. The inconsistency derives from the use of heterogeneous comparative series in the earlier study and of multivariate rather than univariate tests of intrapopulation variation in the later studies. That Leavenworth crania exhibit greater variation than would be expected in a single breeding population is now well established.

References Cited

Abel, A.H.
1939 Tabeau's Narrative of Loisel's Expedition to the Upper Missouri. Norman, Okla.: University of Oklahoma Press.

Allen, W.L., and J.B. Richardson
1971 The Reconstruction of Kinship from Archaeological Data: The Concepts, Methods, and the Feasibility. *American Antiquity* 36:41–53.

Bass, W.M., D.R. Evans, and R.L. Jantz
1971 The Leavenworth Site Cemetery: Archaeology and Physical Anthropology. *University of Kansas Publications in Anthropology* 2.

Deetz, J.
1965 The Dynamics of Stylistic Change in Arikara Ceramics. *Illinois Studies in Anthropology* 4.

Hoffman, J.J.
1977 Archaeological Inference in Societal Modeling: Social Organization of the Bad River Phase. In Trends in Middle Missouri Prehistory: A Festschrift Honoring the Contributions of Donald J. Lehmer. W. R. Wood, ed. *Plains Anthropologist Memoir* 13:21–27.

——, and L.A. Brown
1967 The Bad River Phase. *Plains Anthropologist* 12:323–343.

Howells, W.W.
1973 Cranial Variation in Man: A Study by Multivariate Analysis of Patterns of Differences Among Recent Human Populations. *Papers of the Peabody Museum of Archaeology and Ethnology, Harvard University* 67:1–259.

Hurt, W.R.
1957 The Swan Creek Site 39WW7 Walworth County, South Dakota. Pierre, S.Dak.: Reminder.

Johnston, R.B.
1982 Archaeology of the McClure Site (39HU7) and the Protohistoric Period in the Big Bend Region of South Dakota. *Plains Anthropologist* 27:1–53.

Key, P.J.
1983 Craniometric Relationships Among Plains Indians: Culture-Historical and Evolutionary Implications. *University of Tennessee, Department of Anthropology, Report of Investigations* 34.

——, and R.L. Jantz
1990 Statistical Assessment of Population Variability: A Methodological Approach. *American Journal of Physical Anthropology* 82:53–59.

Konigsberg, L.W.
1988 Migration Models of Prehistoric Postmarital Residence. *American Journal of Physical Anthropology* 77:471–482.

Krause, R.A.
1972 The Leavenworth Site: Archaeology of an Historic Arikara Community. *University of Kansas Publications in Anthropology* 3.

Lane, R.A., and A.J. Sublette
1972 Osteology of Social Organization: Residence Pattern. *American Antiquity* 37:186–200.

Lehmer, D.J.
1971 Introduction to Middle Missouri Archaeology. *National Park Service. Anthropological Papers* 1.

——, and D.T. Jones
1968 Arikara Archaeology: The Bad River Phase. *Smithsonian Institution River Basin Surveys Publications in Salvage Archaeology* 7.

Longacre, W.A.
1964 Sociological Implications of the Ceramic Analysis. In Chapters in the Prehistory of Eastern Arikara, II. P.S. Martin et al., eds. *Fieldiana: Anthropology* 55:155–170.

O'Shea, J.M.
1984 Mortuary Variability: An Archaeological Investigation. Orlando Fla.: Academic Press.

Owsley, D.W. and R.L. Jantz
1978 Intracemetery Morphological Variation in Arikara Crania from the Sully Sites (39SL4), Sully County, South Dakota. *Plains Anthropologist* 23:139–147.

——, S.M. Bennett, and R.L. Jantz
1982 Intercemetery Morphological Variation in Arikara Crania from the Mobridge Site (39WW1). *American Journal of Physical Anthropology* 58:179–185.

——, G.D. Slutzky, M.F. Guagliardo, and L.M. Dietrick

1981   Interpopulation Relationships of Four Postcontact Coalescent Sites from South Dakota. In Progress in Skeletal Biology of Plains Populations, R.L. Jantz and D.H. Ubelaker
eds., *Plains Anthropologist Memoir* 17:31–56.

Parks, D.R.

1979a   The Northern Caddoan Languages: Their Subgroupings
and Time Depths. In Toward Plains Caddoan Origins: A
Symposium. *Nebraska History* 60:197–213.

——

1979b   Bands and Villages of the Arikara and Pawnee. In Toward
Plains Caddoan Origins: A Symposium. *Nebraska History*
60:214–239.

SAS

1985   SAS User's Guide: Statistics. Cary, N.C.: SAS.

Schneider, K.N., and D.J. Blakeslee

1990   Evaluating Residence Patterns Among Prehistoric Populations: Clues from Dental Enamel Composition. *Human
Biology* 62:71–83.

Sigstad, J.S., and J.K. Sigstad

1973   Archaeological Field Notes of W.H. Over. *Office of the South
Dakota State Archaeologist, South Dakota. Research Bulletin 1.*

Wedel, W.R.

1955   Archaeological Materials from the Vicinity of Mobridge,
South Dakota. *Anthropological Papers 45, Bureau of American
Ethnology Bulletin 157:69–188.*

○○○

CHAPTER 17

Metric Variation in the Supraorbital Region in Northern Plains Indians

MARIA S. COLE AND THEODORE M. COLE III

The Supraorbital Region

In addition to the behavioral changes associated with the transition from a hunter-gatherer to an agricultural adaptation, a consistent trend in craniofacial variation has been documented (Frayer 1980). Models developed by Carlson (1976a, 1976b), Carlson and van Gerven (1977), and Larsen (1984) describe a general reduction in the robusticity of the masticatory complex. The progressive gracilization of the facial skeleton is thought to be the result of the changing functional demands placed on the masticatory apparatus by alterations in subsistence strategy. Specifically, less masticatory force is required for food processing with the introduction of softer foods associated with an increased reliance on agriculture.

One aspect of the masticatory apparatus, the supraorbital region or brow ridges, has been suggested to function in the dissipation of stresses engendered during mastication and paramasticatory ("teeth as tools") activities (Biegert 1957, 1963; Endo 1965, 1966, 1967, 1970, 1973; Oyen and Rice 1980; Oyen and Russell 1982; Oyen, Rice, and Cannon 1979; Oyen, Rice, and Enlow 1981; Oyen, Walker, and Rice 1979; Russell 1982, 1983, 1985, 1986a, 1986b; Scott 1963; Weiden-

reich 1941; Wolpoff 1980). Therefore, a reduction in masticatory robusticity would be expected to include brow ridge reduction. This study will examine subsistence-related trends in the supraorbital region for a sample of Northern Plains Indians that exhibits a subsistence shift from hunting and gathering (Plains Woodland tradition) to horticulture (Middle Missouri and Coalescent traditions). Systematic reduction in the demands placed on the masticatory apparatus, and hence the brow ridges, should be evidenced by a progressive reduction in size of the brow ridges from the Woodland to the Coalescent traditions. Furthermore, the brow ridges are notable for consistent sexual dimorphism in humans (Bass 1981; Krogman 1962).

The supraorbital region (fig. 1) is characterized by variable development of two individual segments: the superciliary arch or ridge and the supraorbital arch (Cunningham 1908; Ehara and Seilor 1970; Smith 1976a, 1976b, 1982, 1983, 1984, 1985; Smith and Ranyard 1980). The superciliary arch extends from glabella over the medial one-third to one-half of the orbit. Individuals having strongly developed supraorbital regions may have superciliary arches that are continuous across glabella. Superiorly, the superciliary arch grades into the frontal

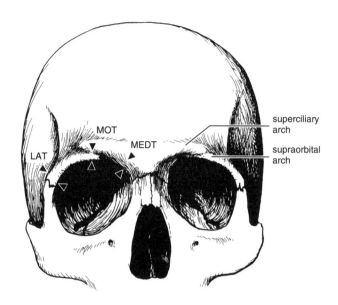

Fig. 1. The supraorbital region. Arrows indicate where measurements are taken. See text for variable abbreviations. Drawn by Luci Betti-Nash.

squama. Typically, the supraorbital arch arises from the supraorbital notch or foramen and extends to the frontozygomatic suture. It often extends medially beneath the lateral portion of the superciliary arch and is separated by a variably pronounced groove, the supraorbital sulcus.

The Study Sample

The sample consists of adult individuals from archaeological sites in central South Dakota and south-central North Dakota. These sites are associated culturally with the Plains Woodland, the Middle Missouri, or the Coalescent traditions (table 1). The traditions are distinguished by differing subsistence strategies. The Woodland tradition dates from A.D. 610 to 1033 (Key 1983) and is characterized by a hunting and gathering economy, with bison the primary large-game animal exploited, along with deer and elk (Lehmer 1954, 1970, 1971; Zimmerman 1985). Wild plant foods also played an important role in the Woodland economy (Zimmerman 1985). The Middle Missouri tradition, which marks the beginning of the Plains Village period, dates from A.D. 900 to 1675 (Key 1983). The Middle Missouri subsistence economy reflected an increased reliance on horticulture, with corn, beans, and squash as the primary crops (Zimmerman 1985). The Coalescent tradition is represented by Arikara crania from Extended, Postcontact, and Disorganized variant sites dating from 1600 to 1832 (Key 1983). As with the Middle Missouri tradition, domesticated plants were an important component of the

Table 1. Sites and Sample Sizes

	Males	Females
Plains Woodland Tradition		
Middle Woodland		
Arbor Hill (39UN1)	1	2
Yankton Mounds (39YK1)	1	0
Terminal Woodland/Great Oasis		
Platte-Winner Bridge (39CH54)	0	1
Ufford Mounds (39CL2)	2	2
Mitchell Mounds (39DV2/3)	1	0
Bloom Village (39HS1)	2	1
Madison Pass Mounds (39LK2)	1	0
Brandon (39MH1)	3	3
Hartford Beach Mounds (39RO4)	2	3
Woodland "B"		
Enemy Swim Lake (39DA3)	1	0
Hofer Mounds (39HT2)	1	1
Newton Hills (39LN10)	0	1
Madsen's Mounds (39RO2)	1	1
Daugherty Mounds (39RO10)	4	3
Buchanan Mounds (39RO3)	3	4
Middle Missouri Tradition		
Initial Middle Missouri		
Twelve Mile Creek (39HT1)	0	2
Extended Middle Missouri		
Fairbanks Village (39SL2)	4	1
Coalescent Tradition		
Extended Coalescent		
Mobridge (39WW1)	4	15
Postcontact Coalescent		
Dinehart's Village (39LM33)	3	1
Cheyenne River (39ST1)	1	0
Stony Point (39ST235)	3	4
Swan Creek (39WW7)	14	11
Disorganized Coalescent		
Leavenworth (39CO9)	2	3

Coalescent diet. Coalescent tribes continued to exploit the bison as the primary game animal, but with increased efficiency following the introduction of the horse around A.D. 1739 (Hurt 1969; Holder 1970).

The sample consists of 54 males and 59 females (table 1).

With only a few exceptions, the discussion of brow ridge size and shape has been qualitative. Landauer (1962) included an ordinal measure of overall brow ridge size in a factor analysis of cranial form in a modern human sample. Aside from this single early study, most of the quantitative concentration on brow ridge size and shape has been focused on fossil human groups, and on Neanderthals and early modern *Homo sapiens* in particular (Simmons, Falsetti, and Smith 1991;

Smith and Ranyard 1980; Smith, Simek, and Harrill 1989). The measurements used in this study were designed to quantify size and shape variation in the supraorbital region. They are adapted from quantitative studies (Harrill 1985; Smith 1976a; Smith and Ranyard 1980; Smith, Simek, and Harrill 1989). The measurements are defined as follows and are illustrated in fig. 1: lateral thickness (LAT)—the thickest point on the lateral segment of the supraorbital arch, lateral to a plane passing through frontotemporale; medial thickness (MEDT)—the thickest point on the superciliary arch lateral to the medial orbital margin; midorbital thickness (MOT)—the point of minimum thickness between the lateral and medial points.

Measurements were taken to the nearest 0.1 millimeter using sliding calipers. Measurements were taken by one observer to eliminate interobserver errors.

It is important to make a distinction between absolute and relative brow ridge sizes. It is possible that two groups could differ in brow ridge size simply because of differences in the size of the entire skull, but with the relative sizes of the brow ridges being the same. However, the hypotheses of subsistence-related gracilization of the face (Carlson 1976a, 1976b; Carlson and van Gerven 1977; Frayer 1980; Larsen 1984) implicitly predict that the *relative* size of the brow ridges (and of the masticatory apparatus in general) will be reduced. Falsetti (personal communication 1990) has reanalyzed data published by Key (1983) and suggests that there is little variation in sex-specific overall cranial size among Plains traditions. Therefore, any size differences observed among traditions in this study will be interpreted as relative size differences.

Methods

The statistical methods used in this are designed to address the following questions: Are there differences in brow ridge size and shape among traditions? Are there differences in brow ridge size and shape between sexes? Are patterns of size and shape variation among traditions and between sexes independent? That is, are patterns of sexual dimorphism consistent across traditions?

Brow ridge size is described by the magnitude of the three thickness measurements (LAT, MOT, and MEDT). These variables are logarithmically transformed, with the logged measurements denoted by an "L" prefix (LLAT, LMOT, LMEDT). To address the questions posed above, the sample was divided into six groups on the basis of tradition and sex: Plains Woodland males and females, Middle Missouri males and females, and Coalescent males and females.

In addition to discussing brow ridge size in terms of individual thickness measurements, a "composite" size variable will be used to describe the overall size of the supraorbital region. The composite variable used is the arithmetic mean of the log-transformed variables (LLAT + LMOT + LMEDT) ÷ 3, which will be referred to as LOGSIZE. This variable will be important for interpreting the results of the multivariate statistical analysis.

Tests for overall heterogeneity among group means are performed using multivariate analysis of variance, with tradition and sex as the main effects. For each effect, the null hypothesis is that there is no difference among group means. Multivariate analysis of variance (MANOVA) is preferred over a separate univariate analysis of variance for each variable because it takes correlations among variables into account. MANOVA assumes both multivariate normality and homogeneity of the within-group variance-covariance matrices (Johnson and Wichern 1982). Preliminary testing indicated that these assumptions are met for the study sample. All MANOVA calculations were performed using the general linear model procedure of the SAS Institute (1982) statistical package.

While MANOVA is designed to determine whether overall differences in group means are present, further analyses are necessary for describing group differences in more explicit terms. Canonical variates analysis (CVA) was utilized as a multivariate statistical method for summarizing the among-group differences in many variables in terms of fewer "composite" variables, which are linear combinations of the original data. CVA recognizes groups that are defined a priori and projects them into a space where among-group variance is maximized relative to within-group variance along a series of orthogonal (statistically independent) axes (Johnson and Wichern 1982). CVA can then be used to determine which original variables are most responsible for producing group differences. All of the CVA calculations were performed using the canonical discriminate analysis procedure of SAS Institute (1982).

Results

Sex- and tradition-specific descriptive statistics for the raw thickness measurements are presented in table 2. The means of the raw thicknesses are displayed in fig. 2.

The multivariate analysis of variance is presented in table 3. Each effect (tradition, sex, and tradition-by-sex interaction) is evaluated using the Wilks's lambda statistic. The significance test for Wilks's lambda approximates an F-distribution (Johnson and Wichern 1982). The MANOVAs indicate that there is significant heterogeneity of group means for both tradition

Table 2. Descriptive Statistics for Raw Measurements and for the Log-Transformed Size Variable

| Tradition | Sex | N | Mean | Lateral Thickness (mm) | |
				Standard Deviation	Range
Plains Woodland	M	23	8.05	1.34	5.0–10.0
	F	21	7.27	1.33	4.9– 9.9
Middle Missouri	M	4	7.15	0.96	5.9– 8.0
	F	3	6.63	0.55	6.0– 7.0
Coalescent	M	27	7.57	1.12	5.5–10.2
	F	34	7.09	1.24	5.0–10.3

| Tradition | Sex | N | Mean | Midorbital Thickness (mm) | |
				Standard Deviation	Range
Plains Woodland	M	23	5.14	1.52	2.8– 8.0
	F	22	4.06	1.06	2.0– 6.1
Middle Missouri	M	4	5.13	0.82	4.2– 6.2
	F	3	4.60	0.52	4.0– 4.9
Coalescent	M	27	5.34	1.05	4.0– 8.0
	F	34	4.49	0.93	2.8– 6.5

| Tradition | Sex | N | Mean | Medial Thickness (mm) | |
				Standard Deviation	Range
Plains Woodland	M	23	17.40	2.20	13.0–21.5
	F	20	14.57	2.64	9.0–19.7
Middle Missouri	M	4	17.98	3.49	16.0–23.2
	F	3	13.93	1.67	12.0–14.9
Coalescent	M	27	16.57	2.13	10.0–21.0
	F	32	14.28	2.20	9.0–20.0

| Tradition | Sex | N | Mean | Logsize | |
				Standard Deviation	Range
Plains Woodland	M	23	2.171	0.172	1.734–2.453
	F	19	2.024	0.180	1.500–2.241
Middle Missouri	M	4	2.154	0.127	2.063–2.341
	F	3	2.014	0.109	1.888–2.079
Coalescent	M	27	2.157	0.122	1.878–2.350
	F	32	2.028	0.136	1.670–2.211

and sex effects. The nonsignificant MANOVA for tradition-by-sex interaction indicates that patterns of sexual dimorphism are consistent across traditions.

The results of the canonical variates analysis are presented in table 4. Because there are three original variables (LLAT, LMOT, and LMEDT), three canonical axes are produced. The first axis accounts for 71.01 percent of the among-group variance. The second axis accounts for nearly all the remaining among-group variance (26.64%), while the third axis accounts for only 2.35 percent. Because of the relatively small amount of variance associated with this final axis, discussions will be confirmed to the first and second axes.

The canonical axes are interpreted in terms of the original logged variables by examining the sample correlations be-

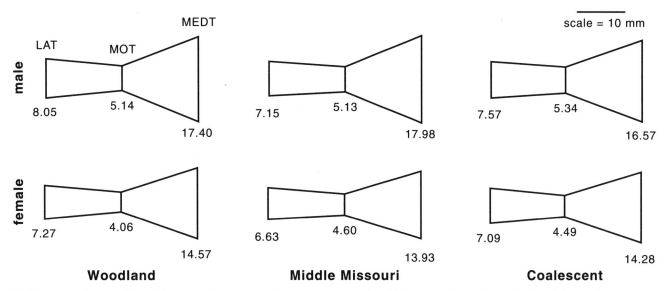

Fig. 2. Schematic diagrams of brow ridge form, using sex- and tradition-specific mean values. Thicknesses are in millimeters. Horizontal distances between measurements are arbitrary.

tween these measurements and the canonical axis scores (table 4). These correlations are known as total canonical structure coefficients (Klecka 1980). The correlations between the logged measurements and the scores on the first canonical axis are all positive, suggesting that variation on the first axis is related to overall size. In fact, if size is characterized as a combination of all variables (sensu Mosimann 1970), this association can be explicitly tested. Correlation of the first axis scores with the logged size variable (LOGSIZE) is 0.814, indicating that groups with more positive mean scores will tend to be absolutely larger. A plot of the group means on the first two canonical axes is presented in figure 3. The means are connected by a minimum spanning tree based on the matrix of Mahalanobis D^2 distances among groups (Sneath and Sokal 1973). This tree connects each group to the groups to which it is most similar. The plot shows that all the male groups have more positive means than the females. The minimum spanning tree suggests that there is more similarity within sexes

than across traditions, with the Coalescent males and females sex means being the most similar within any tradition. This axis can be considered to reflect that part of the among-sample variance that is related to sexual size and shape dimorphism.

The second canonical axis appears to separate traditions on the basis of subsistence strategy. The Plains Village traditions (Middle Missouri and Coalescent), which were characterized by a horticultural economy, have more positive scores on this axis. In contrast, the Plains Woodland groups, characterized by a hunting-gathering economy, have more negative scores. When the correlations between the logged measurements and the scores on the second axis are examined (table 4), a shape contrast is seen between LMOT and both LLAT and LMEDT. LMOT is positively correlated with second axis scores, indicating that midorbital thickness is relatively greater in the Middle Missouri and Coalescent groups than in the Plains Woodland groups. The negative correlations of LLAT and LMEDT with second axis scores indicate that these variables are relatively larger in the Plains Woodland groups. The nonsignificant correlation between LOGSIZE and second axis scores implies that these shape differences are not related to any size differences among traditions.

Interpretation

This research has examined subsistence-related trends in craniofacial form in Northern Plains Indians, with specific interest in the supraorbital region. Studies by Carlson (1976a,

Table 3. Multivariate Analyses of Variance for Log-Transformed Measurements

Source	Degrees of Freedom	Wilks's Lambda	F	Probability
Tradition	6, 200	0.87083	2.39	0.0300
Sex	3, 100	0.83957	6.37	0.0005
Interaction	6, 200	0.9879	0.20	0.9757

Table 4. Canonical Variates Analysis of Logged Measurements

Pooled within-group covariance matrix:

	LLAT	LMOT	LMEDT
LLAT	0.027808		
LMOT	0.020887	0.057802	
LMEDT	0.010375	0.013443	0.025071

Mahalanobis D^2 matrix:

	Plains Woodland male	Plains Woodland female	Middle Missouri male	Middle Missouri female	Coalescent male
Plains Woodland female	1.2855				
Middle Missouri male	0.9534	3.7964			
Middle Missouri female	1.5949	1.1664	1.3894		
Coalescent male	0.7009	6.9826	0.6325	1.1227	
Coalescent female	1.3266	2.1137	2.8366	0.1794	5.1126

Correlations with axis scores:

	LLAT	LMOT	LMEDT	LOGSIZE
Axis 1 (71.01%)	0.3894	0.6114	0.9671	0.8410
Axis 2 (26.64%)	−0.5778	0.3881	−0.2238	−0.0892 ns

Group means of axis scores:

	Axis 1	Axis 2
Plains Woodland male	0.6216	−0.4065
Plains Woodland female	−0.6614	−0.4846
Middle Missouri male	0.9507	0.3537
Middle Missouri female	−0.5422	0.6802
Coalescent male	0.4907	0.2734
Coalescent female	−0.5361	0.2412

1976b; Carlson and van Gerven 1977), Frayer (1980), and Larsen (1984) predict that the introduction of softer foods with the advent of horticulture will result in a progressive gracilization of the masticatory complex. The introduction of a softer diet requires less masticatory force, allowing a decrease in masticatory robusticity, less prognathism, and a more brachycephalic (higher and more rounded) cranial form (Carlson 1976a, 1976b; Carlson and van Gerven 1977). Because the supraorbital region is considered an integral part of the masticatory complex (Ravosa 1988), reduction in this area would also be expected.

For the Northern Plains sample, the Plains Woodland tradition would be expected to possess thicker brow ridges in comparison to later, horicultural groups from the Middle Missouri and Coalescent traditions. However, there is a large degree of overlap in sex-specific means for LOGSIZE (table 2), so that the expectation for reduction in relative size is not met. However, the second canonical axis (table 4 and fig. 3) shows a separation of subsistence groups that is attributed to differences in brow ridge shape. The Plains Woodland groups (with a hunting-gathering economy) possess brow ridges that are thicker both laterally (LLAT) and medially (LMEDT). The horticulturists, who show relative decreases for both of these dimensions, are very slightly thicker midorbitally.

The hypothesis of brow ridge gracilization across the subsistence transition from hunting-gathering to increased horticulture is supported in that the brow ridges decrease in relative size both medially and laterally. This association between subsistence strategy and brow ridge form is empirically based. The theoretical relationships between brow ridge shape and the loads applied to the brow ridges during mastication have yet to be resolved (Picq and Hylander 1989; Russell 1986b; Shea 1986). Therefore, there are no explicit expectations for how the proportions of different

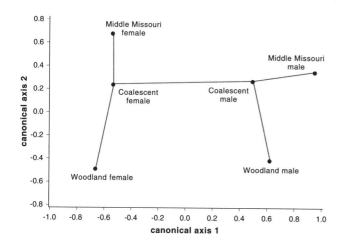

Fig. 3. Plot of first two canonical axes. Group means are connected by a minimum spanning tree.

segments of the brow ridges should vary with differing subsistence strategies.

If the pattern of shape change were consistent with respect to time, the brow ridges of Middle Missouri would be expected to be intermediate in form between the Plains Woodland and the Coalescent. The minimum spanning tree (fig. 3) shows that the Plains Woodland groups are more closely related to the Coalescent means than to the Middle Missouri means. The genetic relationships between the Plains Woodland and Middle Missouri people have yet to be resolved. However, it is clear that the Caddoan-speaking Coalescent groups have separate geographic and genetic origins (Hudson 1976; Key 1983). Therefore, it is possible that the functional "signal" in brow ridge form is confounded with variation related to genetic differences that are unrelated to masticatory function. As an alternative explanation, the relationships between the Middle Missouri and other groups may be distorted slightly as the result of sampling error due to very small sample sizes.

The significant differences in size and shape of the supraorbital region between sexes lead to a potentially valuable means of sex determination in skeletal samples. The effectiveness of the discriminant function (approximately 80%) is not so great as those that can be applied to complete crania (Giles and Elliot 1963; Jantz and Moore-Jansen 1988); however, for many sites (particularly mound burials), it may prove more useful in the sexing of fragmentary or poorly preserved remains.

In conclusion, there are avenues for further research that may lead to a better understanding of the relationship between subsistence and craniofacial form. First, the Northern Plains sample could be temporally and culturally expanded

(perhaps to include Paleo-Indian and Archaic samples), to increase the amount of variation in subsistence strategies. Second, other aspects of the cranial skeleton in Northern Plains Indians have yet to be considered in explicit functional terms. While no clear trend is observed for the supraorbital region, other aspects of masticatory reduction and gracilization, for example, decreased mandibular robusticity, decreased prognathism, and more highly vaulted frontal squama, may exhibit significant subsistence-related trends. Finally, because Plains Village people continued to rely heavily on game (especially bison) as a dietary resource, their adoption of horticulture was not so pronounced as for some other prehistoric Native American cultures, for example, Southwest Indians. Therefore, the relationship between dietary composition and craniofacial form could become clearer with analyses of additional hunting-and-gathering and horticultural groups outside the Northern Plains.

References Cited

Bass, W.M.
    1981   Human Osteology: A Laboratory and Field Manual of the Human Skeleton. Columbia: Missouri Archaeological Society.
Biegert, J.
    1957   Der Formwandel des Primatenschädels und seine Beziehungen zur ontogenetischen (Entwicklung und den phylogenetischen Spezialisationen der Kopforgane). *Gegenbaurs Morphologisches Jahrbuch* 98:77–199.
——
    1963   The Evaluation of Characteristics of the Skull, Hands, and Feet for Primate Taxonomy. Pp. 116–145 in Classification and Human Evolution. S.L. Washburn, ed. Chicago: Aldine.
Carlson, D.S.
    1976a   Temporal Variation in Prehistoric Nubian Crania. *American Journal of Physical Anthropology* 45:467–484.
——
    1976b   Patterns of Morphological Variation in the Human Midface and Upper Face. Pp. 277–299 in Factors Affecting the Growth of the Midface. J.A. McNamara, Jr., ed. Ann Arbor, Mich.: Center for Human Growth and Development.
——, and D.P. van Gerven
    1977   Masticatory Function and Post-Pleistocene Evolution in Nubia. *American Journal of Physical Anthropology* 46:495–506.
Cunningham, D.J.
    1908   The Evolution of the Eyebrow Region of the Forehead, with Special Reference to the Excessive Supraorbital Development in the Neanderthal Race. *Transactions of the Royal Society of Edinburgh* 46:283–311.

Ehara, A., and R. Seilor

1970   Die Strukturen der Überaugenregion bei den Primaten, Deutungen and Definitionen. *Zeitschrift für Morphologie und Anthropologie* 62:1–29.

Endo, B.

1965   Distribution of Stress and Strain Produced in the Human Face by Masticatory Forces. *Journal of the Anthropological Society of Nippon* 73:123–136.

——   1966   Experimental Studies on the Mechanical Significance of the Form of the Human Facial Skeleton. *University of Tokyo, Journal of Facial Sciences, Section V: Anthropology* 3:1–106.

——   1967   Mechanical Analysis of the Form of the Human Facial Skeleton. *VI Congress of the International Sciences of Anthropology and Ethnology* 2:326–353.

——   1970   Analysis of Stress Around the Orbit Due to Masseter and Temporalis Muscles. *Journal of the Anthropological Society of Nippon* 78:251–266.

——   1973   Stress Analysis of the Gorilla Face. *Primates* 14:37–45.

Frayer, D.W.

1980   Sexual Dimorphism and Cultural Evolution in the Late Pleistocene and Early Holocene of Europe. *Journal of Human Evolution* 9:399–415.

Giles, E., and O. Elliot

1963   Sex Determination by Discriminant Function Analysis of Crania. *American Journal of Physical Anthropology* 21:53–68.

Harrill, M.S.

1985   An Analysis of Metric Trends in the Supraorbital Region of Upper Pleistocene European Hominids. (Unpublished Bachelors Thesis, University of Tennessee, Knoxville.)

Holder, P.

1970   The Hoe and the Horse on the Plains: A Study of Cultural Development Among North American Indians. Lincoln: University of Nebraska Press.

Hudson, C.

1976   The Southeastern Indians. Knoxville, Tenn.: University of Tennessee Press.

Hurt, W.R.

1969   Seasonal Economic and Settlement Patterns of the Arikara. *Plains Anthropologist* 14:32–37.

Jantz, R.L., and P.H. Moore-Jansen

1988   A Data Base for Forensic Anthropology: Structure, Content and Analysis. *University of Tennessee. Department of Anthropology Report of Investigations* 47.

Johnson, R.A., and D.W. Wichern

1982   Applied Multivariate Statistical Analysis. Englewood Cliffs, N.J.: Prentice-Hall.

Key, P.J.

1983   Craniometric Relationships Among Plains Indians. *University of Tennessee. Department of Anthropology Report of Investigations* 34.

Klecka, W.R.

1980   Discriminant Analysis. *Sage University Paper Series on Quantitative Applications in the Social Sciences* 19.

Krogman, W.M.

1962   The Human Skeleton in Forensic Medicine. Springfield, Ill.: Charles C. Thomas.

Landauer, C.A.

1962   A Factor Analysis of the Facial Skeleton. *Human Biology* 34:239–253.

Larsen, C.S.

1984   Health and Disease in Prehistoric Georgia: The Transition to Agriculture. Pp. 367–392 in Paleopathology at the Origins of Agriculture. M.N. Cohen and G.J. Armelagos, eds. New York: Academic Press.

Lehmer, D.J.

1954   The Sedentary Horizon of the Northern Plains. *Southwestern Journal of Anthropology* 10:139–159.

——   1970   Climate and Culture History in the Middle Missouri Valley. Pp. 117–129 in Pleistocene and Recent Environments of the Central Great Plains. W. Dort and J.K. Jones, eds. Lawrence: University of Kansas Press.

——   1971   Introduction to Middle Missouri Archeology. Washington: National Park Service.

Mosimann, J.E.

1970   Size Allometry: Size and Shape Variables with Characterizations of the Lognormal and Generalized Gamma Distributions. *Journal of the American Statistical Association* 65: 930–945.

Oyen, O.J., and R.W. Rice

1980   Supraorbital Development in Chimpanzees, Macaques and Baboons. *Journal of Medical Primatology* 9:161–168.

——, R.W. Rice, and M.S. Cannon

1979   Browridge Structure and Function in Extant Primates and Neanderthals. *American Journal of Physical Anthropology* 51: 83–96.

——, R.W. Rice, and D.H. Enlow

1981   Cortical Surface Patterns in Human and Nonhuman Primates. *American Journal of Physical Anthropology* 54: 415–419.

——, and M.D. Russell

1982   Histogenesis of the Craniofacial Skeleton and Models of Facial Growth. Pp. 361–372 in The Effect of Surgical Intervention on Craniofacial Skeleton and Models of Facial Growth. J.A. McNamara, D.S. Carlson, and K.A. Ribbens, eds. Ann Arbor: University of Michigan Press.

——, A.C. Walker, and R.W. Rice
1979 Craniofacial Growth in Olive Babbons (*Papio cynocephalus anubis*): Browridge Formation. *Growth* 43:533–544.

Picq, P.G., and W.L. Hylander
1989 Endo's Stress Analysis of the Primate Skull and the Functional Significance of the Supraorbital Region. *American Journal of Physical Anthropology* 79:393–398.

Ravosa, M.J.
1988 Browridge Development in Cercopithecidae: A Test of Two Models. *American Journal of Physical Anthropology* 76:535–555.

Russell, M.D.
1982 Tooth Eruption and Browridge Formation. *American Journal of Physical Anthropology* 58:59–65.

——
1983 The Functional and Adaptive Significance of the Supraorbital Torus. (Unpublished Ph.D. Dissertation, University of Michigan, An Arbor.)

——
1985 The Supraorbital Torus: "A Most Remarkable Peculiarity." *Current Anthropology* 26:337–360.

——
1986a Response to Shea: "Skull Form and the Supraorbital Torus in Primates." *Current Anthropology* 27:257–260.

——
1986b *In vivo* Testing and Refinement of the Frame Model of the Craniofacial Skeleton. *American Journal of Physical Anthropology* 69:259.

SAS Institute
1982 SAS User's Guide: Statistics. Raleigh: SAS Institute.

Scott, J.
1963 Factors Determining the Skull Form in Primates. *Symposium of the Zoological Society of London* 10:127–134.

Shea, B.T.
1986 On Skull Form and the Supraorbital Torus in Primates. *Current Anthropology* 27:257–260.

Simmons, T., A.B. Falsetti, and F.H. Smith
1991 Frontal Bone Morphometrics of Southwest Asian Pleistocene Hominids. *Journal of Human Evolution* 20:249–269.

Smith, F.H.
1976a The Neandertal Remains from Krapina: A Descriptive and Comparative Study. *University of Tennessee. Department of Anthropology Report of Investigations* 15.

——
1976b A Fossil Hominid Frontal from Velika Pecina (Croatia) and a Consideration of Upper Pleistocene Hominids from Yugoslavia. *American Journal of Physical Anthropology* 44:127–134.

——
1982 Upper Pleistocene Hominid Evolution in South-Central Europe: A Review of the Evidence and Analysis of Trends. *Current Anthropology* 23:667–703.

——
1983 Behavioral Interpretations of Changes in Craniofacial Morphology Across the Archaic/Modern *Homo sapiens* Transition. Pp. 141–163 in The Mousterian Legacy: Human Biocultural Change in the Upper Pleistocene. E. Trinkaus, ed. *British Archaeological Report, International Series* 164.

——
1984 Fossil Hominids from the Upper Pleistocene of Central Europe and the Origin of Modern Europeans. Pp. 137–209 in The Origins of Modern Humans: A World Survey of the Fossil Evidence. F.H. Smith and F. Spencer, eds. New York: Alan R. Liss.

——
1985 Continuity and Change in the Origin of Modern *Homo sapiens*. *Zeitschrift für Morphologie und Anthropologie* 75:147–222.

——, and G.C. Ranyard
1980 Evolution of the Supraorbital Region in Upper Pleistocene Fossil Hominids from South-Central Europe. *American Journal of Physical Anthropology* 53:589–610.

——, J.F. Simek, and M.S. Harrill
1989 Geographic Variation in Supraorbital Torus Reduction During the Later Pleistocene (c. 80,000–15,000 BP). Pp. 172–193 in The Human Revolution: Behavioral and Biological Perspectives in the Origins of Modern Humans. P. Mellars and C. Stringer, eds. Princeton, N.J.: Princeton University Press.

Sneath, P.H.A., and R.R. Sokal
1973 Numerical Taxonomy. San Francisco: W.H. Freeman.

Weidenreich, F.
1941 The Brain and Its Role in the Phylogenetic Transformation of the Human Skull. Paleontologica Sinica, Series D, No. 10.

Wolpoff, M.H.
1980 Paleoanthropology. New York: Knopf.

Zimmerman, L.J.
1985 Peoples of Prehistoric South Dakota. Lincoln: University of Nebraska Press.

○ ○ ○

CHAPTER 18

Size and Shape of the Femur and Tibia in Northern Plains Indians

THEODORE M. COLE III

The adoption of agriculture as a primary means of subsistence marks a major transition in the evolution of a prehistoric culture. Not only does the subsistence pattern change, but also there are usually concomitant transitions in the whole of a prehistoric society, including sociopolitical organization, material culture, the division of labor between sexes and social strata, and demographic profiles (Boserup 1965; Bronson 1975; Cohen 1977; Harris 1965; Steward 1955). Transitions are even evident in the bodies of the early agriculturists themselves (Cohen and Armelagos 1984). Thus, this phase of cultural development provides an important opportunity to study the interactions between cultural and biological evolution.

This study addresses patterns of skeletal variation as the threshold between hunting-and-gathering and horticultural lifeways is crossed. The sample consists of a large number of adult skeletons from prehistoric and early historic American Indian sites in central South Dakota and south-central North Dakota, along the Missouri River. Within the more than 1,200 years spanned by these sites, there was a transition from hunting and gathering to a subsistence strategy that involved increasing reliance on horticulture and concentrated bison hunting.

The bones of the lower limb are especially appropriate for this type of analysis because their lengths are highly correlated with stature (a frequently used estimator of body size), which has been shown to vary across subsistence transitions, and because the shapes of their diaphyseal cross-sections are related to stress resistance during locomotion. Studies by Ruff and colleagues (Brock and Ruff 1988; Ruff 1987; Ruff and Hayes 1983a, 1983b; Ruff, Hayes, and Larsen 1983) and van Gerven, Hummert, and Burr (1989) have linked specific patterns of limb shape to the biomechanical demands of different lifeways and environments.

Size and Shape, Sexual Dimorphism, and Subsistence

Before discussing predictions of specific patterns of size and shape that might be expected to accompany a subsistence transition, basic principles concerning the factors producing these patterns should be addressed. Adult size in archaeological samples is frequently quantified using long bone lengths and stature determinations from regression formulae (Trotter and Gleser 1952; Ubelaker 1978). Several studies (Key 1980;

Meiklejohn et al. 1984) have documented reductions in body size corresponding to subsistence transitions, particularly with the adoption of agriculture. The primary reason cited for this reduction is that the transition to an agricultural way of life is associated with greater environmental stress, due to reductions in available protein or caloric intake (Garn and Clark 1975; Garn and Frisancho 1971; Newman 1975). If this stress slows postnatal growth rates or truncates them prematurely, the net effect is smaller adult body size.

Detrimental environmental effects on growth may affect males and females differently, with females being more resistant to environmental stress than males and more capable of "catch-up" growth if conditions improve (Greulich 1951; Markowitz 1955; Stini 1969, 1972, 1982; see Stinson [1985] for a critical review of these and other references). When a population comes under stress and the growth of males is negatively affected to a greater extent than the growth of females, the net effect is a decrease in sexual size dimorphism (Key 1980; Stinson 1985). Therefore, the first objective of this study is to determine whether the transition from hunting and gathering to horticulture affected the size and size dimorphism of Northern Plains people in a similar fashion.

The bones of the lower limb are shaped to perform several tasks simultaneously and as efficiently as possible (Currey 1984). The femur and tibia must be sufficiently strong to support the body under static loads (supporting the weight of the body when standing), as well as being able to bear the greater forces that occur under dynamic loading (e.g., locomotion). In addition, the shapes of the femur and tibia are influenced by the many muscles that originate from and insert onto them.

If the femur and tibia are modeled as vertical, solid, materially homogeneous columns or beams, then their strength under static (weight-bearing) loads is directly proportional to their cross-sectional area, because the limbs are subjected to axial compressive forces. The compressive stress in a vertical beam is expressed in terms of force per unit area. Therefore, if limbs were designed so that individuals of different weights would experience the same amount of stress in a cross-section, then heavier persons would expect to have proportionately thicker limb bones.

If static loads were the only loads that the lower limb experienced, then cross-sectional area would be the only design parameter that would need to be considered in regulating stress levels. However, bone loading in locomotion is far more complex than under static conditions and cross-sectional shape becomes an important consideration. In locomotion, the lower limb bones tend to bend, which causes greater cross-sectional stresses (tension on the convex aspect and compression on the concave aspect) than in simple compressive loading. Alexander (1968:119) states that a long bone "is probably in most danger of being broken by forces which tend to bend it." Therefore, consideration of strength in bending is of primary importance when diaphyseal form is analyzed in a biomechanical context.

The strength in bending of a bone (that is, its ability to resist bending forces) in a given plane is proportional to its cross-sectional moment of intertia in that plane (Alexander 1968; Currey 1984), which is, in turn, directly proportional to the diameter of the bone cross-section. Therefore, one way in which a bone can be made stronger in bending is to simply add material to the cross-section, making it thicker relative to its length (i.e., more robust). However, added bone means increasing skeletal mass, which increases the energy demands of locomotion (Currey 1984). If there is a particular plane in which bending loads are particularly large or frequent, a more optimal design (one that is both sufficiently strong and energetically efficient) can be produced by keeping the amount of bone in a cross-section constant and "reorganizing" its distribution. For example, if a limb bone is strongly or repeatedly bent in an anteroposterior plane so that it is anteriorly convex during bending, the bending stresses and resulting bone deformation can be reduced by increasing the bone's diameter in that direction. However, if the amount of cross-sectional material is kept constant, the diameter in the mediolateral direction (perpendicular to the plane of bending) must decrease, with a loss of mediolateral bending strength. If directions of bending were highly variable and unpredictable, then this decrease in strength could be disadvantageous. However, if strong or repetitive bending forces are highly patterned and largely confined to a single plane, then the energetic benefits of limiting the mass of the bone will outweigh the risks of not increasing the bone diameter all around.

Work by Ruff and colleagues (Brock and Ruff 1988; Ruff 1987; Ruff and Hayes 1983a, 1983b; Ruff, Hayes, and Larsen 1983) on the cross-sectional geometry of the leg bones of Southwest and Georgia coast Indians has shown that there are specific patterns of bone shape correlated with differences in subsistence activities. In general, they have found that the diaphyses of hunter-gatherers tend to be anteroposteriorly expanded, relative to mediolateral diameter, to a greater extent than for horticulturists. They explain these differences as correlates of the high-magnitude or repetitive stresses in the anteroposterior plane, such as running or carrying heavy loads over long distances that characterize a hunting-gathering life-way. Ruff (1987) has also demonstrated sex differences in cross-sectional shape that tend to decrease in transitions from hunting and gathering to horticulture, and he has related these trends to decreased sexual division of labor.

The measures of shape used in this analysis are descriptive of cross-sections of the femur and tibia, taken at different levels along the shafts of the bones. Femoral and tibial cross-sections are often described in terms of a ratio of anteroposterior (front to back) to mediolateral (side to side) diameters (AP/ML). A ratio of 1.0 indicates that the bone cross-section is circular. Because bending strength is proportional to diameter, a circular bone is equally resistant to bending in all planes. A ratio greater than 1.0 indicates AP expansion (relative to the mediolateral dimension), while mediolateral expansion (relative to the anteroposterior dimension) is indicated by an index less than 1.0 (Ruff 1987). Bone shafts therefore tend to be designed so that the orientation of the greater diameter is indicative of the direction of greatest or most frequent bending stress. A high AP/ML ratio indicates resistance to AP bending; a low AP/ML ratio indicates resistance to mediolateral bending. Indices derived from external diameters of diaphyses are only estimates of cross-sectional properties that are more exactly measured through sophisticated methods such as computed tomography (Jungers and Minns 1979; Ruff and Leo 1986). However, it has been empirically demonstrated that these indices are highly correlated with more precisely measured results and should, therefore, yield comparable interpretations (Jungers and Minns 1979; Ruff 1987).

The second objective of this study is to determine whether the transition from hunting and gathering to horticulture in the Northern Plains results in changes in form in the lower limb. If Ruff's results are used as the basis of expectations for the patterns seen in Northern Plains samples, then hunter-gatherers should tend to have higher midshaft AP/ML ratios than horticulturists, due to more the more strenuous activities associated with hunting and gathering (high peak stresses), as well as the higher repetitive loads associated with routine travel over greater distances. Within subsistence groups, there would be a similar contrast between males and females because of sexual divisions of labor. Sex-specific subsistence behaviors often occur with greater frequency in hunter-gather populations than in agricultural populations (Ruff 1987). Based on this assumption, the degree of sexual dimorphism in shape is expected to be higher in hunters and gatherers (with more division of labor and less sedentism) and lower in horticulturists.

The Study Sample

The sites in this analysis have been divided into three groups (plus one site of uncertain cultural or temporal provenience), based on archaeological affinities. The Woodland sample consists of sites from the Middle Woodland and Terminal Woodland–Great Oasis periods, as well as the earlier (Middle Woodland) Boundary Mounds (32SI1) of the Sonota complex of North Dakota (Neuman 1975). Also included are those sites provisionally designated as "Woodland B" by Blakeslee (this volume). The median dates assigned to these sites range from A.D. 610 to 1033 (Key 1983). The Woodland subsistence base is characterized by a strong dependence on the hunting and gathering of wild foods, supplemented by horticulture on a limited scale (Lehmer 1970; Johnson and Wood 1980).

The Middle Missouri sample includes individuals from the Fairbanks Village site (39SL2) of the Extended Middle Missouri tradition. The median date for this site is A.D. 1550 (Key 1983). The Middle Missouri tradition dates from A.D. 900 to 1675, with the Extended Middle Missouri ranging from A.D. 1100 to 1550 (Key 1983). The Middle Missouri tradition marks the beginning of the Plains Village period (Lehmer 1970; Wedel 1983) and is characterized by the increasing use of cultivated plants, such as maize, beans, squash, and sunflowers (Johnson and Wood 1980). However, there was still a significant dependence on hunting and gathering. The Initial Middle Missouri marked the first permanent villages on the Northern Plains, suggesting the adoption of a more sedentary lifeway (Lehmer 1970). In terms of genetic affinities, the origins of the Middle Missouri people have yet to be fully resolved, although it is possible that the Plains Woodland people contributed to these origins in situ. In terms of later relationships, the Extended Middle Missouri appears to have close affiliations with the historic Siouan-speaking Mandan and Hidatsa (Key 1983).

The Coalescent tradition is represented here by the prehistoric and early historic Arikara tribe, with median site dates ranging from A.D. 1625 to 1817 (Key 1983). While the Coalescent is considered part of the Plains Village period of Northern Plains prehistory along with the Middle Missouri tradition (Wedel 1983), the ultimate origins of the Caddoan-speaking tribes (Arikara, Wichita, and Pawnee) were in Arkansas, Texas, and Louisiana (Hudson 1976). The Coalescent tradition began as Caddoan speakers began to migrate northward along the Missouri River and into the Northern Plains, displacing the endemic populations (e.g., the Mandan) as they went (Jantz 1972). It is important to remember that the term

Coalescent refers to later Plains villagers with common lifeways, but without common genetic origins, so that both Caddoans and some Siouans (the Mandan and Hidatsa) shared a similar way of life (Lehmer 1954; Wedel 1964). The Coalescent tradition is characterized by a subsistence base that was unusual among Native Americans: a combination of intensive maize horticulture and concentrated exploitation of the bison, especially following the introduction of the horse (Hoffman and Brown 1967; Hurt 1969; Johnson and Wood 1980).

The Medicine Creek site (39LM2) is problematic in that the skeletons were excavated from mound burials lacking diagnostic cultural materials. Blakeslee ("The Archaeological Context of Human Skeletons in the Northern and Central Plains," this vol.) suggests that Medicine Creek might be affiliated with the Middle Missouri or Initial Coalescent. Similarly, Key (1983) cited the Medicine Creek burials as having possible ties to the Initial Middle Missouri. Because of the problems of placing Medicine Creek in either a chronological or a cultural context, it will be considered to be separate from any larger cultural group throughout the analysis. The composition of the sample (by site and sex) is presented in table 1.

Fifteen linear measurements of the femur and tibia, from a larger data set developed by Zobeck (1983), were used:

1. Maximum length of the femur (FML)
2. Vertical diameter of the femoral head (VHD)
3. Horizontal diameter of the femoral head (HHD)
4. Subtrochanteric anteroposterior diameter of the femoral shaft (APD)
5. Subtrochanteric mediolateral diameter of the femoral shaft (MLD)
6. Anteroposterior diameter of the femoral midshaft (APS)
7. Mediolateral diameter of the femoral midshaft (MLS)
8. Anteroposterior depth of the lateral femoral condyle (APL)
9. Anteroposterior depth of the medial femoral condyle (APM)
10. Bicondylar breadth of the distal femur (FEB)
11. Maximum length of the tibia (TML)
12. Mediolateral breadth of the proximal tibial epiphysis (BPE)
13. Anteroposterior diameter of the tibial shaft, at the level of the nutrient foramen (APN)
14. Mediolateral diameter of the tibial shaft, at the level of the nutrient foramen (MLM)
15. Mediolateral breadth of the distal tibial epiphysis (BDE)

Table 1. Sites Used in This Study[a]

	Male	Female
Woodland		
Sonota complex		
Boundary Mounds (32SI1)	5	5
Middle Woodland		
Arbor Hill (39UN1)	2	2
Late Woodland–Great Oasis		
Ufford Mounds (39CL2)	14	15
Mitchell Mounds (39DV2/3)	2	0
Split Rock Creek (39MH6)	1	0
"Woodland B"		
Hofer Mounds (39HT2)	0	4
Montrose Mounds (39MK1)	1	2
Madsen's Mounds (39RO2)	1	0
Buchanan Mounds (39RO3)	2	2
Daugherty Mounds (39RO10)	2	0
Middle Missouri		
Extended Middle Missouri		
Fairbanks Village (39SL2)	2	0
Coalescent (Arikara)		
Extended Coalescent		
Anton Rygh (39CA4)	11	9
Scalp Creek (39GR1)	0	2
Sully A (39SL4A)	16	8
Sully D (39SL4D)	13	8
Mobridge I (39WW1)	23	18
Postcontact Coalescent		
Four Bear (39DW2)	3	9
Oahe Village (39HU2)	6	1
Oacoma (39LM26/27)	0	2
Dinehart's Village (39LM33)	6	2
Sully E (39SL4E)	15	8
Cheyenne River (39ST1)	1	1
Leavitt (39ST215)	5	2
Stony Point (39ST235)	3	6
Mobridge II (39WW1)	49	34
Larson (39WW2)	76	69
Swan Creek (39WW7)	12	5
Disorganized Coalescent		
Leavenworth (39CO9)	28	18
Unknown affinity		
Medicine Creek (39LM2)	3	0
Totals	302	232

[a]Because not all measurements were present for all individuals, the sample sizes are maximums based on the largest sample size available for any given measurement.

Measurements were recorded to the nearest millimeter. In most instances, each individual was represented by all 15 measurements. Individuals were sexed using standard methods (Bass 1971; Krogman 1962; Phenice 1969) and those for which sex could not be reliably estimated were deleted from the sample.

Methods

Two different types of comparison were made in this analysis. The first concerns the issue of sexual dimorphism within samples. Sexual dimorphism in size and shape is evaluated within the Woodland and Coalescent groups (there are no females from the Middle Missouri group or the Medicine Creek site). In this way, the effects of subsistence strategies on sexual dimorphism may be tested, with the null hypothesis being that degrees and patterns of sexual dimorphism are the same across archaeological samples. Next, there are sex-specific comparisons among archaeological groups. These tests allow the comparison of groups with different subsistence strategies without the potentially confounding effects of sexual dimorphism. In the among-group comparisons, the sizes and shapes of the Middle Missouri and Medicine Creek males will be compared to the patterns exhibited by the Woodland and Coalescent samples, but these samples are too small to be included in the statistical analyses.

Bone sizes are represented by the 15 measurements, with addition of an estimate of leg length (LEG), produced by adding the maximum lengths of the femur and tibia (when associated). The bone shape variables are designed to reflect cross-sectional properties at the femoral subtrochanter, the femoral midshaft, and the tibial shaft (at the level of the nutrient foramen). At each level, cross-sectional shape is defined as the ratio of the anteroposterior diameter to the mediolateral diameter.

Femoral subtrochanter shape (FSS) is APD divided by MLD. Femoral midshaft shape (FMS) is APS divided by MLS. Tibial shaft shape (TSS) is APN divided by MLM.

Finally, an average robusticity index (Demes and Jungers 1989) is calculated at each level. These indicies are defined as follows.

Average femoral subtrochanter robusticity (AFSR) =
  $100(APD + MLD) \div FML$.
Average femoral midshaft robusticity (AFMR) =
  $100(APS + MLS) \div FML$.

Average tibial shaft robusticity (ATSR) =
  $100(APN + MLM) \div TML$.

These indices serve as measure of average resistance to bending at each level.

Preliminary examination of the data revealed significant departures from normality and from homogeneity of variances among sexes and archaeological groups. Because parametric methods such as analysis of variance (ANOVA) of the raw data are inappropriate under such conditions (Sokal and Rohlf 1981), nonparametric methods were employed. The data were first rank transformed and then subjected to standard analysis of variance, which produces results that are similar to the Kruskal-Wallis test for heterogeneity of group means (Sokal and Rohlf 1981), while offering more powerful tests of significance (Conover and Iman 1981; Maas 1988; Quade 1966; SAS Institute 1982:483). The tests of significance were evaluated using conservative, multiple-case criteria. When a number of tests are performed, it is possible that some of them may be significant by chance alone (Neff and Marcus 1980; Sokal and Rohlf 1981). To reduce this possibility, multiple-case critical values were calculated by taking the desired single-case value of 0.05 and dividing it by the total number of tests. This procedure was done separately for the measures of size (15 measurements plus LEG), cross-sectional shape (three variables), and average robusticity (three variables). Therefore, the critical value for the size comparisons is $0.05 \div 16 = 0.0031$. The critical value for both the shape and average robusticity comparisons is $0.05 \div 3 = 0.0167$.

Results

Sex-specific descriptive statistics for the size and shape variables in the Woodland and Coalescent samples are shown in tables 2 and 3, respectively. The male means for the Middle Missouri sample and the Medicine Creek site are presented in table 4. Analysis of variance tests comparing Woodland males and females (table 5) shows that males are significantly larger than females for each of the 16 size measures at the multiple-case level of significance (0.0031). Table 5 also shows the Woodland sex comparisons of cross-sectional shape where the multiple-case significance level is 0.0167. There is no significant sexual dimorphism in shape at the femoral subtrochanter or at the femoral midshaft. For the shape of the tibial shaft, however, the male sample exhibits a significantly higher mean, indicating that male tibiae are more anteroposteriorly expanded, relative to their mediolateral diameter. In terms of

Table 2. Descriptive Statistics for the Femur and Tibia for the Woodland Sample

		Males				Females		
Variable	N	Mean (mm)	Standard Deviation (mm)	Range (mm)	N	Mean (mm)	Standard deviation (mm)	Range (mm)
Sizes								
FML	22	461.5	18.5	427–493	18	422.5	22.2	384–465
VHD	22	48.8	2.7	43–55	21	42.5	2.4	38–47
HHD	21	48.0	2.8	42–53	18	41.9	2.3	37–46
APD	28	27.0	2.2	23–31	25	24.0	2.0	20–28
MLD	28	35.7	2.0	32–40	26	32.6	1.8	28–35
APS	27	29.4	2.6	24–35	29	25.7	2.1	20–29
MLS	27	28.0	2.2	25–33	29	24.9	1.9	22–30
APL	24	65.4	2.7	61–72	18	60.6	2.7	56–65
APM	22	65.0	4.0	55–71	17	58.8	2.5	55–63
FEB	19	84.6	4.1	77–90	16	73.2	3.2	66–78
TML	25	384.8	12.9	355–408	17	346.8	13.9	328–373
BPE	21	79.9	4.4	73–87	20	70.4	3.3	65–78
APN	28	37.6	1.9	33–41	25	31.2	2.1	26–34
MLM	29	25.0	3.0	21–38	25	22.6	2.1	19–26
BDE	21	52.7	2.8	46–59	17	47.4	2.0	44–51
LEG	12	844.9	32.3	782–901	9	786.0	37.5	729–838
Cross-sectional shapes								
FSS	28	0.76	0.07	0.61–0.88	25	0.74	0.06	0.65–.88
FMS	27	1.05	0.10	0.85–1.28	29	1.03	0.09	0.87–1.23
TSS	28	1.54	0.12	1.32–1.86	25	1.40	0.15	1.13–1.74
Average robusticities								
AFSR	22	13.62	0.46	12.68–14.31	17	13.22	0.56	12.02–14.18
AFMR	22	12.58	0.63	11.42–17.25	18	11.78	0.63	10.76–12.98
ATSR	25	16.19	0.68	14.53–17.25	17	15.43	1.09	13.76–17.56

Table 3. Descriptive Statistics for the Femur and Tibia for the Coalescent Sample

		Males				Females		
Variable	N	Mean (mm)	Standard Deviation (mm)	Range (mm)	N	Mean (mm)	Standard Deviation (mm)	Range (mm)
Sizes								
FML	236	450.6	17.4	400–504	192	415.2	17.3	380–460
VHD	238	47.0	2.1	40–53	191	42.4	2.1	36–49
HHD	238	46.7	2.2	40–54	192	41.9	2.1	36–50
APD	239	25.2	1.7	21–30	193	22.4	1.8	17–28
MLD	239	34.5	2.1	30–41	193	31.1	1.9	26–39
APS	240	30.0	2.2	25–40	194	25.9	2.1	20–33
MLS	240	26.9	1.6	21–33	194	24.4	1.5	20–28
APL	236	66.8	2.9	59–74	191	61.0	3.0	53–70
APM	236	65.9	2.9	58–76	189	59.2	3.3	51–70
FEB	231	83.8	3.4	76–95	185	74.9	3.4	68–87
TML	261	381.5	18.0	299–423	192	348.0	16.1	306–388
BPE	256	78.6	3.2	68–86	189	69.6	3.5	61–79
APN	261	37.8	2.6	28–48	194	31.2	2.5	25–39
MLM	261	23.6	2.1	19–29	194	22.0	2.2	17–29
BDE	257	53.3	2.7	46–61	192	47.3	3.0	36–58
LEG	206	833.5	32.9	748–921	165	763.2	32.6	689–845
Cross-sectional shapes								
FSS	239	0.73	0.06	0.56–.90	193	0.72	0.06	0.58–0.90
FMS	240	1.12	0.09	0.85–1.60	194	1.06	0.09	0.85–1.30
TSS	261	1.61	0.17	1.21–2.18	194	1.43	0.15	1.08–2.18
Average robusticities								
AFSR	236	13.24	0.63	10.98–15.14	192	12.88	0.68	10.74–15.23
AFMR	236	12.63	0.63	10.16–14.35	192	12.11	0.65	10.56–13.70
ATSR	260	16.12	0.99	13.09–22.41	192	15.30	1.03	12.65–18.33

Table 4. Descriptive Statistics for the Femur and Tibia for Males from the Middle Missouri Variant and the Medicine Creek Site

| | | Middle Missouri | | | | Medicine Creek | | |
| | | Mean (mm) | Standard Deviation (mm) | Range (mm) | | Mean (mm) | Standard Deviation (mm) | Range (mm) |
Variable	N				N			
Sizes								
FML	2	459.0	15.6	448–470	3	447.7	4.9	442–451
VHD	2	47.0	1.4	46–48	3	45.7	1.5	44–47
HHD	2	47.0	1.4	46–48	3	45.7	1.5	44–47
APD	2	26.5	0.7	26–27	3	25.3	0.6	25–26
MLD	2	33.0	2.8	31–35	3	36.0	1.0	35–37
APS	2	30.0	4.2	27–33	3	28.7	0.6	28–29
MLS	2	24.0	0.0	24	3	26.7	0.6	26–27
APL	2	67.0	0.0	67	3	64.3	1.5	63–66
APM	2	65.5	0.7	65–66	2	62.5	2.1	61–64
FEB	2	84.0	4.2	81–87	3	81.7	1.5	80–83
TML	2	386.5	23.3	370–403	3	379.3	7.2	371–384
BPE	2	79.5	2.1	78–81	3	77.3	3.1	74–80
APN	2	36.0	0.0	36	3	35.0	2.0	33–37
MLM	2	24.0	2.8	22–26	3	25.3	1.5	24–27
BDE	2	53.5	3.5	51–56	3	50.3	4.0	46–54
LEG	2	845.5	38.9	818–873	3	827.0	12.1	813–834
Cross-sectional shapes								
FSS	2	0.81	0.05	0.77–.84	3	0.70	0.03	0.68–.74
FMS	2	1.25	0.18	1.13–1.38	3	1.08	0.04	1.03–1.12
TSS	2	1.51	0.18	1.39–1.64	3	1.39	0.14	1.30–1.54
Average robusticities								
AFSR	2	12.96	0.33	12.72–13.19	3	13.70	0.28	13.53–14.03
AFMR	2	11.76	0.53	11.38–12.13	3	12.36	0.14	12.20–12.44
ATSR	2	15.53	0.21	15.38–15.68	3	15.90	0.28	15.63–16.19

Table 5. Sex Comparisons of Size and Shape Variables for the Woodland Sample, Using Analysis of Variance of Ranked Data

| | N | | Mean Square | | | |
Variable	Male	Female	Between-Sex	Within-Sex	F	Probability
FML	22	18	2521.6	73.8	34.16	0.0001*
VHD	22	21	4342.4	54.6	79.55	0.0001*
HHD	21	18	3105.8	48.5	64.06	0.0001*
APD	28	25	4434.1	151.0	29.36	0.0001*
MLD	28	26	5691.4	136.8	41.59	0.0001*
APS	27	29	6181.9	152.0	40.66	0.0001*
MLS	27	29	5607.2	161.7	34.68	0.0001*
APL	24	18	2776.7	83.0	33.47	0.0001*
APM	22	17	2330.6	69.3	33.63	0.0001*
FEB	19	16	2590.5	29.3	88.49	0.0001*
TML	25	17	4032.4	53.3	75.60	0.0001*
BPE	21	20	3846.4	48.0	80.17	0.0001*
APN	28	25	8985.8	63.8	140.83	0.0001*
MLM	29	25	2832.2	192.5	14.71	0.0003*
BDE	21	17	2674.1	51.4	52.02	0.0001*
LEG	12	9	359.5	21.6	16.66	0.0006*
FSS	28	25	310.1	236.7	1.31	0.2577
FMS	27	29	68.7	267.9	0.26	0.6146
TSS	28	25	2879.0	186.4	15.44	0.0003*
AFSR	22	17	735.8	113.6	6.48	0.0152*
AFMR	22	18	1654.9	96.7	17.11	0.0002*
ATSR	25	17	827.4	113.6	6.19	0.0171

*Means are significantly different at the multiple-case level.

Table 6. Sex Comparisons of Size and Shape Variables for the Coalescent Sample, Using Analysis of Variance of Ranked Data

| Variable | N | | Mean Square | | F | Probability |
	Male	Female	Between-Sex	Within-Sex		
FML	236	192	3488928.8	7143.6	488.40	0.0001★
VHD	238	191	3790406.1	6389.7	593.20	0.0001★
HHD	238	192	3920295.8	6189.1	633.42	0.0001★
APD	239	193	2660639.6	9159.0	290.49	0.0001★
MLD	239	193	3060421.6	8285.4	369.37	0.0001★
APS	240	194	3446594.2	7637.2	451.29	0.0001★
MLS	240	194	2743684.4	9029.5	303.86	0.0001★
APL	236	191	3414136.1	7154.0	477.24	0.0001★
APM	236	189	3542944.3	6680.0	530.38	0.0001★
FEB	231	185	3875873.2	5086.2	762.04	0.0001★
TML	261	192	3945820.2	8422.9	468.46	0.0001★
BPE	256	189	4592180.6	6154.8	746.11	0.0001★
APN	261	194	4830819.6	6564.7	735.88	0.0001★
MLM	261	194	1075385.3	14594.4	73.69	0.0001★
BDE	257	192	4180990.9	7423.2	563.23	0.0001★
LEG	206	165	2370813.5	5108.0	464.01	0.0001★
FSS	239	193	45411.2	15508.2	2.93	0.0878
FMS	240	194	577406.1	14400.4	40.10	0.0001★
TSS	261	194	1979226.5	12955.0	152.78	0.0001★
AFSR	236	192	440885.9	14301.8	30.83	0.0001★
AFMR	236	192	843428.4	13356.7	63.15	0.0001★
ATSR	260	192	1235763.7	14354.5	86.09	0.0001★

★Means are significantly different at the multiple-case level.

average robusticity, males are significantly more robust in the femoral subtrochanter and femoral midshaft, but there is no significant difference in the tibial midshaft.

The Coalescent sample is similar to the Woodland sample in that the males are significantly larger for each size variable (table 6). The cross-sectional shape comparisons show that, as with the Woodland sample, the Coalescent males have a significantly higher AP/ML ratio for the tibial shaft. In addition, the Coalescent males have significantly higher AP/ML ratios at the femoral midshaft. The shape of the femoral subtrochanter shows no significant sexual dimorphism. The average robusticity was significantly greater in males at all three levels.

An index of sexual dimorphism (Borgognini Tarli and Repetto 1986; Ruff 1987) was used to compare the degrees of sexual dimorphism exhibited by the Woodland and Coalescent samples (table 7 and fig. 1). The sexual dimorphism index (SDI) was calculated as follows:

$$SDI = \frac{(\text{Male Mean} - \text{Female Mean})}{\text{Female Mean}} \times 100$$

where the difference in sex means is expressed as a percentage of the female mean. If the male and female means in a sample are equal, then the SDI will be equal to zero. If the male mean is larger, then the SDI will have a positive value; conversely, this value will be negative in the event of a larger female mean. As an example, an SDI of 10 for a given size measurement indicates that males are, on the average, 10 percent larger than females. The SDI profiles shown in figure 1 approximate each other fairly closely, suggesting that the degree and pattern of size and shape dimorphism is similar in both variants. Relethford and Hodges's (1985) statistic for comparing the degree of sexual dimorphism across groups was used to determine, for each variable, whether one variant is significantly more dimorphic than the other (table 7). While nonparametric statistical methods have been employed thus far, there is no non-parametric alternative for the Relethford and Hodges method. Therefore, instances in which the null hypothesis is rejected (i.e., where the traditions show significantly different degrees of dimorphism) would require cautious interpretation. However, at multiple-case levels of significance (0.0031, 0.0167 and 0.0167 for sizes, shapes, and average robusticities,

Table 7. Sexual Dimorphism Indices of Size and Shape Variables for the Woodland and Coalescent Samples

Variable	Woodland	Coalescent	F	Degrees of Freedom	Probability
FML	9.2	8.5	0.38	1, 464	0.5379
VHD	14.8	10.8	6.13	1, 468	0.0136★
HHD	14.6	11.5	3.12	1, 465	0.0780
APD	12.5	12.5	0.15	1, 481	0.6987
MLD	9.5	10.9	0.27	1, 482	0.6056
APS	14.4	15.8	0.42	1, 486	0.5172
MLS	12.4	10.2	1.70	1, 486	0.1929
APL	7.9	9.5	1.10	1, 465	0.2948
APM	10.5	11.3	0.23	1, 460	0.6318
FEB	15.6	11.9	4.27	1, 447	0.0394★
TML	11.0	9.6	0.65	1, 491	0.4205
BPE	13.5	12.9	0.07	1, 482	0.7915
APN	20.5	17.5	0.08	1, 504	0.7774
MLM	10.6	7.3	1.59	1, 505	0.2079
BDE	11.2	12.7	0.54	1, 483	0.4628
LEG	7.5	9.2	0.59	1, 388	0.4429
FSS	2.7	1.4	0.32	1, 481	0.5719
FMS	1.9	5.7	2.41	1, 486	0.1212
TSS	10.0	12.6	0.74	1, 504	0.3745
AFSR	3.1	2.8	0.04	1, 463	0.8339
AFMR	6.8	4.2	1.83	1, 464	0.1769
ATSR	4.9	5.4	0.04	1, 490	0.8375

★Means are significantly different at the single-case level.

respectively), there were no cases in which the degree of dimorphism was higher in one group than in the other.

Size and shape comparisons of the Woodland and Coalescent males are presented in table 8. Woodland males are significantly larger in two (VHD and APD) of the 16 size measures. Note that

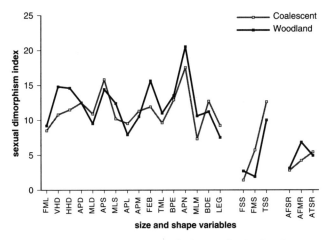

Fig. 1. Sexual dimorphism indices (SDI) for the Woodland and Coalescent samples (table 7).

these significant variables are bone diameters and not bone lengths (i.e., these measurements probably would not contribute to tradition differences in stature). The cross-sectional shape comparisons show that there is a significant difference in the shape of the femoral midshaft, but that the Coalescent sample exhibits the larger AP/ML ratio. The average robusticity of the femoral subtrochanter is greater in Woodland males, but there are no differences at the other levels.

Because of the small sizes of the Middle Missouri and Medicine Creek samples, little can be said for these groups aside from the fact that their values for size and shape fall within the ranges of both the Woodland and Coalescent males. While the Middle Missouri means would be expected to occupy an intermediate condition (in both size and shape) between those of the Woodland and Coalescent, this does not occur with regularity. The most notable characteristic of the Medicine Creek sample is that it tends to be the smallest in nearly all of the size means, although its values overlap with the Woodland and Coalescent samples in all cases.

The female size and shape comparisons are presented in table 9. There are significant differences in two (APD and MLD)

Table 8. Variant Comparisons of Size and Shape Variables for Males, Using Analysis of Variance of Ranked Data

| Variable | N | | Mean Square | | F | Probability |
	Woodland	Coalescent	Between-Tradition	Within-Tradition		
FML	22	236	39051.9	5434.9	7.19	0.0078
VHD	22	238	57490.8	5330.3	10.79	0.0012★
HHD	21	238	28300.4	5404.1	5.24	0.0229
APD	28	239	96289.3	5440.2	17.70	0.0001★
MLD	28	239	49870.0	5672.2	8.79	0.0033
APS	27	240	9532.9	5832.5	1.63	0.2002
MLS	27	240	31546.6	5612.5	5.62	0.0185
APL	24	236	30715.4	5493.0	5.59	0.0188
APM	22	236	2594.5	5516.2	0.47	0.4935
FEB	19	231	5386.0	5181.9	1.04	0.3090
TML	25	261	9497.8	6826.7	1.39	0.2392
BPE	21	256	11772.7	6334.8	1.86	0.1739
APN	28	261	866.2	6874.6	0.13	0.7229
MLM	29	261	48966.7	6713.1	7.29	0.0073
BDE	21	257	8345.0	6364.0	1.31	0.2532
LEG	12	206	6620.8	3965.5	1.67	0.1977
FSS	28	239	29200.8	5869.0	4.98	0.0265
FMS	27	240	63508.2	5736.1	11.07	0.0010★
TSS	28	261	39664.4	6865.2	5.78	0.0169
AFSR	22	236	46562.4	5408.2	8.61	0.0036★
AFMR	22	236	448.5	5588.3	0.08	0.7772
ATSR	25	236	1607.6	6810.6	0.24	0.6274

★Means are significantly different at the multiple-case level.

Table 9. Variant Comparisons of Size and Shape Variables for Females, Using Analysis of Variance of Ranked Data

| Variable | N | | Mean Square | | F | Probability |
	Woodland	Coalescent	Between-Tradition	Within-Tradition		
FML	18	192	6378.8	3677.8	1.73	0.1893
VHD	21	191	251.6	3702.2	0.07	0.7946
HHD	18	192	0.2	3632.5	0.00	0.9935
APD	25	193	55317.4	3632.4	15.23	0.0001★
MLD	26	193	62688.7	3616.1	17.34	0.0001★
APS	29	194	328.2	4072.9	0.08	0.7768
MLS	29	194	7691.3	3990.7	1.93	0.1665
APL	18	191	525.8	3631.7	0.14	0.7040
APM	17	189	667.0	3527.6	0.19	0.6641
FEB	16	185	8678.7	3326.5	2.61	0.1078
TML	17	192	420.1	3670.9	0.11	0.7355
BPE	20	189	6039.5	3613.4	1.67	0.1975
APN	25	194	2504.3	3952.7	0.63	0.4269
MLM	25	194	7224.7	3906.6	1.85	0.1753
BDE	17	192	327.3	3615.5	0.09	0.7638
LEG	9	165	8197.4	2504.0	3.27	0.0721
FSS	25	193	6151.9	3963.5	1.55	0.2142
FMS	29	194	6975.4	4125.8	1.69	0.1949
TSS	25	194	3377.7	4015.2	0.84	0.3601
AFSR	17	192	16851.2	3593.6	4.69	0.0315
AFMR	18	192	14798.6	3639.0	4.07	0.0450
ATSR	17	192	559.8	3672.3	0.15	0.6966

★Means are significantly different at the multiple-case level.

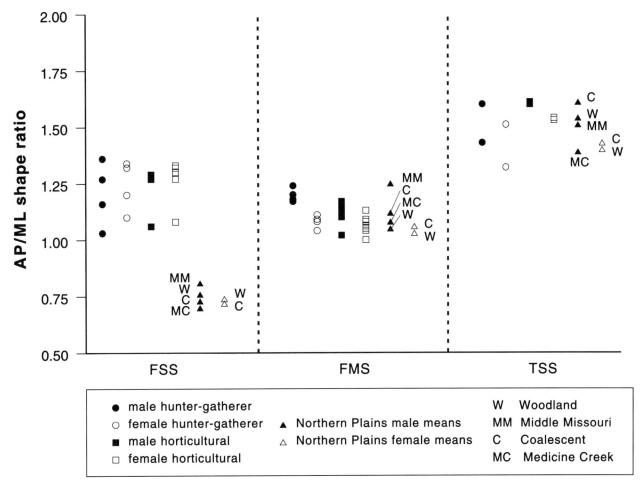

Fig. 2. Comparison of sex-specific means of cross-sectional shape variables for the Northern Plains samples, compared to means reported by Ruff (1987).

of 16 variables, indicating that Woodland females are larger at the level of the femoral subtrochanter. As with males, there is nothing to indicate a difference in stature between the Woodland and Coalescent samples. The cross-sectional shape and average robusticity comparisons show that there are no significant differences between Woodland and Coalescent females.

To consider the Northern Plains sample in a broader comparative context, sex- and tradition-specific means for AP/ML ratios are compared with mean values from other populations, as reported by Ruff (1987:401). These comparisons are summarized in fig. 2. The most striking difference between the Northern Plains samples and other groups is the tendency for a very low AP/ML ratio for FSS. Recall that neither the Woodland nor the Coalescent sample demonstrated significant dimorphism in this shape, in contrast to other groups, where AP/ML ratios were higher in females (Ruff 1987). Ruff attributed this difference to a need for resistance to

relatively greater bending forces in the mediolateral plane at that level, as a consequence of the broader pelvic configuration of females. When compared to females of other groups, Northern Plains males present a "female" condition. For the FMS and TSS, the Northern Plains means overlap those of other samples, although the degree of dimorphism in FMS that was reported by Ruff (1987), and which may be seen for his data in fig. 2, is not evident within the Northern Plains sample.

Interpretation

The objectives of this study were to determine whether the transition from hunting and gathering to a horticultural subsistence strategy in the Northern Plains would have the following effects, with the predictions based on studies of other groups. Is there a reduction in size and in sexual dimorphism in horticulturists? Are there subsistence-related changes (as well as different degrees of sexual dimorphism) in the cross-sectional geometry of the femur and tibia?

The data from the Northern Plains sample studied here produce results that are somewhat different from what has been found in studies of other groups. In terms of size variation (both between sexes and traditions), this study differs from others on two points. First, there were few observed size differences between same-sex samples with different subsistence strategies (i.e., little size reduction as horticulture became increasingly important). Second, the degree of sexual size dimorphism was the same in horticulturists as in hunters and gatherers (who were expected to be more dimorphic).

Why would horticulturists not be smaller and less dimorphic than hunters and gatherers? The reason that size decreases are thought to occur in the transition to horticulture is that the quality of the diet is decreased, with less available protein and fewer available calories (Garn and Clark 1975; Garn and Frisancho 1971; Goodman et al. 1984; Larsen 1984; Newman 1975). However, this study showed few significant size differences between Woodland and Coalescent males and no size differences in females. The lack of a size decrease with the adoption of horticulture may indicate that the stresses associated with subsistence change were not sufficient to have had a significant effect on growth patterns.

The available evidence suggests that the quality of the Arikara diet was fairly good, compared to what might be expected in early horticultural groups (Jantz and Owsley 1984; Lehmer and Jones 1968). Crop yields were sufficiently large to allow the Arikara to use surplus plant foods for trading with other groups (Wood 1980; Zimmerman 1985). Denig (1961:61) suggested that the sedentary settlement patterns of the Arikara allowed them to invest more time and effort in horticulture than neighboring groups:

But owing to their always having a supply of corn on hand, they are not subject to the same vicissitudes of living as other tribes, though they are sometimes hard up for meat. Their stationary habits have taught them a degree of economy in the article of provisions. They do not feast and waste like the migratory tribes [e.g., the Sioux]. All raise some corn, and what little meat they can get on their hunts or around the village is husbanded with great care. Therefore, though not at all times flush, they seldom experience great hunger.

Despite the shift to horticulture, hunting continued to be important to Plains Villagers. While the Arikara were among the most sedentary of Northern Plains tribes, they continued to invest considerable time and effort in bison hunting. In the

early summer and again in late autumn, large groups of Arikara (including women) would depart on long hunts, leaving the old and infirm behind (Hurt 1969). In addition to the bison, the Arikara exploited elk, deer, and pronghorn, as well as game birds and fish (Denig 1961; Hoffman and Brown 1967). In late winter and early spring, meat obtained from hunting was supplemented by snagging drowned bison (in varying states of decay) from the river (Denig 1961; Hurt 1969). Therefore, while their crops provided a large proportion of their food, the hunting and trading of the Arikara seems to have been sufficient to prevent any prolonged, significant nutritional stresses (as judged by a lack of size reduction and no decrease in sexual dimorphism).

The other major aspect of lower limb form to be considered in this study was size and shape variation in the diaphyses of the lower limb bones. Studies of other groups (Brock and Ruff 1988; Ruff 1987; Ruff and Hayes 1983a, 1983b; Ruff, Hayes, and Larsen 1983) demonstrated consistent differences in the cross-sectional geometry of the femur and tibia between hunters and gatherers and horticulturists, as well as between sexes within groups. Such differences in form have been attributed to the biomechancial demands imposed by differing lifeways. However, as with the considerations of size, the shape analyses of the Northern Plains samples often ran counter to patterns seen in other groups.

For females, the lack of significant changes in bone geometry were not altogether surprising, because the activities of females might be less affected by a subsistence shift. Through ethnographic analogy with living hunting and gathering groups, it is assumed that Woodland men devoted much of their time and energy to hunting and traveling, while the women were responsible for the gathering of plant foods, food preparation, and other domestic chores (while traveling less). With the introduction of horticulture, a common assumption is that men contributed more to crop tending and spent less time hunting (with less strenuous travel). Therefore, a change in the "division of labor" really implies a change in the daily activities of males. This idea could be supported by the fact that the tibial shaft (TSS) is more anteroposteriorly expanded in Woodland males, compared to Woodland females, and that Coalescent males are more anterposteriorly expanded than females for both the tibial shaft and the femoral midshaft.

While the sexual division of labor is something that can only be inferred in Plains Woodland groups, there are detailed ethnographic accounts of the Arikara (Denig 1961; Truteau 1912), as well as for other Coalescent Tradition tribes, such as the Hidatsa (Spector 1983). The available information suggests that Coalescent women were responsible for the great majority of horticultural labor, while male responsibilities may not have differed from those of Woodland males. In light of the significant sex differences in FMS and TSS, sex-specific activity patterns may still have been sufficiently different to produce these differences. The strong reliance on female labor in horticultural societies is also not unique to the Plains Coalescent. In a world-wide survey of patterns of sexual division of labor, Murdock and Provost (1973) found that in over two-thirds of the societies surveyed in which the plow was not used for cultivation (i.e., horticultural groups), the majority of the responsibility for planting and harvesting belonged to the women.

The adoption of a horticultural lifeway implies an increasing degree of sedentism, because of the time needed for the planting and harvesting of crops. This implication is supported in the archaeological record of the Plains Village period, where the first permanent villages accompany the adoption of horticulture during the Initial Middle Missouri (Lehmer 1970; Wedel 1983; Zimmerman 1985). However, whole Arikara villages traveled over the Plains twice every year in pursuit of the bison. Therefore, it is possible that the Arikara may have been as mobile, if not more so, during certain times of the year than their Woodland predecessors. Perhaps this could explain why Coalescent male femoral midshafts are more anteroposteriorly expanded than for Woodland or Middle Missouri groups.

Finally, in working with archaeological populations with uncertain genetic relationships, there is the important assumption of genetic homogeneity (Goodman et al. 1984). Throughout this discussion it is assumed that anatomical differences observed among groups are based in responses to different functional demands. However, the possibility remains that observed population differences have a strong genetic component and are not related solely to biomechanical function. This is not to say that "phylogenetic" patterns of size and shape are "nonfunctional." For example, the strong anteroposterior expansion of the Coalescent males is also seen in Southern Plains groups ("Biomechanical Analysis of Northern and Southern Plains Femora: Behavioral Implications," this volume), suggesting the possibility that this pattern could have been present in ancestral groups that may not have participated in identical activity patterns. However, a "phylogenetic" origin for this pattern does not take away from its biomechanical consequences (increase resistance to bending in the AP plane).

In conclusion, there was a greater degree of similarity in bone size and shape than expected, both between traditions and between sexes. These similarities occur despite differences in both subsistence strategy and genetic affinities. The preliminary conclusions reached here are that subsistence-related differences in nutritional quality and locomotion may not have been sufficiently different to produce significant differences in skeletal size and shape. Other trends, such as the mediolateral expansion of the femoral subtrochanter in both sexes of all Northern Plains groups, remain unexplained.

References Cited

Alexander, R.McN.
1968   Animal Mechanics. Seattle: University of Washington Press.

Bass, W.M.
1971   Human Osteology: A Laboratory and Field Manual of the Human Skeleton. Columbia: Missouri Archaeological Society.

Borgognini Tarli, S.M., and E. Repetto
1986   Methodological Considerations on the Study of Sexual Dimorphism in Past Human Populations. Pp. 51–66 in Sexual Dimorphism in Living and Fossil Primates. M. Pickford and B. Chiarelli, eds. Florence, Italy.: Il Sedicesimo.

Boserup, E.
1965   The Conditions of Agricultural Growth. Chicago: Aldine.

Brock, S.L., and C.B. Ruff
1988   Diachronic Patterns of Change in Structural Properties of the Femur in the Prehistoric American Southwest. *American Journal of Physical Anthropology* 75:113–127.

Bronson, B.
1975   The Earliest Farming: Demography as Cause and Consequence. Pp. 53–78 in Population, Ecology, and Social Evolution. S. Polgar, ed. The Hague: Mouton.

Cohen, M.N.
1977   The Food Crisis in Prehistory. New Haven, Conn.: Yale University Press.

——, and G.J. Armelagos
1984   Paleopathology at the Origins of Agriculture. New York: Academic Press.

Conover, W.J., and R.L. Iman
1981   Rank Transformations as a Bridge Between Parametric and Nonparametric Statistics. *The American Statistician* 35:124–129.

Currey, J.
1984   The Mechanical Adaptations of Bones. Princeton, N.J.: Princeton University Press.

Demes, B., and W.L. Jungers
1989   Functional Differences of Long Bones in Lorises. *Folia Primatologica* 52:58–69.

Denig, E.T.
1961   Five Indian Tribes of the Upper Missouri. J.C. Ewers, ed. Norman, Okla.: University of Oklahoma Press.

Garn, S.M., and D.C. Clark

1975   Nutrition, Growth, Development, and Maturation: Findings from the Ten-state Nutrition Survey of 1968–1970. *Pediatrics* 56:306–319.

——, and A.R. Frisancho

1971   Effects of Malnutrition on Size and Skeletal Development. Pp. 84–93 in Proceedings of a Workshop on Problems of Assessment and Alleviation of Malnutrition in the United States. R.G. Hansen and H.N. Munro, eds. Washington: U.S. Government Printing Office.

Goodman, A.H., D.L. Martin, G.J. Armelagos, and G. Clark

1984   Indications of Stress from Bones and Teeth. Pp. 13–49 in Paleopathology at the Origins of Agriculture. M.N. Cohen and G.J. Armelagos, eds. Orlando, Fla.: Academic Press.

Greulich, W.W.

1951   The Growth and Developmental Status of Guamanian School Children in 1947. *American Journal of Physical Anthropology* 9:55–70.

Harris, M.

1965   The Rise of Anthropological Theory. New York: Thomas Y. Crowell.

Hoffman, J.J., and L.A. Brown

1967   The Bad River Phase. *Plains Anthropologist* 12:323–339.

Hudson, C.

1976   The Southeastern Indians. Knoxville: University of Tennessee Press.

Hurt, W.R.

1969   Seasonal Economic and Settlement Patterns of the Arikara. *Plains Anthropologist* 14:32–37.

Jantz, R.L.

1972   Cranial Variation and Microevolution in Arikara Skeletal Populations. *Plains Anthropologist* 17:20–35.

——, and D.W. Owsley

1984   Long Bone Growth Variation Among Arikara Skeletal Populations. *American Journal of Physical Anthropology* 63:13–20.

Johnson, A.E., and W.R. Wood

1980   Prehistoric Studies on the Plains. Pp. 35–51 in Anthropology on the Great Plains. W.R. Wood and M. Liberty, eds. Lincoln: University of Nebraska Press.

Jungers, W.L., and R.J. Minns

1979   Computed Tomography and Biomechanical Analysis of Fossil Long Bones. *American Journal of Physical Anthropology* 50:285–290.

Key, P.J.

1980   Evolutionary Trends in Femoral Sexual Dimorphism from the Mesolithic to the Late Middle Ages in Europe. *American Journal of Physical Anthropology* 52:244.

——

1983   Craniometric Relationships Among Plains Indians. *University of Tennessee Department of Anthropology Report of Investigations* 34.

Krogman, W.M.

1962   The Human Skeleton in Forensic Medicine. Springfield, Ill.: Charles C. Thomas.

Larsen, C.S.

1984   Health and Disease in Prehistoric Georgia: The Transition to Agriculture. Pp. 367–392 in Paleopathology at the Origins of Agriculture. M.N. Cohen and G.J. Armelagos, eds. Orlando, Fla.: Academic Press.

Lehmer, D.J.

1954   The Sedentary Horizon of the Northern Plains. *Southwestern Journal of Anthropology* 10:139–159.

——

1970   Climate and Culture History in the Middle Missouri Valley. Pp. 117–129 in Pleistocene and Recent Environments of the Central Great Plains. W. Dort and J.K. Jones, eds. Lawrence: University of Kansas Press.

——, and D. Jones

1968   Arikara Archaeology: The Bad River Phase. *Smithsonian Institution. River Basin Surveys Publications in Salvage Archaeology* 7.

Maas, M.C.

1988   The Relationship of Enamel Microstructure and Microwear: An Experimental Study of Cause and Effect. (Unpublished Ph.D. Dissertation in Physical Anthropology, State University of New York, Stony Brook.)

Markowitz, S.D.

1955   Retardation of Growth of Children in Europe and Asia During World War II. *Human Biology* 27:258–273.

Meiklejohn, C., C. Schentag, A. Venema, and P. Key

1984   Socioeconomic Change and Patterns of Pathology and Variation in the Mesolithic and Neolithic of Western Europe: Some Suggestions. Pp. 75–100 in Paleopathology at the Origins of Agriculture. M.N. Cohen and G.J. Armelagos, eds. Orlando, Fla.: Academic Press.

Murdock, G.P., and C. Provost

1973   Factors in the Division of Labor by Sex: A Cross-Cultural Analysis. *Ethnology* 12:203–225.

Neff, N.A., and L.F. Marcus

1980   A Survey of Multivariate Methods for Systematics. New York: Privately published.

Neuman, R.W.

1975   The Sonota Complex and Associated Sites on the Northern Great Plains. *Nebraska State Historical Society. Publications in Anthropology* 6.

Newman, M.T.

1975   Nutritional Adaptation in Man. Pp. 210–259 in Physiological Anthropology. A. Damon, ed. New York: Oxford University Press.

Phenice, T.W.

1969   A Newly Developed Visual Method of Sexing of the Os Pubis. *American Journal of Physical Anthropology* 30:297–302.

Quade, D.
1966 An Analysis of Variance for the *k*-Sample Problem. *Annals of Mathematical Statistics* 37:1747–1758.

Relethford, J.H., and D.C. Hodges
1985 A Statistical Test for Differences in Sexual Dimorphism Between Populations. *American Journal of Physical Anthropology* 59:295–298.

Ruff, C.B.
1987 Sexual Dimorphism in Human Lower Limb Structure: Relationship to Subsistence Strategy and Sexual Division of Labor. *Journal of Human Evolution* 16:391–416.

———, and W.C. Hayes
1983a Cross-sectional Geometry of the Pecos Pueblo Femora and Tibiae—A Biomechanical Investigation: I. Method and General Patterns of Variation. *American Journal of Physical Anthropology* 60:359–381.

———, and W.C. Hayes
1983b Cross-sectional Geometry of the Pecos Pueblo Femora and Tibiae—A Biomechanical Investigation: II. Sex, Age, and Side Differences. *American Journal of Physical Anthropology* 60:383–500.

———, W.C. Hayes, and C.S. Larsen
1983 Changes in Femoral Structure with the Transition to Agriculture on the Georgia Coast. *American Journal of Physical Anthropology* 60:247–248.

———, and F.P. Leo
1986 Use of Computed Tomography in Skeletal Structure Research. *Yearbook of Physical Anthropology* 29:181–196.

SAS Institute
1982 SAS User's Guide: Statistics. Cary, N.C.: SAS Institute.

Sokal, R.R., and F.J. Rohlf
1981 Biometry. 2nd. ed. San Francisco: W.H. Freeman.

Spector, J.D.
1983 Male/Female Task Differentiation Among the Hidatsa: Toward the Development of an Archeological Approach to the Study of Gender. Pp. 77–99 in The Hidden Half: Studies of Plains Indian Women. P. Albers and B. Medicine, eds. Lanham, Md.: University Press of America.

Steward, J.
1955 Theory of Culture Change. Urbana, Ill.: University of Illinois Press.

Stini, W.A.
1969 Nutritional Stress and Growth: Sex Difference in Adaptive Response. *American Journal of Physical Anthropology* 31:417–426.

———
1972 Reduced Sexual Dimorphism in Upper Arm Muscle Circumference Associated with Protein-Deficient Diet in a South American Population. *American Journal of Physical Anthropology* 36:341–352.

———
1982 Sexual Dimorphism and Nutrient Reserves. Pp. 391–419 in Sexual Dimorphism in *Homo sapiens*. R.L. Hall, ed. New York: Praeger.

Stinson, S.
1985 Sex Differences in Environmental Sensitivity During Growth and Development. *Yearbook of Physical Anthropology* 28:123–147.

Trotter, M., and G.C. Gleser
1952 Estimation of Stature from Long Bones in American Whites and Negroes. *American Journal of Physical Anthropology* 4:463–514.

Truteau, J.B.
1912 Journal of Jean Baptiste Truteau Among the Arikara Indians in 1795. H.T. Beauregard, ed. *Missouri Historical Society Collections* 4.

Ubelaker, D.H.
1978 Human Skeletal Remains: Excavation, Analysis, and Interpretation. Chicago: Aldine.

van Gerven, D.P., J.R. Hummert, and D.B. Burr
1989 Sexual Dimorphism and Geometry of the Lower Limb in a Medieval Population from Sudanese Nubia. *American Journal of Physical Anthropology* 78:318.

Wedel, W.W.
1964 The Great Plains. Pp. 193–220 in Prehistoric Man in the New World. J.D. Jennings and E. Norbeck, eds. Chicago: University of Chicago Press.

———
1983 The Prehistoric Plains. Pp. 203–241 in Ancient North Americans. J.D. Jennings, ed. New York: W.H. Freeman.

Wood, W.R.
1980 Plains Trade in Prehistoric and Protohistoric Intertribal Relations. Pp. 98–109 in Anthropology of the Great Plains. W.R. Wood and M. Liberty, eds. Lincoln: University of Nebraska Press.

Zimmerman, L.J.
1985 Peoples of Prehistoric South Dakota. Lincoln: University of Nebraska Press.

Zobeck, T.S.
1983 Postcraniometric Variation Among the Arikara. (Unpublished Ph.D. Dissertation in Anthropology, University of Tennessee, Knoxville.)

○○○

CHAPTER 19

Biomechanical Analysis of Northern and Southern Plains Femora: Behavioral Implications

CHRISTOPHER RUFF

Biomechanical beam analysis of long bone diaphyses has been applied with increasing frequency to archaeological samples (Bridges 1989; Brock and Ruff 1988; Kimura 1971; Lovejoy, Burstein, and Heiple 1976; Martin, Burr, and Schaffler 1985; Ruff 1992; Ruff and Hayes 1983a, 1983b; Ruff and Larsen 1990; Ruff, Larsen, and Hayes 1984; Sumner 1984; van Gerven, Hummert, and Burr 1985). The interest in this method of skeletal structural analysis can be attributed to two factors: an appreciation of the advantages of a biomechanical approach over traditional morphometric techniques and technical advances that have greatly facilitated data collection.

In a biomechanical analysis, a long-bone diaphysis is modeled as an engineering beam and certain cross-sectional properties are determined that indicate the rigidity or strength of the beam to resist mechanical forces, or loadings. Assuming that bones are adapted (both genetically and environmentally) to the kinds of mechanical loadings imposed upon them—a principle referred to as Wolff's Law—measuring these structural parameters affords insight into the mechanical environment, and thus behavioral use of the bone during life. This approach also has the advantage of reducing complex variations in bone size and shape to a few easily interpretable parameters with direct functional significance.

Figure 1 is a computer plot of a midshaft femoral cross-section with associated structural properties determined by program SLICE. Bone cortical area (CA) is proportional to simple compressive or tensile strength, while second moments of area (I, with subscripts, and J) are proportional to bending and torsional strengths of the bone at that section. Ratios of second moments of area (I_{max}/I_{min}, I_x/I_y) indicate relative bending strengths in different planes. They may also be considered to represent cross-sectional "shape" variables, since they indicate the relative circularity of distribution of bone in a section (ratios closer to 1 = more circular; see Ruff and Hayes 1983a and Ruff 1987). Theta measures the orientation of greatest bending strength, measured counterclockwise from the mediolateral axis. Total subperiosteal area (TA), medullary area (MA), and percent cortical area (%CA) reflect the relative contraction or expansion of the cortex about its center. Abbreviations and definitions of all sectional properties used in this study are summarized in table 1. More complete discussions of the meaning of these parameters can be found in Lovejoy, Burstein, and Heiple (1976) and Ruff and Hayes (1983a).

Because the distribution of bone within a cross-section is critical in determining its structural and mechanical proper-

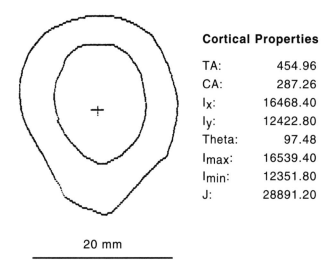

Cortical Properties

TA:	454.96
CA:	287.26
I_x:	16468.40
I_y:	12422.80
Theta:	97.48
I_{max}:	16539.40
I_{min}:	12351.80
J:	28891.20

20 mm

Fig. 1. Femoral midshaft cross-section outline with associated geometric properties determined by program SLICE. See table 1 for definition of properties. I_x and I_y refer to coordinates of the section centroid position (indicated by a cross) not applicable to the present study.

ties, it is important in this type of analysis to obtain as accurately as possible subperiosteal and endosteal boundaries. The simplest approach, and the one used here, is to physically section the bone and directly analyze the cut surface. (If a noninvasive approach is required other techniques are available—Ruff 1989). Once the section boundaries are obtained, they can be analyzed using several automated techniques. Here a modification of the SLICE computer program

Table 1. Cross-Sectional Geometric Properties[a]

CA	Cortical area
MA	Medullary area
TA	Total subperiosteal area
I_{max}	Maximum second moment of area (maximum bending strength)
I_{min}	Minimum second moment of area (minimum bending strenth)
J	Polar second moment of area (torsional or average bending strength)
Theta	Orientation of greatest bending strength (M – L = 0° or 180°)
%CA	Percent cortical area, (CA/TA) · 100
I_{max}/I_{min}	Maximum to minimum bending strength
I_x/I_y	A-P to M-L bending strength

[a]Areas in mm²; second moments of areas in mm⁴; theta in degrees. For group comparisons, all properties except theta and ratios standardized by powers of bone length (length′ as defined in Ruff and Hayes 1983a); areas divided by length² and multiplied by 10^5; second moments of area divided by length⁴ and multiplied by 10^8. Thus, standardized properties are dimensionless.

(Nagurka and Hayes 1980) is used, with x, y boundary point coordinates of the subperiosteal and endosteal surfaces input to the program via a digitizer (Ruff and Hayes 1983a). The technique is rapid and allows analysis of large numbers of cross-sections in a relatively short period of time. Thus, truly demographic studies of variation in these properties can be carried out, in contrast to many earlier studies that included only small samples.

For some types of analyses, for example, comparison of relative bending strengths in different planes (Ruff 1987), raw properties, or ratios of raw properties (table 1) can be used effectively. However, for many kinds of analyses some standardization of raw properties for differences in general body size is necessary. Among Recent period humans, cross-sectional geometric properties of lower limb bones tend to be isometric, or geometrically similar with respect to bone length (Ruff 1984). That is, cross-sectional areas, in linear units squared, vary in proportion to bone length squared, while second moments of area, in linear units to the fourth power, vary in proportion to bone length to the fourth power. Therefore, following Ruff, Larsen, and Hayes (1984), in all of the following comparisons between cultural groups and between the sexes, areas were standardized over bone length², while second moments of area were standardized over bone length⁴ (table 1). It should be noted that the bone length measurement employed here is the length′ dimension defined in Ruff and Hayes (1983a) that does not include the femoral head. In the femur, length′ averages about 5 percent less than maximum length.

The Study Sample

Femora from a total of 129 individuals from the Middle Missouri region (South Dakota) and 18 individuals from the Southern Plains region (Oklahoma) were available for study. A complete listing of specimens by cultural period, site, and sex is given in table 2. All individuals in the sample were adult, that is, over 18 years of age, with fused femoral epiphyses. Sexes and ages were determined using standard forensic methods, with individuals 20 years and older placed into 5-year age groups. Pathological specimens were excluded from the analysis.

For certain analyses the Coalescent sample was divided into earlier (1600–1740) and later (1740–1850) groups (table 2). These correspond approximately to prehorse and posthorse periods on the Northern Plains. Twenty-two individuals from the Middle Missouri region had either unknown or uncertain temporal or cultural affiliation, with most of these assigned to

Table 2. Sample Composition[a]

Cultural-Temporal Provenience	Site Number	Males	Females	Unsexed	Total
Middle Woodland	39YK1		1		1
A.D. 400–900					
Terminal Woodland/Great Oasis	39CH54		1		1
900–1050	39CL2	8	10	1	19
	39GR1		1		1
	39LK2	1	1		2
	39MH1	2			2
	39RO4	4	1		5
	39UN1	2	2		4
Initial Middle Missouri	39DV2	2			2
1000–1250	39HS1	5	2		7
	39HT1/3		1		1
Extended Middle Missouri	39HU1	1	1		2
1200–1600	39SL2	2			2
Extended and early Postcontact Coalescent	39LM33	5	2		7
1600–1740	39WW1	2	4		6
	39HU2	6	1		7
	39WW7	12	5		17
Late Postcontact Coalescent	39CO44	1			1
1740–1850	39ST1		1		1
	39ST235	3	5		8
	39DW2	2	6		8
	39CO9	2	1		3
Post-A.D. 400 ("Woodland B")	39DA3	1			1
	39HT2		4		4
	39LN10		3		3
	39MK1	1	2		3
	39RO2	1			1
	39RO10	1			1
	39RO3	2	2		4
Uncertain or unknown	39LM2A	3			3
	39ST49			1	1
	39WW303		1		1
Southern Plains	34WA5	4	10		14
1200–1300	34GV2	1	3		13

[a]Dates are approximate and refer to these particular samples.

a heterogeneous "Woodland B" group. Since there was only one individual assigned unequivocally to the Middle Woodland, this individual was grouped with the "post-A.D.400" group for statistical analyses. Similarly, the 10 Initial Middle Missouri and four Extended Middle Missouri individuals were grouped with the Terminal Woodland/Great Oasis sample. The five individuals listed as of "uncertain or unknown" cultural-temporal provenience and the other individual with uncertain sex assignment in table 2 were included only in the first, general analysis of the combined Middle Missouri region sample (table 3).

One femur from each individual was sectioned transversely at midshaft, the surface photographed with a superimposed grid and analyzed using a digitizer and program SLICE (see Ruff and Hayes 1983a). The femoral midshaft was chosen for study because it has been included in a large number of previous investigations (Ruff 1987), and because it lies in a skeletal region that is relatively informative with regard to mechanical loadings of the lower limbs and the body in general.

The cross-sectional properties included in the analysis and the size-standardization procedure employed have been described above and are listed in table 1. Bone length is also reported for each group to assess differences in overall body size. In addition, average age at death is listed for the samples since age differences can significantly affect cortical bone geometry (Ruff and Hayes 1983b). Because in all cases these were calculated from five-year grouped data, no standard errors are given for ages. Both right and left sides were used in the analysis (one bone from each individual), but with a preference for lefts, so that the final left/right ratio is about 3/2 over the whole sample and varies somewhat between samples (although no subgroup exceeds about 2/1 in lefts/rights). However, any bilateral differences in structural properties of the femur (Ruff and Hayes 1983b) should be greatly outweighed by differences between groups, so this should not be an important factor in the analysis.

Results

COMPARISONS WITH OTHER GROUPS

To place the results of this study within a larger cultural and geographic context, comparisons between the Middle Missouri and Southern Plains samples and two other North American Indian archaeological samples from the Georgia coast (Ruff, Larsen, and Hayes 1984) and Pecos Pueblo, New Mexico (Ruff and Hayes 1983a) were carried out and are

shown in table 3. Sexes and all cultural-temporal periods represented are combined in each group. The Georgia coast sample is pre-European contact and spans both preagricultural (hunting-gathering-fishing) and agricultural periods, with the majority of remains dating about 500–1500. The Pecos Pueblo sample is late prehistoric and protohistoric, dating about 1300–1650, and was agricultural.

The Middle Missouri sample is the tallest of the four samples, as judged from femoral length (table 3), with the Southern Plains sample close in height to the Georgia coast sample and Pecos Pueblo much shorter. However, the total Middle Missouri sample is slightly weighted toward males, while the Southern Plains sample is heavily weighted toward females (tables 2, 4). Thus, the two Plains samples, when sex-matched, are actually similar in height; and both are taller than the samples from the two other regions.

When standardized for body size differences by dividing by powers of bone length, cross-sectional geometric properties in the four samples are generally quite similar, with the two Plains samples tending to fall intermediate between the Pecos Pueblo and Georgia coast samples. The major exceptions to this are the cross-sectional shape variables of the Southern Plains sample (I_{max}/I_{min}, I_x/I_y) and theta, which are much higher than in other groups. These higher values all indicate relatively greater A-P bending loads in the midshaft femur in the Southern Plains sample.

Table 3. Size-Standardized Cross-Sectional Geometric Properties of the Midshaft Femur

Property	Georgia Coast (n = 40)		Pecos Pueblo (n = 119)		Middle Missouri (n = 127)		Southern Plains (n = 18)	
	Mean	Standard Error	Mean	Standard Error	Mean	Standard Error	Mean	Standard Error
Age	26.6	—	37.0	—	37.0	—	47.6	—
Bone length[a]	407.3	3.9	388.2	2.2	415.2	2.3	403.2	6.2
CA	210.2	6.0	215.6	2.5	209.0	2.7	200.2	7.7
MA	77.3	4.0	86.8	2.5	86.7	2.1	97.1	6.9
TA	287.5	5.3	301.9	2.4	295.8	3.3	297.2	8.9
I_{max}	70.5	3.2	79.0	1.4	74.0	1.9	80.7	5.5
I_{min}	55.6	2.0	57.7	1.0	58.2	1.4	52.9	3.3
J	126.1	5.0	136.6	2.1	132.3	3.2	133.6	8.0
Theta (°)	59.0	6.8	51.6	2.1	64.2	3.2	77.8	4.9
%CA	73.0	1.4	71.6	0.7	70.8	0.6	67.5	2.0
I_{max}/I_{min}	1.26	0.03	1.38	0.02	1.28	0.01	1.56	0.10
I_x/I_y	1.13	0.03	1.10	0.02	1.09	0.02	1.42	0.11

Sources: Ruff and Hayes 1983a, 1983b; Ruff, Larsen, and Hayes 1984.

[a]Bone length in mm, as defined in Ruff and Hayes (1983a); does not include femoral head.

Percent cortical area (CA/TA · 100) is also somewhat low in the Southern Plains sample and somewhat high in the Georgia coast sample, but this is likely a result of the higher and lower average ages at death of these two samples, respectively (table 3) (Ruff and Hayes 1983b). (The age factor would probably not affect the shape variables significantly, since these have not been observed to change greatly with age in the midshaft femur.)

Thus, in terms of femoral structure and lower limb mechanical loadings, the two Plains samples are fairly typical of North American Indians, except that the Southern Plains sample shows evidence of adaptation to relatively increased A-P bending of the femur.

COMPARISONS AMONG CULTURAL-TEMPORAL PERIODS

Length-standardized properties are compared, by sex, among the major cultural groupings within the Plains samples in table 4. One-way analysis of variance, within sex, was carried out to test for differences between group means, using a .05 significance level. Following F tests, two sample t tests were used to identify differences between specific pairs of groups, using the same significance level.

Differences in general body size, as reflected in bone length, are not significant across samples. Differences in the magnitude of cross-sectional areas and second moments of area are

Table 4. Size-Standardized Cross-Sectional Geometric Properties of the Midshaft Femur, by Sex

Property	Terminal Woodland/Great Oasis-Initial and Extended Middle Missouri (n = 25)		Extended and Postcontact Coalescent (n = 33)		Post-A.D. 400 (n = 6)		Southern Plains (Okla.) (n = 5)	
	Mean	Standard Error	Mean	Standard Error	Mean	Standard Error	Mean	Standard Error
Males								
Age	37.3	—	35.0	—	39.8	—	52.0	—
Bone length	427.4	4.8	432.2	3.9	437.3	6.2	431.0	4.4
CA	226.3	7.8	216.3	4.2	224.0	4.8	210.7	6.6
MA	85.6	6.0	91.3	4.1	90.0	8.7	91.1	12.9
TA	311.9	9.9	307.6	6.0	313.9	55.7	301.9	9.4
I_{max}	84.2	6.1	80.2	3.0	83.9	5.1	93.1	8.3
I_{min}	64.6	4.8	62.4	2.2	63.6	2.4	48.5	3.7
J	148.8	10.9	142.6	4.9	147.6	7.1	141.6	7.8
Theta (°)	70.9	6.8	70.2	4.5	77.0	16.0	77.2	5.5
%CA	72.7	1.5	70.6	1.0	71.6	2.2	70.1	3.4
I_{max}/I_{min}[a]	1.32	0.03	1.29	0.03	1.32	0.05	1.97	0.26
I_x/I_y[a]	1.11	0.04	1.18	0.03	1.11	0.08	1.74	0.34
Females								
Age	34.2	—	35.4	—	30.2	—	45.8	—
Bone length	399.6	4.5	394.6	3.2	398.7	5.1	392.5	6.1
CA	196.4	4.9	196.9	5.4	195.7	5.3	196.1	10.3
MA[a]	75.8	3.3	89.4	4.0	84.1	6.3	99.3	8.5
TA	272.3	5.9	286.3	5.2	279.8	8.4	295.5	11.9
I_{max}	62.6	3.1	67.3	2.9	64.5	3.8	76.0	6.6
I_{min}	49.5	2.1	54.0	2.0	52.1	2.7	54.5	4.4
J	112.1	5.0	121.4	4.7	116.5	6.4	130.5	10.8
Theta (°)	51.8	9.6	60.2	7.6	59.0	12.8	78.0	6.6
%CA	72.2	1.0	68.7	1.3	70.2	1.6	66.5	2.4
I_{max}/I_{min}[a]	1.26	0.03	1.25	0.03	1.24	0.03	1.40	0.05
I_x/I_y[a]	0.98	0.04	1.09	0.04	1.02	0.05	1.29	0.06

[a]One-way analysis of variance between cultural periods significant at p < .05.

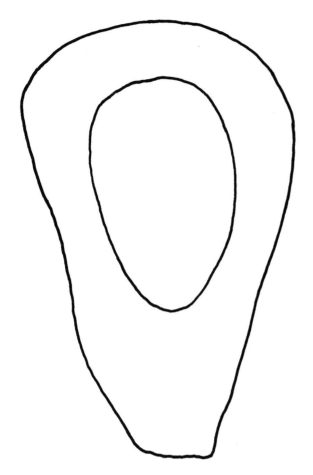

Fig. 2. Tracing of a male Southern Plains femoral midshaft exhibiting extreme values for I_x/I_y and I_{max}/I_{min}, i.e., extreme noncircularity and very large A-P bending strength.

also not significant between groups, except for MA among females. This difference appears to be largely a product of age differences between samples (i.e., the large MA in the older Southern Plains sample), given the marked increase with age in MA observed among females in general (Ruff and Hayes 1983b). The only other significant differences between groups are found in the cross-sectional shape variables: I_{max}/I_{min} and I_x/I_y. The Southern Plains sample is significantly different in this respect from the other samples. Southern Plains males in particular show extremely high values for both I_{max}/I_{min} and I_x/I_y, in fact well above the values for any other population sample reported (Ruff 1987: table 3). An extreme example is illustrated in figure 2, a tracing of the male cross-section with the highest I_x/I_y and I_{max}/I_{min} ratios (both 2.9) of any in the sample. This individual did *not* exhibit any signs of pathology (Douglas Owsley, personal communication 1989).

Percent cortical area shows a near-significant (p < .10) difference between groups among females, with a significant

dip among Coalescent females relative to other period females (p < .05, t test). However, this reflects a relatively expanded cortex in Coalescent females (relatively greater TA and MA) rather than any change in CA itself, which remains virtually constant throughout all periods in females. In fact, due to this outward expansion of the cortex, Coalescent females show the largest values for relative bending and torsional strength (second moments of area) of any of the Middle Missouri groups. The fallacy of using %CA as a general "health status" indicator has been noted (van Gerven, Hummert, and Burr 1985; Ruff and Larsen 1990).

Interestingly, most cross-sectional properties of the "post-A.D. 400" group are intermediate between the other periods and the Coalescent groups, not clustering strongly with either group. Thus, in terms of mechanical loadings and behavioral use of the lower limb, this sample fits the prediction of a heterogeneous group, combining or averaging aspects of the other two groups.

COMPARISONS BETWEEN PREHORSE AND POSTHORSE COALESCENT

Properties for earlier and later Coalescent period samples are shown, by sex, in table 5. No obvious change in bone cross-sectional geometry occurs at the introduction of the horse (no differences in properties reach statistical significance between cultural periods, either using t tests between periods within sex, or 2-way ANOVA of sex and cultural period). Certainly there is no evidence that mechanical loadings of the lower limb decrease in general; if anything areas and second moments of area relative to bone length increase slightly in both sexes (although not significantly). However, males do show a slight (not significant) increase in circularity of the midshaft femur, as reflected in reduced cross-sectional shape ratios, a change that is not paralleled in females.

SEXUAL DIMORPHISM

Sexual dimorphism, expressed as the percentage difference between males and females, is shown in table 6 for some key properties in five Middle Missouri cultural-temporal groupings and the Southern Plains sample.

Sexual dimorphism in general body size (bone length) is relatively similar in all groups (small variations probably reflect sampling error). However, sexual dimorphism in both cross-sectional size and shape relative to bone length shows distinct temporal and geographic differences. Sexual dimorphism in length-standardized cross-sectional size (CA and *J*) declines

Table 5. Size-Standardized Cross-Sectional Geometric Properties of the Midshaft Femur, by Sex

	Males				Females			
	Prehorse (n = 25)		Posthorse (n = 8)		Prehorse (n = 12)		Posthorse (n = 13)	
Property	Mean	Standard Error	Mean	Standard Error	Mean	Standard Error	Mean	Standard Error
Age	35.0	—	37.0	—	31.9	—	38.5	—
Bone length	432.2	3.9	434.4	6.3	390.1	4.0	398.8	4.9
CA	215.7	5.1	218.3	7.3	192.2	8.8	201.2	6.5
MA	89.8	4.7	95.9	8.4	88.7	6.1	90.1	5.5
TA	305.6	6.8	314.2	12.7	280.9	9.3	291.3	5.1
I_{max}	79.8	3.4	81.6	6.9	64.0	4.8	70.5	3.4
I_{min}	61.5	2.5	65.2	4.4	52.9	3.4	55.0	2.1
J	141.2	5.6	146.8	10.5	116.9	8.0	125.5	5.3
Theta (°)	68.4	5.0	75.5	10.8	67.2	12.6	53.8	9.0
%CA	70.8	1.2	69.8	1.7	68.4	2.0	69.0	1.8
I_{max}/I_{min}	1.30	0.30	1.25	0.07	1.21	0.04	1.28	0.04
I_x/I_y	1.19	0.03	1.14	0.07	1.10	0.05	1.08	0.06

from Terminal Woodland/Great Oasis and the Middle Missouri periods to Coalescent, and within Coalescent from prehorse to posthorse periods. The Southern Plains sample shows even smaller male-female differences in relative cross-sectional size. Similarly, sexual dimorphism in the two cross-sectional shape indices declines between earlier and later Middle Missouri region groups (with a transient increase in the prehorse Coalescent). However, here the Southern Plains sample deviates markedly from the other groups, with extremely high sexual dimorphism in shape, at or above the limits recorded for any other population sample (Ruff 1987). The post-A.D. 400 group is also intermediate between the Terminal Woodland–Middle Missouri and Coalescent groups in terms of sexual dimorphism.

Thus, in the Middle Missouri region males and females tend to become more similar through time in femoral structure and inferred mechanical loading of the lower limb. In contrast, in the Southern Plains, while the overall *magnitude* of loading tends to be fairly similar in males and females, the *type* of loading shows a large difference, with male femora being much more adapted to high A-P bending loads.

Interpretation

The cultural and behavioral interpretations of these data are limited by several factors. First, only one skeletal area—the femoral midshaft—was sampled. While this provides a good index of general use of the lower limb and general activity

Table 6. Sexual Dimorphism in Some Size-standardized Cross-sectional Geometric Properties of the Midshaft Femur in the Middle Missouri and Southern Plains

	Percent Sexual Dimorphism: [(Male-Female)/Female] · 100					
Property	Terminal Woodland/Great Oasis–Initial and Extended Middle Missouri	Total Coalescent	Prehorse Coalescent	Posthorse Coalescent	Post-A.D. 400	Southern Plains
Bone length	7.0%	9.7	10.8	8.9	9.7	9.8
CA	15.2	9.9	12.2	8.5	14.5	7.4
J	32.7	17.5	20.8	17.0	26.7	8.5
I_{max}/I_{min}	4.8	3.2	7.9	−2.4	6.5	41.4
I_x/I_y	13.3	8.3	7.5	5.4	8.9	34.6

level, it would also have been interesting and informative to have included bone sections from other regions of the skeleton, particularly the upper limb (Bridges 1989; Ruff and Larsen 1990). Second, while the total sample is large, some of the samples become quite small when broken down by cultural-temporal period and sex, with less than 10 individuals per group (tables 3, 4), leading to increased probabilities of sampling error (Ruff 1987). It is also unfortunate that with the exception of a single individual no well-defined Middle Woodland population samples were available for measurement, since these would have provided a greater contrast in subsistence strategy and behavior. Finally, other than a few relatively general summaries, a complete synthesis of the archaeological record for the Plains region has not yet been carried out, particularly with regard to subsistence strategy and behavior, so that it is difficult to tie the present information into a more general cultural-behavioral framework. Thus, for these reasons the interpretations offered here should be viewed only as preliminary hypotheses to be further tested when additional skeletal and archaeological data from this region become available.

Taken as a whole, the Northern and Southern Plains samples are taller than two other samples from the Southwest (Pecos Pueblo) and Southeast (Georgia coast) (Ruff and Hayes 1983a; Ruff, Larsen, and Hayes 1984), but when standardized for differences in bone length, femoral "robusticity" (CA and J) is similar across all four regions. This is perhaps not surprising, given that all of these samples represent primarily later prehistoric and protohistoric populations with mixed agricultural-nonagricultural subsistence economies (even the Pecos Pueblo "agricultural" sample actually engaged in a significant amount of hunting—Ruff and Hayes 1983a). If the Georgia coast sample is broken down into preagricultural and agricultural groups, the two Plains samples are more similar in robusticity to the preagricultural group (and to Pecos Pueblo). The general mechanical demands of life were probably similar at Pecos Pueblo and among hunter-gatherers from the Georgia coast, and these demands decreased among the coastal agriculturists (Ruff, Larsen, and Hayes 1984). In this context the Plains individuals, even the later more agricultural ones, appear to have had a relatively rigorous life, which accords with ethnohistoric evidence (Hurt 1969). Bridges (1989) also found that the adoption of agriculture did not result in a decrease in mechanical loading of the skeleton in an interior (Tennessee River Valley) sample.

In terms of the types of mechanical loadings on the lower limb (i.e., the I_x/I_y or I_{max}/I_{min} ratios), the Middle Missouri and Southern Plains region samples are quite distinct, with the

Middle Missouri sample falling closer to the Pecos Pueblo and Georgia coast samples and the Southern Plains sample falling well above the range of any of the others. When considered by subsistence strategy, the Middle Missouri region sample is most similar in this regard to Georgia coast *agriculturists* (and to Pecos), again according with a previous hypothesis that types (although not necessarily levels) of activity would be more similar under similar subsistence economies (Ruff, Larsen, and Hayes 1984). The Southern Plains sample clearly falls with hunter-gatherers in this respect (Ruff 1987), an apparent paradox.

In terms of temporal-cultural change on the Plains, the clearest trend is for Middle Missouri region samples to exhibit progressively less sexual dimorphism through time in both the overall magnitude and the types of mechanical loadings on the femur. Again the Southern Plains sample is different in showing extreme sexual dimorphism in the types (although not general levels) of mechanical loadings of the femur.

In a study of a number of population samples from a wide geographic and temporal range, it was shown that cross-sectional shape differences (I_x/I_y and I_{max}/I_{min}) in the femur and tibia are partly sex related, but that the degree of sexual dimorphism varies systematically according to subsistence strategy (Ruff 1987). Specifically, male lower limb bones tend to be adapted for relatively greater A-P bending (i.e., are less round and more A-P "elongated" or M-L "flattened") in the region about the knee, from the mid-femur through the mid-tibia. This sex difference is very marked in hunter-gatherers (extending back to the Middle Paleolithic), declines in agriculturists, and essentially disappears in modern industrial people. Based on both ethnographic and kinesiological observations, it appears that the degree of sexual dimorphism in this structural feature is related to the degree of sexual differentiation in activity (primarily subsistence) tasks, with greater mobility and long distance travel by hunter-gatherer males leading to relatively greater A-P bending strength, and with sexual differences in this feature declining with the adoption of more sedentary (and less sex-specific) behavioral patterns.

In this context, temporal and geographic variation in sexual dimorphism in femoral structure in the Plains samples may be informative with regard to changes in subsistence strategy and sexual division of labor in these populations. Figure 3 shows the sexual dimorphism in femoral midshaft I_x/I_y of the Terminal Woodland/Great Oasis-Initial Middle Missouri-Extended Middle Missouri sample, the earlier (prehorse) and later (posthorse) Coalescent samples, and the Southern Plains sample relative to other population samples, grouped by subsistence strategy. The Terminal Woodland and Middle Missouri

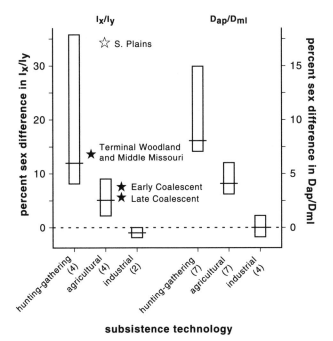

Fig. 3. Percent sex difference [(male-female)/female · 100] in two indices of relative A-P/M-L bending strength of the midshaft femur: I_x/I_y and D_{ap}/D_{ml}, the ratio of A-P to M-L external diameters. Bars show ranges of variability and median values for comparative sample means from other regions, grouped by subsistence category. Numbers indicate number of population samples in each category. (Adapted from Ruff 1987.)

sample falls close to the median of hunter-gatherers, the two Coalescent samples fall within the range of agriculturists, with the earlier Coalescent in the upper part of this range, and the Southern Plains sample falls just within the upper end of the known range for hunter-gatherers.

These results are consistent with a view of Terminal Woodland–Initial Middle Missouri populations as essentially hunter-gatherers in subsistence strategy, despite possible minor dependence on crop cultivation (Henning 1981; Lehmer 1971:31; Zimmerman 1985:77; Donald Blakeslee, personal communication 1989). The very small sample of Extended Middle Missouri individuals placed within this group for statistical analysis (table 2) does not seem to be different from the earlier sample in this regard, which could reflect the continued importance of hunting and a relatively mixed economy extending through the Middle Missouri cultural tradition (Lehmer 1971:65, 109). However, more individuals from the Middle Missouri cultural tradition will be needed to test this possibility.

The results are also concordant with the evidence for increasing intensification of agriculture among Coalescent population samples in the Northern Plains (Owsley 1991;

"Antelope Creek Phase Subsistence: The Bone Chemistry Evidence," this vol.). All the Coalescent samples date from the late prehistoric or protohistoric periods (table 2; Owsley 1991; a few postdate 1800 and thus are technically historic) during which horticultural activities in this region intensified over previous periods. Since women did most of the planting (Hurt 1969), this would have increased general mechanical loads on their skeletons, and thus could explain the temporal increase in robusticity (length-standardized CA and J) of their femora observed here, a change not observed among males (tables 4, 5). On the other hand, while bison and other hunting continued and was mainly a male occupation, it may have decreased in relative importance until the advent of the horse in the middle of the eighteenth century. Increased bison hunting on horseback (Holder 1970:112) would not be expected to produce the typical increase in I_x/I_y found among male hunter-gatherers who travel great distances on foot (see Ruff 1987). In fact, horse riding could conceivably produce higher M-L loadings of the femur and might have contributed to the small decline in the I_x/I_y index among posthorse period males (table 5). Thus, sexual dimorphism in mechanical loadings and femoral cross-sectional shape continued to decline during the late Postcontact Coalescent in the Middle Missouri region.

The situation was apparently quite different in the Southern Plains region, at least at the two Oklahoma sites reported here. Although these were relatively late (1200–1300), well within the agricultural period for this region, they exhibit a degree of sexual dimorphism in bone shape close to the upper limit for hunter-gatherers (fig. 3). It is possible that sampling error (only five males) could account for this apparent paradox. However, if this result is validated in a larger sampling from this region and time period, it could indicate a very unusual behavioral pattern, with generally high levels of mobility in both males and females, but particularly high levels among males. Further speculation on this difference is outside the scope of this investigation, but at the least, the present data indicate significant variation in mechanical loading and behavioral use of the lower limb among Plains Village sites, with a possible North-South dichotomy.

The study results are consistent with Owsley's (1991) study of femoral cortical thickness in late prehistoric, protohistoric, and historic Arikara. In his larger sample, which included many of the same sites as this study, medial and lateral cortical thickness, measured radiographically, reached its maximum in the early protohistoric period (1650–1740) but did not decline significantly until the historic period (post-1800). Total M-L subperiosteal breadth increased throughout the time span sampled, except among historic period males. Thus, as in the present study, the introduction of the horse at about 1740 had no dramatic effect on femoral structure. Also, the increase in TA and second moments of area (which follows from subperiosteal expansion) observed here between pre- and posthorse periods parallels Owsley's reported temporal increase in subperiosteal breadth in his larger sample. He also observed no large changes in bone length (general body size) over his samples. Sample sizes in this study are too small to allow a further breakdown by finer temporal periods, as Owsley did, so that it is not possible to further explore the effects of European contact with this data set (i.e., comparisons of late prehistoric with early protohistoric, and late protohistoric with historic periods).

The heterogeneity of the post-A.D. sample of skeletal material from the Middle Missouri region is supported by the present results, since their cross-sectional properties fall at about the mean for the other samples analyzed. There probably are some Woodland period sites in this sample, but any distinguishing features of these individuals are apparently swamped by the rest of the (temporally later) sample. It is also possible that they are not significantly different in subsistence strategy and mechanical loadings of the femur from the succeeding Terminal Woodland/Great Oasis period sample. A sample of indisputable Middle Woodland period origin from this region would be very useful in this regard.

Conclusions

Biomechanical analysis can form an important complement to traditional osteometric studies of long bone morphology, by providing additional structural information that can be used to reconstruct mechanical loadings on the bone during life, and thus past behavioral patterns. In this study cross-sectional geometric properties of the midshaft femur were used to help interpret the behavior of pre- and protohistoric Plains Village samples from the Middle Missouri region and a smaller Southern Plains sample. Within the limitations of the data, the following tentative conclusions can be drawn from the results of the analysis.

Plains Villagers had a relatively rigorous lifeway, similar in terms of overall activity level to hunter-gatherers from the Georgia coast or the Pecos Pueblo sample from New Mexico. In the Middle Missouri region, *types* of activities in the population as a whole were most similar to agricultural groups from other regions. However, in some ways, particularly with respect to sexual division of labor, incipient or early horticulturists (Terminal Woodland/Great Oasis and Middle

Missouri traditions) were more similar to hunting-gathering groups from other areas, indicating that the initial adoption of agriculture had a minimal effect on at least this aspect of social behavior. Later groups (Coalescent tradition) show evidence of a reduction in the sexual division of labor with increasing intensification of agriculture, a process that continued through the protohistoric period. It is possible that the use of the horse for hunting of bison in the late Protohistoric period may have contributed to a continuing decline in sexual dimorphism of lower limb mechanical loadings through a reduction in long-distance foot travel by males.

In the Southern Plains (Oklahoma) region, some later prehistoric populations may have been highly mobile, at least during parts of the year. Marked differences in mobility between males and females were also present. Perhaps a different sexual division of labor was characteristic of these populations than those of the Northern Plains, with more long-distance migration of the population as a whole as well. Larger samples with greater time-depth from this region and other areas of the Plains are necessary to further test and extend these hypotheses.

Kelly Goulette provided assistance in tracing the sections and entering data for statistical analyses.

References Cited

Bridges, P.S.
    1989 Changes in Activities with the Shift to Agriculture in the Southeastern United States. *Current Anthropology* 30:385–394.
Brock, S.L., and C.B. Ruff
    1988 Diachronic Patterns of Change in Structural Properties of the Femur in the prehistoric American Southwest. *American Journal of Physical Anthropology* 75:113–127.
Henning, E.R.P.
    1981 Great Oasis and the Middle Missouri Tradition. Pp. 33–38 in The Future of South Dakota's Past (Special Publication 2). L.J. Zimmerman and L.C. Stewart, eds. Sioux Falls, S.Dak.: South Dakota Archaeological Society.
Holder, P.
    1970 The Hoe and the Horse on the Plains. Lincoln: University of Nebraska Press.
Hurt, W.R.
    1969 Seasonal Economic and Settlement Patterns of the Arikara. *Plains Anthropologist* 14:32–37.
Kimura, T.
    1971 Cross-section of Human Lower Limb Bones Viewed from Strength of Materials. *Journal of the Anthropological Society of Nippon* 79:323–336.

Larsen, C.S., Schoeninger, M.J., Hutchinson, D.L., Russell, K.F., and C.B. Ruff

 1990 Beyond Demographic Collapse: Biological Adaptation and Change in Native Populations of La Florica. Pp. 409–428 in Columbian Consequences, Vol. 2: Archaeological and Historical Perspectives on the Spanish Borderlands. D.H. Thomas, ed. Washington: Smithsonian Institution Press.

Lehmer, D.J.

 1971 Introduction to Middle Missouri Archaeology. Washington: National Park Service.

Lovejoy, C.O., Burstein, A.H., and K.G. Heiple

 1976 The Biomechanical Analysis of Bone Strength: A Method and Its Application to Platycnemia. *American Journal of Physical Anthropology* 44:489–506.

Martin, R.B., D.B. Burr, and M.B. Schaffler

 1985 Effects of Age and Sex on the Amount and Distribution of Mineral in Eskimo Tibiae. *American Journal of Physical Anthropology* 67:371–380.

Nagurka, M.L., and W.C. Hayes

 1980 An Interactive Graphics Package for Calculating Cross-sectional Properties of Complex Shapes. *Journal of Biomechanics* 13:59–64.

Owsley, D.W.

 1991 Temporal Variation in Femoral Cortical Thickness of North American Plains Indians. Pp. 105–110 in Human Paleopathology: Current Syntheses and Future Options. D. Ortner and A.C. Aufderheide, eds. Washington: Smithsonian Institution Press.

Ruff, C.B.

 1984 Allometry Between Length and Cross-sectional Dimensions of the Femur and Tibia in *Homo sapiens*. *American Journal of Physical Anthropology* 65:347–358.

 ——

 1987 Sexual Dimorphism in Human Lower Limb Bone Structure: Relationship to Subsistence Strategy and Sexual Division of Labor. *Journal of Human Evolution* 16:396–416.

 ——

 1989 New Approaches to Structural Evolution of Limb Bones in Primates. *Folia Primatologica* 53:142–159.

 ——

 1992 Biomechanical Analyses of Archaeological Human Material. Pp. 41–62 in The Skeletal Biology of Past Peoples. S.R. Saunders and A. Katzenberg, eds. New York: Alan R. Liss.

 ——, and W.C. Hayes

 1983a Cross-sectional Geometry of Pecos Pueblo Femora and Tibiae—A Biomechanical Investigation. I: Method and General Patterns of Variation. *American Journal of PHysical Anthropology* 60:359–381.

 ——, and W.C. Hayes

 1983b Cross-sectional Geometry of Pecos Pueblo Femora and Tibiae—A Biomechanical Investigation. II: Sex, Age, and Side Differences. *American Journal of Physical Anthropology* 60:383–400.

 ——, and C.S. Larsen

 1990 Postcranial Biomechanical Adaptations to Subsistence Changes on the Georgia Coast. *Anthropological Papers of the American Museum of Natural History* 68:94–120.

 ——, Larsen, C.S., and W.C. Hayes

 1984 Structural Changes in the Femur with the Transition to Agriculture on the Georgia Coast. *American Journal of Physical Anthropology* 64:125–136.

Sumner, D.R.

 1984 Size, Shape, and Bone Mineral Content of the Human Femur in Growth and Aging. (Unpublished M.A. Thesis, University of Arizona, Tucson.)

van Gerven, D.P., Hummert, J.R., and D.B. Burr

 1985 Cortical Bone Maintenance and Geometry of the Tibia in Prehistoric Children from Nubia's Batn el Hajar. *American Journal of Physical Anthropology* 66:275–280.

Zimmerman, L.J.

 1985 Peoples of Prehistoric South Dakota. Lincoln, Neb.: University of Nebraska Press.

CHAPTER 20

○○○

Growth and Dental Development in Arikara Children

RICHARD L. JANTZ AND DOUGLAS W. OWSLEY

Research involving growth of long bones in children found in American Indian skeletal samples has faced several serious problems. Consequently, the use of children's long bones as indicators of growth sufficiency is rarely attempted, even though growth is sensitive to environmental influences, and children from birth to two years of age are generally the most numerous segment of skeletal collections. These problems have been described (Jantz and Owsley 1984; Johnston 1968; Sundick 1978). The specific problem addressed in this paper concerns the relationship between dental age and long bone length. Although chronological age is not usually known for archaeological samples, it is possible to explore the consequences of different dental aging schedules for assessment of long bone growth.

It is generally agreed that dental calcification is the indicator of developmental age least likely to be affected by environmental disturbances and to be most highly correlated with chronological age. The most commonly used aging standards are those of Schour and Massler (1944) and Moorrees, Fanning, and Hunt (1963a, 1963b). The latter standards are preferred because they provide age means and ranges for each stage of tooth development. Merchant and Ubelaker (1977) have shown that different age criteria applied to the same data can yield different growth curves.

Application of these commonly used White-based standards to American Indian children may not be appropriate. It is well known that development and eruption schedules may exhibit marked interpopulation differences, as such variation has been repeatedly documented (Dahlberg and Menegaz-Bock 1958; Moorrees 1957; Troddon 1982). Further, using Moorrees, Fanning, and Hunt's (1963a) standards on different teeth can produce age estimates differing by as much as two years (Owsley and Jantz 1983a). Unfortunately, the lack of comprehensive chronological standards documenting rates of tooth formation in Native American populations has provided little alternative for determination of age, yet accurate assessments of age are essential for many kinds of studies, including research in demography, paleopathology, growth, and forensic sciences.

Ubelaker (1989) produced a type of Schour and Massler (1944) chart visually presenting dental eruption and formation for American Indian and other non-White dentitions. Data for the chart were compiled from a worldwide survey of the literature. The result is an improvement that addresses the problem of interpopulation variability and the need for group-specific standards. This report presents a new approach for deriving schedules of deciduous dental development that are specific to an American Indian population, the Arikara of

Table 1. Dental Development Stages of Moorrees, Fanning, and Hunt (1963a, 1963b)

Stage	Description
1	Coalescence of cusps
2	Cusp outline complete
3	Crown ½ complete
4	Crown ¾ complete
5	Crown complete
6	Initial root formation
7	Initial cleft formation
8	Root length ¼
9	Root length ½
10	Root length ¾
11	Root length complete
12	Apex ½ closed

Table 2. Sample Size by Tooth and Development Stage

Stage		Femur	Tibia	Humerus	Radius
dc	2	24	20	23	24
	3	53	51	55	47
	4	22	18	18	18
	5	14	13	14	10
	6	23	19	27	18
	7	—	—	—	—
	8	21	24	24	19
	9	39	29	36	32
	10	20	17	22	19
	11	15	14	17	11
	12	25	27	29	27
dc Totals		256	232	265	225
dm1	2	15	15	13	17
	3	78	75	82	74
	4	64	54	59	48
	5	30	31	27	27
	6	15	12	14	11
	7	13	9	13	7
	8	37	28	35	23
	9	30	24	31	23
	10	24	22	28	22
	11	25	20	18	19
	12	20	18	24	20
dm1 Totals		351	308	344	291
dm2	2	77	71	81	73
	3	42	33	38	30
	4	22	18	20	17
	5	21	22	28	14
	6	25	21	24	16
	7	36	26	32	27
	8	22	20	24	19
	9	31	26	28	26
	10	15	12	15	14
	11	17	14	19	14
	12	10	10	11	7
dm2 Totals		318	273	320	257

South Dakota. These schedules are then used to study variation in long bone growth among different Arikara groups.

Sample Sizes and Primary Data

The sample consists of those children with measurable long bone diaphyses and with one or more of the following deciduous mandibular teeth: canine (dc), first molar (dm1), or second molar (dm2). These three deciduous teeth are the only ones for which Moorrees, Fanning, and Hunt (1963b) present age distributions for developmental stages. Table 1 shows their stage descriptions, together with the stage numbers used to identify them. Long bone measurements and dental ratings were performed by Owsley. (Measurements of the femur, tibia, humerus, and radius were used.) Left bone lengths were preferred, although rights were substituted in cases of better preservation. Dental ratings were based on loose teeth from damaged mandibles and from periapical radiographs when the teeth were in the alveolar sockets. Owsley and Jantz (1983a) describe the dental rating procedure in detail. Table 2 gives the sample sizes for each long bone for each dental stage. The samples shown in Table 2 are drawn from South Dakota Coalescent tradition sites containing appropriate long bones and teeth. These sites have been described in Jantz and Owsley (1984).

Developing an Arikara Dental Standard

Since the approach employed is complicated and a full description has not been published, it is presented here in some detail, with particular attention to critical assumptions.

(Owsley and Jantz 1983a have published a preliminary description, and Hyman 1987 has developed the method.) Jantz and Owsley (1985) have used ages derived from the method in a study of childhood mortality.

There are four steps to the procedure. The first is to estimate the birth length of each long bone using the perinatal distribution of bone lengths. The second is to use ages associated with developmental stages to derive an estimate of birth length. The estimate is obtained by fitting long bone lengths to the dental ages using a second degree polynomial. These two independent estimates of birth length are compared. The third step is to adjust the dental ages so that they produce birth lengths of long bones in agreement with those derived from the perinatal distribution. The fourth step is to we compare the growth curves obtained using dental ages to growth data for Whites and further adjust the dental ages so that all teeth yield growth curves of similar shape.

ESTIMATION OF BIRTH LENGTH USING PERINATAL DISTRIBUTIONS

A demographic assumption is used for the first part of the procedure. In a normal preadult mortality distribution, infants at the time of birth have the highest probability of dying; therefore, frequency histograms of long bone lengths should yield modes corresponding to birth. The length identified as the mode for each long bone can be taken as the best estimate of bone length at birth. Stewart (1979) employed this rationale to derive birth lengths of long bones.

Figure 1 gives the frequency histograms of the femur, tibia, humerus, and radius. All perinatal infants with the appropriate

bone were used to construct these histograms, whether they possessed teeth or not. The sample sizes used to determine these histograms numbered between 344 (tibia) and 414 (femur). The femur histogram yields a distinct peak at 77 millimeters, but there is a broad zone ranging from 74 to 80 millimeters that includes a large proportion of the femora. The tibia histogram produces high, nearly identical modes at 68 and 69 millimeters, with high frequencies ranging between 63 and 72. The humerus histogram shows no distinct mode at a single value. Rather, there is a broad mode of similar frequencies ranging from 65 to 70 millimeters. The radius histogram has high frequency values in the range of 55 to 58 millimeters.

In all these distributions, the low frequencies for bones shorter than the modal values represent premature births, or infants that were small for gestational age (Owsley and Jantz 1985). Low frequencies for bones longer than the modal values represent postnatal deaths. Because preterm, term, and postterm infants are not distinguishable, the mean birth

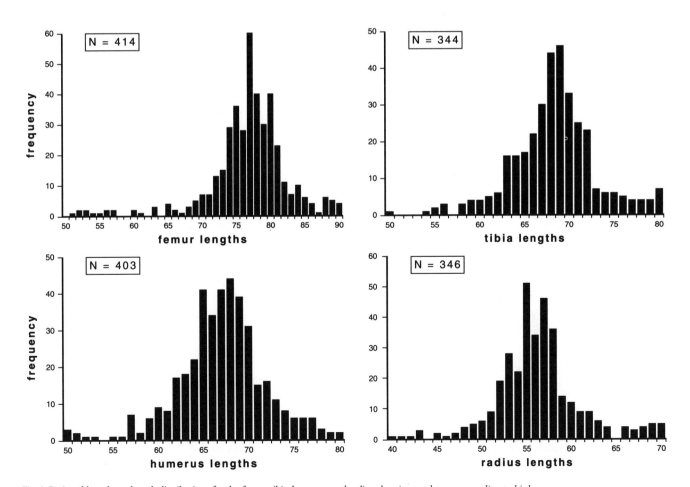

Fig. 1. Perinatal long bone length distributions for the femur, tibia, humerus, and radius, showing modes corresponding to birth.

lengths of these bones cannot be estimated. However, taking the approximate midpoint of the modes as reasonable estimates of the means results in the following: femur = 77 millimeters, tibia = 68.5 millimeters, humerus = 67 millimeters, and radius = 56 millimeters.

BIRTH LENGTHS FROM DENTAL AGES

Table 3 gives the descriptive statistics for bone length for each stage of deciduous tooth development. The ages given for each stage are the mean ages found in the Boston White sample (sexes combined) (Moorrees, Fanning, and Hunt 1963b). The greatest frequencies are found in the ages of 0.075–0.25, ages assigned to dc stage 2, dm1 stages 3 and 4, and dm2 stage 2 (table 2). Using the same argument applied to long bone distributions in the preceding section, that is, that birth is the time of highest mortality, the data suggest that American Indian dental development precedes that of Boston Whites by as much as 0.25 years at birth. The birth lengths of long bones estimated from the frequency distribution (fig. 1) agree most closely with ages from 0.075 to 0.15 years, further suggesting precocious dental development in the Arikara.

Table 3. Mean Bone Diaphyseal Lengths for Three Deciduous Teeth

Stage		Moorrees, Fanning, and Hunt's Age	Femur X	Femur Standard Deviation	Tibia X	Tibia Standard Deviation	Humerus X	Humerus Standard Deviation	Radius X	Radius Standard Deviation
dc	2	0.15	76.33	3.38	67.50	2.98	66.22	2.57	54.50	2.26
	3	0.25	78.85	4.69	69.51	3.42	68.55	3.39	56.57	2.52
	4	0.45	85.64	7.02	75.72	5.92	73.50	5.71	59.50	4.22
	5	0.675	99.50	8.09	85.31	9.59	85.36	6.11	64.70	5.08
	6	0.85	110.91	9.09	94.11	6.98	90.67	7.42	71.83	4.45
	7	—	—	—	—	—	—	—	—	—
	8	1.00	135.05	8.84	112.25	6.92	108.96	8.62	84.09	4.61
	9	1.275	147.90	14.09	122.21	10.66	116.47	8.29	90.66	7.43
	10	1.875	166.80	11.35	139.76	9.13	129.50	8.19	98.42	5.67
	11	2.00	175.07	11.43	143.57	11.03	135.94	9.48	100.45	5.37
	12	2.50	203.44	23.31	168.78	20.16	153.55	15.17	116.93	12.06
dm1	2	0.00	77.13	3.85	67.80	3.39	66.39	2.63	54.94	2.15
	3	0.175	76.64	3.51	67.37	3.10	66.94	2.95	55.16	2.76
	4	0.25	79.42	4.95	69.81	4.13	68.88	3.66	56.63	2.88
	5	0.40	88.03	7.27	78.68	7.78	77.44	7.14	61.15	5.19
	6	0.55	101.27	5.86	86.33	4.38	84.43	2.98	67.73	3.00
	7	0.60	109.77	7.42	93.22	7.17	89.23	4.64	73.43	5.35
	8	0.70	120.95	8.97	102.25	8.87	97.11	6.21	77.70	5.40
	9	0.925	131.53	9.92	110.38	6.59	106.45	5.79	84.61	3.93
	10	1.15	137.29	13.02	113.91	8.28	111.61	9.65	86.05	6.68
	11	1.25	147.32	14.12	121.15	11.25	114.22	8.60	89.74	7.92
	12	1.55	164.70	12.07	136.50	11.33	130.08	12.01	96.50	6.00
dm2	2	0.075	77.14	3.03	67.76	3.07	66.94	2.94	54.66	2.41
	3	0.25	84.00	6.90	73.39	5.26	71.68	4.48	58.77	3.66
	4	0.45	93.64	7.18	80.67	6.80	80.80	6.37	63.71	5.01
	5	0.70	111.14	7.61	92.82	6.12	89.46	4.99	71.93	4.94
	6	0.90	120.36	9.23	102.10	8.18	97.25	7.21	76.44	7.36
	7	0.95	126.83	8.88	108.50	6.33	104.56	7.92	82.48	3.84
	8	1.30	137.91	12.20	113.85	9.29	108.67	7.44	85.26	5.60
	9	1.525	149.41	10.45	121.92	9.62	116.36	7.39	90.73	6.71
	10	1.85	163.67	16.82	139.25	10.80	128.40	8.58	98.00	7.46
	11	1.975	168.35	13.49	139.64	9.39	134.16	12.47	99.79	4.23
	12	2.40	180.30	12.53	150.10	9.89	137.91	9.00	107.14	5.08

Table 4. Regression Parameters for Arikara, Denver, and Fels Samples

Bone	Coefficient	Arikara			Denver	Fels
		dc	dm1	dm2		
Femur	b_0	61.13	64.26	71.31	79.26	—
	b_1	71.48	75.68	60.73	64.24	—
	b_2	−6.07	−7.01	−6.11	−8.76	—
Tibia	b_0	56.44	58.55	63.65	64.37	69.84
	b_1	53.24	56.87	45.66	50.95	57.23
	b_2	−3.52	−4.56	−3.81	−6.60	−8.30
Humerus	b_0	55.94	58.04	63.01	66.05	—
	b_1	51.37	54.23	42.99	44.28	—
	b_2	−5.90	−5.31	−4.43	−6.30	—
Radius	b_0	47.73	48.75	51.95	54.91	53.02
	b_1	35.18	40.71	31.84	29.29	32.35
	b_2	−3.20	−6.09	−3.83	−4.06	−4.56

The bone distributions exhibit an anomaly. Stage 2 of dm1 bone lengths exceeds stage 3 lengths in the femur and the tibia. What accounts for the anomaly is unknown; it affects age estimates derived later for dm1.

The relationship between bone length and age was explored further by fitting a second degree polynomial to the data, where y = bone length, x = dental age, and x^2 = dental age^2. The mean bone lengths were fitted to age and age^2 weighting by sample size rather than by using individual data. The regression parameters are the same in both cases, but using the mean eliminates variation within age categories, thus elevating the R^2 (proportion of explained variation by age). Regression lines were determined for each bone for each deciduous tooth. Bone length regressions were calculated on chronological age from the growth status in Denver, Colorado (Maresh 1970), and Fels Research Institute, Yellow Springs, Ohio (Gindhart 1973). Table 4 gives the estimated regression parameters.

The Y intercept (b_0 in table 4) is the regression estimate of bone length at birth (age = 0). It should be emphasized that the Arikara estimates were generated from the Moorrees, Fanning, and Hunt ages, and that the Denver and Fels regressions were based on chronological age. The Denver and Fels birth lengths are extrapolations, as measurements in these studies began at two months and one month, respectively. There is considerable variation among groups in estimates of b_0. For all bones, Arikara dc and dm1 estimates for b_0 are

markedly lower than the dm2 estimate, which, in turn, is less than for Denver or Fels.

Variation among estimates will exist to the extent that ages from Moorrees, Fanning, and Hunt depart systematically from chronological ages. Variation among the three Arikara estimates, where dc and dm1 differ from dm2, suggests that Arikara developmental timing differs from the White standards used to assign ages. The lower birth length estimates of Arikara, compared to Denver and Fels, suggest that Arikara dental development is precocious, Arikara children being smaller at given dental stages than White children. Most important, the birth lengths derived from dental age regressions differ markedly from those obtained from the mortality modes.

Table 5 gives Arikara birth length data estimated from Moorrees, Fanning, and Hunt dental age regressions and from the mortality modes. Denver and Fels birth lengths are estimated from chronological age regressions. The British lengths are direct, in utero, radiographic measurements for specific perinatal ages (Russell et al. 1972). These data permit evaluation of the various Arikara estimates.

Arikara birth lengths estimated from the mortality modes agree well with the Denver and Fels regression estimates. The radiographic estimates are somewhat larger than either of these. However, the Arikara estimates based on dental age regressions are unrealistically small. This finding results from precocious dental development schedules in Arikara dentitions relative to Whites.

Table 5. Estimates of Arikara Bone Lengths at Birth Compared to White Estimates

Population/Method	Femur	Tibia	Humerus	Radius
Arikara dc/regression	61.13	56.44	55.94	47.73
Arikara dm1/regression	64.26	58.55	58.04	48.75
Arikara dm2/regression	71.31	63.65	63.01	51.95
Arikara/Mortality mode	77.0	68.5	67.0	56.0
Denver/regression	79.26	64.37	66.05	54.91
Fels/regression	—	69.84	—	53.02
British/radiography[a]				
36 weeks	79.00	67.20	67.90	54.00
37 weeks	80.70	70.20	68.50	55.10
38 weeks	80.10	69.70	70.30	54.80
39 weeks	81.70	72.10	69.60	56.30
40 weeks	84.50	74.30	70.50	56.10
41 weeks	80.90	72.40	70.50	55.70
42 weeks	84.80	73.40	76.90	57.70

[a]Russell et al. (1972).

AGE ADJUSTMENT OF ARIKARA GROWTH CURVES

Figure 2 shows the Arikara fitted growth curves calculated from the quadratic equations given in table 4. The fitted Denver curve is also presented. All four bones yield a consistent pattern that can be described as follows: the dm2 line closely approximates the Denver line, beginning slightly below the Denver line, ultimately crossing it, and ending slightly above it. The dc and dm1 lines also begin below the Denver line but exhibit rapid increase in bone length, ending with bone lengths greater than either dm2 or Denver.

Variation in the shape of the regression lines permits a further inference concerning variation among teeth in development schedules. The shorter bone lengths at birth result from overaging of Arikara infants due to their precocious dental development. Precocious development, particularly in dc and dm1, is also evident for the first six months to one year, where predicted bone lengths for Arikara are below those for Denver, and also those predicted for dm2. However, after about one year, dc and dm1 predicted bone lengths exceed those of Denver children. This unreasonable situation suggests that Arikara dm1 and dc development lags behind Moorrees, Fanning, and Hunt's standards, resulting in underaging of Arikara children.

An assumption becomes necessary to develop more appropriate ages for Arikara dental stages. One of the Arikara teeth must be selected as the one that provides the most realistic model for Arikara long bone growth. As previously noted, dm2 yields a curve that is nearly parallel to that of Denver,

differing mainly in the intercept. Thus the assumption is that Arikara and Denver children exhibit similar growth for the first two years of life. Acceptance of this assumption allows a simple adjustment to Moorrees, Fanning, and Hunt ages that will yield the appropriate length at birth for Arikara long bones. This adjustment is made for dm2 using the femur, as it produces the most clearly defined mortality mode.

The adjustment is obtained by finding the constant that, when subtracted from developmental ages, yields a regression intercept of 77 millimeters, the length at birth of Arikara femora estimated from the mortality distribution. The solution is 0.095 years. This constant was subtracted from each Moorrees, Fanning, and Hunt age and new regressions calculated. Table 6 shows the results. The regression equation estimates of b_1 and b_2 are virtually unchanged, for a constant was subtracted from the age variable. The adjustment was necessary to produce a femur intercept of 77, which has been achieved, within rounding error. Application of the femur-derived age adjustment to the humerus, radius, and tibia yields intercepts that closely approximate the birth lengths estimated from the mortality modes. Thus, if Arikara teeth attained their developmental stages 0.095 years earlier (slightly more than one month), the resulting regression estimates of birth lengths agree with the birth lengths estimated from the perinatal modes.

Figure 3 shows the fitted regression lines for the four long bones using adjusted dm2 ages for Arikara. The Denver regression lines are shown for comparison, and for the tibia and radius, the Fels growth lines are also shown. The Arikara and

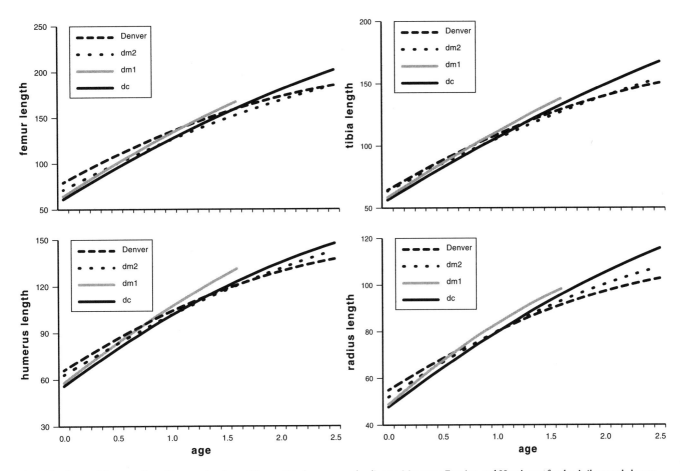

Fig. 2. Fitted second degree polinomial regression lines of femur, tibia, humerus, and radius on Moorrees, Fanning, and Hunt's ages for the Arikara and chronological age for Denver Whites.

Denver fitted lines for the femur are similar, the Arikara being slightly shorter than those for Denver at all ages up to two years, where they are roughly equal. The humerus line for Arikara children surpasses that for Denver children at about 1.5 year of age. The tibia curves for Fels children are consistently above those for Denver children, with the Arikara close to those for Denver. After about 1.5 years, the Arikara have slightly longer bones than the Denver children but shorter bones than those in the Fels sample. The radius curves are similar for all three groups, those for the Arikara being slightly longer than for either White sample.

Using the assumption that dm2 yields the most reasonable growth pattern for Arikara children allows easy adjustment of dm2 ages, which, when used as predictors of bone length, give appropriate birth lengths and a curve similar to those for Denver and Fels children. However, the dc and dm1 ages still produce a regression line that differs markedly from those of dm2, Denver, and Fels. Using the assumption that dm2 ad-

justed ages are accurate models for Arikara growth, it is possible to bring the dc and dm1 ages into line with dm2 ages. This procedure is accomplished algebraically, using the quadratic equation

$$x = [b \pm \sqrt{(b^2 - 4ac)}] / 2a$$

where x = age, b = 59.57 (b_1), a = −6.11 (b_2), and c = 77.03 (b_0) minus the mean bone length per dental stage. The constants are from the adjusted dm2 ages shown in table 6. Solving the

Table 6. Fitted Regression Lines Using dm2 Adjusted Ages

Coefficient	Femur	Tibia	Humerus	Radius
b_0	77.03	67.95	67.06	54.94
b_1	59.57	44.93	42.15	31.12
b_2	−6.11	−3.81	−4.43	−3.83

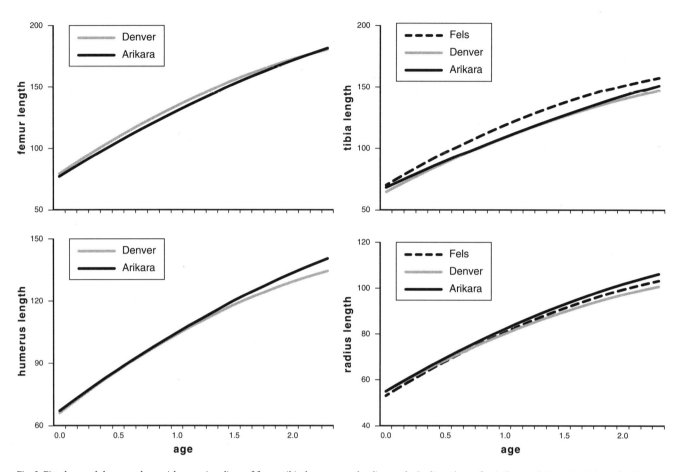

Fig. 3. Fitted second degree polynomial regressions lines of femur, tibia, humerus, and radius on dm2 adjusted ages for Arikara and chronological age for Denver and Fels populations.

equation for each dental stage will yield ages that, when used in the polynomial regression, will model long bone growth identical to dm2. Table 7 presents the new ages and Moorrees, Fanning, and Hunt ages.

The Arikara adjusted ages differ considerably from the Whites' ages. Arikara ages show early precocity, reaching the early stages as much as 0.3 years (3.6 months) sooner than Whites for dc stage 4 (root initial). By the end of their development, however, both dc and dm1 for Arikara are behind Whites' ages by as much as 0.62 years (almost 7.5 months for dc).

Application of the Dental Standard

The adjusted ages reflect both the timing differences of individual teeth and their interrelationships. Data on different teeth should now yield the same age for the same individuals. Age can be derived by assigning each tooth an age from

table 7 and averaging over the number of teeth present, which allows maximization of sample size, because individuals with one, two, or three teeth can be assigned an age. If these age adjustments are accurate, regressions estimated from these ages will have the same parameters as the dm2 regressions shown in table 6. A brief example demonstrates the way that these dental ages can be employed to study growth variation in young children and provides a test of the age adjustments.

Variation in bone length among the three archaeological variants of Extended, Postcontact, and Disorganized Coalescent tradition was examined by means of the comparative research design used previously to evaluate growth variation in Arikara children (Jantz and Owsley 1984). Assignments of sites to variants is the same as in Jantz and Owsley (1984), except for the addition of the Four Bear site (39DW2) to the Disorganized Coalescent. Four Bear represents a period long after contact when the stress of interaction with Europeans was intensifying (see Owsley and Jantz 1985). For arguments

Table 7. Arikara Adjusted Ages Compared to Moorrees, Fanning, and Hunt (1963a, 1963b) Ages for Each Tooth Stage

Tooth	Stage	Arikara	MFH
dc	2	−0.110	0.150
	3	0.030	0.250
	4	0.146	0.450
	5	0.395	0.675
	6	0.606	0.850
	7	—	—
	8	1.097	1.000
	9	1.387	1.275
	10	1.863	1.825
	11	2.097	2.000
	12	3.120	2.500
dm1	2	0.002	0.000
	3	−0.007	0.175
	4	0.040	0.250
	5	0.188	0.400
	6	0.430	0.550
	7	0.585	0.600
	8	0.804	0.700
	9	1.022	0.925
	10	1.146	1.150
	11	1.373	1.125
	12	1.806	1.550
dm2	2	−0.020	0.075
	3	0.155	0.250
	4	0.355	0.450
	5	0.605	0.700
	6	0.805	0.900
	7	0.855	0.950
	8	1.205	1.300
	9	1.430	1.525
	10	1.755	1.850
	11	1.880	1.975
	12	2.305	2.400

for inferring health and nutritional status of Arikara groups assigned to these three variants, see Jantz and Owsley (1984) and Owsley (1985, 1992).

Table 8 gives the least square equations from regressing bone length onto age and age^2 for the total sample and for each variant. Regression parameters for all four bones are similar to those for dm2 (compare with table 6). Minor differences can be accounted for by increased sample sizes. Most important, birth length, as inferred from the *Y* intercept, now agrees well with the estimates of birth length obtained from the mortality modes.

Equations for individual variants show no impressive deviation in slope. The most consistent difference relates to the lower intercept associated with the Disorganized Coalescent. This difference occurs in all bones. The R^2 values are uniformly high, the highest values typically associated with the femur. This approach yields a slight improvement over R^2 values obtained using individual tooth regressions and Moorrees, Fanning, and Hunt's (1963a, 1963b) ages, which range from 0.89–0.93 (Hyman 1987). Individual variants exhibit no marked differences, although the R^2 values associated with the Disorganized Coalescent tend to be higher than those of the other two variants.

Extensive application of this method has yet to be undertaken. Children of the Disorganized Coalescent variant have the shortest bones at birth, and those of the Postcontact Coalescent, the longest. By 1.5 years of age, the children of the Disorganized Coalescent have caught up, and thereafter, little difference among variants occurs. This result would support earlier arguments that the stress of contact had negative consequences for Arikara children, including depressed growth during the prenatal period in the Disorganized Coalescent population (Jantz and Owsley 1984; Owsley and Jantz 1985).

Interpretation

The approach presented here allows modification of Moorrees, Fanning, and Hunt's dental ages in a manner that more closely approximates chronological age in Arikara children. The age adjustments have two effects: all stages of dm2 and the early stages of dc and dm1 are attained earlier by Arikara children than by White children, and the later stages of dc and dm1 are reached later by Arikara than by White children. The results on age obtained with this method suggest that deciduous teeth of Arikara do not develop in relation to one another in the same way as do those of the children used in establishing the White standards.

The age adjustment allowing Arikara children to reach the early development stages sooner than White children is based on an identification of birth length from mortality modes of long bones. The assumption required is that the mortality modes provide a reasonable estimate of bone length at birth. Birth lengths estimated in this manner agree with estimates from samples of White children, and there is no reason to believe that Arikara children begin life significantly smaller than do White children. Data on birth lengths of modern Indian infants is not available, but it is well known that they are heavier at birth than White infants (Adams and Niswander 1973).

Table 8. Polynomial Equations Showing Relationships Between Age and Bone Length

		Total	Disorganized Coalescent	Postcontact Coalescent	Extended Coalescent
Femur	N	402	60	221	120
	b_0	76.709	74.978	77.623	76.301
	b_1	57.700	59.178	57.932	55.752
	b_2	−6.915	−6.964	−7.286	−5.842
	R^2	0.943	0.962	0.945	0.942
Tibia	N	350	48	200	101
	b_0	67.599	67.083	68.324	67.272
	b_1	45.057	42.706	45.070	44.945
	b_2	−5.367	−3.858	−5.738	−4.721
	R^2	0.931	0.951	0.936	0.951
Humerus	N	398	59	226	112
	b_0	67.012	65.460	67.707	66.591
	b_1	41.529	42.574	41.779	39.425
	b_2	−5.394	−5.745	−5.739	−3.692
	R^2	0.939	0.952	0.939	0.937
Radius	N	334	45	192	96
	b_0	55.316	54.015	55.514	54.975
	b_1	30.534	31.153	31.223	29.472
	b_2	−4.513	−4.599	−4.790	−4.059
	R^2	0.933	0.942	0.937	0.947

The second effect of the age adjustments prolongs the developmental period for dc and dm1. The analysis has shown that dc and dm1 have a more extended development than dm2, so an adjustment is required to obtain the same age estimate from different teeth. The assumption here is that dm2, after the initial adjustment described previously, tracks chronological age better than does dm1 or dc. Support for this assumption derives from the close approximation of the dm2 growth curve to that of Denver White children. The adjusted dc and dm1 ages shown in table 7 now yield comparable bone lengths for comparable ages, which they do not when White developmental standards for ages are used.

The main objection that might be raised to this assumption is that no evidence suggests that Arikara children should have the same rate of growth as Denver White children, particularly in the later stages spanning one through three years of age. Most studies comparing archaeological American Indian children to well-nourished White controls find that the long bones of the American Indians are shorter than those of Whites (Johnston 1962; Mensforth et al. 1978; Y'Edynak 1976). These studies use ages based on White dental standards and usually postulate some degree of nutritional or disease stress. The pattern of dental development seen in the Arikara,

if applicable to other American Indian populations, could also explain the early retardation in growth and later recovery observed at Libben site, Ohio (Lovejoy, Russell, and Harrison 1990; Mensforth et al. 1978), or tibia lengths at birth, at Libben and Carlston Annis, Kentucky (Mensforth 1985), that are considerably shorter than those of the Arikara. Lovejoy, Russell, and Harrison (1990) explicitly assume that Libben children and White children are coequal at birth with respect to dental development. They argue that advanced dental development leading to overaging of Libben children is unlikely to explain the early depression of their growth velocity. Results reported here call these assumptions into question.

The assumption that the Arikara exhibit patterns of growth similar to well-nourished White children is supported by the absence of significant evidence for nutritional stress until late in the Postcontact period, after 1780 (Owsley 1992). The indications from recent growth studies suggest that well-nourished American Indian children do not differ markedly from their White counterparts during the first several years (Eveleth and Tanner 1976; Johnston et al. 1978). In earlier populations, Sundick (1978) found that Indian Knoll children showed growth patterns nearly identical to medieval Germans until puberty.

Even if the argument that Arikara growth patterns are similar to those seen in White children is not accepted, the approach outlined here still provides a valuable tool for investigating developmental relationships among teeth. It is obvious that different teeth should give the same age, on average, if the relationships with chronological age are correct. Arikara permanent teeth are characterized by developmental differences that, when White age standards are used, lead to age variation among teeth. Results show that dc and dm1 are delayed relative to dm2. Even though the sequence of developmental events may be nearly identical in Whites and Indians, as Scuilli (1990) has argued for Late Archaic skeletons from Ohio, the absolute times separating different events could differ substantially from those of Whites. Using Moorrees, Fanning, and Hunt's ages, one observes, for example, that dc and dm2 reach stage 12 at about the same age. Using Arikara adjusted ages, dm2 stage 12 is attained at 0.8 years before dc stage 12. Whatever the actual ages at which these stages are reached in the Arikara, it will always be necessary for dc to reach stage 12 later than dm2.

Application of this method to determination of age of children's skeletons provides a more objective measure than has often been the case. The method is explicit and does not involve subjective weighting of different teeth. Different investigators will arrive at the same ages for the same developmental stages; therefore, this method can provide a basis for assessing growth performance in small samples such as the one studied by Tiffany et al. (1988).

The principal problem at this stage is the limitation to three deciduous teeth. It should be possible to add early-forming permanent teeth, such as the first molar (M1), as there is considerable overlap in developmental schedules. However, the farther from the relatively reliable relationship between dental maturity and bone length established at birth, the more conjectural the exercise becomes. One could adjust M1 to the deciduous dental standard employed here during the common period of development, but extrapolating to later stages of M1 development would require further assumptions about growth in size beyond three years of age. Sampling also becomes more difficult as probability of death diminishes from infancy to late childhood.

References Cited

Adams, M.S., and J.D. Niswander
   1973 Birth Weight of North American Indians: A Correction and Amplification. *Human Biology* 45:351–358.

Dahlberg, A.A., and R.M. Menegaz-Bock
   1958 Emergence of the Permanent Teeth in Pima Indian Children: A Critical Analysis of Method and an Estimate of Population Parameters. *Journal of Dental Research* 35:1123–1140.

Eveleth, P.B., and J.M. Tanner
   1976 Worldwide Variation in Human Growth. Cambridge: Cambridge University Press.

Gindhart, P.S.
   1973 Growth Standards for the Tibia and Radius in Children Aged One Month Through Eighteen Years. *American Journal of Physical Anthropology* 39:41–48.

Hyman, S.A.
   1987 The Relationship Between Dental Age and Long Bone Growth in Arikara Infants. (Master's Thesis in Anthropology, University of Tennessee, Knoxville.)

Jantz, R.L., and D.W. Owsley
   1984 Long Bone Growth Variation Among Arikara Skeletal Populations. *American Journal of Physical Anthropology* 63:13–20.

——
   1985 Patterns of Infant and Early Childhood Mortality in Arikara Skeletal Populations. Pp. 209–213 in Status, Structure and Stratification, Proceedings of the Sixteenth Annual Conference, Chacmool, The Archaeological Association of the University of Calgary. M. Thompson, M.T. Garcia, and F.J. Kense, eds. Calgary, Alberta: University of Calgary.

Johnston, F.E.
   1962 Growth of the Long Bones of Infants and Young Children at Indian Knoll. *American Journal of Physical Anthropology* 20:249–254.

——
   1968 Growth of the Skeleton in Earlier Peoples. Pp. 57–66 in The Skeletal Biology of Earlier Human Populations. D.R. Brothwell, ed. *Symposia for the Study of Human Biology* 8.

——, J.I. McKigney, S. Hopwood, and J. Smelker
   1978 Physical Growth and Development of Urban Native Americans: A Study in Urbanization and Its Implications for Nutritional Status. *American Journal of Clinical Nutrition* 31:1017–1027.

Lovejoy, C.O., K.F. Russell, and M.L. Harrison
   1990 Long Bone Growth Velocity in the Libben Population. *American Journal of Human Biology* 2:533–541.

Maresh, M.M.
   1970 Measurements from Roentgenograms, Heart Size, Long Bone Lengths, Bone, Muscle and Fat Widths, Skeletal Maturation. Pp. 155–200 in Human Growth and Development, by R.W. McCammon. Springfield, Ill.: Charles C. Thomas.

Mensforth, R.P.
   1985 Relative Tibia Long Bone Growth in the Libben and Bt-5 Prehistoric Skeletal Populations. *American Journal of Physical Anthropology* 68:247–262.

——, C.O. Lovejoy, J.W. Lallo, and G.J. Armelagos

1978   The Role of Constitutional Factors, Diet and Infectious Disease in the Etiology of Porotic Hyperostosis and Periosteal Reactions in Prehistoric Infants and Children. *Medical Anthropology* 2:1–59.

Merchant, V.L., and D.H. Ubelaker

1977   Skeletal Growth of the Protohistoric Arikara. *American Journal of Physical Anthropology* 46:61–72.

Moorrees, C.F.A.

1957   The Aleut Dentition. Cambridge, Mass.: Harvard University Press.

——, E.A. Fanning, and E.E. Hunt

1963a Age Variation of Formation Stages for Ten Permanent Teeth. *Journal of Dental Research* 42(6):1490–1502.

1963b Formation and Resorption of Three Deciduous Teeth in Children. *American Journal of Physical Anthropology* 21:205–213.

Owsley, D.W.

1985   Postcontact Period Nutritional Status and Cortical Bone Thickness of South Dakota Indians. Pp. 199–207 in Status, Structure and Stratification, Proceedings of the Sixteenth Annual Conference of the Archaeological Association of the University of Calgary. M. Thompson, M.T. Garcia, and F.J. Kense, eds. Calgary, Alberta: University of Calgary.

1992   Temporal Variation in Femoral Cortical Thickness of North American Plains Indians. Pp. 105–110 in Human Paleopathology: Current Syntheses and Future Options. D.J. Ortner and A.C. Aufderheide, eds. Washington: Smithsonian Institution Press.

Owsley, D.W., and R.L. Jantz

1983a Formation of the Permanent Dentition in Arikara Indians: Timing Differences That Affect Dental Age Assessments. *American Journal of Physical Anthropology* 61:467–471.

1983b Developmental Timing of the Deciduous Dentition in American Indians. (Paper presented at the 35th Annual Meeting of the American Academy of Forensic Aciences, Cincinnati, Ohio.)

——

1985   Long Bone Lengths and Gestational Age Distributions of Post-contact Period Arikara Indian Perinatal Infant Skeletons. *American Journal of Physical Anthropology* 68:321–328.

Russell, J.G.B., A.E. Mattison, W.T. Easson, D. Clark, T. Sharp, and J. McGough

1972   Skeletal Dimensions as an Indication of Foetal Maturity. *British Journal of Radiology* 45:667–669.

Schour, I., and M. Massler

1944   *Development of the Human Dentition*. 2nd ed. Chicago: American Dental Association.

Sciulli, P.W.

1990   Deciduous Dentition of a Late Archaic Population of Ohio. *Human Biology* 62:221–245.

Stewart, T.D.

1979   Essentials of Forensic Anthropology. Springfield, Ill.: Charles C. Thomas.

Sundick, R.I.

1978   Human Skeletal Growth and Age Determination. *Homo* 29:228–249.

Tiffany, J.A., S.J. Schermer, J.L. Theler, D.W. Owsley, D.C. Anderson, E.A. Bettis, and D.M. Thompson

1988   The Hanging Valley Site. *Plains Anthropologist* 33(120):219–259.

Trodden, B.J.

1982   A Radiographic Study of the Calcification and Eruption of the Permanent Teeth in Inuit and Indian Children. *Archaeological Survey of Canada, National Museum of Man, Mercury Series.* Paper No. 112. Ottawa.

Ubelaker, D.H.

1989   Human Skeletal Remains: Excavation, Analysis, Interpretation. 2nd ed. Chicago: Aldine.

Y'Edynak, G.

1976   Long Bone Growth in Western Eskimo and Aleut Skeletons. *American Journal of Physical Anthropology* 45(3):569–574.

ooo

Subsistence Strategies and Dietary Assessments

CHAPTER 21

○○○

Stable Isotopes on the Plains: Vegetation Analyses and Diet Determinations

LARRY L. TIESZEN

Ratios of the natural abundances of stable isotopes have great value for geochemical and other physical science investigations. Bender (1968) noticed a systematic relationship between photosynthetic reduction pathways (C_3 and C_4 systems) and the stable isotopic ratios of carbon in grasses. This predictive relationship, and the realization that the ratios labeled the organic matter and, therefore, could be exploited as natural and quantitative tracers, stimulated totally new approaches to both ecological and archaeological research. These new approaches have been most useful in paleoecological research, plant physiological ecology, climatic interpretations, and dietary reconstructions for humans and other animals.

This review summarizes what is known about the ecology of stable isotopes in the Great Plains. The assumption is that stable isotopic approaches can be used to explore current questions and hypotheses in Great Plains archaeology and paleoecology. Questions about the integral roles of diet and climate in cultural change have long been of interest to archaeologists. Among the principal topics for research are: dietary dependence on bison; the role of migratory versus residential herds; relationships among climatic change, change

in vegetation, and subsistence; specific time of the origin of agricultural dependency; quantitative dependence on maize horticulture; and the impact of dependence on maize horticulture on subsistence strategies in the Great Plains. The application of stable isotopic approaches will help to refine understanding of these relationships and to interpret cultural change in this region.

Several elements exist in stable isotopic forms (see Ehleringer and Rundel 1989), five of which are of principal use for archaeological and environmental reconstructions (table 1). Oxygen and hydrogen ratios provide information about the terrestrial moisture status of continental areas, but they are outside the scope of this paper. Sulfur is frequently used to distinguish terrestrial from aquatic, especially marine, food sources, as these signals are often distinctive. In special cases, sulfur is also used in tracing food webs in complex aquatic systems. Sulfur analyses generally require significant amounts of hair, keratin, or other sulfur-rich material. Because skeletal remains are low in sulphur, they are rarely useful in archaeological reconstructions. Thus, in the Great Plains, nitrogen and carbon have the broadest application. As more is known about carbon, this review focuses on the use of natural abundances

Table 1. Forms of Stable Isotopes Used in Archaeological and Environmental Research

Element	Stable Isotopes	Molecule Measured
Carbon	^{13}C, ^{12}C	CO_2
Nitrogen	^{15}N, ^{14}N	N_2
Sulfur	^{34}S, ^{32}S	SO_2
Oxygen	^{18}O, ^{16}O	CO_2
Hydrogen	^{2}H, ^{1}H	H_2

of carbon for climatic and archaeological interpretations in Plains grasslands.

The grasslands of the world represent one of the most widespread natural vegetation systems, accounting for about 25 percent of the natural land surface (Shantz 1954; Tieszen and Detling 1983). The existing systems account for about 16 percent of net annual primary production of vegetation. Although grasslands can be developed and maintained as successional communities by burning, grazing, mowing, or other agricultural practices, the geographical distribution of most of the world's grasslands is controlled primarily by climate. Grasslands occur in areas having one or more periods during the year when availability of water declines below that needed for forests, but they receive sufficient precipitation to maintain graminoids as the dominant or codominant life form.

In North America, the grasslands of the Great Plains extend from south-central Texas north to southern Manitoba and central Alberta. Although there is a substantial replacement of species along this broad latitudinal distribution, the grasslands maintain three recognizable, although arbitrary, growth forms. The higher precipitation along the eastern margin of the grassland supports the Tallgrass Prairie (dominants from 1 to 1.5 m tall), a productive system in which precipitation of 60–90 centimeters usually exceeds evaporation. Little of this component remains today, for it has been displaced by managed agricultural systems. The Shortgrass Prairie (dominants from <0.5 m tall) is distributed along the dry west side where precipitation is far less than evaporation and results in a common cessation of growth in midsummer when the system becomes parched. The Mixed-grass Prairie occupies the intermediate zones and includes a broad belt covering most of the Dakotas, Nebraska, and Kansas and extending south into Texas. Local topographic and soil features often cause a mosaic pattern of these grassland types in any given area. Primary production of vegetation is largely controlled by available

moisture and varies markedly from near 600 grams per square meter in the east to < 150 g/m^2 in the Shortgrass Prairie of the west (Sala et al. 1988).

Grasslands are of special interest because the two families (Poaceae and Cyperaceae) that often dominate the vegetation have the highest frequencies of C_4 species. In fact, some 50 percent of the species in each family are of the C_4 photosynthetic type. Because graminoid-dominated terrestrial systems occur across the broad temperature range from equatorial tropics to polar tundras, physiological differences in C_3 and C_4 plants become especially significant.

Carbon Isotope Fractionation

Carbon exists in nature in several isotopic forms that differ only in the number of neutrons they possess. The stable (nonradioactive) forms, ^{13}C and ^{12}C, are particularly relevant to research on vegetation and diet: ^{12}C is the most abundant, representing nearly 99 percent of the earth's carbon; ^{13}C forms most of the remainder. The ratio of ^{13}C to ^{12}C is used to express differences in abundances. This ratio is measured with an isotope ratio mass spectrometer in which the ratios of the two masses of a sample are compared to a standard and are expressed as a delta ^{13}C value in units of ‰.

$$\delta^{13}C = \frac{^{13}C/^{12}C_{sample} - {^{13}C/^{12}C_{standard}}}{^{13}C/^{12}C_{standard}} \times 10^3 ‰ \qquad (1)$$

A carbonate sample, Pee Dee Formation, from South Carolina is the accepted standard. Most naturally occurring carbon is depleted in ^{13}C relative to this standard. Carbon dioxide (CO_2) in air, for example, is about $-8.0‰$; however, this value is changing in the modern atmosphere because of anthropogenic factors.

It has been known (Nier and Gulbransen 1939) that ^{13}C is depleted in plants relative to carbonates and air, and the mechanism accounting for fractionation during CO_2 uptake and reduction is now understood (Farquhar 1980; Farquhar, O'Leary, and Berry 1982; O'Leary 1981; Vogel 1980). Discrimination among isotopes could occur during any of the processes illustrated in figure 1 for a C_3 plant. Farquhar has formalized the control by the following relationship, which emphasizes the relatively small fractionation associated with diffusion and the potentially large discrimination caused by Rubisco, the carboxylating enzyme in C_3 plants.

$$\delta^{13}C_{pl} = \delta^{13}C_{air} - a - (b - a) \, C_i/C_a \qquad (2)$$

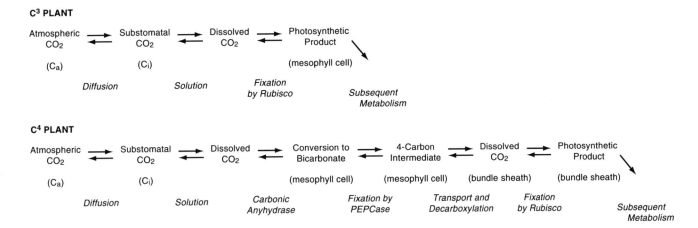

Fig. 1. Pathway of carbon dioxide from bulk air to fixed organic molecules in C_3 and C_4 species. Note the similar components in the pathways and the addition of fixation by PEPCase from bicarbonate in C_4 plants. The four-carbon product is then transferred to the bundle sheath cell and decarboxylated. Rubisco now fixes the CO_2 from a relatively closed pool of CO_2, more or less effectively negating any additional fractionation by Rubisco.

where:

pl   = plant
a = fractionation associated with diffusion 4.4‰
b = fractionation by Rubisco to excess CO_2 = ca. 28‰
C_i = internal leaf CO_2 concentration
C_a = air CO_2 concentration
$\delta^{13}C_{air}$ = isotopic value of air (bulk atmosphere) = −8.0‰.

Plants that take up CO_2 by the C_4 mechanism discriminate less in part because phosphoenolpyruvate (PEP) carboxylase takes up bicarbonate and produces 4-carbon molecules that deliver CO_2 to a closed pool inside the parenchymatous bundle sheath (PBS) cells, thereby preventing further fractionation by RuBP carboxylase. Other complications of fractionation in C_4 are addressed by Farquhar (1983; Farquhar, Ehleringer, and Hubick 1989) and O'Leary (1988). In addition to stomatal and enzymatic components, dissolution and hydration of CO_2 and CO_2 leakage from PBS cells are important. The model to explain isotopic values in C_4 plants is

$$\delta^{13}C_{pl} = \delta^{13}C_{air} - a - (b4 + b3 \varnothing - a)\, C_i/C_a \qquad (3)$$

where:

b4   = the net fractionation associated with PEP carboxylation (−5.7‰)
b3   = the actual fractionation by Rubisco carboxylation (30‰)

$\varnothing$ = the fraction of carbon fixed by PEP carboxylase, which leaks out of the bundle sheath.

In essence, the delta value will be less sensitive to C_i/C_a than in C_3 plants. Furthermore, $\delta^{13}C$ values should become more negative with water stress or other environmental factors that reduce C_i instead of less negative as in C_3 plants. The field data (O'Leary 1988; Tieszen and Boutton 1989) show less variation in C_4 plants but also show significant genetic variation from species to species (Hesla, Tieszen, and Imbamba 1982).

It is obvious that the $\delta^{13}C$ values will be largely a function of the photosynthetic pathway, although they may also be sensitive to any environmental factors that affect the parameters indicated in equation (3). The principal factor controlling ^{13}C depletion is the photosynthetic pathway (e.g., Smith and Epstein 1971). Consequently, bimodal distributions of ^{13}C values result and group around generally accepted mean values between −26 and −28‰ for C_3 plants and −12 and −14‰ for C_4 plants. These values vary as a direct function of the ambient $\delta^{13}C$ value for CO_2, which is normally around −8‰ (for discussion, see O'Leary 1981). Respiratory release of CO_2 (from ^{13}C-depleted organic matter) lowers this ambient value. On a global scale, the reduction is small but significant (Keeling, Mook, and Tans 1979). When free mixing with the atmosphere is restricted, as in growth chambers, greenhouses, or closed canopy understories, ambient CO_2 can become depleted in ^{13}C, resulting in more negative values for both C_3 and C_4 plants.

Thus, two broad patterns of fractionation associated with the photosynthetic types have been identified, although the specific values can be modified slightly by both genetic and environmental components. The field verification of these broad patterns has provided a powerful research approach that is increasing fundamental understanding of ecology, especially in grassland systems. There are several reasons for the effectiveness of this approach. First, the particular ratio or delta values can serve as a label and can be transmitted to herbivore- or detritivore-based trophic levels, making possible the assessment of the quantitative contributions of C_3 and C_4 plants to herbivores and carnivores, as well as to below-ground consumers. Furthermore, the direct assessment of the assimilation of energy by animals and the determination of the source of soil organic matter (SOM) are now possible. Second, isotopic ratios accumulate over time as normal constituents of carbon skeletons, thereby providing time-integrated estimates of various processes. These estimates include "life-time" assessments of assimilation, long-term accumulation of SOM, and the degree of chronic water stress in C_3 plants. Third, the label can be preserved in organic materials that are often resistant to diagenetic change. Therefore, it is possible to use this approach for short-term, historical, and paleoecological assessments.

Determinants of Isotopic Discrimination

VARIATION IN THE ATMOSPHERIC VALUE

As noted in equation (2), the $\delta^{13}C_{pl}$ value is a direct function of the $\delta^{13}C_{air}$. This atmospheric value varies in predictable ways, and this variation must be recognized when using carbon isotope values to estimate diets. The most obvious source of current variation is respiratory release of CO_2 (from ^{13}C-depleted organic matter) in systems that do not mix freely with the atmosphere. When free mixing is restricted, as in closed canopy understories, ambient CO_2 can become depleted in ^{13}C, resulting in higher negative values for both C_3 and C_4 plants. The magnitude of this $\delta^{13}C$ profile in closed forest canopies can be as great as 8‰ (air = −16‰) and can account for plant values as negative as −36‰ (Medina et al. 1986; van der Merwe and Medina 1989). This depletion and its transmission to other trophic levels must be taken into account in any assessment of diet for forest-dwelling hunters, gatherers, and horticulturists. This problem is minimal in the Great Plains because of the short grass canopy, but the potential change of this value in closed forest should be understood.

Over geological and historical time, $\delta^{13}C_{air}$ has not been constant (Chisholm 1989). The anthropogenic addition of CO_2 into the atmosphere has depleted atmospheric CO_2 of ^{13}C, largely as a result of the combustion of fossil fuels ($\delta^{13}C$ ca. −28‰), and enhanced decomposition associated with agriculture and deforestation. The ice core data on CO_2 (Friedli et al. 1986) for Antarctica show a preindustrial (before A.D. 150) CO_2 concentration of about 280 ppm and a $\delta^{13}C$ value of −6.45‰. This value is in reasonable agreement with the trend derived from tree ring data (Keeling, Mook, and Tans 1979) showing $\delta^{13}C$ becoming more negative by 0.69‰ in the 22 years between 1955 and 1977. With a conservative estimate for today's value at −8.0‰ and for pre-1800 CO_2 at −6.49‰, significant adjustments are necessary for making dietary estimates. This anthropogenic alteration of atmospheric CO_2 makes the reconstruction of past diets and other paleoecological interpretations based on carbon isotopes more difficult, as each 1‰ change in an end member whose span is 15‰ represents an error of nearly 6.5 percent in any reconstruction. At this time it appears that carbon fixed during the Holocene and before 1800 is about 1.5‰ more positive than modern values. This is in general agreement with Marino and McElroy (1991).

This anthropogenic effect helps explain the positive values that have been reported for human material and maize in North America. Wagner (1988) lists several sites with maize values between −8.7 and −9.3‰, and the review of maize data (Tieszen and Fagre 1993a) shows similarly positive values in archaeological samples from Chile and the United States. Because simulated charring confirms the absence of a carbonization effect (Marino and DeNiro 1987) and similar biochemical variation is shown in archaeological and modern specimens, the positive archaeological maize was in fact no more positive than modern maize once adjusted for the anthropogenic effect. The comparison (Tieszen and Fagre 1993a) did show genetic variation in maize but established that there was no difference among the mean values of dent, flint, flour, and other types (table 2). Modern maize averaged −11.2 ± .03‰ in the Great Plains, −11.0 ± .07‰ in Mexico, and −10.7 ± .02‰ in Florida, overlapping the −9.3‰ to −11.1‰ range reported initially by Lowdon (1969) for maize in Canada. Primitive varieties collected from Plains Indians and grown under modern conditions (M. Scullin, personal communication 1990) possess isotopic values similar to modern maize.

REVIEW OF ENVIRONMENTAL SENSITIVITY

Several components of equation (2) are potentially sensitive to environmental factors, and they might also be subject to genetic variation and selection. Thus, both environmental effects within species and genetically based differences among

Table 2. Carbon Isotopic Comparison of Maize Types

Seed Type	Mean	Standard Error
CIMMYT[a]		
Dent	−10.96	0.138
Flint	−11.13	0.075
Flour	−10.61	0.198
Goodman[b]		
Dent	−10.64	0.073
Flint	−10.71	0.041
Flour	−10.70	0.239

[a]From the collections of Centro Internacional de Mejoramiento de Maiz y Trigo grown in Mexico.

[b]From the collections of Goodman grown in Florida.

species can be expected. To what extent are these known, and to what extent does this potential variation in the isotopic signal affect archaeological interpretations? The major environmental factors affecting carbon isotopic values in C_3 plants are summarized in table 3, based on Tieszen (1991). The value for "a" should be a physical constant independent of environmental effects or selection pressure. Less certain are the enzymatic components that determine the magnitude of "b"; however, there appears to be little variation of this value in higher plants. Thus, it is the C_i/C_a ratio that is important in determining the variation in $\delta^{13}C$ of C_3 plants.

Table 3. Important Environmental Factors That Affect Carbon Isotopic Values in C_3 Plants and Maximum Expected Range from Generalized Mean for These Plants[a]

Environmental Context	Maximum Range of ^{13}C Value	Ecological Context
Recycling respired CO_2	8	Dense and closed canopies
Reduced light	5 to 6	Dense and closed canopies
Increased water stress	3 to 6	Open and arid environments
Increased osmotic stress	5 to 10	Osmotically impacted areas

[a]The effect of most of these environmental factors will result in slight departures from the plant's mean value. These ranges estimate maxima under extreme situations. Temperature, inorganic nutrient supply, CO_2 partial pressure, and other factors will also affect carbon isotope values (Tieszen and Archer 1990).

The C_i/C_a ratio is largely a function of C_i, for C_a is generally constant in natural systems that mix freely with the atmosphere. C_i, then, is determined principally by the relative importance of diffusional and enzymatic control over the photosynthetic rate. Diffusional control is modulated by factors that affect stomatal opening, including light, water stress, and C_i itself. The in-situ enzymatic activity is also modulated by irradiance, nutrient status, and temperature, among other factors. The data in table 3 describe the potential size of these factors and the most likely mechanism for changing C_i. It is important that archaeologists recognize that variations in isotopic values in source plants can be as large as 5 to 10‰ but will probably vary less in nature, perhaps as little as 2‰. Water stress is likely to account for most of the environmentally induced variation in natural systems, especially in the Great Plains.

Sources of Variation in Carbon Isotopic Composition

LATITUDINAL AND ALTITUDINAL GRADIENTS

In addition to the effect of specific environmental factors on discrimination within individual plants, it is important to know that C_3 and C_4 species are not distributed at random in the Great Plains. These distributions determine the menus available for any localized group. In the grassland biome, many grasses are C_4, and the isotopic values in bison should reflect the mixture of C_3 and C_4 species in their habitat.

Temperature is the main factor controlling the distribution of C_3 and C_4 species. C_3 species increase in the flora with either an increase in altitude or latitude (Terri and Stowe 1976; Tieszen et al. 1979). At low altitudes in the tropics (for example, Kenya), all grasses in open savannas are C_4 and nearly all shrubs and trees are C_3. Above 1,800 meters, C_4 grasses begin to be replaced by C_3 grasses and at 3,000 meters all species are C_3. Boutton, Harrison, and Smith (1980) show a similar change with altitude in southeast Wyoming. The most striking pattern in the Great Plains is the increase in C_3 presence with an increase in latitude. The floristic data (Terri and Stowe 1976) show 68 to 82 percent C_4 species in the southwest and south Texas, 35 percent in South Dakota, and decreasing composition into Canada. The floristic composition predicted by Terri's regressions is nearly identical to the actual composition, 36 percent determined at the Ordway Prairie in northern South Dakota (Ode, Tieszen, and Lerman 1980). The distribution of C_3 and C_4 species in the sedge family is not so clearly established. All members of the genus

Carex should be C_3 regardless of latitude (Hesla, Tieszen, and Imbamba 1982). However, Cyperus, common in moist and warm habitats but not in uplands, could be either C_3 or C_4.

Generalist consumers of grass biomass should show a modern isotopic signal that reflects these mixtures of C_3 and C_4 species. However, it should be recognized that the broad floristic composition does not necessarily have to reflect the actual biomass production at any site. The carbon isotope values of the soil organic matter and soil carbonates along this broad transect (Cerling et al. 1989) correspond with the expected floristic composition, thereby suggesting that the floristic data show promise of predicting biomass amounts.

Because the latitudinal composition of the grasslands in the Great Plains is largely controlled by temperature, there is no certainty that the modern distribution existed at any time during the Holocene. In fact, vegetation values at any specific geographic location probably varied as temperatures during the Holocene varied. In South Dakota, for example, values should have been more negative during cold periods of the Holocene reflecting a higher percentage C3 species, and more positive during hotter periods when the percentage of C3 species was lower. This temporal variation again complicates the potential isotopic signal available to humans through bison and other herbivores.

SEASONALITY

Because temperature has a pronounced effect on the distribution of C_3 and C_4 grasses, and because a large part of the Great Plains has a mixed flora of these two types, it is likely that the grasslands would show a seasonal displacement in the growth and production of these two types. This seasonal displacement of activity has been observed and quantified in the Ordway Prairie in northern South Dakota (Ode, Tieszen, and Lerman 1980). In this part of the Great Plains, the productive growing season for native grasses extends from the beginning of April until the end of October. In early spring and late fall, all the biomass produced has a C_3 carbon isotopic signal of about −26‰. As summer develops, the proportion of C_3 biomass in the vegetation decreases, and the proportion of C_4 signal increases until the July-August period, when the signal approaches −20‰, roughly 50 percent C_3 and 50 percent C_4 in upland communities. The response pattern is similar in lowland communities, but the contribution of C_4 species is much less.

Large mobile herbivores can use a large number of community types. Studies document the extent of variation in carbon isotopic signals among different communities and the relationship of this array to the feeding behavior and isotopic signals incorporated in free-ranging herbivores. Figure 2 describes the areal extents of different communities at Wind Cave National Park, South Dakota, and the integrated isotopic signal available to herbivores throughout an entire year.

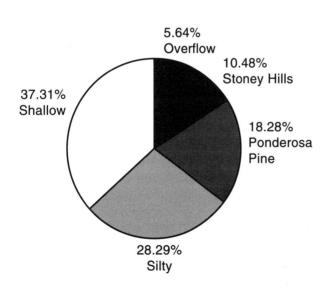

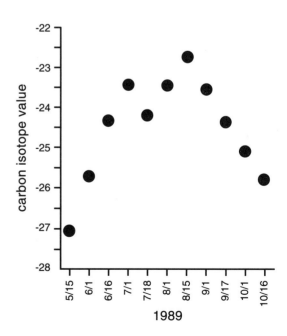

Fig. 2. Areal composition of the five main community types at Wind Cave National Park, S.Dak., and the estimated seasonal isotopic composition of the grass biomass available to grazers. (From Tieszen et al. 1988.)

These communities vary in their production as well as their composition. Overflow and silty communities are highly productive and show little contribution of C_4 biomass. Nevertheless, the weighted averages for carbon isotopic signals show a pattern similar to that described for Ordway. Bison, or other herbivores, have access to C_4 signals for a short time during the growing season. During the rest of the year only C_3 green biomass is available. A similar seasonally changing signal is likely throughout the region of major overlap, with the contribution of C_4 forms diminishing to the north, and that of C_3 forms to the south.

Nearly six months of the year are too cold to be productive in much of the Great Plains, with significant consequences for all herbivores (Speth and Spielmann 1983). The alternatives available to them include subsistence on the remaining low levels and, probably, low quality of biomass, or migration to an area that provides better resources, probably to the south. The extent of long-distance migration by herbivores, especially among bison, is the subject of debate (Chisholm et al. 1986; Epp 1988; Hanson 1984). Bison can survive winter periods in the Northern Great Plains but often do so with considerable weight loss. Bison tissues would reflect the isotopic signals available during assimilation of secondary biomass instead of a simple integration of the yearly average available in their range. Presumably, isotopic signals are only transferred when ingested biomass is used in assimilation not simply for maintenance.

TOPOGRAPHIC AND SOIL EFFECTS

In addition to changes in community composition with latitude and altitude, similar changes occur with soil types and topographic position. In north-central South Dakota, for example, the composition of the prairie changes from the wetter lowlands to the drier uplands. At Ordway Prairie (fig. 3), communities in the lowlands are dominated by C_3 species, with few C_4 species present. The prairie communities on the drier south-facing hillsides and hilltops, however, have more C_4 species. These mesoscale distributions are most clearly related to moisture availability, with C_4 plants most common where moisture stress is greatest. This pattern is typical of both the Great Plains (Barnes, Tieszen, and Ode 1983; Ode, Tieszen, and Lerman 1980) and tropical grasslands at intermediate altitudes where C_3 and C_4 plants coexist.

In the Great Plains, localized salinity can lead to water stress conditions in which C_4 plants, for example, *Spartina pectinata* and *S. gracilis, Distichlis spicata,* and Muhlenbergia sp., often

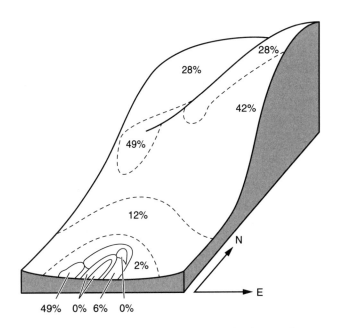

Fig. 3. Generalized representation of the distribution of C_4 biomass, showing percentages, in a mixed prairie in Ordway Prairie, S.Dak. as related to topographic position. (Adapted from Barnes, Tieszen, and Ode 1983.)

dominate. Areas of substantial water evaporation and apparent withdrawal of moisture from the nearby lowlands are, therefore, characterized by large saline areas dominated by these species and zones of C_4 plants next to the edges of wetlands and ephemeral ponds. Where salt stress is not great, all species in the wetter lowland areas (wetlands) are likely to be C_3, including the common grasses, Scolochloa, Phragmites, Calamagrostis, Hierochloe, and other plants such as cattails, rushes, and most sedges.

FOREST PRAIRIE COMPARISONS

Although C_4 photosynthesis is highly polyphyletic and is present in at least 17 families, there are only two families in which C_4 species are as common as C_3 species: the grass family and the sedge family. C_3 plants have higher quantum yields than C_4 plants; therefore, C_3 plants tend to outcompete C_4 plants whenever light is limiting, as happens in ecological systems with well-developed canopies. The C_4 syndrome is essentially absent from tree growth forms, except some unusual species of Euphorbia and a few species from a salt-affected area of Asia. Few shrubs and forbs are C_4, especially in the Great Plains grasslands. Thus, to the extent that the Great Plains consist of grasslands with margins of woodlands or forests, and to the extent that scattered forested areas occur within the grasslands, consumers would have access to a C_3 dominated system or a grassland with a mixture of C_3 or C_4

species. With the exception of some species of Muhlenbergia, all species in forested areas will probably be C_3 and have very negative signals. These negative values will characterize all gathered plants, as well as herbivores feeding there, or any plants that might be under a closed canopy. Furthermore, the relative scarcity of C_4 forbs and shrubs in the prairies means that most nongrass foods gathered in grassland systems will also have C_3 isotopic ratios, although perhaps a few per mil more positive than forest species. Similarly, prairie browsers might have C_3 signals as opposed to grazers, which would reflect the mixture of C_3 and C_4 grasses.

In desert areas more of these growth forms will possess C_4 photosynthesis. The other growth form that could be common and that could change the isotopic signal available to consumers is the one associated with CAM (crassulacean acid metabolism) plants. These plants are nearly always associated with a succulent growth form typified by cacti. Thus, in the drier areas of the Great Plains, and even to a significant extent in the Tallgrass prairie, these species will be present. Although they will rarely contribute large amounts of biomass in any grassland system, they are significant because they were often consumed directly by humans. Their isotopic ratios are generally similar to C_4 species. Some species, however, are facultative CAM plants, and when moisture is adequate and other conditions are appropriate, the signal can reflect a C_3 pattern of CO_2 uptake.

Intraspecific Variation in Isotopic Composition

VARIATION ALONG TOPOGRAPHIC AND MOISTURE GRADIENTS

Water stress results in some stomatal closure that, with irradiance still high, results in reduced C_i/C_a ratios and decreased discrimination against ^{13}C. The $\delta^{13}C$ value becomes more positive. Among 30 cultivars of wheatgrass, a common genus in the Northern and Eastern Great Plains, delta values can range as much as 6‰ (Johnson et al. 1990). As water availability often limits plant growth, substantial variation is likely across the range of mesic to xeric habitats, as shown for desert regions (Ehleringer and Cooper 1988) where plants from presumed drier habitats had the highest positive values. Plants from the driest habitats had isotopic values of −24.4; those from the wetter topographic positions reflected higher C_i/C_a ratios and had a delta value of −26.6‰. Data from the Great Plains are rare; however, comparative studies between the Northern Great Plains and Inner Mongolia, China, show a similar pattern.

Tieszen and Bingyu (1990) sampled fully expanded leaves of five dicotyledons and five grasses throughout one growing season. All species showed large variation in the stable isotopic value throughout the season yet strong consistency within duplicates (fig. 4). The four C_3 grasses had a similar seasonal pattern, with the greatest depletion (most negative values) in early spring. Leaves then became more positive and attained the highest values between July 18 and August 15, after which they again became more negative. The four dicots differed from the grasses by showing less variation, around 2‰, but a similar seasonal pattern. At Makoce Washte, eastern South Dakota, all species were sampled along three transects that traversed wetland, low prairie, slopes, and upland prairie. Mature leaves were sampled in late June and again during the second week in August. The results demonstrate a topographic (moisture) effect similar to that shown in desert areas (fig. 5). C_3 plants ranged from the most negative value of −27.0‰ at the wetland habitat to −26.3‰ on the upland. In August, the pattern was identical with a range from −26.4‰ to −27.5‰. Statistical analysis using analysis of variance showed that position was significant ($p < .0001$), time of season was not; there were no significant differences between grasses and forbs. Among the C_4 plants, position, plant type, or time of season did not make a significant difference. Thus, in these prairies, species carbon isotope values are likely to vary about 1‰ across topographic positions and probably will be accompanied also by seasonal variation within given C_3 species that could be nearly 2 or 3‰. This variation is probably associated with the greater development of water stress during midsummer because of limited soil water availability and high atmospheric demand. High irradiance, as well, would contribute to slightly more positive values.

The relationship between water stress and decreased fractionation has potential application for paleoclimatological reconstructions. If carbon fixed during a prolonged drought period is preserved, it should retain the isotopic signature reflecting that period of low C_i/C_a. Tree rings were sampled from several oak trees along the eastern fringes of the prairie (Sioux Falls, South Dakota). Figure 6 plots the mean ring widths and isotope values from 1989 to 1930. Both show marked changes during the dry years of the 1930s, and the regression relating width to isotopic value is strong. Although there are problems associated with tree ring analyses (Francey and Farquhar 1982; Francey and Hubick 1988), it should be possible to gain information about moisture status from wood or other carbon fragments associated with human sites.

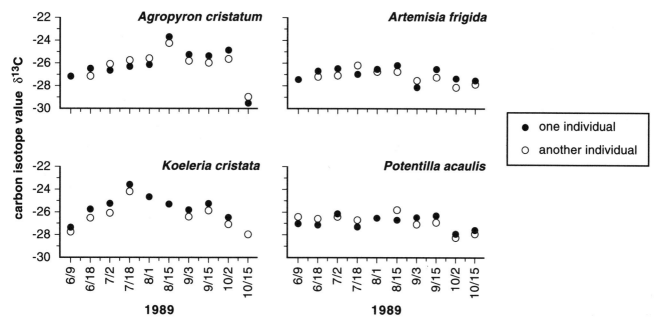

Fig. 4. The effect of time of season on the carbon isotopic signal of representative temperate zone grasses and forbs in native Inner Mongolia grasslands. Data represent bulk tissue from the most recently expanded leaves of two individuals. (Adapted from Tieszen and Bingyu 1990.)

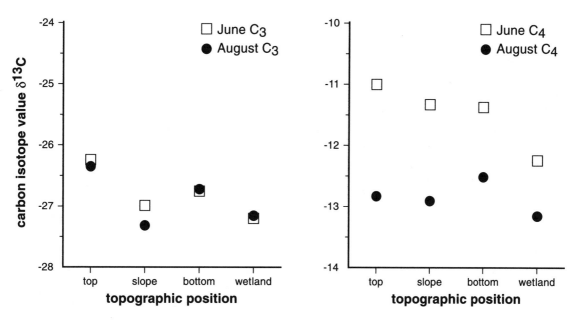

Fig. 5. The relationship between topographic position and mean isotope values for all species in four transects in spring and mid-summer, 1990. Data represent bulk tissue from recently expanded leaves at each location and include 250 individuals.

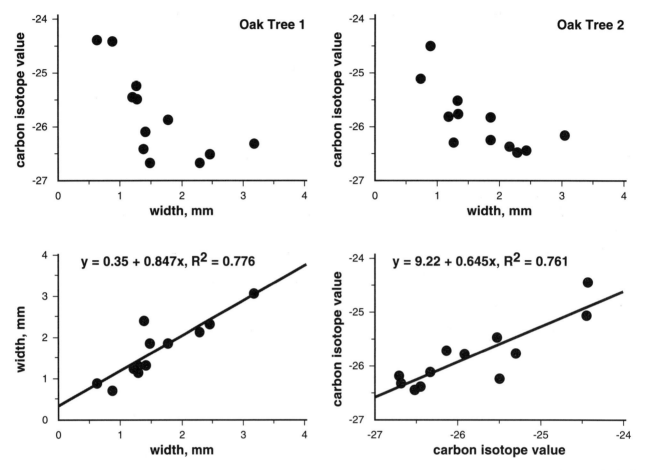

Fig. 6. Comparison of tree-ring width and bulk carbon isotope values for select years between 1930 and 1989 in *Quercus macrocarpa* (bur oak) in an upland oak savanna in southeastern S.Dak. Pooled data for both species produced an R^2 of 0.5 for the linear regression of isotope value versus width. Lower graphs regress tree 1 against tree 2.

SPECIES VARIATION

There is discrimination within C_3 and C_4 groups that is genetically based but not well understood. At Makoce Washte, for example, $\delta^{13}C$ values ranged from −29.2‰ to −24.1‰ across all species. It is not known if species with large or small discrimination are distributed differently. Ecologically, such relationships might be expected, as the isotope values reflect the C_i/C_a ratio, hence efficiency of water use. That these differences are genetically based is suggested by the consistency of the ranking of the species through time (table 4). Six of the 12 species with the most discrimination in June are also the ones with the most in August, and eight of the ones with the least discrimination in June also have the least in August. The range in isotopic values is large, and selectivity by herbivores, including humans, could lead to dietary values that deviate from the mean.

A similar range of values among species characterized each grassland community in Inner Mongolia as well. There, species of Festuca and Stipa tended to the positive. Also, communities distributed along alluvial deposits near streams were on average 1‰ more negative than other grassland communities (Tieszen and Bingyu 1990) in more mesic sites, similar to the results at Makoce Washte.

There are also differences among C_4 species. Side oats grama tends to be more negative, around −14, than big bluestem, little bluestem, or Indian grass, which are about −12‰. Values for modern maize seeds range between −10.7 and −11.2‰, but such comparisons should be interpreted with care, for seeds do not necessarily have the same isotopic composition as leaves. In maize, for example, leaves appear to be about 1‰ more negative than seeds (Lowdon 1969; Tieszen and Fagre 1993a).

Table 4. Species with Most Positive and Most Negative Carbon Isotope Values During June and August at Makoce Washte, South Dakota[a]

Species	June Samples[b]	August Samples[b]
Most Negative		
False boneset	−27.3	−27.5
Junegrass	−27.4	−27.0
Heath aster	−27.4	−27.9
Slender wheatgrass	−27.5	−27.9
Common yarrow	−27.6	−29.0
Missouri goldenrod	−27.6	−29.0
Curled dock	−27.9	−28.9
Foxtail barley	−28.1	−28.2
Sweet clover	−28.2	—
Silky aster	−28.3	−27.6
Purple prairie clover	−28.5	—
White prairie clover	−29.2	−28.5
Most Positive		
Kentucky bluegrass	−25.8	−24.5
Horsetail	−24.5	−24.8
Leadplant	−25.3	−24.9
Chenopod	—	−25.0
Wild onion	—	−25.2
Meadow anemone	−25.3	−25.2
Prairie coneflower	−27.0	−25.2
Small panic grass	−26.1	−25.4
Annual milkweed	−25.6	−25.5
Maximillian sunflower	—	−25.7
Ground cherry	−26.1	−25.8
Wild rose	−25.5	−25.9

[a]The most negative samples are arranged in increasing order based on the June sample period; the most positive samples are arranged on the basis of the August sample period.

[b]Italics = value that is not among that group of 12 at that time.

PLANT PART AND BIOCHEMICAL VARIATION

There is some variation among plant biochemicals and plant parts. DeNiro (DeNiro and Epstein 1977) showed that lipids are generally depleted in ^{13}C. Consequently, it is likely that tissues that have high concentrations of lipids will be more negative than other tissues in that same individual. Again, there are few data from which to draw generalizations. Some detailed comparisons of plant parts in four prairie grasses and one dicot showed that differences in plant parts were usually statistically significant and sometimes large (fig. 7). Young leaves, old leaves, and dead leaves are generally more negative than other parts, as illustrated by *Agropyron cristatum*. Stems are typically more positive than leaves. The reproductive structures of *Stipa grandis* and *Agropyron cristatum* show the most dramatic enrichment. The seeds (including spikelets) are 5‰ more positive than their corresponding leaves. Differences in plant parts are sometimes small as in *Mellisetus ruthenica*, where the maximum difference ranges from 1.6‰ to as much as 6‰.

What can account for these large differences in the isotopic values of plant parts? Figure 8 illustrates some of the complexity that determines the isotopic value of a menu item. First, discrimination during photosynthesis is variable, depending on the C_i/C_a ratio. The early products of photosynthesis are then metabolized into storage and structural components in the leaf. If there is any discrimination as these biochemical components are synthesized, the leaf tissue will vary. Thus, leaves with high concentrations of lipids should be more negative than those with low lipid concentrations. These early synthesized products must now be translocated to other plant parts where they are again used for the synthesis of storage or structural components. During these enzymatic and transport reactions further discrimination can occur. Little is known about any of these reactions.

DeNiro and Epstein (1977, 1978) have established that lipids in plants are depleted in ^{13}C, and Benner et al. (1987) showed large differences in plant biochemicals, with lignin depleted by 2 to 6‰ relative to whole plant material, and by 4 to 7‰ relative to cellulose, which was slightly enriched relative to bulk plant material. It is important to determine how biochemical components vary as a means of better understanding the fidelity of the signal transfer to consumers. These analyses (fig. 9) are similar to those shown by Winkler et al. (1978), but any absolute interpretation is often difficult because of the absence of a clear and independent reference from which to evaluate enrichment or depletion. Lipids usually show the most depletion, as expected; however, proteins are depleted from 1‰ in grasses in the Great Plains and Kenya compared to 2‰ in lab chow and some seeds. Spartina possesses depleted lignin in both live and dead tissue. Other grasses show lignin depletion as well, but not to the extent found in Spartina. Nakamura et al. (1982) examined commercial foodstuffs and suggested a general depletion of ^{13}C in proteins in terrestrially derived foods. Reported data vary, and a systematic study of isotopic composition of modern and archaeological analogues should be undertaken.

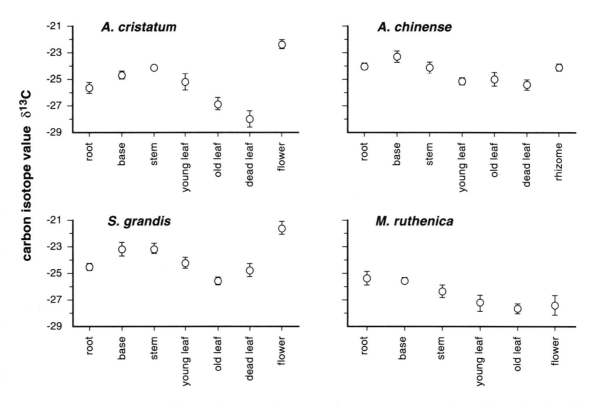

Fig. 7. The variation in carbon isotope value in bulk tissues from various plant compartments in three grasses and one legume from an Inner Mongolia grassland. Points represent the means and standard errors of eight individuals. "Flower" = grass caryopsis and legume seed. (Adapted from Tieszen and Bingyu 1990.)

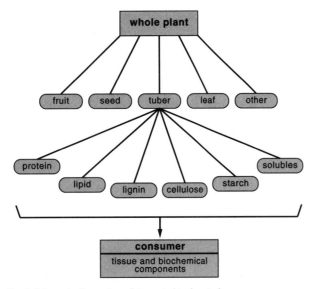

Fig. 8. Schematic illustration of the main biochemical components present in each of the major plant compartments. Since each biochemical may possess a distinct isotopic ratio, the bulk isotopic value for any compartment will reflect the mass balance of its constituent parts, as well as any fractionation as a result of respiration and translocation processes.

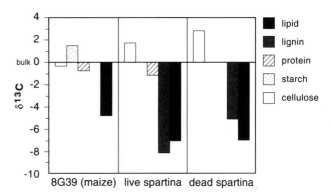

Fig. 9. Carbon isotope values of the main biochemical constituents of live and dead leaves of *Spartina pectinata* and a typical maize seed. Grass leaves contained insufficient starch for accurate analysis.

Isotopic Analysis of Consumers

LABEL TRANSFER: THEORY, RESULTS, AND DIET-COLLAGEN SPACING

Although there is some variation in the $\delta^{13}C$ values of the two modal groups, C_3 and C_4 plants, the successful application of these isotopic signals for dietary analysis has been unprecedented. The broad carbon isotope patterns are transmitted to consumers (DeNiro and Epstein 1978; Tieszen et al. 1983) and through other trophic levels, although the transfer of the isotopic signal from diet is tissue specific (Tieszen et al. 1983). There is also some evidence that quality of diet, and even animal size or digestive system, may affect the fidelity of this transfer. Since collagen and bioapatite are the two materials of most usefulness for archaeological reconstructions, it is the relationship of their isotopic signals to diet that is of greatest concern.

The model proposed by Krueger (Krueger and Sullivan 1984) best describes what factors might account for the diet, collagen, and bioapatite spacings, that is, the departure of isotope values in collagen and bioapatite from bulk diet carbon. The model is based on a theoretical assessment of the biochemical disposition of ingested organic molecules. Krueger and Sullivan suggest that when protein is readily available, the amino acids are incorporated into collagen, and when protein is in short supply, as may often be the case for herbivores, some amino acids will be synthesized from ingested carbohydrates. The result in herbivores is an approximate 5‰ enrichment of ^{13}C in collagen over diet. Because carnivores have excess protein in the diet, collagen can be synthesized directly; therefore, Krueger and Sullivan propose no enrichment. The relationship between collagen isotopic values and diet differs greatly between herbivores and carnivores. Tieszen (1991) has suggested that the difference may reflect diet quality instead of trophic position, with quality referring to the adequacy of protein in the diet. High quality diets should show little fractionation; low quality diets should provide a collagen-diet spacing near 5‰.

The bioapatite isotope value should also vary as a function of diet. Carnivores will probably use ingested lipids and protein for energy metabolism. Since the carbonate in bioapatite is synthesized from blood bicarbonate (produced by cellular respiration), bioapatite should reflect the depleted nature of dietary lipids. In contrast, herbivores will use carbohydrates for energy metabolism and for some protein synthesis. Therefore, bioapatite-collagen spacing is expected to be less for carnivores than herbivores.

BISON TISSUE FRACTIONATION

To determine the relationships among various tissue types for Plains bison and other human resources and the diet-collagen spacing, samples from bison and other animals from free-ranging habitats were obtained, where a reasonable estimate of their lifetime diets was possible. Figure 10 presents the stable isotopic values for a wide array of tissue types for a bison, a mule deer, and a Canada goose from central South Dakota. This bison from an open range near the Missouri River near Pierre, South Dakota, has a pattern of tissue variation similar to that of "obligate" grazers in East Africa. In the grazers—wildebeest, kongoni, and bison—the collagen is enriched relative to all other tissues, even other protein-rich tissues like hoof, horn, muscle, and hair. Tieszen and Fagre (1993b) found, in experimental work, that muscle tissue is often about 2‰ depleted relative to collagen. Estimates of the seasonal dietary intake for the East African grazers are reasonably good. The estimate of −11.3‰ suggests a collagen-diet spacing of 4.6‰ to 4.9‰. Exact dietary estimates for the entire year for the bison were lacking but were probably near −24.7‰. This estimate yields a diet-collagen spacing of 4.9‰ as well. However, the amount of depletion by lipids in the bison was small, a likely consequence of death late in the fall after seasonal consumption of C_4 plants. The figure also illustrates that the African mixed feeders have tissue spectra similar to grazers, although the range among tissue types is not so great. The Canada goose suggests a dietary input largely from C_3 sources because of its collagen value, near −20‰. The relatively small spacing between the fat and collagen in this specimen suggests a recent input of C_4 material, probably maize in the fall of the year. This inference is further supported by an unusually positive value for the liver carbon isotope. Liver tissue turns over rapidly, probably because of glycogen utilization and replacement. A migrant goose in spring might well have the same collagen value but could have a different signal in its fat and liver.

SEASONALITY AND LIFETIME INTEGRATED VALUES

A more detailed analysis of bison feeding behavior and integrated collagen values was undertaken at Wind Cave National Park. Collagen was examined from bones of 19 bison, all of which were born and died without supplemental feed. The bones were left at the site of death for detailed taphonomic studies. They were analyzed for carbon isotopes as illustrated in table 5. Collagen yields ranged between 4.1 and 12.0 percent, the carbon composition of the "collagen" analyzed was

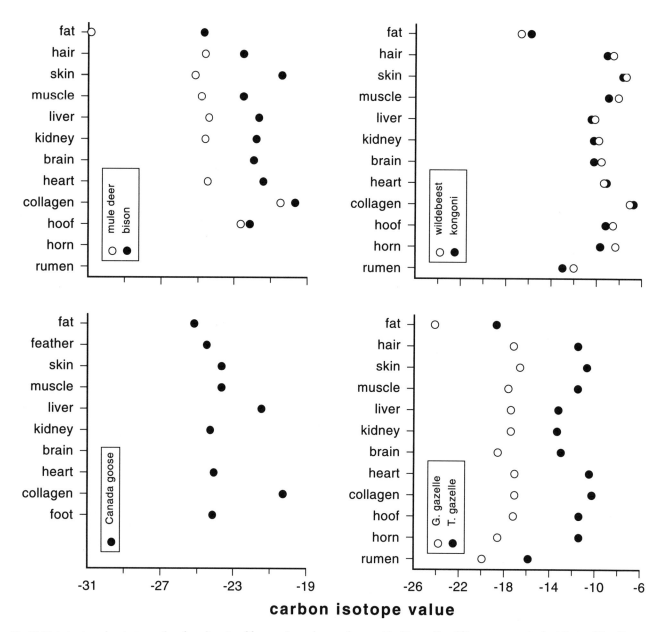

Fig. 10. Variation in carbon isotope values for a diversity of free-ranging and unsupplemented herbivores. East African grazers and mixed feeders (N = 4) were collected from Hopcraft's ranch each of Nairobi, modern bison from Houck's ranch near Pierre, S.Dak., mule deer from Wind Cave National Park, and goose from the Missouri River.

Table 5. Carbon and Nitrogen Isotope Analysis of Bone Collagen from Wind Cave National Park[a]

Species	Carbon to Nitrogen	Mean Yield %	δ¹³C ‰	δ¹⁵N ‰
Bison (N = 19)	3.22	6.5	−18.7 ± 0.2	6.4 ± 0.23
Elk (N = 19)	3.3	9.3	−19.0 ± 0.2	7.0 ± 0.3

[a]Bones were collected in situ from natural deaths after 2 to 11 years of exposure.

between 39.4 and 49.6 percent, and the carbon to nitrogen molar ratios were between 3.2 and 3.4. The pseudomorph of collagen was usually subjectively placed among the two best categories on a scale of 1 to 5. Thus, the collagen is of high quality and should be free from significant diagenetic alteration. The carbon isotopic values showed small variation, with a mean of −18.7‰. Regression analysis showed no relationship between the carbon isotope value and age (2 to 15 years) at death, years (2 to 11) of bone exposure, or sex. Similar results, with a mean of −19.0‰, characterized the elk data from this same site. Again, there were no significant relationships with age, exposure period, or sex. Furthermore, a comparison of the isotope data for the bison and elk show that their carbon isotope values are not distinguishable.

The nitrogen isotope values for bison and elk are also similar. The mean for elk, 7.0‰, is not different from the mean for bison, 6.4‰. Again, there was no statistical relationship between the nitrogen isotope values in bison and elk and age at death, exposure period, or sex. These comparisons from Wind Cave suggest that during the period sampled by these natural deaths, individuals possessed similar carbon and nitrogen isotope ratios, indicating that dietary assimilation throughout this period was similar within each species. As this isotopic technique only assesses assimilation of carbon and nitrogen isotopic forms, it seems that elk and bison may compete for similar photosynthetic types during most of the year.

The carbon isotope values from bone collagen for bison and elk are probably an integration of the C_3 and C_4 sources of organic matter that were assimilated during growth. Because collagen turnover is slow, this integrated carbon signal must reflect a reasonable estimate of the seasonal inputs during these periods. From the detailed work at Wind Cave, it is known that some herbivores show significant seasonality in their dietary inputs and that others do not (fig. 11). In a detailed documentation of lifetime vegetation utilization, fresh feces were sampled at biweekly and monthly intervals. In combination with a detailed assessment of the availability of C_3 and C_4 plant biomass in each of the major communities, seasonal selectivity can be as estimated. It is immediately clear that pronghorn are selecting vegetation that is even more negative than the average C_3 grass and that at no time during the year do they show any use of C_4 species. Pronghorn should possess a bone collagen value of about −23‰. Although mule deer could not be sampled with this detailed frequency, the data suggest that they have a seasonal pattern similar to pronghorn. During July, for example, when C_4 biomass is most available, fecal samples from 10 deer averaged −26.0‰.

In contrast to the consistent pattern of the pronghorn bison and elk, prairie dogs show strong seasonal trends. Prairie dogs use some vegetation in mid-winter, which is again quite negative, presumably either frozen dicot material or stored foods. During the growing season, they begin to rely on other species and near early August approach 50 percent use of C_4 grasses. Bison rely on C_3 grasses until early June. During July and into early August the fecal value is just below −20‰. Thus, for somewhat over one month they show a 45 percent dependence on C_4 vegetation. This finding confirms a similar pattern described in north-central South Dakota (Tieszen et al. 1980). Elk show a similar pattern, with the following significant differences. The lower values in mid-winter suggest a greater reliance on plants from the forest understory, and the lower values in mid-summer suggest a lesser dependence on C_4 at this time than is the case with bison.

These results clearly show that the major herbivores in a specific system can have distinct carbon isotope values. The fecal samples also suggest that the collagen values obscure (or integrate) the dynamic seasonal dietary patterns. Bison horns increase in size as the animal grows, and the horn case of keratin must expand and develop as the bone of the horn grows. This horn case has the appearance of rings that overlap from the inside of the case to the outside. These probably represent growth rings, with each ring showing the expansion during one year. Thus, the innermost ring represents the last year of growth, and the oldest years are both external and near the tip of the horn. In fact, the oldest years may be lost as the horn is worn. The innermost four rings from a bison collected at Wind Cave were sampled by dividing the ring cross-section into six segments, each of which was excised, ground, and analyzed. It is clear from fig. 12 that there is a cyclical pattern in the carbon signal, which is interpreted as a seasonal signal. The innermost layer of each ring is the most positive, with the exception of the oldest ring. The second through fifth intervals are usually more negative. In the year ending with layer "B," for example, the most recent layer of this ring has a value of −18.6‰. The next layer is the lowest in that ring at −21.5 and is followed by layers at −21.4, −20.5, −20.3, −20.4‰. There is then an abrupt jump to −18.0‰. This pattern could represent an annual growth ring, with the last part of the year at position "B" and the first part of the year at the layer next to "C," the last position of the previous year. If this interpretation is correct, it suggests that most of the horn case is synthesized in spring, with values indicative of C_3 input, and that only the last segment of each ring shows substantial C_4 input; thus the horn case probably stops growing sometime near the end of summer.

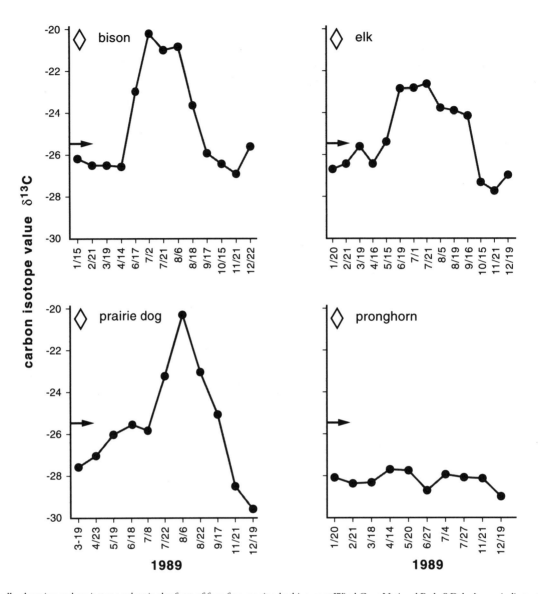

Fig. 11. Seasonally changing carbon isotope values in the feces of four free-ranging herbivores at Wind Cave National Park, S.Dak. Arrow indicates the yearly weighted mean carbon isotope value of the green biomass. Diamond represents the value expected on the basis of floristic composition of the grasses. Each point represents the mean of eight individual samples.

A primary objective was to identify a tissue that reflected seasonal input to test hypotheses about enrichment of ^{15}N during food or water deprivation. The field results from Africa (Heaton et al. 1986) suggest that animals from arid habitats have high values of $\delta^{15}N$. Tieszen (1991) suggested that this finding could indicate periods of food shortage and tissue recycling—an analogue of another trophic transfer of organic matter—instead of a direct effect of water shortage and stress. Since bison on the Plains often lose substantial weight in winter (A.A. Steuter, personal communication 1990), this tissue breakdown could be interpreted as enriched ^{15}N values in the tissues that are simultaneously synthesized. Figure 12

plots the $\delta^{15}N$ values for these same horn case samples. The results show no clear annual cyclicity in the nitrogen isotope data. There is a marked change (1.75 per mil) in the isotope value from the beginning of the most recent year and the end of the previous year; thus the data provide no evidence in support of a seasonal ^{15}N enrichment with seasonal food shortage. Yet, the horn case does record one distinct departure from the mean. Without the date of death of this animal, there is no way of knowing what environmental conditions might be associated with or have influenced the findings.

The average value for the carbon isotope is −20.0‰, slightly lower than the collagen mean for bison of −18.7. This

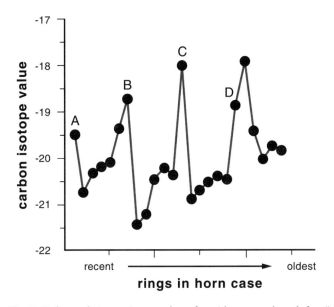
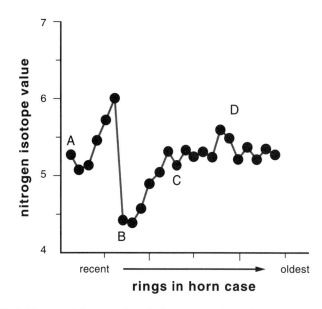

Fig. 12. Carbon and nitrogen isotope values of a serial sequence through four "rings" of a bison keratin horn case from the innermost portion to the outermost. Each ring was subdivided into six portions for analysis. Letters designate the innermost portion of each ring.

difference is consistent with the difference between collagen and hair in bison and African grazers. Experimental work also shows muscle protein that is about 2‰ more negative than collagen. The mean value for ^{15}N of 4.0 is also similar to the mean collagen value for bison from Wind Cave. A comparison of the yearly averages in the horn (table 6) shows a range of 1.1‰ for carbon and only 0.6‰ for nitrogen. Presumably, the carbon difference reflects differences in assimilation during those two years.

Some additional collagen data were obtained from sites in South Dakota: bison from Ordway Prairie in north-central South Dakota were −19.2‰, and bison from Houck's ranch in the central part of the state along the Missouri River near Pierre were −19.7‰ (more negative than the −15.7‰ reported by Boutton, Lynott, and Bumsted 1991 for one bison from the Crow Creek site).

Table 6. Mean Carbon and Nitrogen Isotope Values for Each Putative Annual Ring of Bison Horn Illustrated in Figure 12

Annual Ring	δ^{13}C	δ^{15}N
A (recent)	−20.0	6.7
B	−20.4	6.0
C	−20.2	6.5
D (oldest)	−19.3	6.5

LATITUDINAL VARIATION IN MODERN VALUES

An attempt was made to identify all possible sources of free-ranging bison that exist without supplemental feed as a step toward predicting vegetation and inferring climate, based on stable carbon isotopic signatures. The data for U.S. collections (fig. 13) show a clearly defined latitudinal trend. The bone collagen carbon isotope values from Oklahoma were −13.1‰, whereas those from Montana were as negative as −22‰. Individuals from Konza Prairie, Kansas, were more positive than those from Oklahoma, probably reflecting the dominance of big bluestem (C_4) at Konza and the availability of closed forests with C_3 plants at Oklahoma. These values cannot be related to the available mix of C_3 and C_4 biomass, but overall relationships with latitude and temperature are obvious. Therefore, it should be possible to examine bone collagen from bison through the Holocene and to make reasonable estimates of vegetation changes during that epoch.

HOLOCENE ISOTOPE CHANGES

The collagen from bison reflect the isotopic composition of the vegetation assimilated during growth and development. If the availability of C_3 and C_4 biomass changes through time, the signals from these forms should be recorded in the collagen, and should indicate past vegetation assemblages and some aspects of past climate. McKinnon's (1986) analysis of bison at

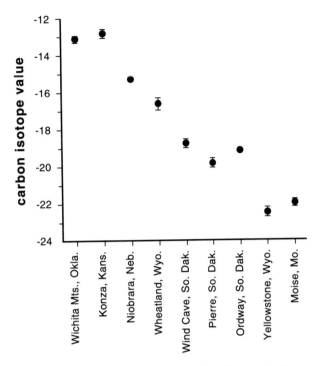

Fig. 13. Mean carbon isotope values for bone collagen from modern free-ranging bison in natural systems. Diets are believed to be unsupplemented. N ranges from 1 to 19.

Head Smashed In, Alberta, Canada, includes 44 individuals within the last 6,000 years. Individual values range 3.6‰ around the long-term mean of −19.6‰. The excursions from the mean for the site showed some consistency; however, values often differed by 2‰ or more within a 300-year period. On the basis of these departures from the mean value, McKinnon proposes various periods of more C_4 and less C_4

vegetation in the vicinity. The periods 3750–3550 B.C., 3150–1300 B.C., and A.D. 1200–1450 appear to have greater than normal amounts of C_4 vegetation, and the periods around 550 B.C. and A.D. 950 have greatly reduced amounts or none.

Table 6 presents some collagen and bioapatite carbon isotope values for bison material from South Dakota. The bone collagen values from one site, Oakwood Lake, range from −15.6‰ to −20.6 (table 7). The Smiley Evans and the White-cap specimens are near the positive end of the Oakwood Lake range and are more positive than modern material from Wind Cave, Houck's ranch, or Ordway Prairie. The bioapatite values are around 9‰ enriched relative to collagen, supporting theory, which suggests a large collagen-bioapatite spacing for obligate herbivores.

It is difficult to know whether the excursions found by McKinnon (1986) and variations here are an accurate reflection of changing climatic or vegetation patterns. Bison are mobile grazers, and the individual values could reflect a real climatic change or they could represent a sojourner from some different vegetation system. Chisholm (Chisholm et al. 1986) has used carbon isotope ratios to infer that bison migrated between the plains and parklands in Alberta but that the Peace River bison did not. The captive herd of bison at Wind Cave possesses similar variation in the isotopic signal even though all individuals have access to the identical vegetation types. Dominance relationships and individual behavioral patterns may result in different selectivity patterns and different isotopic compositions. To make climatic reconstructions with confidence, it must be determined whether the variation between sample dates is significantly different from that possible at one sample time. At present, it is unknown

Table 7. Bone Collagen Carbon Isotope Values and Radiocarbon Dates from Bison at South Dakota Sites

| Site | Bone Collagen | | Bioapatite |
	Date	^{13}C, ‰	^{13}C, ‰
Oakwood Lake (39BK7)			
#A2231	280 B.C. ± 245	−20.6	—
#A2226	220 B.C. ± 100	−17.4	—
#A2230	A.D. 215 ± 90	−16.1	−7.2
#A2227	A.D. 250 ± 95	−15.8	−6.8
#A2229	A.D. 250 ± 90	−15.9	−6.6
#A2224	A.D. 370 ± 140	−15.6	−6.7
#A2223	A.D. 570 ± 290	−17.6	—
#A2222	A.D. 730 ± 305	−18.0	—
Smiley Evans (39BV2)	A.D. 1000 ± 140	−15.2	—
Whitecap (39WW43)	5170 B.C. ± 60	−16.7	—

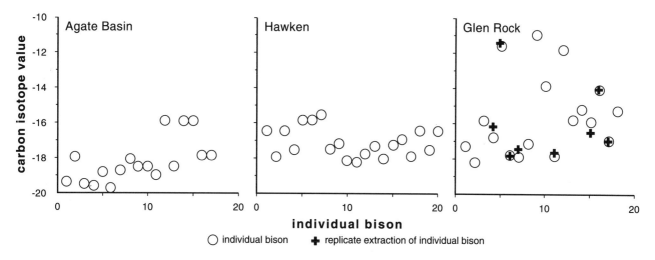

Fig. 14. Individual bone collagen values for bison from three archaeological sites spanning the Holocene. In all cases C/N values were between 3.0 and 3.6, %C was 38 to 48, and pseudomorphs were present after extraction of ethylenediamine-tetraacetic acid.

what the variation is in free-ranging bison at one point in time. A larger number of replicates from a short time interval (a few decades) is needed to derive an acceptable mean for that period, as the vegetation can respond quickly to changing temperature and moisture conditions. Excellent time controls probably will be required to definitively establish migratory patterns or changing climates.

A study of Holocene bison illustrates this need. In an attempt to reconstruct the Holocene changes in the carbon isotopic composition of collagen, a large number of bison from various kill sites was sampled. These sites range from the Mill Iron site, 9390 B.C., to A.D. 1750. Figure 14 shows the range of variation within three sample periods. Agate Basin (8730–8480 B.C.) material, which includes specimens from Agate Basin Level, Hell Gap, and Folsom and spans more than 300 years, has an average value of −18.2‰, but three specimens are as positive as −16‰. Hawken, a mid-Holocene site (4450–4050 B.C.), has a mean of −17.2‰, and Glen Rock, a recent site (A.D. 1670–1740), has a mean of −15.6‰. Some of the specimens at Glen Rock are as positive as −11‰. This range of carbon isotopic values must represent natural variation in bison at those times for the replicate extractions are nearly identical in all cases. The ANOVA for these three sites shows that groups are significant (F = 11.69, p = .0001). All groups are statistically different except Agate Basin and Hawken. Although all the analyses are not yet complete, a linear regression for over 200 bison spanning the Holocene shows a distinct trend, with an approximate 2.5‰ increase from Mill Iron to modern specimens. Nevertheless, it is clear

that excursions during short time intervals will require a large number of samples, which should be individually dated.

This variation has not been observed during the Holocene for $\delta^{15}N$. These sites possess similar nitrogen isotope values (Agate Basin $\delta^{15}N$ = 7.1 ± .17‰; Glen Rock = 6.3 ± .47‰; Hawken = 6.9 ± .23‰). The ANOVA for these three groups indicates that there are no differences (F = 2.06, p = .15). The preliminary review of all data from the bison kill sites shows no change among 200 individuals through the Holocene. The values for these prehistoric materials are also similar to the mean for modern bison material from Wind Cave.

Conclusion

The application of stable isotopic procedures is becoming well established in ecological and archaeological research. The increased availability of the isotope ratio mass spectrometer, the expanding data base of isotopic information, the testing of hypotheses based on empirical data with laboratory experimentation, and a generation of scientists who understand isotopic technology all combine to suggest that rapid advances in understanding of archaeological, paleoecological, and ecological phenomena will occur. It is clear that the two major photosynthetic groups have distinct isotopic ratios and are differently distributed in relation to temperature, moisture, and irradiance. Further, certain plant growth forms are exclusively C_3. Thus, in the grasslands of North America a quantitative change in C_3 and C_4 abundance can be predicted from north to south and calibrated to temperature. Forested systems also possess C$_3$ signals. Because the specific carbon isotopic value for any plant is subject to environmental modification, end-members are not sufficiently constant for exact dietary reconstruction, but quantitative understanding of the environmental effects provides some assurance of the reliability of these values.

Yet to be established are the exact relationships among floristic composition, biomass production, and the assimilation of isotopic signals by consumers. Further analyses of free-ranging animals on natural systems will define some of these relationships. The experimental assessment of diet quality and isotopic fractionation will be invaluable. Uncertainty about the diet-collagen spacing and its relationship to diet in herbivores, omnivores, and carnivores should receive high priority in future research if dietary patterns are to be integrated accurately. It is important to continue to gather isotopic data on both bone collagen that is well characterized and bioapatite, as a possible basis for quantifying direct herbivory and carnivory, as well as distinguishing a C$_4$ signal from maize versus bison.

It is not clear to what extent nitrogen isotope data will become important in the Great Plains. Local applications will be needed, and a trophic transfer amplification should help validate inferences about the amount of carnivory estimated from narrow bioapatite-collagen spacing. The few data on nitrogen suggest a high similarity of values both spatially and through the Holocene.

The papers in this section underscore the importance of the detailed understanding of the ecologic, geographic, and temporal variations in both carbon and nitrogen isotopes. The focus on specific sites also indicates that the isotopic reconstruction of diets, or climates, on the Plains is in its infancy, and generalizations for Plains cultures cannot yet be proposed.

Tuross and Fogel present information from the Northern Plains for the Sully site, an important site, containing the largest earthlodge village along the Missouri River. Their data argue strongly for bison as a substantial component of dietary intake; and the authors stress the necessity for a thorough database of isotopic information on potential resources available during the Holocene epoch. Temperature differences during various periods of the Holocene could have resulted in significant changes in vegetation composition and therefore isotopic values of bison. These climate-related changes will confound attempts at dietary analyses unless well-dated specimens and a bison database of high time resolution are available. The significance of the nitrogen enrichment with passage of organic matter through trophic levels is also evident in their work. Tuross and Fogel show conclusively that nursing infants

possess elevated δ^{15}N values, an elevation that may serve as a nursing marker. The power of this isotopic approach becomes apparent because scientists can make hypotheses concerning the collagen-apatite spacing on these individuals, which can be tested. All individuals with elevated δ^{15}N values should also possess large collagen-apatite spacing.

The final contribution, also site specific, is from the Southern Plains. Habicht-Mauche, Levendosky, and Schoeninger present collagen isotope data from the Antelope Creek phase that are notable for their very positive carbon values. These values, around −7‰ to −8‰, surely circumscribe the range of resources used by these people. They relied heavily on C$_4$ plants directly or supplemented with varying amounts of bison, the only large mammal grazer of consequence. The study illustrates the inability to define specific food items on the basis of stable isotopes alone. A more detailed understanding of the relationships between diets and isotopic values in collagen coupled with a detailed understanding of the isotopic resource base on the Plains through time hold the promise for significant improvements in comprehending diets and culture on the Plains.

This research was supported by grants from the National Science Foundation (RUI-BSR-8813598; USE-8851442; REU-BBS-8804021 and 8712603). The Research Corporation and the Augustana Research Artist Fund (ARAF) were instrumental in providing support for the acquisition and operation of the mass spectrometer and for various local projects.

References Cited

Barnes, P.W., L.L. Tieszen, and D.J. Ode
1983   Distribution, Production and Diversity of C3 and C4 Dominated Communities in a Mixed Prairie. *Canadian Journal of Botany* 61:741–751.

Bender, M.M.
1968   Mass Spectrometric Studies of Carbon 13 Variations in Corn and Other Grasses. *Radiocarbon* 10:468–472.

Benner, R., M.L. Fogel, E.K. Sprague, and R.E. Hodson
1987   Depletion of 13C in Lignin and Its Implications for Stable Carbon Isotope Studies. *Nature* 329:708–710.

Boutton, T.W., A.T. Harrison, and B.N. Smith
1980   Distribution of Biomass of Species Differing in Photosynthetic Pathway Along an Altitudinal Transect in Southeastern Wyoming Grassland. *Oecologia* 45:287–298.

——, M.J. Lynott, and M.P. Bumsted
1991   Stable Carbon Isotopes and the Study of Prehistoric Human Diet. *Critical Reviews in Food Science and Nutrition* 30:373–385.

Cerling, T.E., J. Quade, Y. Wang, and J.R. Bowman
   1989 Carbon Isotopes in Soils and Paleosols as Ecology and Paleoecology Indicators. *Nature* 341:138–139.

Chisholm, B.S.
   1989 Variation in Diet Reconstructions Based on Stable Isotopic Evidence. Pp. 10–37 in The Chemistry of Prehistoric Human Bone. T.D. Price, ed. New York: Cambridge University Press.

——, J. Driver, S. Dube, and H.P. Schwarcz
   1986 Assessment of Prehistoric Bison Foraging and Movement Patterns via Stable-carbon Isotopic Analysis. *Plains Anthropologist* 31:193–205.

DeNiro, M., and S. Epstein
   1977 Mechanism of Carbon Isotope Fractionation Associated with Lipid Synthesis. *Science* 197:261–263.

——
   1978 Influence of Diet on the Distribution of Carbon Isotopes in Animals. *Geochimica et Cosmochimica Acta* 42:495–506.

Ehleringer, J.R., and P.W. Rundel
   1989 Stable Isotopes: History, Units, and Instrumentation. Pp. 1–15 in Stable Isotopes in Ecological Research. *Ecological Studies* 68. P.W. Rundel, J.R. Ehleringer, and K.A. Nagy, eds. New York: Springer-Verlag.

Epp, H.T.
   1988 Way of the Migrant Herds: Dual Dispersion Strategy Among Bison. *Plains Anthropologist* 33:309–320.

Farquhar, G.D.
   1980 Carbon Isotope Discrimination by Plants: Effects of Carbon Dioxide Concentration and Temperature via the Ratio of Intercellular and Atmospheric CO_2 Concentrations. Pp. 105–107 in Carbon Dioxide and Climate: Australian Research. G.I. Pearman, ed. Canberra: Australian Academy of Science.

——
   1983 On the Nature of Carbon Isotope Discrimination in C_4 Species. *Australian Journal of Plant Physiology* 10:205–206.

——, J.R. Ehleringer, and K.T. Hubick
   1989 Carbon Isotope Discrimination and Photosynthesis. *Annual Review of Plant Physiology and Plant Molecular Biology* 40:503–537.

——, M.H. O'Leary, and J.A. Berry
   1982 On the Relationship Between Carbon Isotope Discrimination and the Intercellular Carbon Dioxide Concentration in Leaves. *Australian Journal of Plant Physiology* 9:121–137.

Francey, R.J., and G.D. Farquhar
   1982 An Explanation of $^{13}C/^{12}C$ Variations in Tree Rings. *Nature* 297:28–31.

——, and K.T. Hubick
   1988 Tree-ring Carbon-isotope Ratios Re-examined. *Nature* 333:712.

Friedli, H., H. Lotscher, H. Oeschger, U. Siegenthaler, and B. Stauffer
   1986 Ice core record of the $^{13}C/^{12}C$ Ratio of Atmospheric CO_2 in the Past Two Centuries. *Nature* 324:237–238.

Hanson, J.R.
   1984 Bison Ecology in the Northern Plains and a Reconstruction of Bison Patterns for the North Dakota Region. *Plains Anthropologist* 29:93–113.

Heaton, T.H.E., J.C. Vogel, G. von la Chevallerie, and G. Collett
   1986 Climatic Influence on the Isotopic Composition of Bone Nitrogen. *Nature* 322:822–823.

Hesla, B.I., L.L. Tieszen, and S.K. Imbamba
   1982 A Systematic Survey of C_3 and C_4 Photosynthesis in the *Cyperaceae* of Kenya, East Africa. *Photosynthetica* 16:196–205.

Johnson, D.A., K.H. Asay, L.L. Tieszen, J.R. Ehleringer, and P.G. Jefferson
   1990 Carbon Isotope Discrimination: Potential in Screening Cool-season Grasses for Water-limited Environments. *Crop Science* 30:338–343.

Keeling, C.D., W.G. Mook, and P.P. Tans
   1979 Recent Trends in the $^{13}C/^{12}C$ Ratio of Atmospheric Carbon Dioxide. *Nature* 277:121–123.

Krueger, H.W., and Charles H. Sullivan
   1984 Models for Carbon Isotope Fractionation Between Diet and Bone. In Turnland, J.R. and P.E. Johnson, *Stable Isotopes in Nutrition, American Chemical Society Symposium Series* 258:205–220.

Lowdon, J.A.
   1969 Isotopic Fractionation in Corn. *Radiocarbon* 11:391–393.

Marino, B.D., and M.J. DeNiro
   1987 Isotopic Analysis of Archaeobotanicals to Reconstruct Past Climates: Effects of Activities Associated with Food Preparation on Carbon, Hydrogen and Oxygen Isotope Ratios of Plant Cellulose. *Journal of Archaeological Science* 14:537–548.

——, and M.B. McElroy
   1991 Isotopic Composition of Atmospheric CO_2 Inferred from Carbon in C_4 Plant Cellulose. *Nature* 349:127–131.

McKinnon, N.A.
   1986 Paleoenvironments and Cultural Dynamics at Head-Smashed-In Buffalo Jump, Alberta: The Carbon Isotope Record. (Unpublished Master's Thesis, University of Calgary, Calgary, Alberta.)

Medina, E., G. Montes, E. Cuevas, and Z. Rokzandic
   1986 Profiles of CO_2 Concentration and $\delta^{13}C$ Values in Tropical Rain Forests of the Upper Rio Negro Basin, Venezuela. *Journal of Tropical Ecology* 2:207–217.

Nakamura, K., D.A. Schoeller, F.J. Winkler, and J.H. Schmidt
   1982 Geographical Variations in the Carbon Isotope Composition of the Diet and Hair in Contemporary Man. *Biomedical Mass Spectrometry* 9:390–394.

Nier, A.V., and E.A. Gulbransen
   1939 Variations in the Relative Abundance of the Carbon Isotopes. *Journal of the American Chemical Society* 61:697–698.

Ode, D., L.L. Tieszen, and J.C. Lerman

1980 The Seasonal Contribution of C_3 and C_4 Plant Species to Primary Production in a Mixed Prairie. *Ecology* 61:1304–1311.

O'Leary, M.H.

1981 Carbon Isotope Fractionation in Plants. *Phytochemistry* 20:553–567.

———

1988 Carbon Isotopes in Photosynthesis. *BioScience* 38:328–335.

Sala, O.E., W.J. Parton, L.A. Joyce, and W.K. Lauenroth

1988 Primary Production of the Central Grassland Region of the United States. *Ecology* 69:40–45.

Shantz, H.L.

1954 The Place of Grasslands in the Earth's Cover of Vegetation. *Ecology* 35:142–145.

Smith, B.N., and S. Epstein

1971 Two Categories of $^{13}C/^{12}C$ Ratios of Higher Plants. *Plant Physiology* 47:380–384.

Speth, J.D., and K.A. Spielmann

1983 Energy Source, Protein Metabolism, and Hunter-gatherer Subsistence Strategies. *Journal of Anthropological Archaeology* 2:1–31.

Terri, J.A., and L.G. Stowe

1976 Climatic Patterns and Distribution of C_4 Grasses in North America. *Oecologia* 23:1–12.

Tieszen, L.L.

1991 Natural Variations in the Carbon Isotope Values of Plants: Implications for Archaeology, Ecology, and Paleoecology. *Journal of Archaeological Sciences* 18:227–248.

———, and S. Archer

1990 Isotopic Assessment of Vegetation Changes in Grassland and Woodland Systems. Pp. 293–321 in Plant Biology of the Basin and Range. *Ecological Studies* 80. New York: Springer-Verlag.

———, and S. Bingyu

1990 Stable Carbon Isotopic Variation Among Plants of the Inner Mongolian Grasslands. Pp. 273–287 in Reports from the Inner Mongolia Grassland Ecosystem Research Station of Academia Sinica by Y. Ba and P. Keli. Beijing: Science Press.

———, and T.W. Boutton

1989 Stable Carbon Isotopes in Terrestrial Ecosystem Research. Pp. 167–195 in Stable Isotopes in Ecological Research. *Ecological Studies* 68. P.W. Rundel, J.R. Ehleringer, and K.A. Nagy, eds. New York: Springer-Verlag.

———, T.W. Boutton, K.G. Tesdahl, and N.A. Slade

1983 Fractionation and Turnover of Stable Carbon Isotopes in Animal Tissues: Implications for $\delta^{13}C$ Analysis of Diet. *Oecologia* 57:32–37.

———, and J.K. Detling

1983 Productivity of Grassland and Tundra. Pp. 173–203 in Encyclopedia of Plant Physiology New Series, Volume 12D: Physiological Plant Ecology IV. O.L. Lange, P.S. Nobel, C.B. Osmond, and H. Ziegler, eds. Berlin: Springer-Verlag.

———, and T. Fagre

1993a Carbon Isotopic Variability in Modern and Archaeological Maize. *Journal of Archaeological Sciences* 20.

———, and T. Fagre

1993b Effect of Diet Quality on the Isotopic Composition of Respiratory CO_2, Bone Collagen, Bioapatite, and Soft Tissues. In Prehistoric Human Bone: Archaeology at the Molecular Level. J.B. Lanbert and G. Grupe, eds. Berlin: Springer-Verlag.

———, M. McElroy, S. Archer, and R.W. Klukas

1988 Vegetation Units at Wind Cave National Park for Use in Stable Isotopic Interpretations of Diets. *Proceedings of the South Dakota Academy of Sciences* 67:84–99.

———, D.J. Ode, P.W. Barnes, and P.M. Bultsma

1980 Seasonal Variation in C3 and C4 Biomass at the Ordway Prairie and Selectivity by Bison and Cattle. Pp. 165–174 in Proceedings of the 7th North American Prairie Conference by C.L. Kucera. Springfield, Mo.

———, M.M. Senyimba, S.K. Imbamba, and J.H. Troughton

1979 The Distribution of C_3 and C_4 Grasses and Carbon Isotope Discrimination Along an Altitudinal and Moisture Gradient in Kenya. *Oecologia* 37:337–350.

van der Merwe, N.J., and E. Medina

1989 Photosynthesis and 13C/12C Ratios in Amazonian Rainforests. *Geochimica et Cosmochimica Acta* 53:1091–1094.

Vogel, J.C.

1980 Fractionation of the Carbon Isotopes During Photosynthesis. Berlin: Springer-Verlag.

Wagner, G.E.

1988 The Implications of the Adoption of Northern Flint Corn. In Agricultural Adaptations to Marginal Areas of the Upper Midwest, Society for American Archaeology 53rd Annual Meeting, April 27–May 1, 1988, Phoenix, Ariz.

Winkler, F.J., E. Wirth, E. Latzko, H.L. Schmidt, W. Hoppe, and P. Wimmer

1978 Influence of Growth Conditions and Development on δ ^{13}C Values in Different Organs and Constituents of Wheat, Oat, and Maize. *Zeitschrift Pflanzenphysiologie* 87: 255–263.

CHAPTER 22

○○○

Stable Isotope Analysis and Subsistence Patterns at the Sully Site

NOREEN TUROSS AND MARILYN L. FOGEL

In the seventeenth and eighteenth centuries, the bluffs overlooking the Missouri River in the Dakotas were home to the members of the Mandan, Arikara, and Hidatsa tribes. Villages were scattered the length of the river, and the tribal population numbered tens of thousands (Holder 1970). These Indians were among the last large group to encounter Europeans, and by the early nineteenth century, disease and violence had reduced tribal numbers to a few thousand (Rogers 1990). This chapter describes dietary patterns interpreted from stable carbon and nitrogen values of bone collagen from one group of Arikara at the Sully site (39SL4), South Dakota.

The Sully site has been described as the largest earthlodge village on the Missouri. The site, 4,000 feet long and 1,500 feet wide, contained 300–400 houses at the height of its occupation (Bass 1964; Wedel 1961). Inhabited by the Arikara tribe from 1650 to 1733, Sully is one of 90 archaeological sites of the Postcontact Coalescent period (Fawcett 1988). The Sully site was excavated in the 1950s and 1960s as part of the River Basin Survey Program sponsored by the Smithsonian Institution and the National Park Service (Bass 1964; Lehmer 1971; Owsley 1992; Owsley and Jantz 1978).

Two factors strongly affected the lives of the inhabitants of the Sully site: bison and cold temperatures. These two variables interacted and ultimately became encoded in the human bone chemistry through the diet. The changes in collagen isotopic values, particularly $\delta^{15}N$, are examined as a function of age in infants and young children, and interpreted as a tracer for breastfeeding duration and weaning strategies in this population.

Ecological Background and Isotopic Consequences

The Plains, bounded by the Rocky Mountains and fading into the eastern woodlands, has been considered "a single physiographic unit with the associated typical climate and relatively uniform floral and faunal population" (Holder 1970). This assumption cannot be maintained in a consideration of subsistence based on stable isotope analyses. The foundations of the human food chain during the Plains Village period were horticulturally derived plants such as beans, squash, and corn, as well as the native plants utilized by people directly and secondarily through the ingestion of large herbivores, such as bison.

Variations in Holocene climate can be expected to affect the isotopic baselines for the flora and fauna in the Plains ("Stable Isotopes on the Plains: Vegetation Analyses and Diet Determinations," this vol.). It is likely that in the period in which the Sully site was inhabited by the Arikara, the temperature of the area was, on average, colder than today. The earth's climate is thought to be affected by the sun's luminosity, and the last prolonged period of low sunspot activity, called the Maunder minimum (1645–1715), occurred during a period known as the Little Ice Age (Jones and Wigley 1990).

General climate trends in the Plains during the Little Ice Age are discussed by Bamforth (1988, 1990). An analysis of vegetation types in the Plains since the last glacial maximum suggests a trend of average temperature increase through the Holocene up to the Neo-Boreal or Little Ice Age, when the number of boreal species indicates a decline in average temperature (Wendland, Bean, and Semken 1987). A decrease in mean annual temperature, largely a reflection of colder winters, would have resulted in lower forage production and possibly a shortened growing season.

Although the evidence for drought in the Plains is controversial (Bamforth 1990), a simulation analysis on Northern Plains moisture data assigns a 250–300 year cycle to the 1930s drought (Eddy and Cooter 1978). This cyclical pattern would put the early Sully site habitation in a severe drought interval. The adaptation of bison to these climatic changes would have included increased dispersion of herds during the winter months in search of food and a longer period of seasonal nutritional stress (Bamforth 1988). A combination of lower mean annual temperature and a decline in rainfall that resulted in a shortened growing season would have compromised the ability of the Sully site Arikara to buffer a loss of bison with horticulturally derived foodstuffs. Indeed, the growing season on the Northern Plains is sufficiently short (on the order of 60 days) that dependence on bison during the height of the Little Ice Age could have been greater among these people than among those who preceded or followed them.

The consistent availability of bison to Plains inhabitants has been questioned based on an analysis of faunal lists from the Southern Plains (Dillehay 1974). An examination of bison bone densities from an archaeological site (41TG91) in Tom Green County, Texas, documents variability in human utilization of bison from 600 B.C. to A.D. 1650 (Creel, Scott, and Collins 1990).

In the Plains, the background flora is a mixture of C_3 and C_4 grasses that forms the subsistence base for all grazing herbivores. There is a general pattern of north to south in-crease in the amount of C_4 grasses that is largely a function of temperature (Terri and Stowe 1976). In assessing the isotopic baseline of the flora, changes in mean annual temperature could be expected to alter the relative proportion of C_3 and C_4 grasses in the Plains. In the Dakotas, today, the percentage of C_4 grasses is quite high: one study of a mixed prairie found that C_4 grasses accounted for 36 percent of the biomass (Tieszen et al. 1980). Within one prairie, the C_4 grass abundance varied topographically from 0 to 49 percent (Barnes, Tieszen, and Ode 1983), and seasonally, peaking in the summer months (Tieszen and Boutton 1989; "Stable Isotopes on the Plains: Vegetation Analyses and Diet Determinations," this vol.).

The north to south cline in C_4 grasses is reflected in the bone collagen of the bison. Archaeologically recovered bison bones from Canadian and Montana sites contain $\delta^{13}C$ values that indicate little C_4 intake, −17.3‰ to −18.9‰ (Chisholm 1986). The Sully site is about −17.5. In northern Texas, values have been recorded at −11.2‰ ("Antelope Creek Phase Subsistence: The Bone Chemistry Evidence," this vol.), and in central Texas, the bison bone collagen is indistinguishable from maize stable carbon values at −7.0 (Stafford et al. 1991). Chisholm et al. (1985) utilized the lack of C_4 grasses in parts of Canada to examine foraging and movement patterns of prehistoric bison.

Bison migrations and availability, the variation in C_3 and C_4 grasses in the micro and macroenvironments of the Plains, as well as seasonal changes in the amount of C_3 and C_4 grasses available, all add complexity to interpreting human stable isotope values. A few key pieces of the isotopic puzzle are missing. Nevertheless, scientists assume that a wide range in faunal stable isotope values due to nutritional stress and an increase in foraging range could lead to increased variability in human stable isotope values from a single site. Although the use of stable carbon isotopes to determine the temporal introduction of maize has been successful against a background of largely C_3 groundcover (Smith 1989; Vogel and van der Merwe 1978), the complication of a substantial and variable C_4 grass component throughout the Plains will, at a minimum, complicate the interpretation of isotopic results as regards maize consumption.

Materials and Methods

Collagen prepared by decalcification with tetrasodium ethylenediaminetetraacetic acid (EDTA) was prepared from small (< 1 inch) pieces of rib from 36 individuals from the Sully site (Tuross, Fogel, and Hare 1988). The sample consisted of eight adults and 28 children under five years of age. Dental calcification ages after Moorrees, Fanning, and Hunt (1963a, 1963b) were provided by Douglas W. Owsley of the Department of Anthropology, Smithsonian Institution.

The collagen was combusted at 900°C for one hour in the presence of copper and cupric oxide wire and cooled at a controlled rate. Gases were cryogenically distilled, and stable carbon and nitrogen isotope ratios were obtained on gas source mass spectrometers.

Results and Interpretation

There is a combination of evidence in the stable isotope values from human bone collagen at the Sully site that is consistent with substantial dietary reliance on bison meat. First, $\delta^{15}N$ in the adult human bone collagen is enriched relative to bison bone collagen values by an average of 3.8‰ (table 1). The magnitude of the increase suggests that humans were eating food with an average $\delta^{15}N$ range of 7–8‰ (table 1, fig. 1) (DeNiro and Epstein 1981). Although plant $\delta^{15}N$ values can vary widely, a range of vegetation from the Plains averaged 3.9‰ (Stafford et al. 1991), while Sully bison collagen averaged 7.4‰.

Second, the average collagen $\delta^{13}C$ value from the adult humans is −13.4‰. It has been suggested (Hare et al. 1991; Lee-Thorp, Sealy, and van der Merwe 1989; Schwartz et al. 1985; van der Merwe and Vogel 1978; "Antelope Creek Phase Subsistence: The Bone Chemistry Evidence," this vol.) that the $\delta^{13}C$ fractionation in the bone collagen of omnivores is in the range of +2 to +5 relative to the food source (fig. 1). Using a diet-collagen spacing of +5, and the notation after Schwartz et al. (1985),

$$\Delta_{dc} = \delta_{diet} - \delta_{collagen}$$

the predicted δ value of the aggregate human diet at Sully would have a value of −18.3 ± 1.5‰ (fig. 1). The bison bone excavated from the Sully site had an average $\delta^{13}C$ bone collagen value of −17.4‰, reflecting C_4 grasses in the diet. The difference between the $\delta^{13}C$ of bone and that of meat is on the order of −2‰ (DeNiro and Epstein 1978, 1981; Hare et al. 1991). Therefore, within the standard deviation of the analysis, no additional C_4 (e.g., maize) component in the diet need be invoked in order to account for the average human bone collagen $\delta^{13}C$ values of −13.4‰ (fig. 1).

This is not to suggest that maize was absent from the horticultural base of the peoples at the Sully site. As early as 1734 there are reports of excess production of maize for trade

Table 1. Sully Site Human and Bison $\delta^{15}N$ and $\delta^{13}C$ Collagen Values

Sample No.	Age at Death (yrs)	$\delta^{15}N$ Collagen	$\delta^{13}C$ Collagen
Infants and Children			
381359	0.0	9.8	
381461	0.0	10.0	
381324	0.0	12.1	
381446	0.1	11.4	−11.2
381416	0.2	11.9	
381335	0.3	11.7	
381368	0.4	13.3	
381466	0.5	12.6	−11.1
381437	0.5	13.3	
381419	0.6	13.3	
381367	0.6	14.0	−14.0
381331	0.6	11.8	
381439	0.9	12.9	
381408	1.0	14.0	−11.0
381381	1.0	13.3	−11.2
381370	1.0	12.9	−13.5
381444	1.3	12.3	−12.2
381414	1.4	13.0	−12.6
381334	1.6	11.2	
381399	2.1	10.2	−13.7
381387	2.5	12.3	−12.6
381366	3.1	9.5	−13.5
381362	4.2	9.4	−18.9
381380	4.6	10.1	
381349	4.6	10.8	−11.7
381445	4.6	10.6	−16.3
381418	4.6	9.0	−12.9
381440	5.0	10.1	−13.3
Adults			
381341		10.9	−12.1
381345		10.6	−11.8
381342		11.0	−16.2
381357		11.8	−14.2
381354		11.8	−11.8
381352		10.8	−13.3
381332		10.9	−13.8
381330		11.7	−14.1
Mean +1 standard deviation		11.1 + 0.5	−13.4 + 1.5
Bison			
1		6.8	−16.9
2		9.3	−17.5
3		6.1	−17.9

by the tribes of the upper Missouri (Ewers 1968), and the importance of maize in Arikara culture is well known (Rogers 1990). Other plants at Sully include pumpkin, black cherries, peppers, chenopodium, and grapes. Faunal remains revealed deer, antelope, bison, dog, jackrabbit, woodchuck, fox, coyote,

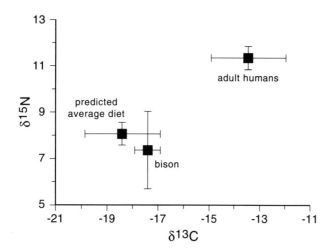

Fig. 1. Mean ± 1 standard deviation of collagen $\delta^{13}C$ and $\delta^{15}N$ from adult human and bison bone at Sully, S. Dak. The predicted carbon and nitrogen isotopic values for the average human diet at Sully is based on a fractionation from diet to bone collagen of +3‰ for $\delta^{15}N$ and +5‰ for $\delta^{13}C$.

otter, prairie dog, cottontail, catfish, and mussels. The point of the analysis of the human collagen stable isotope values is to suggest, first, that both the carbon and nitrogen isotopic data are consistent with major utilization of bison by the Sully site inhabitants and, second, that the C_4 ground cover obscures the ability to quantitate, even crudely, the use of maize at this site.

A third reason for suggesting that bison was the major food of humans at the Sully site relates to the variability in the $\delta^{13}C$ values of the adult humans. One effect of climate change during the Sully site habitation would have been to enlarge bison foraging ranges with the expected outcome of increased variability in the carbon isotope values in both humans and bison. The $\delta^{13}C$ values of the adult bone collagen from the Sully site ranged from −11.8‰ to −16.2‰ (table 1). These carbon values contrast with the consistency of the $\delta^{15}N$ data, which had a range of 1.2‰ and a coefficient of variation of 4 percent. This pattern of variable carbon and invariant nitrogen isotopic values is also observed in the Glen Rock bison population, which dates to approximately the same time as the Sully site habitation ("Stable Isotopes on the Plains: Vegetation Analysis and Diet Determinations," this vol.). The $\delta^{13}C$ bone collagen values of all the humans and bison from the Sully site are intermediate to pure C_3 and C_4 values, indicating that a C_4 dietary input from a variety of prairie grasses is observed even as far north as the Dakotas.

The temporal effect of climate change on bison bone collagen $\delta^{13}C$ has been documented by Stafford et al. (1991) at Lubbock Lake in Texas. Collagen $\delta^{13}C$ values range from −6.7‰ in the most recent bison (200 years ago) to −18.2‰ in bison that date to the terminal Pleistocene at 10,500 B.C.

During the last 700 years, when maize horticulture was introduced into the Plains, bison bone collagen from the Lubbock Lake site averaged −8.1‰, thus adding another major C_4 isotopic dietary input to the human subsistence base. The $\delta^{15}N$ values in bison bone collagen also varied temporally, although the causative factors are not well understood (Stafford et al. 1991). Variation in carbon and nitrogen isotopic values can derive from a defined food source (e.g., bison), but it is not well known whether the quality and quantity of the human diet affects the fidelity of the isotopic signature encoded in human bone collagen.

The two component model, such as was used to analyze paleodiet in southern Ontario by Schwartz et al. (1985), cannot be used to determine maize intake at Sully because of the contribution of the bison $\delta^{13}C$ values. A study of archaeologically associated fauna in southern Ontario confirmed that only dog and raccoon contribute mixed C_3 C_4 values to the isotopic pool (Katzenberg 1989). Katzenberg notes the difficulty in ascribing human collagen $\delta^{13}C$ values in the −11‰ range to large amounts of maize in the diet when the $\delta^{15}N$ values indicate a major dependence on animal products.

In a study of adult human bone collagen $\delta^{13}C$ values from the Initial Coalescent site, Crow Creek, Bumsted (1984) reported a more positive average of −11.5‰ as compared to the Sully average of −13.5‰. In addition, the standard deviation of the collagen $\delta^{13}C$ of the Crow Creek population is half that of the adult Sully population. These differences are consistent with a milder and less variable climate in the northern Plains just prior to the Little Ice Age.

An attempt to model a three-component system of dietary input based on C_3 plants, C_4 plants, and meat using algebraic and graphic representations led Bumsted (1984) to suggest that the human collagen $\delta^{13}C$ values from Crow Creek support an interpretation of a 78–90 percent maize diet. However, there is an error in bisecting the triangular coordinate graphing system with the observed $\delta^{13}C$ from human bone collagen (Bumsted 1984:125). If instead, the calculated $\delta^{13}C_{diet}$ is used in the triangular graph employed by Bumsted, any combination of C_3, C_4, and meat diets can be supported by the Crow Creek data, and human diets dominated by maize are no more likely than a diet largely based on bison meat. Bumsted (1984) utilized only stable carbon collagen values in her analysis and did not have the substantial benefit that $\delta^{15}N$ data adds.

A few caveats must be offered. Simplistic modeling or mass balance approaches, while commonly done in isotopic paleodietary interpretations, require many assumptions, only some of which have been stated here (Bumsted 1984; Schwartz et al.

1985). The relative digestibility and bioavailability of the foods in question could dramatically alter this analysis. Maize is an incomplete food source to humans, deficient in the essential amino acid lysine and difficult to digest in large amounts. These factors would lead to maize being underrepresented in the stable isotope values of human bone collagen. Conversely, meat serves as a complete protein source for humans and may be overrepresented in collagen isotopic values, particularly in regard to nitrogen.

In addition, many C_3 foods were eaten by the Plains people. If a substantial portion of the bone collagen carbon derives from C_3 foods, then maize intake would have to be invoked, even in a simple mass balance calculation, to account for the observed human collagen stable isotope values. The C_3 isotopic input could well include deer (Drass and Flynn 1990), but faunal bone counts do not exist for the Sully site, making it difficult to assess this parameter.

The isotopic analysis of skeletal remains from the Postcontact Coalescent Sully site agrees with the emphasis that Plains archaeologists have put on the importance of bison in human subsistence (Bamforth 1987; Ewers 1968; Gunnerson 1972; Parmalee 1979; Speth 1983). Speth (1983) has outlined the metabolic stress that can result when humans are forced to rely on a largely meat-based diet. Unlike the situation in the Arctic, Plains Indians had a variety of carbohydrate sources that could be utilized for protein sparing. However, the recent history of the Plains, with massive crop failures (Bowden et al. 1981), suggests that occasionally during the Sully occupation, horticulturally derived products could have been in short supply.

Breastfeeding and Weaning

The $\delta^{15}N$ values in the bone collagen of the Sully site infants and young children exhibit the fractionation that is the result of breast milk ingestion (Fogel, Tuross, and Owsley 1989) (table 1). Figure 2 illustrates the maintenance of the adult $\delta^{15}N$ in infants up to approximately three months of age. Although infants are breastfed at birth, there is a lag in the increase in $\delta^{15}N$ due to the time it takes for newly synthesized proteins to reflect nutritional input. The nursing-derived values are apparent by three months of age, maximize at one year, then decline to the adult values. Between three months and two years of age the $\delta^{15}N$ is on average 1.6 ‰ enriched relative to the adult population (p < .001). After two years of age the $\delta^{15}N$ of bone collagen declines to an average of 10.2‰, which is significantly lower than the adult population (p < .02).

Examining isotopic values in bone collagen as a function of age at death has led to the development of a nitrogen isotopic

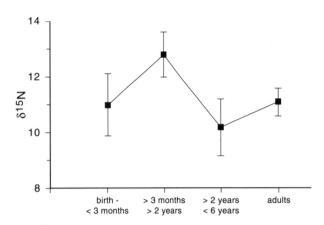

Fig. 2. $\delta^{15}N$ (mean ± 1 standard deviation) of bone collagen as related to age. Adults vs. >3 months and <2 years, p < .001; adults vs. 2–5 years, p < .02, Student's t test. Age determinations based on dental development after Moorrees, Fanning, and Hunt (1963a, 1963b).

tracer that determines the full breastfeeding duration of infants. At the Sully site, women breastfed their infants for one year without introducing any substantial amount of an alternative nitrogen source. All substitute foods were probably limited by the mother in order to maintain infant reliance on breast milk. If maize had been used in large amounts as an early weaning food, one would predict that the $\delta^{13}C$ of the infant collagen would be less negative than the adult value, and that the $\delta^{15}N$ value would be less positive than the fully breastfed infant, or even the adult population. The bone collagen $\delta^{13}C$ values of infants under two years of age are not significantly different from the adult values, although the variation in $\delta^{13}C$ values in this adult population may make this a less than optimal study area for this analysis (table 1). The stable nitrogen isotopes also indicate that maize was not introduced to any great extent up to age two (fig. 2).

From age two to five years, however, the $\delta^{15}N$ values fall below that of the adult population (p < .02). In addition, the $\delta^{13}C$ of these young children was even more variable than the adults (fig. 3). The decline in $\delta^{15}N$ to a value less than that of the adult population suggests that these young children were eating, on average, less meat than their elders. One reasonable interpretation is that these young children ate more fruits and vegetables than did the adults. The decline in $\delta^{15}N$ from a high in the three months to two-year-old group of 12.8‰ to a low in the two- to five-year-old group of 10.2‰ (p < .001) is affected not only by diet but also by bone collagen turnover. The rate of growth declines after the first year of life (Sinclair 1969), and it is anticipated that dietary input will take longer to become recorded in bone collagen as growth slows. As an example, it is assumed that adult bone collagen is a reflection

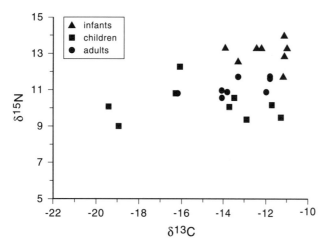

Fig. 3. Stable nitrogen and carbon isotopic values of human bone collagen of infants, children, and adults from the Sully site, S.Dak.

of approximately 20 years of dietary input due to the low turnover of collagen once the skeleton stops growing. The average $\delta^{15}N$ of 10.2‰ in the toddler population is an aggregate value that includes some of the elevated nursing-based signal from their infant years. In summary, the nitrogen input to these toddlers had a $\delta^{15}N$ value that is substantially less than 7‰ and was probably due to one or more plant sources.

Conclusions

Stable nitrogen and carbon analyses of bone collagen from human skeletal remains have contributed to knowledge of paleodiet. The combination of information in carbon and nitrogen isotopes increases the possibility of arriving at reasonable paleodietary interpretations in complex ecosystems. At the Sully site, the stable isotope data of bone collagen is consistent with a major reliance by humans on bison meat. Nitrogen isotopic values in infant bone collagen reveal the persistence of breastfeeding as the sole source of dietary nitrogen up to one year of age, and carbon and nitrogen isotopes may provide useful information on the weaning strategies of the population.

References Cited

Bamforth, D.B.

1987   Historical Documents and Bison Ecology on the Great Plains. *Plains Anthropologist* 32:1–16

——

1988   Ecology and Human Organization on the Great Plains. New York: Plenum Press.

——

1990   An Empirical Perspective on Little Ice Age Climatic Change on the Great Plains. *Plains Anthropologist* 35:359–366.

Barnes, P.W., L. Tieszen, and D.J. Ode

1983   Distribution, Production and Diversity of C3 and C4-dominated Communities in a Mixed Prairie. *Canadian Journal of Botany* 61:741–751.

Bass, W.W.

1964   The Variation in Physical Types of the Prehistoric Plains Indians. *Plains Anthropologist Memoir* 1:70–145.

Bowden, M.J., R.W. Kates, P.A. Kay, W.E. Riebsame, R.A. Warrick, D.L. Johnson, H.A. Gould, and D. Weiner

1981   The Effect of Climate Fluctuations on Human Populations: Two Hypotheses. Pp. 479–513 in Climate and History. T.M.L. Wigley, M.J. Ingram and G. Farmer, eds. Cambridge: Cambridge University Press.

Bumsted, M.P.

1984   Human Variation: $\delta^{13}C$ in Adult Bone Collagen and the Relation to Diet in an Isochronous C4 (Maize) Archaeological Population. Thesis # LA-10259-T. Los Alamos: Los Alamos National Laboratory.

Chisholm, B., J. Driver, S. Dube, and H. Schwartz

1985   Assessment of Prehistoric Bison Foraging and Movement Patterns via Stable-Carbon Isotopic Analysis. *Plains Anthropologist* 29:193–205.

Creel, D., R.F. Scott, and M.B. Collins

1990   A Faunal Record from West Central Texas and Its Bearing on Late Holocene Bison Population Changes in the Southern Plains. *Plains Anthropologist* 35:55–69.

DeNiro, M.J., and S. Epstein

1978   Influence of Diet on the Distribution of Carbon Isotopes in Animals. *Geochimica Cosmochimica Acta* 42:495–506.

——

1981   Influence of Diet on the Distribution of Nitrogen Isotopes in Animals. *Geochimica Cosmochimica Acta* 45:341–351.

Dillehay, T.D.

1974   Late Quaternary Bison Population Changes on the Southern Plains. *Plains Anthropologist* 19:180–196.

Drass, R.R., and Flynn, P.

1990   Temporal and Geographic Variations in Subsistence Practices for Plains Villagers in the Southern Plains. *Plains Anthropologist* 35:175–191.

Eddy A., and A. Cooter

1978   A Drought Probability Model for the USA Northern Great Plains. Norman, Okla.: University of Oklahoma Press.

Ewers, J.C.

1968   Indian Life on the Upper Missouri. Norman, Okla.: University of Oklahoma Press.

Fawcett, W.B.

1988   Changing Prehistoric Settlement Along the Middle Missouri River: Timber Depletion and Historic Context. *Plains Anthropologist* 33:67–94.

Fogel, M.L., N. Tuross, and D.W. Owsley
 1989 Nitrogen Isotope Tracers of Human Lactation in Modern and Archaeological Populations. *Annual Report of the Director Geophysical Laboratory of the Carnegie Institution of Washington* 89:111–117.
Gunnerson, D.A.
 1972 Man and Bison on the Plains in the Protohistoric Period. *Plains Anthropologist* 17:1–10.
Hare, P.E., M.L. Fogel, T.W. Stafford, A.D. Mitchell, and T.C. Hoering
 1991 The Isotopic Composition of Carbon and Nitrogen in Individual Amino Acids Isolated from Modern and Fossil Proteins. *Journal of Archaeological Science* 18:277–292.
Holder, P.
 1970 The Hoe and the Horse on the Plains. Lincoln: University of Nebraska Press.
Jones, P.D., and T.M.L. Wigley
 1990 Global Warming Trends. *Scientific American* 263:84–91.
Katzenburg, A.
 1989 Stable Isotope Analysis of Archaeological Faunal Remains from Southern Ontario. *Journal of Archaeological Science* 16:319–329.
Lee-Thorp J., J. Sealy, and N.J. van der Merwe
 1989 Stable Carbon Isotope Ratio Differences Between Bone Collagen and Bone Apatite, and Their Relationship to Diet. *Journal of Archaeological Science* 16:585–599.
Moorrees, C.F.A., E.A. Fanning, and E.E. Hunt, Jr.
 1963a Formation and Resorption of Three Deciduous Teeth in Children. *American Journal of Physical Anthropology* 21:205–213.

——

 1963b Age Variation of Formation for Ten Permanent Teeth. *Journal of Dental Research* 42:1490–1502.
Owsley, D.W.
 1992 Demography of Prehistoric and Early Historic Northern Populations. Pp. 75–86 in Disease and Demography in the Americas. J.W. Verano and D.H. Ubelaker, eds. Washington: Smithsonian Institution Press.
——, and R.L. Jantz
 1978 Intracemetery Morphological Variation in Arikara Crania from the Sully Site (39SL4), Sully County, South Dakota. *Plains Anthropologist* 23:139–147.
Parmalee, P.W.
 1979 Inferred Arikara Subsistence Patterns Based on a Selected Faunal Assemblage for the Mobridge Site, South Dakota. *Kiva* 44:191–218.
Rogers, J.D.
 1990 Objects of Change. Washington: Smithsonian Institution Press.

Schwartz, H.P., J. Melbye, M.A. Katzenberg, and M. Knyl
 1985 Stable Isotopes in Human Skeletons of Southern Ontario: Reconstructing Paleodiet. *Journal of Archaeological Science* 12:187–206.
Sinclair, D.
 1969 Human Growth After Birth, London: Oxford University Press
Smith, B.
 1989 Origins of Agriculture in Eastern North America. *Science* 216:1567–1571.
Speth, J.
 1983 Bison Kills and Bone Counts, Chicago: University of Chicago Press.
Stafford, T.W., Jr., M.L. Fogel, K. Brendel, and P.E. Hare
 1991 Late Quaternary Paleoecology of the Southern High Plains Based on Stable Carbon and Nitrogen Analyses of Fossil Bison Collagen. (Manuscript in authors' possession.)
Terri, J.A., and L.G. Stowe
 1976 Climatic Patterns and Distribution of C4 Grasses in North America. *Oecologia* 23:1–12.
Tieszen L.L., and T.W. Boutton
 1989 Stable Carbon Isotopes in Terrestrial Ecosystem Research. Pp. 167–195 in Stable Isotopes in Ecological Research. P.W. Rundel, J.R. Ehleringer and K.A. Nagy, eds. New York: Springer-Verlag.
Tieszen, L.L., D.J. Ode, P.W. Barnes, and P.M. Bultsma
 1980 Seasonal Variation in C3 and C4 Biomass at the Ordway Prairie and Selectivity by Bison and Cattle. Pp. 165–174 in *Proceedings of the 7th North American Prairie Conference*. C.L. Kucera, ed. Springfield, Mo.
Tuross, N., M. Fogel, and P.E. Hare
 1988 Variability in the Preservation of the Isotopic Composition of Collagen from Fossil Bone. *Geochimica et Cosmochimica Acta* 52:929–935.
van der Merwe, N.J., and J.C. Vogel
 1978 ^{13}C Content of Human Collagen as a Measure of Prehistoric Diet in Woodland North America. *Nature* 276:815–816.
Wedel, W.R.
 1961 Prehistoric Man on the Great Plains. Norman, Okal.: University of Oklahoma Press.
Wendland, W., A. Bean, and H.A. Semken, Jr.
 1987 Evaluation of Climatic Changes on the North American Great Plains Determined from Faunal Evidence. Pp. 460–469 in Late Quaternary Mammalian Biogeography and Environments of the Great Plains and Prairies. R.W. Graham, H.A. Semken, and M.A. Graham, eds. Springfield, Ill.: Illinois State Museum.

○○○

CHAPTER 23

Antelope Creek Phase Subsistence: The Bone Chemistry Evidence

JUDITH A. HABICHT-MAUCHE, ALYTIA A. LEVENDOSKY, AND
MARGARET J. SCHOENINGER

There is much to be learned about the people who inhabited late prehistoric Plains Village sites in the Canadian and North Canadian river drainages in the Oklahoma and Texas Panhandle. Today this area is agriculturally marginal, yet archaeological remains of villages suggest that farmers survived there for several hundred years without irrigation (Lintz 1984, 1986). The dates of occupation are uncertain, as dating has been based largely on correlations with intrusive Southwest pottery. These correlations and a few radiocarbon dates indicate that these sites, assigned to the Antelope Creek phase, were occupied between approximately 1200 and 1450 (Baerreis and Bryson 1966; Bryson, Baerreis, and Wendland 1970). Diagnostic of the phase is the use of stone-slab wall foundations in building construction. This construction method has been identified in various settlement types, from single-room dwellings to villages containing more than 35 living rooms. There is also variation among villages, with some consisting of free-standing, one-room dwellings and others of contiguous, multi-room structures. Certain diagnostic artifacts, such as heart-shaped cordmarked ceramic jars, link these various settlement types into a single phase (Lintz 1984, 1986).

Antelope Creek Subsistence

Most evidence, although indirect, indicates a mixed economy (Lintz 1984). A specialized chipped-stone tool kit, including beveled knives, side and end scrapers, and a variety of drill forms, indicates that hunting and hide processing were important activities in Antelope Creek society. Bone digging-stick tips and bison-scapula hoes show that horticulture was also a feature of the subsistence strategy. Basin metates and one-handed manos, found on a number of sites, could have been used to process a variety of domesticated or wild plant resources.

Unfortunately, little direct evidence of Antelope Creek subsistence practices have been recovered from the archaeological sites. Few macrobotanical or microbotanical samples have been systematically analyzed (Dean 1986) and faunal collections for only a few sites have been adequately described (e.g. DeMarcay 1986; Duffield 1970; Keller 1975). In the assemblages that have been analyzed, bison is by far the most common animal represented. Charred maize has been recovered from most sites (Dean 1986; Duffield 1964; Holden 1933; Johnson 1939; Studer 1934a). The presence of cobs and cupules suggests that at least some of the grain was raised locally. Rare finds of wild plant foods indicate that gathered wild foods were also used (Dean 1986; Green 1967; Keller 1975). The relative importance of each of these food items has been difficult to determine, although the consensus is that primary dependence on maize horticulture and bison hunting was supplemented by variable amounts of wild plants and small game (Lintz 1984).

The findings from interdisciplinary studies of climatic trends in the Woodland and Prairie Plains regions of Oklahoma (Albert 1981; Farley and Keyser 1979; Lintz and Hall 1983) and in the Southwest (Euler et al. 1979; Jelinek 1967; Schoenwetter and Dittert 1968) complicate the determination of subsistence patterns in the Southern High Plains. Such studies (summarized by Lintz 1984, 1986, 1991) indicate that relatively moist conditions characterized this portion of the continent during the first millenium of the present era, but that some time between A.D. 1100 and 1300 drought gradually set in and probably continued into the sixteenth century. Although no detailed climatic studies have been conducted in the Southern High Plains, it is generally assumed that the same general climatic regime characterized this area as those east and west of it.

Lintz (1984, 1986, 1991), in interpreting the effect of changing climatic conditions, reasons that decreasing precipitation during the twelfth and thirteenth centuries probably led to decreasing stream flow across the entire Southern Plains. However, seep and spring water availability on the High Plains would have been relatively unaffected because the source of this water is the fossil reserves of the Ogallala aquifer. These water resources may have been an important factor in the sudden appearance of Antelope Creek farmers on the Southern High Plains during the thirteenth century.

As climatic conditions continued to deteriorate during the fourteenth century, the viability of this already marginal subsistence strategy could have been severely jeopardized. If periodic crop failures decreased the predictability, reliability and overall productivity of local horticulture, expansion of alternative food acquisition methods would have been necessary. In the short term, hunting could have improved as herds congregated near waterholes and springs near agricultural villages. Eventually hunting also would have been negatively affected by this increasing drought as the overall size and range of natural grazing and foraging habitats changed.

Given the overall marginality of the region, as well as the probable deterioration of climatic conditions, it is surprising that the archaeological record indicates that Antelope Creek populations increased throughout the fourteenth century. This trend is reflected in an increase in both mean living room size and mean total indoor space recorded for late (1350–1500) compared with early (1200–1350) subphase sites (Lintz 1986). A growing population would have further strained the already dwindling food resources of the area.

Two changes in settlement pattern, possibly related to changing climate, appear toward the end of the fourteenth century. First is a move away from the main valley of the Canadian River toward the lateral tributaries. This shift could reflect the abandonment of marginal farmland along the river in favor of fields located adjacent to reliable spring-fed tributary streams (Etchieson 1981; Hughes et al. 1977; Lintz 1986). Concurrently, marked change in settlement organization as hamlets consisting of single, large, contiguous, multifamily structures, such as Alibates 28-Unit I and Antelope Creek 22, were abandoned in favor of others made up of dispersed clusters of isolated, single-family dwellings similar to Alibates 28-Unit II. Lintz (1991) suggests that this pattern reflects an increase in seasonal mobility related to a more intensive use of secondary wild resources during the late subphase of Antelope Creek culture. He reasons, further, that such a shift in subsistence scheduling may have led to decreased community investment in the construction and maintenance of large, permanent agricultural villages.

Antelope Creek communities may have experienced low-level warfare and raiding throughout their existence. Evidence includes the presence of burned structures at numerous sites (Krieger 1946; Lintz 1986; Studer 1934a, 1934b), physical indications of trauma (Eyerly 1907; Green 1967; Holden 1929; Patterson 1975), and the placement of defensive structures along the periphery of settlement clusters (Lintz 1986). Thus, many of the physical manifestations of Antelope Creek culture appear to represent adaptations to endemic environmental and population stress. This stress seems to have reached a critical point around the middle of the fourteenth century when radical changes occurred in regional settlement pattern and community structure. In regard to subsistence and diet, Lintz (1986) has suggested that increasing population combined with deteriorating climatic conditions may have depleted two primary food sources—bison meat and maize. To counteract the potential nutritional effects of long-term population and environmental stress, Antelope Creek communities could have diversified their basic subsistence strategy to include a greater reliance on secondary meat sources, such as deer and antelope, and on seasonally available wild plants.

The objectives of this study were, first, to outline the basic diet of the people at Antelope Creek sites and, second, to identify any change in subsistence strategy during the time of occupation. The relative importance of the various foods, such as plant versus animal, or domesticated versus wild, is difficult to assess using archaeological data (Smith 1979; cf. Wetterstrom 1986). Bone composition offers the possibility of detailed information on prehistoric diets. In additional, the diets of specific individuals or subgroups of individuals can be estimated, which is not possible using faunal and floral remains. Thus, it becomes possible to identify associations between diet and physical and social attributes such as status, age, sex, or general health.

Materials and Methods

Bone samples from 29 individuals assigned to the Antelope Creek phase were obtained from the Panhandle-Plains Historical Museum in Canyon, Texas. The individuals were recovered from five sites along the Canadian River in the Texas Panhandle: Antelope Creek 22, Antelope Creek 22A, Alibates 28 (Unit I and Unit II) (Baker and Baker 1941), a cemetery associated with the Mathews site, and the Parcell site cemetery.

Unfortunately, no chronological data of any kind are available from the Mathews and Parcell sites; therefore, temporal trends are based exclusively on the Antelope 22 and 22A and Alibates 28-Units I and II samples. The dating of the skeletal remains from Alibates 28 is somewhat ambiguous. From evidence that all but two burials at Alibates 28-Unit I were excavated from above room floors, Lintz (1986) concluded that they are probably associated with the later occupation at Alibates-Unit II. Although there are no radiometric dates from either site, both the architecture and artifact assemblage from Unit II indicate that the village was occupied during the late subphase. Based on these interpretations, the samples from both units were considered together as representative of the late period.

The dating of the burials from Antelope Creek 22 and 22A is also problematical. C.R. Lintz (personal communication 1989) believes that the burials recovered from Antelope Creek

22A are probably part of the same resident population as the burials from the adjacent site of Antelope Creek 22 because some of the burials at the former site were placed above floors and superimposed in walls. No absolute dates exist for these sites, but, architecturally, Antelope Creek 22 is a contiguous structure which is considered diagnostic of the early subphase. However, there is a high percentage of Southwest trade goods at the site, suggesting the late subphase. For the purposes of this report, the burials from Antelope Creek 22 and 22A are considered as representative of the early subphase population, but in the absence of precise dating, this assumption is debatable.

Four elements of bone composition were analyzed in this study: carbon, nitrogen, strontium, and zinc. The stable carbon isotope ratio (expressed as $\delta^{13}C$ in units ‰) in bone collagen was used to indicate use of bison meat and maize relative to other animals and wild plants. Plants differ in their ratios of two stable carbon isotopes ($^{13}C/^{12}C$) according to the type of photosynthetic pathway they use (see summary in O'Leary 1988). The majority of edible wild plants in the Panhandle region use a method of photosynthesis that results in a huge depletion of the heavier isotope (^{13}C) in the plant's tissues relative to its concentration in atmospheric CO_2. These plants are called C_3 and have $\delta^{13}C$ values around −28‰ as compared with −7‰ in atmospheric CO_2 (O'Leary 1988). Maize and certain other wild plants (table 1) use a different method of photosynthesis that results in less depletion of ^{13}C relative to the concentration in the atmosphere. They are referred to as C_4 plants and have $\delta^{13}C$ values around −12‰. Succulents, like cacti, belong to a third photosynthetic group known as CAM (crassulacean acid metabolism) plants, which have $\delta^{13}C$ values equivalent to C_4 plants, or values somewhere between those from C_3 and C_4 plants, depending on environmental growth conditions.

Empirical evidence indicates that animal tissues (including bone collagen) have stable isotope ratios which reflect the observed differences in plant stable isotope ratios (Bender, Baerreis, and Stevenson 1981; DeNiro and Epstein 1978; van der Merwe 1982). In other words, the ratio of stable carbon

Table 1. Some Edible C$_4$ and CAM Plants Available to Antelope Creek Phase Populations

Plant Name	Part Used	Used As	Sources
Amaranthus retroflexus (redroot pigweed)	Young plant, leaves, seeds	Greens, pot herb, parched and ground for flour	Lintz 1986
Atriplex canescens (four-wing saltbush)	Seeds	Meal, parched	Lintz 1986
Portulaca oleracea (common purslane)	Young plant leaves	Greens, pot herb	Dean 1986
Panicum obtusum (vine mesquite)	Seeds	Flour	Lintz 1986
Sporobolus cryptandrus (sand dropseed)	Seeds	Parched, ground for flour	Lintz 1986
Opuntia sp. (prickly pear)	Fruits, buds, flowers, seeds	Food	Lintz 1986

isotopes in the flesh and bone collagen of animals feeding on C_3 plant material has a C_3 signature of carbon isotopes whereas the ratio in animals feeding on C_4 plants reflects the C_4 signature (Tieszen et al. 1983; Vogel 1978).

The stable nitrogen isotope ratio (expressed as $\delta^{15}N$ in units ‰) in bone collagen and the zinc and strontium concentrations in bone mineral were measured as indicators of the amount of meat relative to plant material in human diet. Foods derived from animal sources often differ from those obtained from plants in both strontium and zinc concentrations (Elias, Hirao, and Patterson 1982; Schroeder, Tipton, and Nason 1972; Sillen and Kavanagh 1982; Underwood 1977), as well as in the relative ratio of stable nitrogen isotopes in their proteins (Schoeninger and DeNiro 1984; Wada 1980). As with carbon, the ratio of stable nitrogen isotopes and the concentration of strontium and zinc in the bones of known herbivores and carnivores reflect the differences in isotopic ratio and trace element concentration between plants and animals when these occur (DeNiro and Epstein 1981; Morgan and Schoeninger 1989; Schoeninger 1979, 1985; Sillen and Kavanagh 1982). Therefore, it is theoretically possible to determine the relative significance of certain classes of food resources (i.e. meat versus plants, domesticated versus wild plants) in the prehistoric diets of the Antelope Creek phase inhabitants through the chemical analysis of their skeletal remains. These data can be used to study variability among individuals, as well as changes in basic subsistence strategies between the early and late portion of the phase. A shift in subsistence strategy should be reflected in the bone composition signatures. For example, because most of the edible wild plants on the Southern High Plains belong to the C_3 group, and deer, antelope, and other small mammals forage primarily on C_3 plants, increasing use of these resources through time should result in a lower (more negative) $\delta^{13}C$ value for the late subphase sample as compared to the early subphase sample.

Samples of ground bone were prepared from twenty-nine individuals representing 18 adults and 11 sub-adults. Eight of the individuals could be identified as males; 12 were females. Most of the samples were ribs, although a few long bones and skull fragments were included. Most of the samples were well-preserved, although some had a hard mineral deposit, possibly caliche, on the exposed surfaces. Bone samples were cleaned mechanically and cancellous bone was removed. The remaining cortical bone was cleaned in distilled, deionized water in a ultrasonic cleaner. After drying to a constant weight in a low-temperature oven, each bone sample was ground either in a Spex freezer mill at liquid nitrogen temperatures or by hand with a mortar and pestle.

Each sample was divided into two aliquots, one for trace element analysis and the other for stable isotope analysis. Sample preparation for trace elements zinc and strontium analysis followed procedures described by Schoeninger (1981). Bone samples were analyzed for zinc and strontium concentrations using a Perkin-Elmer atomic absorption spectrophotometer (Model 3030). Strontium analysis was performed with a nitrous oxide/acetylene flame while air/acetylene was used for the zinc analysis. Results from the analysis of nine preparations of the I.A.E.A. bone standard H5 were as follows: strontium range = 92–100 parts per million (ppm), mean value = 96 ppm; and zinc range = 82–106 ppm, mean value = 96 ppm. Published values for the standard are strontium range = 88–105 ppm, mean value = 96 ppm; zinc range = 84–95 ppm, mean value = 89 ppm.

Stable isotope analysis was performed on the remaining aliquot of each ground bone sample. Collagen was extracted, combusted, and the resulting CO_2 and N_2 gas separated and purified cryogenically in a vacuum system (see Schoeninger and DeNiro 1984). Gas samples were analyzed by mass spectrometry to determine isotopic ratios of $^{13}C/^{12}C$ and $^{15}N/^{14}N$ respectively; the standard for carbon is PDB (peedee belumnite) (‰) and for nitrogen, AIR (ambiant inhalable reservoir) (‰). Precision for $\delta^{15}N$ was ±0.2‰ and for $\delta^{13}C$ was ±0.1‰.

Results

STRONTIUM AND ZINC

The bones of humans or other animals whose diets consist primarily of plants should contain relatively higher strontium concentrations than those of species whose diets consist of either a broad mix of plants and animals or primarily animals (Schoeninger 1979; Sillen and Kavanagh 1982). Table 2 presents the strontium concentrations (reported as "parts per million in ash") for the Antelope Creek samples. The mean value for the entire sample is 1,374 ppm, which is more than four times higher than the mean value of samples from Pecos Pueblo (Spielmann, Schoeninger, and Moore 1990), an intensive horticultural site. The marked difference between the Pueblo and Plains Village sites could be the result of differences in the concentration of strontium in the soil of the two regions. The strontium/calcium ratio in surface water on the Southern High Plains (13:1) is the highest recorded anywhere in the United States (Sillen and Kavanagh 1982). There is also a great deal of variation among the six Antelope Creek samples (table 3). If the bone strontium levels are reflecting surface water or soil strontium concentration, the results indi-

Table 2. Zinc and Strontium Concentrations in Antelope Creek Phase Samples

Sample No.	Site	Zinc (ppm)	Strontium (ppm)	Sex	Age
MS2901	Mathews	101	748	M	Adult
MS2902	Parcell	100	513	?	Infant
MS2903	Parcell	151	1280	?	Adolescent
MS2904	Parcell	107	926	F	Adult
MS2905	Parcell	41	1188	F	Adult
MS2906	Parcell	50	938	F	Adult
MS2907	Parcell	73	1188	F	Adult
MS2908	Parcell	190	861	F	Adult
MS2909	Antelope Creek 22A	174	2454	F	Adult
MS2910	Antelope Creek 22A	218	[a]	?	Child
MS2911	Antelope Creek 22A	334	2064	M	Adult
MS2912	Antelope Creek 22A	130	2243	F	adolescent
MS2913	Antelope Creek 22A	201	1470	F	Adult
MS2914	Antelope Creek 22A	361	1615	M	Adult
MS2915	Antelope Creek 22A	175	1333	M	Adult
MS2916	Antelope Creek 22A	250	2922	F	Adult
MS2917	Antelope Creek 22	286	952	M	Adult
MS2918	Antelope Creek 22	242	2707	M	Adult
MS2919	Antelope Creek 22	146	1993	?	Child
MS2920	Antelope Creek 22	250	2413	M	Adult
MS2922	Antelope Creek 22	228	2278	?	Adolescent
MS2923	Alibates 28, I	841[b]	804	F	Adolescent
MS2924	Alibates 28, I	391	1054	F	Adult
MS2925	Alibates 28, I	131	810	?	Child
MS2926	Alibates 28, I	150	740	?	Child
MS2927	Alibates 28, I	295	920	?	Child
MS2928	Alibates 28, II	179	1393	F	Adult
MS2929	Alibates 28, II	115	438	?	Child
MS2930	Alibates 28, II	327	162	M	Adult
Mean		193	1374		
Standard deviation		94	742		
Coefficient of variation		49%	54%		

[a]This value was outside the linear range of the instrument.

[b]This value is abnormally high, not included in the following analysis.

cate that there is a high degree of variation in environmental levels of strontium within the Canadian River valley. The means for Antelope Creek 22 and Antelope Creek 22A, located only 50 meters apart, are nearly identical, yet their means differ significantly (over 1,000 ppm) from the other, more distant sites.

In contrast to the trophic level distribution for strontium, lower zinc values are expected with a more herbivorous diet and higher values with a more carnivorous diet (Beck 1985; Morgan and Schoeninger 1989). The zinc concentra-

tions in bone from the Antelope Creek sites are within the range previously observed in modern animals (Morgan and Schoeninger 1989). However, the zinc results show the same pattern as the strontium data with a great deal of variation among samples (table 2). The results of a comparison among sites (see table 3) suggest that the variation clusters according to site.

The inordinately high strontium concentrations and broad range of geographic variability in both strontium and zinc measured in the Antelope Creek samples could reflect differ-

Table 3. Comparison of Trace Element Concentrations Among Antelope Creek Sites

	Mathews	Parcell	Antelope Creek 22A	Antelope Creek 22	Alibates 28
Strontium					
Mean	748	985	2014	2069	850
Standard deviation		262	576	675	373
Coefficient of variation		27%	29%	33%	47%
N	1	7	7	5	8
Males	1	0	3	3	1
Females	0	5	4	0	3
Zinc					
Mean	102	102	230	230	227
Standard deviation		54	81	52	109
Coefficient of variation		53%	35%	23%	48%
N	1	7	8	5	7
Males	1	0	3	3	1
Females	0	5	4	0	2

ences which existed between living populations, but it is more likely that they result from diagenetic changes in bone composition after burial (Lambert et al. 1982). Grupe and Piepenbrink (1989) have demonstrated that in soils enriched in strontium and zinc, contamination of bone by fungi can result in an enrichment of both elements in bone by several orders of magnitude. Given this ambiguity it is impossible to draw any conclusions regarding Antelope Creek diet based on these data.

STABLE NITROGEN ISOTOPE RATIOS

The results on nitrogen isotopes are presented in table 4. The overall mean of the nitrogen values from the Antelope Creek bone samples is 9.4‰, with a standard deviation of 1.1‰ and a coefficient of variation of 12 percent. This coefficient of variation is much higher than that previously observed within a population of small mammals all fed the same diet (<4%, DeNiro and Schoeninger 1985). On the assumption that humans eating a monotonous diet would exhibit similar coefficients, it appears that some degree of dietary variation existed among individuals in Antelope Creek society.

A statistical comparison of the adult male and female samples (table 5) indicates that there is a significant difference in the mean stable nitrogen isotope ratios between these two subgroups of the population, with the males being more positive on average than the females. In addition, the females have a higher coefficient of variation,

indicating a much greater range of individual dietary variability among them. A comparison of the mean stable nitrogen isotope values among sites (table 6) does not reveal any significant differences. These results suggest that differences in diet between men and women are more important in determining variation in nitrogen isotope values than either changes in diet through time or differences among geographic areas. Even so, it is impossible to infer the nature of these presumed dietary differences.

In contrast to expectations, the $\delta^{15}N$ values for both plant and animal foods are roughly equivalent (table 7). There is variation among the small number of food items selected for analysis and when more plants and animals are analyzed, the range of variation probably will increase. If the observation of a consistent relationship between diet and collagen $\delta^{15}N$ values in animals (DeNiro and Epstein 1981) holds true for humans, the variation among the people buried at these sites must indicate differences in diet. At this time the specific food items responsible for such variation cannot be identified.

STABLE CARBON ISOTOPE RATIOS

The overall mean for the stable carbon isotope ratios is −8.0‰ with a standard deviation of 1.0‰ and a coefficient of variation of 12.6 percent (table 4). Such a high coefficient of variation indicates that the diet of these people was varied, because a sample from a population eating a uniform diet would be expected to yield a coefficient of

Table 4. Stable Carbon and Nitrogen Isotope Ratios for Antelope Creek Phase Samples

Sample No.	Site	$\delta^{13}C$ (‰)	$\delta^{15}N$ (‰)	Sex	Age
MS2901	Mathews	−7.7‰	10.5	M	Adult
MS2903	Parcell	−6.4	7.1	?	Adolescent
MS2904	Parcell	−11.2	8.3	F	Adult
MS2905	Parcell	−9.4	9.4	F	Adult
MS2906	Parcell	−7.6	9.8	F	Adult
MS2907	Parcell	−7.6	9.1	F	Adult
MS2909	Antelope Creek 22A	−8.3	9.8	F	Adult
MS2910	Antelope Creek 22A	−7.6	10.4	?	Child
MS2911	Antelope Creek 22A	−8.2	9.2	M	Adult
MS2912	Antelope Creek 22A	−8.2	6.6	F	Adolescent
MS2914	Antelope Creek 22A	−7.8	9.9	M	Adult
MS2915	Antelope Creek 22A	—	10.2	M	Adult
MS2916	Antelope Creek 22A	−8.9	9.2	F	Adult
MS2917	Antelope Creek 22	−7.5	10.4	M	Adult
MS2918	Antelope Creek 22	−7.8	10.1	M	Adult
MS2919	Antelope Creek 22	−7.6	—	?	Child
MS2920	Antelope Creek 22	−8.2	9.3	M	Adult
MS2922	Antelope Creek 22	−6.9	9.0	?	Adolescent
MS2923	Alibates 28, I	−8.8	8.8	F	Adolescent
MS2924	Alibates 28, I	−7.8	9.7	F	Adult
MS2925	Alibates 28, I	−9.4	7.1	?	Child
MS2926	Alibates 28, I	−7.8	10.0	?	Child
MS2927	Alibates 28, I	−7.6	11.1	?	Child
MS2928	Alibates 28, II	−7.7	9.8	F	Adult
MS2930	Alibates 28, II	−8.3	10.0	M	Adult

variation of only around 2 percent in $\delta^{13}C$ (DeNiro and Schoeninger 1985). A comparison between sexes (table 5) indicates no significant difference between the mean stable carbon isotope ratios of men and women from Antelope Creek sites. This implies that the relative ratio of C_4 and C_3 components in the diets of both groups was about equal. The reason for the lack of statistical significance is the large standard deviation in the female sample. The coefficient of variation for the female sample (19%) is high and suggests individual variation among the diets of Antelope Creek women. There is no significant difference in stable carbon isotope ratios among sites (table 6). Consequently, there appears to have been no change in the relative ratio of C_4 and C_3 components in Antelope Creek diets between the early (Antelope Creek 22 and Antelope Creek 22A) and late (Alibates 28) subphases.

Table 5. Comparison of Stable Isotope Ratios in Adults from Antelope Creek[a,b]

	Male ($\delta^{15}N$)	Female ($\delta^{15}N$)	Male ($\delta^{13}C$)	Female ($\delta^{13}C$)
Mean	9.9	9.4	−7.9	−8.6
Standard deviation	0.5	0.5	0.3	1.6
Coefficient of variation	4.8%	5.6%	3.8%	19.0%
N	8	8	7	8

[a]t-Test of difference in means ($\delta^{15}N$) between males and females: t = 2.24, df = 14. This is significant at the $p \leq .05$ level.

[b]t-Test of difference in means ($\delta^{13}C$) between males and females: t = 1.6, df = 15. This is not significant at the $p \leq .05$ level.

Table 6. Comparison of Stable Isotope Ratios from Antelope Creek Sites[a,b]

	Mathews	Parcell	Antelope Creek 22	Antelope Creek 22A	Antelope Creek 22A and 22	Alibates
$\delta^{15}N$ *(AIR)* ‰						
Mean	10.5	8.7	9.7	9.3	9.5	9.5
Standard deviation	—	1.1	0.7	1.3	1.1	1.1
Coefficient of variation	—	22.2%	6.8%	13.8%	12.6%	16.8%
N	1	5	4	7	11	7
Male	1	0	3	3	6	1
Female	0	4	0	3	3	3
$\delta^{13}C$ *(PDB)* ‰						
Mean	−7.7	−8.4	−7.6	−8.2	−7.9	−8.2
Standard deviation	—	1.9	0.5	0.5	0.5	0.7
Coefficient of variation	—	22.0%	6.2%	5.5%	6.7%	8.2%
N	1	5	5	6	11	7
Male	1	0	3	2	5	1
Female	0	4	0	3	3	3

[a]t-Test of difference between means from early subphase (Antelope Creek 22 + 22A) and late subphase (Alibates 28) samples: t = 0.0, df = 16. This is not significant at the p ≤ .05 level.

[b]t-Test of difference between means from early subphase (Antelope Creek 22 + 22A) and late subphase (Alibates 28) samples t = 0.9, df = 16. This is not significant at the p ≤ .05 level.

Interpretation

Because the variation in $\delta^{13}C$ values from food items is patterned, it is possible to estimate the relative ratio of these foods in the diet of the sampled population. Indirect evidence indicates a variety of food items in Antelope Creek diet: bison, antelope, deer, cottontail and jackrabbits, turtle, a variety of birds (including wild turkey), and mussels have all been recov-

ered from archaeological contexts (Duffield 1964; Holden 1933; Johnson 1939; Studer 1934a). Duffield (1970) identified the skeletal remains of 19 mammal species, 13 bird species, six amphibians, as well as a variety of reptiles, fish and mollusks from Antelope Creek phase sites in the Texas Panhandle. Despite the broad range of species represented, it was estimated that bison contributed between 80 to 100 percent of the potential available meat weight at these sites with deer and

Table 7. Elemental and Isotopic Composition of Selected Antelope Creek Diet Items

	$\delta^{15}N_{(AIR)}$ ‰			$\delta^{13}C_{(PDB)}$ ‰		
	N	Mean	Range	N	Mean	Range
Fauna						
Mule deer (*Odocoileus hemionus*)	3	3.9	3.5 to 5.0	3	−20.7	−22.1 to −19.5
Pronghorn antelope (*Antilocapra americana*)	3	8.0	6.3 to 9.0	3	−20.2	−20.5 to −19.9
Bison (*Bison bison*)	3	5.6	5.1 to 5.9	3	−11.2	−11.2 to −10.9
Flora						
Maize kernels (*Zea mays*)	2	7.0	6.3 to 7.6	2	−11.2	−11.3 to −11.2
Beans (*Phaseolus vulgaris*)	2	5.4	5.3 to 5.6	2	−24.8	−25.1 to −24.6
Amaranth seeds	1	9.0	—	1	−11.3	—
Chenopodium seeds	1	8.1	—	1	−25.5	—
Prickly pear (*Opuntia* sp.)	—	—	—	1	−12.3	—

Sources: Speilmann, Schoeninger, and Moore 1990; John Speth, personal commnication 1989.

antelope contributing only 20 percent and under 2 percent, respectively (Duffield 1970). A similar pattern can be seen in the data from Landergin Mesa where bison remains outnumber deer and antelope on the order of two to one (DeMarcay 1986).

In regard to plants, in addition to maize, Keller (1975) reports remains of squash and beans at Black Dog Village, but these were not charred and could represent modern intrusives. A single domesticated bean (*Phaseolus vulgaris*) was recovered from excavations on Landergin Mesa (Dean 1986). Chenopodium-amaranth pollen has been identified in samples from Landegin Mesa (Dean 1986) but could reflect the intrusion of weedy plants at the site during periods of abandonment. Other wild food remains have revealed the use of acorns (Quercus spp.), hackberry (Celtis sp.), mesquite (Prosopis sp.), wild buckwheat (Eriogoum sp.), cattail stems (Typha sp.), plums (Prunus sp.), persimmons (Diospyros spp.), prickly pear (Opuntia spp.), Indian mallow (Abutilon sp.), narrowleaf yucca buds (*Yucca angustifolia*), Portulaca, and Chenopodium (Dean 1986; Green 1967; Keller 1975). Most of these plants were of minimal economic utility and would not be expected to be a major constituent of Antelope Creek diet. An exception is prickly pear, which, reportedly, was an important seasonal food for groups living in this area of the Texas Panhandle during the Protohistoric period (Hammond and Rey 1927).

As part of a related study in the Southwest, food items from Pecos Pueblo were analyzed (Spielmann, Schoeninger, and Moore 1990). Some, presented in table 7, are thought to be of dietary importance in the Panhandle. In contrast to that study, which included bison from both the Central and Southern plains, only three bison from the Southern Plains appear in table 7. Bison on the Southern High Plains grazed on approximately 75 to 80 percent C_4 grasses and sedges, but farther north, where more C_3 grasses constitute the groundcover, these grasses provide a greater percentage of bison diet (Peden 1972; L.L. Tieszen, personal communication 1987). The $\delta^{13}C$ values of the bison bone collagen (−9.6, −9.2, and −8.9‰) reflect dietary composition. (It should be noted that the values presented in table 7 are estimated flesh values rather than measured bone collagen values, based on 2‰ difference—Medaglia, Little, and Schoeninger 1989.) If the Antelope Creek people ate mainly Southern Plains bison, samples recovered from the Southern Plains should be more representative of their diet. A sample of prickly pear cactus was analyzed for its stable carbon isotope ratio. The $\delta^{13}C$ value of −12.3‰ is similar to that measured in the maize samples.

The data indicate that both the fauna and the flora divide into two groups on the basis of their stable carbon isotope ratios. Of the fauna of economic importance, only bison has a C_4 signature. The estimated value for bison meat on the Southern Plains lies between −12 and −11‰. Of the plant samples, maize, amaranth, and prickly pear would contribute a C_4 signature to human bone collagen. The maize and amaranth samples have $\delta^{13}C$ values of about −11‰, and that of prickly pear is close to −12‰. Although there is little paleobotanical evidence for its use by Antelope Creek populations, amaranth commonly occurs as an opportunistic weed associated with agricultural fields (Gish 1982). Its seeds are easily gathered and can be parched and ground into a nutritious flour. Prickly pear fruits could have been gathered seasonally and stored dry, and would have been sources of calories and vitamin C. The leaves could have been gathered year round but would have provided little more than bulk to the diet.

The average $\delta^{13}C$ value for the Antelope Creek sample is −8.0‰. As the difference between bone collagen and diet is about 5‰ (DeNiro and Epstein 1978; Vogel 1978), the $\delta^{13}C$ value for Antelope Creek diet was probably around −13‰, indicating that approximately 85 to 95 percent of the Antelope Creek diet consisted of maize, cactus, amaranth (or other C_4 plants) and bison meat, all of which have a C_4 signature. Surveys of human diet indicate that intake levels of meat, worldwide, are strikingly constant at about 10–15 percent of total calories (Degarine 1978). Speth and Spielmann (1983) suggest that people may have eaten higher percentages of meat at times of scarcity of other food resources, yet, the upper limit appears to be between 20 and 40 percent of total calories, for death from protein poisoning results beyond 50 percent (Noli and Avery 1988). "While the limits have never been clearly defined by experimentation, the highest figure for a specific diet that has actually been recorded is 15–25%" (Noli and Avery 1988:397, citing McClellan and Du Bois 1930; McClellan, Spencer, and Falk 1931) of total calories from meat. Even if bison supplied 25 percent of the calories in the diet of the Antelope Creek phase people, more than half the calories (>60%) must have been supplied by maize, cactus, or other C4 plants such as amaranth (Schoeninger 1989).

Although present at most Antelope Creek sites, microbotanical remains of charred maize are not abundant, nor are agricultural implements (i.e., digging sticks and hoes) and processing implements (i.e., grinding stones) common. The unpredictability of climatic conditions on the Southern High Plains would have made maize horticulture a fairly risky enterprise for Antelope Creek communities. The growing season is within the range necessary for maize, but early frosts can have severe impact on productivity from one year to the next. The region, on average, receives little more than the required 18 inches of summer rain needed for a successful maize crop and droughts of varying severity are a common occurrence (Lintz 1986). There is no evidence for the construction of water control devices of any kind, nor is irrigation feasible in the area because of erratic stream flow and the brackish character of much of the stream water, especially during summer months. Finally, garden plots would have been restricted to a small number of locations near springs and along the margins of stabilized sand dunes (Lintz 1986). These factors, together with the stable carbon isotope data, suggest that the subsistence strategies of Antelope Creek phase populations included the seasonal gathering of edible succulents and weedy C_4 plants.

Data on diet in the Southern Plains were compared to data on diet in the Southwest. A random sample of 10 individuals from the complete Antelope Creek data set was generated using a random number table. Figure 1 presents these data compared with a similarly generated random sample (n = 10) from a study of diet at Pecos Pueblo (Spielmann, Schoeninger, and Moore 1990) and Hawikuh, a protohistoric Zuni Pueblo in western New Mexico (Schoeninger, Tauber, and DeNiro 1983). The total sample from Hawikuh consisted of 10 indi-

viduals (constituting the constraint on the number of samples used in the comparative plot).

The Panhandle data suggest that the population varied in its dependence on C_4 food components when compared with settled Pueblo agriculturalists. The data for most individuals overlap with the Pecos values, but two of the 10 have $\delta^{13}C$ values that indicate a diet consisting of lower amounts of food with C_4 signatures. There are also 2 of the 10 samples from Antelope Creek that have more positive carbon isotope values than those from the two Pueblos. This variability probably reflects the overall marginality of the Panhandle Plains environment, which could have fostered a broader, more flexible and more individualistic subsistence strategy than that practiced by the communal farming villages of the Southwest. It should be noted that in one respect the diet at Pecos Pueblo is closer to that of the Plains Villagers than to that of their Pueblo neighbors to the west. Both the Pecos and the Antelope Creek samples have relatively high nitrogen values in comparison to Hawikuh. To interpret this finding as reflecting greater emphasis on hunting and meat consumption in populations living along the western margins of the High Plains would be premature; further analyses of food items from each geographic area are necessary to justify such a conclusion.

Conclusion

The results of trace element and stable isotope analyses of human bone samples from late prehistoric Antelope Creek phase sites in the Texas Panhandle reveal several interesting patterns. First, the results for nitrogen indicate statistically significant differences in the diets of males and females. The results for nitrogen and carbon also show a much broader range of internal variability among the female samples as compared to the male samples from the same population (fig. 2). In general, these differences between sexes appear to be a far more important source of variability within the sample as a whole than are differences over time and geographic location.

Second, the carbon isotope analysis suggests that, on average, some 90 percent of the Antelope Creek diet consisted of maize, bison meat, prickly pear cactus, and amaranth, all of which have a C_4 signature. The remaining 10 percent probably consisted of a variety of wild plants and game, such as antelope and deer, which have a C_3 signature. These results support archaeological interpretations of Antelope Creek phase subsistence as a broad-based economy that included a mix of hunting, foraging, and horticulture (Lintz 1991). Un-

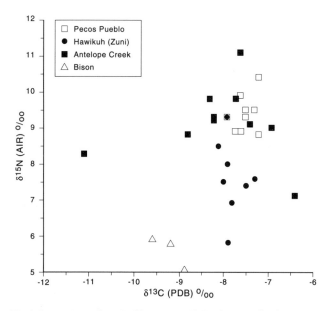

Fig. 1. Comparison of two Pueblo groups with Antelope Creek. There is greater variation among the Antelope Creek samples, suggesting that the dietary adaptation among these people varied to a greater extent than among the Pueblo groups. The $\delta^{13}C$ values indicate a heavy reliance upon C_4 plants and bison. In the area of the Antelope Creek sites, maize, amaranth, and cactus have $\delta^{13}C$ values of C_4 plants. Thus, the Antelope Creek people subsisted on variable amounts of bison, maize, amaranth, and cactus.

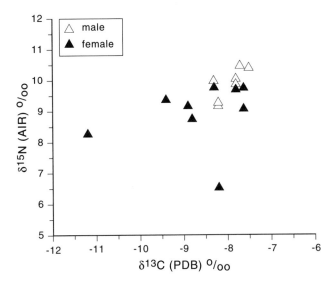

Fig. 2. Comparison of carbon and nitrogen isotope values of males and females from Antelope Creek sites. Females demonstrate greater variability than the males.

fortunately, with bone composition analysis it not possible to determine the relative importance of bison hunting versus maize agriculture in Antelope Creek subsistence. Based on nutritional requirements for carbohydrates and avoidance of protein poisoning, most ingested calories were surely from plants. Given the relative marginality of the Southern High Plains for maize horticulture, a significant portion of the C_4 signature could result from dependence on gathered cactus and other C_4 wild plants (i.e., amaranth and grasses) in addition to bison, rather than from domesticated maize. An alternative interpretation is that Antelope Creek individuals may have supplemented local maize production through trade with Pueblo farmers. The relatively low frequency of Southwest trade goods recovered from early subphase sites (Lintz 1986) does not support this explanation of the high $\delta^{13}C$ values recorded for the early sample.

Assuming that Antelope Creek 22 and Antelope Creek 22A date to the early period and that Alibates 28 dates to the late subphases, there are no indications from human bone composition analysis of greater use of secondary meat sources such as deer, antelope, or other smaller game during the late subphase. Paleoecological and archaeological evidence suggests that the Antelope Creek people were adapting to conditions of increasing climatic and population stress during the late fourteenth century. More secondary plant foods such as cactus and amaranth could have been gathered more intensively to replace maize. The stable carbon isotope values can not distinguish among these plant foods.

These data can be interpreted in several ways. First, the climatic changes recorded for adjacent regions may not have affected the agricultural productivity and foraging capacity of the people of the Southern High Plains to the degree previously predicted. Secondly, Antelope Creek people may have been able to ameliorate these changes by intensifying agricultural production in selected, fertile, well-watered areas as is suggested by the shift in settlement distribution during the late subphase. Thirdly, they could have increased their dependence on other wild C_4 and CAM plants. Fourth, Antelope Creek communities may have ameliorated the effects of local food shortages through trade with neighboring horticultural groups. This strategy would explain the increased number of Southwest trade goods recovered from Antelope Creek sites dated after 1350 (Lintz 1986).

It is not possible, based on either the archaeological evidence or the bone composition results, to choose among these alternatives. Probably no single explanation fully accounts for Antelope Creek subsistence during the late occupation of the Panhandle Plains. What is clear it that by the end of the fifteenth century the broad-based farming, hunting, and foraging economy, described here for the Antelope Creek phase, disappeared from the Southern High Plains.

References Cited

Albert, L.
    1981 Ferndale Bog and Natural Lake: Five Thousand Years of Environmental Change in Southeastern Oklahoma. *Studies in Oklahoma's Past* 7.

Baerreis, D.A., and R.A. Bryson
    1966 Dating the Panhandle Aspect Cultures. *Bulletin of the Oklahoma Anthropological Society* 14:105–116.

Baker, E., and J. Baker
    1941 Final Report. Archaeological Survey O.P.-665-66-3-404, State Application 30976. (Unpublished manuscript on file at the Panhandle-Plains Historical Museum, Canyon, Texas.)

Beck, L.
    1985 Bivariate Analysis of Trace Elements in Bone. *Journal of Human Evolution* 14(5):493–502.

Bender, M.M., D.A. Baerreis, and R.L. Stevenson
    1981 Further Light on Carbon Isotopes and Hopewell Agriculture. *American Antiquity* 46:346–353.

Bryson, R.A., D.A. Baerreis, and W.M. Wendland
    1970 The Character of Late-Glacial and Post-Glacial Climatic Changes. Pp. 53–77 in Pleistocene and Recent Environments of the Central Great Plains, W. Dort, Jr. and J.K. Jones, eds. (Special Publication 3.) Lawrence, Kans.: University of Kansas, Department of Geology.

Dean, G.
1986   The Archeobotany of Landergin Mesa. (Manuscript on file at the Office of the State Archeologist, Texas Historical Commission, Austin.)

Degarine, I.
1978   Variability and Constancy of Feeding Behavior in Man. P. 146 in *Recent Advances in Primatology* 1. D.J. Chivers and J. Hevheut, eds. London: Academic Press.

DeMarcay, G.B.
1986   Vertebrate Fauna from Landergin Mesa: An Antelope Creek Period Village Site. (M.A. Thesis in Anthropology, Texas A&M University, College Station.)

DeNiro, M.J., and S. Epstein
1978   Influence of Diet on the Distribution of Carbon Isotopes in Animals. *Geochimica et Cosmochimica Acta* 42:495–506.

———
1981   Influence of Diet on the Distribution of Nitrogen Isotopes in Animals. *Geochimica et Cosmochimica Acta* 45:341–351.

———, and M.J. Schoeninger
1985   Stable Carbon and Nitrogen Isotope Ratios of Bone Collagen: Variations Within Individuals, between Sexes and Within Populations Raised on Monotonous Diets. *Journal of Archaeological Science* 10:199–203.

Duffield, L.F.
1964   Three Panhandle Aspect Sites at Sanford Reservoir, Hutchinson County, Texas. *Bulletin of the Texas Archeological Society* 35:19–81.

———
1970   Some Panhandle Aspect Sites in Texas: Their Vertebrates and Palaeoecology. (Ph.D. Dissertation in Anthropology, University of Wisconsin, Madison.)

Elias, R.W., Y. Hirao, and C.C. Patterson
1982   The Circumvention of the Natural Biopurification of Calcium Along Nutrient Pathways by Atmospheric Inputs of Industrial Lead. *Geochimica Cosmochimica Acta* 46:2561–2580.

Etchieson, G.M.
1981   Archaeological Survey at Lake Meredith Recreation Area, Moore and Potter Counties, Texas. Amarillo: U.S. Department of the Interior, Water and Power Resources Service, Southwest Region.

Euler, R.C., G.J. Gumerman, T.V. Karlstrom, J.S. Dean, and R. Hevly
1979   The Colorado Plateaus: Cultural Dynamics and Paleoenvironment. *Science* 205(4411):1089–1101.

Eyerly, T.L.
1907   The Buried City of the Panhandle. *Transactions of the Kansas Academy of Science* 21(1):219–228.

Farley, J.A., and J.D. Keyser
1979   Little Caney River Prehistory: 1977 Field Season. *University of Tulsa Laboratory of Archaeology Contributions in Archaeology* 5.

Gish, J.W.
1982   Appendix D. Pollen Results from the Tierra Blanca Site, Northwestern Texas Panhandle. Pp. 384–402 in Intersocietal Food Acquisition Among Egalitarian Societies: An Ecological Study of Plains/Pueblo Interaction in the American Southwest by K.A. Spielmann (Ph.D. Dissertation in Anthropology, University of Michigan, Ann Arbor.)

Green, F.E.
1967   Archaeological Salvage in the Sanford Reservoir Area. National Park Service Report 14-10-0333-1126.

Grupe, G., and H. Piepenbrink
1989   Impact of Microbial Activity on Trace Element Concentrations in Excavated Bones. *Applied Geochemistry* 4:293–298.

Hammond, G.P., and A.G. Rey, eds. and trans.
1927   The Gallegos Relation of the Rodriquez Expedition to New Mexico. *Historical Society of New Mexico Publications in History* 4.

Holden, W.C.
1929   Some Explorations and Excavations in Northwest Texas. *Bulletin of the Texas Archeological and Paleontological Society* 1:23–35.

———
1933   Excavations at Saddleback Ruin. *Bulletin of the Texas Archeological and Paleontological Society* 5:39–52.

Hughes, J.T., H.C. Hood, B.P. Newman, and P.B. Hughes
1977   *Final Report on an Archaeological Survey of the Red Deer Creek Watershed in Gray, Roberts, and Hemphill Counties, Texas.* Canyon, Tex.: West Texas State University, Killgore Research Center.

Jelinek, A.
1967   A Prehistoric Sequence in the Middle Pecos Valley, New Mexico. *University of Michigan. Museum of Anthropology Papers* 31.

Johnson, C.S.
1939   A Report on the Antelope Creek Ruin. *Bulletin of the Texas Archeological and Paleontological Society* 11:190–202.

Keller, J.E.
1975   The Black Dog Village Site: A Panhandle Aspect Manifestation in Hutchinson County, Texas. *Texas Highway Department Publications in Archaeology, Report* 5. Austin.

Krieger, A.D.
1946   Culture Complexes and Chronology in Northern Texas. *University of Texas Publication* 4640.

Lambert, J.B., S. Vlasak, A.C. Thometz, and J.E. Buikstra
1982   Comparative Study of the Chemical Analysis of Ribs and Femurs in Woodland Populations. *American Journal of Physical Anthropology* 59:289–294.

Lintz, C.R.
1984   The Plains Villagers: Antelope Creek. Pp. 325–346 in The Prehistory of Oklahoma. R. Bell, ed. Orlando: Academic Press.

―――

1986 Architecture and Community Variability Within the Antelope Creek Phase of the Texas Panhandle. *Studies in Oklahoma's Past* 14.

―――

1991 Texas Panhandle-Pueblo Interactions from the 13th through 16th Centuries. Pp. 89–106 in Farmers, Hunters, Colonists: Interactions between the Southwest and Southern Plains. K.A. Spielman, ed. Tucson: University of Arizona Press.

――, and S.A. Hall

1983 The Geomorphology and Archaeology of Carnegie Canyon. Fort Cobb Laterals Watershed, Caddo County, Oklahoma. *Oklahoma Conservation Commission. Archaeological Research Report* 10.

McLellan, W.S., and E.F. Du Bois

1930 Clinical Calorimetry 45. Prolonged Meat Diets with a Study of Kidney Function and Ketosis. *Journal of Biological Chemistry* 87:651–668.

――, H.J. Spencer, and E.A. Falk

1931 Clinical Calorimetry 47. Prolonged Meat Diets with a Study of the Respiratory Metabolism. *Journal of Biological Chemistry* 93:419–434.

Medaglia, C., E.A. Little, and M.J. Schoeninger

1989 Late Woodland Diet on Nantucket Island (Massachusetts): A Study Using Stable Isotope Ratios. (Paper presented at Society for American Archaeology, Atlanta, Ga.)

Morgan, M., and M.J. Schoeninger

1989 Zinc and Strontium as Dietary Indicators in a Modern Tropical Community. *American Journal of Physical Anthropology* 78(2):276.

Noli, D., and G. Avery

1988 Protein Poisoning and Coastal Subsistence Strategies. *Journal of Archaeological Science* 15(4)395–401.

O'Leary, M.

1988 Carbon Isotopes in Photosynthesis. *BioScience* 38(5):328–336.

Patterson, D.K.

1975 An Analysis of Human Skeletal Material from The Antelope Creek Focus Sites of Northern Texas. (M.A. Thesis in Anthropology, Eastern New Mexico University, Portales.)

Peden, D.G.

1972 The Trophic Relations of *Bison bison* to the Shortgrass Plains. (Ph.D. Dissertation in Ecology, Colorado State University, Fort Collins.)

Schoeninger, M.J.

1979 Diet and Status at Chalcatzingo: Some Empirical and Technical Aspects of Strontium Analysis. *American Journal of Physical Anthropology* 51:295–309.

―――

1981 The Agricultural "Revolution": Its Effect on Human Diet in Prehistoric Iran and Israel. *Paleorient* 7:73–92.

1985 Trophic Level Effects on 15N/14N and 13C/12C Ratios in Bone Collagen and Strontium Levels in Bone Mineral. *Journal of Human Evolution*, 14:419–447.

―――

1989 Reconstructing Prehistoric Human Diet. Pp. 38–67 in The Chemistry of Prehistoric Human Bone. T. Price, ed. Cambridge: Cambridge University Press.

――, and M.J. DeNiro

1984 Nitrogen and Carbon Isotopic Composition of Bone Collagen in Terrestrial and Marine Vertebrates. *Geochimica et Cosmochimica Acta* 48:625–639.

――, H. Tauber, and M.J. DeNiro

1983 15N/14N Ratios of Bone Collagen Reflect Marine and Terrestrial Components of Prehistoric Human Diet. *Science* 220:1381–1383.

Schoenwetter, J., and A. Dittert

1968 Ecological Interpretation of Anasazi Settlement Patterns. Pp. 41–66 in Anthropological Archaeology of the Americas. B. Meggers, ed. Washington: Anthropological Society of Washington.

Schroeder, H.A., I.H. Tipton, and A.P. Nason

1972 Trace metals in Man: Strontium and Barium. *Journal of Chronic Disorders* 25:491–517.

Sillen, A., and M. Kavanagh

1982 Strontium and Paleodietary Research: A Review. *Yearbook of Physical Anthropology* 25:67–90.

Smith, B.D.

1979 Measuring the Selective Utilization of Animal Species by Prehistoric Human Populations. *Antiquity* 44:155–160.

Speth, J.D., and K.A. Spielmann

1983 Energy Source, Protein Metabolism, and Hunter-gatherer Subsistence Strategies. *Journal of Anthropological Archaeology* 2:1–31.

Spielmann, K.A., M.J. Schoeninger, and K. Moore

1990 Plains-Pueblo Interdependence and Human Diet at Pecos Pueblo, New Mexico. *American Antiquity* 55(4):745–765.

Studer, F.V.

1934a Texas Panhandle Culture Ruin No. 55. *Bulletin of the Texas Archaeological and Paleontological Society* 6:80–96.

―――

1934b Hunting Indians in the Panhandle-Plains Museum. *Panhandle-Plains Historical Review* 7:79–94.

Tieszen, L.L., T.W. Boutton, K.G. Tesdahl, and N.G. Slade

1983 Fractionation and Turnover of Stable Carbon Isotopes in Animal Tissues: Implications for 13C Analysis of Diet. *Oecologia* 57:32–37.

Underwood, E.J.

1977 Trace Elements in Human and Animal Nutrition. 4th ed. New York: Academic Press.

van der Merwe, N.J.

1982   Carbon Isotopes, Photosynthesis and Archaeology. *American Scientist* 70:596–606.

Vogel, J.C.

1978   Isotopic Assessment of the Dietary Habits of Ungulates. *South African Journal of Science* 74:298–301.

Wada, E.

1980   Nitrogen Isotope Fractionation and Its Significance in Biogeochemical Processes Occurring in Marine Environ-ments. Pp. 375–398 in Isotope Marine Chemistry. E.D. Guldherg, Y. Hovihe and K. Saruhashi, eds. Tokyo: Vchida Rokakuho.

Wetterstrom, W.

1986   Food, Diet, and Population at Prehistoric Arroyo Hondo Pueblo, New Mexico. (Arroyo Hondo Archaeological Series.) Santa Fe, N.Mex.: School of American Research Press.

○○○

PART 5

Warfare on the Plains

○○○

CHAPTER 24

Plains Warfare and the Anthropology of War

CLAYTON A. ROBARCHEK

Although Plains specialists have, over the past century, amassed an immense amount of data concerning precontact and postcontact warfare, this research has not, by and large, had a major impact on the development of anthropological theories of warfare. The reasons for the relative neglect of data from the Plains are primarily historical. This neglect has excluded from consideration an enormous amount of material that, as the chapters in this volume demonstrate, has the potential to greatly expand the understanding of the sources and dynamics of warfare in prestate societies. This chapter will sketch an outline of anthropological thinking about warfare and suggest how the rich data on Plains warfare can facilitate theoretical development by providing a unique laboratory for the generation and testing of anthropological theories of "primitive," "prestate," or "preindustrial" war.

Anthropological Approaches to the Explanation of War

The twentieth century has seen a rapid decline in the incidence of prestate warfare (both small-scale raiding and large-scale war) as traditional societies have steadily been brought

under the effective military and political control of state systems. Paradoxically, as the incidence of such warfare has declined, there has been an increase in interest on the part of anthropologists in explaining it.

A number of models have been applied to the problem of discovering the causes of warfare in these societies. Through the 1950s, explanations were directed toward the explanation of warfare in specific societies, in a framework that took culture as a given and accounted for war either as an expression of a generalized culture pattern, theme, or value (Benedict 1934; Spicer 1947; Wilson 1958), as an expression of aggressive impulses generated in social interaction (Ellis 1951; Murphy 1957; Steward and Faron 1959), or as an attempt to realize specific cultural objectives (Evans-Pritchard 1957; Smith 1951; Speier 1941; Swanton 1943; Turney-High 1949). As a consequence of this focus on culture-specific explanations, little progress was made in the direction of formulating general theories of prestate warfare. (For more detailed discussions of the history of anthropological theorizing about warfare, see Ferguson 1984; Otterbein 1973; Robarchek 1989.)

In the decade of the 1960s, the subject of warfare as a general phenomenon began to draw increased attention from anthropologists. This was sparked in part by the appearance of several popular books and was nurtured by the sociopolitical climate of the times. These works, especially those by Robert Ardrey (1961, 1966), Desmond Morris (1967), and Konrad Lorenz (1966), saw the causes of warfare in a predisposition to aggressiveness rooted in the genetic heritage of humanity, a product of biological adaptations for innate aggression or territorial behavior made in the evolutionary career of the human species. This argument was widely resisted by most anthropologists, and a spirited counterattack was launched against the ethological paradigm (Alland 1972; Montague 1968, 1978). The ensuing debate, although inconclusive, spurred an increased interest in both theory and research on warfare on the part of anthropologists.

The resurgent interest in field research on warfare and on the generation and testing of more general theories soon became concentrated in those few areas where primitive warfare persisted or had only recently ceased, most notably in New Guinea and Amazonia. These areas, increasingly the second, have come to be the foci of anthropological attempts to explain the origins and persistence of prestate war such that, by the 1970s, ethnographic research and debate on the subject had come to be concentrated almost exclusively on peoples such as the Yanomamo (Chagnon 1967, 1968a; Harris 1974; Lizot 1977), Jivaro (Bennett Ross 1980; Harner 1972; Ross 1978), Sharanahua (Siskind 1973), Guahibo (Morey 1972), Mae Enga (Meggitt 1977), and Gebusi (Knauft 1987). The concentration of research and debate in these two areas has meant that, with few exceptions, the rich data from the Plains region have largely been ignored in theory building.

The narrowing of the areal focus of anthropological research on warfare to Amazonia and New Guinea was accompanied by a shift in theoretical perspectives with the emergence to prominence in the 1970s of two opposing paradigms for the explanation of war: a materialist model with ecological and sociobiological variants, and a sociocultural-motivational model.

MATERIALIST APPROACHES

The ecological approach sees warfare as part of a mode of adaptation to particular environmental conditions (Vayda 1961). Explanations are cast in terms of ecological variables such as population density and resource availability. Warfare is seen as an adaptive response to ecological conditions such as population pressure and limited resources, functioning to increase access to resources (Goldman 1963; Lathrap 1968; Morey and Marwitt 1975; Siskind 1973), to create a "no man's land" where hunting pressures are relieved allowing prey

species to replenish their numbers (Bennett Ross 1980; Harris 1977), or to limit populations either directly through battle deaths or indirectly through functional links with practices such as female infanticide (Divale 1970; Divale and Harris 1976; Harris 1971, 1972, 1977).

A number of formulations have been advanced holding protein to be the critical limiting resource, especially in the Amazon, and arguing that important sociocultural elements, often including warfare, were ecologically adaptive responses to low protein availability (Bennett Ross 1980; Gross 1975; Harris 1971, 1974, 1979; Meggers 1971; Ross 1978, 1979, 1980; Siskind 1973). The scarcity of data offered in support of most of these formulations has provided the impetus for a substantial amount of field research directed toward establishing or testing one or another of the links in the hypothesized causal chains, most commonly the assertion of protein scarcity in Amazonia (Beckerman 1979, 1980; Berlin and Markell 1977; Chagnon and Hames 1979; Hames 1980; Johnson 1982; Johnson and Behrens 1982; Lizot 1977; Milton 1984; Vickers 1980). The bulk of this research shows that Amazonian societies, by and large, have more than adequate protein intakes; thus, it offers little support to the protein scarcity hypothesis or to the more general ecological-functional model of warfare.

The explanation of warfare in biological terms reappeared in a somewhat more sophisticated form with the emergence of sociobiology, to which the earlier ethological approach had given rise. This model holds that a wide range of cultural behaviors, from altruism to warfare, can be explained by reference to some sort of selection for behaviors that increase adaptive fitness. Although the extreme claims of genetic determinism made by some of sociobiology's early proponents have been substantially moderated by later researchers, the attempt to explain human violence and war in terms of strategies for maximizing inclusive fitness continues (Chagnon 1988; Robarchek 1989; Wilson and Daly 1985).

SOCIOCULTURAL AND MOTIVATIONAL APPROACHES

Where the materialist approaches see society and culture as dependent variables, the sociocultural and motivational approaches see these as independent variables. Explanations focus on the proximate causes of warfare: the attainment of cultural values, such as prestige, the advancement of the interests of the fraternal group, and so on, or the expression of psychological dispositions such as hostility deriving from socialization. The explanations that they offer are largely cast in terms of sociocultural variables such as kinship, residence patterns, or socialization practices.

Fraternal interest group theory, for example, sees social-structural variables as crucial, arguing that the existence of localized groups of related men with common interests is predictive of high rates of feuding and/or warfare (Otterbein 1968, 1985; Otterbein and Otterbein 1965; Thoden van Velzen and van Wetering 1960). Socialization theories of violence and war, on the other hand, link male aggressiveness to factors such as harsh socialization and an emphasis on obedience and punishment (Ross 1985a, 1985b).

The variables hypothesized by the various sociocultural and motivational approaches can, at least in principle, be identified cross-culturally, promising a more general approach to the explanation of warfare in sociocultural terms than that provided by the culture-specific approaches (Chagnon 1967, 1968a, 1986b; Kiefer 1969; Koch 1970; Otterbein 1968; Sahlins 1961). Although these approaches continue to inspire theory and research, it has been the materialist models, both ecological and sociobiological, that have provided the dominant paradigms shaping anthropological thinking about warfare in the 1980s.

Explanations of Plains Warfare

The study of Plains warfare has followed a similar course. Reflecting the theoretical orientation of the times, the early ethnographies of Plains Indian warfare tended to be largely descriptive, and their explanations culture-specific, accounting for warfare largely in terms of the motives voiced by the people themselves: prestige, revenge, and so on (Lowie 1920; Wissler 1940; cf. Newcomb 1950).

It is important to note this emphasis on the part of the early ethnographers. As the study of warfare in the Plains and elsewhere has gotten removed from the people who were actually doing it (as it has become less the province of ethnography and more the province of ethnology, archaeology and history), the explanations of it have become more impersonal and abstract, couched in terms of the working out of logics of ecology, biology, or social structure in which human motives and concerns have little or no causal relevance (Harris 1974; Newcomb 1950). It was a great deal more difficult for the ethnographer whose informants described to him the reasons why they engaged in warfare to dismiss those reasons as irrelevant epiphenomena.

In the 1940s and 1950s, with the deaths of the informants who were the last direct links to the warfare pattern, research interests shifted to other topics: acculturation, culture and

personality, and so on. With relatively few exceptions, Plains warfare disappeared as a discrete area of study.

One exception is Newcomb's (1950) examination of Plains warfare. Adopting the culturological approach of White (1947), the forerunner of Harris's (1968) ecological functionalism, Newcomb saw warfare as "a function of sociocultural systems . . . and individuals are regarded as being no more than the means through which these systems attain their ends" (1950:317). His conclusion, not surprising given his definition of warfare as armed conflict over valued resources, saw the causes of Plains warfare in migrations and subsequent competition over horses and hunting territories, although he also emphasized the importance of the historical context of Plains warfare.

When warfare reemerged in the 1960s as a subject for anthropological investigation, field research on warfare had shifted to Amazonia and New Guinea, and subsequent theory-building largely ignored the rich body of ethnographic, ethnohistoric, and archaeological material from the Plains. There were also few attempts to apply the theories that were being developed elsewhere to an explanation of Plains warfare. Biolsi (1984) stands out as an exception. Although operating within the ecological-functional framework, he argues that "resource competition and warfare . . . were multi-factorial phenomena involving the conjunction of ecological and cultural factors" (Biolsi 1984:143), and he calls for an approach that attends to the roles of the environment, cultural imperatives, and social behavior in engendering competition and warfare. Like Newcomb, he emphasized the historical context and saw the causes of war as lying in competition over resources, especially horses and hunting rights, but he also recognized that ecological constraints are not absolute but depend on their cultural interpretation. He specifically emphasized the role of culture in defining scarcity and the need for competition and in defining relations between groups and, thereby, the existence or nonexistence of states of war between groups.

Theoretical Issues in the Explanation of War

This, in very brief summary, sketches the course of anthropological thinking with regard to warfare. To return to the objective of this introduction, the question here is: what does research from the Plains have to contribute to it? Perhaps the place to begin is to ask what an adequate theory of war should look like.

Spiro (1967) argues that to ask about the cause of any social behavior is to ask two very different kinds of questions: what is its origin? and why does it persist? The first of these is a historical question, requiring a specification of the historical conditions that generated the specific cultural institution. The second is a motivational question requiring an analysis of the reasons why people perform the behavior and, thereby, maintain and continue the institution. The historical or archaeological data necessary to answer the first question will not answer the second, and the synchronic functional and motivational data necessary to the second will not answer the first. Neither, by itself, provides a causal explanation, and answering both requires some specification of how the purported ultimate historical causes are translated into current motivations, the proximate causes of action. Much (but by no means all) of the controversy over the explanation of warfare derives from the confusion of these two questions and from failure to recognize the differences in the nature of the data required to answer them.

None of the current approaches is, as currently phrased, capable of accounting for both the origin and the persistence of warfare, either in specific societies or in general. Theories of warfare based almost entirely on synchronic data offer "explanations" that require assumptions about historical events and processes that, in most cases, cannot be supported.

In the case of the dominant materialist approaches, there are two problems: the assumption that historical causes can be inferred from present consequences and the lack of any means for the articulation of purported "final causes" (for example, population regulation or increased inclusive fitness) that exist outside of consciousness, with the human goals, purposes, and intentions that are the proximate causes of all human behavior, including warfare.

The fact that ecological determinists and sociobiologists are frequently in disagreement should not obscure the fundamental assumptions that they share. Foremost among these is the assumption that the ultimate causes of warfare are in the immediate material realm—food, offspring, land, or other scarce resources—rather than in the realm of ideas and ideals, beliefs and values, purposes and intentions, that many anthropologists call culture. Methodologically, this is reflected in the identification of the material consequences of warfare, for example, increased protein intake, population limitation, or sexual conquests, as its historical cause. Data concerning the material effects (or functions) of warfare are adduced as evidence of the historical conditions that gave it rise; Harris (1979) sees population limitation as the cause of Yanomamo war, and Chagnon (1968a) sees it in a drive toward the maximization of offspring.

Since human beings are not automata responding blindly to biological or ecological contingencies, any factor that is purported to have causal efficacy must in some way articulate with human motivational complexes if it is to find behavioral expression. No accounting of the material correlates of warfare can truly explain it unless they somehow articulate with the decisions, intentions, and goals of those who engage in it. That is a crucial problem with most ecological and sociobiological explanations: not that they are necessarily wrong, but that neither specifies any means for the articulation of the preferred extrinsic "causes" with human intentions and consciousness, the proximate causes of human action.

Both the ecological and the sociobiological approaches purport to identify the ultimate causes of warfare, treating sociocultural and motivational variables as epiphenomena. In contrast, the various sociocultural and motivational approaches stress the proximate causes of warfare. They document the culturally structured motives, goals, and intentions of the actors that serve to maintain the warfare pattern. Like the materialist approaches, they rely almost entirely on synchronic data. As with increased protein intake or inclusive fitness maximization, current motives and functions cannot be assumed, in the absence of historical evidence, to be relevant to the origins of the cultural pattern—to the biological, ecological, and sociocultural contexts in which it arose.

In formulating theories, both approaches have relied heavily on research in Amazonia and New Guinea, research that has provided a wealth of ethnographic data on the practice of warfare, but with very little temporal depth. It is in this regard that research on warfare in the Plains is particularly relevant, since it presents resources not available in most other areas where warfare has been studied. Most important, it offers a truly long-term historical perspective on the phenomenon.

In the Plains, the range of data—ethnographic, historical, ethnohistorical, and archaeological—that can be brought to bear on the problem of warfare is unsurpassed anywhere in the world. There is an immense body of historical and ethnohistorical data—firsthand reports by traders, trappers, explorers, and adventurers—dating from almost the first contacts with the European world; and there are rich ethnographic accounts of the historic warfare period based on the testimony of those who participated in it. Moreover, a century of archaeological research has provided a body of data dating back 10,000 years, and a great deal of archaeological material yet remains for the testing of particular hypotheses. In short, where current theories of warfare are flawed by a lack of historical context, research in the Plains, drawing both on the ethnographic present and the historic and prehistoric past, is ideally suited to address some of the central theoretical and empirical issues in the anthropology of war. This can be clearly seen in the papers in this volume. They present data that are immediately relevant to many of the theoretical issues discussed above, and they point the way toward future utilization of Plains research for the generation and testing of anthropological theories of war.

Blakeslee, in seeking to integrate these diverse studies, notes the apparent spatial and temporal variation in the intensity of violence that these papers reveal ("The Archaeological Context of Human Skeletons in the Northern and Central Plains," this vol.). This ranged from small-scale raiding prior to Plains Village 1, to wholesale slaughter in Plains Village 2, to large-scale slave raids and massacres in the historic period. Presumed areal variation in the intensity of warfare between the Central and Northern Plains (previously inferred largely from the presence of fortifications in the latter area and their absence in the former) may, he suggests, be more apparent than real, more a function of the distribution and defensibility of land than of the intensity of conflict. Nonetheless, he notes a genuine decrease in the intensity of warfare in the north under the Extended Coalescent occupation, the so-called Pax La Roche (Caldwell 1964:3).

Owsley ("Warfare in Coalescent Tradition Populations of the Northern Plains," this vol.) argues that warfare in the contact period did not represent a qualitative change from earlier times, and he shows that warfare in the Northern Plains, thoroughly documented for the historic and protohistoric periods, was well established prehistorically as well. He argues that it fluctuated in intensity over time, and he presents dramatic evidence of a considerable time-depth for large-scale hostilities, documenting massacres from the Middle Missouri through postcontact periods. He also shows the persistence of scalping as a cultural practice associated with warfare through the protohistoric and historic periods.

That argument is strengthened by Hollimon and Owsley ("Osteology of the Fay Tolton Site: Implications for Warfare During the Initial Middle Missouri Variant," this vol.), who present graphic evidence of violent conflict from the Fay Tolton site, a fortified Plains Village site in South Dakota and the northernmost Initial Middle Missouri site known. Skeletal remains of five individuals recovered from burned dwellings show a range of traumatic, presumably warfare-related, injuries including perimortem burning, cranial fractures, scalping, and decapitation.

Bovee and Owsley ("Evidence of Warfare at the Heerwald Site," this vol.), and Owsley, Mann, and Baugh ("Culturally Modified Human Bones from the Edwards I Site," this vol.), summarizing data from a number of Late Prehistoric and Protohistoric sites in the Southern Plains, provide evidence of the widespread areal and temporal distribution of a warfare pattern that included the taking of scalps and, perhaps, trophy heads.

Olsen and Shipman ("Cutmarks and Perimortem Treatment of Skeletal Remains on the Northern Plains," this vol.) likewise present evidence of the historical depth of warfare, including scalping and trophy taking, from the Late Woodland through the Disorganized Coalescent periods. They also document variation in the intensity of warfare over time: although some evidence of scalping occurs in the Late Woodland and Middle Missouri sites, the osteological evidence of battle injuries and of perimortem mutilations indicative of the taking of trophy heads, feet, and noses increases after the Initial Coalescent.

Brooks ("Warfare on the Southern Plains," this vol.), presenting data from Plains Village period sites in the Southern Plains, provides further evidence of the areal breadth of warfare in the Plains. He shows that although warfare apparently never reached the levels of intensity that developed to the north, it was (at least in the form of small-scale raiding) widespread in the Southern Plains. He also suggests that the intensity of its expression may have varied over time, perhaps in relation to socioeconomic changes.

Ewers's chapter ("Women's Roles in Plains Indian Warfare," this vol.), uniquely valuable for its ethnographic content, provides rich data on the place of women in the warfare complex and describes the importance of motives of revenge and prestige seeking. He also shows that new motives (or perhaps the intensification of old ones) such as captive taking, grew out of the contact situation and its consequences, which included massive depopulation as a result of introduced diseases and the development of a market in slaves.

Conclusion

The data presented in these chapters were not collected with reference to specific warfare hypotheses; nonetheless, they make important contributions to theorizing about warfare in the Plains, and about preindustrial warfare generally. The evidence presented here calls into question some of the most prominent explanations of such warfare, and it also implicitly suggests some directions that more productive approaches might take.

It is, for example, clear from the archaeological and bioarchaeological material (and this is perhaps the most significant empirical implication of the data presented by these papers) that culturally patterned violent conflict among different social groups—warfare—has a long history, two or more millennia in the Plains ("Disease Profiles of Archaic and Woodland Populations in the Northern Plains," this vol.).

Moreover, examination of the archaeological record clearly shows that this violence was not simply opportunistic instrumental behavior invented in each generation. Rather, these data suggest that this was an identifiable and persistent tradition, a culture complex involving the importance of raiding, scalps and other physical trophies and, by implication, probably the perduring motives of prestige and revenge, motives whose importance has been clearly documented for the historic period. This was, in short, a regional cultural institution, a complex of values, ideas and behaviors that persisted for at least two thousand years. Given this historical depth, the warfare of the historic and protohistoric periods could not have had, contrary to Newcomb's (1950) argument, its origins in European contact, in waves of migration generated by it, or in competition for horses. The warfare complex long predates all of these. Although warfare was (as Ewers documents) altered, intensified, and turned to new uses in the contact period, its roots lie far deeper in the past.

Similarly, the clear evidence of this long history argues strongly against some of the basic premises of ecological-functional theories of warfare. The Plains warfare complex clearly persisted over several radical transformations in ecological adaptations, from hunting and gathering to settled horticulture and back to nomadic big game hunting, all of which argues strongly against theories that see the causal roots of warfare in the ecological requirements of particular subsistence strategies.

It is also difficult to see how the long-term persistence of a warfare complex such as this, yet one that varied dramatically in the intensity of its expression over time and space, can be explained within the framework of sociobiology, an approach that sees warfare as the outcome of a strategy for maximizing individual inclusive fitness, a biologically based propensity that, presumably, remains a constant over time and in different populations.

Finally, these data similarly raise questions for sociological approaches that find the sources of war in the internal dynamics of particular social systems. Many researchers have noted associations and have suggested causal connections between warfare and various aspects of social organization. Fraternal interest group theory sees intragroup violence as a concomitant of the existence of residence groups of agnatically related men who stand together in opposition to other, similar, groups (Otterbein 1968; Thoden van Velsen and van Wetering 1960). Others have postulated a causal relationship between

larger-scale (intergroup) warfare and social structural features (such as matrilocal residence) that create networks of obligations that cross-cut agnatic ties to permit the mobilization of larger groups for extended campaigns (Colson 1953; Murphy 1957). Still others have reversed the causal sequence, holding warfare to be an independent variable that determines the form of social organization (Divale 1974; Harris 1977). Yet, in the Plains, the warring societies of the historic and protohistoric periods encompassed virtually the entire possible range of diversity of descent and residence systems—patrilineal, matrilineal, matrilocal, virilocal, and so on, through most of the known permutations. Moreover, the wide range of sociopolitical systems involved in the warfare complex— from the highly ranked social stratification of the Pawnee to the acephalous egalitarianism of the Eastern Shoshone— similarly argues against any simple social structural explanation of warfare and suggests that the relationship of social structural variables to warfare can only be understood as part of a much wider (and most probably hierarchically interrelated) complex of causal relations set within specific ecological and cultural-historical contexts.

These chapters thus point the way toward the use of archaeological and bioarchaeolgical data from the Plains to provide the temporal dimension necessary for a test of extant assumptions and hypotheses about warfare in the Plains and elsewhere. One of the most important of these assumptions is that warfare necessarily derives from resource competition. First articulated for the Plains by Newcomb (1950), this idea is so widely accepted that it virtually constitutes a truism. The argument has become circular, with resource competition frequently inferred directly from evidence of the ocurrence of warfare, even in the absence of any independent evidence of resource scarcity (Zimmerman 1985).

This assumption has both synchronic and diachronic implications, both of which are amenable to testing with the kinds of data and techniques presented in these papers. Synchronically, it implies that warfare should, in specific instances, be asssociated with evidence of resource scarcity. Given the levels of technological and sociopolitical development of these societies, such scarcity should, if it was adaptively significant, be manifested in evidence of environmental, especially dietary, stress. Diachronically, one would expect to find covariation over time between the intensity of warfare and intensity of such stress.

The techniques employed and the data presented in these papers are ideally suited to the testing of these kinds of hypotheses. Detailed analyses of archaeological populations, such as those conducted by Owsley, by Olsen and Shipman, and by Bovee and Owsley document the frequency of warfare-induced trauma and provide a basis for assessing both the intensity of warfare in specific periods and variations in intensity over time. Bioarchaeological analyses of dental and osteological materials in terms of diet and paleopathology promise to provide evidence of the degree of environmental stress to which populations would have been subjected as a consequence of the scarcity of protein or other dietary resources. (These kinds of analyses promise to be of even greater value with the application of techniques and technologies that are making it possible to draw more specific information about behavior, diet, demographics, and, perhaps, even social organization, from dental and osteological materials [Schneider and Blakeslee 1990].)

On the side of theory building, these papers demonstrate that warfare in the Plains was a cultural and regional phenomenon. Endemic warfare was a permanent cultural fact that, once begun, was a part of the context of all that followed, an important component of the culturally constituted reality within which all the other changes—including those of the protohistoric and historic periods in modes of subsistence, social organization, and so on—occurred. The dynamic and adaptive character of this persisting culture complex is apparent in Ewers's description) of how the preexisting warfare complex was turned to addressing the opportunities and constraints of these new situations, including depopulation and the development of a slave trade. In these specific instances, the cultural fact of the preexistence of the warfare complex was, contrary to its place in the sociobiological and ecological-functional models, both logically and temporally primary, and the material objectives—functions—to which it was turned were secondary; they were the effects, not the causes of the existence of warfare.

There is every reason to assume that the dynamism and adaptability of warfare in the historic period was typical of earlier periods. It is clear that the intensity of violence varied widely over time and that there were periods when, at least in particular areas, the level of violent conflict was quite low. The Pax La Roche of the Extended Coalescent has, for example, long been recognized. Sully village (39SL4) was apparently unfortified, and the skeletal remains lack evidence of scalping or other traumatic injuries common in so many other sites. At other times, as local populations sought to deal with new challenges and opportunities (those presented, for example, at the onset of the Initial Coalescent), the warfare complex, with its attendant values and goals, was an important component of the cultural and behavioral repertoire. Thus the intense warfare of the protohistoric and historic periods was, at least in part, a precipitate of its own history.

All of this recalls Biolsi's (1984:162) conclusion that "it is perhaps wise to underscore the role of cultural factors in determining the ecological niche of Great Plains mounted hunters . . . the niche is determined as much by the given behavior of the adapting unit as it is by the nature of the habitat." It argues that a comprehensive explanation of warfare in the Plains (and probably of warfare everywhere else) will require, in addition to a much more sophisticated understanding of the ecological and biological parameters and of their interactions with psychological and social variables, a much wider cultural and historical perspective than has generally been employed in the past.

Field and library research on the anthropology of war has been supported by research grants from the Harry Frank Guggenheim Foundation, whose support is gratefully acknowledged.

References Cited

Alland, A.
  1972   The Human Imperative. New York: Columbia University Press.

Ardrey, R.
  1961   African Genesis. New York: Dell.

——
  1966   The Territorial Imperative. New York: Athenium.

Beckerman, S.
  1979   The Abundance of Protein in Amazonia: A Reply to Gross. *American Anthropologist* 81(3):533–560.

——
  1980   Fishing and Hunting by the Bari of Colombia. Pp. 66–70 in Working Papers on South American Indians 2. R.B. Hames, ed. Bennington, Vt.: Bennington College.

Benedict, R.F.
  1934   Patterns of Culture. Boston: Houghton Mifflin.

Bennett Ross, J.
  1980   Ecology and the Problem of the Tribe: A Critique of the Hobbesian Model of Preindustrial Warfare. Pp. 33–60 in Beyond Myths of Culture. E.B. Ross, ed. New York: Academic Press.

Berlin, E.A., and E.K. Markell
  1977   An Assessment of the Nutrition and Health Status of an Aguaruna Jivaro Community, Amazonias, Peru. *Ecology of Food and Nutrition* 6:69–81.

Biolsi, T.
  1984   Ecological and Cultural Factors in Plains Indian Warfare. Pp. 141–168 in Warfare, Culture and Environment. R.B. Ferguson, ed. Orlando, Fla.: Academic Press.

Chagnon, N.
  1967   Yanomamo: The Fierce People. *Natural History* 76(1):22–31.

——   1968a Yanomamo Social Organization and Warfare. Pp. 109–159 in War: The Anthropology of Armed Conflict and Aggression. M. Fried, M. Harris, and R. Murphy, eds. Garden City, N.Y.: The Natural History Press.

——   1968b Yanomamo: The Fierce People. New York: Holt, Rinehart and Winston.

——   1988 Life Histories, Blood Revenge and Warfare in a Tribal Population. *Science* 239(4843):985–992.

——, and R.B. Hames
    1979 Protein Deficiency and Tribal Warfare in Amazonia: New Data. *Science* 203(4383):910–913.

Colson, E.
    1953 Social Control and Vengeance in Plateau Tonga Society. *Africa* 23(3):199–211.

Divale, W.
    1970 An Explanation for Primitive Warfare: Population Control and the Significance of Primitive Sex Ratios. *New Scholar* 2:173–192.

——   1974 Migration, External Warfare, and Matrilocal Residence. *Behavior Science Research* 9:75–133.

——, and M. Harris
    1976 Population, Warfare and the Male Supremacist Complex. *American Anthropologist* 78(3):521–538.

Ellis, F.H.
    1951 Patterns of Aggression and the War Cult in the Southwestern Pueblos. *Southwestern Journal of Anthropology* 7(2):177–201.

Evans-Pritchard, E.E.
    1957 Zande Border Raids. *Africa* 27(3):217–231.

Ferguson, R.B.
    1984 Introduction: Studying War. Pp. 1–81 in Warfare, Culture and Environment. B. Ferguson, ed. Orlando, Fla.: Academic Press.

Goldman, I.
    1963 The Cubeo: Indians of the Northwest Amazon. Urbana: University of Illinois Press.

Gross, D.R.
    1975 Protein Capture and Cultural Development in the Amazon Basin. *American Anthropologist* 77(3):526–549.

Hames, R.B.
    1980 Game Depletion and Hunting-zone Rotation Among the Ye-Kwana and Yanomamo of Amazonas, Venezuela. Pp. 31–66 in Working Papers on South American Indians 2. R.B. Hames, ed. Bennington, Vt.: Bennington College.

Harner, M.J.
    1972 The Jivaro, People of the Sacred Waterfalls. New York: Doubleday.

Harris, M.
    1968 The Rise of Anthropological Theory. New York: Crowell.

——   1971 Culture, Man and Nature. New York: Crowell.

——   1972 Warfare, Old and New. *Natural History* 81(3):18–20.

——   1974 Cows, Pigs, Wars and Witches: The Riddles of Culture. New York: Vintage.

——   1977 Cannibals and Kings. New York: Random House

——   1979 The Yanomamo and the Causes of War in Band and Village Societies. Pp. 122–132 in Brazil: Anthropological Perspectives. M. Margolis and W.E. Carter, eds. New York: Columbia University Press.

Johnson, A.
    1982 Reductionism in Cultural Ecology: The Amazon Case. *Current Anthropology* 23(4):413–428.

Johnson, A., and C. Behrens
    1982 Nutritional Criteria in Machiguenga Food Production Decisions: A Linear Programming Analysis. *Human Ecology* 10(2):167–189.

Kiefer, T.M.
    1969 Tausug Armed Conflict: The Social Organization of Military Activity in a Phillipine Moslem Society. *Philippine Studies Program, Research Series* 7.

Knauft, B.H.
    1987 Reconsidering Violence in Simple Human Societies: Homicide Among the Gebusi of New Guinea. *Current Anthropology* 28(4):457–497.

Koch, K.-F.
    1970 Cannibalistic Revenge in Jale Warfare. *Natural History* 79(2):40–50.

Lathrap, D.W.
    1968 The "Hunting" Economics of the Tropical Forest Zone of South America: An Attempt at Historical Perspective. Pp. 23–29 in Man the Hunter. R. Lee and I. Devore, eds. Chicago: Aldine.

Lizot, J.
    1977 Population, Resources and Warfare Among the Yanomamo. *Man* 12(3–4):497–517.

Lorenz, K.
    1966 On Aggression. New York: Harcourt, Brace and World.

Lowie, R.
    1920 Primitive Society. New York: Boni and Liveright.

Meggers, B.J.
    1971 Amazonia: Man and Culture in a Counterfeit Paradise. Chicago: Aldine.

Meggitt, M.
    1977 Blood Is Their Argument: Warfare Among Mae Enga Tribesmen of the New Guinea Highlands. Palo Alto, Calif.: Mayfield.

Milton, K.
   1984   Protein and Carbohydrate Resources of the Maku Indians of Northwestern Amazonia. *American Anthropologist* 86(1):7–27.
Montague, A., ed.
   1968   Man and Aggression. New York: Oxford University Press.

——
   1978   Learning Non-Aggression. New York: Oxford University Press.
Morey, R.V.
   1972   Warfare Patterns of the Colombian Guahibo. Pp. 58–68 in *Proceedings of the 39th Annual Congress of Americanists,* Vol. 4. Lima.
——, and J.P. Marwitt
   1975   Ecology, Economy and Warfare in Lowland South America. Pp. 439–450 in War: Its Causes and Correlates. M.A. Nettleship, R.D. Givens, and A. Nettleship, eds. The Hague: Mouton.
Morris, D.
   1967   The Naked Ape. New York: Dell.
Murphy, R.F.
   1957   Intergroup Hostility and Social Cohesion. *American Anthropologist* 59(6):1018–1035.
Newcomb, W.W., Jr.
   1950   A Re-examination of the Causes of Plains Warfare. *American Anthropologist* 52(3):317–330.
Otterbein, K.
   1968   Internal War: A Cross-cultural Study. *American Anthropologist* 70(2):277–289.

——
   1973   The Anthropology of War. Pp. 923–958 in Handbook of Social and Cultural Anthropology. J. Honigmann, ed. Chicago: Rand McNally College Publishing.

——
   1980   Internal War: A Cross-Cultural Study. Pp. 204–223 in The War System: An Interdisciplinary Approach. R.A. Falk and S.S. Kim, eds. Boulder, Colo.: Westview Press.

——
   1985   The Evolution of War: A Cross-Cultural Study. 2nd ed., New Haven: HRAF.
——, and C.S. Otterbein
   1965   An Eye for an Eye, a Tooth for a Tooth: A Cross-Cultural Study of Feuding. *American Anthropologist* 67(6):1470–1482.
Robarchek, C.A.
   1989   Primitive Warfare and the Ratomorphic Image of Mankind. *American Anthropologist* 91(4):903–920.
Ross, E.B.
   1978   Food Taboos, Diet and Hunting Strategy: The Adaptation to Animals in Amazonian Cultural Ecology. *Current Anthropology* 19(1):1–16.

——
   1979   Reply to Lizot: C.A. Comment. *Current Anthropology* 20(1):151–155.

——
   1980   Introduction. In Beyond Myths of Culture. E.B. Ross, ed. New York: Academic Press.
Ross, M.H.
   1985a The Limits to Social Structure: Social Structural and Psychocultural Explanations for Political Conflict and Violence. *Anthropological Quarterly* 59(4):171–176.

——
   1985b Internal and External Conflict and Violence: Cross-cultural Evidence and a New Analysis. *Journal of Conflict Resolution* 29:547–579.
Sahlins, M.
   1961   The Segmentary Lineage: An Organization of Predatory Expansion. *American Anthropologist* 63(2):322–345.
Schneider, K.N., and D. Blakeslee
   1990   Evaluating Residence Patterns Among Prehistoric Populations: Clues from Dental Enamel Composition. *Human Biology* 62(1):71–83.
Siskind, J.
   1973   Tropical Forest Hunters and the Economy of Sex. Pp. 226–240 in Peoples and Cultures of Native South America. D.R. Gross, ed. Garden City, N.Y.: Natural History Press.
Smith, M.
   1951   American Indian Warfare. *Transactions of the New York Academy of Sciences* 13:348–365.
Speier, H.
   1941   The Social Types of War. *American Journal of Sociology* 46:445–454.
Spicer, E.H.
   1947   Yaqui Militarism. *Arizona Quarterly* 3:40–48.
Spiro, M.E.
   1967   Burmese Supernaturalism. Englewood Cliffs, N.J.: Prentice-Hall.
Steward, J., and L.C. Faron
   1959   Native Peoples of South America. New York: McGraw-Hill.
Swanton, J.R.
   1943   Are Wars Inevitable? Washington: The Smithsonian Institution.
Thoden van Velsen, H.U.E., and W. van Wetering
   1960   Residence, Power Groups and Intra-societal Aggression: An Enquiry into the Conditions Leading to Peacefulness within Non-stratified Societies. *International Archives of Ethnography* 49:169–200.
Turney-High, H.H.
   1949   Primitive War: Its Practices and Concepts. Columbia: University of South Carolina Press.
Vayda, A.P.
   1961   Expansion and Warfare Among Swidden Agriculturalists. *American Anthropologist* 63(2):346–358.

Vickers, W.T.
    1980 An Analysis of Amazonian Hunting Yields as a Function of Settlement Age. *Working Papers on South American Indians* 2. Bennington, Vt.: Bennington College.

White, L.A.
    1947 Culturological vs. Psychological Interpretations of Human Behavior. *American Sociological Review* 12:3–15.

Wilson, M., and M. Daly
    1985 Competitiveness, Risk-taking and Violence: The Young Male Syndrome. *Ethology and Sociobiology* 6(2):59–73.

Wilson, H.C.
    1958 Regarding the Causes of Mundurucu Warfare. *American Anthropologist* 60(6):1193–1196.

Wissler, C.
    1940 Indians of the United States. Garden City, New York: Doubleday.

Zimmerman, L.J.
    1985 Peoples of Prehistoric South Dakota. Lincoln: University of Nebraska Press.

CHAPTER 25

○ ○ ○

Warfare on the Southern Plains

ROBERT L. BROOKS

Warfare on the Southern Plains is well documented in the ethnological literature (Newcomb 1950; M. Wedel 1982), which addresses the numerous intertribal conflicts that prevailed among the Wichita, Osage, Comanche, Pawnee, and Apache during the historic era. What is not so apparent is that this conflict was just as prevalent in protohistoric and prehistoric times. There are two reasons for this omission. First, there has been an absence of systematic studies of human skeletal remains for the Southern Plains region (Owsley, Marks, and Manheim 1989), which has limited opportunities for identifying cases of violent death. Only with comparative studies by bioarchaeologists has the evidence of these conflicts been observed in the osteological data ("Evidence of Warfare at the Heerwald Site," this vol.). Second, the level of warfare on the Southern Plains never reached the pervasive and regional intensity expressed on the Northern Plains (Owsley, Berryman, and Bass 1977).

In 1987–1988, a bioarchaeological synthesis of the Southern Plains was undertaken (Owsley and Jantz 1989; Owsley 1989; Owsley, Marks, and Manheim 1989). Work consisted of a literature review as well as a reanalysis of skeletal collections in Oklahoma and Texas. Traumatic injuries resulting from

warfare or other forms of hostilities were observed in the skeletal sample.

This chapter attempts to characterize the extent and nature of conflict on the Southern Plains during the Plains Village period. This cultural unit, beginning around A.D. 800 and ending by 1500, was selected because it contains the most extensive collection of archaeological data within the region and because bioarchaeological analysis has been focused on the skeletal population of this taxonomic unit. Cultural complexes reviewed for evidence of warfare and conflict include the Antelope Creek phase, the Zimms complex, and the Washita River phase, which are summarized in "Southern Plains Cultural Complexes," this volume.

The Antelope Creek Phase

Considerable evidence exists regarding warfare and conflict during the Antelope Creek phase. Bioarchaeological studies have revealed some individuals with skeletal trauma suggestive of violent death (Patterson 1974; Texas Archaeological Society 1969). An analysis of skeletal remains from the Antelope Creek 22 site (41HC23) resulted in the identification of two individuals with physical injuries suggestive of conflict

(Patterson 1974). One of these is an adult male (Burial 22A-B4) with a perforation in the right scapula; the other is an adult female (Burial 22A-B6) with a perforation of the third segment of the sternum. Although Patterson does not equate these injuries with combat wounds, it is suspected that they resulted from other than natural causes (Douglas Owsley, personal communication 1989).

The most conclusive data are derived from the Footprint site (41PT25), where the remains of 11 adults, 6 subadults, and 4 infants were found in three bell-shaped pits within a burned subterranean structure (Green 1967:138). These remains were disarticulated and intermixed among the three pits with some of the remains being charred from intense heat. It is unclear whether the charred remains reflect intentional cremation or indirect effects from the pit being left open during burning of the structure (Lintz 1986:168). Other disarticulated remains were found in a layer of clean sand and gravel overlying the house floor but underneath charred timbers from the burned roof. In another pit within the structure, a cluster of 10 adult skulls was found, one with an attached cervical vertebrae and a flint knife of Alibates chert underlying the skull. One of these individuals also displayed a healed puncture wound (from an arrowpoint?) on the left side of the cranium (Patterson 1974:175). Lintz (1986:1986) suggests the skulls of these individuals were dismembered prior to the decomposition of connective tissue. The absence of additional skeletal elements also indicates that this dismemberment occurred outside rather than within the structure. Based on Green's data, Lintz (1986:170) has reconstructed a possible sequence of events to account for this pattern. The initial subterranean room was occupied, and the subfloor pits served as an ossuary for the resident Antelope Creek phase population. The occupation ended in violence with some if not all the local Antelope Creek group being slaughtered and partially dismembered during a raid by another group. Somewhat later, sand and gravel fill was added over the floor and portions of the dismembered Antelope Creek individuals were interred in this fill but prior to burning of the structure. Trophy skulls were obtained either from individuals killed during the attack or during subsequent retaliatory raids.

Archaeological data to document better evidence of warfare is less conclusive. Burned structures have often been attributed to raiding parties. However, other factors can lead to the burning of structures. These include natural fires (brush or prairie fires and lightning), accidents stemming from sparks in internal hearths, fires set to rid buildings of vermin, and intentional burning of dwellings as part of the mortuary ritual following the death of a house resident. With the exception of

the one structure at the Footprint site, there is no evidence for conflict in association with the burning of residential dwellings (Lintz 1986:247–248). However, Lintz (1986:248) has noted numerous house burnings at sites surrounding the Alibates chert quarries. This may be a function of intergroup or intragroup disputes over the use of the quarries. Or it may reflect the greater use of these settlements because of their proximity to the quarries.

There are indications of defensive features at Antelope Creek settlements where some sites apparently functioned as defensive lookouts. Along the western perimeter of the Antelope Creek phase, four sites occur on high mesas: Saddleback Mesa (41OL1) (Studer 1931), Landegrin Mesa (41OL2) (Texas Historical Commission 1984), Mesa Alamosa (41OL8) (Marmaduke and Whitsett 1975), and Congdon Butte (LA 1994) (Studer 1931). In the east two such promontories served as defensive outlooks: Lookout Ruin (41HC29) and Arrowhead Peak (41HC19) (Lintz 1986:251). These sites may have functioned like perimeter outposts in historic times; they were perhaps positioned to spot external raiding parties, thus providing more time in which to develop defensive strategies. The location of these settlements also gives some indications for directionality in encounters with external groups. However, the difference in the number of such lookout sites in the west compared to the east may be a matter of opportunity (high mesas) rather than a real difference in the intensity of conflict on the eastern and western borders.

The Zimms Complex

Because of the limited number of sites and their small size, less information is available on potential warfare and conflict for the Zimms complex. However, the information that has resulted from bioarchaeological analysis is intriguing. Preliminary reports attested to a violent death for at least one individual from the Wickham #3 site (34RM29) (Wallis 1984:5–7). When three burials from this site were reanalyzed, an adult male was found to have a projectile point embedded in the sternum and fragments of a second point embedded in the bicipital groove of the right humerus. This individual also exhibited two cutmarks on the inferior surface of the right clavicle. A puncture wound to the right scapula and a notch in a rib similar to that caused by an arrowpoint noted in the initial report on this burial are now thought to represent postmortem damage. A second individual exhibited cutmarks on the skull indicative of scalping (Douglas Owsley, personal communication 1989).

Unlike the situation within the Antelope Creek phase, there is not much archaeological evidence to strengthen the presence of external or internal conflict. Structures at the Zimms and Hedding sites exhibit evidence of burning, but there is little to suggest that the fire was other than an accidental occurrence or intentionally set by village residents. Most Zimms complex sites also occur on ridges or high terraces above minor streams, thus setting up a defensive mechanism with the intent being to avoid detection by other groups living in the region, for example, Washita River phase peoples. Certainly, the small size of the settlements would put Zimms complex peoples at a disadvantage in any hostilities. However, this settlement distribution may also be a reflection of their subsistence strategies.

The Washita River Phase

As was the case with the Zimms complex, information on warfare and conflict within the Washita River phase has been drawn primarily from bioarchaeological analyses. Data compiled from this research presents a picture of conflict extending across the area encompassed by this cultural pattern. Bioarchaeological analyses of four sites within the Washita River phase area have been used in this study: the Grant, Heerwald, McLemore, and Nagle sites.

In the westernmost part of the Washita River phase, evidence from the Heerwald site (34CU27) in Custer County attests to violent death among members of this Washita River phase community. Excavations at the Heerwald site (Shaeffer 1966) resulted in the recovery of three individuals placed in a large pit—a young, adult female, a child, and a near-term fetus. Analysis of the adult female revealed that she had been shot at least twice. One arrowpoint lodged in a thoracic vertebra and the second point shattered the right scapula, cut through a rib, and passed through soft tissue before exiting the body. This individual also displayed scalping cutmarks on the cranium ("Evidence of Warfare at the Heerwald Site," this vol.). No evidence of combat trauma was observed on the child.

At the McLemore site (34WA5) 55 individuals were excavated from approximately 50 burials within a cemetery area, making it one of the most comprehensive skeletal data sets for the Southern Plains (Brues 1962; Owsley and Jantz 1989). Only three display evidence of possible trauma associated with conflict. These examples include a young adult female with an arrowpoint embedded in a thoracic vertebra and two individuals with fractured skulls (Brues 1962:73). Reanalysis of the fractured crania shows these to be postdepositional

conditions and not a result of violence (Douglas Owsley, personal communication 1989). There is also no apparent evidence for scalping among these or other individuals. Considering the size of the McLemore burial sample, there is not compelling evidence for extensive warfare.

The third site analyzed for the Washita River phase is the Grant site (34GV2) (Sharrock 1961). Restudy of the skeletal remains from the Grant site has resulted in the identification of 15 individuals (Owsley and Jantz 1989), only one of which exhibits trauma suggestive of a combat wound. Burial 10, an adult male, has a fracture of the left parietal. This fracture is a roughly circular depression measuring approximately 15 millimeters in diameter. There is no evidence of radiating fractures, and it does not appear to be a severe injury. It is not thought to have been the cause of death (Douglas Owsley, personal communication 1989). This is probably a combat injury.

The fourth site with implications for group conflict is the Nagle site (34OK4) (Brues 1957). The remains from the Nagle site do not represent a Washita River phase population. However, it is possible that remains at this site are a consequence of warfare with Washita River phase people.

The Nagle site contains 20 individuals—four adult males, three adult females, three adults of undetermined sex, three subadults, and seven infants and children (Owsley and Jantz 1989). Unlike other skeletal samples discussed in this chapter, the Nagle burials represent solely a cemetery site. There is no associated habitation debris, and the burials were placed in a low area adjacent to the North Canadian River, a location not considered favorable for settlement. Analysis of the Nagle burials based on burial furniture revealed that they are most likely a group of Caddoans, possibly from the Spiro site (34LF6) (Robert E. Bell, personal communication 1989). Study of the skeletal remains (Brues 1957; Douglas Owsley, personal communication 1989) reinforced this view. People from the Nagle site exhibit evidence of malnutrition as well as low adaptive efficiency as reflected by a variety of infectious diseases (cf. Burnett 1988). Based on the characteristics of the osteological remains and the the nature of the grave goods, it appears that the Nagle people were a refugee population from the Spiro site. The people from Nagle may represent a lineage or population group that was forced to emigrate from Spiro. As a displaced population on the Southern Plains, they probably would have been perceived as an invading group.

The traumatic death of an adult male (Burial 10) from the Nagle site attests to the fact that the intrusion of these Caddoans was challenged by some Plains Villagers (Washita River phase people ?). This individual was found with four arrowpoints within the thoracic cavity. The points were made of Alibates chert from the Texas panhandle. The use of this material supports the notion that the responsible party was native to the Southern Plains. In addition to his violent death, he had also been scalped.

Archaeological data to qualify the extent of warfare during the Washita River phase is lacking. Only a limited number of houses have been excavated, and few of these appear to have been burned as a result of conflict. At the Arthur site (34GV32) where five houses were excavated, the only house with clear evidence of burning was either accidentally burned or was burned as a result of the death of a house resident (Brooks 1987:107). There is also no evidence in the Washita River phase for defensive enclosures such as those used by the Wichita in protohistoric and historic times (Bell, Jelks, and Newcomb 1967).

The density of Washita River phase settlements may have had some effect on the potential for intergroup conflict. This cultural complex contained a large resident population that was concentrated in the Washita River valley. This numerical strength served as a deterrent to attack by external groups. Although it is possible that the Washita River phase represents more than one phase (or society), it is likely that these people had strong cultural ties that promoted alliances against common foes.

An Evaluation of the Evidence for Conflict

Two schools of thought exist on causal explanations for Plains warfare (cf. Biolsi 1984). Linton (1936), Wissler (1940), and others attributed these conflicts to the militaristic and competitive nature of Plains societies. Another reason couched in terms of a "psychological image" was Ewers's (1975:397–398) suggestion that ethnocentrism and revenge played important roles in fostering conflict. A second school championed materialistic causes of warfare, arguing that defense of territory and competition for critical resources—horses, bison, fertile soils, and water—were the principal causes of intergroup conflict (Biolsi 1984:144–162; Newcomb 1950). Both perspectives recognized a distinction between large-scale warfare and small-scale hostilities (Biolsi 1984:143). The intensity of the conflict was also recognized as contributing to different causal explanations. For example, diminishing resources might lead to widespread warfare whereas horse raiding reflected small-scale hostilities.

These explanations of Plains warfare were drawn primarily from historic, ethnohistoric, and ethnographic data. It is more difficult to reconstruct the reasons for warfare during pre-

historic times. Before proposing causal explanations for warfare between prehistoric Plains societies, it is necessary that the extent of the conflict be identified and classified as constituting large-scale warfare or small-scale hostilities. Various categories of information can be used to establish the nature of the conflict setting. Archaeological concerns include destruction of dwellings and villages and evidence of fortifications or other defensive architecture. Bioarchaeological evidence consists of traumatic injuries resulting from combat, for example, fractures, puncture wounds, embedded projectile points, and cutmarks reflecting scalping, mutilation, or dismemberment. The spatial distribution reflected in the archaeological and bioarchaeological data must also be given critical evaluation.

The three Southern Plains village societies discussed in this paper have been analyzed using these criteria. The Antelope Creek phase represents the only case where both archaeological and bioarchaeological data support a context for moderate to large-scale conflict. The archaeological evidence consists of numerous burned structures and the presence of sites that may have functioned as defensive outposts. Bioarchaeological evidence consists of individuals from at least three sites with traumatic injuries due to combat (Antelope Creek 22, Footprint, and the Big Blue Cemetery). In addition to combat wounds, the remains at the Footprint site point to mutilation and decapitation (trophy skulls). Both decapitation and mutilation are common traits in Northern Plains warfare (Owsley, Berryman, and Bass 1977:124–125), but it is difficult to establish whether it is more likely to occur in large-scale warfare than in small-scale hostilities. Based on evidence from the Northern Plains (Gregg et al. 1981; Owsley, Berryman, and Bass 1977), it would appear that the more intensive pattern of large-scale warfare is more apt to generate this type of combat behavior. The only correlate to this type of combat behavior on the Southern Plains is the ritualistic cannibalism practiced by the Wichita in the eighteenth century (Bell, Jelks, and Newcomb 1967:326).

The spatial distribution of warfare during the Antelope Creek phase is also revealing. Although defensive outposts are found on both the eastern and western perimeters of Antelope Creek, they are more numerous on the western frontier. Additional evidence for conflict in terms of burned houses and violent deaths is also primarily found in the western portion of the territory traditionally identified with this society. In fact, little evidence exists for conflict in the east, with exception of the outposts at Lookout Ruin and Arrowhead Peak.

The context for large-scale warfare during the Zimms complex is less convincing, although the situation is distorted due to limited data. Two burials show evidence of violent death and conflict. Considering the small size of the Zimms complex settlements, this may represent a substantial segment of a hamlet's population. The Zimms settlement pattern may reflect an attempt to avoid detection by other groups. These people apparently lacked the numbers to successfully engage in warfare. Because their territory lies between that of groups of the Antelope Creek and Washita River phases (cultures with numerical superiority and greater population aggregation), it would have been imprudent to engage these groups in large-scale conflict (or even small-scale hostilities). On the other hand, these groups might have found it relatively easy to conduct raids against the small, isolated homesteads of the Zimms complex.

Data on hostilities are indicative of moderate levels of small-scale conflict during the Washita River phase. Evidence for violent death exists at the Heerwald and McLemore sites. Information from the Nagle site also provides documentation for hostilities against a Caddoan population entering the area. However, the Washita River phase lacks evidence of large-scale warfare. Given that the McLemore and Grant sites represent two of the larger skeletal samples from the Southern Plains villages, they are remarkably free of violent death; only one death among 70 individuals can be attributed to violence. There is also little in the way of archaeological data to support an argument for warfare. Instances of burned houses are uncommon, although this may reflect the limited number of excavated structures. There is also no suggestion of defensive architecture such as that encountered in the Antelope Creek phase or during the protohistoric period. The spatial distribution of violent deaths again reveals a pattern focused on the periphery of this society. Perhaps the population size and density served as a deterrent in respect to conflict with external groups. Analysis of the Nagle site burials also suggests that Southern Plains villagers were sensitive to encroachments on their territory, in this case, the eastern frontier.

Southern Plains village hostilities were essentially small-scale conflicts rather than the large-scale warfare observed on the Northern Plains during this time. Moreover, most of the conflict occurred on the borders of the two larger groups, the Antelope Creek and Washita River phases. Considering the size of their villages and the relative density of settlements, it is not surprising that most of the hostilities were found along the frontier rather than in the heartland of these societies where they could marshal a sizable force of adult males for armed conflict.

Despite the relative similarity in patterns of conflict on the Southern Plains during the Plains Village period, it is quite possible that these small-scale hostilities in frontier settings were derived from different causes. In the case of the Washita River phase, it is proposed that these conflicts reflect boundary maintenance. With the Nagle site, a good case can be made for this defensive strategy on the eastern boundary. The Nagle site people probably were a displaced Caddoan population with women and children, moving into an area some 275 kilometers from their cultural homeland. Their intrusion might be considered an invasion rather than simply a raiding episode. Along the western boundary, it is possible that small-scale conflict was taking place with people of the Zimms complex. The Zimms complex occupies an area adjacent to the Washita River phase with a somewhat different settlement-subsistence strategy suggesting different cultural affinities. Zimms complex settlements were too small to have represented a serious threat to the Washita River phase villages. On the other hand, the Zimms people probably did encroach on the hunting territories of Washita River phase groups. This competition over hunting territory may have resulted in small-scale conflict (raiding) between the two groups. Raiding is also the only type of conflict that the Zimms complex groups with their limited population aggregation could have successfully pursued.

The situation is somewhat different for the Antelope Creek phase people. First of all, the most intensive warfare pattern found in the region is along their western border. Lintz (1986:251–252), although considering a number of alternative warfare models, appears comfortable with the idea of a Puebloan group from the Chaco Canyon area moving into the Middle Rio Grande valley and disrupting established relationships between Southern Plains and Puebloan groups. One group that may have been involved in this turmoil was an eastern Mogollon group occupying the Sierra Blanca region of southeastern New Mexico and the Texas panhandle. In this instance, it may be that trading in valuable commodities such as bison meat and hides represented the motive for warfare. Another resource possibly competed for is Alibates chert, a high quality stone used in the manufacture of chipped-stone tools. Certainly, the Antelope Creek phase people were so concerned that they constructed defensive lookouts along their western frontier for protection.

Summary

Conflict on the Southern Plains at this time has been found to be primarily small-scale in context. However, some evidence on the western extent of the Antelope Creek phase points to greater intensity. Most conflict also appears to occur in frontier settings. This conflict has been attributed to both boundary maintenance and to trade relationships. Although these patterns are not strongly manifested in the Plains Village period, they become stronger in historic times. By the Protohistoric period, villages are found with entrenchments and fortifications and well-documented evidence of persistent and intensive conflict. These conflicts focus not only on the trade of critical commodities and the defense of hunting territories but also on the presence of newcomers to the Southern Plains, nomadic Athapaskan-speaking groups with economic and cultural systems significantly different from the resident Southern Plains villagers. In the eighteenth and nineteenth centuries, White explorers and traders used these conflicts to exploit the resources of the region.

References Cited

Bell, R.E., E.B. Jelks, and W.W. Newcomb
  1967 A Pilot Study of the Wichita Indian Archaeology and Ethnohistory. (Report submitted to the National Science Foundation, Washington.)

Biolsi, T.
  1984 Ecological and Cultural Factors in Plains Indian Warfare. Pp. 141–168 in Warfare, Culture, and Environment. R.B. Ferguson, ed. New York: Academic Press.

Brooks, Robert L.
  1987 The Arthur Site: Settlement and Subsistence Structure at a Washita River Phase Village. *Oklahoma Archeological Survey, Studies in Oklahoma's Past* 15.

Brues, A.M.
  1957 Skeletal Material from the Nagle Site. *Bulletin of the Oklahoma Anthropological Society* 5:93–99.

——
  1962 Skeletal Material from the McLemore Site. *Bulletin of the Oklahoma Anthropological Society* 10:69–78.

Burnett, B.A.
  1988 Bioarcheological Synthesis. Pp. 193–220 in Human Adaptation in the Ozark-Ouachita Mountains. G. Sabo III, A.M. Early, J.C. Rose, B.A. Burnett, J. Voegele, and J.P. Harcourt, eds. Fayetteville, Ark.: Arkansas Archeological Survey.

Ewers, J.C.
  1975 Intertribal Warfare as the Precursor of Indian-White Warfare on the Northern Great Plains. The Western Historical Quarterly 6:397–410.

Green, F.E.
  1967 Archaeological Salvage in the Sanford Reservoir Area. (National Park Service Report 14-10-0333-1126, Washington.)

Gregg, J.B., L. Zimmerman, J.P. Steele, H. Ferwerda, and P.S. Gregg
  1981 Ante-mortem Osteopathology at Crow Creek. *Plains Anthropologist* 26:287–300.

Linton, R.
  1936 The Study of Man. New York: Appleton Press.

Lintz, C.R.
  1986 Architecture and Community Variability Within the Antelope Creek Phase of the Texas Panhandle. *Oklahoma Archeological Survey, Studies in Oklahoma's Past* 14.

Marmaduke, W.S., and H. Whitsett
  1975 Reconnaissance and Archaeological Studies in the Canadian River Valley. Canadian Breaks, a Natural Area Survey Pt VII. Austin: University of Texas, Division of Natural Resources and Environment.

Newcomb, W.W.
  1950 A Re-examination of the Causes of Plains Warfare. *American Anthropologist* 52:317–330.

Owsley, D.W.
  1989 The History of Bioarchaeological Research in the Southern Great Plains. Pp. 123–136 in From Clovis to Comanchero: Archeological Overview of the Southern Great Plains. J.L. Hofman, R.L. Brooks, and D.W. Owsley, eds. *Arkansas Archeological Survey Research Series* 35.

——, and R.L. Jantz
  1989 A Systematic Approach to the Skeletal Biology of the Southern Plains. Pp. 137–156 in From Clovis to Comanchero: Archeological Overview of the Southern Great Plains. J.L. Hofman, R.L. Brooks, and D.W. Owsley, eds. *Arkansas Archeological Survey Research Series* 35.

——, H.E. Berryman, and W.M. Bass
  1977 Demographic and Osteological Evidence for Warfare at the Larson Site, South Dakota. Pp. 119–131 in Trends in Middle Missouri Prehistory: A Festschrift Honoring the Contributions of Donald J. Lehmer. W.R. Wood, ed. *Plains Anthropologist Memoir* 13.

——, M.K. Marks, and M.H. Manhein
  1989 Human Skeletal Samples in the Southern Great Plains Study Area. Pp. 111–122 in From Clovis to Comanchero: Archeological Overview of the Southern Great Plains. J.L. Hofman, R.L. Brooks, and D.W. Owsley, eds. *Arkansas Archeological Survey Research Series* 35.

Patterson, D.K.
  1974 An Analysis of Human Skeletal Material from Antelope Creek Focus of Northern Texas. (Unpublished Masters Thesis in Anthropology, Eastern New Mexico University, Portales.)

Shaeffer, J.B.
  1966 Salvage Archaeology in Oklahoma, Vol. II. Papers of the Oklahoma Archaeological Salvage Project, Nos. 18–21. *Bulletin of the Oklahoma Anthropological Society* 14:1–86.

Sharrock, F.W.
  1961 The Grant Site of the Washita River Focus. *Bulletin of the Oklahoma Anthropological Society* 9:1–66.

Studer, F.V.

1931 Some Field Notes and Observations Concerning Texas Panhandle Ruins. Pp. 131–145 in Archaeology of the Arkansas River Valley. W.K. Moorehead, ed. London: Oxford University Press.

Texas Archaeological Society

1969 Big Blue Creek Cemetery, Field Notes and Excavations Forms from Crew Members. (Notes on file at the Panhandle-Plains Historical Society, Archaeological Library, Canyon, Tex.)

Texas Historical Commission

1984 Completion Report (Project: Landegrin Mesa). (Report submitted to the National Register of Historic Places, Project No. 48-84-OJB-48.11.)

Wallis, C.S., Jr.

1984 Summary of Notes and Earlier Analysis of the Wickham #3 Site, 34Rm-29, Roger Mills County, Oklahoma. *Bulletin of the Oklahoma Anthropological Society* 33:1–22.

Wedel, M.

1982 The Wichita Indian in the Arkansas River Basin. Pp. 118–134 in Plains Indian Studies: A Collection of Essays in Honor of John C. Ewers and Waldo Wedel. D.H. Ubelaker and H.J. Viola, eds. *Smithsonian Contributions to Anthropology* 30.

Wissler, C.

1940 Indians of the United States. Garden City, N.Y.: Doubleday Press.

CHAPTER 26

○ ○ ○

Women's Roles in Plains Indian Warfare

JOHN C. EWERS

Most students of Plains Indians have recognized warfare as a significant aspect of Plains life in the eighteenth and nineteenth centuries, and they have tended to treat warfare as a men's activity. Well then, what about the drawing by a Cheyenne Indian in a ledger book (fig. 1)? It pictures an Indian woman, nude to the waist and clutching her rifle. But how accurate is it as an interpretation of women's roles in Plains Indian warfare?

Evidence demonstrates that women were much involved in a number of ways besides providing encouragement to their menfolk. Women's roles were both passive and active ones. They exulted in the thrill and excitement of victory; they also suffered the humiliation and agony of defeat.

In 1832 the American artist George Catlin found it difficult to accept the accuracy of the war honors story of the Mandan Four Bears, told on a painted robe he gave to Catlin (fig. 2). Could Four Bears have been so lacking in chivalry as to kill enemy women? Indeed Catlin reported: "I incurred his ill-will for a while by asking him whether it was manly to boast of taking the scalps of women? And his pride prevented him from giving me any explanation or apology. The interpreter, however, explained to me that he had secreted himself in the most daring manner, in full sight of the Ojibbeway [Chip-

pewa] village, seeking to avenge a murder, where he remained six days without sustenance, and then killed two women in full view of the tribe, and made his escape, which entitled him to the credit of a victory, though his victims were women" (Catlin 1841, 1:154).

Four Bears was not the only prominent chief to record with pride his killing of enemy women. Running Antelope, one of the chiefs among the Hunkpapa Sioux before Sitting Bull gained a prominent position in that tribe, compiled a record of killing 10 men and 3 women in the year 1856 (fig. 3).

Ledger drawings by late nineteenth-century Cheyenne warriors portray women's deaths in warfare. A drawing in the Crazy Dog Ledger portrays a mounted Cheyenne warrior delivering an apparently fatal lance thrust to the breast of a Crow woman (Powell 1981, 1:142). Another drawing pictures a Cheyenne warrior chasing and killing two Kiowa women (fig. 4).

There is an earlier reference to a shift from the killing to the capture of enemy women during the historic period. David Thompson, a pioneer fur trader on the Canadian plains, told of a meeting of Piegan chiefs and warriors in 1783 or 1784 after that tribe had suffered population losses in the smallpox epidemic of 1781. At that meeting a chief stated that

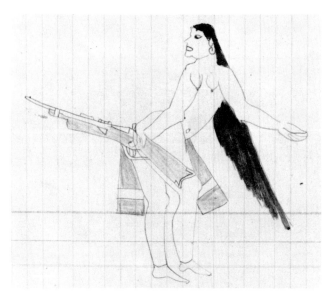

Fig. 1. A warrior woman, as drawn by a Cheyenne artist before 1889. (National Anthropological Archives, Smithsonian Institution: Manuscript 166,032.)

smallpox was a punishment for their having killed so many in warfare.

The chief suggested that in the future enemy women [young women] must all be saved and adopted i.e. brought to our camps, and be adopted amongst us, to be our people, and make us more numerous and stronger than we are. Thus the Great Spirit will see that when we make war we will kill only those who are dangerous to us, and make no more ground red with blood than we can help, and the Bad Spirit will have no more power over us. . . . everyone signified his assent to the Old Chief, and since that time, it has sometimes been acted on, but more with the women than the boys and while it weakens our enemies it makes us stronger (Thompson 1916:339).

Observe that David Thompson reported that the old chief's sage advice "has sometimes been acted on." Actually the killing

Fig. 2. Mandan Chief Four Bears killing two Chippewa women. Painted on a buffalo robe prior to 1832. (Catlin 1841, 1: plate opp. p. 154, fig. 10.)

Fig. 3. Hunkpapa Chief Running Antelope's record of his killing 10 enemy men and 3 women in 1856. (Mallery 1893: fig. 816.)

of women persisted in intertribal warfare on the northern Plains into the second half of the nineteenth century.

The fur trader Edwin T. Denig, while in charge of the American Fur Company's post of Fort Union at the mouth of the Yellowstone River during the 1850s, wrote: "The Assiniboin, Blackfeet, Sioux, Cree, and Arikara also kill women and children and dance as much for their scalps as for those of men" (Denig 1930:552). At the same time Denig recognized that the Crows didn't kill enemy women and children. Why this difference? At that time the Crows were a relatively small tribe, but they occupied one of the best hunting grounds on the Northern Plains. They were surrounded by four larger enemy tribes—the Sioux, Blackfeet, Cheyenne, and Eastern Shoshone. They needed to increase their number while they fought desperately for survival. So they captured rather than killed the women and children of enemy tribes who fell into their hands.

Nevertheless, it is probably true throughout most of the historical period of intertribal warfare on the Great Plains that Indian women had more reason to fear being taken captive than being killed. Early in the historic period young Indian women captives became valuable pawns in intertribal trade, passing from the west to the more easterly tribes and to White traders at their early outposts in the wilderness.

There were said to have been Blackfeet and Gros Ventre women captives among the English on Hudson's Bay before Anthony Hendry (1907:339) became the first Englishmen to explore westward to the Upper Saskatchewan River in 1754. He reported seeing "many fine girls who were captives" in the camps of those Indians. In 1772 Mathew Cocking found young people of both sexes taken as slaves and adopted into Gros Ventre families "who have lost their children, either by war or sickness" (Cocking 1908:111). During the 1770s the

Fig. 4. Cheyenne killing of 2 Kiowa women in a Cheyenne ledgerbook, pencil and crayon, 1881. (Frontier Army Museum, Ft. Leavenworth, Kans.: LEAV 66.50.1.)

elder Alexander Henry saw Blackfeet women and children who were slaves among the Assiniboin (Henry 1809:312). And during the first decade of the nineteenth century the younger Alexander Henry found that the Cree and Assiniboin still referred to the Blackfeet and Gros Ventre as "Slaves" (Henry and Thompson 1897:312).

During the late seventeenth and early eighteenth centuries, the Illinois Indians made something of a business of capturing women and children from the Plains tribes and passing them on to other Indians and French outposts farther east. These captives came to be known by the French word *pani,* often translated as Pawnee. However, the *pana* women and boy who were given to Réné-Robert Cavelier, sieur De LaSalle in 1682 were probably members of the Wichita tribe. The boy claimed that he had been passed eastward as a captive from tribe to tribe over a period of years before he was given to LaSalle (Wedel 1988:53–74).

The Wichita, too, captured enemy women. "The chief object of [their] war expeditions was the taking of scalps and capture of women to be used as slaves. The hereditary enemies of the Wichita were the Apache, Osage, and Tonkawa" (Dorsey 1904:7).

In the southwestern Plains the Kiowa and Comanche took many captives from enemy tribes and from the Mexicans to strengthen their diminishing numbers during the nineteenth century. During the 1850s Indian Agent Robert S. Neighbors observed that the "Comanche sometimes take women prisoners, in which case their chastity is uniformly not respected" (Neighbors 1852:132). At nearly the same time the Lipan Apache women were "noted for their prettiness and good features. On this account the Comanches have often made war upon the Lipans so as to take their women as prisoners" (Bollaert 1850:277).

The best and most detailed description of intertribal slave-raiding of Plains Indian women appears in the accounts of Illinois Indian raids on the Pawnee and Quapaw, about the year 1700 (Pease and Werner 1934:375–388). Similarities in the organization and procedures between those early slave raids and the later horse raids of Plains Indians suggest that the raid for captives may have furnished the model for the horse raid of the Plains Indians (Ewers 1955:311).

Although all Plains Indian women may have had reason to fear being killed or captured by the enemy, not all of them were content to stay home and pray for the safe return of their fathers, brothers, or husbands while the men were off raiding their enemies. There is ample evidence that a number of women of many tribes joined raiding parties and took active parts in them.

As early as 1751 the governor of New France, in a letter to the French minister, described a combined Comanche and Wichita attack on the Osage in which he stated "their women go to war with them" (La Jonquire 1908:88). In 1820 Capt. John Bell of Maj. Stephen H. Long's exploring expedition, returning overland from the Rocky Mountains down the Arkansas River valley, reported meeting three returning war parties from three different tribes of the Southern Plains. The first, composed of eight men and a woman of the Arapaho, was returning from an unsuccessful horse raid upon the Pawnee. The second, "about 40 men and 4 or 5 squaws" of Cheyenne, was returning with a Pawnee scalp. And the third, a party of "30 men and 5 squaws," were Comanche who had been badly beaten in a fight with the Otoe (Bell 1957:207–210, 221–222, 224–225).

A journal written at Fort Clark on the Upper Missouri for the date of April 24, 1839, reported the arrival at that trading post of "a war party of Arikaras on their way to the Pawnees to steal horses composed of 42 men and 2 women" (Chardon 1932:193).

A Kiowa woman accompanied her husband on a raid into Mexico in 1854, and another woman of that tribe joined a party of 37 men to avenge an enemy killing of her husband (Nye 1962:95, 227). The literature provides numerous references to women of the so-called hostile tribes who fought alongside men against the Army of the United States during the 1860s and 1870s (Powell 1981, 2:964).

The Sioux artist, Amos Bad Heart Bull, drew the picture of an outward-bound Sioux war party leaving their home camp on foot (fig. 5). The partisan in the lead carries the pipe. The two women bringing up the rear carry packs on their backs as do the men. A note on this drawing in Lakota translates "women also go along." This was a small war party, comprising only six men and two women. The two women were probably wives of two of the men on the expedition.

Graphic portrayals of women warriors in action against their enemies are exceedingly rare. Father Nicolas Point, a pioneer Roman Catholic missionary among the tribes of the

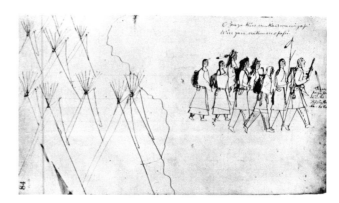

Fig. 5. An outward-bound Sioux war party of 6 men and 2 women pictured by Amos Bad Heart Bull, detail. (Blish 1967:fig. 88. © 1967 University of Nebraska Press.)

Northern Rockies during the 1840s, learned of Kuiliy, "a young Pend d'Oreille woman renowned for intrepidity in battle," who led a party of men of her tribe in the destruction of a Blackfeet war party (Point 1967:158). Father Point's drawing of a woman warrior in action may have been intended to picture Kuiliy (Point 1967:fig. 156).

Members of several Plains Indian tribes recalled successful women leaders of war parties. Two outstanding examples have become heroines of historical novels—Woman Chief (Capps 1979) and Running Eagle (Schultz 1919). There can be no doubt that both these women were successful war leaders. The trader Edwin T. Denig knew Woman Chief well during the 1850s and was the first to write of her successes as a war leader (Denig 1961:195–200). A Gros Ventre by birth, she was taken prisoner by the Crow Indians at the age of 12 and grew up to become a Crow war leader and to gain chiefly recognition in that tribe, only to be killed by her own people when she attempted to pay them a friendly visit. Denig learned that an Assiniboin woman who sought to emulate Woman Chief's success as a warrior was killed on her first expedition against the enemy.

The Piegan war leader, Running Eagle, came into prominence somewhat later. Weasel Tail, a Blood Indian, gained some knowledge of her through Old Chief White Grass, who had accompanied Running Eagle on several expeditions. Weasel Tail's account did not jibe with that of Schultz (1919) on a number of points. He said that when she was young, she married a Piegan, but her husband was killed by the Crows. She sought help from Sun to avenge her husband's death. Sun told her "I will give you great power in war, but if you have intercourse with any other man, you will be killed."

Running Eagle was a large woman. On the warpath she wore men's leggings, a sort of undershirt doubled over like a diaper, a woman's dress, and a blanket coat.

Weasel Tail said that the men who followed her on war parties respected her highly. She was not proud. She always insisted that she was a woman, and she cooked for her war parties and mended the men's moccasins. When one of the men protested that it was not right for the party leader to do that kind of work she replied, "I am a woman. Men don't know how to sew."

Weasel Tail said that Running Eagle was successful on repeated raids on the horse herds of the Flathead Indians west of the Rockies. When those Indians learned that it was a woman who had been leading those raids, they determined to kill her. One time she entered a Flathead camp for horses when the Flatheads were on the lookout for a strange woman. A man saw her, and in his Salish language asked her name. She did not answer but backed away. He lifted his gun and shot her dead.

Some Blackfeet claimed that Running Eagle had not been faithful to her vow to the Sun: that she had sexual relations with one of the men of her war parties. "That was why she was killed" (Ewers 1941–1944).

Marked differences of opinion have been expressed about the social roles of these women warriors. Capps (1979:vii) said that Woman Chief "defied the limitations placed upon her sex and made the fierce warriors of the northern plains respect her." On the other hand, Beatrice Medicine, a Sioux anthropologist, after reviewing the literature on Plains Indian woman warriors, concluded that the warrior role was not an unwomanly one, but it was an alternative one which the individual woman might accept if she so chose (Albers and Medicine 1983:274–275).

What is known of these woman warriors does not suggest that they were sexual deviants. They did have to be powerfully motivated to assume a warrior's role in a culture where the great majority of women did not. A strong motivation was an important factor in the making of outstanding male warriors also. For example, White Quiver, who became a successful horse raider, was spurred on by the fact that his father was killed by Crow Indians; most of his daring raids were on Crow camps (Ewers 1955:191–193).

An examination of the literature on Plains Indians reveals relatively little evidence of the torture of prisoners such as was common among the tribes east of the Mississippi in historic times. There is considerable evidence of the mutilation of dead enemies by Plains Indians and of women playing active roles in that mutilation.

The classic case involved the Blackfeet in their defense of an Assiniboin-Cree dawn attack upon a small camp of Piegan just outside the walls of the American Fur Company's post of Fort McKenzie near the mouth of the Marias on August 28, 1833. This was the action the German naturalist, Prince Maxmilian of Wied-Neuweid and his artist companion, Karl Bodmer, witnessed from the raised platform behind the stockade, and the one Bodmer illustrated in a view that portrays the intensity of the action and the use of a variety of deadly weapons at very close range.

After the attackers were driven off, Maxmilian sought to obtain the skull of one of the enemy who been killed. He found "The scalp had already been taken off, and several Blackfeet had engaged in venting their rage on the dead body. The men fired their guns at it; the women and children beat it with clubs, and pelted it with stones, the fury of the latter was particularly directed against the privy parts" (Maximilian 1906, 23:149).

The action of older women in emasculating the dead bodies of enemy males was well documented in the writings of other careful observers of Plains Indian warfare as far back as the 1790s. Jean-Baptiste Truteau, an experienced French trader and keen observer of the tribes of the Middle Missouri, described the frenzied mutilation of dead enemies by elderly Indian women: "I have seen these furious old hags near their dwelling themselves cut off the hands, limbs, [and] the virile parts of the dead enemies, hang them around the neck and at the ears, and dance thus at all the lodge doors of the village" (Wedel 1989:100).

The literature contains numerous references to the roles Plains Indian women played in the postraid victory celebration of their people. In the scalp dance it was customary for women to stand in the center displaying the trophies their husbands or other male relatives had taken in the recently concluded action. The scalps were held high, attached to the upper ends of slender willow poles (fig. 6).

Despite the heavy emphasis upon the scalp, it was not the only part of an enemy that Plains Indians took as a trophy. Other extremities—most commonly hands—were severed from the fallen body, carried home, displayed in the victory dance, then thrown away. In a Cheyenne drawing of a scalp dance that followed the Indian victory over Gen. George Custer's cavalry on the Little Big Horn in June 1876, one woman holds a hand tied to the upper end of her pole (Powell 1981, 2:981).

The widow of a warrior who failed to return from a raid against the enemy took no part in the public celebrations. Left alone, she went into extended mourning, cutting her long hair, and in some cases sacrificing a finger or scarifying her legs and arms. She would encourage her male relatives to avenge her loss in raids against the tribe that took her

Scalp Dance.

Drawn by an Assiniboine warrior Fort Union.

Nov. 10. 1853.

Fig. 6. Scalp Dance, drawn by an Assiniboine warrior at Fort Union, 1853. (Pen and ink in National Anthropological Archives, Smithsonian Institution: Manuscript 2600-B-1.)

husband's life. She herself might accompany one of those revenge raids.

Weasel Tail possessed a remarkably accurate memory of the details of his own experiences:

A lot of the old timers took their wives on war parties. Their wives wanted to go. But usually only a woman who as yet had no children would go on a war party with her husband. My wife was in five fights with me. She carried a revolver—a six shooter. Once she took a horse with a saddle, a bag of ammunition, and a war club on it. She said she loved me, and if I was to be killed she wanted to be killed with me.

I was frequently a leader of a war parties. On those parties my wife didn't have to do the cooking or other chores. We took boys 14 to 20 years old who cooked, rustled food and firewood for us in my day (Ewers 1941–1944).

Weasel Tail recalled that Red Crow, a Blood head chief, had a wife named Sings Before who took a gun from the enemy while on a war party with her husband. Weasel Tail named several Piegan men who took their wives on war parties. One of them was Young Bear Chief, whose wife, Annie Elk Hol-

lering in the Water Bear Chief, accompanied him on several war parties and had taken things from the enemy (fig. 7) (Ewers 1941–1944).

Wades in the Water, a full-blood Piegan, was probably the last man of his tribe to take an enemy scalp in intertribal warfare. He was a young teenager at the time, and the action was a small-scale one against some Assiniboins. After he took the scalp of a fallen Assiniboin, his older brother, who was close by, told him to cut off the enemy's hand at the wrist. This he did, and his brother tied the wrist trophy to the bridle of Wades in the Water's horse for the return to camp. The hand was carried in a victory dance, and then thrown away (Ewers 1941–1944).

Weasel Tail stated that the Blackfeet tribes did not ordinarily mutilate the dead. "If a man had a brother or a son killed by the enemy, and he went on a war party to avenge that killing, and one of the enemy was killed, this relative would mutilate the dead body. . . . But if there was no revenge [motive] there was no mutilation."

During World War II, the Sun Dance experienced a revival on the Blackfeet Reservation. Traditionally the pledger of the Sun Dance was a woman of unquestionable virtue who

Fig. 7. Annie Bear Chief, a Piegan woman who went on war parties with her husband when a young woman. (Photograph by John C. Ewers, 1943.)

vowed to Sun that she would give the ceremony in return for Sun's help to her. During those war years, the pledger asked Sun for the safe return of the young Blackfeet who were serving in the armed forces. The wife of Swims Under, the pledger of the Sun Dance in 1943, on the climactic day of the ceremony, faced the sun in the western sky, held toward it a piece of the sacred tongue, and prayed for the welfare of her people and the safe return of their servicemen.

But what of those Blackfeet men who did not return? The old people consoled the mothers of those young men with a traditional saying: "It is better for a man to die in battle than of old age or sickness."

Proof that that belief was an old and widespread one among Plains Indians appears in the 1796 writings of Jean-Baptiste Truteau:

I myself have seen, when I resided for three consecutive years at the home of the nation of *Panis Republicains* [Pawnee] fathers and mothers sing near the bodies of their sons that had been brought back to the village to be interred, sons who had been killed in a battle between the *Halitannes* [Comanche] and the *Republicains* on open prairie at some distance from their summer hunting camp, which episode I witnessed. These women, mothers of the young men who were killed, holding a bow in one hand and an arrow in the other, sang near the bodies of their sons an air both gay and martial, thanking them for having given them [the mothers] the satisfaction of seeing them die at the hands of the enemy while fighting valiantly for the defense of their country, a death a thousand times preferable to the fate of him who on a wretched mat expires consumed by some deadly disease (Wedel 1989:107).

References Cited

Albers, P., and B. Medicine
  1983 The Hidden Half: Studies of Plains Indian Women. Washington: University Press of America.
Bell, J.R.
  c1957 Journal of Captain John R. Bell. H.M. Fuller and L.R. Hafen, eds. Glendale, Calif.: A.H. Clark.
Bad Heart Bull Amos
  1967 A Pictographic History of the Oglala Sioux. Text by Helen H. Blish. Lincoln: University of Nebraska Press.
Bollaert, W.
  1850 Observations of the Indian Tribes of Texas. *London Ethnological Society Journal* 2.
Capps, B.
  1979 Woman Chief. Garden City, N.Y.: Doubleday.
Catlin, G.
  1841 Letters and Notes on the Manners, Customs, and Condition of the North American Indians. 2 vols., London: Published by the author and printed by Tosswill and Myers.
Chardon, F.A.
  1932 Chardon's Journal at Fort Clark, 1834–1838. Pierre, South Dakota. A.H. Abel, ed. Pierre, S.Dak.: Lawrence K. Fox, Superintendant, Department of History.
Cocking, M.
  1908 An Adventurer from Hudson Bay: Journal of Mathew Cocking from York Factory to the Blackfeet Country, 1772–1773. L.J. Burpee, ed. *Transaction of the Royal Society of Canada* ser. 3, vol. 2.

Denig, E.T.

1930   Indian Tribes of the Upper Missouri. J.N.B. Hewitt, ed. Pp. 375–628 in *46th Annual Report of the Bureau of American Ethnology for the Years 1928–1929.*

—

1961   Five Indian Tribes of the Upper Missouri: Sioux, Arikaras, Assiniboines, Cress, Crows. J.C. Ewers, ed. Norman, Okla.: University of Oklahoma Press.

Dorsey, G.A.

1904   The Mythology of the Wichita. Washington: Carnegie Institution of Washington.

Ewers, J.C.

1955   The Horse in Blackfeet Indian Culture. With Comparative Material from Other Western Tribes. *Bureau of American Ethnology Bulletin* 159.

Hendry, A.

1907   York Factory to the Blackfeet Country: The Journal of Anthony Hendry 1754–55. L.J. Burpee, ed. *Transaction of the Royal Society of Canada,* ser. 3, vol. 1.

—

1809   Travels and Adventures in Canada, and the Indian Territories Between the Years 1760 and 1776. New York: I. Riley.

Henry, A., and D. Thompson

1897   New Light on the Early History of the Greater Northwest. The Manuscript Journals of Alexander Henry. . . . and of David Thompson. . . . 1799–1814. 3 vols. E. Coues, ed. New York: F.P. Harper.

La Jonquire, P.J. de T.

1908   September 25, 1751, to French Minister in The French Regime in Wisconsin. *Wisconsin Historical Society Collections* 10.

Mallery, G.

1893   Picture-writing of the American Indians. Pp. 3–807 in *10th Annual Report of the Bureau of American Ethnology for the Years 1888–1889.*

Maximilian, Prince of Wied-Neuwied

1906   Travels in the Interior of North America. Early Western Travels 1748–1846. R.G. Thwaites, ed. Vols. 22–25. Cleveland: Arthur H. Clark.

Neighbors, R.S.

1852   The Na-u-ni, or Comanches of Texas; Their Traits and Beliefs, and Their Division and Intertribal Relations. Pp. 125–134 in Historical and Statistical Information Respecting the History, Condition, and Prospects of the Indian Tribes of the United States, vol. 2. Henry R. Schoolcraft, ed. Philadelphia: Lippincott, Grambo.

Nye, W.S.

1962   Bad Medicine and Good: Tales of the Kiowas. Norman, Okla.: University of Oklahoma Press.

Pease, T.C., and R.C. Werner, eds.

1934   Memoir of De Gannes concerning the Illinois Country. *Collections of the Illinois State Historical Library* 23, French Ser., vol. 1.

Point, N.

1967   Wilderness Kingdom, Indian Life in the Rocky Mountains: 1840–1847. J.P. Donnelly, trans. New York: Holt, Rinehart and Winston.

Powell, P.J.

1981   People of the Sacred Mountain. 2 vols. New York: Harper & Row.

Wedel, M.

1988   The Wichita Indians 1541–1750, Ethnohistorical Essays. *Reprints in Anthropology* 38. Lincoln, Neb.: J and L Reprint.

—

1989   Manuscript Translation of Jean-Baptiste Truteau, Abridged Description of the Upper Missouri, addressed to M. Zenon Truteau, Lt. Governor of the Western Part of the Illinois Country. (Original in Archives of the Seminary of Quebec.)

○○○

CHAPTER 27

Warfare in Coalescent Tradition Populations of the Northern Plains

DOUGLAS W. OWSLEY

This chapter examines the incidence of violent death in South Dakota during the late prehistoric, protohistoric, and early historic periods as manifested by the presence of perimortem cuts on the cranial vault caused by scalping. The primary objective is to determine whether the frequency of traumatic death varied temporally and geographically, with measurable change occurring as a result of indirect Euro-American contact. Data for skeletal samples recovered from archaeological sites representing the Extended, Postcontact, and Disorganized variants of the Coalescent tradition are compared through diachronic analysis.

Scalping was a longstanding practice in the Northern Plains. A basic question is whether it offers a useful indicator of the frequency of warfare. The significance of scalping in Plains Indian society, based on the ethnohistoric record and archaeological evidence, suggests that the pattern and intensity of violence changed over time.

As the European population increased in the Great Plains, relations with Native Americans deteriorated. For the Arikara, overt hostility began in the 1820s with attacks on fur traders, in particular the 1823 attack on traders who were led by Gen. (in the Missouri militia) William H. Ashley, his fur-trading associate, Andrew Henry, and about 90 men (Zimmerman 1985; Bass, Evans, and Jantz 1971). In reprisal, the federal government sent the 6th Regiment, under the command of Col. Henry Leavenworth, accompanied by a contingent of irregulars from the Missouri Fur Company and by 400 to 500 Dakota Sioux, to subdue this rebellion. Leavenworth village was shelled in 1823.

The Plains Indian wars during the last half of the nineteenth century involved army operations against other tribes as well, the best known being the Battle of the Little Bighorn in Montana (Custer's Last Stand) (Utley 1988). However, even before direct involvement of the United States military, documents for the eighteenth century mention that intertribal conflict was frequent. Tribal migrations from the north and east, particularly from the Great Lakes region, followed the fur trade wars and the development of a militarily oriented, nomadic, bison-hunting Plains culture. Siouan groups with horses had crossed the Missouri River by 1750 (Zimmerman 1985).

Cultural interaction between the more sedentary village populations and the equestrian tribes frequenting the Missouri Valley resulted from their participation in an extensive trading network. During the protohistoric period, the Arikara were well established as middlemen in an exchange of agricultural products, horses, guns, and other artifacts of European derivation. The Cheyenne, Assiniboine, and Sioux were drawn to the villages because of opportunities for trading.

From another perspective, the agricultural surpluses, numerous horses, and other supplies proved to be attractive booty, making the farming villages prime targets for raids. Historical literature reveals ample evidence of pressure, hostility, and intermittent warfare between the Arikara and other groups. Their enemies included at various times the Assiniboine, Crow, Mandan, Hidatsa, and, particularly, the Sioux (Owsley, Berryman, and Bass 1977).

Aggression between tribal groups was usually small-scale, with raids involving only a few warriors whose objective was to steal horses or avenge prior grievances. Occasionally, large military units of several hundred warriors assembled to attack a village. Travelers to the Missouri Valley reported seeing the ruins of destroyed Arikara villages. The Meriwether Lewis and William Clark journals provide an example: "A little above our encampment the ricaras had formerly a large village on each side which was destroyed by the Sioux. There is remains of five other villages on the S.W. side below the Cheyenne river and one on Lehocatts Isld. all those villages have been broken up by the Sioux" (Thwaites 1959: 360).

Direct incursions of Euro-Americans into South Dakota and the earlier migrations of nomadic Plains Indians represented only the most recent expression of geographic expansion and the displacement of resident populations. Even in prehistoric times, major population movements characterized this region. The apparent frequency of historically documented warfare tends to overshadow the occurrence of similar episodes during the protohistoric and prehistoric periods. Archaeologists and osteologists have become increasingly aware of the evidence of violent, often lethal, conflict in precontact centuries. The evidence is varied and includes changes in settlement patterns and population distributions; village architectural features, especially fortification systems; and destruction of villages. The presence of village defensive systems has been the primary basis for inferring the frequency of warfare in the Northern Plains. For example, Caldwell (1964:1) points out that fortifications reflect "not only changes in the pattern of warfare, but suggest profound changes in the orientation of Plains cultural groups as well." In addition, paleopathological evidence of conflict, consisting of skeletal injuries and indications of violent death, corroborates and strengthens the archaeological and sociohistorical findings.

Village Fortifications and Changing Geographic Distributions

Village fortification systems in the Dakotas changed dramatically over the past millennium. They often consisted of defensive systems of moats, palisades, bastions, and use of strategic features in the natural terrain. Elaborate fortifications began with the Middle Missouri tradition, a nonindigenous culture with roots in the Prairie-Plains border area of southwestern Minnesota and northwestern Iowa (Key 1983). Responding to intense pressure, apparently from other Mississippian-influenced cultures similar to their own, villages were often heavily fortified and positioned on promontories where steep bluffs afforded protection (Zimmerman 1985). The Oneota, located to the south and east, were a potential threat. A raiding pattern of warfare, resulting in a high incidence of violent death among young adults, was a major problem for some Oneota populations (Milner, Anderson, and Smith 1991).

Central Plains tradition villages in Nebraska were loosely organized, with widely scattered houses lacking any special arrangement or fortifications (Zimmerman 1985). After 1150 (with the primary push after 1250), Central Plains groups moved north up the Missouri River, coming into contact and, eventually, competition and conflict with long-established, resident, Middle Missouri villagers. This migration, probably resulting from drought or some other natural environmental condition, led to the development of the Coalescent tradition (a blending of the Central Plains and Middle Missouri cultures), beginning with the Initial Coalescent variant.

Early Initial Coalescent sites, like Central Plains tradition villages in Nebraska, were loosely organized, with scattered lodges, and unfortified (Zimmerman 1985). Eventually, the density of lodges increased and fortifications became necessary. The Initial Coalescent became dominant and expanded throughout South Dakota, developing and continuing as the Extended Coalescent, among which were the ancestors of the historic Arikara.

The Initial Middle Missouri variant disappeared as a cultural entity shortly after the emergence of the Initial Coalescent, and a related culture, the Extended Middle Missouri variant, withdrew into North Dakota. The Extended Coalescent peoples resumed the Central Plains settlement pattern, with houses scattered over large areas. These rural hamlets were not totally undefended, and occasionally clusters of houses were surrounded by a simple palisade with one or two bastions and a ditch. "It does not appear that serious thought was given to enfilades and the bastions seem to be little more than gestures toward an old tradition" (Caldwell 1964:3).

Villages in the Grand-Moreau region in South Dakota were fortified, "suggesting contact/conflict with the late Extended Middle Missouri groups coming down from the north" (Key 1983:22). Because so many villages were unfortified, the Extended Coalescent has been referred to as the period of the Pax La Roche, a time of political quiescence, which only later was disrupted by the appearance of European and Dakotan influences in the eighteenth century (Caldwell 1964:3).

The compact, historic villages of the Arikara, Mandan, and Hidatsa observed by the fur traders were fortified, but special defensive features such as bastions were usually absent and the ditch and stockade were fairly modest. Caldwell (1964:4) notes that:

The renewed emphasis upon fortifications seems to coincide with increasing pressures by hunting groups, who by late [18th] century had become aggressive horsemen. The changed nature of the fortifications may not be solely the result of progressive disarray, rather it probably reflects the changed nature of warfare. One might infer that previously, conflict had been internecine, fought between tightly organized, well supplied groups of villagers. Although this sort of thing doubtlessly continued, the raids of the hunters, reasoning from historic accounts, were probably hit and run affairs, sporadic transient attacks by nomads raiding for food or merely for the sake of fighting. Thus defensive fortifications of a minimal sort would have been entirely satisfactory.

Osteological Evidence for Warfare

The osteological evidence for warfare is dramatic because it documents catastrophic episodes in which entire villages were destroyed and the inhabitants massacred. The Initial Coalescent site of Crow Creek (39BF11) (Willey 1982, 1990) and the Extended Middle Missouri site of Fay Tolton (39ST11) provide graphic examples. As many as 500 people were killed at Crow Creek and their bodies mutilated and scalped. A few skeletons provided evidence of old physical trauma (healed fractures, projectile injuries, and nonlethal scalpings) suggesting a history of violence (Gregg et al. 1981).

At Larson (39WW2), a Postcontact Coalescent site, commingled and partially disarticulated human skeletons were found on the floors of earthlodges that had collapsed due to burning. Musket balls and copper arrow points were found in direct association, and the skeletons showed evidence of scalping, depressed fractures of the crania, traumatic dental avulsions, and mutilation (Owsley, Berryman, and Bass 1977). Men, women, and children were scalped, the youngest about

five years old. Several males were decapitated, which partially accounts for the absence of many skulls.

The evidence for small-scale feuding and raiding, as well as for large-scale warfare, demonstrates that culturally patterned violent conflict among different social groups has a long history, a millennium or more, in the Plains. Moreover, the archaeological and bioarchaeological data clearly show that this violence was not simply opportunistic instrumental behavior invented anew in each generation. Rather, these data indicate that this tradition was identifiable and persistent, a pattern that included raiding, scalping, and the taking of other physical trophies, and, by implication, probably the perduring motives of prestige and revenge, whose importance has been clearly documented for the historic period. In sum, warfare was a regional-cultural institution, a complex of values, ideas, and behaviors that persisted for at least 1,000 years (Robarchek et al. 1991:14).

Given this background, many questions about the nature and frequency of intertribal warfare during the prehistoric and early historic transition arise:

1. Do human skeletal remains (from cemeteries) provide additional evidence of traumatic injury resulting from violence?
2. Who were the casualties? That is, what do the data on casualties reveal about age, sex, and geographical distribution of the victims?
3. Is there a marked difference in patterns of warfare in the early historic period compared to prehistory?

A possible osteological indicator that could be used to study the nature and occurrence of warfare in Plains Indians and to provide answers to these questions is the presence of cuts on the cranial vault that suggest scalping.

Origin and History of Scalping

WHAT IS SCALPING?

Scalping, the forcible removal of all or part of the scalp (Nadeau 1941), was a form of mutilation practiced on fallen enemies from ancient times (see, for example, Reese 1940; Axtell and Sturtevant 1980). Hamperl (1967:630) defines scalping anatomically as "incising the skin over the skull down to the galea and the periosteum with a sharp object in a circular manner. The soft tissue can then be quickly removed from the cranial vault." He notes further that if the cutting instrument is not sharp it must be applied with considerable force to cut through the tissue to the bone and usually leaves marks similar to those of a saw on the cranial vault. If the victim survives, a shallow, smooth but uneven depression in the skull results, with only remnants of sutures in the scalped area. This depression is the end result of a sequence of changes beginning with exfoliation of necrotic bone, development of new spongy bone tissue, and, finally, the regeneration of epidermis closing the wound (Hamperl and Laughlin 1959).

Using documentary accounts of scalping practices among tribes of North American Indians, Nadeau (1941) described a number of variations. First, scalping could be simple, if only the scalp was taken, or compound, if ears, eyes, or parts of the face and neck were removed with the scalp. The amount taken varied greatly, from the entire scalp to a small, circular section near the crown of the head, the scalplock. Further, sometimes several small sections would be removed from the same head, particularly if more than one warrior participated in felling the victim. After the introduction of firearms, it was often difficult to determine who was responsible for a killing, and several warriors might each remove a piece of scalp; Nadeau (1941) calls this multiple scalping. The choice piece, the part at the crown of the head, was left for the chief or the man who had struck or shot first. In rare cases, called incomplete, the scalp was left attached at the back of the neck, a variation associated with torture of captives rather than action during or immediately after battle.

The techniques and tools of scalping also varied, as indicated in the documentary accounts of early explorers summarized by Nadeau (1941). The most common method was to make a circular incision with a sharp instrument of shell, reed, stone, steel, or other material, to pull or pry up a section of skin at the edge of the incision, to grasp it firmly, and to pull the incised section free. Another method, called sabrage, omitted the circular incision. Instead, the hair was seized and pulled violently to loosen a section of skin from the bone. With a knife wielded like a saber or sickle, the loosened section was sliced away. This method always yielded only a small area of scalp and injured the table of the skull, as some periosteum was removed with the scalp. A third method involved use of the teeth. After incising the skin around the area to be removed, if the victim was bald or had a shaved head so that pulling the hair was not feasible as a means of lifting the scalp, the aggressor used his teeth to grasp the skin at the edge of the incision and to tear off the scalp. Some of the sources cited by Nadeau (1941) indicated that particular tribes always used their teeth in scalping, even when the victim had a full head of hair or a scalplock.

WHEN AND WHERE DID SCALPING BEGIN?

Although the previous analysis of the nature and techniques of scalping was based on descriptions of the practice among tribes of Indians in North America, the practice was not limited to this continent or to the relatively recent past. Among those who have traced the origins and occurrence of scalping are Reese (1940), Owsley and Berryman (1975), and Axtell and Sturtevant (1980). The first documentary account is that of Herodotus in the fifth century B.C.; he describes the Scythian custom of decapitating a victim, then cutting the skin around the head, taking hold of the scalp, and shaking it off. Scalps were hung from the bridle of a warrior's horse, and Herodotus states that whoever had the greatest number of such head skins was judged the bravest man (Reese 1940).

Xenophon also refers to the practice in describing the March of the Ten Thousand from Mesopotamia back to Greece. In their travels through the wild lands of what is now Eastern Turkey and Soviet Armenia and among the mountains bordering the Black Sea, Xenophon reported that men separated from the main body of the army were likely to be set on by wild tribes, slain, and their hair taken (Murray 1964). The Biblical Apocrypha offers further evidence of the antiquity of scalping. In II Maccabees, Chapter 7, scalping was one of the tortures inflicted on Jewish captives in the third century B.C. by order of the Persian king Antiochus Epiphanes.

The great Byzantine general Belisarius, sent by the emperor Justinian in the sixth century A.D. to regain North Africa from the Vandals and Italy from the Ostrogoths, had under his command many auxiliary troops and mercenaries whom he regarded as barbarians, such as Huns and Herulians. The general was appalled at the scalping of fallen enemy officers by some of his troops among whom were Goths as well as eastern tribes (Murray 1964). Scalping was "a rite in the ancient Germanic code of the Visogoths, where the decalvare of the enemy is described as *capillos et cutem detrahere*" (Reese 1940:7). References to scalping are found in the archives compiled by Flodoard of Rheims (A.D. 891–966), who reported that Anglo-Saxons and Francs scalped their enemies. Thereafter, no additional references to scalping occur in European documents until the era of exploration of the New World. In fact, the early explorers and settlers had difficulty finding words to describe the practice when they first encountered it among the Indians. As there was no terminology to describe scalping in English, French, or Spanish, they used words ambiguously or invented new ones to express their meaning. Though such atrocities as disemboweling, beheading, and drawing and quartering were commonplace in sixteenth to eighteenth-century Europe, scalping seems to have disappeared; that is, no records of it have been found after the ninth century (Axtell and Sturtevant 1980).

A large body of literature documents scalping at the time of initial European contact with various tribes of aboriginal peoples of North America, from the Caribbean Islands to Mexico and Guatemala, to Florida, and northward to Canada (Axtell and Sturtevant 1980:461). Evidence of scalping is not limited to accounts of early explorers and settlers. Osteological evidence (France 1988; Hoyme and Bass 1962; Neiburger 1989; Neuman 1940; Owsley and Berryman 1975; Snow 1941, 1942; Willey and Bass 1978) indicates that the practice was present as early as A.D. 600 during the Woodland and later Mississippian cultural periods. Radiocarbon samples from the site where a scalped skull described by Neiburger (1989) was found yielded dates of A.D. 490–580. Nieburger (1989:207) concludes: "This Indian Warrior was killed and scalped 900 years before European explorers first visited the Americas. . . . [and that] scalping was actively practiced by the residents of North America as it was throughout the rest of the world." Willey and Bass (1978:6) also found evidence "that the scalping tradition had common elements across the eastern United States at least from Virginia to Kansas and from South Dakota to possibly Alabama." Such osteological evidence consists of circular or successive cuts or scratches on the skull vaults of victims who had been killed and lesions on the skulls of victims who survived scalping long enough to allow the bone tissue partially to regenerate (Axtell and Sturtevant 1980). The evidence also shows that scalping was not limited to young male warriors; all—old and young, male and female—could be scalped. In fact, Swanton (1946) notes that among some tribes such as the Creek, scalps of women and children were symbols of greater valor than those taken on the battlefield, for the warrior or raider had to go into enemy territory to get them.

Though scalping existed prior to European contact (some have hypothesized that it came to North America with the peoples of the Far East who first crossed the Bering Strait—Murray 1964), the introduction of steel knives and firearms, and the offering of bounties for scalps—at first for Indian scalps but subsequently for those of White enemies as well—led to the spread and intensification of this practice. Not only did the French and English encourage scalping during the series of wars throughout the colonial era, but in the Revolutionary War, both the English and the colonists offered bounties for scalps. Henry Hamilton, lieutenant governor of Upper Canada, was known as the "hair-buyer general" (Reese 1940:17).

WHAT IS THE CULTURAL SIGNIFICANCE OF SCALPING?

The Indians had a long tradition of scalping, a set of rituals and motives that were a part of tribal culture and varied form one tribe to another. Axtell and Sturtevant (1980:461–462) list some of the rituals associated with it. They note

that the actual removal of an enemy's head-skin was firmly embedded among other customs that could hardly have been borrowed from the European traders and fishermen who preceded the earliest European authors. The elaborate preparation of the scalps by drying, stretching on hoops, painting, and decorating; special scalp yells when a scalp was taken and later when it was borne home on raised spears or poles; the scalplock as men's customary hairdress; scalp-taking as an important element in male status advancement; occasionally nude female custodianship of the prizes; scalp dances; scalps as body and clothing decorations; scalps as nonremunerative trophies of war to be publicly displayed on canoes, cabins, and palisades; elaborate ceremonial treatment of scalps integrated into local religious beliefs; and the substitution of a scalp for a living captive or its adoption to replace a deceased member of the family—all these appear too varied, too ritualized, and too consistent with other native cultural traits over long periods of white contact to have been recent and foreign introductions by Europeans.

The taking of scalps as trophies in battle, evidence of bravery and prowess in warfare, appears to have been the most frequent and widespread practice. However, the discovery of the remains of scalped individuals who had received mortuary rites and burial, sometimes with gravegoods, at sites not associated with violence, suggested other cultural motives for scalp-taking and uses of scalps than as trophies. The scalp had a supernatural or religious significance in many tribes. For example, among the Pueblo peoples scalps were associated with sacrifices and ceremonies to bring rain, some scalps even being referred to as seed or water beings, with power over weather conditions (Allen, Merbs, and Birkby 1985). In the southeastern United States, when the scalp figured in offerings to a supernatural being, there was usually a medicine man or specially appointed group to handle the scalp and conduct the ceremonies in which it played a part. Often, too, scalps were closely associated with the spirits of members of the tribe, symbolizing the souls of the dead. Among the Chickasaw, the ghosts of those whose death in battle had not been avenged could only be appeased by placing scalps on top of their former homes (Owsley and Berryman 1975).

Scalps also had therapeutic significance. Allen, Merbs, and Birkby (1985:24) mention as examples that "The Navaho believed that scalp chewing would cure a toothache, and, at Isleta, pieces of scalp were chewed, mixed with mud and wrapped in a corn husk, as medicine against anxiety or to relieve longing for a dead relative." They also note that scalping itself could have been a form of therapy for severe headaches and for diseases and injuries involving the head.

Related to the use of pieces of scalp in various therapeutic brews was a kind of sympathetic magic. Among the Hopi, pieces of scalp were fed to young boys to make them brave. In addition, the scalp was sometimes regarded as an amulet or protective charm. The scalplock, a braid or lock of hair growing from the crown of the head, was often painted and decorated with ornaments denoting honors and achievements; it came to be symbolic of a man's life and had special significance when still attached to its owner as well as when taken as a trophy of war (Allen, Merbs, and Birkby 1985).

Not just the scalp but a person who survived scalping had a variety of cultural associations. Dorsey (1904), Gilmore (1933), and Parks (1982) are among those who have examined the Arikara legends surrounding the scalped man. In the Arikara language, to scalp was synonymous with to ruin, and a man who survived scalping was considered no longer quite human. He had to lead a solitary existence apart from the tribe. The scalped man "made a shelter for himself in some isolated place far away from the villages and the customary resorts of his people. He cunningly concealed his dwelling to keep it from being seen by anyone who chanced to pass by. Since he was regarded as a dead man and a ghost, the sight of him would have been a shock and an offense to the living" (Gilmore 1933:30). The scalped man lived in a cave, generally on a steep hill, with the entrance camouflaged. The Pawnee, according to Parks (1982), covered the floor of the cave with wild sage, built a fireplace in the center, and had either a spring or a cistern to supply water. Near the source of water was an altar of buffalo skulls.

Descriptions of dress varied, but often the scalped man wrapped himself in animal hides and kept his head covered to conceal his wound. Among the Pawnee the head covering was white cloth; among the Arikara, a cap, usually of coyote skin.

The scalped man became the focus of many legends and myths. Believed to have supernatural powers, it was said that "he travelled at night as a spirit and was able to take scalps, capture horses, and catch eagles without difficulty" (Parks 1982:52). He also had the power to bring good fortune in battle and to heal the sick, and these powers, which he could confer on others, were the subjects of many legends. In addition to legends relating to then-contemporary life and events, the scalped man figured in mythology having to do with the origin of the world, the occurrence of the seasons, and the nature of death and the spirit world.

Yet another dimension to the lore of the scalped man, and quite different from the mythological and legendary persona, was the comic folktale, with the scalped man as a trickster, the hero of some farcical episode, often of a sexual nature. Occasionally, a scalped woman also figured in such humorous tales.

Finally, again in contrast to the serious and beneficent role usually ascribed to the scalped man, he was sometimes viewed as a malevolent sort of bogeyman who moved about dark, isolate areas at night and might well steal from or harm individuals.

SCALPING AS AN INDICATOR OF PLAINS WARFARE

The process of scalping usually results in cuts on the cranial vault. Such marks provide a useful indicator of Plains Indian warfare. As early ethnographies of Plains Indians and the ethnohistorical record indicate, scalping a defeated enemy was an activity commonly associated with tribes of the historic period. Wilson (1924:163), for example, quoted one of his informants, Wolf Chief, a Hidatsa man born around 1849, as follows: "When an enemy fell, the first man to strike coup on his body cut out the crown; and the others who also struck coup would in a twinkling strip the whole skull of the scalp."

In coup warfare, honors were accorded warriors who touched an enemy or captured weapons or horses (Lowie 1920). Although the scalping of an enemy frequently occurred, "Neither the killing nor the scalping was regarded as an especially creditable act. The chief applause was won by the man who first could touch the fallen enemy" (Grinnell 1910:297). Scalps were taken as trophies and regarded as emblems of victory, "a good thing to carry back to the village to rejoice and dance over" (Grinnell 1910:303). However, expeditions were often organized for the purpose of revenge and scalping. For most Plains tribes, the hair had an important relationship with the lifeblood of a warrior. "Unlike customs found in other areas in North America, there were none associated with the removal of any curse connected with the scalp on the Great Plains. The main emphasis was on a display of triumph" (Taylor 1975:71).

During the Postcontact period, the pattern of intertribal warfare changed. "In early days, the spirit of the widespread Scalp Raid prevailed but then as the horse increasingly dominated the culture, the Horse Raid became progressively popular and the desire to organize Scalp Raids decreased" (Taylor 1975:34).

The antiquity of scalping in the Central and Northern Plains is demonstrated by examples from prehistoric sites, including Blood Run (13LO2) (Schermer 1987) and Hanging Valley (13HR28) in western Iowa (Tiffany et al. 1988), the Sargent Ossuary (25CU28) and Wallace Mound (25SY67) in Nebraska (O'Shea and Bridges 1989; Snow 1942), the Fordville Mounds (32WA1) in North Dakota (Williams 1991), and Crow Creek (Willey 1982, 1990) and Fay Tolton in South Dakota. The Hanging Valley site dates to the Middle Woodland period, A.D. 200–700; Fordville Mounds represents a Late Woodland cemetery complex.

For a number of reasons, the incidence of scalping provides a conservative estimate of the frequency of warfare and violence along the Missouri Trench:

1. Casualties of warfare were not always scalped (Grinnell 1910:297).
2. Other forms of mutilation included decapitation and dismemberment of limbs, hands, and feet (Grinnell 1910). As determined from cuts on occipital bones and cervical vertebrae, one fourth of the people killed at Crow Creek were decapitated (Willey 1990). Similarly, the crania of several victims of the Larson massacre are unaccounted for (Owsley, Berryman, and Bass 1977). The study collections include decapitated individuals (not counted) whose heads were apparently taken as trophies (e.g. Feature 201, Burial 55G from Larson).
3. Scalps may have been taken without leaving cut marks. At Crow Creek, cuts caused by scalping were found in 95 percent of the frontal bones; however, only 38 percent were identified in the Postcontact Larson Village sample (Willey 1990). This difference in frequency may be due to the kinds of knives used at these sites. Experiments (Hamperl 1967) have shown that metal knives are less likely to produce cuts in the bone than blades made of stone.
4. Some childhood fatalities can be attributed to warfare at the massacre sites of Crow Creek, Fay Tolton, and Larson. The youngest person scalped in the Larson Village series was five years old (Owsley, Berryman, and Bass 1977). Scalped children are also present in cemetery samples (e.g., a scalped six-year-old from Mobridge, Burial 11521) but are not included in this study.
5. Some individuals were killed when hunting or raiding away from their villages, and their bodies were not recovered for burial. This possibility may be especially true for males, although the sex ratio for the total collection does not suggest underrepresenation.

Despite these limitations, a systematic survey of adult crania was undertaken to collect data on scalping that, together with data from other sources, would provide a fuller picture of Plains warfare.

Skeletal Samples

The analysis was based on the examination of 751 crania of individuals more than 10 years of age (i.e., second molars erupted). The sample represents 15 archaeological sites and includes 365 males, 357 females, and 29 individuals for whom sex could not be determined. The sites were located in two contiguous geographical regions of the Middle Missouri valley (Lehmer 1971). The Bad-Cheyenne region (N = 242) extends north from the mouth of Bad River near the center of South Dakota to the old Cheyenne Indian Agency. The Grand Moreau region (N = 509) continues upriver and terminates about 15 miles below the North Dakota–South Dakota border. These spatial divisions provide a basis for determining regional differences in the frequency of warfare.

Chronologically, the data represent late prehistoric, protohistoric, and early historic period Plains Village populations circa A.D. 1600 to 1832. Site samples were grouped according to archaeological variant as: Extended Coalescent (about 1550–1675), Mobridge (39WW1), Sully (39SL4), and Anton Rygh (39CA4); Postcontact Coalescent (about 1675–1780), Black Widow Ridge (39ST203), Cheyenne River (39ST1), Four Bear (39DW2), Larson (39WW2), Leavitt (39ST215), Mobridge, Oahe Village (39HU2), Second Hand (39PO207), Spiry-Eklo (39WW3), Stony Point Village (39ST235), Swan Creek (39WW7), Sully, and Walth Bay (39WW203); or Disorganized Coalescent (about 1800–1832), Leavenworth (39CO9). Mobridge and Sully include both Extended and Postcontact cemetery components, such that eight individuals could not be assigned to specific cultural categories. Victims of the Larson village massacre were excluded from this analysis.

This sample does not include crania with cuts caused by mortuary practices that involved defleshing of the body (e.g., Bass and Phenice 1975). Included, however, are three individuals displaying evidence of cranial infection subsequent to scalping (39WW2, F201 Burial 6B, 39CA4 "XX," and 39SL4 F16 5227 [381356]).

The risk of being scalped was about the same for both sexes. A total of 41 (5.5%) crania had cuts, 23 (6.7%) males and 18 (5.3%) females (fig. 1). Nearly all examples came from northern sites of the Grand-Moreau region (7.7%) in contrast to rare occurrences in the Bad-Cheyenne region (0.8%) (fig. 2). The difference is highly significant (chi-square = 14.8,

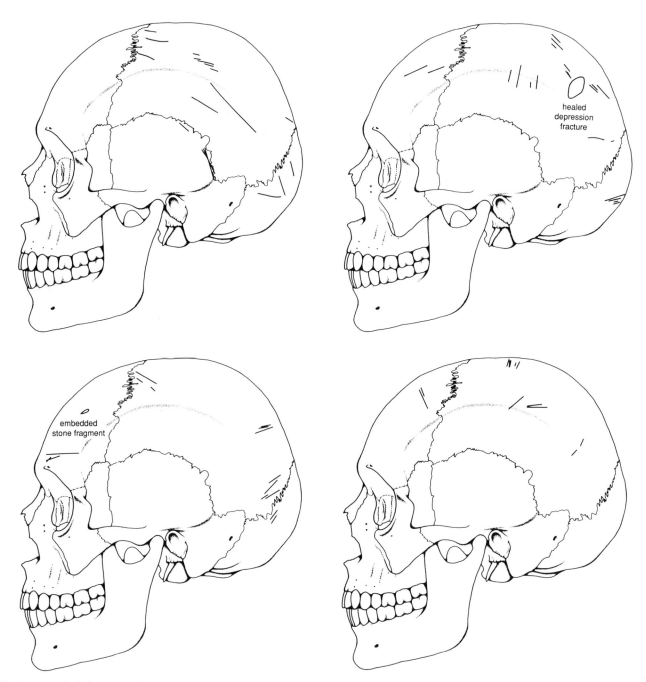

Fig. 1. Cuts on skulls from 4 sites. Top left, cuts on the right parietal, temporal and occipital of an adult male from the Leavenworth site (Feature 120, Burial 2A); 21 discrete cuts were identified. Top right, cuts on the frontal, left parietal, and occipital of a 14- to 17-year-old female from Anton Rygh (No. 670); the vault contains 36 cuts. Bottom left, cuts on the right side of the skull of a male aged 17 to 19 years from Larson (Feature 201, Burial 146B); 26 cuts are present. The tip of a stone projectile or knife is embedded in the right frontal. Bottom right, cuts on the frontal and left parietal of a young adult female from Mobridge (W.H. Over collection, No. 11425); 18 cuts are present on the frontal and left and right parietals. A blow to the back of the head produced a depressed, ovoid-shaped, perimortem skull fracture measuring 24.5 by 32 mm.

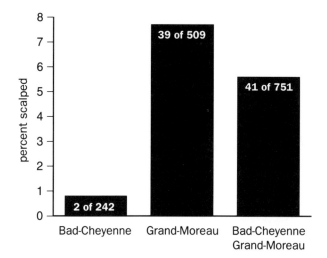

Fig. 2. Numbers of scalped skulls identified in two Middle Missouri regions.

DF = 1, P = .00). Figure 3 shows the occurrence of scalped skulls by archaeological variant. The overall trend (sexes combined) through time reflects a slight, but not significant, increase in the frequency of scalping during the early historic period (chi-square = 2.1, DF = 2, P = .35). However, this pattern results from a threefold increase for males, whereas the number of scalped females is reduced by half.

Table 1 shows the age distributions of the 23 scalped males and 18 females and the percentages in each age category who were scalped. Most (69.5%) of the males were aged 20 to 34 years, indicating the loss of young warriors killed during raids

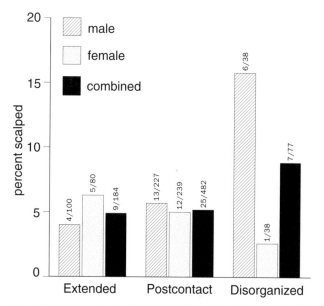

Fig. 3. Distribution of scalped skulls by Coalescent tradition variants and sex. The category "combined" includes crania with sex undetermined; a few individuals could not be assigned to a specific archaeological variant.

or in defense of the village. Given the small sample sizes, a sex-related difference in these mortality distributions cannot be clearly demonstrated. However, a slightly lower percentage (55.5%) of females was assigned to this age category. Women were likely to be attacked while gathering firewood or working in the fields, tasks in which all age groups participated and thus were equally at risk. The deaths of 24 percent of the males aged 20 to 24 years and 17.1 percent of those aged 25 to 29 years can be attributed to warfare. The percentage of violent deaths in each age interval for females was much lower and more evenly distributed across categories.

Equal numbers of male and female scalping victims were buried in cemeteries, reflecting conflict in close proximity to the villages, probably from intermittent raids. Some males were probably killed away from the villages, and their remains not recovered for burial in the cemetery, but deaths remote from the home village appear to have been infrequent. Continuing losses and lack of recovery would produce a disproportionate sex ratio, with fewer males than females, a pattern that was not observed. Both males and females were at risk of violent death and of being scalped. Sex-related vulnerability changed through time, increasing markedly for males while decreasing slightly for females. Differences among the female samples may simply reflect sampling variation.

Interpretation

The findings provide evidence that small-scale warfare was fairly common during all variants of the Coalescent tradition of the Northern Plains. On occasion, the level of warfare escalated and entire villages were destroyed and the inhabitants massacred (Crow Creek, Fay Tolton, Larson). This pattern was long-established and did not change dramatically during the early historic period. It can be traced to the earliest migrations of the ancestors of the Arikara up the Missouri River into territory occupied by Middle Missouri tradition peoples. As emphasized by Robarchek et al. (1991:14), the roots of Plains Indian warfare are deep in the prehistoric past: "warfare of the historic and protohistoric periods could not, contrary to Newcomb's (1950) argument, have its origins in European contact, in waves of migration generated by it, or in competition for horses. The warfare complex predates all of these."

The marked difference in the frequency of scalping between Grand-Moreau and Bad-Cheyenne sites indicates much greater safety for villagers located in the southern district. The Pax La Roche, as inferred by the lack of fortifications and a less structured settlement pattern, aptly applies to

Table 1. Ages of Scalped Individuals[a]

	Males			Females		
	Scalped	N	%	Scalped	N	%
10–14	1 (4.3%)	11	9.1	0	7	0.0
15–19	2 (8.7%)	25	8.0	4 (22.2%)	60	6.7
20–24	6 (26.1%)	25	24.0	4 (22.2%)	55	7.3
25–29	7 (30.4%)	41	17.1	2 (11.1%)	32	6.3
30–34	3 (13.0%)	59	5.1	4 (22.2%)	42	9.5
35–39	0	62	0.0	1 (5.6%)	53	1.9
40–49	3 (13.0%)	70	4.3	2 (11.1%)	45	4.4
50+	1 (4.3%)	31	3.2	1 (5.6%)	33	3.0
Total	23	324		18	327	

[a]Age assessments were not available for the total sample.

southern sites, which were generally not exposed to warfare. This distinct gradient, with few scalped individuals in the south, implies that most warfare was intertribal in nature, rather than intratribal. Grand-Moreau villages were located along the northern boundary of the Arikara. Northern sites were fortified because the risk of attack was much greater along this frontier zone, presumably initially from Middle Missouri tradition villages located to the north, and eventually from nomadic groups coming from the north and east. By the nineteenth century, nearly all horticultural villages along the Missouri River were fortified with wooden palisades (Ahler, Thiessen, and Trimble 1991). The western migration and increasing presence of adversarial Siouan groups posed a threat to the sedentary villagers. The arrival of the Sioux is indicated by the increased numbers of scalped males found in the Disorganized Coalescent sample.

Georgia Phillippi and Beth Bowman assisted with data collection and analysis. Age determinations for the Mobridge collection were provided by Ann Palkovich.

References Cited

Ahler, S.A., T.D. Thiessen, and M.K. Trimble
   1991 People of the Willows. Grand Forks, N.Dak.: University of North Dakota Press.
Allen, W.H., C.F. Merbs, and W.H. Birkby
   1985 Evidence for Prehistoric Scalping at Nuvakwewtaqa (Chavez Pass) and Grasshopper Ruin, Arizona. Pp. 23–42 in Health and Disease in the Prehistoric Southwest. C.F. Merbs and R.J. Miller, eds. *Arizona State University Anthropological Research Papers 34.*
Axtell, J., and W.C. Sturtevant
   1980 The Unkindest Cut, or Who Invented Scalping? *The William and Mary Quarterly* 37:451–472.

Bass, W.M., D.R. Evans, and R.L. Jantz
   1971 The Leavenworth Site Cemetery: Archaeology and Physical Anthropology. Appendix by D.H. Ubelaker. *University of Kansas Publications in Anthropology* 2.
——, and T.W. Phenice
   1975 Prehistoric Human Skeletal Material from Three Sites in North and South Dakota. Pp. 106–140 in The Sonota Complex and Associated Sites on the Northern Great Plains by R.W. Neuman. Lincoln: Nebraska State Historical Society.
Caldwell, W.W.
   1964 Fortified Villages in the Northern Plains. *Plains Anthropologist* 9:1–7.
Dorsey, G.A.
   1904 Traditions of the Arikara. Washington: Carnegie Institution.
France, D.L.
   1988 A Human Burial from Dolores County, Colorado. *Colorado Bureau of Land Management. Cultural Resource Series* 24.
Gilmore, M.R.
   1933 The Plight of Living Scalped Indians. *Papers of the Michigan Academy of Science, Arts, and Letters* 19:39–45.
Gregg, J.B., L.J. Zimmerman, J.P. Steele, H. Derwerda, and P.S. Gregg
   1981 Ante-mortem Osteopathology at Crow Creek. *Plains Anthropologist* 26–94:287–300.
Grinnell, G.B.
   1910 Coup and Scalp Among the Plains Indians. *American Anthropologist* 12:296–310.
Hamperl, H.
   1967 The Osteological Consequences of Scalping. Pp. 630–634 in Diseases in Antiquity. D. Brothwell and A.T. Sandison, eds. Springfield, Ill.: C.C. Thomas.
——, and W.S. Laughlin
   1959 Osteological Consequences of Scalping. *Human Biology* 31:80–89.

Hoyme, L.E., and W.E. Bass

1962 Human Skeletal Remains from the Tollifero (Ha6) and Clarksville (Mc14) Sites, John H. Kerr Reservoir Basin, Virginia. *Bureau of American Ethnology Bulletin* 182:329–400.

Key, P.J.

1983 Craniometric Relationships Among Plains Indians. *University of Tennessee, Department of Anthropology. Investigations Report* 34.

Lehmer, D.J.

1971 Introduction to Middle Missouri Archeology. Washington: U.S. Department of the Interior. National Park Service.

Lowie, R.H.

1920 *Primitive Society.* New York: Boni and Liveright.

Milner, G.R., E. Anderson, and V.G. Smith

1991 Warfare in the Late Prehistoric West Central Illinois. *American Antiquity* 56:581–603.

Murray, K.D.I.

1964 Who Started Scalping? *The West* 1:30–31, 54.

Nadeau, G.

1941 Indian Scalping. Technique in Different Tribes. *Bulletin of the History of Medicine* 10:178–194.

Neiburger, E.J.

1989 A Prehistoric Scalping: 600 A.D. *Central States Archaeological Journal* 36:204–208.

Neuman, G.K.

1940 Evidence for the Antiquity of Scalping from Central Illinois. *American Antiquity* 5:287–289.

Newcomb, W.W., Jr.

1950 A Re-examination of the Causes of Plains Warfare. *American Anthropologist* 52:317–330.

O'Shea, J.M., and P.S. Bridges

1989 The Sargent Site Ossuary (25CU28), Custer County, Nebraska. *Plains Anthropologist* 34:7–21.

Owsley, D.W., and H.E. Berryman

1975 Ethnographic and Archaeological Evidence of Scalping in the Southeastern United States. *Tennessee Archaeologist* 31:41–58.

——, H.E. Berryman, and W.M. Bass

1977 Demographic and Osteological Evidence for Warfare at the Larson Site, South Dakota. *Plains Anthropologist* 22(78):119–131.

Parks, D.R.

1982 An Historical Character Mythologized: The Scalped Man in Arikara and Pawnee Folklore. Pp. 47–58 in Plains Indian Studies: A Collection of Essays in Honor of John C. Ewers and Waldo R. Wedel. D.H. Ubelaker and H.J. Viola, eds. Washington: Smithsonian Institution Press.

Reese, H.H.

1940 The History of Scalping and Its Clinical Aspects. Pp. 3–16 in The 1940 Yearbook of Neurology, Psychiatry and Endocrinology. Chicago: The Year Book Publishers.

Robarchek, C.A., D.J. Blakeslee, A.H. Rohn, and P.H. Moore-Jansen

1991 A Bioarchaeological and Ethnohistorical Approach to the Comparative Study of Warfare. (Manuscript on file, Department of Anthropology, Wichita State University, Wichita, Kansas).

Schermer, S.J.

1987 Human Skeletal Remains from 13LO2, the Blood Run National Historic Landmark Site 1984–1986. *Research Papers. Miscellaneous Reports on Iowa Archaeology* 12:61–81.

Snow, C.E.

1941 Possible Evidence of Scalping at Moundville. Pp. 55–57 (Paper 15) in Anthropological Studies at Moundville, Part II. Mobile: Alabama Natural History Museum.

——

1942 Additional Evidence of Scalping. *American Antiquity* 7:398–400, 401.

Swanton, J.R.

1946 War. Pp. 686–701 in Indians of the Southwestern United States. *Bureau of American Ethnology Bulletin* 137:686–701.

Taylor, C.

1975 The Warriors of the Plains. London, New York, Sydney, and Toronto: Hamlyn Publishing Group.

Thwaites, R.G., ed.

1959 Original Journals of Lewis and Clark Expedition 1804–1806. Vols. 1, 5. New York: Antiquarian Press.

Tiffany, J.A., S.J. Schermer, J.L. Theler, D.W. Owsley, D.C. Anderson, E.A. Bettis, III, and D.M. Thompson

1988 The Hanging Valley Site (13HR28): A Stratified Woodland Burial Locale in Western Iowa. *Plains Anthropologist* 33(120):219–259.

Utley, R.M.

1988 Indian-United States Military Situation 1848–1891. Pp. 163–184 in Handbook of North American Indians, vol 4. W.E. Washburn, ed. Washington: Smithsonian Institution.

Willey, P.

1982 Osteology of the Crow Creek Massacre. (Unpublished Ph.D. Dissertation in Physical Anthropology, University of Tennessee, Knoxville.)

——

1990 Prehistoric Warfare on the Great Plains. New York: Garland.

——, and W.M. Bass

1978 A Scalped Skull from Pawnee County. *Kansas Anthropological Association Newsletter* 24:1978.

Williams, J.A.

1991 Evidence of Scalping from a Woodland Cemetery on the Northern Plains. *American Journal of Physical Anthropology* Supplement 12 (AJPA Annual Meeting Issue):184.

Wilson, G.L.

1924 The Horse and the Dog in Hidatsa Culture. In *Anthropological Papers of the American Museum of Natural History* 15. Pt. 2.

Zimmerman, L.J.

1985 Peoples of Prehistoric South Dakota. Lincoln: University of Nebraska Press.

○ ○ ○

CHAPTER 28

Osteology of the Fay Tolton Site: Implications for Warfare During the Initial Middle Missouri Variant

SANDRA E. HOLLIMON AND DOUGLAS W. OWSLEY

Archaeological research on prehistoric peoples in the Middle Missouri Valley of South Dakota suggests that warfare often resulted from population movement into and within this area. The prehistoric cultures of the Middle Missouri region have been divided into a number of taxonomic units. The first semisedentary village cultures in this area belong to the Plains Village pattern. Within this taxonomic unit, the Middle Missouri and Coalescent cultural traditions have been recognized and subdivided into variants (Lehmer 1971). The earliest variants are the Initial Middle Missouri, A.D. 900–1400; the Extended Middle Missouri, A.D. 1100–1550, and the Initial Coalescent, A.D. 1300–1550. Archaeological evidence indicates that Initial Middle Missouri groups were the first horticultural villagers in the Middle Missouri region (Wood 1976), who were subsequently displaced by Initial Coalescent people migrating into this area (Zimmerman 1985).

Evidence of Warfare

Lehmer (1971) suggests that people of the Initial and Extended Middle Missouri variants came into contact between A.D. 1100 and 1300 and, citing the number of fortified sites in the contact zone, that this interaction resulted in conflict. Extended variant villagers from North Dakota apparently followed the Missouri River southward into Initial Middle Missouri territory in South Dakota; the people of the Initial Coalescent moved northward from the central Plains. Archaeological evidence, such as extensive site fortifications, abandoned sites, and changing settlement distributions, in conjunction with osteological data on trauma and violent death, supports the claim that the interaction among the people of the three variants was characterized by instability and intergroup conflict (Zimmerman 1985).

Fortified villages in defensive positions occur in both the Initial Middle Missouri and Initial Coalescent variants (Ludwickson, Blakeslee and O'Shea 1987; Zimmerman 1985). That the southernmost Initial Middle Missouri and the northernmost Initial Coalescent villages were fortified suggests that conflict occurred along the contact zone between indigenous Initial Middle Missouri groups and intrusive Initial Coalescent populations. In addition, many Initial Middle Missouri villages were abandoned at the beginning of the Initial Coalescent variant, suggesting that Middle Missouri groups were forced out by the Initial Coalescent population movement (Johnson 1977; Lehmer 1971).

Another possibility is that conflict occurred between culturally or biologically related groups as a result of compression of territory and competition over scarce resources. According to Zimmerman (1985), changing climatic conditions may have limited essential resources available to the incoming populations, leading to intragroup warfare over scarce resources and arable land. However, evaluation of this climate model casts doubt on the validity of this assumption (Blakeslee 1990).

The Crow Creek site (39BF11) provides persuasive evidence of warfare at an Initial Coalescent site. This village was fortified and contained at least 50 lodges, many of which were burned (Kivett and Jensen 1976). The inhabitants were massacred in approximately A.D. 1325 (Willey 1982). The commingled skeletons of at least 486 people were buried in the fortification ditch, and many of these showed evidence of perimortem mutilation, such as scalping, dismemberment, and decapitation. The osteological data also suggest that the massacre was not an isolated incident of aggression, as some skeletons displayed bony remodeling, indicating healing of traumatic injuries received before the individuals were killed in the attack that destroyed the village. Two people had been scalped previously, and a third skull exhibited a healed fracture, probably the result of intergroup violence.

Olsen and Shipman ("Cutmarks and Perimortem Treatment of Skeletal Remains on the Northern Plains," table 1, this vol.) support the existence of intergroup violence based on their examination of skeletal samples from 12 sites. They record osteological indications of scalping, defleshing, disarticulation, and blows to the head; and they attribute the initial increase in violence in the Middle Missouri area to conflict between Initial Middle Missouri and Initial Coalescent groups.

Osteological evidence of warfare during the Initial Middle Missouri variant has not been systematically evaluated, as few skeletons are available for examination. Burial customs of the Middle Missouri tradition are not well known, although it has been suggested that these people practiced scaffold burial, defleshing, and other forms of secondary burial (Lehmer 1971; Ludwickson, Blakeslee and O'Shea 1987; Zimmerman 1985). Skeletal remains from the Fay Tolton village offer a unique opportunity to augment understanding of the incidence and nature of conflict during the Initial Middle Missouri variant.

The Fay Tolton Site

Fay Tolton (39ST11) is a fortified Plains Village site on the west bank of the Missouri River in central South Dakota (Lehmer 1971). It is the northernmost Initial Middle Missouri village (Wood 1976) and dates to the Anderson phase, A.D. 950 to 1250. Originally, it consisted of at least 33 houses, but much of the site was lost through slumping into the Missouri River. In 1957, two houses and part of the fortification ditch, which was eight feet wide and six feet deep, were excavated (Cottier and Cottier 1976). A test trench (5 by 50.8 feet) revealed no firm evidence of a palisade or stockade in the ditch. House 1, near the center of the village, and House 2, near the fortification ditch in the southern part of the site, had been burned, and both contained human skeletons.

Despite the size of the site, Fay Tolton appears to have been only briefly occupied. The amount of surface and house refuse and the general lack of artifacts (especially pottery) point to a brief occupation (Wood 1976).

The depositional context of the Fay Tolton skeletons suggests that these people were the victims of a raid (Butler 1976). The two adult males were awkwardly positioned in cache pits within the earthlodges (fig. 1). The two young females and the child were lying in a corner near the lodge entrance on a floor surrounded by debris that accumulated when the lodge burned (figs. 2–3). The presence of skeletons in the lodges and their positions are unusual. These individuals were not intentionally buried, but instead appear to have been killed in the houses, which were then burned.

PALEOPATHOLOGY AND PERIMORTEM MUTILATION

Bass and Berryman (1976) have provided preliminary descriptions of the human skeletal remains. Age and sex of the skeletons were determined by visual inspection, as follows:

House 1, Burial 1A, probable female, 14 to 16 years of age
House 1, Burial 1B, possibly female, 10 to 12 years of age
House 1, Burial 1C, sex unknown, 5 to 7 years of age
House 1, Burial 2, male, 25 to 29 years of age
House 2, Burial 3, male, 25 to 29 years of age

Of the five individuals excavated, two skeletons are partially burned (Burials 1B and 1C), two show indications of perimortem alteration (Burials 1C and 3), two display evidence of

Fig. 1. Skeletons deposited in cache pits, Fay Tolton site.

antemortem trauma (Burials 1C and 2), and one (Burial 1B) suffered a perimortem injury.

The color, distribution, and size of the charred areas on the skeletons indicate that the bodies had not decomposed prior to burning. Relatively little of either skeleton is burned, and the uneven pattern of color and exfoliation indicate that soft tissues were present and that the temperature of the fire was low, because of limited fuel or an oxygen-poor environment (Holck 1986).

The outer table of the left parietal of Burial 1B exhibits blackened, burned bone. As a result of burning, the outer table of the left parietal boss has exfoliated in a circular pattern, exposing the diploe. The left half of the frontal bone is missing. Skeleton 1B has the tip of a projectile point embedded in the anterior surface of the distal right tibia 1.8 centimeters above the joint surface. The point broke upon impact. This wound occurred at the time of death, as the bone shows no signs of remodeling or infection.

Burial 1C was located partially underneath Burial 1B (figs. 2–3) and exhibits similar burning on the cranium. The left half of the frontal is blackened, as are the broken distal ends of the

Fig. 2. Lodge floor with Burials 1A, 1B, and 1C and artifacts in situ, Fay Tolton site.

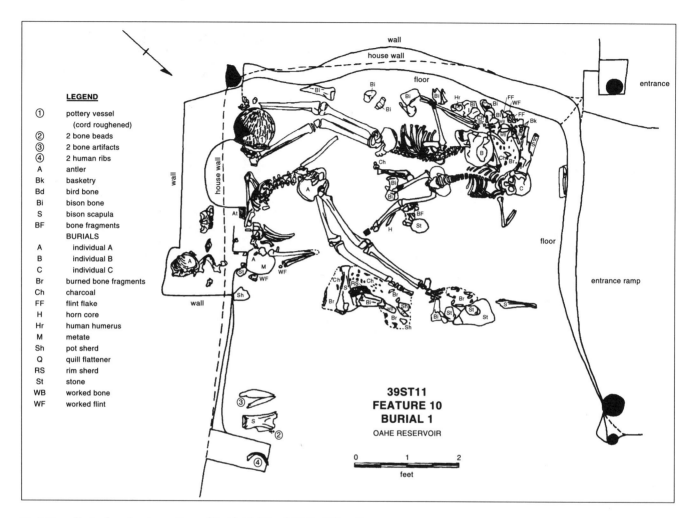

Fig. 3. Plan of lodge floor showing positions of Burials 1A, 1B, and 1C, Fay Tolton site.

right radial and ulnar shafts. The forearms were raised upward (in situ), placing them in proximity to the cranium and adjacent to an unidentified item that was burning. The discoloration extends into the inner cortices. The same pattern of burned exposed cortex is visible on the proximal left ulna. The distal left radius displays a small area of burning, but the burned area does not extend to the exposed inner cortex.

Both hands of Burial 1C are missing. The radii and ulnae were broken in the same place, such that the resulting fragments are of equal length. The color and jagged contour of the fractures indicate that they are not recent.

A number of explanations may be posited for this evidence. One possibility is that some postdepositional occurrence removed the forearms and hands prior to archaeological excavation. The fact that no material from this portion of the lodge floor was recovered archaeologically supports this explanation (see fig. 3).

Another possibility is that the wrists and hands were consumed in the fire, and that the resulting fragments of highly calcined bone were not recovered. This explanation is not consistent with the pattern of material distributed on the lodge floor.

A third and more likely interpretation is that the forearms were intentionally broken in order to remove the hands. However, the lack of cuts on the forearms of Burial 1C argues against this explanation. A case of hand dismemberment was found at the Postcontact Coalescent Larson site (39WW2) (Owsley, Berryman, and Bass 1977). This example exhibited cuts on the forearms, in contrast to Burial 1C.

Burial 3 appears to have been decapitated prior to being placed in a cache pit (Butler 1976). The cranium, mandible, and several cervical vertebrae are missing. (That these elements were present but not excavated is unlikely, as the recovery of small and fragmentary bones from the lodge, as well as available photographs, indicate complete excavation.) The most superior cervical vertebra (C3) displays no cuts.

Antemortem evidence suggesting interpersonal violence includes a pair of healed depressed fractures on the cranium of an adult male, and areas of cranial necrosis from scalping in the child. The cranium of Burial 2 (male, aged 25 to 29 years) displays a healed depressed fracture (14 by 14 mm) on the left parietal immediately adjacent to the sagittal suture and 18 millimeters above the lambda. The depth of the fracture is 1.5 millimeters. The fracture and the surrounding area of disorganized bone are roughly circular in shape. A second fracture lies on the right parietal between the sagittal suture and the parietal boss. This circular depression fracture measures 3.7 by 2.4 millimeters and is less than 1 millimeter deep.

The cranium of a 5- to 7-year-old child (Burial 1C) exhibits cuts and lesions caused by scalping. The degree of bone necrosis and reaction indicates that the child survived for at least two weeks after the incident (Lent Johnson, personal communication 1991). Large areas of necrotic bone are located on the left parietal and left portion of the occipital (fig. 4). The area of necrosis on the occipital bone, below the lambdoidal suture, has a well-defined sharp border, but on the superior portion of the left parietal and adjacent to the sagittal suture, its margins are sloping and ill-defined. The bone is porous and irregular, and the resorptive lesions have affected both the inner and outer tables in several areas. Most of the outer table has exfoliated but the majority of the inner table is intact. Only a few areas of the endocranium are perforated.

Three islands of normal cortical bone, exhibiting 20 cuts, lie within the area of necrosis (fig. 4). The margins of these islands are well-defined and irregular in contour. The largest island is located on the occipital, between the lambda and the external occipital protuberance. The outer surface of this bone has three cuts, ranging in length from 7.4 to 16.9 millimeters. The other two islands are located on the left parietal; one lies on the parietal eminence, and the other is located immediately superior to the lambdoidal suture. These two areas exhibit a total of 17 cuts, ranging in length from 3.0 to 17.5 millimeters. The parietal island adjacent to the lambdoidal suture has a round resorptive lesion on its superior border. This lesion has perforated the inner and outer tables. The outer table surrounding the three islands has been lost due to osteoclastic activity resulting in an irregular and pitted diploe.

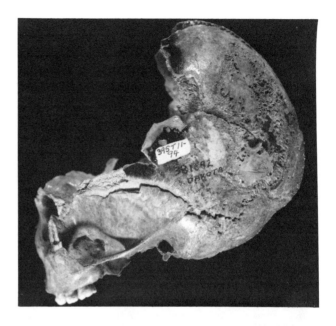

Fig. 4. Burial 1C showing necrotic areas on left parietal and occipital. Closeup of left parietal (bottom) shows cuts and necrosis. Fay Tolton site.

Other Partially Healed Scalpings

Scalping involves the forcible removal of all or part of the soft tissue (hair, scalp, and periosteum) on the cranial vault (Hamperl 1967; Nadeau 1941). If death does not result from associated injuries or infection, and cranial bleeding is not excessive, an individual can survive, and healing can occur. Complications from scalp avulsion include bleeding, infection (often causing meningitis), and sloughing of exposed bone (McGrath 1983:679).

After trauma to the scalp's blood supply, the reactive process begins with increased vascularization to the traumatized area. The accelerated blood flow stimulates osteoclastic activity causing bone resorption along the periphery of the injury. As the response proceeds, there is exfoliation of necrotic bone, eventually progressing to the development of new granulation tissue (spongy bone), and finally the regeneration of epidermis closing the wound (Hamperl and Laughlin 1959).

Well-healed scalping wounds have been noted in several Northern Plains sites, including Crow Creek (Willey 1982), Spiry-Eklo (39WW3) (Hamperl and Laughlin 1959), Mobridge (39WW1), and Anton Rygh (39CA4). Two individuals with partially healed scalped crania from other Plains sites provide a basis for comparison with the Fay Tolton child. These examples display similar features, including areas of necrosis and outer table erosion, in addition to the formation of granular, disorganized bone. Cuts are present on both crania. A young female (age 15 to 17 years) from the Sully site

(39SL4) in South Dakota, which dates to the Postcontact Coalescent variant, A.D. 1650–1725) (Owsley and Jantz 1978), has a narrow groove encircling the cranial vault. This groove is an osteoclastic response initiated by trauma to the scalp's blood supply, and it ranges in width from 1.9 to 8.8 millimeters. The ring lies immediately superior to the external occipital protuberance, follows the right and left temporal lines, and crosses the right and left frontal bosses (fig. 5). Within it are several islands of necrotic bone, the largest of which is located at the lambda. The largest necrotic area displays sharp borders, and at its center is an area of porous, spongy bone. This area measures 48 by 38 millimeters, and it is 5.5 millimeters deep.

Lying along the sagittal suture is a small island of necrotic bone, with dimensions of 15 by 25 and a depth of 5.2 millimeters. It has sharp, irregular borders, extending to the inner table, which is intact. A third island of necrosis is located on the frontal, immediately anterior to the coronal suture, left of the bregma. This area is shallow (less than 1 millimeter deep), has well-defined margins, and measures 22 by 29 millimeters. Porous bone is evident within this area.

Numerous cuts are present on the outer table within the osteoclastic ring. Several small cuts (less than 2 millimeters in length) can be seen on the left portion of the occipital, immediately below the lambdoidal suture. Numerous longer cuts (4 to 14 millimeters) on the right parietal boss run parallel to the coronal suture. Other cuts on the right parietal are immediately adjacent and parallel to the sagittal suture. These cuts are approximately 11 millimeters in length. Cuts on the frontal bone are located on both bosses, along the

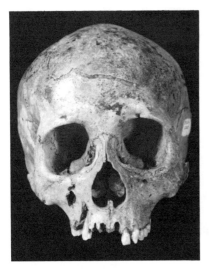  

Fig. 5. Sully site female displaying osteoclastic ring on the frontal. Necrotic areas and possible infection are seen on sagittal and lambdoidal sutures (center). Closeup shows osteoclastic ring and cuts on frontal (right).

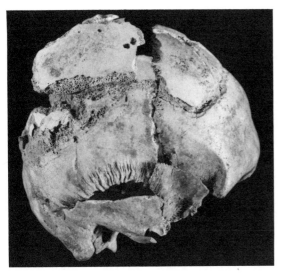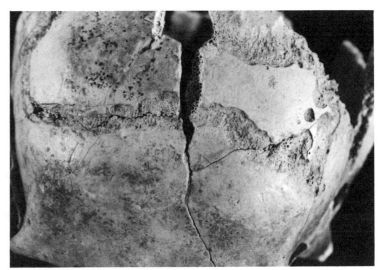

Fig. 6. Female displaying osteoclastic areas on right parietal and frontal. Closeup (right) shows osteoclastic ring on frontal, Wallace Mound site.

midsagittal plane (anterior to an island of necrotic bone at the bregma), and above the right temporal line (fig. 5).

A second example of partially healed scalping comes from the Wallace Mound (25SY67) in Sarpy County, eastern Nebraska. The cultural affiliation of this site is the Nebraska phase of the Central Plains tradition, A.D. 1050–1400). This female was aged between 16 and 18 years using dental development standards (Moorrees, Fanning, and Hunt 1963). The cranium is in poor condition and is missing large portions of the left and right parietals. Despite the postdepositional breakage and erosion, evidence of bony reaction can be seen. A ring of osteoclastic resorption encircles the vault, and this pattern of response resembles the Sully cranium (fig. 6). This ring has sharp borders and runs superior to the right temporal line. On the left parietal, the ring lies on the temporal line. On the frontal, it lies superior to the frontal bosses. The margins of the lytic area are poorly defined on the occipital due to extensive osteoclastic action superior to the external occipital protuberance.

There are several areas of necrosis within the resorptive groove, but the generally poor condition of the bone makes identification of these areas difficult. Within the borders of the necrotic ring, it appears that the outer table has exfoliated on the frontal, along the coronal suture, and on the right parietal and occipital. In these regions, diploe has been exposed. There is also exposed diploe on the left temporal, but most of this bone is missing, making it difficult to assess the extent of response. Four small areas of outer table have sloughed off, leaving round pits less than two millimeters in diameter on the frontal and right parietal.

Six cuts are visible on the remaining areas of outer table on the frontal bone. These cuts lie within the osteoclastic ring and range in size from 1.7 to 16.5 millimeters.

This cranium exhibits greater osteoclastic reaction than that observed in the Sully example. This individual may have lived longer after injury than the Sully female, allowing greater opportunity for the reactive process to progress. Large amounts of cranial bone have been lost in the Wallace Mound female, suggesting that posttraumatic infection may have accelerated the process. Similarly, the Fay Tolton child shows extensive bone loss indicating secondary infection. In contrast, the more limited circumferential depression surrounding the avulsed area on the Sully cranium can be attributed primarily to osteoclastic resorption associated with hyperemia at the periphery of the injury (Lent Johnson, personal communication 1991).

Scalping Practices in the Northern Plains

Scalping was a prehistoric practice having great antiquity in the Northern Plains. Two cases of scalping in North Dakota from the Archaic (6000 B.C.–A.D. 500) Bahm site (32MO97) and one from the Woodland (A.D. 1–900) site of Blasky Mound in the Fordville Mounds (32WA1) are described in this volume ("Disease Profiles of Archaic and Woodland Populations in the Northern Plains"). Another Woodland example was found at the Hanging Valley site (13HR28) in Iowa, dated from A.D. 190 to 310 (Tiffany et al. 1988).

Scalping figures prominently in the ethnohistoric literature of the Pawnee and Arikara (Parks 1982). The "scalped man" became a character in Arikara and Pawnee folklore, assuming various guises, including a bogeyman, a historical or comic figure, and a bestower of supernatural power (Parks 1982). The legendary figure was regarded with an ambivalent combination of fear and admiration, because he was endowed with miraculous powers (Dorsey 1906; Parks 1982). Parks (1982) suggests that the mythical figure of the scalped man had its basis in reality. The Arikara word for scalping literally means to ruin. Those who survived were considered no longer human (Gilmore 1933; Parks 1982). They were relegated to a distinct class and were forced to live solitary lives on the margins of society. They could not return to society because their disfigurement would be ridiculed, and they were active only at night when they could not be seen (Parks 1982).

The identification of individuals with completely or partially healed scalping wounds within a village or cemetery context (Crow Creek, Sully, Anton Rygh, and Spiry-Eklo) seems inconsistent with the historic folklore. Perhaps the practice of banishment was more typical of the early historic period or an age or gender association is indicated (that is, scalped women were not exiled). An evaluation of other known cases of this type is needed in order to discern possible patterns with regard to variables such as geographical region, population, time period, age, and sex.

Assessments of Plains Warfare

Examples of osteological studies include the analysis of skeletal remains from the Larson (Owsley, Berryman, and Bass 1977), Heerwald ("Evidence of Warfare at the Heerwald Site," this vol.), and other Northern Plains sites ("Cutmarks and Perimortem Treatment of Skeletal Remains on the Northern Plains," this vol.). Such analyses indicate that intergroup conflict on the Northern Plains extends from prehistoric times to the nineteenth century. Evidence of warfare has been described at the Bahm site, at the Initial Coalescent Crow Creek site (Willey 1982), and at the Wright site (25NC3) (Lower Loup phase of the Coalescent tradition, about 1750) (Grange 1968:30).

At Fay Tolton, two skeletons show evidence of antemortem trauma and two display evidence of perimortem alteration. Furthermore, Skeleton 1B has a projectile point embedded in a lower leg bone. This injury, although by itself not fatal, provides evidence that the Fay Tolton village was attacked. This female may have taken refuge in the lodge after being wounded. Specific causes of death could not be discerned, as other cuts, unhealed fractures, or fatal projectile point injuries were not apparent on any of the remains. The villagers could have been trapped as earthlodges burned and the roofs collapsed, or they might have died as a result of other trauma not reflected in their bones. The absence of certain bones and the archaeological context suggest that some of the bodies were mutilated. These osteological data are consistent with previous analyses in indicating that warfare was a feature of prehistoric Plains society during this period.

References Cited

Bass, W.M., and H.E. Berryman
    1976 Physical Analysis. Pp. 29–31 in Fay Tolton and the Middle Missouri Variant. W.R. Wood, ed. *Missouri Archaeological Society Research Series* 13.

Blakeslee, D.J.
    1990 Modeling the Abandonment of the Central Plains: Radiocarbon Dates and the Origin of the Initial Coalescent. (Manuscript in possession of the author.)

Butler, W.B.
    1976 Human Skeletal Remains. Pp. 27–29 in Fay Tolton and the Middle Missouri Variant. W.R. Wood, ed. *Missouri Archaeological Society Research Series* 13.

Cottier, J.W., and R.L. Cottier
    1976 Site Description. Pp. 2–8 in Fay Tolton and the Middle Missouri Variant. W.R. Wood, ed. *Missouri Archaeological Society Research Series* 13.

Dorsey, G.A.
    1906 The Pawnee: Mythology (Part I). Washington: Carnegie Institution of Washington.

Gilmore, M.R.
    1933 The Plight of Living Scalped Indians. *Papers of the Michigan Academy of Science, Art and Letters* 19:39–45.

Grange, R.T., Jr.
    1968 Pawnee and Lower Loup Pottery. *Nebraska State Historical Society Publications in Anthropology* 3.

Hamperl, H.
    1967 The Osteological Consequences of Scalping. Pp. 630–634 in Diseases in Antiquity. D. Brothwell and A.T. Sandison, eds. Springfield, Ill.: Charles C. Thomas.

——, and W.S. Laughlin
    1959 Osteological Consequences of Scalping. *Human Biology* 31: 80–89.

Holck, P.
    1986 Cremated Bones: A Medical-Anthropological Study of an Archaeological Material on Cremation Burials. (*Antropologiske Skrifter* 1.) Oslo: University of Oslo, Anatomisk Institutt.

Johnson, A.M.

1977 Testing the Modified Initial Middle Missouri Variant. *Plains Anthropologist* 22(78):14–20.

Kivett, M.F., and R.E. Jensen

1976 Archaeological Investigations at the Crow Creek Site (39BF11). *Nebraska State Historical Society Publications in Anthropology* 7.

Lehmer, D.J.

1971 Middle Missouri Archeology. *National Park Service Anthropological Papers* 1.

Ludwickson, J., D. Blakeslee, and J. O'Shea

1987 Missouri National Recreational River: Native American Cultural Resources. *Wichita State University Publications in Anthropology* 3.

McGrath, M.H.

1983 Scalping: The Savage and the Surgeon. *Clinics in Plastic Surgery* 10(4):679–688.

Moorrees, C.A., E.A. Fanning, and E.E. Hunt, Jr.

1963 Age Variation of Formation Stages for Ten Permanent Teeth. *Journal of Dental Research* 42(6):1490–1502.

Nadeau, G.

1941 Indian Scalping: Technique in Different Tribes. *Bulletin of the History of Medicine* 10:178.

Owsley, D.W., H.E. Berryman, and W.M. Bass

1977 Demographic and Osteological Evidence for Warfare at the Larson Site, South Dakota. *Plains Anthropologist Memoir* 13:119–131.

———, and R.L. Jantz

1978 Intracemetery Morphological Variation in Arikara Crania from the Sully Site (39SL4), Sully County, South Dakota. *Plains Anthropologist* 23(80):139–147.

Parks, D.A.

1982 An Historical Character Mythologized: The Scalped Man in Arikara and Pawnee Folklore. Pp. 47–58 in Plains Indian Studies: A Collection of Essays in Honor of John C. Ewers and Waldo R. Wedel. D.H. Ubelaker and H.J. Viola, eds. Washington: Smithsonian Institution Press.

Tiffany, J.A., S.J. Schermer, J.L. Theler,

D.W. Owsley, D.C. Anderson, E.A. Bettis, III, and

D.M. Thompson

1988 The Hanging Valley Site (13HR28): A Stratified Woodland Burial Locale in Western Iowa. *Plains Anthropologist* 33(120):219–259.

Willey, P.

1982 Osteology of the Crow Creek Massacre. (Unpublished Ph.D. Dissertation in Anthropology, University of Tennessee, Knoxville.)

Wood, W.R., ed.

1976 Fay Tolton and the Middle Missouri Variant. *Missouri Archaeological Society Research Series* 13.

Zimmerman, L.J.

1985 Peoples of Prehistoric South Dakota. Lincoln: University of Nebraska Press.

CHAPTER 29

○○○

Evidence of Warfare at the Heerwald Site

DANA L. BOVEE AND DOUGLAS W. OWSLEY

Warfare as practiced in the Great Plains has been documented archaeologically and osteologically at a number of Northern and Central Plains sites (Owsley, Berryman, and Bass 1977; Rose et al. 1984; Willey 1982; Zimmerman et al. 1981). The results of the reexamination of previously described skeletal remains from a terminal Late Prehistoric Southern Plains burial are presented here. There is evidence in the Heerwald burial of small-scale warfare.

The Heerwald site (34CU27) is located in Custer County, west-central Oklahoma, on the south side of Turkey Creek, a tributary of the Washita River (Brighton 1951; Drass, Baugh, and Flynn 1987; Shaeffer 1965). Testing conducted in the northern portion of the site in 1983 yielded corrected radiocarbon dates of A.D. 1377 ± 52, 1380 ± 50, and 1535 ± 115 reported for samples derived from two features (Drass, Baugh, and Flynn 1987). The 1535 ± 115 and the 1380 ± 50 dates are derived from sampling the same feature. Elimination of charred corn from a second sample submitted for analysis yielded the date of 1380 ± 50. The northern and southern portions of the site were shown to be contiguous spatially and temporally on the basis of assemblage characteristics. Artifact and feature comparisons with contemporaneous Plains Village sites showed that Heerwald represents a subvariant of the Washita River phase (Drass, Baugh, and Flynn 1987).

Archaeology of the Burial

The Heerwald burial was excavated in 1957. The partial, well-preserved skeletons of a near-term fetus, a young adult female, and a child of unknown sex, incorrectly identified as an adolescent by Shaeffer (1965), were recovered from a single circular burial pit. The archaeological context is reported in Shaeffer (1965), and a brief description of each skeleton is presented in an appendix (Brues 1965a). The uncalibrated radiocarbon date for the burial is A.D. 1300 ± 80 (Beta-57894), as adjusted for the C^{13}/C^{14} ratio.

The burial pit (Shaeffer 1965:110) was circular, approximately three feet in diameter, with straight sides and a level floor:

The close-flexed position of the [adult female] skeleton was additionally contorted by the neck being turned so that the face was down while the hips were twisted in the opposite direction and faced up. Across the back and side of the woman was the extended skeleton of an adolescent child with its head resting on the open right hand of the adult so that the two heads were side by side. Underneath the adult pelvis, but not in the prenatal position, were found the well-preserved bones of the fetus (Shaeffer 1965:113).

A large well-made Harrell-type projectile point was recovered from between the ribs of the adult opposite the first lumbar vertebra. A smaller Harrell point was deeply embedded in the first lumbar (Shaeffer 1965:116). Shaeffer, noting that Harrell points were common at Heerwald, stated that it was impossible to determine whether intra- or intervillage violence was responsible for the woman's death. At the time of Shaeffer's investigation, the prevailing view was that burials within villages were rare in central and western Oklahoma. When present, as at Heerwald and Hubbard (34BK4), they involved subadults or adults in unusual burial positions. Shaeffer (1965, 1966) conjectured that these individuals were buried under crisis-related circumstances, as rapidly as possible, and with little ceremony. Limited comparative data were available in the Southern Plains.

Skeletal Inventory

Brues (1965a) described the fetal skeleton as nearly complete. However, little of this skeleton could be located for reanalysis (Julie Droke, personal communication 1988). A left scapula and a right mandible fragment lacking tooth buds were found in a bag labeled "unidentified fragments from Burial 1." The mandible fragment represents approximately half of the right corpus. From its overall size, fetal age is estimated to be eight uterine months (Fazekas and Kósa 1978). This corresponds to the age assessment of the complete skeleton (Brues 1965a).

The child is represented by the cranial vault missing the face and mandible, the left scapula and clavicle, the partial right scapula, a fragment of the left humerus, most of the vertebrae and ribs, partial innominates, the complete sacrum, and hand and foot bones. Dental remains include a maxillary left central incisor, a maxillary right deciduous second molar, a maxillary right permanent first molar, unerupted maxillary left canine, first premolar and second molar, a mandibular right canine, and a mandibular left deciduous first molar. The age of this individual was 5.5–6.5 years, as determined from dental calcification standards (Moorrees, Fanning, and Hunt 1963). There are no carious lesions on the teeth, although there are moderate calculus deposits.

The adult is represented by the frontal, the temporals, the parietals, and other fragmentary portions of the cranium. The maxilla is missing the right canine, the right first and second premolars, the left central incisor, and the left canine. The mandible shows postmortem loss of the left canine, left first and second premolar, the left second molar, the right canine, and right first premolar.

Postcranial remains include the left humerus, radius, ulna, clavicle, scapula, and femoral head; left and right innominate; sacrum, sternum; complete vertebrae and ribs; and hand

bones. Sex of the adult was determined to be female on the basis of pelvic morphology and cranial and postcranial robusticity (Acsádi and Nemeskéri 1970; Bass 1987; Krogman 1962; Phenice 1969; Ubelaker 1978). The assessment of degenerative changes in the pubic symphysis and the auricular surface of the ilium, dental attrition, and epiphyseal and cranial suture closure suggest an age of 18–22 years (Bass 1987; Brooks 1955; Brothwell 1981; Gilbert and McKern 1973; Krogman 1962; Lovejoy et al. 1985; Meindl et al. 1985; Smith 1984). Ectocranial porosis of the frontal, parietal, and occipital bones is evident, and the parietals show slight hyperostotic thickening.

There is a large crown-destroying carious lesion on the maxillary right first molar. Moderate calculus deposits were observed on most teeth. The alveolar bone of the maxillary right second premolar is perforated from a periapical abcess. Dental attrition is moderate to heavy. The teeth are worn flat with dentine exposure on all teeth. There is slightly heavier attrition on the left side, probably reflecting a response to the pain engendered by the maxillary right molar carie and right maxillary alveolar abscess. Dental hypoplasia in the mandibular central and lateral incisors indicate that childhood stress occurred at the ages of 1.5–2.0 years, 2.0–2.5 years, 2.5–3.0 years, and 3.0–3.5 years (Murray 1988).

Several skeletal elements, particularly the long bones, are missing. It is impossible to determine whether the disarticulation occurred prior to burial or reflects postburial events.

Evidence of Violence

The adult female skeleton has numerous signs of violent death. The Harrell point in the first lumbar vertebra is embedded in the anterior centrum at the superior margin of the body (fig. 1). The position and orientation of the arrowpoint indicate abdominal entry a few inches above and to the left of the navel, with penetration of the stomach, possibly the pancreas, and certainly the aorta. The recovery of the other Harrell point in the lower thoracic region implies that it was lodged in soft tissue. In addition, there is a deep, triangularly incised cutmark on the inferior margin of the left second rib at a distance of eight centimeters from the head of the rib (fig. 2). The cut is steep-sided on the ventral side, growing increasingly broad and splintered from the ventral to the dorsal rib surfaces, extending up approximately one-quarter the width of the rib. On the dorsal rib surface, there is a circular spalling of the bone with a slight perimortem fracture extending medially from the cut approximately 1.75 centimeters.

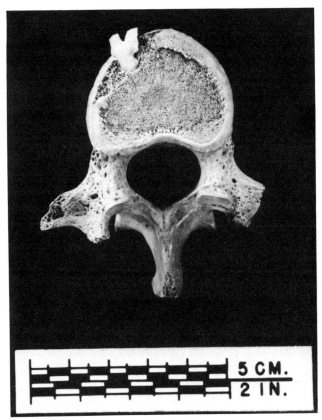

Fig. 1. First lumbar vertebra of the adult female from the Heerwald site showing the embedded Harrell point.

The left scapula is damaged, with a large triangular section missing between the spine inferiorly and the vertebral border laterally. Perimortem fractures radiate from the damaged area of the scapular body. The pattern of fracturing suggests that force was exerted on the ventral surface of the body (fig. 3). From the configuration and depth of the cutmark on the rib and the scapular fractures, a third projectile point apparently penetrated the left shoulder below the clavicle, knicking the inferior margin of the rib and piercing the lung before exiting the back.

Cutmarks on the preserved cranial portions indicate that this woman was scalped. Thirty cutmarks cross the squamous part of the frontal bone in a horizontal band paralleling the

Fig. 2. Cutmark on the left second rib of the adult female.

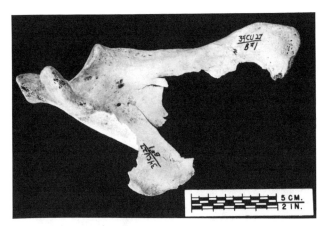

Fig. 3. Fractured left scapula of the adult female.

supraorbital margin (fig. 4). Continuing in roughly the same orientation, there are five cuts on the right parietal below and parallel to the superior temporal line, four short cuts on the right temporal near the squamous suture, 10 on the occipital fragment, and 11 on the left parietal fragment. The cutmarks are relatively short, ranging in length from 0.13 to 2.32 centimeters. The consistent horizontal orientation of the cutmarks on this cranium describes a rough circle.

Shaeffer (1965) cites the unusual position of the individuals within the pit as evidence that interment was carried out hastily, without the normal rituals. The near-term fetus was located beneath the adult female, and the child's body was sprawled across the adult. The degree of flexure necessary to accommodate the three bodies within the pit is reflected in the extreme contortion of the adult body. Indeed, there is evidence that force was applied to hyperabduct and twist the spine to the right side. The superior portion of the right transverse process of the twelfth thoracic vertebra was crushed by the right inferior facet of the eleventh thoracic vertebra. Perimortem damage to these vertebrae occurred as the trunk was rotated, leaving the pelvis face-up while the upper torso was twisted into the face-down position (fig. 5).

There is no osteological evidence of violence in the juvenile skeleton. The absence of many elements, particularly the long bones, is enigmatic given the presence of most of the bones of the axial skeleton, the cranium, and hand and foot bones.

The coburial of several individuals suggests that all died during the same episode of violence. It is possible, even probable, that the woman was in her third trimester of pregnancy. However, the relationship of the adult and the fetus cannot be demonstrated on the basis of the existing evidence. There are other examples in the Washita River phase of the

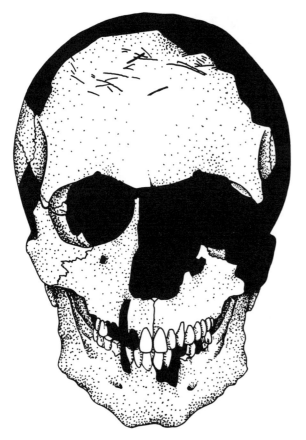

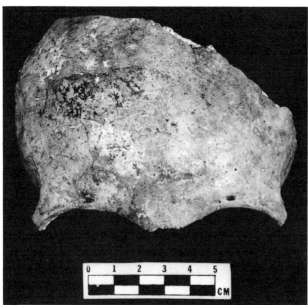

Fig. 4. Cutmarks on the frontal bone of the adult female. Drawing by Mary Lee Eggert.

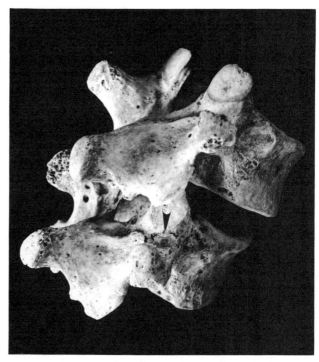

Fig. 5. Perimortem damage to the eleventh and twelfth thoracic vertebrae of the adult female.

co-burial of young adult females and infants (Brues 1962; Pillaert 1963), but none of these burials includes a third individual or evidence of violent death.

Violence at Other Southern Plains Sites

Burials with indicators of violence possibly associated with death have been reported at a small number of Late Prehistoric/Early Protohistoric period Southern Plains sites (table 1). The table lists individuals, their reported ages and sexes, and the specific observations that have been interpreted as evidence for violence. Detailed documentation is not available for many of these burials.

The cemetery at the McLemore site (34WA5) provides the largest comparative sample for the Washita River phase. The radiocarbon dates for McLemore indicate that its occupation was roughly contemporaneous with that at Heerwald (Drass, Baugh, and Flynn 1987; Pillaert 1963). Three individuals in the cemetery were reported to have osteological signs of violent death (Brues 1962; Pillaert 1963). Two of them, burials #23 and #34, had perimortem cranial fractures, and a third, #13, identified as a young male, had a Washita point embedded in a thoracic vertebra (Brues 1962). Reexamination of these skeletons indicates that the cranial fractures observed in

Table 1. Late Prehistoric Southern Plains Sites with Reported Violence-Related Trauma

Site	Burial Number	Sex/Age	Nature of Trauma	References
McLemore (34WA5)	13	Male/20	Arrowpoint in vertebra	Pillaert 1963; Brues 1962
	23	Female/26	Perimortem cranial fracture	
	34	Male/35–50	Perimortem cranial fracture	
Heerwald (34CU27)	1	Female/22–25	Arrowpoint in vertebra, scalping	Shaeffer 1965; Brues 1965a
Hedding (34WD2)	4	Unknown/adult	Charred bone	Shaeffer 1965; Brues 1965b
	5	Female/30–40	Charred bone	
Wickham #3 (34RM29)	1	Male/adult	Arrowpoint in sternum	Wallis 1984
	2	Male/adult	Scalping	
Canadian (34CN7)	1	Unknown/adult	Disarticulation	Anonymous 1957
Edwards I (34BK2)	1	Female/adult	Defleshed cranium	"Culturally Modified Human Bones from the Edwards I Site," this vol.
Nagle (34OK4)	10	Male/30	Five arrowpoints in burial, scalping	Shaeffer 1957; Brues 1957
Shackleford (41SF00)	1	Unknown/child	Mandible only	Forrester 1951
	1	Male/20	Disarticulation; cutmarks on bone	
	1	Male/18	Arrowpoint in bone	
Footprint (41PT25), Structure 1	1	MNI[a] = 7	Disarticulation, charred bone	Green 1967; Lintz 1986; Patterson 1974
	2	MNI[a] = 7	Disarticulation, charred bone	
	3	MNI[a] = 7	Disarticulation, charred bone	
	4	10 adults	Disarticulation, crania only	
Big Blue Cemetery (A678)	?	?/?	Arrowpoints in burial	Lintz 1986
Tarbox (41HC2)	?	?/adult	Isolated cranium	Holden 1929; Lintz 1986
Handley Ruins (410C1)	?	?/adult	Arrowpoint in bone	Eyerly 1912; Lintz 1986
Harrell (41YN1)	1	Female/adult Female?/adult Unknown/adult	Arrowpoints in mass burial	Hughes 1942
	2	Female/adult Female/adult Female?/adult Unknown/adult Unknown/infant	Arrowpoints in mass burial	
Red Ochre (41PR12)	2	Female/adult	Arrowpoints in burial	Everett 1989

[a]MNI = minimum number of individuals.

#23 and #34 represent postmortem breakage rather than perimortem fractures (Owsley and Jantz 1989). As for #13, on the basis of pelvic morphology, cranial characteristics, and general skeletal robusticity, this individual is a young adult female. The projectile point, embedded in an upper thoracic vertebra, is the only osteological evidence of violence present in this skeleton. Individual #13 was buried facedown (Pillaert 1963). This observation seemingly supports Shaeffer's suggestion that unusual burial positions and violence may be associated. However, the excavation record and field map indicate that the excavator was not certain of the burial position and

that the burial was disturbed (Bell 1960). Only one other burial, #20, was recovered in the facedown position. In contrast to #13, this young adult female was flexed and provided no bioarchaeological evidence of violence. Thus, there seems to be little consistency in the relationship between unusual burial position and violent death at McLemore.

Five adult crania from the Nagle site (34OK4) were examined for cutmarks. One of the three males, Burial #10, has cuts indicative of scalping. This individual was buried in a flexed position, like the other intact burials at Nagle. Four Harrell points were retrieved from within the thoracic cavity and one against the lower left leg. Correlation of assemblage features seems to place Nagle in the late thirteenth to early fourteenth century, with close ties to the Caddoan cultures to the southeast (Shaeffer 1957).

Salvage excavation at the Wickham #3 site (34RM29) uncovered the cremated remains of two individuals with osteological evidence of violence. The adult male in Burial #1 has a Washita-type point penetrating the sternum from the dorsal side. Other evidence of violence includes two Washita-type point fragments recovered from within the chest cavity and an old arrowpoint wound on the right proximal humerus with a fragment of the point visible in the healed bone (Wallis 1984). Burial #2 was more extensively damaged by looters, but portions of the skeleton including part of the skull were recovered. Examination indicates that the remains are those of a young adult male who was scalped. Archaeological evidence and differences in burial practice indicate that the Wickham #3 people are of the Zimms complex, a cultural group occupying a restricted area northwest of the Washita River groups ("Southern Plains Cultural Complexes," this vol.).

Burials were reported as having projectile points embedded in bone or in direct association with the skeletons at three Antelope Creek phase sites—Big Blue Cemetery (SARE-242), Handley Ruins (410C1), and Footprint (41PT25) (Lintz 1986; Patterson 1974). Lintz (1976) has addressed the issue of warfare and has presented evidence of increasing population stress from diminishing resources caused by deteriorating climatic conditions. At the Footprint site, the scattered and partially articulated remains of at least 32 individuals were recovered from three subfloor pits and the fill within a burned structure; a fourth pit in the structure contained 10 crania, thought to represent trophy skulls (Green 1967; Lintz 1986; Patterson 1974).

Conclusions

Among Washita River phase burials, the Heerwald burial is unique in its association of violent death, co-burial of several individuals, and unusual burial position. Cutmarks indicative of scalping have not been reported for skeletal samples of any other culturally affiliated Washita River phase groups.

At Heerwald, there is no good contextual or osteological evidence of large scale warfare. On the other hand, the level of violence and the patterned nature of the scalping indicate that this is something more than the result of a domestic brawl. The best interpretation is that this situation provides good evidence of small-scale, intergroup conflict. This conflict may have taken the form of a raid, with a small, organized band

intent on inflicting damage on the Heerwald group, or it may simply represent the result of an opportunistic encounter between hostile groups. That only typical Washita River phase projectile points were recovered from the burial suggests that the conflict may have arisen between culturally allied groups.

In the regions peripheral to this area, there is evidence of conflict with the Washita River people. On the basis of osteological evidence provided by Brues and point-type identification, Shaeffer (1957:99) suggested that the culturally Southeast-affiliated Nagle site people were in conflict with a Washita River focus group to the west. The occurrence of Washita River point types and the scalping at the Wickham #3 site support the hypothesis that the conflict occurred at the peripheries of the Washita River focus. Further analysis of the Nagle skeletal series may elucidate the morphological relationships among these Plains Village groups and thereby clarify the movement of groups. Lintz (1986) interprets the burned structure at the Footprint site as evidence of a raid. The 10 crania found concentrated in a single pit, which is distinct from the other burial pits in the burned structure, may represent trophy skulls collected in retaliation. He supports his contention that the skulls are derived from an outside group by citing the results of population divergence studies. The crania from the burned structure are unlike other Antelope Creek crania and, in fact, exhibit closest affinity to Washita River skulls, specifically those of the McLemore cemetery (Lintz 1986; McWilliams and Johnson 1979). However, given the small samples available for comparison, it is unclear to what extent Antelope Creek and Washita River crania can be distinguished statistically.

Northern Plains populations provide an interesting contrast with the Southern Plains. At the roughly contemporaneous Crow Creek site (39BF11), 90 percent of the minimum of 486 individuals were scalped (Willey 1982). A similar pattern is reflected at the Larson site (39WW2), a village that dates to the protohistoric period (Owsley, Berryman, and Bass 1978). These skeletal samples indicate warfare on a grand scale. Such dramatic examples are not evident on the Southern Plains.

The opportunity to reexamine previously described samples has provided new evidence regarding the incidence and practice of warfare in the terminal Late Prehistoric period in the Southern Plains. Researchers must be alert to possible signs of violence when dealing with both newly excavated and long-curated skeletal materials.

The authors thank the Oklahoma Museum of Natural History and Julie Droke, Collections Manager, for loan of the Heerwald skeletons. Robert Brooks and Timothy Baugh provided archaeological and environmental data that enhanced the interpretation of the osteological data. Christopher Lintz offered additional data and insight on Southern Plains warfare. James Everett provided the data for 41PR12.

References Cited

Acsádi, G., and J. Nemeskéri
  1970 History of Human Life Span and Mortality. Budapest: Academiai Kiado.
Anonymous
  1957 34CN7 Unpublished Burial Data. (Form on file at Oklahoma Archaeological Survey, Norman, Okla.)
Bass, W.M.
  1987 Human Osteology. 3rd ed. Columbia: Missouri Archaeological Society.
Bell, V.
  1960 34WA5 Unpublished Burial Data. (Form on file at Oklahoma Archaeological Survey, Norman, Okla.)
Brighton, H.D.
  1951 Archaeological Sites in Custer County, Oklahoma. *Texas Archeological and Paleontological Society Bulletin* 22:164–187.
Brooks, S.T.
  1955 Skeletal Age at Death: The Reliability of Cranial and Pubic Age Indicators. *American Journal of Physical Anthropology* 13(4):567–597.
Brothwell, D.R.
  1981 Digging Up Bones: The Excavation, Treatment, and Study of Human Skeletal Remains. Ithaca, N.Y.: Cornell University Press.
Brues, A.M.
  1957 Skeletal Material from the Nagle Site. *Bulletin of the Oklahoma Anthropological Society* 5:101–108.

  1962 Skeletal Material from the McLemore Site. *Bulletin of the Oklahoma Anthropological Society* 10:69–78.

  1965a Skeletal Material from Site CU-27. *Bulletin of the Oklahoma Anthropological Society* 13:127–128.

  1965b Skeletal Material from Site WD-2. *Bulletin of the Oklahoma Anthropological Society* 13:145.
Drass, R., T.G. Baugh, and P. Flynn
  1987 The Heerwald Site and Early Plains Village Adaptations in the Southern Plains. *North American Archaeologist* 8(2):151–190.
Everett, J.
  1989 Two Red Ochre Burials from 41PR12, Parker County, Texas. (Unpublished manuscript on file, Smithsonian Institution, Washington.)

Eyerly, T.L.
  1912 The Buried City of the Panhandle. *The Archaeological Bulletin* 3(1):1–5.
Fazekas, I.G., and F. Kósa
  1978 Forensic Fetal Osteology. Budapest: Académiai Kiadó.
Forrester, R.E., Jr.
  1951 A Series of Eighteen Indian Skeletons Excavated in Shackelford County, Texas. *Bulletin of the Texas Archeological and Paleontological Society* 22:132–143.
Gilbert, B.M., and T.W. McKern
  1973 A Method for Aging the Female Os Pubis. *American Journal of Physical Anthropology* 38(1):31–38.
Green, F.E.
  1967 Archeological Salvage in the Sanford Reservoir Area. *National Park Service Report* #14-10-0333-1126. Washington.
Holden, W.C.
  1929 Some Explorations and Excavations in Northwest Texas. *Bulletin of the Texas Archeological and Paleontological Society* 1:23–35.
Hughes, J.T.
  1942 An Archaeological Report on the Harrell Site of North-Central Texas. (Unpublished Masters Thesis in Anthropology, University of Texas, Austin.)
Krogman, W.M.
  1962 The Human Skeleton in Forensic Medicine. Springfield, Ill.: Charles C. Thomas.
Lintz, C.R.
  1986 Architecture and Community Variability Within the Antelope Creek Phase of the Texas Panhandle. *Oklahoma Archaeological Survey, Studies in Oklahoma's Past* 14.
Lovejoy, C.O., R.S. Meindl, R.R. Pryzbeck, and R.P. Mensforth
  1985 Chronological Metamorphosis of the Auricular Surface of the Ilium. *American Journal of Physical Anthropology* 68(1):15–28.
McWilliams, K.R., and J.L. Johnson
  1979 Physical Evidence on the Origins and Fate of the Panhandle Aspect People. *Plains Anthropologist* 24(85):249–253.
Meindl, R.S., C.O. Lovejoy, R.P. Mensforth, and R.A. Walker
  1985 A Revised Method of Age Determination Using the *Os pubis* with a Review and Tests of Accuracy of Other Current Methods of Pubic Symphyseal Aging. *American Journal of Physical Anthropology* 68(1):29–45.
Moorrees, C.F.A., E.A. Fanning, and E.I. Hunt
  1963 Age Variation of Formation Changes of Ten Permanent Teeth. *Journal of Dental Research* 42:1490–1502.
Murray, S.
  1988 Hypoplasia Age Correlation. (Unpublished document on file, Smithsonian Institution, Washington.)
Owsley, D.W., H.E. Berryman, and W.M. Bass
  1977 Demographic and Osteological Evidence for Warfare at the Larson Site, South Dakota. *Plains Anthropologist Memoir* 13:119–131.

——, and R.L. Jantz

1989 A Systematic Approach to the Skeletal Biology of the Southern Plains. Pp. 137–156 in From Clovis to Comanchero: Archeological Overview of the Southern Great Plains. J.L. Hofman, R.L. Brooks, and D.W. Owsley, eds. *Arkansas Archeological Survey. Research Survey Series* 35.

Patterson, D.

1974 An Analysis of the Human Skeletal Material from the Antelope Creek Focus of Northern Texas. (Unpublished Master's Thesis in Anthropology, Eastern New Mexico University, Portales.)

Phenice, T.W.

1969 An Analysis of the Human Skeletal Material from the Burial Mounds in North Central Kansas. *University of Kansas Publications in Anthropology* 1.

Pillaert, E.E.

1963 The McLemore Site of the Washita River Focus. *Bulletin of the Oklahoma Anthropological Society* 11:1–114.

Rose, J.C., M.K. Marks, M. Kay, and

E.B. Riddick, Jr.

1984 Analysis of Human Osteological Remains from Multi-county Areas, South Dakota. (Final Report, Contract DACW45-83-M-2506.) Omaha, Nebr.: U.S. Army Corps of Engineers, Omaha District.

Shaeffer, J.B.

1957 The Nagle Site, Ok-4. *Bulletin of the Oklahoma Anthropological Society* 5:93–99.

——

1965 Salvage Archaeology in Oklahoma, vol. I. Papers of the Oklahoma Archaeological Salvage Project, 8–15. Reprinted in the *Bulletin of the Oklahoma Anthropological Society* 13:77–151.

——

1966 Salvage Archaeology in Oklahoma, vol. II. Papers of the Oklahoma Archaeological Salvage Project, 18–21. Reprinted in the *Bulletin of the Oklahoma Anthropological Society* 14:1–86.

Smith, B.H.

1984 Patterns of Molar Wear in Hunter-Gatherers and Agriculturalists. *American Journal of Physical Anthropology* 63(1):39–56.

Ubelaker, D.H.

1978 Human Skeletal Remains. Washington, D.C.: Taraxacum.

Wallis, C.S., Jr.

1984 Summary of Notes and Earlier Analysis of the Wickham #3 Site, 34Rm-29, Roger Mills County, Oklahoma. *Bulletin of the Oklahoma Anthropological Society* 33:1–29.

Willey, P.

1982 Osteology of the Crow Creek Massacre. (Unpublished Ph.D. Dissertation in Anthropology, University of Tennessee, Knoxville.)

Zimmerman, L.J., T. Emerson, P. Willey, M. Swegle, J.B. Gregg, P. Gregg, E. White, C. Smith, T. Haberman, and M.P. Bumsted

1981 The Crow Creek Site (39BF11) Massacre: A Preliminary Report, Contract DACW45-78-C-0018. Omaha, Nebr.: U.S. Army Corps of Engineers, Omaha District.

ooo

Culturally Modified Human Bones from the Edwards I Site

DOUGLAS W. OWSLEY, ROBERT W. MANN, AND
TIMOTHY G. BAUGH

The Edwards I site (34BK2), located on the North Fork of the Red River in southwest Oklahoma, was a fortified village. Although occupied during the Washita River phase (A.D. 1250–1450), the principal occupation of this site occurred during the protohistoric Wheeler phase (A.D. 1450–1750). When the artifact assemblage from Edwards I was described, it was initially assigned to the Edwards complex (Baugh 1982). The protohistoric period has been divided into the Edwards complex and the Wheeler complex (Hofman 1984). Reexamination has resulted in the combination of these two complexes into the Wheeler phase (Baugh 1986). However, this taxonomic reassignment has not been universally accepted, and the site is still identified by some investigators as one of the type sites of the Edwards complex (Hofman 1989). Distinctive lithic implements include unnotched (Fresno), side-notched (Washita), basally notched (Garza), and both side-notched and basally notched (Harrell) triangular projectile points. Other bone tools include flake-based drills, ensiform pipe drills, diamond-beveled Harahay knives, small end scrapers, and side scrapers. The ceramics are predominantly plain wares (such as Edwards Plain and Little Deer Plains types). Bone implements include bison metatarsal fleshers, bison scapula hoes, and, more rarely, bison tibia digging stick tips.

Like the people of the earlier Washita River phase, whose economy was based mainly on horticulture and hunting (Drass and Moore 1987; Drass and Swenson 1986; Drass, Baugh, and Flynn 1987), the Wheeler phase occupants also farmed, but they placed greater emphasis on hunting bison and on trade with the Pueblos. Polychrome glaze ceramics, obsidian, and turquoise provide evidence of trade (Baugh 1982; Baugh and Nelson 1987). Despite this shift in the economy, the Wheeler phase adaptation reflects cultural continuity with the preceding Plains Caddoan Washita River phase, as shown by, for example, ceramic typology and technology and house styles.

Distinctive features from two of the Wheeler phase sites are the large circles characterized by surface remains of bison bone and large concentrations of artifacts. Because of the large quantities of bone, the circles can be readily identified by aerial photography. Archaeological testing of these features revealed that they are circular trenches, two meters across at the top and tapering to about one meter at their lower levels, which are about one meter below the ground surface (Baugh 1986). Measurements made from aerial photography and actual field mapping showed the diameter of these circular trenches to be about 50 meters. An intensive magnetic survey indicated that the original backdirt from the trench was thrown to the inside of the circle, creating a low embankment or parapet into which posts could have been placed to form a protective stockade and redoubt (Baugh 1986; Weymouth 1981); however, there is no evidence that any structures or other major features existed within these circles. Baugh (1986) interprets these circular trenches with parapets as fortifications.

There is a striking similarity between these protohistoric, circular features and those described in the eighteenth century by Spaniards at the Taovaya Wichita village on the north bank of the Red River. The earliest mention of this village is an account of an attack on the Wichita, who were hosting a contingent of Comanche allies in 1759, by Diego Ortiz Parrilla:

It was noticed by all, that the huts which formed the village occupied a large area and that there was a great number of them. They were situated at the edge of the river and the populated land ran from east to west. And one could see that one part of this village was the part which was fortified and that the other part was uninhabited; all the inhabitants having run to the site of the fort. One could clearly see the enemy's remuda which was protected by some corrals of palisade . . . (Newcomb and Field 1967:261–262).

Antonio Trevino, who was captured by the Wichita a few years after the Spanish attack on the Taovaya village, provides a more detailed description:

In the middle of (this settlement) is the fortress they built to resist Colonel Don Diego Ortiz Parrilla's campaign. It is made of split logs, which the Indians have placed separate one from the other in order to make use of muskets, the weapons they use, through them. . . . Said fortress is completely surrounded on the outside by an earthen rampart, close to more than a vara and a third in height [a little less than four feet], which serves them as an entrenchment, and, about four paces to the east and west, a very deep trench made so that one can come close to (the fortress) on horseback. Inside there are four subterranean apartments occupying all of its circumference, into which all of the people who cannot help with the defense of the said settlement retreat in time of invasion (Newcomb and Field 1967:323–324).

This description, except for the four subterranean compartments, appears to match the protohistoric structures revealed by the archaeological investigations of the Edwards I and Duncan (34WA2) sites in western Oklahoma (Baugh 1986).

Four human bones (one frontal, one ulna, and two femora) were recovered from the fill of the fortification trench, which also contained items such as bison bone, lithic artifacts, and pottery sherds that can be correlated with the Wheeler phase occupation of the site. The location for each of these bones (based on 6-inch arbitrary levels) was as follows: frontal, S11-L13, level 8; ulna, S27-R5, level 7; femur rasp, N1-L8, level 5; and femur section, N1-L8, level 7. These isolated elements, from separate levels between 30 and 48 inches below ground surface and located in three different squares, were the only human remains found at Edwards I.

The fragmentary bones represent more than one adult and exhibit cuts ranging from slight scratches to deep grooves. The number, location, and depth of the cuts on the ulna and frontal bones indicate that they were defleshed, but the pattern of cuts on the femora suggest modifications that have functional significance.

Four Modified Human Bones

FRONTAL BONE

The incomplete but well-preserved frontal bone includes portions of the right eye orbit, sinus, and coronal suture (fig. 1). The sharp upper margin of the orbit, small frontal sinuses, flat browridges, slight degree of frontal curvature, and small size suggest that this bone belonged to a female (Bass 1987; Stewart 1979). The lack of Pacchionian pits, an open coronal suture, and thick diploe place its age in the young adult range (Stewart 1979; Krogman and Iscan 1986). The outer surface of the bone is marked with more than 70 short, shallow scratches and cuts. There are a few clusters of parallel cuts, mostly in the central portion of the bone, but the major cuts on the frontal do not appear to be patterned. The close proximity of the cuts along the coronal suture indicates that many of the cuts crossed the suture onto both parietals.

The appearance of these cuts at the microscopic level is shown in figure 1 using scanning electron microscopy. The photograph shows parallel striations within the groove typical of known cutmarks (Olsen and Shipman 1988). Apart from obvious cuts, extremely fine striae are also present on the frontal, and these are consistent with marks produced by sedimentary abrasion.

RIGHT ULNA

The right ulna lacks both the proximal and distal ends, with 16.6 centimeters of the shaft remaining intact. Although

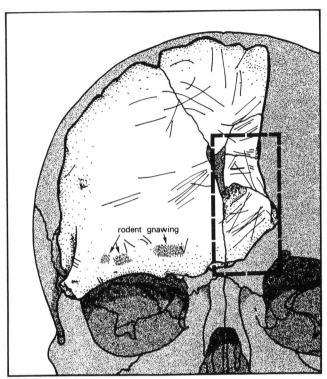

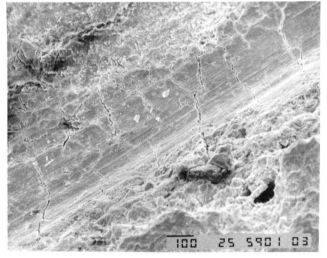

Fig. 1. Frontal bone with approximately 70 shallow cuts over much of its outer surface. Above, photograph. Top right, drawing depicting the cuts. Bottom right, area examined using scanning electron microscopy. Fine parallel striations are evident within a cut in the frontal bone; the scale is 100 microns. (Oklahoma Museum of Natural History, Norman: Specimen No. 246. Drawing by Mary Lee Eggert.)

incomplete, the general size and slight muscle attachment sites suggest that this bone is from an adult female (Krogman and Iscan 1986; Stewart 1979). The bone appears healthy and shows no sign of disease or trauma. The well-preserved cortex exhibits two types of cuts on all surfaces of the shaft: small cuts (slices might be a more descriptive term), and long parallel cuts or striations (resembling scratches more than cuts). There are 15 short cuts clustered in two areas—

10 on the posterior surface at the level of, but not on, the supinator crest, and five along the posteromedial surface approximately one third of the distance from the proximal end. Three of the cuts are perpendicular to the long axis of the shaft, two are parallel, and 10 are oblique. In contrast, the striations appear as superficial scratches running parallel to the long axis of the shaft. Most traverse the length of the shaft as either continuous or interrupted lines.

RIGHT FEMUR

This partial right femur, which includes most of the diaphysis, was recovered from about 42 inches below the surface. Both ends of the shaft show postmortem breakage and loss, with the proximal end missing from below the lesser trochanter and the distal end from the metaphysis downward. Comparison of size, cortical thickness, and general robusticity of this bone with other Native American femora from the Plains suggests that it probably was that of a young to middle-aged adult female. The bone appears healthy, with no apparent disease, trauma, or deformity. The cortex is weathered from prolonged exposure and damaged by root invasion.

The linea aspera, a muscle attachment ridge running along the posterior surface of the shaft, exhibits 31 deep cuts from 5 to 13 millimeters in length and approximately one millimeter in width and depth (fig. 2). Nine of the 31 cuts are concentrated within a 2.5 centimeter area of the midshaft, with the remainder irregularly spaced along both ends of the diaphysis. All the cuts originate on the linea aspera and extend medially along the convex medial surface. (The cuts cross perpendicular to the long axis of the diaphysis and are irregularly spaced.) There is one other shallow cut on the anterior surface of the shaft near the proximal end.

RIGHT FEMUR

This bone, in a fair to good state of preservation, consists of 15.2 centimeters of the shaft. There are a number of postmortem weathering cracks extending along the length and depth of the shaft. The proximal and distal ends are missing due to postmortem breakage. The overall shape, robusticity, and cortical thickness suggest an adult female.

Approximately one-half of the circumference of the diaphysis displays seven parallel grooves in its anterior surface. The grooves are uniform (1.6 mm) in width, V-shaped in cross-section, and vary in length from three to four centi-

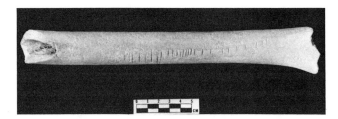

Fig. 2. Right human femur with irregularly spaced cuts along its posterior surface. (Oklahoma Museum of Natural History, Norman: Specimen No. 181.)

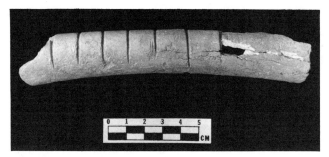

Fig. 3. Right human femur showing the widely spaced, deep grooves along the anterior surface (musical rasp?). (Oklahoma Museum of Natural History, Norman: Specimen No. 300.)

meters (fig. 3). The distance between the grooves ranges between 13 and 18 millimeters with an average of 14.7. Each groove was produced by multiple cuts. The uniform surface of the deepest portion of each groove suggests finishing with an abrasive device of narrow diameter. The surface bone in the grooves is darker in color than that of the surrounding cortex, possibly reflecting compaction that occurred as the grooves were abraded. In a few instances, there are shallow cuts adjacent to the deep grooves. The proximal diaphysis is missing, and it is possible that there were additional grooves at this end. The distal end is more nearly complete, with the grooves terminating approximately 4.7 centimeters from the end.

This bone is highly polished along the surface that contains the incised grooves, and the central portion of the groove walls shows differences in wear. Striations paralleling the long axis of the bone indicate the direction of abrasion. In contrast, the cortex on either side of the grooves is dull, weathered, and cracked.

Modified Human Bone and Scored Bone Artifacts

NORTH AMERICA AND MESO-AMERICA

The archaeological and ethnographic records for Central and North America provide many examples of objects made from human bone at widely dispersed sites. Excavations at seven sites in British Columbia, dating from 1000 B.C. to A.D. 500, revealed 12 worked pieces of human skulls, four altered long bones, and nine complete or partial skeletons with modified skulls or long bones. Three of the long bones were modified for use as tools, while the other items seem to have had no utilitarian function and were presumably associated with rituals (Cybulski 1978). Human bone artifacts were reported at the Saint Lawrence Iroquoian Roebuck site in Ontario (Jamieson 1983). These included: skull gorgets, awls made from ulnae, beads from fibulae, and several long bones with their ends removed by cutting. The gorgets had smooth rounded edges, and one was decorated with five straight parallel lines on the convex surface. Perforations on the edges would have permitted attachment to hides or other clothing, or the attachment of one disk to another to form a rattle. Several ulnae were ground to a point and polished; they could have been used to punch holes in birchbark or as daggers. A bead was manufactured by cutting off the ends of a fibula and hollowing the medullary cavity.

Some of the most diverse examples come from the Hopewell Mounds in Ohio. Baby (1961), when excavating prehistoric Indian burials under part of the Bourneville mound, found a bone whistle fashioned from the right radius of a 40- to 50-year-old female. This bone whistle was found in association with copper artifacts, beads, and grizzly bear teeth. A portion of the distal radius had been removed to form this whistle, and copper bands were placed near the end of the polished bone, into which a triangular opening and elliptical perforations had also been made. A geometric design covered the entire posterior surface—a mixture of cross-hatched lobes, tear-shaped forms, and circles, which were common in Hopewell designs. Baby (1956) also described an unusual artifact from Burial 13 of the Mound City Group—a mask and headdress fashioned from parts of a human skull (including a large portion of the frontal, the right and left maxillae, the zygomatic arches, as well as parts of the temporals and parietals). All had been ground, scraped, and polished, with drilled perforations at the edges to permit attachment of a hood that covered the head.

Other excavations of the Hopewell mounds reported incised human maxillary bones and perforated cranial bones that had been placed in burials, as well as bone awls and shuttles, and a tool made from a fragment of a human ulna to one end of which a piece of meteoritic iron had been attached (Moorehead 1922). Most decorated bone artifacts found in Ohio Hopewell sites were made from human bone (Willoughby and Hooton 1922).

Data and artifacts from six Hopewell sites were reexamined in an effort to determine the origin of the polished, drilled, and decorated human skulls. Because the modified skulls were predominantly those of young adults, rather than individuals of advanced age, Seeman (1988) concluded that these were trophy heads taken in battle, rather than revered ancestors. Seeman (1988) also concluded that these were tangible signs to potential allies of success in battle and served as a means of promoting intergroup peace. The pattern of embellishment of human bones and their use in the production of rattles, flutes,

gorgets, and tubes was in some way related to a changing pattern of subsistence from migratory hunting and gathering to settlement in one location. With the establishment of a fixed community came increasing emphasis on ceremony and ritual, involving the use of such special objects.

Daggers made from a human femur and two fibulae were found at Key Marco, Florida (Gilliland 1975). Numerous specialized human bone artifacts have been found in cemetery sites in Kleberg County along the south Texas coast, with occasional examples known from other areas in south Texas and coastal Tamaulipas, Mexico (Hester 1969a, 1969b). These objects include tubular beads made from long bones, mouthpieces made from ulnae to be used on stone pipes (one was found in place, with unattached "spares" nearby), and a bone tube made from a humerus shaft and decorated with zigzag lines, reddish pigment, and 33 shallow notches. This tube may have been a rasplike instrument.

The Clarksville and Tollifero sites in Virginia (Hoyme and Bass 1962) have yielded long bones, a cranium, and an innominate decorated with incised markings; metatarsals, a metacarpal and navicular, and a left pubis with holes cut in them; a notched clavicle; and a spine from which the dorsal surfaces and lateral processes of all vertebrae were removed.

In studying a Hopi site in Arizona, Turner and Morris (1970) found not only decapitated, dismembered, and mutilated human bones but also bones that had been carefully reamed and fashioned into scoops.

Meso-America has produced a number of unusual human bone artifacts. Two exquisitely decorated human femora adorned with intricate designs were discovered at the site of Chiapa de Corzo, Chiapas, Mexico (Dixon 1959; Agrinier 1960). On each is a pair of human figures, one below and upside down in relation to the other, the space around and between them being filled with scroll and disk ornamentation. One figure on each bone wears an elaborate beaded mask; below and inverted to this design on one bone is a serpent-headed figure, and on the other, a profile of a human face. These carved bones date from the early Proto-Classic period, A.D. 1–100, and were probably made for ritual use. Other human bone artifacts from Chiapas include human femora fashioned into tubes with a spout at one end. As the Maya are said to have used water held in bones for a kind of "baptismal" ritual, Agrinier (1960) suggests the possibility of a similar use. He experimented with trying to reproduce the low relief designs with which two of the "tubes" were decorated using tools available to Proto-Classic artisans (flint, obsidian, and chalcedony) and concluded that fresh bone must have been employed. Rasp or grating instruments made from human long bone shafts and flutes made from humeri were described by Marti (1955).

The skull seems to have been a prized part of the human skeleton, with the maxilla and mandible being only somewhat less so. In regard to the mandible, one of the most unusual examples is from the undisturbed fill below a rooffall at the Quandahl Rockshelter (13WH35) in northeastern Iowa (Mallam 1979). The mandible of a human male had been separated into two sections at the symphyseal line. Each ramus was removed by cutting the bone below the condylar and coronoid processes. The edges were then ground and smoothed, and four perforations were made, two with a tapered drill and two by enlarging the mental foramen by chipping. A cord passed through these holes would link the two sections, which could be worn as a pendant. A similar mandible pendant had been reported from the Sister Creeks Mounds in Illinois (Cole and Deuel 1937).

Another unusual ornament made from a human mandible was collected in Arizona. The jaw is covered with beaded and painted buckskin and suspended from a cord on which alternating beads and human teeth are strung. It may have been made from the lower jaw and teeth of an enemy slain in battle (National Museum of Natural History specimen 248935).

So-called trophy skulls and skulls modified for display are often reported. For example, Powell (1977) describes a "Plaza of Skulls" from the Crenshaw (3MK16) site (A.D. 900–1400) in southwest Arkansas. Powell examined eight of these skulls, two of which were female; no defleshing or scraping marks were noted on the skulls. Apparently, these crania were buried with the flesh still covering the bone and the mandible in normal articulation. Such practices were noted for the historic Hasinai by Spanish priests who described the ceremonies accompanying the burial of heads taken in raids during the seventeenth century.

A modified cranium was found in eastern Iowa in a Hopewell(?) mound overlooking the Mississippi River at the Lowry Farm site (13MC4) (Hodges 1989; Pratt 1876; Schermer and Owsley 1989–1990). Left and right parietals, and the frontal, minus the supraorbital ridge were present. Seven semicircular holes were drilled around the margin of the bones, possibly for the removal of disks. These roundels ranged in diameter from approximately 18 to 36 millimeters. Although the removed sections were not recovered, disks, which perhaps were similar in function and origin, were found in 1935 in Mound 8 of the Deppe Group (13JK11) in east Iowa (Schermer and Owsley 1989–1990). Two roughly circular disks, made from a parietal (likely) or frontal bone measuring 4.7 by 4.0 centimeters and 2.8 by 2.2 centimeters, were found

along with solitary bones and several bundle burials. These pieces have sharp, uneven edges without polish, suggesting discard without further modification after removal from the vault. Field notes also mention a partial humerus with two notches cut into it (Schermer and Owsley 1989–1990; letter from Ellison Orr to Charles R. Keyes, May 5, 1935—in the office of the State Archaeologist of Iowa, Iowa City).

Feagins (1989) described cuts on a fragment of a human skull found on the surface of a large habitation site in northwest Missouri (23PL44), at which there were several prehistoric occupations—Middle and Late Archaic, Early and Middle Woodland, and Mississippian. This fragment was from the central part of the frontal, and on it were more than 70 fine cuts typical of marks produced by chert tools. Also from Missouri, a partially burned incomplete skull bowl with a polished edge on the occipital was recovered at the Utz site (23SA2) (Wedel 1986). Utz is identified as an Oneota period site dating between A.D. 1400–1750.

Two prehistoric (Woodland or Mississippian period) skull artifacts, oval disks cut from a right parietal bone and a frontal, were reported (Williams 1975) at a site (40KN23) in eastern Tennessee along the Tennessee River. The edges of both bones had been ground and the surfaces polished. Both were drilled, but there was no indication of abrasion adjacent to the perforations. Noting that human bone artifacts were not common in the Tennessee Valley region, and in attempting to place these finds in context, Williams (1975) referred to a Late Archaic period human skull bowl found at site 1CT27 in Alabama (Webb and DeJarnette 1942). In addition, gorgets made from human skulls have been reported by Webb and Baby (1957) in their study of Late Adena and Hopewell sites in Ohio.

GREAT PLAINS

Cuts on human crania have been reported in cases of scalping in the Great Plains (Owsley, Berryman, and Bass 1977; Willey 1992). Cranial and postcranial cuts also have been documented in cases associated with Woodland period mortuary practices that involved disarticulation and defleshing of the dead (Bass and Phenice 1975). Phenice (1969) described cranial alterations found during the excavation of 17 sites in north-central Kansas. Openings had been cut into the occipitals of eight crania, and there was no evidence of healing—no resorption or remodeling. The openings appeared to have been made after death; thus, therapeutic trephination seemed unlikely. The edges of the holes in the occipitals were polished, suggestive of wear. Phenice (1969) states that these

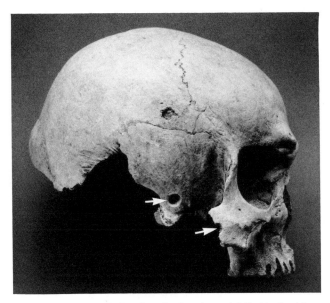

Fig. 4. Sully site trophy skull with perforations (arrows) drilled in the right temporal and malar. (University of Tennessee, Knoxville, Department of Anthropology: Specimen No. 9909.)

modified skulls could have been displayed on pegs attached to a wall and might only have been so displayed on ceremonial occasions.

Trophy skulls have been reported in a few sites such as Footprint (41PT25) in the Texas Panhandle (Lintz 1986), Blood Run (13LO2) in northwest Iowa (Schermer 1987), and with Omaha (25DK2A-S22, S24, S25; Nebraska State Museum field notes dated 1939, Lincoln) and Pawnee (25WT-S2, Nebraska State Historical Society field notes dated March 27, 1941, Lincoln) burials in Nebraska. However, intentionally incised or modified human bones are rare in Plains archaeological sites.

Among the few examples of modified crania that have been reported are two worked human crania from Upper Republican (Central Plains tradition, 25FT13, 25HN36, about A.D. 1050–1250) sites in Nebraska (Roll 1968; Wedel 1986). Both calvaria were found in trash pits. Four cranial vaults from the Crow Creek site (39BF11) (Initial Coalescent, A.D. 1325) massacre bone bed display cuts, cut edges, and, in two cases, polish from wear, suggesting purposeful modification (Willey 1992). A trophy skull with two drill holes in the right temporal and zygomatic bones was recovered at the Postcontact Coalescent tradition Sully site (39SL4) in South Dakota (fig. 4). The Sully trophy skull is that of a male 35 to 45 years of age. Most of the occipital bone, both temporals, and the entire cranial base are missing. Small portions of both eye orbits, the nasal bones, and the right zygomatic arch are also

missing. The right temporal and malar bones exhibit circular, conoidal-shaped (i.e., inwardly beveled) drill holes. The perforation in the temporal, immediately superior to the right temporomandibular eminence, measures eight millimeters (diameter) in the external table and five millimeters internally. The right malar bone is broken (and missing) through the middle of a drill hole that measures six millimeters in diameter. This perforation is also inwardly beveled with its widest portion being the external margin. There is no evidence of disease or premortem trauma visible on the skull.

The appearance of the perforations indicates that a conoidally shaped implement was used to drill the holes from the external surface. Although the drill only partially perforated the inner surface of the temporal bone, the inner margin of the hole is slightly beveled and polished, indicating modification after the skull was broken or abrasion caused by a suspension cord. No other cuts or cultural modifications were noted.

The cranium of a male(?) aged 12 to 14 years from the Broken Kettle site is a trophy associated with the Mill Creek culture in western Iowa. Two small burr holes measuring 6.7 and 7.5 millimeters externally are present in the frontal bone, probably for suspension (fig. 5). The holes are located high on

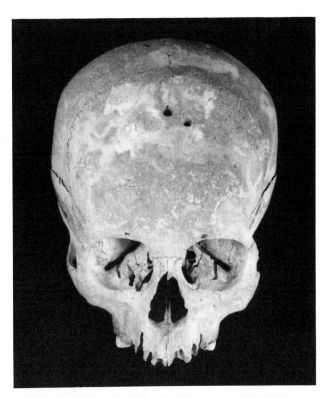

Fig. 5. Trophy skull from the Broken Kettle site with two drill holes in the frontal bone. (Iowa State Historical Society, Iowa City, Keyes Collection: 13PM1, Pli-2212.)

the frontal about three centimeters anterior to bregma. Trauma to the frontal resulted in an oblong depressed fracture that measures 3.8 by 1.7 centimeters. The skull shows occipital deformation, which is rarely seen in Plains groups or the Oneota, suggesting that this individual was from a Mississippian group (S. Schermer, personal communication 1990). An etched cranial fragment from the Dixon Village site (13WD8), an Oneota village dated to A.D. 1100–1400, is intricately covered with diamond-shaped designs and a four-sided star (S. Schermer, personal communication 1990). These artifacts represent the few known culturally modified human bones recovered from the Great Plains.

Behavioral and Cultural Interpretation

Cuts on adult cranial and postcranial bones recovered during 1968 excavations at the Edwards I site provide evidence of dismemberment and defleshing, followed by intentional modification of some bones. The bones represent at least two adults, both probably female. The frontal (fig. 1), ulna, and right femur (fig. 2), which has posterior surface cuts on the linea aspera, are similar in age (young adult), coloration, and general robusticity. These bones could represent the disarticulated skeletal elements of the same person.

The location, distribution, and number of cuts can be used to distinguish between meticulously defleshed crania and those scored through the processing of scalping. The number and apparent randomness of cuts on the frontal make it apparent that systematic defleshing of the bone, not scalping, was the objective. Generally, scalped skulls show fewer cuts and these are clustered, exhibiting a distinctive circumferential pattern (Allen, Merbs, and Birkby 1985; Hamperl and Laughlin 1959; Hoyme and Bass 1962) that is quite different from the cuts on this frontal. Often, a scalped frontal bone shows cuts that originate at the temporal line, extend to approximately halfway between the hairline and the browridges, and terminate at the opposing temple. Similar cuts are then made that circumscribe the parietals and occasionally the occipital. Cuts on the Edwards I frontal are found on the forehead, beginning at the level of the anatomical landmark glabella.

Table 1 provides data to illustrate that the process of defleshing generally results in more cuts than scalping. This tabulation gives the numbers of distinct cuts observed in several scalped crania from Oklahoma (Heerwald and Nagle sites, "Evidence of Warfare at the Heerwald Site," this vol.; Owsley 1989) and South Dakota (Anton Rygh, Sully, and Mobridge sites, "Warfare in Coalescent Tradition Populations

Table 1. Number of Cuts on Cranial Bones from Selected Sites

| Site | Feature | Specimen No. | Frontal | Parietal | | Temporal | | Occipital |
				L	R	L	R	
Oklahoma								
34BK2	—	246	71	—[a]	—	—	—	—
34CU27	—	1A	30	11	5	—	4	10
34OK4	—	10	12	17	2	3	20	0
North Dakota (Woodland)								
39SI1	03	3E	29	8	5	36	2	0
39SI1	03	6B	4	2	23	11	70	0
39SI1	03	9A	34	16	9	0	—	0
39SI1	03	13	32	20	54	6	—	40
South Dakota (Coalescent)								
39WW1	101	27F	11	0	7	3	0	0
39WW1	201	11C	7	0	0	0	—	0
39WW1	101	29D	0	29	0	0	0	14
39CA4	101	13	1	12	6	0	0	2
39CA4	101	13	1	12	6	0	0	2
39CA4	—	670	2	14	14	0	0	6
39CA4	—	4859	0	0	5	0	0	0
39CA4	101	12	0	2	0	0	0	0
39SL4	116	5227	37	2	27	0	0	5

[a]Bone not present for examination.

of the Northern Plains," this vol.). Comparable data for cut crania from a mortuary process of disarticulation and defleshing are available for the Woodland period Boundary Mound 3 (39SI1) (Neuman 1975; Owsley 1985–1990). The partial frontal from Edwards I has more cuts (N = 71) than any other specimen. Note that the number of cuts on the frontals of the scalped crania ranges between 0 and 37, with eight of the 10 examples having 12 or fewer cuts. On average, defleshed specimens have higher numbers of cuts, with some bones having as many as 70 cuts.

Short cuts on the ulna suggest defleshing by slicing or sawing, while the longer, longitudinally oriented, parallel striations indicate scraping, possibly with a knife blade. The muscles and tendons of the right arm were first cut away, then the periosteum (the tight, durable sheath covering the cortex) was removed by scraping. The overall pattern suggests meticulous defleshing shortly after death. Similar striations have been observed in Woodland period skeletons from the Central and Northern Plains that were defleshed prior to burial (Bass and Phenice 1969; Owsley 1985–1990). Our experience with modern forensic cases, autopsies, and human decay studies supports this conclusion. Had the ulna been left to decay before the periosteum was removed, the soft tissues would have dried and hardened. At this stage of decomposition, the periosteum can be stripped like dried sinew, with less need for scraping. However, if defleshing was performed while the tissues were fresh, vigorous scraping would have been necessary to remove the tightly adhering periosteum.

A search of the literature for specimens comparable to the two femora revealed few reports of similarly altered bone. Notched sticks and similar nonhuman bone artifacts fashioned from deer (or antelope) and bison ribs have been identified as sounding rasps (fig. 6a–b). These bones "show a glossiness along the middle of the scored surface, and in a few instances the cuts at this zone have been partially rubbed or worn away" (Wedel and Hill 1942:95; see also Lehmer 1971). Rasplike objects that lack surface polish have been related to the production of certain styles of paddle-marked pottery decoration (fig. 6c–d) with discontinuous corrugations or plaited effects (Wedel and Hill 1942). The similarity of the Edwards I notched femur (fig. 3) to nonhuman modified bones reported in the literature suggests that it could be a musical rasp. One noteworthy difference is that the spacing between the grooves in this femur is much wider than the animal bone rasps in figure 6a–b.

The utilitarian, ceremonial, or symbolic value of the femur in figure 2 is not known. The location of the cuts, confined to the linea aspera, indicates that the bone was held in position

Fig. 6. Animal ribs modified for functional use. a–b, Scored deer or antelope ribs used as musical rasps, from Kansas (National Museum of Natural History, Smithsonian: 388658, 388659). c–d, Bison ribs with cuts probably used as paddles to decorate pottery, from South Dakota (National Museum of Natural History, Smithsonian: 325506).

and cut for a specific purpose. No other Wheeler phase artifacts are similar, and comparable examples have not been reported.

In the Southern Plains during the protohistoric period, several groups of people interacted in a variety of ways. Archaeologists have identified three cultural complexes in this region: the Wheeler phase in Oklahoma and Texas, and the Garza and Tierra Blanca complexes in the Oklahoma and Texas panhandles (Baugh 1986; Habicht-Mauche 1987, 1988; Hofman 1989). Because bison hunting was basic to the adaptive strategy of each of these cultures, scholars have tended to treat them as intertwined or closely related. For example, Gunnerson and Gunnerson (1971), Gunnerson (1987), and Hofman (1984), in their ethnohistorical accounts, argue that the Wheeler phase represents an Apache occupation in the southern mixed-grass prairies: "The similarity of the majority of the ceramics to pottery identified elsewhere as Apache supports such an identification for the complex" (Gunnerson 1987:111). However, these assemblages may reflect the activities of the Wichita or Wichita-related Caddoans (Hofman 1989).

A more detailed analysis of ceramics of the Edwards Plain type and Washita River types (especially Lee Plain) points to a gradual transition from the Early Plains Village to the later Edwards Plain ware (Swenson 1986). Support for this hypothesis appears in the Habicht-Mauche (1988) study of Plains Village ceramics and other behavioral indicators in the Southern Prairie Plains. "General similarities in artifact assemblages, ceramic technology, settlement patterns, and basic subsistence strategies suggest a continuity of culture in this area from at least Washita River times through the historic period" (Habicht-Mauche 1988:159). This cultural continuity includes the more westerly Garza complex people, who may represent the ethnohistoric Teya (Baugh 1982, 1986; Habicht-Mauche 1987, 1988) and a more western Plains Caddoan adaptation. Such an adaptation should be more closely examined in other regions of the prairie plains margin of Kansas, Nebraska, and Colorado where the Dismal River aspect is commonly encountered.

This assertion is not to say that the Apache were not in the Southern Plains. The most probable candidate for an archaeological correlation with the Southern Athapaskans is the Tierra Blanca complex people. This affiliation is based on the comparison of ceramic types, especially Tierra Blanca plain. Although clear differences exist between the faint-striated ceramic wares of the Southwest and Tierra Blanca Plain, there can be little doubt that the technological and functional attributes of the Tierra Blanca type were derived not from the Plains but from the Pueblo peoples (Baugh and Eddy 1987; Habicht-Mauche 1987, 1988). Only an immigrating group of hunters and gatherers, rather than indigenous farmers, would need to develop such a technology for the processing and storage of food. From such evidence, it can be argued that the people of the Wheeler phase and Garza complex represent a continuum of Plains Caddoans, from east to west across the Southern Plains, who tended to rely increasingly on bison hunting. The Southern Athapaskans are represented by the Tierra Blanca complex, which dates about 1450–1650 in the protohistoric era (Gunnerson 1956; Habicht-Mauche 1988).

Questions concerning population origins and relationships, as traced from the Historic period into prehistory, are problematical and require further study (e.g., Hofman 1989). Archaeologically, the Edwards I people probably are the antecedents of the Wichita; and human bone deformation among this group, for which the present study of artifacts from the Edwards site provides evidence, appears to have been an old cultural pattern. The occurrence of purposefully modified bones may relate to cultural practices documented ethnohistorically and is relevant to discussions concerning tribal identification.

The Wichita are said to have practiced ritual cannibalism (Margry 1886; Newcomb and Field 1967; Sandoval 1749), possibly a relatively old cultural practice among these Southern Plains people. The earliest ethnohistoric account of cannibalism among these Plains Caddoans is that of Bernard de La Harpe, who was exploring the Arkansas River in 1719 to establish commercial and political ties with the Wichita. At that time, de La Harpe was given a young Lipan Apache slave who had one finger missing from each hand as a symbolic indicator that this captive eventually would be eaten by the

Wichita. These fingers had already been consumed by the Tawakoni. The leader of this Tawakoni band of the Wichita apologetically informed de La Harpe that he would have been given more slaves if he had arrived earlier and that at least 17 Lipans had been eaten in a ceremony about a month earlier (Margry 1886:292; Newcomb and Field 1967:326). In 1749, Felipe Sandoval, a Spaniard in the employment of the French, noted that the Wichita "eat all prisoners of war, since their favorite dish is human flesh. During my stay with them (20 days) I saw them eat a fifteen-year-old girl and an infant whom they had captured from another nation" (Sandoval 1749; also cited in Newcomb and Field 1967:326). One of the latest references to such practices among the Wichita was that of the trader J. Gaignard, who stated in 1773: "They are brave, and go to their enemies to steal horses and capture slaves. When they take a slave capable of returning they broil him and eat him" (Bolton 1914:85; also cited in Newcomb and Field 1967:326).

Although Sjoberg (1953:95–96; see also Newcomb 1961:126) maintains that the Lipan Apache ate the remains of Comanche captives, others dispute such unverified claims. The likelihood that Southern Athapaskans engaged in such practices seems remote, for, as Opler (1982:140) has pointed out, "The Apache fear of death, the corpse, and the ghost is extreme, and it inspires practices such as hasty burial, avoidance of the burial site, destruction of the personal property of the deceased, refusal to utter the name of the deceased, purification measures to keep the ghost at a distance, and many others." Opler (1982) states that preparation and burial of the body were conducted by elders who had less to fear from contamination than younger individuals. Once placed in the ground, the ghost of the deceased was ordered to depart quietly and not to disturb any of its relatives. The burial party returned to camp by an alternative route to confuse the roaming spirit, with purification rites immediately following their return. Bathing, sprinkling pollen, and rubbing cedar smoke over one's body were means of cleansing and removing the contaminating and polluting elements (Opler 1945). Thus, fear and avoidance of a corpse were typical behaviors among all the Apachean groups.

Even more terrifying than the corpse to the Athapaskans was the human head. Opler (1940:49), for example, notes that while scalps were taken by the Lipan during the historic period, this activity was done by burning the flesh rather than by means of direct contact with the head such as cutting would require. "The corpse, and particularly the skull, was considered a source of danger and contamination; the word for skull symbolizes not only the corpse but all the material and polluting aspects of death. It was believed hazardous even to get too close to the dead. Fainting spells, insanity, and facial paralysis could result from such exposure or contact. Consequently the body was prepared and disposed of with all dispatch" (Opler and Bittle 1961:384). From this perspective, the probability, or even the possibility, of an Apache engaging in the defleshing of a cranium or the carving of human remains would be extremely unlikely. This prohibition is not limited to the Apacheans alone but reflects a general Athapaskan behavioral pattern. These considerations lead to the conclusion that the altered bones from the Edwards I site are the work of one or more individuals of a Plains Caddoan group rather than a Southern Athapaskan group.

The following individuals provided help: Julie Droke, Collections Manager, Oklahoma Museum of Natural History, loan of the skeletal elements; Sandra L. Olsen, scanning electron microscopy and interpretation; Robert L. Brooks, Gail D. Potter, John Ludwickson, Karl J. Reinhard, and Shirley J. Schermer, background information.

References Cited

Agrinier, P.
1960 The Carved Human Femurs from Tomb 1, Chiapa de Corzo, Chiapas, Mexico. *Papers of the New World Archaeological Foundation* 5:1–28. Orinda.

Allen W.H., C.F. Merbs, and W.H. Birkby
1985 Evidence for Prehistoric Scalping at Nuvakwewtaqa (Chavez Pass) and Grasshopper Ruin, Arizona. Pp. 23–42 in Health and Disease in the Prehistoric Southwest. C.F. Merbs and R.J. Miller, eds. *Arizona State University Anthropological Research Papers* 34. Tempe.

Baby, R.S.
1956 A Unique Hopewellian Mask—Headdress. *American Antiquity* 21(3):303–305.

1961 A Hopewell Human Bone Whistle. *American Antiquity* 27(1):108–110.

Bass, W.M.
1987 Human Osteology: A Laboratory and Field Manual. 3rd ed. Columbia: Missouri Archaeological Society.

——, and T.W. Phenice
1975 Prehistoric Human Skeletal Material from Three Sites in North and South Dakota. Pp. 106–140 in The Sonota Complex and Associated Sites on the Northern Great Plains. R.W. Neuman, ed. *Nebraska State Historical Society Publications in Anthropology* 6.

Baugh, T.G.
1982 Edwards I (34BK2): Southern Plains Adaptations in the Protohistoric Period. *Oklahoma Archaeological Survey. Studies in Oklahoma's Past* 8.

1986 Culture History and Protohistoric Societies in the Southern Plains. In Current Trends in Southern Plains Archaeology. T.G. Baugh, ed. *Plains Anthropologist Memoir* 21: 167–187.

——, and F.W. Eddy
1987 Rethinking Apachean Ceramics: The 1985 Southern Athapaskan Ceramics Conference. *American Antiquity* 52(4):793–798.

——, and F.W. Nelson, Jr.
1987 New Mexico Obsidian Sources and Exchange on the Southern Plains. *Journal of Field Archaeology* 14:313–329.

Bolton, H.E.
1914 Athanase de Mezières and the Louisiana-Texas Frontier, 1768–1780, vol. 2. Cleveland, Ohio: Arthur H. Clark.

Cole, F.C., and T. Deuel
1937 Rediscovering Illinois. Chicago: University of Chicago Press.

Cybulski, J.S.
1978 Modified Human Bones and Skulls from Prince Rupert Harbour, British Columbia. *Canadian Journal of Archaeology* 2:15–32.

Dixon, K.A.
1959 Two Carved Human Bones from Chiapas. *Archaeology* 12(1):106–110.

Drass, R.R., and M.C. Moore
1987 The Linville II Site (34RM492) and Plains Village Manifestations in the Mixed Grass Prairie. *Plains Anthropologist* 32(118):404–418.

——, and F.E. Swenson
1986 Variation in the Washita River Phase of Central and Western Oklahoma. *Plains Anthropologist* 31(111):35–49.

——, T.G. Baugh, and P. Flynn
1987 The Heerwald Site and Early Plains Village Adaptations in the Southern Plains. *North American Archaeologist* 8(2):151–190.

Feagins, J.D.
1989 Prehistoric Treatment of a Human Skull from Northwest Missouri. *Missouri Archaeological Society Quarterly* 6(2):4–5.

Gilliland, M.S.
1975 The Material Culture of Key Marco, Florida. Gainesville: University Presses of Florida.

Gunnerson, D.A.
1956 The Southern Athabascans: Their Arrival in the Southwest. *El Palacio* 63:346–365.

Gunnerson, J.H.
1987 Archaeology of the High Plains. *Bureau of Land Management. Cultural Resource Series* 19.

——, and D.A. Gunnerson
1971 Apachean Culture: A Study in Unity and Diversity. Pp. 7–27 in Apachean Culture History and Ethnology. K.H.

Basso and M.E. Opler, eds. *University of Arizona Press Anthropological Papers* 21.

Habicht-Mauche, J.A.

1987 Southwestern-style Culinary Ceramics on the Southern Plains: A Case Study of Technological Innovation and Cross-cultural Interaction. *Plains Anthropologist* 32(116): 175–189.

1988 An Analysis of Southwestern Style Utility Ware Ceramics from the Southern Plains in the Context of Protohistoric Plains-Pueblo Interaction. (Unpublished Ph.D. Dissertation in Anthropology, Harvard University, Cambridge.)

Hamperl, H., and W.S. Laughlin

1959 Osteological Consequences of Scalping. *Human Biology* 31:80–89.

Hester, T.R.

1969a Human Bone Artifacts from Southern Texas. *American Antiquity* 34(3):326–328.

1969b Archeological Investigations in Kleberg and Kenedy Counties, Texas in August, 1967. *State Building Commission Archeological Program Report* 15.

Hodges, D.C.

1989 Cranial Fragment from the Lowry Farm Site 13MC4. *Office of the State Archaeologist,* Research Papers 14(3):58–59. Iowa City.

Hofman, J.L.

1984 The Western Protohistoric: A Summary of the Edwards and Wheeler Complexes. Pp. 347–362 in Prehistory of Oklahoma. R.E. Bell, ed. New York: Academic Press.

1989 Protohistoric Culture History on the Southern Great Plains. Pp. 91–100 in From Clovis to Comanchero: Archeological Overview of the Southern Great Plains. J.L. Hofman, R.L. Brooks, and D.W. Owsley, eds. *Arkansas Archeological Survey Research Series* 35. Fayetteville.

Hoyme, L.E., and W.M. Bass

1962 Human Skeletal Remains from the Tollifero (Ha6) and Clarksville (Mc14) Sites, John H. Kerr Reservoir Basin, Virginia. *Bureau of American Ethnology Bulletin* 182:329–400.

Jamieson, J.B.

1983 An Examination of Prisoner-sacrifice and Cannibalism at the St. Lawrence Iroquoian Roebuck Site. *Canadian Journal of Archaeology* 7(2):159–175.

Krogman, W.M., and M.Y. Iscan

1986 The Human Skeleton in Forensic Medicine. 2nd ed. Springfield, Ill.: Charles C. Thomas.

Lehmer, D.J.

1971 Introduction to Middle Missouri Archeology. *National Park Service. Anthropological Papers* 1.

Lintz, C.R.

1986 Architecture and Community Variability Within the Antelope Creek Phase of the Texas Panhandle. *Oklahoma Archeological Survey Studies in Oklahoma's Past* 14.

Mallam, R.C.

1979 A Cut and Perforated Human Mandible from the Quandahl Rockshelter, Winneshiek County, Iowa. *Journal of the Iowa Archeological Society* 26:30–36.

Margry, P., ed.

1886 Découvertes et etablissements des Français dans l'ouest et dans le sud de l'Amérique Septentrionale (1614–1754). 6 vols. Paris.

Marti, S.

1955 Instrumentos musicales precortesianos. Mexico City: Instituto Nacional de Antropologia e Historia.

Moorehead, W.K.

1922 The Hopewell Mound Group of Ohio. *Publications of the Field Museum of Natural History, Anthropological Series* 6(5): 79–178.

Neuman, R.W.

1975 The Sonota Complex and Associated Sites on the Northern Great Plains. *Nebraska State Historical Society Publications in Anthropology* 6.

Newcomb, W.W.

1961 The Indians of Texas: From Prehistoric to Modern Times. Austin: University of Texas Press.

——, and W.T. Field

1967 An Ethnohistoric Investigation of the Wichita Indians in the Southern Plains. Pp. 240–395 in A Pilot Study of Wichita Indian Archeology and Ethnohistory. R.E. Bell, E.B. Jelks, and W.W. Newcomb, eds. Norman, Okla.: Final Report for Grant GS-964 to National Science Foundation.

Olsen, S.L., and P. Shipman

1988 Surface Modification on Bone: Trampling Versus Butchery. *Journal of Archaeological Science* 15:535–553.

Opler, M.E.

1940 Myths and Legends of the Lipan Apache Indians. *Memoirs of the American Folklore Society* 36.

1945 The Lipan Apache Death Complex and Its Extensions. *Southwestern Journal of Anthropology* 1:122–141.

1982 The Scott County Pueblo Site in Historical, Archaeological, and Ethnological Perspective. Pp. 135–144 in Pathways to Plains Prehistory. D.G. Wyckoff and J.L. Hofman, eds. *Oklahoma Anthropological Society Memoir* 3.

——, and W.E. Bittle

1961 The Death Practices and Eschatology of the Kiowa Apache. *Southwestern Journal of Anthropology* 17(4):383–394.

Owsley, D. W.

1989 The History of Bioarcheological Research in the Southern Great Plains. Pp. 123–136 in From Clovis to Comanchero:

Archeological Overview of the Southern Plains. J.L. Hofman, R.L. Brooks, and D.W. Owsley, eds. *Arkansas Archeological Survey Research Series* 35.

——

1985–1990   Osteological Data. (On File in Department of Anthropology, National Museum of Natural History, Smithsonian Institution, Washington.)

——, H.E. Berryman, and W.M. Bass

1977   Demographic and Osteological Evidence for Warfare at the Larson Site, South Dakota. *Plains Anthropologist Memoir* 13:119–131.

Phenice, T.W.

1969   An Analysis of the Human Skeletal Material from Burial Mounds in North Central Kansas. *University of Kansas Publications in Anthropology* 1.

Powell, M.L.

1977   Prehistoric Ritual Skull Burials at the Crenshaw Site (3 MI 6), Southwest Arkansas. *Bulletin of the Texas Archeological Society* 48:111–118.

Pratt, W.H.

1876   Report of Explorations of the Ancient Mounds at Toolesboro, Louisa County, Iowa. *Proceedings of the Davenport Academy of Natural Sciences for 1867–1876. Women's Centennial Association* 1:106–111.

Roll, T.E.

1968   Upper Republican Cultural Relationships. (Unpublished M.A. Thesis, Department of Anthropology, University of Nebraska, Lincoln.)

Sandoval, F.

1749   Deposition, Archivo General de Mexico, Provincias Internas, XXXVII, 1749 (W.E. Dunn Transcripts), Bexar Archives. Austin, Tex.: University of Texas Library.

Schermer, S.J.

1987   Human Skeletal Remains from 13L02, the Blood Run National Historic Landmark Site. *Miscellaneous Reports on Iowa Archaeology* 12(1).

——, and D.W. Owsley

1989–1990   Osteological Data. (On File in Office of the State Archaeologist of Iowa, Iowa City.)

Seeman, M.F.

1988   Ohio Hopewell Trophy-skull Artifacts as Evidence for Competition in Middle Woodland Societies Circa 50 B.C.– A.D. 350. *American Antiquity* 53(3):565–577.

Sjoberg, A.F.

1953   Lipan Apache Culture in Historical Perspective. *Southwestern Journal of Anthropology* 9:76–98.

Stewart, T.D.

1979   Essentials of Forensic Anthropology. Springfield, Ill.: Charles C. Thomas.

Swenson, F.E.

1986   A Study in Cultural Adaptation to Climatic Shifts on the Southern Plains: Washita River Phase and Edwards Complex Cultural Continuity. (Unpublished Masters Thesis in Anthropology, University of Oklahoma, Norman.)

Turner, C.G. II, and N.C. Morris

1970   A Massacre at Hopi. *American Antiquity* 35(3):320–331.

Webb, W.S., and R.S. Baby

1957   The Adena People No. 2. Columbus: The Ohio Historical Society.

Webb, W.S., and D.L. DeJarnette

1942   An Archeological Survey of Pickwick Basin in the Adjacent Portions of the States of Alabama, Mississippi, and Tennessee. *Bureau of American Ethnology Bulletin* 129.

Wedel, W.R.

1986   Central Plains Prehistory: Holocene Environments and Culture Change in the Republican River Basin. Lincoln, Nebr.: University of Nebraska Press.

——, and A.T. Hill

1942   Scored Bone Artifacts of the Central Great Plains. *Proceedings of the United States National Museum* 92(3141): 91–100.

Weymouth, J.W.

1981   Magnetic Surveys on the Edwards I (34BK2) and the Taylor (34GR8) Sites in Western Oklahoma. (Manuscript on file, Oklahoma Archaeological Survey, Norman, Okla.)

Willey, P.

1992   Prehistoric Warfare on the Great Plains: Skeletal Analysis of the Crow Creek Massacre Victims. New York: Garland.

Williams, L.C.

1975   Human Skull Artifacts. *Tennessee Archaeologist* 31(1): 33–36.

Willoughby, C.C., and E.A. Hooton

1922   The Turner Group of Earthworks, Hamilton County, Ohio. *Papers of the Peabody Museum of American Archaeology and Ethnology, Harvard University* 8(3).

○ ○ ○

CHAPTER 31

Cutmarks and Perimortem Treatment of Skeletal Remains on the Northern Plains

SANDRA L. OLSEN AND PAT SHIPMAN

In this chapter, three hypotheses are explored: that the frequency of intertribal conflict rose at about the time the Arikara moved into the area; that replacement of the Mandan by the Arikara at this time might be reflected in a lowered frequency of secondary burials; and that, in most cases, modification due to funerary practices could be distinguished from that caused by events related to intergroup conflict.

The study sample was selected from the entire W.H. Over collection by Douglas Owsley to span a large time range and to include both typical and exceptional examples. A few specimens that were not part of the Over Collection were also included, such as those from Boundary Mound (32SI1). This analysis is best seen as a pilot study to document mortuary practices, tool use on human bodies, and conflict among Northern Plains Indian populations through the examination of bone modification patterns.

It is important to note that our sample does not reflect the chronological record of a single ethnic group. Tribal affiliation is uncertain for the Woodland sites, but by the Middle Missouri tradition, evidence indicates the villages were ancestral Mandan. By the Initial Coalescent, the Arikara were moving in and largely displacing the Mandan.

The significant changes in cutmarks and other surface modifications through time emphasize both the shift in funerary traditions in the area and the conflicts arising from the influx of the ancestral Arikara. Although the Woodland and ancestral Mandan people practiced secondary burial, there appears to be a decline in this tradition in later Arikara sites. The term "secondary burial" is used to refer to collections of disarticulated human bones that were secondarily deposited after the flesh was removed either with tools or through decomposition (Ubelaker 1978).

"Ossuary burial practice may be described generally as the collective, secondary deposit of skeletal material representing individuals initially stored elsewhere." The term ossuary is often "restricted to those secondary deposits that probably represent the periodic redisposal of individuals, which took place after a culturally-prescribed number of years" (Ubelaker 1974:8).

In the case of the Woodland and ancestral Mandan people of South Dakota, it is thought that individuals were initially either placed on a scaffold above ground or were deposited in temporary graves before being interred in mounds.

Although it is beyond the scope of this chapter to elaborate on the various kinds of evidence for intertribal conflict between the Mandan and the intruding Arikara during the Coalescent period, it is clear that battle-related injuries and perimortem mutilation dramatically increased after the arrival of the Arikara.

Although this study focuses on the location and nature of the cutmarks, it also incorporates essential data gathered by Douglas Owsley, Richard Jantz, Donald Blakeslee, and others regarding available ethnohistoric descriptions, the archaeological context, relative completeness of skeletons, and degree of articulation for each burial. All these lines of evidence have been considered in the interpretations of bone modifications in the sample. Those interpretations have been extended to the remainder of the Over Collection. Activities that are represented in the surface modifications in the Over Collection include secondary burial practices, battle or other traumatic injuries, and perimortem mutilation like scalping and vigorous dismemberment of bodies with a large ax. Although some of the marks in this collection might have been caused by cannibalism, there is no particular evidence to support this interpretation. The use of human bones for artifact manufacture appears to have been rare in this sample. Worked cranial bones were reported at Crow Creek, but these specimens were not examined.

Materials and Methods

The sample consists of 85 replicas of bone surfaces from 38 individuals, derived from 12 sites. These sites span a range of time from the Middle Woodland tradition (at about A.D. 400), through the Middle Missouri, up to the Disorganized

Coalescent, and ending at about 1832 (table 1). A range of approximately 1,400 years in a moderately restricted geographic region is represented.

In the course of this study, cutmarks or other surface alterations on the bones were replicated by making silicone rubber impressions, from which epoxy resin casts were made (see Rose 1983). The casts were then coated with gold-palladium and examined by light and scanning electron microscopy at low magnification (generally less than 500 times). The purposes for making replicas of surface modifications were to facilitate examination in a scanning electron microscope and because the skeletal material was to be reburied.

This study builds on previous research on bone surface modifications aimed at distinguishing between marks caused by different cultural and natural processes (Olsen 1988; Olsen and Shipman 1988; Shipman, Fisher, and Rose 1984; Shipman and Rose 1984, 1988). With this background research, it was possible to distinguish between marks produced by a variety of ancient tools, including those made of both stone and metal; marks made by natural processes like sedimentary abrasion, carnivore or rodent gnawing, and root etching; and marks made during excavation.

Of great assistance in the study are data provided by Douglas Owsley and Robert Mann on the age and sex of the individuals examined and inventories of the elements collected. They also compiled cutmark "maps" that show the

Table 1. Sample Examined in This Study

Tradition	Variant	Phase	Site	Individuals	Replicas	Defleshed	Disarticulated	Open Foramen Magnum	Scalp	Head Blow	Knife or Arrow Wound
Woodland	Middle	Sonota	Enemy Swim	4	9	5	1	2			
			Boundary Mound	6	7	4	1				
	Late Late	Loseke Creek	Split Rock Creek	4	11	4	1	1			
Middle Missouri	Initial	Over	Mitchell Mounds (39DV2/3)	1	1	1					
			Twelve Mile Creek	1	1	1				1	
	Extended	Thomas Riggs	McKensey Village (39AR201)	5	10	1	3				
Coalescent	Initial	?	Crow Creek	1	8	1					
	Extended and Postcontact	La Roche and Le Beau	Mobridge	3	7	1			2	1	1
			Anton Rygh	2	3		1		1	1	2
	Postcontact	Le Beau	Larson	7	20		2		7	2	4
			Swan Creek	1	1		1		1		1
	Disorganized	Arikara	Leavenworth	3	7		1		3		1
			Total	38	85	18	11	3	14	5	9

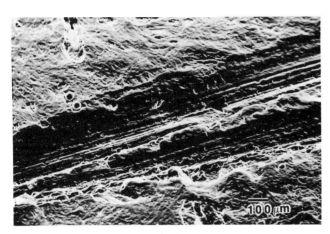

Fig. 1. Cutmarks on a left parietal of a male, aged 40–49 years, from Larson (Burial 62B), made with a retouched stone tool during scalping. Scanning electron micrograph.

Fig. 3. Chopmark on lesser trochanter of femur of teenager of indeterminate sex from Crow Creek. Numerous depressed fractures (arrows) along the lower margin of the mark are typical of chopping. Scanning electron micrograph.

precise location, the orientation, and occasionally the length of all marks on the Over specimens, including those replicated for further study.

Although the purpose or intent of any particular mark cannot be known with certainty, it was found that characteristics of the marks, such as morphology, size, frequency, location, and orientation on the bone, are useful in deducing the activities that led to the creation of individual marks. When this information is combined with the archaeological context, cultural affiliation, and skeletal completeness, it is possible to present reasonable interpretations of the modifications.

Marks found on the specimens were made with a variety of implements, including retouched stone tools such as knives (fig. 1) and scrapers (fig. 2), large implements like axes (fig. 3), and, in one instance from Leavenworth, a metal knife (fig. 4). Some skeletons bore possible wounds from stabbing or projectile points. In a few cases, small pieces of flint, probably derived from projectile points or knives, were found embedded in bone. Blunt objects, perhaps wooden clubs, were

Fig. 2. Scraping done with a stone tool on a right parietal of a female, aged 40–44 years, from the Anton Rygh site (Burial 4859), probably made during scalping.

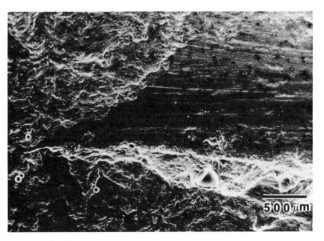

Fig. 4. Cutmark made by a metal knife on a left parietal of a male (Burial 13), aged 30–34 years, from the Leavenworth site. Scanning electron micrograph.

Table 2. Characteristics Associated with Secondary Burial and Conflict

Secondary Burial	Conflict
1. Partial skeleton	1. Mostly complete skeleton
2. High cutmark frequencies: up to hundreds on one bone	2. Few cutmarks: often less than 20
3. Defleshing marks on cranium	3. Scalping marks on cranium
4. Mandibular marks common	4. Mandibular marks usually absent
5. Postcranial cutmarks abundant	5. Postcranial cutmarks infrequent
6. Patterned orientation and distribution of postcranial marks	6. Variable orientation and distribution of postcranial marks
7. Type of marks: cutmarks scraping, enlarging of foramen magnum	7. Type of marks: cutmarks, chopmarks, ax wounds, blows, embedded flint, stabbing or projectile point wounds

employed to fracture the skulls of the enemy at some of the massacre sites.

Two major categories of marks occur on skeletons from this sample, which are interpreted as representing secondary burial, on the one hand, and the effects of intergroup conflict, on the other. Table 2 summarizes the characteristics observed to be associated with each of these activities. Figures 5 through 8 show cutmark maps illustrating various aspects of these patterns. The differences between the two patterns are striking in the Over Collection.

Secondary Burial

In this sample, secondary burials occur from Middle Woodland through the Extended Coalescent sites and are absent from the later Arikara sites of the Postcontact and Disorganized Coalescent. Skeletons from secondary burial contexts (i.e., partial, disarticulated inhumations in mounds) possess two kinds of marks, often in abundance and widely distributed over the skeleton. These marks are interpreted as ones associated with defleshing and disarticulation and occur on both the cranium and postcranial skeleton.

DEFLESHING

Defleshing is usually represented by short, fine cutmarks or broader scraping over the surfaces of bones caused when a

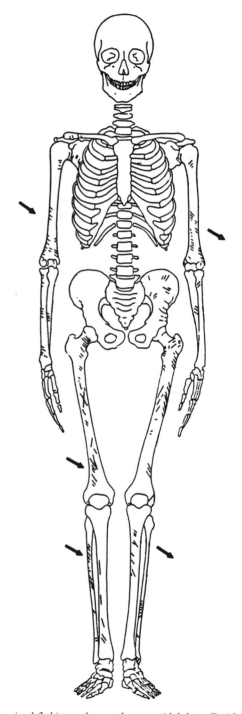

Fig. 5. Extensive defleshing marks on male postcranial skeleton (Burial 6), aged 30–34 years, from Boundary Mound, demonstrating a strong pattern of orientation of cuts on limb bones (arrows indicate predominant orientation).

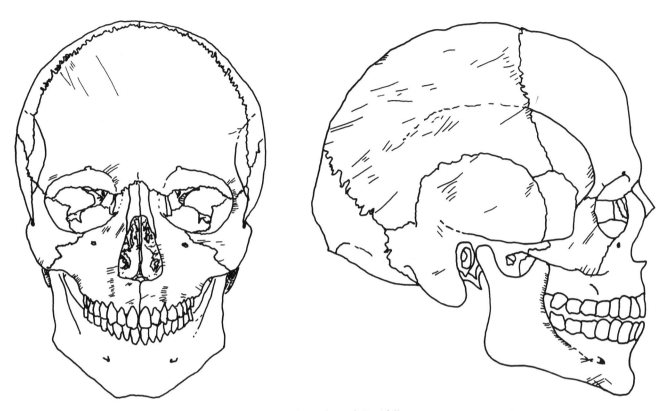

Fig. 6. Defleshing marks on skull of adult, aged about 23 years, from Split Rock Creek (Burial 8).

sharp tool is used to remove soft tissue adhering to the bone. Such marks frequently appear in clusters, an indication that repeated strokes were necessary to successfully clean the bone. Defleshing marks are similar to filleting marks reported on archaeological animal bones (Olsen 1987) where whole muscles are removed for transport or for drying or smoking. The difference is that defleshing marks can occur anywhere on the bone where skin, muscles, tendons, ligaments, periosteum, or any other soft tissue attaches, whereas filleting marks are usually concentrated at the points of origin and insertion of muscles and tendons. Defleshing marks are occasionally found densely distributed over much of the surface of the bone, indicating an almost compulsive need to thoroughly remove all the soft tissue (fig. 5). In one case, the tibia of an individual (not from this sample) recovered from the Boundary Mound site bore traces of over 500 separate cutmarks.

Defleshing marks on the cranium chiefly represent the skinning process and are hence similar to scalping. However, scalping marks are usually more restricted in their distribution, whereas defleshing marks can occur on the face and basicranium, as well as the scalp region (fig. 6). Multiple short, straight marks around the orbital margins and nasal aperture and on the canine eminences are not uncommon in secondary burials. The abundance of cutmarks indicates that removing the flesh of the nose, around the orbits, and along the jaw was often difficult. Horizontally oriented marks on the buccal surface of the ascending ramus of mandibles were primarily for removal of the masseter muscle.

DISARTICULATION

Disarticulation is indicated by fine cutmarks located on or adjacent to articular surfaces of bones. These represent the use of a sharp tool to cut through skin, tendons, and ligaments at the joint to segment the body into smaller parts. Since human bones in mounds in this region are frequently found disarticulated, it is assumed that the natural cleaning processes were often expedited by the use of butchering tools prior to depositing the bones in the mound.

The combination of defleshing and disarticulating marks on the skeletons from these early mounds is best explained by

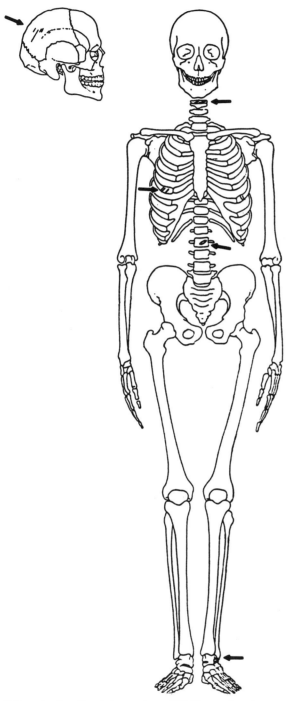

Fig. 7. Example of conflict victim: a male, aged 20–24 years, from the Larson site (Burial 55I), exhibiting evidence of scalping, attempted decapitation, multiple stabbings in the thoracic region, an embedded projectile point or knife in a vertebra, and possible removal of the foot as a trophy.

the idea that the bones were cleaned and carefully prepared sometime after death and before they reached their final disposition in the mound. Sometimes the bone surfaces show changes typical of weathering that must have occurred prior to the formation of cutmarks, a good indication that cleaning of the skeleton sometimes occurred well after death and exposure of the bones to sunlight. In other cases, including a femur from Boundary Mound, the weathering appears to have taken place after the cutmarks were made (fig. 9), a situation that implies that some cleaning occurred before the bones were removed from exposure to the sun for final burial. The relationship between weathering and cutmarks on human bones recovered from burial mounds suggests that the bodies were placed on scaffolds or otherwise exposed to sunlight for a period of time sufficient enough for ultraviolet damage to have occurred on the bone, and that at intervals during the time of exposure the decomposing flesh was removed from the bones and discarded.

Defleshing marks associated with secondary burial reveal additional information about mortuary practices. Inspection of cutmark maps drawn on outlines of articulated skeletons (fig. 5) shows pronounced orientation of the cutmarks on the long bones. Individuals processing corpses probably moved several times during the procedure in order to be able to reach various parts of the body, but there are indications that the cutting tool was held in a consistent manner and that an individual long bone was usually attacked from one primary position. If it could be established that the body was lying in a supine position while the anterior surface was being cleaned, as seems likely, then handedness of the tool-user could be inferred. In this situation, a righthanded person processing the corpse would create oblique cutmarks on the anterior surface of right long bones that are oriented on an axis that is inferior medially and superior laterally (fig. 5). Long bones on the body's left side would show marks in the same orientation, which, because it is the mirror image, is superior medially and inferior laterally. Forearms (radii and ulnae) frequently show more variable cutmark orientations than upper arm or upper leg segments, as if the forearm could be manipulated and turned about freely. This would suggest that either the cuts were made soon after death or that the elbow joint was severed prior to processing.

There is evidence that crania were occasionally severed from the spine during defleshing. Such is the case with a young male from Split Rock Creek (39MH6) (Burial 7) that has numerous cuts on one occipital condyle, the supraoccipital and the basiocciput. Disarticulation marks on the mandibular condyles also occur with frequency.

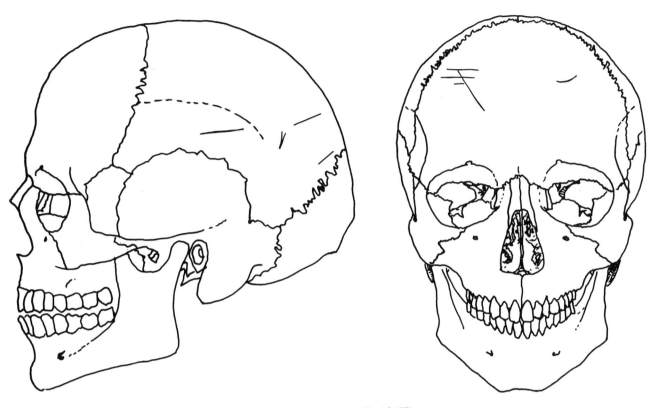

Fig. 8. Scalping marks on the cranium of a male, aged 40–49 years, from the Larson site (Burial 62B).

FORAMEN MAGNUM OPENING

Opening of the foramen magnum was noted in three individuals from Enemy Swim (39DA3) (Burial 15119 and 15124) and Split Rock Creek (Burial 7). All these crania showed signs of having been extensively defleshed, with cutmarks about the braincase, face, and mandible. If the breaks that enlarged the foramen magnum were culturally inflicted, then it is likely they served to facilitate brain removal during the cleaning process.

Secondary burial was inferred to have been conducted on nine males, five females, and four persons of indeterminate sex. Individuals subjected to secondary burial were both adult and juvenile, some skeletons being those of very young children (less than 3 years old) who were spatially associated with adult skeletons.

CONCLUSIONS FOR SECONDARY BURIAL

Evidence for secondary interment is reflected in disarticulation and defleshing cutmarks from the Woodland sites, through the Middle Missouri, and into the Initial and Extended Coalescent. None of the very late specimens was judged to have been secondarily buried. Most of the sites yielding skeletons determined to have been secondarily buried are either Woodland or ancestral Mandan, but Crow Creek (39BF11) and Mobridge (39WW1) are both identified as ancestral Arikara. The burial pattern at Crow Creek was atypical for this region. Secondary burial is reported for the Mandan in the ethnographic literature, but there is disagreement about the existence of secondary burial among the Arikara (Gilbert and Bass 1967; Lehmer 1971; Orser 1980; Ubelaker and Willey 1978, and references cited therein).

Conflict-Related Traumas

Skeletons bearing marks interpreted as the result of conflict were usually relatively complete in terms of the body parts preserved, with the possible exception of some of the small or more fragile elements. Individuals killed in conflict commonly bore only scalping marks on the cranium, although some also possessed a few marks on the postcranium. These

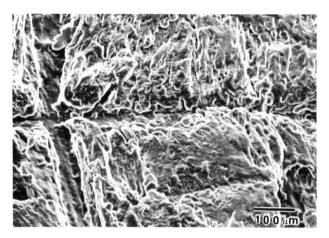

Fig. 9. Weathering damage overlying two cutmarks (horizontal grooves) on femur of a female, aged 18–20 years, from Boundary Mound (Burial 8). Scanning electron micrograph.

postcranial marks have been interpreted as stabbing wounds, arrow wounds, the severing of limbs for the taking of trophies (fig. 7), or violent dismemberment to hack up the body into segments, as in the case of Burial 50 from the Leavenworth site (39CO9).

In this sample, the earliest evidence for a conflict-related trauma is a head blow on the cranium of Burial 48 from the Twelve Mile Creek site (39HT1). Although some small amount of intervillage conflict probably occurred at this relatively early date, the incidence of conflict-related injury and mutilation increases markedly from the Initial Coalescent onward. Recognition of these features is facilitated by the relative completeness of skeletons and the rarity of heavy bone modification due to secondary burial preparation. The high frequency of battle injuries at Crow Creek and Larson (39WW2), two massacre sites, has been documented (Owsley, Berryman, and Bass 1977; Zimmerman et al. 1980). Thus, the first dramatic rise in violence appears to be attributable to conflict between different indigenous groups (possibly the ancestral Mandan and Arikara) who were vying for resources, rather than between Europeans and Indians during the contact period.

SCALPING

Scalping marks are typically a series of short, straight or slightly curved marks, around the crown of the head (fig. 8). They are commonly found in the forehead region of the frontal, on the lateral surfaces of the parietals, occasionally as low as the temporals (especially at the suprameatal crest), and on the occipital (sometimes as low as the nuchal crest). Marks are not expected to be present on the face below the brow ridges or on the mandible. None of the scalping marks in this sample encircles the cranium continuously nor are they normally long, sweeping strokes that could be joined up visually to reconstruct one smooth action. Most frequently, marks are present only on the parietals. Figure 8 shows a skull of an adult male from the Larson site that is interpreted as possessing typical scalping marks. Examples of scalping from the Over Collection are very similar to those illustrated and described from the sites of Nuvakwewtaqa and Grasshopper in Arizona (Allen and Merbs 1985).

BLUNT-FORCE TRAUMA

Five individuals from four sites in this sample exhibited cranial fractures caused by a powerful blow with a blunt object (fig. 10). All but two of these fractures are located on individual parietals. One of the exceptions is a female skull from Larson (Burial 307) that received a blow farther forward that fractured an area involving the frontal, malar, and temporal, as well as part of the parietal. The second is a female skull from the Anton Rygh site (39CA4) (Burial 4859) that has two possible blows—one to the posterior part of the right parietal, zygomatic, and mandible; and another to the left mandible. A female from the Larson site (Burial 120B) exhibits a long,

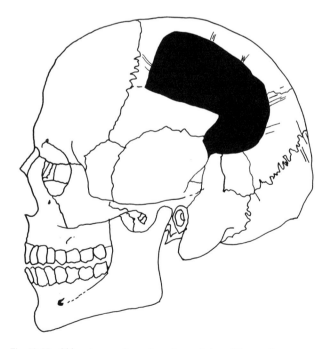

Fig. 10. Head blow to a cranium of a male, aged about 22 years, from Mobridge (Burial 29D). Numerous cutmarks around the fracture were probably made during scalping.

narrow entry wound in the superior surface of the right parietal that was probably made by a sharp weapon like an ax. All these crania bear evidence of scalping, and the frequency of cutmarks around the wounds suggests difficulty in removing the scalp intact from the damaged part of the cranium. Death by traumatic blows to the head was noted in the burial records at a number of sites in the Over Collection beyond this sample, including the Mobridge, Anton Rygh, Larson, and Leavenworth sites. At Mobridge, as many as seven crania of men, women, and a child were damaged in this manner. From the nature of the fractures, this massacre seems to have been conducted with clubs or similar blunt instruments, rather than axes.

KNIFE OR PROJECTILE POINT WOUNDS

Possible stabbing or projectile point wounds are undocumented in this sample before the Extended Coalescent, after which they appear in numerous individuals. These marks may serve as good indicators of increased intergroup conflict, since they are less likely to occur by other means. The two types of marks are combined here because it is not an easy task to distinguish between them. Both may appear as a V-shaped notch in the margin of a bone, such as a rib, or as a small lenticular depressed fracture on bone surfaces. Grazing wounds inflicted with a knife or projectile would be difficult to distinguish from cutmarks created by other perimortem activities like secondary burial preparation. Knife or projectile point wounds have been recorded on ventral surfaces of ribs at Mobridge (Burial 27F), Anton Rygh (Burial 13), and Larson (Burials 50G, 55I, 62B, and 146B); and on ventral surfaces of vertebrae at Larson (Burial 50G).

If impact is forceful or of high velocity, the tip of either a knife or a projectile point may penetrate the bone, snap off, and remain embedded in the wound. Studies comparing location and depth of penetration might enable researchers to differentiate between these two forms of injury, but at present it seems prudent to combine them into one category of bone modification. Embedded tips of flint weapons have been identified in the bones of four males from the Larson site. A lumbar vertebra and the sacrum of one individual (Burial 50G) who was wounded several times in the abdomen, a rib and a lumbar vertebra of another (fig. 7), and a clavicle of a third (Burial 38A) all bore wounds that retained pieces of flint inside. A fourth male (Burial 146B) had a piece of flint embedded in his frontal, as well as having been stabbed in the chest and scalped. A left and a right rib from a male (Burial 33) from Swan Creek (39WW7) and a distal radius from

Leavenworth (Burial 50) likewise exhibited wounds with embedded flint. These are almost certainly the results of combat rather than simple defleshing marks since considerable force would be required to puncture the bone and break the tips off of either projectile points or knives.

TROPHY-TAKING OR MUTILATION

Some individuals show marks that may have been associated with either mutilation or the taking of trophies during conflict. The capturing of trophies during battle in the Plains has been well-documented in literature, but it is less commonly recognized in the archaeological record. The most frequently observed trophies were enemy scalps, but occasionally heads or other body parts were appropriated.

The atlas of an adult male from the Larson site (Burial 55I) individual (fig. 7) had two cuts, perhaps made in an unsuccessful attempt to decapitate him. At the Leavenworth site, the scalped cranium and the atlas of a young male (Burial 00201) were found without a body. One explanation for the presence of this isolated specimen is that it, too, was a trophy head taken during intertribal conflict. Marks around the nasal aperture of crania from Mobridge (Burial 38D), initially thought to represent removal of the nose as a possible trophy, are more reliably attributed to defleshing associated with secondary burial since there are also marks near the orbit and on the forehead.

The most frequent examples in Arikara individuals were cuts at the knee or the foot. There are specimens with cuts on the posterior surface of the distal femur from the Anton Rygh (Burial 13) and Larson (Burial 38A) sites. At both Larson (Burial 55I) and Swan Creek (not this sample), at least one individual had deep cuts through the tarsals that indicate an attempt to remove a foot. The burial records do not report the presence or absence of foot elements below the talus, so it is not possible to know if the foot was actually removed in either case.

The best example of dismemberment of a violent nature occurred at the Leavenworth site, where a male in his early twenties (Burial 50) was hacked up with an axe or similar chopping tool. Deep chopping marks were located at the right shoulder, both hips, both knees, and the right ankle. A piece of embedded stone was found in the distal radius and the individual was scalped, as well.

Dismemberment inflicted in the heat of battle is not easily distinguished from disarticulation of decomposed bodies as a part of mortuary practices surrounding secondary burial. Deciphering the cause of disarticulation marks relies, in part, on their context and whether there are other indications of either secondary burial or conflict. Although individual marks may not always allow differentiation, those found on partial, disarticulated skeletons belonging to Woodland or ancestral Mandan cultures are more likely to represent mortuary practices, whereas those in the more complete Arikara burials may have occurred during battle.

CONCLUSIONS FOR CONFLICT-RELATED TRAUMAS

Within this sample, 10 males, 5 females, and one individual of indeterminate sex demonstrated cases of conflict-related traumas. The tendency for males to exhibit more "battle-inflicted" perimortem damage to their skeletons is borne out in the records for the whole Over Collection. Although scalping is probably the most reliable and most easily recognized expression of intergroup conflict, it is also important to be able to recognize the cause of death in many instances. The wounds observed here indicate that several kinds of weapons were employed, including stone-tipped arrows, stone and metal knives, axes or other chopping implements, and blunt instruments such as wooden clubs.

Summary

This study suggests that frequencies, locations, and orientations of surface marks can be used along with skeletal completeness to interpret the activities that gave rise to these modifications to human skeletal remains. Marks in the sample from the Over Collection were made by a variety of stone and metal tools.

Two distinct patterns were found in the Over Collection material, interpreted as being secondary burial, on the one hand, and conflict-related injuries, on the other. Defleshing of the cranium for secondary interment gave rise to different patterns of cutmarks than did scalping. Although there was a clear rise in evidence for conflict through time, the initial appearance of conflict-related injuries substantially predated European contact. There was also a decline in the incidence of secondarily buried individuals through time, which probably reflects changes in the ethnic composition of the sample from predominantly ancestral Mandan to predominantly ancestral Arikara.

More males than females were secondarily buried, according to this small sample. Both adults and children were secondarily buried. Details of the strategy of defleshing and of the handedness of those processing corpses for secondary burial were deduced in a few cases. Weathering appears to

have occurred before and after cutmarks were made, indicating that the bodies were laid outdoors in at least some cases and that the cleaning of the bones was a long process.

Differences were found in conflict-related injuries between males and females, with males demonstrating a higher frequency of these injuries than females. However, it is clear that both sexes bore cutmarks and traumatic injuries that were highly likely to be associated with conflict. In this sample, no such injuries were found on children.

Given the issues of reburial of bones, it is more important than ever that scientists record as much information as possible about human osteological material from archaeological sites. This study has demonstrated the need for complete recording of the presence or absence of all elements, whether they were found in articulation, whether fractures appear to be perimortem or merely postdepositional, and, most important, whether surface alterations like cutmarks are present. Without the diligent recording of all observed cutmarks, fractures, puncture wounds, chopmarks, scraping, and so forth by Owsley, Mann, and others, this study would have been impossible. Much more work can continue in this area of research on the Over Collection despite reburial because of the existence of such detailed records. This study also shows the importance of taking molds and casts of surface modifications so that types of marks, orientation, directionality, handedness, and other features can be gleaned from material that, in its original state, is no longer available to scientists.

References Cited

Allen, W.H., and C.F. Merbs
  1985 Evidence for Prehistoric Scalping at Nuvakwewtaqa (Chavez Pass) and Grasshopper Ruin, Arizona. Pp. 22–42 in Health and Disease in the Prehistoric Southwest. C.F. Merbs and R.J. Miller eds. *Arizona State University Anthropological Research Papers* 34.

Gilbert, B.M., and W.M. Bass.
  1967 Seasonal Dating of Burials from the Presence of Fly Pupae. *American Antiquity* 32(4):534–535.

Lehmer, D.J.
  1971 Introduction to Middle Missouri Archaeology. *National Park Service Anthropological Papers* 1.

Olsen, S.L.
  1987 Magdalenian Reindeer Exploitation at the Grotte des Eyzies, Southwest France. *Archaeozoologia* 1:171–182.

———
  1988 The Identification of Stone and Metal Tool Marks on Bone Artifacts. Pp. 337–360 in Scanning Electron Microscopy. S.L. Olsen, ed. *British Archaeological Reports International Series* 452.

——, and P. Shipman

1988 Surface Modification on Bone: Trampling versus Butchery. *Journal of Archaeological Science* 15:535–553.

Orser, C.E.

1980 Toward a Partial Understanding of Complexity in Arikara Mortuary Practice. *Plains Anthropologist* 25(88):113–120.

Owsley, D.W., H.E. Berryman, and W.M. Bass

1977 Demographic and Osteological Evidence for Warfare at the Larson Site, South Dakota. *Plains Anthropologist Memoirs* 13:119–131.

Rose, J.J.

1983 A Replication Technique for Scanning Electron Microscopy: Applications for Anthropologists. *American Journal of Physical Anthropology* 62(3):255–263.

Shipman, P.L., D.C. Fisher, and J.J. Rose

1984 Mastodon Butchery: Microscopic Evidence of Carcass Processing and Bone Tool Use. *Paleobiology* 10(3):358–365.

——, and J.J. Rose

1984 Cutmark Mimics on Modern and Fossil Bovid Bones. *Current Anthropology* 25(1):116–117.

——, and J.J. Rose

1988 Bone Tools: An Experimental Approach. Pp. 303–335 in *Scanning Electron Microscopy*. S.L. Olsen, ed. *British Archaeological Reports International Series* 452.

Ubelaker, D.H.

1974 Reconstruction of Demographic Profiles from Ossuary Skeletal Samples: A Case Study from the Tidewater Potomac. *Smithsonian Contributions to Anthropology* 18.

——

1978 Human Skeletal Remains. Excavation, Analysis, Interpretation. Chicago: Aldine.

——, and P. Willey

1978 Complexity in Arikara Mortuary Practice. *Plains Anthropologist* 23:69–74.

Zimmerman, L.J., T. Emerson, P. Willey, M. Swegle, J.B. Gregg, P. Gregg, E. White, C. Smith, T. Haberman, and P. Bumstead

1980 The Crow Creek Site (39 BF 11) Massacre: A Preliminary Report. Vermillion, S.Dak.: University of South Dakota Archeology Laboratory.

PART 6

○○○

Conclusion

CHAPTER 32

○○○

An Overview of Great Plains Human Skeletal Biology

DOUGLAS H. UBELAKER

In 1980 Richard L. Jantz and I edited a volume synthesizing much of the then-active research in the human skeletal biology of past populations of the Great Plains (Jantz and Ubelaker 1981a). That volume culminated from a 1978 symposium held at the Plains Conference in Denver, Colorado. In that work, William M. Bass (1981) related that when he initiated his research in the Plains region during the late 1950s, relatively little analysis had been conducted on Plains human samples. To a large extent stimulated by Bass, Plains physical anthropology expanded rapidly during the next 20 years. Large, well-documented skeletal samples from diverse time periods and localities were acquired, and they attracted a number of increasingly sophisticated physical anthropologists.

By the time of the 1978 symposium in Denver, tentative synthesis was made possible by a sizeable literature and a growing and increasingly complex research effort. That symposium touched on the major research efforts at the time: population relationships, mortuary practices, disease, demography, and biocultural interpretations. As editors and symposium organizers, Jantz and I were impressed by how much had been learned during the previous 20 years but equally impressed at the intensity of the field and how fast it appeared to be changing. In our closing editorial comments we noted: "It

is clear that we have learned a great deal in the past 20 years, but it is even clearer that a great deal more can be learned to the benefit of all with an interest in Plains prehistory" (Jantz and Ubelaker 1981b:2). However, we did not imagine that the field would change so much in the ensuing 10 years.

Two major developments have transformed the nature of research on archaeologically recovered samples of human remains from the Great Plains. The first involves a new battery of research techniques, mostly chemical in nature, that allow new types of problems to be investigated. In our 1978 gathering, the innovations were primarily a population approach to disease and demography and the use of multivariate statistics and high-speed computers to address issues of population relationships. These techniques continue to evolve and be used, but the battery of chemical approaches and functional analysis of structure allow research to be directed at dietary patterns, the timing and nature of infant weaning, and related problems. Techniques and problem orientations unheard of in 1978 are now routine. Some of the best of this research is presented within the essays of this volume.

The second unpredicted factor in Plains research today is the negative reaction of contemporary American Indians to the excavation and study of human remains. In 1978 problems resulting from this concern were sporadic and largely confined to the Plains area. Today, this concern has spread throughout the United States, resulting in national legislation and many state laws that threaten to dramatically reduce excavation of human remains from archaeological sites and to empty museums of their collections of human remains.

As unsettling as this political process has been for archaeologists and physical anthropologists, a silver lining has emerged. The crisis atmosphere surrounding many collections has, to some extent, stimulated scientists and funding agencies to intensify their study of human remains. In some cases, this effort has focused considerable scientific attention on collections that until then had been studied only minimally. Such threatened collections have, on occasion, brought scientists together for interdisciplinary studies that would not otherwise have taken place. The resulting research experience not only generates new data for future interpretation but also stimulates current multidisciplinary problem-oriented research.

This volume is a case in point. Research culminating in this volume was stimulated by the new state law in South Dakota calling for the transfer of the William H. Over collection of human skeletal remains to contemporary American Indians. This large, diverse, and well-documented Plains collection had been studied minimally before and was scheduled for imminent transfer. With support from the National Science Foundation, the University of Tennessee, and the Smithsonian Institution, Douglas Owsley organized a major interdisciplinary effort to study the material. Much of that research is summarized in this volume. However, because the research was both documentary and problem oriented, it needed to be framed in broad context. The resulting volume moves far beyond reporting on the Over collection and toward a new synthesis of Plains human skeletal biology. This work builds on and complements our efforts in 1978, but, reflecting the new techniques of the times, moves a quantum level beyond.

Chronology

Documentation and chronological interpretation remain the foundation of collection-oriented research. To allow research interpretation, each museum object (or in the context of this volume, each human skeleton), must be placed in correct or reasonable temporal and spatial context. Only with such documentation can interpretation on temporal change and spatial variation proceed. Appropriately, essays by Owsley and Jantz, Blakeslee, Brooks, and Snortland on archaeological provenience introduce the 28 following essays in this volume and provide the needed framework. The Blakeslee essay is especially informative in not only providing a chronological framework for the Northern and Central Plains but also pointing out the difficulty in relating this framework in all situations to historically documented groups, linguistic categories, and ancestral trees. The three central themes explored by Blakeslee—migration, warfare, and subsistence—are woven through most of the essays in this volume.

Discussion of migration patterns features a general south-to-north movement of Plains people, especially seen with the Arikara. Peoples of Kansas City Hopewell appear to represent a separate migration, but the source remains elusive. Late Woodland samples from Nebraska and the entire Middle Missouri tradition appear to have an eastern origin. The Steed-Kisker complex is best related to Mississippian influence to the south. The discussion challenges physical anthropologists to sort out the evidence for migration vis-à-vis local continuity using available skeletal samples.

As Snortland points out, the problem is complicated in that some mortuary sites are quite complex and may present a specialized cultural assemblage difficult to relate to data from non-mortuary sites. Her study of Northern Plains burial mounds indicates some may have been reused over a 600-year period and involve complex interpretations of intrusive burials and a mixture of burial customs that differ from those employed in other related areas.

Population Relationships and Biomechanics

As noted by Jantz, measurements have long been utilized to elucidate problems in human skeletal biology. Following this tradition, Key turns to multivariate analysis of crania to examine population relationships in the northern and central Plains. In the Northern Plains, Key traces biological continuity back to the Archaic. This ancestral relationship is less clear in the Central Plains, but Key sees a deep regional differentiation between Woodland groups from the Northern and Central Plains. His data suggest population movement beginning in the Late Woodland. During Middle Woodland times, Key's data differentiate three biological groups on the upper Plains: Kansas City Hopewell, the Keith and Valley complexes on the Central Plains, and the Sonota complex on the Northern Plains.

Multivariate analysis offers the potential not only to assess population relationships but also to identify individual outliers that may represent individuals from other populations. Jantz and Owsley offer an example of this methodology in identifying both morphologically and statistically the cranium of a White man, apparently a trader, in the Swan Creek sample.

The date of Swan Creek of 1675 to 1725 clearly pulls back the date of the earliest known European contact in the area, previously thought to have been the La Vérendrye brothers' expeditions of 1742 and 1743.

Using similar methodology, Byrd and Jantz document biological groupings within the skeletal sample recovered from the Leavenworth site, South Dakota. In the salvage excavation of the Leavenworth site cemetery in 1965, William Bass inaugurated the skeletal recovery program that stimulated much of the research detailed in this volume. Twenty-seven years later, two of his academic descendents show how computer-assisted analysis and a keen sense of research design can discover intrasample variation that confirms hypotheses of social heterogeneity generated from other subdisciplines of anthropology. Leavenworth was a single site, but it housed the remnants of previously distinct groups who apparently retained some intragroup variation when it came time for burial.

A methodological problem addressed indirectly in this volume involves sorting out the genetic and environmental contributions to skeletal morphology. Key, Owsley, and Jantz assume the environmental contribution to cranial morphology is minimal and use cranial measurements to assess genetic relationships. In contrast, T. Cole and Ruff reverse this logic by assuming postcranial size and robusticity is largely environmentally shaped. Minimal differences in the size and shape of the femur and tibia in northern Plains Indians suggest to Cole lack of variation in diet and locomotory stress and a minimal sexual division of labor. Looking at the supraorbital region in samples from the Northern Plains, Cole and Cole use metric analysis to document sexual variation and find differences in shape that correlate with differences in subsistence.

Ruff's biomechanical analysis of Northern and Southern Plains femora reveals evidence of a comparatively rigorous lifestyle. His comparison of femora between the Northern and Southern Plains reveals less sexual dimorphism in the former. His data support a temporal increase in intensive agriculture among Coalescent samples in the Northern Plains. Agriculturally active females show an increase in bone robusticity, while male robusticity declines. Femoral architecture in the Southern Plains suggests high levels of mobility through time and maintenance of a hunter-gatherer type subsistence. Ruff's comparisons of subsistence among Plains, eastern, and southwestern United States samples seem to be complicated by genetic differences among the diverse populations sampled. However, his inferences on diet in the Southern Plains match those suggested by Brooks, who argues that populations in the eastern portion of the Southern Plains ate primarily corn, beans, and squash, while bison became more important in the west.

Interpretations of Subsistence

From archaeological evidence, Blakeslee notes more of a temporal change in subsistence to the north, where long-distance hunts for bison were always important but, through time, cultigens became more important to Plains village populations. Diet in the Middle Missouri shows more variety than in later Coalescent samples.

The volume also presents exciting new chemical evidence for subsistence in the Plains. Tieszen summarizes the theoretical issues and development in the Great Plains of stable isotope analysis, currently the most applicable area of chemical research. The potential of this research is both far-reaching and exciting, but, as Tieszen notes, accuracy depends upon sophisticated interpretation of the environment of the time, growth of the individuals involved, and the archaeological contexts of the samples. Clearly, an assemblage of data is becoming available for the Plains that will allow chemical approaches to be interpreted into research designs aimed at reconstructing subsistence patterns, seasonal shifts in food procurement, and related issues.

Working with Southern High Plains samples, Habicht-Mauche, Levendosky, and Schoeninger find that, although trace element analysis for strontium and zinc is attractive theoretically, it appears vulnerable to post-mortem taphonomic change that masks reliable interpretation of subsistence. In contrast, carbon and nitrogen stable isotope ratios in bone collagen seem immune from postmortem factors and suggest that females had a more varied diet than males but, overall, diet consisted of meat supplemented with seasonal gathering of C_4 plants.

Working with northern Plains samples from the Arikara Sully site (A.D. 1650–1733), Tuross and Fogel utilize stable isotope analysis to suggest substantial dietary reliance upon bison. Tuross and Fogel further indicate from isotopic analysis of infant and child bones that infants were breastfed for one year and then gradually weaned until age five on a diet high in vegetable and fruit products.

Warfare and Cultural Inferences

Brooks and Blakeslee cite abundant evidence for increasing hostility and violence through time throughout the Plains. In the Southern Plains, the temporal increase was restricted to frontier areas, apparently in the form of small-scale hostilities in competition for resources and border control.

Farther north in the Plains Village I period, Blakeslee reports fortified sites in the Northern but not in the Central Plains. Coalescent traditions in Plains Village 2 show abundant evidence for warfare, most dramatically at the massacre site of Crow Creek. Evidence of violent conflict is detected archaeologically in the Extended Coalescent as well. In fact, warfare in the Plains became so institutionalized that Robarchek considers it a "longstanding cultural tradition."

Exploring the dimensions of Plains warfare, Ewers notes that not only were women killed and captured during Plains warfare, but also they were at times participants in raiding parties as well as related rituals. According to ethnohistoric records, scalps were occasionally removed from female victims.

Bovee and Owsley report archaeological evidence for such an example from the Heerwald site, dating from the Washita River phase of the Early Plains Village period in west-central Oklahoma. An adult female skeleton displayed projectile points in the ribs and vertebrae. Small incisions on the cranial vault offer unmistakable evidence for scalping. Bovee and Owsley further report that interpopulation violence was widespread throughout the northern Plains but localized in the Southern Plains. The number of osteologically documented deaths from warfare in the Northern Plains during the late prehistoric and early historic periods is fairly large. Although both males and females were victims, the age-dependent risk was different. Most males showing cutmarks from scalping were young adults aged 15 to 30 years. In contrast, the age profile for women lacks a specific peak for young adults with older females also represented. This contrast reflects sex-related activities with different risks of being killed by an enemy.

Olsen and Shipman offer abundant evidence for cutmarks on the Over material from the Northern Plains. Their careful analysis of a variety of incisions identifies the tools involved (stone blades, scrapers, axes, metal knives). Cutmarks are found in remains ranging temporally from Woodland to historic. Analysis reveals a temporal shift from defleshing and disarticulation as a mortuary practice at early sites to evidence for violence in later sites. Additional evidence is reported by Owsley for the Coalescent tradition of the Northern Plains and by Hollimon and Owsley for the Initial Middle Missouri material from the Fay Tolton site. Their discoveries document the long tradition of warfare, including scalping, in the Plains.

Not all cut bones reflect violence or mortuary customs. Owsley, Mann, and Baugh report on culturally modified human bones from the Edwards I site, a fortified village in southwestern Oklahoma. This Southern Plains site dates to A.D. 1450–1750 and produced four bones with cultural modifications. Study of the cutmarks suggests some likely were produced by intentional defleshing while one modified femur may have functioned as a musical instrument. The essay illustrates the many ways human bones have been modified and used in North America as well as the difficulties in interpreting cutmarks on bone.

Disease

As noted by Ortner, careful description and caution in interpretation are in order to avoid the pitfalls in paleopathology. Jantz and Owsley sharpen the tools of paleopathological analysis by providing a new innovative system of assessing dental development and chronological age at death. The method assumes that the peak of infant mortality is at or about the moment of birth. They produce the expected finding that Arikara dentitions develop earlier than modern Whites, but they also find variability in the relative development of different teeth.

Williams reports on research in the Northern Plains indicating that health of Archaic and Woodland populations was good compared to later populations. He found periodontal disease to be a problem, but frequencies of caries and hypoplasia were relatively low. The temporal trend of increasing morbidity matches those suggested for many other parts of the New World, apparently reflecting the stress and morbid conditions associated with increasing population density, sedentism, conflict, and diet of diminishing quality.

Schermer, Fisher, and Hodges report evidence for endemic treponematosis in prehistoric western Iowa. Evidence for the disease in four of eight adults from a Late Archaic Early Woodland component at the Pooler site argues for treponemal disease in Iowa at 610 B.C. This report joins a growing literature suggesting treponemal disease has a New World origin. The date is among the earliest reported for treponemal disease in the Americas.

In contrast, Kelley, Murphy, Levesque, and Sledzik argue that pulmonary tuberculosis was a major factor in mortality at the Arikara sites. Rib lesions offer the primary evidence. Few could doubt that tuberculosis was a health problem at these sites since the disease is firmly documented to be of New World origin and also is known to have been a major problem among Plains Indians throughout the historic period. The importance of tuberculosis as a factor in mortality vis-à-vis other diseases is more problematic since many of the other diseases likely were present but would have left little or no imprint on bone tissue.

Mann, Owsley, and Reinhard also report evidence for tuberculosis along with otitis media and other problems from two child skeletons dating 1780 to 1820 (Nebraska) and 800 to 1100 (Oklahoma). Their work further documents the occurrence of these disease conditions in the Plains; it also shows the value of careful description and how modern clinical data can be utilized to explain ancient diseases.

Willey and Hofman call attention to interproximal grooves in the Over material. These grooves are of minimal importance as factors in morbidity or mortality, but their interpretation has attracted considerable anthropological attention. The Over samples produced 32 such grooves in 15 individuals. Willey and Hofman argue, along with others in the literature, that the grooves were produced in an attempt by the individuals to relieve pain associated with dental disease. The authors speculate that the grooves were produced by or with the use of herbal medicines such as black sampson (*Echinacea angustifolia*).

Discussion of disease in the Great Plains moves to the historic period with Trimble's essay on the spread of smallpox in the early nineteenth century. Trimble's work suggests how smallpox mortality among Plains Indians may have been shaped both by a purposeful inoculation program as well as by differences in lifestyle. The essay also demonstrates how newly discovered primary historical data can contribute to enhanced understanding of historical biological events, such as epidemics.

Finally, Gill reminds us that scholarship in archaeologically recovered human remains from the Plains need not be confined to American Indians. Gill's study of samples of historic pioneers of European descent documents the brutality and violence of pioneer life. Clearly the Plains continued to offer a rigorous lifestyle well into the historic period.

New Directions

Scholarship in this volume moves well beyond what anyone could have predicted 10 years ago. The volume represents, first, a testimonial to the information that can be harvested from skeletal samples, such as those in the Over collection; second, the potential of physical anthropology to contribute to an understanding of population dynamics and history; and third, the changing, increasingly complex nature of science.

As this volume goes to press, laboratories and computers are churning with new techniques and new approaches to interpretation. Scientists are rapidly developing the research capability to isolate DNA from archaeologically recovered bone. Once realized, this technique could revolutionize procedures and scholars' ability to ascertain population relationships through time. Many of the evolutionary relationships hinted at in this volume through multivariate analysis of bone measurements or through other archaeological resources could be clarified or even resolved if this technology becomes available.

Chemical analysis of bone already offers exciting information not available only a few years ago, but the potential of this new field has only begun to be tapped. Research in detecting immunoglobulins can decipher the secrets of individual disease history. Current debates on the interpretation of skeletal lesions could be completely superseded by test-tube diagnoses of the chemical imprints of disease.

As the expertise in anthropology, biochemistry, demography, and related fields continues to grow and interrelate, new research problems and solutions will result. Likely, we will continue to find that bones hold the answers to an increasing number of key archaeological and historical questions.

Ironically, as research capability is advancing at an unprecedented pace, so is the loss of human remains from museums and laboratories. Of course, it can be argued convincingly that this volume was stimulated by the political crisis behind that exodus. However, it is also clear that the next generation of scientists will be faced with a more limited database than is now available. The scientific community must show sensitivity to concerns of contemporary American Indians about their ancestry and the new laws must be followed. However, I hope that the value of scientific analysis, demonstrated so thoroughly in this volume, will convince those involved to encourage analysis and to allow meaningful samples to be retained for future study. The history of Plains Indians and all American Indians is rich and complex. The story deserves to be told as accurately and completely as possible.

References Cited

Bass, W.M.
  1981 Skeletal Biology on the United States Great Plains: A History and Personal Narrative. Pp. 3–18 in Progress in Skeletal Biology of Plains Populations. *Plains Anthropologist Memoir* 17, 26(94, Part 2).

Jantz, R.L., and D.H. Ubelaker, eds.
  1981a Progress in Skeletal Biology of Plains Populations. *Plains Anthropologist Memoir* 17, 26(94, Part 2).

Jantz, R.L., and D.H. Ubelaker
  1981b Introduction. Pp. 1–2 in Progress in Skeletal Biology of Plains Populations. *Plains Anthropologist Memoir* 17, 26(94, Part 2).

ooo
Contributors

Dr. Timothy G. Baugh
Western Cultural Resource Management
1715A Bloomfield Highway
Farmington, N.Mex. 87401

Dr. Donald J. Blakeslee
Department of Anthropology
Wichita State University
Wichita, Kans. 67208-1595

Ms. Dana L. Bovee
21 Lawlor Avenue
Toronto, Ontario M4E 3L8
Canada

Dr. Robert L. Brooks
Oklahoma Archaeological Survey
University of Oklahoma
1808 Newton Drive, Room 116
Norman, Okla. 73019

Mr. John E. Byrd
Department of Anthropology
University of Tennessee
Knoxville, Tenn. 37996

Dr. Maria S. Cole
Division of Mammals
National Museum of Natural History
Smithsonian Institution
Washington, D.C. 20560

Dr. Theodore M. Cole III
Department of Cell Biology and Anatomy
School of Medicine
The Johns Hopkins University
725 North Wolfe Street
Baltimore, Md. 21205

Dr. John C. Ewers
4432 26th Road North
Arlington, Va. 22207

Dr. A.K. Fisher
Deceased

Mrs. Marilyn L. Fogel
Geophysical Laboratory
Carnegie Institution of Washington
5251 Broad Branch Road NW
Washington, D.C. 20015

Dr. George W. Gill
Department of Anthropology
University of Wyoming
P.O. Box 3431
Laramie, Wyo. 82701

Dr. Judith A. Habicht-Mauche
Board of Studies in Anthropology
University of California at Santa Cruz
Santa Cruz, Calif. 95064

Dr. D.C. Hodges
Department of Anthropology
Northern Illinois University
Dekalb, Ill. 60115

Dr. Jack L. Hofman
Department of Anthropology
University of Kansas
622 Fraser
Lawrence, Kans. 66045

Dr. Sandra E. Holliman
25050 Coast Highway 1
Jenner, Calif. 95450

Dr. Richard L. Jantz
Department of Anthropology
University of Tennessee
Knoxville, Tenn. 37996

Dr. Marc A. Kelley
1523 Hidden Terrace
Santa Cruz, Calif. 95062

Dr. Patrick J. Key
The Key Company, Ltd.
P.O. Box 776
Excelsior, Minn. 55331-0776

Ms. Alytia A. Levendosky
Department of Psychology
University of Michigan
580 Union Drive
Ann Arbor, Mich. 48109-1346

Ms. Dianne R. Levesque
Department of Anthropology
University of Tennessee
Knoxville, Tenn. 37996

Mr. Robert W. Mann
U.S. Army Central Identification Laboratory
Fort Kamehameha, Building 45
Hickam AFB, Hawaii 96853-5000

Mr. Sean P. Murphy
Department of Anthropology
University of Tennessee
Knoxville, Tenn. 37996

Dr. Sandra L. Olsen
Department of Paleobotany
Carnegie Museum of Natural History
4400 Forbes Avenue
Pittsburgh, Pa. 15213

Dr. Donald J. Ortner
Department of Anthropology
National Museum of Natural History
Smithsonian Institution
Washington, D.C. 20560

Dr. Douglas W. Owsley
Department of Anthropology
National Museum of Natural History
Smithsonian Institution
Washington, D.C. 20560

Dr. Karl J. Reinhard
Department of Anthropology
University of Nebraska
Lincoln, Nebr. 68588-0368

Dr. Clayton A. Robarchek
Department of Anthropology
Wichita State University
Wichita, Kans. 67208

Dr. Christopher Ruff
Department of Cell Biology and Anatomy
School of Medicine
The Johns Hopkins University
725 North Wolfe Street
Baltimore, Md. 21205

Mrs. S.J. Schermer
Office of the State Archaeologist
Eastlawn Building
University of Iowa
Iowa City, Iowa 52242

Dr. Margaret J. Schoeninger
Department of Anthropology
University of Wisconsin
Madison, Wis. 53706

Dr. Pat Shipman
Department of Cell Biology and Anatomy
School of Medicine
The Johns Hopkins University
725 North Wolfe Street
Baltimore, Md. 21205

Mr. Paul S. Sledzik
National Museum of Health and Medicine
Armed Forces Institute of Pathology
Washington, D.C. 20306

Ms. J. Signe Snortland
State Historical Society of North Dakota
North Dakota Heritage Center
612 East Boulevard Avenue
Bismarck, N.Dak. 58505

Dr. Larry L. Tieszen
Department of Biology
Augustana College
29th Street and Summit Avenue
Sioux Falls, S.Dak. 57197

Dr. Michael K. Trimble
U.S. Army Corps of Engineers
St. Louis District Planning Division
1222 Spruce Street
St. Louis, Mo. 63103

Dr. Noreen Tuross
Conservation Analytical Laboratory
Smithsonian Institution
4210 Silver Hill Road
Suitland, Md. 20746

Dr. Douglas H. Ubelaker
Department of Anthropology
National Museum of Natural History
Smithsonian Institution
Washington, D.C. 20560

Dr. P. Willey
Department of Anthropology
Chico State University
Chico, Calif. 95929

Dr. John A. Williams
Department of Anthropology
University of North Dakota
Grand Forks, N.Dak. 58202

Index